Why Do You Need This New Edition?

If you're wondering why you need this new edition of *Texas Government*, here are six good reasons!

1. A "Breaking News" feature has been added to each chapter. Each box includes a short "news story" followed by a question-answer section that applies core concepts to analyses of contemporary issues. Topics include the recent rise in oil production, healthcare reform, the abortion sonogram legislation, water conservation strategies in El Paso, and more.

2. "Around the Nation" boxes have been updated to reflect current hot topics in state politics across the nation, including immigration reform in Arizona and minor political parties' increasing presence on New York ballots.

3. In light of Texas' most recent census, Chapter 1 focuses on rapid population growth in Texas and Chapter 7 addresses redistricting in Texas using data from the 2010 census. Chapters 12 and 13 also touch on population trends by discussing the impact of the high school dropout rate on the state's economic future and the governor's efforts to reform higher education.

4. The issue of healthcare reform and its impact on Texas state government is explored in Chapter 3.

5. Chapter 4 explores the effects of the 2010 election on party balance in Texas and looks forward to the upcoming congressional and presidential elections by tackling the Tea Party movement. Chapter 9 continues this discussion in an examination of Rick Perry's presidential campaign.

6. This edition includes full coverage of Texas's major legislative decisions in 2011, including the influence of small-government conservative groups (Chapter 5) and the failure of the legislature to pass sanctuary-cities legislation in its 2011 session (Chapter 8). Also, Chapter 13 examines efforts to balance the budget in 2011 without raising taxes or dipping into the Rainy Day Fund.

D1450034

PEARSON

Texas Government

POLICY AND POLITICS

Twelfth Edition

NEAL TANNAHILL
Houston Community College

PEARSON

Boston   Columbus   Indianapolis   New York   San Francisco   Upper Saddle River
Amsterdam   Cape Town   Dubai   London   Madrid   Milan   Munich   Paris   Montreal   Toronto
Delhi   Mexico City   São Paulo   Sydney   Hong Kong   Seoul   Singapore   Taipei   Tokyo

Executive Editor: Reid Hester
Supplements Editor: Emily Sauerhoff
Senior Marketing Manager: Lindsey Prudhomme
Production Manager: Bob Ginsberg
Project Coordination, Text Design, and Electronic Page Makeup:
    S4Carlisle Publishing Services
Cover Design Manager/Cover Designer: John Callahan
Cover Photo: Lanier/iStockphoto
Senior Manufacturing Buyer: Roy L. Pickering, Jr.
Printer and Binder: RR Donnelley & Sons Company/Crawfordsville
Cover Printer: Lehigh Phoenix

Credits and acknowledgments borrowed from other sources and reproduced, with permission, in this textbook appear on the appropriate page within text or on page 407.

Library of Congress Cataloging-in-Publication Data
Tannahill, Neal R., date.-
    Texas government : policy and politics/Neal Tannahill. — 12th ed.
      p. cm.
    ISBN-13: 978-0-205-25172-8
    ISBN-10: 0-205-25172-2
    1. Texas—Politics and government—1951—Textbooks. 2. Local government—Texas—Textbooks.
    3. Political planning—Texas—Textbooks. I. Title.
JK4816.T36 2013
320.4764—dc23

10 9 8 7 6 5 4 3 2—DOC—15 14 13 12

ISBN 10:   0-205-25172-2
ISBN 13: 978-0-205-25172-8

Brief Contents

Contents

CHAPTER 3 • The Federal Context of Texas Policymaking   55

CHAPTER 4 • Political Participation   77

Chapter 5 • Interest Groups   97

Chapter 6 • Political Parties   117

Chapter 7 • Elections   143

CHAPTER 11 • City Government   263

CHAPTER 12 • Counties, School Districts, and Special Districts   297

Preface

Textbooks should be designed with students in mind. I have written this textbook in a clear, straightforward fashion so students can easily understand concepts even if they have little background knowledge of Texas government and politics. I have also done my best to present the subject in an interesting fashion. Texas government is not boring, and Texas government textbooks should not be boring either.

NEW TO THIS EDITION

This edition of *Texas Government* includes a number of changes designed to reflect recent political developments, take account of the latest developments in scholarly research, and respond to requests from faculty using the textbook:

Introduction: Discusses the nationwide reduction in the number of death sentences assessed and executions carried out.

Chapter 1: The new opener focuses on rapid population growth in Texas. A new *Around the Nation* feature addresses immigration reform in Arizona. The chapter is updated to account for the latest census data. The *Breaking News* feature discusses rising oil production in Texas after decades of decline.

Chapter 3: The new opener focuses on the impact of healthcare reform legislation on Texas state government. The *Breaking News* feature discusses the lawsuits filed by Texas and other states seeking to overturn healthcare reform on constitutional grounds.

Chapter 4: The new opener focuses on the Tea Party movement as an example of grassroots participation in Texas politics. The *Breaking News* feature looks at the adoption of Voter ID by the Texas legislature.

Chapter 5: The new opener considers the influence of small-government conservative groups on the legislature in 2011. The *Breaking News* feature examines the passage of abortion sonogram legislation in the 2011 session of the Texas legislature.

Chapter 6: The new opener focuses on the party balance after the 2010 election. The *Breaking News* feature looks at the decision of two Democratic members of the Texas House to switch political parties. The *Around the Nation* feature focuses on minor political parties in New York.

Chapter 7: The new opener discusses redistricting in Texas following the 2010 census. The *Breaking News* feature examines the various lawsuits filed against the Texas redistricting plan.

Chapter 8: The new opener examines the failure of the legislature to pass sanctuary-cities legislation in its 2011 session. The *Breaking News* feature explores the legislature's failure to adopt guns-on-campus legislation.

Chapter 9: The new opener discusses state regulation of hydraulic fracking. The *Breaking News* feature focuses on the presidential run of Governor Rick Perry.

Chapter 10: The new opener previews a case before the Texas Supreme Court concerning water rights. The *Breaking News* feature discusses a constitutional amendment designed to address water development in the state.

Chapter 11: The *Breaking News* feature discusses water conservation strategies in El Paso.

Chapter 12: The new opener discusses the impact of the high school dropout rate on the state's economic future. The *Breaking News* feature looks at the new lawsuit that has been filed against the state's system for funding public education.

Chapter 13: The new opener discusses the governor's efforts to reform higher education. The chapter examines the efforts of the legislature to balance the budget in 2011 without raising taxes or dipping into the Rainy Day Fund. The *Breaking News* feature focuses on accounting gimmicks used to keep the budget in balance.

Chapter 14: The new chapter opener discusses the closure of a state prison in Sugar Land. The *Breaking News* feature considers the decision of the Texas Department of Corrections to serve inmates only two meals a day on weekends.

FEATURES

The text includes a number of features designed to help students learn and help instructors teach:

- **What We Will Learn.** Each chapter begins with questions that focus on the topics covered in the chapter. Each chapter concludes with a What We Have Learned section that presents the answers to each of the questions.

- **Key Terms.** Words and phrases that have a specific meaning in the context of the subject matter appear in bold type, followed by a clear, straightforward definition. Students should not memorize the definitions of the terms, but rather learn what they mean in the context of the chapter and be able to define and explain them in their own words. The list of terms at the end of each chapter helps students study by focusing their attention on important concepts.

- **Multiple-Choice Questions.** I have created a set of 25 multiple-choice questions for each chapter. Students can use the questions to help them master course material.

- **Around the Nation.** Each chapter includes a short essay about politics and government in another state. Students will better understand Texas government and politics in comparison with other state governments.

- **Breaking News.** Each chapter includes a short "news story" followed by a question-answer section that applies core concepts to analyses of contemporary issues.
- **Getting Involved.** Each chapter includes a feature telling students how they can get involved in their communities, the college, and their government by doing volunteer work, joining an interest group, or becoming a court-appointed special advocate, for example.
- **Glossary.** The textbook contains a glossary that includes the definitions of the key terms listed in the text. If students forget what a term means, they can look it up quickly in the glossary without having to search for it in the text.
- **What Is Your Opinion?** The text includes a number of questions asking students their opinion about some of the political controversies discussed in the text. The questions are designed to be interesting and thought provoking.
- **Instructor's Manual/Test Bank.** The Instructor's Manual includes chapter outlines, chapter summaries, teaching suggestions, ideas for student projects, and discussion questions. The Test Bank contains hundreds of challenging multiple-choice, short-answer, and essay questions with an answer key.
- **PowerPoints.** Available for download at www.pearsonhighered.com/irc, this text-specific package provides a basis for your lecture with PowerPoint slides for each chapter of the book.
- **My Test.** This flexible, Web-based test-generating software includes all questions found in the Test Bank and allows instructors to create their own personalized exams, edit the existing test questions, and even add new questions. Other special features of this program include random generation of test questions, creation of alternate versions of the same test, scrambling of question sequence, and test preview before printing. Available at www.pearsonmytest.com/irc (access code required).
- **Study Site.** A website is available to provide both students and instructors with additional resources. The site includes practice test questions, a syllabus builder, links to relevant sites on the Internet, and more. It can be accessed at **www.pearsontexasgovernment.com.**
- **MySearchLab with eText.** This interactive website features an eText that is identical in content and design to the printed text, access to the EBSCO ContentSelect database and multimedia, and step-by-step tutorials which offer complete overviews of the entire writing and research process. MySearchLab is designed to amplify a traditional course in numerous ways or to administer a course online. Additionally, MySearchLab offers chapter-specific content such as learning objectives, quizzes, media, and flashcards to enrich learning and help students succeed.

ACKNOWLEDGMENTS

Many persons contributed significantly to the writing and production of this book. Reid Hester, Emily Sauerhoff, and the other professionals at Pearson gave me sympathetic and professional help from the edition's beginning to its completion. I am also grateful to the scholars who reviewed the manuscript. Their comments proved invaluable in preparing the final text.

I am grateful to the government faculty at Houston Community College for their friendship and support. I have learned most of what I know about teaching from them. Thank you Ghassan Abdallah, Cecile (Cammy) Artiz, Evelyn Ballard, Max Beauregard, Harold "Hal" Comello, Dale Foster, Larry Gonzalez, Mark Hartray, Thomas Haymes, Edmund "Butch" Herod, Brenda Jones, Aaron Knight, Heidi Lange, Gary LeBlanc, Raymond Lew, Joe C. Martin, Vinette Meikle Harris, David Ngene, Carlos Pierott, Donna Rhea, John Speer, Jaye Ramsey Sutter, John Ben Sutter, R. Mark Tiller, Steven Tran, Linda Webb, and Celia Wintz.

Finally, I wish to dedicate this book to Anup Bodhe, Anderson Brandao, Jason Orr, Kim Galle, Hal Stockbridge, and Aaron Zambrano.

NEAL TANNAHILL
Houston Community College
neal.tannahill@hccs.edu

Introduction
The Policymaking Process

CHAPTER OUTLINE

The Stages of the Policymaking Process

    The Context of Policymaking

    Agenda Setting

    Policy Formulation

    Policy Adoption

    Policy Legitimation

    Policy Implementation

    Policy Evaluation

    Policy Change

The Dynamics of the Policy Process

    Policy Cycles

    Issue Networks

    Policymaking and Politics

Why Study Texas Government?

What We Have Learned

WHAT WE WILL LEARN

After studying the Introduction, you should be able to answer the following questions:

1. What are the stages of the policymaking process?

2. What are the political dynamics of the policymaking process?

3. Why is it important to study state and local government in Texas?

exas leads the nation in executions. Between 1977 and mid-2011, the state of Texas put to death 467 convicted murderers, more than any other state and more than a third of the total executions nationwide.[1] In May 2011, 304 men and 10 women awaited execution on death row at the Allan B. Polunsky Unit of the state prison system in Livingston.[2] Only California has more people on death row than Texas.[3]

Capital punishment The death penalty.

Capital punishment, the death penalty, is controversial. Death penalty advocates contend that a criminal who takes a life should pay for the crime with his or her own life. The death penalty protects law-abiding citizens by permanently removing violent criminals from society. The fear of the death penalty deters potential criminals from committing murder. Death penalty proponents believe that an execution enables the family members of a murder victim to reach closure and go on with their lives. In contrast, death penalty opponents call capital punishment a barbaric relic of the nineteenth century, pointing out that the United States is the only Western democracy that still uses the death penalty against criminal defendants. Instead of deterring crime, they say, the death penalty may increase the violent crime rate by cheapening the value of human life. The opponents of capital punishment also charge that it is biased because most of the persons who are sentenced to death and actually executed are poor, uneducated members of racial and ethnic minority groups.

THE STAGES OF THE POLICYMAKING PROCESS

Public policy What government officials choose to do or not to do about public problems.

Policymaking process A logical sequence of activities affecting the development of public policies.

The death penalty is an example of a **public policy**, which is what government officials choose to do or not to do about public problems. Texas and 33 other states have responded to the problem of violent crime by adopting the death penalty. No state carries out the policy more aggressively than Texas. The **policymaking process** is a logical sequence of activities affecting the development of public policies. A study of capital punishment in Texas from a policy perspective examines the context for making a policy to address the issue of violent crime. It considers how and why violent crime became an issue of public concern and the process through which the state formulated and adopted a policy on capital punishment. The study discusses the actions taken by public officials to ensure that the policy is perceived as legitimate. It examines the implementation of the death penalty, evaluates its effectiveness at reducing violent crime, and assesses its impact on the state. Finally, the study discusses policy change.

The Context of Policymaking

The policymaking process takes place within a cultural, socioeconomic, legal, and political context. The policymaking context is not one of the stages of the policymaking process; rather, it is the background in which the policymaking process takes place. It helps determine the problems that government attempts to solve, the set of policy alternatives that government decision-makers will be willing to consider, the resources available to government to address the problems, and the relative strength of the political forces involved in the policymaking process.[4]

The most important contextual factors influencing capital punishment in Texas are (1) the legal and constitutional setting, and (2) public attitudes toward violent crime and the death penalty. The state's death penalty statute must meet the constitutional standards set by federal and state courts. Because of the high stakes involved, defendants sentenced to death typically appeal their convictions through the state and federal court systems. Frequently, Texas has changed its capital punishment policy to conform to state and, especially, federal court rulings. The U.S. Supreme Court has ruled, for example, that the execution of persons who are mentally retarded violates the U.S. Constitution, forcing Texas to commute the sentences of several death row inmates.[5] The state's death penalty policy also reflects public opinion. Texas is the nation's death penalty leader because capital punishment is more popular in Texas than it is in most other states. According to public opinion polling data, 78 percent of Texans support the death penalty, compared with only 18 percent who oppose it. The rest are undecided.[6]

Agenda Setting

Agenda setting
The process through which issues become matters of public concern and government action.

Official policy agenda Those problems that government officials actively consider how to resolve.

Agenda setting is the process through which issues become matters of public concern and government action. Those problems that government officials actively consider how to resolve are part of the **official policy agenda.** Not all problems become the object of government action. In short, agenda setting is the process through which issues become part of the official policy agenda.

Capital punishment has been part of the official policy agenda in Texas for decades. More than 40 years ago, state policymakers rewrote the state's capital punishment law to satisfy the objections of the U.S. Supreme Court. In subsequent years, state officials have considered a broad range of death penalty issues, including streamlining the appeals process and providing post-conviction DNA analysis for death row inmates. In 2005, for example, the Texas legislature amended the state's death penalty statute to give juries the option of sentencing convicted capital murderers to either death or life in prison without the possibility of parole. The latter punishment replaced the option of life in prison with the possibility of parole after 40 years.

At any one time, the official policy agenda contains a relatively small number of major issues. In recent years, the official policy agenda for Texas state government has included the following issues:

- **Funding public education**—How can the state ensure that local school districts have adequate funding to provide a quality education to the state's school children and that the money is collected fairly?
- **Educational accountability**—How can taxpayers be sure that they are getting their money's worth for the school taxes they pay?
- **Property tax reform**—How can the state protect property owners from rapidly rising property taxes without undermining the ability of local governments to fund the essential services they provide?
- **Insurance reform**—What steps can the state take to ensure that Texas homeowners are able to purchase home insurance at affordable rates?

- **Water resources**—What steps should the state take to ensure that Texans continue to have an adequate supply of water?
- **Transportation**—What steps should state government take to address the state's transportation needs?
- **Electricity deregulation**—How can the state ensure that consumers will have an adequate supply of electricity at affordable rates?
- **Border security**—What actions can state government take to prevent the spread of organized criminal activity from Mexico into Texas?

As students of Texas government, we ask how each of these issues became part of the official policy agenda. Who raised each issue? What actions did individuals and groups take to get their issues addressed by government? Did other individuals and groups attempt to keep these issues off the official policy agenda? Why did the former succeed and the latter fail?

Agenda setting not only identifies problems for government attention but also defines the nature of the problems, and therefore the eventual direction of a policy solution. Capital punishment, for example, can be defined in different terms. Death penalty advocates prefer to focus on the seriousness of violent crime and the length of delay between a death sentence and its imposition. In contrast, the opponents of capital punishment emphasize racial disparities in sentencing, the risk of executing an innocent person, and the relative cost of capital punishment compared with the expense of life in prison without parole. Whether state government attempts to streamline the appeals process to make it easier to carry out the death penalty, adopts reforms to protect against bias, or even eliminates capital punishment altogether depends on the way the issue is defined.

 WHAT DO YOU THINK?

Do you support the death penalty? Why or why not?

Policy Formulation

Policy formulation
The development of strategies for dealing with the problems on the official policy agenda.

Policy formulation is the development of strategies for dealing with the problems on the official policy agenda. Once an issue becomes part of the official policy agenda, individuals and groups, both inside and outside of government, develop and propose approaches for addressing the problem. Defense attorneys, victims' rights organizations, legislators, prison officials, criminologists, prosecuting attorneys, civil rights activists, prison reformers, and the news media may all be involved in formulating policies affecting the death penalty.

Scholars who study public policymaking identify two models of policy formulation. The rational comprehensive model of policy formulation assumes that policymakers establish goals, identify policy alternatives, estimate the costs and benefits of the alternatives, and then select the policy alternative that produces the greatest net benefit. In contrast, the incremental model of policy formulation assumes that policymakers, working with imperfect information, continually adjust policies in pursuit of policy goals that are subject to periodic readjustment. Most political scientists believe that the rational comprehensive model is an unrealistic approach to policy formulation except when dealing with technical questions of limited scope. They believe that the incremental model of policy formulation more closely reflects the real world of public policymaking in which political actors disagree about policy goals, information about policy alternatives is imperfect, and resources to achieve goals are limited.

Consider the death penalty. Policymakers and other participants in the debate over the death penalty disagree about the goals of capital punishment and its effectiveness. Some participants in the policymaking process favor the death penalty in order to deter crime, whereas others seek to punish offenders. Still others hope to minimize the application of the death penalty or eliminate it altogether. They argue that life in prison without possibility of parole achieves societal goals without the state taking life.

Scholars also disagree about the effect of capital punishment on the murder rate and its impact on society. The nature of the death penalty makes it difficult, if not impossible, to assess its impact with precision. How do we place a value on the life of a convicted murderer or the murder victim? In practice, current death penalty policy reflects a compromise developed by policymakers with different personal values, working with imperfect information, and facing conflicting political pressures on an emotional issue.

Policy Adoption

Policy adoption
The official decision of a government body to accept a particular policy and put it into effect.

Policy adoption is the official decision of a government body to accept a particular policy and put it into effect. For example, the legislature passes and the governor signs a bill. The Texas Supreme Court issues a major ruling. A city council passes an ordinance. In practice, major government policies frequently reflect adoption decisions made at different points in time by different units of government. The legislature and the governor enacted the state's basic death penalty statute in 1973. They subsequently adopted amendments changing the method of execution from the electric chair to lethal injection, expanding the list of capital crimes, modifying appeals procedures, and providing juries with the sentencing option of life in prison without possibility of parole as an alternative to the death penalty.

Policy Legitimation

Policy legitimation
The actions taken by government officials and others to ensure that most citizens regard a policy as a legal and appropriate government response to a problem.

Policy legitimation refers to the actions taken by government officials and others to ensure that most citizens regard a policy as a legal and appropriate government response to a problem. In Texas, the governor, legislators, and judges defend capital punishment as an appropriate policy in light of the state's murder rate. They discuss the issue from the perspective of the victims of crime rather than the possibility that the state may have executed innocent persons. In contrast, critics of the death penalty point to a number of high-profile incidences of wrongful convictions. In 2010, for example, state officials ordered the release of Anthony Graves, who had spent 18 years in prison, including 14 years on death row, for a crime that prosecutors now admit that he did not commit.[7]

Policy Implementation

Policy implementation is the stage of the policy process in which policies are carried out. Implementation involves government officials as well as individuals and groups outside of the government. Numerous political actors participate in the implementation of the state's death penalty policy:

- District attorneys determine whether to ask for the death penalty in a particular capital murder case.
- Juries and judges decide whether to sentence a convicted defendant to death or life in prison without parole.
- State and federal judges hear appeals.
- Lawyers from the office of the attorney general represent the state in court during the appeals process.
- Private defense attorneys represent the defendant during the appeals process.
- The Board of Pardons and Paroles entertains requests for clemency.
- The governor may grant a 30-day reprieve on the execution of a death sentence and must concur with a decision of the Board of Pardons and Paroles to grant clemency.
- Officials in the Texas Department of Corrections carry out death sentences.

Implementation is an essential part of the policy process. Sometimes policymakers misjudge the nature of a problem or underestimate the resources needed for its solution. As a result, the policy may evolve far differently in operation than what its architects intended or expected. Consider the implementation of capital punishment in Texas. Because of the length of the appeals process, the average stay on death row in Texas is 10.6 years.[8] In 2011, the death row inmate with the longest tenure was Raymond Riles of Harris County, who was first sentenced to death in 1975.[9] The opponents of the death penalty argue that appeals are necessary to ensure that innocent people are not put to death. In contrast, critics charge that the current system is unfair to the relatives of murder victims and inhumane to people awaiting execution.

⟨?⟩ WHAT DO YOU THINK?

Do convicted murderers spend too much time on death row before their sentences are carried out?

The implementation of the state's capital punishment statute varies from county to county. Many small counties rarely, if ever, send anyone to death row because they cannot afford the expense of conducting a capital murder trial, which can cost the county $1.2 million in trial expenses alone, not including the cost of subsequent mandatory appeals. A non-death-penalty murder case typically costs county government less than $10,000.[10] The overwhelming majority of the state's death row inmates are from urban counties. Those counties have the most people and the most murders, of course, but county governments in urban areas also have the resources to pay the considerable costs of trials and appeals.

The national trend is toward fewer death sentences and fewer executions. Since 2000, the number of death sentences issued by juries nationwide has fallen in half, from 224 in 2000 to 112 in 2009. The decline in death sentences has been even more dramatic in Texas, down from 34 death sentences assessed in 2000 to only 8 in 2009.[11] Figure I.1 graphs the number of executions carried out nationally and in Texas from 2000 to 2010. Although the number of executions nationwide is in decline, Texas continues to carry out 18 to 26 executions a year, a rate that has held fairly steady since 2005.

Juries nationwide are giving fewer death sentences because of a decline in support for the death penalty. In the mid-1990s, national opinion surveys found that death penalty supporters outnumbered opponents by a lopsided margin of 80 percent to 16 percent. Although recent national polls indicate that capital punishment remains popular, the ratio of supporters to opponents is closer, 64 percent to 29 percent.[12] Some observers believe that public support for capital punishment has slipped because of publicity surrounding the release of prison inmates, including some on death row, after DNA testing proved their innocence.[13]

Texas juries are assessing the death penalty less frequently not because of public opinion, but because of the impact of the life-without-parole option and a reduction in the murder rate. Richard Dieter, the head of the Death Penalty Information Center, believes that life without parole gives Texas jurors a more attractive sentencing

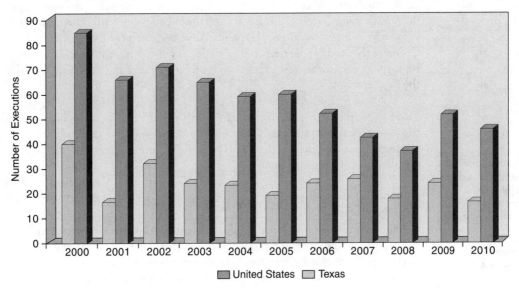

FIGURE I.1   Executions in the USA and Texas, 2000–2010.

option than life imprisonment. "When you present life without parole to juries," he says, "it lifts any confusion they might have about whether someone is ever going to walk the streets again."[14] Finally, the murder rate in Texas has declined, reducing the pool of potential death row inmates. According to the Texas Department of Public Safety, the number of murders committed in Texas fell from 2,149 in 1993 to 1,327 in 2009.[15]

Policy Evaluation

Policy evaluation
The assessment of policy.

Policy evaluation is the assessment of policy. It involves questions of equity, efficiency, effectiveness, and political feasibility. Equity is the concept that similarly situated people be treated the same. In other words, is the death penalty assessed in an even-handed fashion without regard to the gender, race, ethnicity, or financial status of the criminal and the victim? Research on capital murder cases held in Harris County between 1992 and 1999 finds that convicted capital murderers were six times more likely to get a death sentence when they killed married whites or Latinos with college degrees and no criminal records than when they murdered poorly educated unmarried African Americans with criminal records.[16]

Efficiency is a comparison of a policy's costs with the benefits it provides. Because of the cost of trials and appeals in death penalty cases, capital punishment is actually several times more expensive than imprisoning a criminal for 40 years or more. Nonetheless, the supporters of capital punishment believe that the costs of the legal process need to be balanced against the benefits of permanently eliminating a violent criminal from society.

Effectiveness is the extent to which a policy achieves its goals. Does the death penalty deter violent crime? Recent research on the death penalty in Texas concludes that the number of homicides committed in the state declines by 0.5 to 2.5 in the month immediately following an execution compared with other months. Consequently, as many as 60 people may be alive because of the Texas death penalty. Critics of the study argue that studies evaluating the deterrent effect of capital punishment are suspect because executions are relatively rare and many factors influence the murder rate.[17]

Political feasibility pertains to a policy's ability to obtain public support. The Texas legislature will never repeal the death penalty as long as public opinion in the state supports capital punishment as strongly as it does today. Furthermore, the interest groups that defend the death penalty are more influential than the groups opposed to capital punishment.

Empirical analysis
A method of study that relies on experience and scientific observation.

Normative analysis A method of study that is based on certain values.

Evaluation can be either empirical or normative. An **empirical analysis** is a method of study that relies on experience and scientific observation. Empirical research on capital punishment finds that Texas juries are no more likely to sentence convicted murderers to death than are juries in other states. Rather, Texas is the national capital punishment leader because it is a populous state with a relatively high murder rate and because state authorities are willing to carry out executions.[18] In contrast to an empirical study, a **normative analysis** is a method of study that is based on certain values. A normative analysis of the death penalty might consider the morality of the policy and the fairness of its implementation. It examines whether the death penalty is right or wrong, good or bad, fair or unfair.

Policy evaluation sometimes highlights the distinction between policy outputs and policy outcomes. Whereas **policy outputs** are actual government policies, **policy outcomes** are the situations that arise as a result of the impact of policy in operation. Consider the distinction between policy outputs and outcomes as far as capital punishment is concerned. Thirty-four states have capital punishment laws on the books, a policy output. In practice, however, many states seldom, if ever, carry out executions, a policy outcome. In 2010, only 12 states conducted executions.[19]

Policy outputs
Actual government policies.

Policy outcomes
The situations that arise as a result of the impact of policy in operation.

Policy change
The modification of policy goals and means in light of new information or shifting political environments.

Policy Change

Policy change refers to the modification of policy goals and means in light of new information or shifting political environments. Policy change is frequently the result of policy evaluation. Programs that are successful may no longer be needed; unsuccessful programs may be eliminated because of their failure. Partially successful programs or programs with unintended negative consequences may be modified in hopes of improving their operation. Texas juries, aware that numerous death sentences have recently been overturned based on new evidence, such as DNA testing, are choosing the life-in-prison-without-parole option rather than the death penalty.

THE DYNAMICS OF THE POLICY PROCESS

Policymaking is more complex than the policy process would suggest at initial glance.

Policy Cycles

Policy cycle The passage of an issue through the policy process from agenda setting through policy change.

The term **policy cycle** refers to the passage of an issue through the policy process from agenda setting through policy change. Issues do not always travel smoothly through the policy cycle, moving from one stage to the next. No clear lines of separation can be drawn among the stages of the policy process. For example, the stages of agenda setting and policy formulation sometimes overlap. For example, some religious leaders in Texas have called for a moratorium on executions in Texas to allow time to review death penalty convictions because they believe that the capital punishment process is seriously flawed. The religious leaders are attempting to both raise an issue (the danger that the state may execute an innocent person) and propose a solution (a moratorium on the implementation of the death penalty to allow time to review questionable convictions). Similarly, policy implementation often has an aspect of policy adoption to it, as agencies fill in the details of policies adopted by legislative bodies. Policy evaluation occurs throughout the policy process, not just at its end.

Not every issue completes the policy cycle. Issues may be raised to the official policy agenda and policies formulated but then forgotten as the attention of the general public and government officials turns to other, more pressing problems.

Sometimes public officials, interest group spokespersons, or individual citizens succeed in keeping an issue in the public eye until a policy solution is adopted and implemented. A triggering mechanism, such as a dramatic event, a news media report of a scandal, is often necessary to force a public policy response to an issue.

Finally, some issues, particularly major, controversial issues, such as the death penalty, travel through the policy process again and again over an extended period of time. The issue of capital punishment has arisen repeatedly because of court rulings, controversies over the guilt or innocence of particular death row inmates, public concern over crime rates, complaints about the length of time between sentencing and execution, and candidates using the issue to score political points during an election campaign. As long as the public remains deeply divided over capital punishment, the death penalty is likely to be a recurring item on the state's official policy agenda.

Issue Networks

Issue network A group of political actors that is concerned with some aspect of public policy.

The policymaking process involves a broad range of political actors, including government officials, the institutions of government, individual policy activists, political parties, the news media, and interest groups. Political scientists use the term **issue network** to describe a group of political actors that is concerned with some aspect of public policy. District attorneys, victim rights organizations, defense attorneys, organizations opposed to capital punishment, legislators concerned with criminal justice issues, state and federal judges, the governor, and the members of the Board of Pardons and Paroles constitute the issue network for capital punishment in Texas. Issue networks vary from issue to issue. Although not all participants in an issue network are equally influential, no one individual or group is usually able to dominate policymaking on the issue. Instead, policy reflects the result of conflict (and occasionally compromise) among the participants.

Policymaking and Politics

Politics The process that determines who will occupy the roles of leadership in government and how the power of government shall be exercised.

Politics is the process that determines who will occupy the roles of leadership in government and how the power of government will be exercised. Politics exists because individuals and groups have different interests and different views about public policy. For example, the decision of county government officials to widen and extend a road might please land developers who hope to build a shopping center alongside the road but displease area homeowners who do not want additional traffic in their neighborhoods. The developers and the homeowners would oppose each other on this issue because their interests clash. Individuals and groups may also disagree on policy questions because their values differ. Whereas some people believe that the death penalty is morally wrong, other individuals think that it is morally just.

Political actors compete to shape public policy in ways that conform to their interests and values. Individuals and groups attempt to push issues on which they want government action to the forefront of the official policy agenda while diverting attention from matters on which they prefer that the current policy remain unchanged.

Once an issue is part of the official policy agenda, political actors seek to influence the policy formulation process in ways that further their interests. Individuals and groups who support the policy work for its adoption, whereas those who oppose the policy try to defeat it. Even after a policy is adopted, individuals and groups work to shape public attitudes toward the policy during the legitimation stage. Conflict continues during implementation, with competing interests attempting to shape implementation in ways beneficial to them. Individuals and groups evaluate policies in accordance with their own perspectives, creating feedback designed to support the policy's continuance, encourage its revision, or urge its repeal. Policy change may or may not occur, depending on the relative political strength of the forces engaged.

WHY STUDY TEXAS GOVERNMENT?

Public opinion polls show that many Americans are cynical about government and uninterested in the way it works. Only a fourth of the public trusts the federal government to do what is right most of the time.[20] Many people question the relevance of government to their daily lives and express little interest in public affairs. College students often tell their professors that they have registered for a course in Texas government only because it is required. They frankly admit that they have little interest in the subject and doubt that they will learn anything beneficial. International students, in particular, question the value of a class in Texas government.

Nonetheless, Texas government is profoundly important to the lives of Texas residents, regardless of their ages, backgrounds, and careers. State and local government in Texas provides a broad range of essential services, including law enforcement, fire protection, education, highways, mass transportation, welfare, job training, parks, airports, water and sewage treatment, libraries, and public hospitals. Students attending public colleges and universities benefit directly from state-supported higher education. Everyone living in Texas needs to understand state and local laws and regulations concerning such matters as driver's licenses, automobile purchases, and renters' rights.

Laws and regulations adopted by state and local governments affect all Texans. Cities enact and enforce zoning ordinances, fire codes, and building codes to regulate land use and construction within city limits. Federal and state regulations affect air and water quality. The state criminal law governs many aspects of personal behavior. State agencies establish educational and technical requirements that must be fulfilled before individuals can engage in certain occupations and professions. College students take courses in Texas government because the Texas legislature requires that public college and university students complete six semester-hours in American national, state, and local government, including study of the Texas Constitution.

 **WHAT DO YOU THINK?**

Do you agree with the legislative requirement that college students must complete six semester hours in political science?

Texans pay for government through taxes and fees. State government and many local governments levy sales taxes on the retail purchase of a broad range of items. Property owners pay property taxes to municipalities, school districts, counties, and some other units of local government. Texans also pay fees to state and local governments in order to drive an automobile, operate a business, practice their profession, sell liquor, obtain a marriage license, and go hunting or fishing.

State and local government impacts not just individuals but society as a whole. In general, the actions of state and local governments affect the business climate in Texas, which in turn helps determine whether new companies relocate to the state and whether firms already here expand their operations. Education, healthcare, welfare assistance, good roads, public transportation, sanitation, recreation facilities, law enforcement, environmental regulations, and fire protection make the state a better place in which to live and work. Tax rates and the impact of individual taxes on different income groups affect the distribution of wealth in society and influence the state's economy.

Students benefit from courses in Texas government because they can learn not just how state and local governments affect their lives but also how they can influence public policy in the state. The essence of American democracy is that citizens govern themselves through their elected officials. Texans have the right (some would say *obligation*) not just to vote but also to communicate their policy preferences to their representatives. Government officials are responsive to the demands and requests of their constituents, especially officials at the state and local levels who work directly with individual citizens on a regular basis.

WHAT WE HAVE LEARNED

1. What are the stages of the policymaking process?

The policymaking process is a logical sequence of activities affecting the development of public policies. The policymaking process takes place within a context of factors, including the social, economic, political, and cultural contexts. It includes seven stages: agenda setting, policy formulation, policy adoption, policy legitimation, policy implementation, policy evaluation, and policy change.

2. What are the political dynamics of the policymaking process?

Policymaking is more complex than the policy process would suggest at initial glance. Policy cycles, issue networks, and politics all play a role in the process. The passage of an issue through the policy process from agenda setting through policy change is a policy cycle. The policymaking process involves a broad range of political actors, including government officials, the institutions of government, individual policy activists, political parties, the news media, and interest groups. Political scientists use the term *issue networks* to describe this phenomenon. The policymaking process also involves politics, which is the process that determines who will occupy the roles of leadership in government and how the power of government will be exercised.

3. Why is it important to study state and local government in Texas?

Texas government is profoundly important to the lives of Texas residents, regardless of their ages, backgrounds, and careers. State and local governments provide a wide range of services.

Laws and regulations adopted by state and local governments affect all Texans. Texans pay for government through taxes and fees. State and local government impacts not just individuals but society as a whole by affecting the business climate and the quality of life for people living in the state. Students benefit from courses in Texas government because they can learn not just how state and local governments affect their lives but also how they can influence public policy in the state.

KEY TERMS

agenda setting	policy adoption	policy legitimation
capital punishment	policy change	policy outcomes
empirical analysis	policy cycle	policy outputs
issue network	policy evaluation	policymaking process
normative analysis	policy formulation	politics
official policy agenda	policy implementation	public policy

NOTES

1. Death Penalty Information Center, "Executions by State," available at www.deathpenaltyinfo.org.
2. Texas Department of Criminal Justice, "Offenders on Death Row," available at www.tdcj.state.tx.us.
3. California Department of Corrections, available at www.cdcr.ca.gov.
4. Michael E. Craft and Scott R. Furlong, *Public Policy: Politics, Analysis, and Alternatives*, 3rd ed. (Washington, DC: CQ Press, 2010), pp. 10–15.
5. *Atkins v. Virginia*, 536 U.S. 304 (2002).
6. Jim Henson, "The Polling Center: Voter Empathy," *Texas Tribune*, February 23, 2010, available at www.texastribune.org.
7. Brian Rogers and Cindy George, "Prisoner Ordered Free from Texas' Death Row," *Houston Chronicle*, October 28, 2010, available at www.chron.com.
8. Texas Department of Criminal Justice, "Execution Statistics," available at www.tdcj.state.tx.us/stat/annual.htm.
9. Texas Department of Criminal Justice, "Offenders on Death Row," available at www.tdcj.state.tx.us/
10. Logan Carver, "Death Penalty Cases More Expensive than Lifetime Imprisonment, but Local CDA Says Cost Never a Consideration," *Lubbock Avalanche-Journal*, December 13, 2009, available at www.lubbockonline.com.
11. Death Penalty Information Center, "Death Sentences in the United States from 1977 by State and by Year," available at www.deathpenaltyinfo.org.
12. Frank Newport, "In U.S., 64% Support the Death Penalty in Cases of Murder," November 8, 2010, available at www.gallup.com.
13. Max B. Baker, "Texas Still Leads in Executions, but the Numbers Are Down Here and Across the Nation," *Fort Worth State Telegram*, December 11, 2008, available at www.star-telegram.com.
14. Quoted in John Moritz, "The Life Penalty," *Texas Observer*, November 28, 2008, p. 16.
15. Texas Department of Public Safety, "Crime in Texas Annual Report," various years, available at www.txdps.state.tx.
16. Peggy O'Hare, "Study Figures Odds of Killer Getting Death," *Houston Chronicle*, March 5, 2010, p. B5.
17. Michael Graczyk, "Texas Study: Death Penalty Deters Killers," *Houston Chronicle*, January 7, 2010, p. B2.
18. Adam Liptak, "Study Revises Texas's Standing as a Death Penalty Leader," *New York Times*, February 14, 2004, available at www.nytimes.com.
19. Death Penalty Information Center, available at www.deathpenaltyinfo.org.
20. "Trust the Federal Government, 1958–2008," *The ANES Guide to Public Opinion and Electoral Behavior*, available at www.electionstudies.org.

Chapter 1

The People, Economy, and Political Culture of Texas

CHAPTER OUTLINE

The People of Texas
    Population Size and Growth
    Population Diversity
    Population Distribution
    Religious Belief and Practice

The Texas Economy
    An Economy in Transition
    Wealth, Poverty, and Healthcare

Political Culture

What We Have Learned

WHAT WE WILL LEARN

After studying Chapter 1, you should be able to answer the following questions:

1. How is the population of Texas described in terms of size, diversity, distribution, and religious beliefs?

2. How does the economy of Texas compare with the economies of other states in terms of household income, poverty rates, and health insurance coverage?

3. How do political scientists describe the political culture of Texas?

The population of Texas is growing rapidly. Between 2000 and 2010, the state's population increased by 4.3 million people, from 20.8 million to 25.1 million, for a growth rate of 21 percent. Among the 50 states, only California, with a population of 37.3 million, is larger. Although some relatively small states (Nevada, Idaho, Arizona, and Utah) grew at a faster percentage pace than Texas, no other state came close to adding as many people. In fact, about a quarter of the nation's total population growth during the decade took place in Texas.[1]

Rapid population growth presents both opportunities and challenges for policymakers. On the one hand, population growth has led to greater representation for Texas in Congress, a bigger share of federal grant money, and an enlarged tax base. Because the U.S. Constitution bases each state's representation in the U.S. House of Representatives on its population, relatively rapid population growth in Texas translates into more representation in Congress. Texas gained four House seats after the 2010 Census, giving the state 36 seats in the U.S. House. Population growth also means an increase in federal financial aid because Congress bases funding for many grant programs on population. Furthermore, population growth has generally meant a larger tax base for state and local governments. With more consumers to buy products, sales tax receipts have risen. On the other hand, population growth also presents policy challenges. Rapid population growth has placed a considerable strain on public services in Texas. More people mean more automobiles on city streets and freeways, more garbage to be collected and disposed of, more children to be educated, and more subdivisions for local law enforcement agencies to police.

The discussion of population growth in Texas and its impact on state and local governments illustrates the importance of the demographic, economic, and cultural context of policymaking in Texas. The first section of this chapter profiles the people of Texas, considering the size of the state's population, population growth, population diversity, and the geographic distribution of the state's people. It also discusses the religious faith and practice of the people of the state. The second section of the chapter examines the state's economy, looking at economic trends, personal income, poverty, and health insurance coverage. The final section of the chapter addresses the subject of political culture.

The People of Texas

The population of Texas is one of the largest and most diverse of any state in the nation.

Population Size and Growth

Figure 1.1 traces the growth of Texas's population decade by decade from the 1970s through 2010 and compares the population growth rate of Texas with the growth rate for the United States as a whole. As the figure shows, the state's population expanded the most rapidly between 1970 and 1980, growing at an annual rate of 2.7 percent. Texas's population growth rate fell just below 2 percent a year in

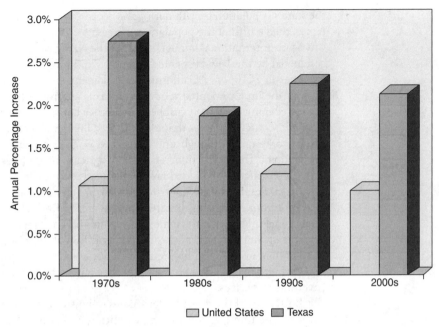

FIGURE 1.1   Average Annual Population Growth.

the 1980s before rebounding to grow at a rate of 2.3 percent a year in the 1990s. The growth rate between 2000 and 2010 was 2.1 percent. Throughout the period, the population of the **Lone Star State,** which is a nickname for Texas, increased more rapidly than did the population of the nation as a whole.

Both natural population increase and immigration contribute to population growth in Texas. **Natural population increase,** the extent to which live births exceed deaths, accounted for 55 percent of the state's population growth between 2000 and 2010.[2] Texas is tied with Alaska for the second highest birthrate in the nation, just behind Utah. In 2009, the Texas birthrate was 16.2 babies for every 1,000 people.[3] Because the state's population is relatively young (a median age of 33.6 compared with a national average of 37.2),[4] the proportion of women of childbearing age is relatively high. The state's ethnic composition also contributes to rapid population growth. The birthrate for Mexican American women, particularly recent immigrants, is more than 50 percent higher than the birthrates for Latino women who are not of Mexican origin and for women who are African American or white.[5] The relatively high birthrate for Hispanic Texans also reflects the average age for Latinos in the state, which is 27, compared with the average age of the state's white population, which is nearly 40, just past the prime childbearing years.[6]

The state's population also grows because of immigration. Between 2000 and 2010, Texas recorded a net gain of 1.9 million residents from international and domestic immigration combined. Domestic immigration accounted for a fourth of the state's population growth during the decade, whereas international immigration represented a fifth of the population increase.[7]

Many international immigrants enter the country illegally. According to a study conducted by the Pew Hispanic Center, 1.7 million undocumented residents lived in Texas in 2010; only California had a larger number of unauthorized residents. Most of the undocumented residents of Texas are from Mexico, with a majority of the rest coming from the Caribbean and other Latin American countries. The Pew Hispanic Center estimates that unauthorized immigrants constitute 9 percent of the Texas workforce. Although undocumented workers are employed in all sectors of the economy, the largest numbers work in agriculture, grounds keeping and maintenance, construction, and food preparation and serving.[8]

Illegal immigration is controversial. Critics charge that undocumented workers take jobs from American citizens while overcrowding schools and hospital emergency rooms. They add to traffic congestion and contribute to the crime problem. In contrast, immigration advocates contend that the United States benefits from immigration, even illegal immigration. They argue that undocumented workers fill jobs that citizens do not want and that they pay more in taxes than they receive in government services.

Both sides of the debate offer studies to bolster their position on illegal immigration. The Immigration Reform Coalition of Texas, a group opposed to illegal immigration, has published a report concluding that unauthorized immigrants cost the state $4.5 billion to $5 billion a year, mostly to educate their children and pay for their healthcare.[9] In contrast, Americans for Immigration Reform, an organization formed by business interests that benefit from immigration, released a study estimating that the mass deportation of undocumented workers from Texas would cost the state's economy more than $220 million a year along with 1.1 million jobs.[10]

The Texas Comptroller of Public Accounts, meanwhile, has published a relatively balanced report assessing both the costs and benefits of illegal immigration in Texas. On one hand, the report finds that undocumented workers add to the state's economy and pay more money in state taxes than they receive in services. Illegal immigrant workers and their families boost the Texas economy by $17.7 billion a year through their purchases of goods and services. They also pay more taxes to state government than they receive in state services—$1.58 billion in sales, excise, and motor vehicle taxes paid compared with $1.16 billion in state services for education, healthcare, emergency medical services, and incarceration. On the other hand, illegal immigrants are a drain on local governments because of the expense to local governments to provide healthcare services and law enforcement. The report found that illegal immigrants pay $513 million a year in local sales and property taxes while receiving $1.44 billion in local services.[11]

Because of immigration, Texas has a large and diverse foreign-born population. The four million foreign-born residents in Texas make up 16 percent of the state's population. The foreign-born population of Texas is younger, poorer, and less well educated than are the state's native-born residents. Most of the state's foreign-born residents are not American citizens.[12]

Half of the public school students in the state of Texas are Latino.

Population Diversity

The population of Texas is quite diverse. In fact, more than half of Texans (55 percent) are members of racial and ethnic minority groups. According to the 2010 Census, the population of Texas is 45 percent white (not Hispanic), 38 percent Latino, 12 percent African American, 4 percent Asian American, and 1 percent other.[13] Although most Latino residents of Texas are Mexican American, the state's Hispanic population includes significant numbers of people who trace their ancestries to Cuba, El Salvador, or other Latin American countries. Similarly, the state's Asian population includes, from largest to smallest in terms of population, Asian Indians, Chinese, Filipino, Korean, and Vietnamese Americans.[14]

Almost all of the population growth of Texas between 2000 and 2010 came in the state's minority communities. The Latino population increased by 42 percent during the decade, the African American population grew by 24 percent, and the size of the state's Asian community increased by 72 percent. In contrast, the white population increased by only 4 percent.[15] The minority population grew more rapidly than the white population because it is younger and has higher birthrates. Most immigrants to the state are minority group members as well.

Texas's ethnic communities are distributed unevenly across the state. Most African Americans live in the rural areas and small towns of East Texas, along the Gulf Coast, and in metropolitan areas. Houston and Dallas are home to a third of the state's African American population. Although Latinos live in every part of the

AROUND THE NATION

Immigration Reform in Arizona

Arizona has enacted the nation's strictest and most controversial immigration law. The purpose of the measure is to identify, prosecute, and deport illegal immigrants. The law makes failure to carry immigration papers a crime for noncitizens and it empowers the police to stop individuals if an officer has a "reasonable suspicion" that the person may be undocumented.

The Arizona law grew out of frustration with the failure of the federal government effectively to address the issue of illegal immigration. Arizona is a border state with Mexico and has become a gateway for illegal immigration and an avenue for narcotics smuggling. Many Arizonans worry that the drug violence south of the border may spill into their state.

The Arizona immigration measure unleashed a firestorm of controversy. President Barack Obama suggested that it was irresponsible, and some opponents demanded that conventions boycott Arizona.[*] Critics declared that the law was an invitation for **racial profiling,** which is the practice of a police officer targeting individuals as suspected criminals on the basis of their race or ethnicity. Furthermore, they say, the law will undermine law enforcement in the state. Police will be distracted from their real work of fighting violent crime and undocumented immigrants will no longer feel comfortable reporting crimes or cooperating with police.[†]

The defenders of the law believe that it is a reasonable effort to address a serious problem. They note that the requirement that noncitizens carry their immigration papers mirrors federal law. The police cannot stop people because of the color of their skin or their accent, because Arizona Governor Jan Brewer has signed an executive order making it illegal to consider race and ethnicity in the measure's enforcement.[‡]

Most of the provisions of the Arizona law have yet to go into effect because of a legal challenge filed by the federal government. The lawsuit argues that the Arizona statute violates U.S. law that gives the federal government exclusive authority to regulate immigration. A federal judge blocked enforcement of the law until the legal challenge could be heard by the courts. Most legal observers believe that the U.S. Supreme Court will eventually rule on the matter.[§]

The legal challenge to Arizona's immigration suit has not prevented other states from adopting their own immigration measures, and some states have taken an even more aggressive approach. Alabama, for example, bars illegal immigrants from enrolling in any public college after high school. The Alabama measure also makes it a crime to rent to illegal immigrants.[**]

QUESTIONS

1. If the courts allow Arizona and other states to enforce their immigration laws, do you think large numbers of undocumented workers and their families will leave the country?
2. What are the advantages and disadvantages of individual states having their own immigration policies?
3. If you were a member of the Texas legislature, would you vote for or against an Arizona-style law? What is the reasoning behind your answer?

---

[*] Randal C. Archibald, "Arizona Enacts Stringent Law on Immigration," *New York Times*, April 23, 2010, available at www.nytimes.com.

[†] Jim Wallis, "Arizona's Immigration Bill Is a Social and Racial Sin," *Huffington Post*, April 21, 2010, available at www.huffingtonpost.com.

[‡] Kirk Adams, "The Truth Behind Arizona's Immigration Law," *Washington Post*, May 28, 2010, available at www.washingtonpost.com.

[§] Paul Davenport, "Arizona Wants Speedy Ruling on Immigration Law," May 10, 2011, available at www.news.yahoo.com.

[**] Julia Preston, "In Alabama, a Harsh Bill for Residents Here Illegally," *New York Times*, June 3, 2011, available at www.nytimes.com.

Racial profiling
The practice of
a police officer
targeting individuals
as suspected criminals
on the basis of their
race or ethnicity.

state, they are more numerous in South Texas and West Texas, especially along the Mexican border. San Antonio, El Paso, Corpus Christi, Brownsville, McAllen, and Laredo all have Hispanic majorities.[16] Asians are clustered in the Gulf Coast region, whereas many Texans of German and Czech descent live in the Hill Country in Central Texas. More than 90 percent of the state's foreign-born residents, regardless of racial/ethnic origin, live in metropolitan areas.[17]

The average age of the state's population varies by region and the type of community. Areas with a large Latino population tend to be younger than areas where the population is mostly white. In some parts of South Texas, the average age is less than 30. Urban centers tend to be relatively young as well. For example, the average age in Harris County is 32.2, more than a year less than the average age statewide. In contrast, the population of the Hill Country (in Central Texas), Panhandle, and West Texas (except for El Paso) is relatively old.[18]

Population Distribution

The population of Texas is not evenly distributed across the state. The most populous regions are Central, South, North, and East Texas and the Gulf Coast region. Between 2000 and 2010, 37 of the state's 254 counties clustered around Houston, Dallas-Fort Worth, the Hill Country, and the Rio Grande Valley grew between 20 and 82 percent. In contrast, 79 counties, mostly in West Texas, lost population during the decade.[19]

Texas is an urban state, with 85 percent of its population living in metropolitan areas. Table 1.1 identifies the largest cities in the state, showing their population in 2010 and their rate of population growth since the 2000 Census. Three Texas cities—Houston, San Antonio, and Dallas—are among the 10 largest cities in the United States. Houston is the fourth largest, San Antonio the seventh, and Dallas the ninth. Many Texas cities are also growing rapidly. As Table 1.1 shows, San Antonio, Austin, Fort Worth, El Paso, Corpus Christi, and Plano grew by 10 percent or more between 2000 and 2010.

TABLE 1.1   Population and Growth Rates for Texas Cities

City	2010 Population	Percentage Increase between 2000 and 2010 Censuses
Houston	2,099,000	7.5 %
San Antonio	1,327,000	16.0
Dallas	1,198,000	0.8
Austin	790,000	20.4
Fort Worth	741,000	38.6
El Paso	649,000	15.2
Arlington	365,000	9.8
Corpus Christi	305,000	10.0
Plano	260,000	17.0
Laredo	236,000	33.7

Source: U.S. Census Bureau, available at www.census.gov.

Much of the growth in metropolitan areas has taken place in the suburbs rather than the inner cities. In the Dallas-Fort Worth area, Collin and Denton counties grew by more than 50 percent between 2000 and 2010. Rockwell County increased by 81 percent. In the Houston area, Montgomery County grew by more than 60 percent; Fort Bend increased by more than 50 percent.[20]

 WHAT DO YOU THINK?

By law everyone who graduates from a public high school in Texas is charged in-state tuition, whether they are in the United States legally or not. Do you agree with this policy? Why or why not?

Religious Belief and Practice

Texans are more religious than people in the nation as a whole. According to the U.S. Religious Landscape Survey conducted by the Pew Forum on Religion & Public Life, the state's residents are more likely to say that religion is important in their lives and to participate in religious activities than are Americans as a whole. Considering the following data:

- 77 percent of Texans are "absolutely certain" of their belief in God compared with a national figure of 71 percent;
- 67 percent of Texans say that religion is "very important" in their lives compared with a national figure of 56 percent;
- 47 percent of Texans attend religious services at least once a week compared with a national figure of 39 percent; and
- 66 percent of Texans indicate that they pray at least once a day compared with a national figure of 58 percent.

In terms of religious affiliation, evangelical Protestants (Southern Baptists, Assemblies of God, etc.) are more numerous in Texas than they are nationally, 34 percent in Texas compared with 26 percent in the nation as a whole. Mainline Protestants (Presbyterians, Methodists, Episcopalians, etc.) are less numerous, 15 percent in Texas versus 18 percent nationally. At 24 percent, the presence of Catholics in Texas is the same as their presence nationwide. Finally, fewer Texans (12 percent) are religiously unaffiliated than are people in the nation as a whole (16 percent).[21]

THE TEXAS ECONOMY

The Texas economy is a key part of the policymaking context.

An Economy in Transition

For most of Texas's history, the state's economy was based on the sale of agricultural commodities and raw materials. In the nineteenth century, cotton and cattle formed the basis of economic activity. Unfortunately for the state, neither product provided the necessary foundation for a manufacturing boom. Texas exported most of its ginned cotton for clothing production to other states or countries. Meanwhile, cattle ranchers drove their herds to railheads in Kansas for shipment to stockyards in the Midwest.

In 1901, oil was discovered at Spindletop near Beaumont. Subsequently, oil and gas deposits were found throughout the state and Texas became the nation's leading producer of oil and gas. In contrast to other commodities, oil spawned huge processing industries, including pipelines and refineries. The growth of petroleum-related businesses helped move the majority of Texans into urban areas by the 1950s.

Having an economy built on agriculture and oil had a major impact on the state's development. In the nineteenth century, Texas's economic health depended on the prices of cotton and cattle. For much of the twentieth century, the state's economy rose and fell in line with oil prices. Because commodity prices tend to fluctuate widely, Texas's economic history was one of booms and busts as prices for Texas products soared or collapsed. The state's economy boomed in the 1970s and early 1980s, for example, as oil prices rose to around $40 a barrel. The economy sagged in the mid-1980s as the price of oil dipped to less than half its earlier level.

The nature of the state's economy has contributed to a relatively lopsided distribution of income. Even though Texas has been a rich state, most Texans have not

East Texas oil fields in 1903.

been wealthy. Although agriculture and oil were sources of significant wealth for the state's major landowners and big oil producers, more Texans were farm workers and oil-field roughnecks than large landowners or oil producers. Workers in these industries historically were poorly organized and poorly paid, at least in comparison with workers in the auto assembly plants or steel mills of the northern states. Because people employed in industrial plants work together in close proximity, it is easier for them to organize and form unions to demand higher wages and better working conditions than it is for farm workers and oil-field roughnecks who are dispersed, working outdoors.

The Texas economy is changing. As Figure 1.2 demonstrates, Texas oil production fell steadily for years before recently trending upward because of improved production techniques and the incentive of high prices. Natural gas production has risen as well after a long period of decline. Despite the recent production increases, oil and gas tax revenues play a less important role in the state's financial picture than before. Since the early 1970s, the proportion of state revenues generated by oil and gas production taxes has declined from more than 20 percent to just over 7 percent in 2011.[22]

The Texas economy is more diverse than ever before. Although agriculture and energy are still important features of the state's economic picture, other industries play a major role, including aeronautics, defense, computer technology, healthcare, communication, insurance, entertainment, and tourism. The largest companies headquartered in Texas (as measured by annual revenue) are Exxon Mobil, ConocoPhillips, AT&T, Valero Energy, Marathon Oil, Dell, Sysco, Enterprise Products Partners, Plains All American Pipeline, and AMR.[23]

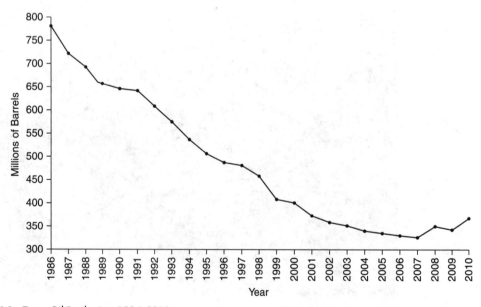

FIGURE 1.2 Texas Oil Production, 1986–2010.

High-technology industries Industries based on the latest in modern technology, such as telecommunications and robotics.

Minimum wage The lowest hourly wage that an employer can pay covered workers.

The economic changes that are taking place in the state affect the Texas workforce. The most rapidly growing components of the state's economy involve health-care and **high-technology industries,** those industries based on the latest in modern technology, such as telecommunications and robotics. These fields employ workers with technical knowledge and a capacity to learn new skills as technology changes. Texans who meet these criteria have a bright economic future. In 2011, medical professionals, lawyers, geoscientists, business managers, engineers, computer scientists, and some college faculty in Texas enjoyed annual salaries in excess of $100,000.[24] In contrast, unskilled workers were lucky to find jobs that paid much more than **minimum wage,** which is the lowest hourly wage that an employer can pay covered workers. Texas is tied with Mississippi for the highest percentage of workers earning minimum wage—9.5 percent of hourly workers. The median wage for hourly workers in Texas is $11.20 compared with $12.50 nationally.[25]

BREAKING NEWS!

Texas Oil Production Is on the Rise

After decades of decline, oil production in Texas has begun to increase. In 2010, 158,451 oil wells pumped 357 million barrels of oil. Not since 2003 have so many wells produced so much oil in the state of Texas. Moreover, petroleum geologists now estimate that the state has 5.5 million barrels of crude oil reserves, the highest estimate since 1997.*

Discussion

Does the increased production reflect the discovery of new oil fields in Texas? Yes and no. New production is coming from shale formations, especially the 400-mile long Eagle Ford shale formation that runs from South Texas near Laredo to East Texas. Geologists have known about shale oil for a long time, but only recently have technological breakthroughs and high energy prices made shale oil production both feasible and profitable.† Production is also rising in some old fields in West Texas, including some that have been in operation since the 1920s. Conventional methods of oil production typically produce only a fraction of a field's oil. Secondary methods substantially increase output, but still leave a good deal of oil behind. The latest production surge is the result of enhanced recovery methods, including the injection of large quantities of carbon dioxide, steam, and other chemicals into the field.‡

Why is all of this happening now? Production is rising because of new technologies and energy prices hovering around $100 a barrel. High oil prices give energy companies an incentive to re-develop old fields and exploit shale oil. Technological advances make the development possible.

Is Texas heading for a new energy boom? Shale oil development has the potential to be huge. Manuj Nikhanj, the vice president of Ross Smith Energy Group of Calgary, Alberta, Canada, is optimistic: "You could eventually see 20,000 to 30,000 wells drilled in the play. You could have more than 10 billion barrels of oil through time."**

How would that affect the state's economy? It would mean faster economic growth, with thousands of new jobs. It would also mean increased tax revenue for state and local government.

---

* Texas Railroad Commission, "Oil Production and Well Counts, 1935–2010," available at www.rrc.state.tx.us.

† Vicki Vaughan, "Eagle Ford's Calling Card: Help Wanted," *Houston Chronicle*, May 22, 2011, available at www.chron.com.

‡ Brett Clanton, "Coaxing Along a Geriatric Field," *Houston Chronicle*, June 26, 2011, pp. D1, D3.

** Quoted in Vaughan, "Eagle Ford's Calling Card."

Texas is a low-wage state because its people are poorly educated. More than 10 percent of Texans age 25 and older have less than a ninth-grade education compared with 6 percent nationwide. Only 26 percent of the state's adults are high school graduates; the national figure is 29 percent. Meanwhile, the college graduation rate in Texas is 25 percent compared with a 29 percent figure nationwide.[26]

Wealth, Poverty, and Healthcare

Gross state product (GSP)
The total value of goods and services produced in a state in a year.

Texas is a big state with a big economy. In 2010, the Texas **gross state product (GSP)**, which is the total value of goods and services produced in a state in a year, stood at $1.3 trillion.[27] Only California had a larger state economy than Texas.[28] If Texas were an independent nation, it would have the 15th biggest economy in the world.[29]

Recession An economic slowdown characterized by declining economic output and rising unemployment.

The Texas economy has been growing at a more rapid pace than the national economy. Figure 1.3 compares the annual growth rate of the Texas economy with the rate of economic growth for the entire nation from 2000 through 2010. As the figure indicates, the economic growth rate in Texas exceeded the national growth rate in 8 of the 11 years shown. In particular, the recession of 2008 and 2009 was less severe in Texas than in the nation as a whole. A **recession** is

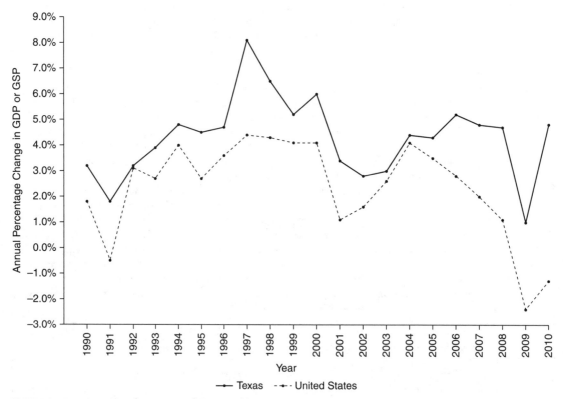

FIGURE 1.3 Economic Growth Rate, United States and Texas.

an economic slowdown characterized by declining economic output and rising unemployment.

Nonetheless, Texas is a relatively poor state, at least in terms of individual and family income. The median annual household income in Texas in 2010 was $47,445 compared with a national figure of $49,445. Texas ranked 29th among the 50 states. The states with the highest levels of household income were Massachusetts, Connecticut, and Maryland. In contrast, Mississippi, Arkansas, and Tennessee had the lowest income levels.[30]

Household income varies with race and ethnicity. The median income for white families nationwide in 2010 was $54,620 compared with $37,759 for Latino households, $32,068 for African American households, and $64,308 for Asian households.[31] Professor Stephen Klineberg, a Rice University sociologist, attributes the income disparity among ethnic and racial groups to a historic lack of access to quality education for African Americans and Latinos compared with whites and Asian Americans. Because the economy is changing, relatively few high-paying jobs are now available for people with weak job skills. "The good jobs that used to pay good money for unskilled or semi-skilled work are much harder to find these days," he explains.[32]

The income differential among the rich, the poor, and those in the middle in Texas is relatively large. According to a report jointly published by the Center on Budget and Policy Priorities and the Economic Policy Institute, the top one-fifth of Texas families has an annual income of $118,971, whereas the middle one-fifth of Texas families earns $41,015 a year. The average annual income for the bottom one-fifth of families is $14,724. The income gap between the top and the middle is greater in Texas than in any other state, whereas the gap between the top and the bottom is second only to that in the state of New York.[33] Analysts attribute the income gap to Texas having a large population of poorly educated people, including many immigrants from Mexico, who are unable to find good-paying jobs.[34]

 WHAT DO YOU THINK?

Should the government adopt policies designed to narrow the wealth and income gaps between the poorest and wealthiest segments of the population?

Poverty line The amount of money an individual or family needs to purchase basic necessities, such as food, clothing, healthcare, shelter, and transportation.

The poverty rate is relatively high in Texas. The government measures poverty on the basis of subsistence. By the official government definition, the **poverty line** is the amount of money an individual or a family needs to purchase basic necessities, such as food, clothing, healthcare, shelter, and transportation. The actual dollar amount varies with family size and rises with inflation. In 2011, the poverty line stood at $22,350 for a family of four.[35] The poverty rate in Texas in 2010 was 18.4 percent compared with a rate of 15.1 percent for the United States as a whole. Texas had the seventh highest poverty rate among the 50 states. Whereas Connecticut, Wyoming, and Wisconsin have the lowest poverty rate in the nation, Mississippi and Louisiana have the worst.[36]

Poverty is concentrated among racial minorities, single-parent families headed by women, and the very young. In 2010, the national poverty rate for whites was 9.9 percent compared with 27.4 percent for African Americans, 26.6 percent for Latinos, and 12.1 percent for Asians and Pacific Islanders. In addition, 22 percent of the nation's children under age 18 lived in poor families, whereas 31.6 percent of families headed by women with no husband present earned incomes below the poverty line.[37]

Texas has the highest percentage of residents without health insurance in the nation. Nearly 24.6 percent of Texas adults lack health insurance coverage compared with a national average of 16.3 percent. The states with the fewest people without health insurance coverage are Massachusetts, Hawaii, and Maine. The states that join Texas with the largest percentage of uninsured residents are New Mexico, South Carolina, Nevada, and Mississippi.[38] Texas also trails the national average in the percentage of children without health insurance coverage, 15.4 percent in Texas compared with a national average of 9.8 percent.[39] Most Texans without insurance are employed in low-wage jobs that do not provide health coverage. They and their families must do without health-care, pay for health services out of pocket, or go to hospital emergency rooms. A recent study finds that Texas leads the nation in the percentage of residents who avoid physicians because they cannot afford care. The state is in the bottom tier of states in preventive care for diabetics and dental checkups.[40] Texas has the second lowest percentage of immunized children, 75 percent, just above Nevada, which has an immunization rate of 71 percent.[41] It also has the third highest teen birthrate in the nation, behind Mississippi and New Mexico. The teen birthrate in Texas is 64 births for every 1,000 teenage girls compared with a national teen birthrate of 43 per 1,000.[42] Moreover, 23 percent of teen mothers in Texas are giving birth to their second, third, or even fourth child, giving the state the highest percentage of repeat teenage mothers in the nation.[43]

These sorts of data on health insurance, poverty rates, and income distribution trigger lively policy debates. Some policy analysts believe that the government should adopt policies designed to improve the lives of ordinary Texans. They favor government-sponsored health insurance programs, increased spending for education, and legislation to raise the state minimum wage. In contrast, other policy analysts argue that government programs hurt poor families by damaging the economy and thus limiting job growth. The best way to improve conditions for low- and middle-income people, they say, is to allow the market to work.

The state's high teen birthrate has sparked debate about sex education in the state. A number of observers believe that the high teenage birthrate is an indication that the state's abstinence-only approach to sex education is a failure. School districts in Texas are not required to teach sex education at all; however, if they do, they must present abstinence as the preferred choice for unmarried persons of school age. If a school district chooses to teach about contraception, it must allow parents to remove their children from the class and it must teach that contraception methods have failure rates. Critics of the state's sex education policy favor a balanced approach that combines information about contraception with an emphasis on abstinence. They believe that students need to know about birth control because abstinence-only is not a realistic approach for everyone. They point to research indicating that Texas teenagers are more likely to have sex and less likely to use condoms than their counterparts in states with comprehensive sex education programs.[44] In contrast, the defenders of the state's sex education policy stress that abstinence is the only foolproof way to prevent pregnancy. They oppose teaching youngsters about contraception because they do not want to give the impression that the state condones premarital sex. The Texas legislature apparently agrees with the proponents of abstinence-based sex education, and consistently defeats legislative efforts to require Texas public schools to include information about contraception in their sex education curricula.[45]

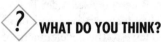 **WHAT DO YOU THINK?**

Is abstinence-only education the correct approach in Texas?

POLITICAL CULTURE

Political culture
The widely held, deeply rooted political values of a society.

Individualistic political culture
An approach to government and politics that emphasizes private initiative with a minimum of government interference.

Moralistic political culture
An approach to government and politics in which people expect government to intervene in the social and economic affairs of the state, promoting the public welfare and advancing the public good.

Political culture refers to the widely held, deeply rooted political values of a society. Professor Daniel Elazar identifies three strains of political culture found in the United States: individualistic, moralistic, and traditionalistic.[46] The **individualistic political culture** is an approach to government and politics that emphasizes private initiative with a minimum of government interference. This political culture stresses the importance of the individual and private enterprise. In this view of society, the role of government should be limited to protecting individual rights and ensuring that social and political relationships are based on merit rather than tradition, family ties, or personal connections. Elazar says that individualistic political culture developed from the eighteenth- and nineteenth-century business centers in New York, Philadelphia, and Baltimore and spread westward through the central part of the nation. Immigrants from areas dominated by the individualistic political culture settled in the northern and central parts of Texas in the mid-nineteenth century.

The **moralistic political culture** is an approach to government and politics in which people expect government to intervene in the social and economic affairs of the state, promoting the public welfare and advancing the public good. Participation in political affairs is regarded as one's civic duty. Elazar says the moralistic political culture developed from Puritanism (a religious reform movement) and New England town meetings and spread westward through the northern part of the nation and down the West Coast. Texas has received relatively little immigration from areas where the moralistic political culture was important.

The **traditionalistic political culture** is an approach to government and politics that sees the role of government as the preservation of tradition and the existing social order. Government leadership is in the hands of a social elite, and the level of participation by ordinary citizens in the policymaking process is relatively low. The government's role is to protect and preserve the existing social order. Elazar says that the traditional form of political culture developed from the plantation society of the South and spread westward through the southern states. Many immigrants from areas where the traditionalistic political culture was strong settled in East Texas.

Traditionalistic political culture
An approach to government and politics that sees the role of government as the preservation of tradition and the existing social order.

Civic culture A political culture that is conducive to the development of an efficient, effective government that meets the needs of its citizens in a timely and professional manner.

Elazar believes that the political culture of Texas is a hybrid, including both traditionalistic and individualistic elements, and he identifies some aspects of state politics that reflect these two strains of political culture. Texas's traditionalistic political culture, Elazar says, is represented in the state's long history as a one-party state, low levels of voter turnout, and social and economic conservatism. Elazar identifies the state's strong support for private business, opposition to big government, and faith in individual initiative as reflections of Texas's individualistic political culture.

Political scientists Tom W. Rice and Alexander F. Sundberg take a different approach to political culture. They focus on the concept of **civic culture,** which is a political culture that is conducive to the development of an efficient, effective government that meets the needs of its citizens in a timely and professional manner. States with a civic culture have innovative and effective governments, they say, whereas states without a strong civil culture have governments that are less responsive to citizen demands.

Rice and Sundberg identify four elements of a civic culture:

- **Civic engagement:** Citizens participate in the policymaking process in order to promote the public good.
- **Political equality:** Citizens view each other as political equals with the same rights and obligations.
- **Solidarity, trust, and tolerance:** Citizens feel a strong sense of fellowship with one another, tolerating a wide range of ideas and lifestyles.
- **Social structure of cooperation:** Citizens are joiners, belonging to a rich array of groups, from recreational sports teams to religious organizations.

Texas is forty-third among the 50 states in its level of civic culture. Rice and Sundberg found that most of the civic states are located in the north, running from New England to the Northwest. In contrast, most southern states are low in civic culture.[47]

Political culture is a useful concept for students of public policy because it leads them to focus on a state's history and development as important factors

GETTING INVOLVED
Volunteering

Everyone should do volunteer work, especially college students. Volunteering is a way to give back to the community for the kindness of others. People who volunteer develop an attachment to their community by learning about the problems in their area and helping solve them. Furthermore, volunteer work is a rewarding experience.

Your community has many fine organizations that welcome volunteers, including hospitals, schools, nursing homes, and animal shelters. Your college may have a service-learning program that matches volunteers with organizations needing help. Contact the organization of your choice and find out the procedures for volunteering. Even if you are able to put in only a few hours between semesters or on an occasional weekend, you will benefit from the experience.

It's your community—get involved!

influencing politics and policy. Scholars who study the American states recognize variations in political behavior and beliefs among different regions of the country that can be explained on the basis of political culture. The concepts developed by Elazar and the team of Rice and Sundberg are useful tools for understanding policy differences among states that cannot be explained simply on the basis of socioeconomic factors.

WHAT WE HAVE LEARNED

1. How is the population of Texas described in terms of size, diversity, distribution, and religious belief?

Texas is the second most populous state in the nation, behind California. It is also one of the fastest growing states. Both natural population increase and immigration, legal and illegal, fuel the state's population growth. The population of Texas is quite diverse, with no one racial/ethnic group in the majority. The state's minority populations accounted for almost all of the population growth between 2000 and 2010. The suburban counties of the state's big cities and the Rio Grande Valley are areas of strong population growth, but the Panhandle and most of West Texas are growing slowly or even losing population. Texans are more religious than people in the nation as a whole.

2. How does the economy of Texas compare with the economies of other states in terms of household income, poverty rates, and health insurance coverage?

Historically, the Texas economy has been based on the sale of agricultural commodities and raw materials. Cotton and cattle were king in the nineteenth century; oil and gas in the twentieth century. Fluctuating commodity prices meant the Texas economy alternated between boom and bust. The nature of the state's economy has contributed to a relatively lopsided distribution of income. Today, the most rapidly growing segments of the economy are healthcare and high-tech industry. Although the Texas economy generally grows at a faster pace than the national economy, Texas is a relatively poor state with a median household income below the national average. Hourly wage rates lag behind the national average. African Americans and Latinos have lower average incomes and higher poverty rates than do whites and Asians. The income differential among the rich, the poor, and those in the middle in Texas is relatively large. Texas also has the highest percentage of residents without health insurance in the nation. Texas's status as a relatively poor state with incomes and healthcare coverage below the national average can be attributed to low levels of educational attainment among the state's population.

3. How do political scientists describe the political culture of Texas?

Political culture refers to the widely held, deeply rooted political values of a society. Professor Elazar identifies three strains of political culture found in the United States: individualistic, moralistic, and traditionalistic. He believes that the political culture of Texas is a hybrid, including both traditionalistic and individualistic elements. Political scientists Rice and Sundberg focus on the concept of civic culture, a political culture that is conducive to the development of an efficient, effective government that meets the needs of its citizens in a timely and professional manner. Texas is 43rd among the 50 states in its level of civic culture.

KEY TERMS

civic culture

Gross state product (GSP)

high-technology industries

individualistic political culture

Lone Star State

minimum wage

moralistic political culture

natural population increase

political culture

poverty line

racial profiling

recession

traditionalistic political culture

NOTES

1. U.S. Census Bureau, "2010 Census Demographic Profiles," available at http://2010.census.gov.
2. Jeannie Kever and R.G. Ratcliffe, "Texas Snares 4 House Seats," *Houston Chronicle*, December 22, 2010, pp. A1, A5.
3. National Center for Health Statistics, "Births, by Race and Hispanic Origin of Mother, and Birth and Fertility Rates: United States, Each State and Territory, Preliminary 2009," National Vital Statistics Reports, available at www.cdc.gov.
4. Jeannie Kever, "Census Shows Ever-Changing Face of Texas," *Houston Chronicle*, May 26, 2011, p. A1.
5. U.S. Census Bureau, "Total Fertility Rate by Race and Hispanic Origin," available at www.census.gov.
6. Jim Getz, "Census: Texas Adds Almost 2 Million Hispanics since 2000," *Dallas Morning News*, May 1, 2008, available at www.dallasnews.com.
7. Kever and Ratcliffe, "Texas Snares 4 House Seats," p. A5.
8. Pew Hispanic Center, "Unauthorized Immigrant Population: National and State Trends, 2010," February 1, 2011, available at http://pewhispanic.org.
9. Elaine Ayala, "Study: Illegal Immigration Costs State Billions," *Houston Chronicle*, April 24, 2009, available at www.chron.com.
10. Brandi Grissom, "Report Says Loss of Undocumented Workers to Cost Trillions," *El Paso Times*, May 21, 2008, available at www.elpasotimes.com.
11. Texas Comptroller of Public Accounts, "Undocumented Immigrants in Texas: A Financial Analysis of the Impact to the State Budget and Economy," December 2006, available at www.window.state.tx.us.
12. Pew Hispanic Center, "Statistical Portrait of the Foreign-Born Population in the United States, 2009," available at http://pewhispanic.org.
13. U.S. Census Bureau, "2010 Census Data," available at http://2010census.gov.
14. Kever, "Census Shows Ever-Changing Face of Texas," p. A8.
15. U.S. Census Bureau, "2010 Census Data," available at http://2010census.gov.
16. U.S. Census Bureau, "Percent of Population by Race and Hispanic or Latino Origin, for States, Puerto Rico, and Places of 100,000 or More Population: 2000," available at www.census.gov.
17. U.S. Census Bureau, "Profile of the Foreign-Born Population in the United States: 2000," available at HYPERLINK "http://www.census.gov"
18. Kever, "Census Shows Ever-Changing Face of Texas," p. A1.
19. *Texas Weekly*, February 21, 2011, available at www.texasweekly.com.
20. Ibid.
21. Pew Forum on Religion & Public Life, "Religious Landscape Survey," available at http://religions.perforum.org.
22. Texas Comptroller of Public Accounts, *Fiscal Notes*, May 2011, available at http://www.window.state.tx.us.
23. "Fortune 500, 2011" CNN Money, available at http://money.cnn.com.
24. Texas Workforce Solutions, "Wage Information Network," available at www.texasindustryprofiles.com.
25. Patrick Danner, "Lone Star State Ties Mississippi in Low Pay Count," *Houston Chronicle*, March 29, 2011, p. B6.
26. Jeannie Kever, "Census Reveals Layers of Data," *Houston Chronicle*, December 15, 2010, p. A1.
27. Texas Comptroller of Public Accounts, "Texas Ahead: Gross State Product and Income," available at www.texasahead.org.
28. U.S. Census Bureau, "Gross Domestic Product by State in Current Dollars, 2008" *The 2011 Statistical Abstract*, available at www.census.gov.
29. U.S. Census Bureau, "Gross National Income by Country," *The 2011 Statistical Abstract*, available at www.census.gov.
30. U.S. Census Bureau, "Income, Poverty and Health Insurance in the United States: 2010," available at www.census.gov.
31. Ibid.
32. Quoted in David Plesa, "Racial Income Gap Widens," *Houston Post*, April 16, 1993, p. A-1.
33. Center on Budget and Policy Priorities, "Income Inequality Grew Across the Country over the Past Two Decades," available at www.cbpp.org.

34. Asher Price and Claire Osborn, "Texas Leads Nation in Upper and Middle Income Gap," *Austin American-Statesman*, January 28, 2006, available at www.statesman.com.

35. U.S. Department of Health and Human Services, "The 2011 HHS Poverty Guidelines," available at www.hhs.gov.

36. U.S. Census Bureau, "Income, Poverty and Health Insurance in the United States: 2010."

37. U.S. Census Bureau, "Income, Poverty, and Health Insurance Coverage in the United States: 2010."

38. Ibid.

39. National Center for Health Statistics, "National Health Interview Survey," available at www.cdc.gov.

40. Richard S. Dunham and Lynsi Burton, "Health Care Debate Highlights Texas Paradoxes," *Houston Chronicle*, October 16, 2009, p. A19.

41. Corrie MacLaggan, "Report: Texas Ranks in Bottom 10 States for Percentage of Children in Poverty," *Austin American-Statesman*, June 27, 2006, available at www.statesman.com.

42. "Texas has 3rd Highest Teen Birthrate Among States, Study Says," *Fort Worth Star-Telegram*, July 26, 2010, available at www.star-telegram.com.

43. Robert T. Garrett, "Dallas Leads Nation in Repeat Teen Births, Study Finds," *Dallas Morning News*, September 1, 2009, available at www.dallasnews.com.

44. Melissa Mixon, "Sex Education: Does Teaching Abstinence Work?" *Austin American-Statesman*, July 13, 2008, available at www.statesman.com.

45. Michelle de la Rosa, "Sex Education Bill Going Nowhere," *San Antonio Express-News*, May 6, 2009, available at www.mysanantonio.com.

46. Daniel Elazar, *American Federalism: A View from the States*, 2nd ed. (New York: Crowell, 1972), pp. 84–126.

47. Tom W. Rice and Alexander F. Sundberg, "Civic Culture and Government Performance in the American States," *Publius: The Journal of Federalism* 27 (Winter 1997): 99–114.

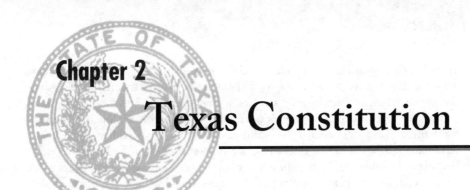

Chapter 2

Texas Constitution

CHAPTER OUTLINE

State Constitutions

Background of the Texas Constitution

Constitutional Convention of 1875

Overview of the Texas Constitution

Constitutional Change
    Change Through Amendment
    Change Through Practice and Experience

Change Through Judicial Interpretation
Constitutional Revision

Individual Rights and the Texas Constitution

What We Have Learned

WHAT WE WILL LEARN

After studying Chapter 2, you should be able to answer the following questions:

1. How do state constitutions compare and contrast with the U.S. Constitution?

2. What is the historical background of the Texas Constitution?

3. What were the goals of the majority of delegates at the state constitutional convention of 1875, and how did those goals affect the document they drafted?

4. What are the principal features of the Texas Constitution?

5. What are the means through which the Texas Constitution changes?

6. What role do Texas courts and the Texas Constitution play in the protection of individual rights?

Is gambling a solution to the state's budget problem? In 2011, the governor and the legislature faced a budget gap of $27 billion between expected revenues and the money needed to fund public services at their current levels for the upcoming two-year budget period. Gambling proponents argued that the introduction of casino gambling in Texas along with the addition of slot machines (called video lottery terminals) at horse and dog tracks would generate as much as $3 billion a year to help close the budget gap. Gambling is a voluntary tax, they said; no one pays unless he or she chooses to play. Legalized gambling creates jobs and attracts visitors with money to the state. It also provides a local alternative for Texans who have been traveling to neighboring states to visit casinos. In contrast, the opponents of legalized gambling believe that it creates a morally corrupting climate that is associated with social problems, such as crime, bankruptcy, and gambling addiction. Furthermore, the introduction of casinos and other gambling establishments to an area hurts small businesses because people spend their money gambling rather than purchasing goods and services.[1]

Gambling proponents failed to make any headway in 2011, despite the state's difficult budget picture, not just because of political opposition but also because the Texas Constitution prohibits gambling. The expansion of gambling in the state takes more than passage of ordinary legislation; instead it requires the adoption and ratification of a constitutional amendment, and that is more difficult to achieve. Ordinary legislation requires majority-vote approval of the Texas House and Texas Senate. After the measure passes the legislature it goes to the governor, who can sign it into law or allow it to become law without signature. If the governor issues a veto, the legislature can override the veto by a two-thirds vote of the House and Senate. In contrast, the adoption of a constitutional amendment requires a two-thirds vote by the Texas House and the Texas Senate and then ratification by a majority of voters in a special constitutional amendment election. Gambling expansion failed in the 2011 session of the Texas legislature, just as it has failed before, because proponents were unable to muster the two-thirds vote necessary to put the issue to the voters.

The Texas Constitution sets the ground rules for policymaking by defining the process for policy adoption. It creates the branches of government and establishes processes for passing ordinary legislation and adopting constitutional amendments. Because the Constitution prohibits gambling, legislators who want to expand legalized gambling in the state to increase revenues will have to round up two-thirds majorities in the Texas House and Texas Senate and then persuade a majority of voters to approve the measure as well.

This chapter examines the Texas Constitution as an important element of the context for policymaking in the Lone Star State. The chapter begins with a discussion of the role of state constitutions in general. It explores the background of the Texas Constitution, describes the constitutional convention of 1875, and presents an overview of the document. The chapter discusses constitutional change and the role the Texas Constitution plays in protecting individual rights. Finally, the chapter examines the impact of the Texas Constitution on the policymaking process.

STATE CONSTITUTIONS

Constitution A fundamental law by which a state or nation is organized and governed.

Bicameral legislature A legislative body with two chambers.

Separation of powers The division of political authority among legislative, executive, and judicial branches of government.

Plural executive The division of executive power among several elected officials.

Unicameral legislature A legislative body with one chamber.

A **constitution** is the fundamental law by which a state or nation is organized and governed. The U.S. Constitution is the fundamental law of the United States. It establishes the framework of government, assigns the powers and duties of governmental bodies, and defines the relationship between the people and their government. Similarly, a state constitution is the fundamental law for a state. The U.S. Constitution and the state constitutions together provide the total framework for government within the United States.

State constitutions resemble the U.S. Constitution in some respects but differ in others. The framers of the U.S. Constitution based the document on the principle of separation of powers, with a strong chief executive, a **bicameral legislature** (which is a legislative body with two chambers), and a judiciary appointed for life. Although every state constitution provides for the **separation of powers** (which is the division of political authority among the legislative, executive, and judicial branches of government), many state documents differ from the national constitution in important details. A number of state constitutions, including the Texas Constitution, give their governor fewer official powers than the U.S. Constitution grants the president. Indeed, the constitutions of Texas and several other states weaken their governors through means of the **plural executive,** which is the division of executive power among several elected officials. Most state constitutions, including the Texas Constitution, provide for the election of judges. One state, Nebraska, has a **unicameral legislature,** which is a legislative body with one chamber.

Some state constitutions reflect a different approach to democracy than the U.S. Constitution embodies. The U.S. Constitution creates a **representative democracy** or a **republic,** which is a political system in which citizens elect representatives to make policy decisions on their behalf. The framers of the U.S. Constitution believed

GETTING INVOLVED
Joining a Student Club or Organization

If you join a student organization, you will enjoy college more and probably earn better grades as well. Joining a club will give you the chance to make new friends with similar interests and become acquainted with a faculty advisor outside the classroom setting. Because you will be better connected to the school, you will be more likely to stay in college and finish your education.

Colleges and universities typically offer a range of student clubs and organizations. Students at your school may participate in such organizations as an international student association, Campus Crusade for Christ, chess club, Young Democrats, Young Republicans, choir, gay/lesbian/bisexual student association, black student union, bridge club, Muslim student association, computer science club, Jewish life organization, Latino student association, karate club, pre-medical society, Catholic Student Union, math club, and Asian student association. The student life office at your college will have a list of student groups active on your campus.

It's your college—get involved!

Representative democracy or **republic** A political system in which citizens elect representatives to make policy decisions on their behalf.

Direct democracy A political system in which the citizens vote directly on matters of public concern.

Initiative process A procedure whereby citizens can propose the adoption of a policy measure by gathering a prerequisite number of signatures. Voters must then approve the measure before it can take effect.

Statutory law Law made by a legislature.

Constitutional law Law that involves the interpretation and application of the constitution.

that elected representatives were needed to act as a buffer between the people and government policies. In contrast, some state constitutions include certain elements of **direct democracy,** which is a political system in which the citizens vote directly on matters of public concern. Almost half the states (but not Texas) provide for the **initiative process,** a procedure whereby citizens can propose the adoption of a policy measure by gathering a prerequisite number of signatures. Voters must then approve the measure before it can take effect. State officials then place the measure on the ballot for approval by the voters. Citizens can use the initiative process either to adopt measures or to repeal legislation enacted through the legislative process. Voters in California, Oregon, and other states with the initiative process have used it to make policy decisions concerning such issues as state tax rates, bilingual education, gay and lesbian rights, insurance rates, term limits for elected officials, and the provision of public services to illegal immigrants.

In contrast to the U.S. Constitution, state constitutions have a quality of impermanence to them. Although the present state constitution of Massachusetts was written in 1780, only six state constitutions now in effect were drafted before 1850. The average state constitution lasts for 70 years.[2] Nonetheless, about one-fourth of the states have adopted new constitutions since World War II. Furthermore, most states have changed constitutions several times. Louisiana, for example, has had 11 constitutions; Georgia has had 10.[3]

Most state constitutions have more amendments than the U.S. Constitution, which has only 27. In contrast, the average state constitution has been amended nearly a hundred times. At the high end, the Constitution of South Carolina has been changed formally more than 450 times.[4] The California Constitution has more than 500 amendments.[5]

Finally, state constitutions are on average four times longer than the U.S. Constitution. The Alabama Constitution, at 310,000 words, is the longest constitution in the nation, compared with only 7,400 words in the U.S. Constitution. The Texas Constitution is 93,000 words.[6] The length of state constitutions reflects the broader scope of state policy responsibilities compared with those of the national government. State constitutions deal with some matters not discussed at all in the U.S. Constitution, such as the structures, functions, and finances of local governments. State constitutions consider other issues, such as elections and land management, in greater detail than they are covered in the national document.

State constitutions also generally include numerous miscellaneous provisions that might be called "super legislation." These measures are the same quality and type as **statutory law** (law made by a legislature) but for historical or political reasons are upgraded to **constitutional law,** which is law that involves the interpretation and application of the constitution.[7] The South Dakota Constitution, for example, provides for state hail insurance; the Oklahoma Constitution requires that home economics be taught in public schools.[8] Some critics of the Texas Constitution believe that issues such as the expansion of legalized gambling should be addressed through the legislative process rather than addressed in the state constitution.

Because the Texas Constitution prohibits gambling, Texas legislators who want to legalize casino gambling in the state have to push for a constitutional amendment rather than just the passage of ordinary legislation.

BACKGROUND OF THE TEXAS CONSTITUTION

Jacksonian democracy The philosophy (associated with President Andrew Jackson) that suggested the right to vote should be extended to all adult male citizens and that all government offices of any importance should be filled by election.

Suffrage The right to vote.

Texans adopted their first state constitution in 1845, when the Lone Star State joined the Union. As with most other state constitutions written in the first half of the nineteenth century, the Texas Constitution of 1845 was patterned after the U.S. Constitution. Following the national model, it created a government with legislative, executive, and judicial branches. Similar to the U.S. Constitution, the Texas Constitution of 1845 was a document of broad, general principles that allowed state government leeway to deal with policy problems as they arose. The voters would select the governor, lieutenant governor, and members of the legislature. The governor would then appoint other state executive officials and members of the state judiciary.

In 1850, Texas amended the state constitution to provide for the election rather than appointment of state judges and most executive officeholders. The change reflected the principle of **Jacksonian democracy,** the philosophy (associated with President Andrew Jackson) that suggested the right to vote should be extended to all adult male citizens and that all government offices of any importance should be filled by election. The advocates of Jacksonian democracy believed that government is made responsive to the people through broad-based **suffrage,** which is the right to vote, and the **long ballot,** an election system that provides for the election of nearly every public official of any significance.

Long ballot An election system that provides for the election of nearly every public official of any significance.

When Texas joined the Confederacy in 1861, the state changed its constitution. The new document pledged the state's allegiance to the Confederacy and included a strong prohibition against the abolition of slavery. Otherwise, the Constitution of 1861 closely resembled its predecessor.

In 1866, with the war lost, Texas rewrote its constitution once again in hopes of rejoining the Union under President Andrew Johnson's reconstruction plan. This new constitution repealed secession, repudiated the war debt, and recognized the supremacy of the U.S. Constitution. Although the document abolished slavery, it fell short of granting full equality to former slaves. African Americans could not testify in court cases unless other African Americans were involved, and they were denied the right to vote. In most other respects, though, the Constitution of 1866 simply reenacted provisions of the 1845 document.

The Texas Constitution of 1866 was short lived. By the time of its adoption, the Radical Republican majority in Congress had taken control of Reconstruction from President Johnson. The **Radical Republicans** were members of the Republican Party who wanted sweeping social change to take place in the South after the Civil War. Congress passed legislation over President Johnson's veto declaring that Texas and the other states of the Confederacy could not reenter the Union until they granted African Americans the right to vote, ratified the Thirteenth and Fourteenth Amendments to the U.S. Constitution, and drafted new state constitutions acceptable to Congress.

Radical Republicans Members of the Republican Party that wanted sweeping social change to take place in the South after the Civil War.

Because Union troops occupied Texas, the state had little choice but to accept the demands. Ninety Texans, representing a broad range of political factions, gathered in convention in June 1868 to draft another state constitution. The convention was a stormy one, with the delegates unable to agree on a document. In 1869, the military commander of Texas intervened to gather the bits and pieces the convention had produced into a single document. The U.S. Congress accepted this new constitution and Texas was readmitted to the Union in 1870.

The Texas Constitution of 1869 created an active state government. Reverting to the procedure established in the original state constitution of 1845, it provided for the gubernatorial appointment rather than election of judges and most executive branch officials. It established annual sessions of the legislature and authorized increased salaries for state officials. The constitution also included a compulsory school attendance law and provided for state supervision of education.

For most white, ex-Confederate Texans, the Constitution of 1869 represented defeat and humiliation. Many Texans regarded the document not as a Texas constitution at all but a document imposed on them by outside forces. Radical Republican Governor E. J. Davis held office under this constitution, and the two were closely linked in the minds of the ex-Confederate Texans who considered Davis arrogant and corrupt. In particular, Democrats criticized the Davis administration for excessive spending, taxation, and borrowing.

Defenders of the Davis administration argued that the policies adopted by the governor and the Republican legislature were an appropriate effort to help the state recover from the Civil War. Under Davis, the state undertook programs to promote railroad construction, build an extensive network of roads, and construct a free public school system. Furthermore, Democratic Governor Richard Coke and the Democratic majority in the legislature who succeeded the Republicans in office were no more successful at dealing with the state's financial problems than their predecessors. The state **budget deficit,** the amount of money by which annual budget expenditures exceed annual budget receipts, was higher in 1875 and 1876 under Coke than it had been in 1872 and 1873 under Davis.[9]

Budget deficit The amount of money by which annual budget expenditures exceed annual budget receipts.

Nonetheless, the association of the Texas Constitution of 1869 with Reconstruction guaranteed strong Democratic support for a new document. When Democrats regained control of state government in 1872 and 1873, their first priority was to draft a new constitution for Texas. Governor Coke and Democratic legislative leaders initially proposed that the state legislature write a new constitution. When legislators deadlocked over a new document, however, the governor and the Democratic leaders had no choice but to call for the election of delegates to a state constitutional convention.

 WHAT DO YOU THINK?

Do you agree with the political philosophy underlying the concept of Jacksonian democracy?

CONSTITUTIONAL CONVENTION OF 1875

In the fall of 1875, 90 Texans gathered in Austin to draft a new constitution for the state. Although a number of Republicans, including several African Americans, served as convention delegates, most of the delegates were white Democrats. Farmers, ex-Confederate officers, and lawyers were all well represented at the convention. The largest organized group of delegates was the Texas Patrons of Husbandry, better known as the **Grange,** an organization of farmers. Indeed, "retrenchment and reform," the Grangers' slogan, became the watchword of the convention.

Grange An organization of farmers.

The Grangers' slogan embodied two basic goals: to restrict the size and scope of state government and to control the excesses of big business. Most of the delegates at the convention wanted to restrain a state government that they believed was too large and expensive. To accomplish this task, the delegates abandoned one constitutional tradition while reinstating another. On one hand, the authors of the new constitution turned away from the pattern initially established in the Texas Constitution of 1845 of a general document phrased in broad terms, favoring instead a restrictive constitution of great length and detail. On the other hand, the delegates returned to the tradition of Jacksonian democracy, reinstating the long ballot and shortening the terms of office for elected officials.[10]

The convention restricted the authority of every branch and unit of Texas government. The new constitution weakened the office of governor by cutting the governor's salary and reducing the term of office from four to two years. It restricted the governor's power of appointment by creating a plural executive, which divided executive power among several elected officials, including a lieutenant governor, attorney general, comptroller, treasurer, and a land commissioner. Executive officials elected independently from the governor would owe no allegiance to the governor. Indeed, they might be political rivals. The governor could appoint a number of lesser officials, but they would have little incentive to follow the governor's lead because the governor had no power to remove them before the end of their terms.

The constitution's framers reduced the power of the legislature by cutting its meeting time and restricting the scope of its policymaking authority. They limited regular sessions of the legislature to 140 calendar days, every other year. They reduced legislative salaries and required that the legislature adopt a balanced budget unless four-fifths of the membership agreed to deficit spending. Furthermore, by including long, detailed sections on education, finance, railroad regulation, and similar matters in the constitution, the framers forced legislators to propose constitutional amendments if they wanted to adopt policy changes in many areas.

The authors of Texas's new constitution employed several devices for reducing the power of the judicial branch of state government. They divided the state's court system into two segments, limiting the types of cases individual courts would be authorized to hear. In the best tradition of Jacksonian democracy, they provided for the election of judges to relatively brief terms. The framers also reduced judicial discretion by writing a long, detailed constitution that left relatively little room for judicial interpretation.

The framers of the Texas Constitution did not overlook local government. They specified the forms local governments must take and restricted local authority to levy taxes, provide services, adopt regulations, and go into debt. In many instances, local officials would have to ask the state legislature for permission to adopt even relatively minor policies. Changing local political structures would frequently necessitate a constitutional amendment.

Another major goal of the Granger-dominated convention was to control the excesses of big business. Consider the constitutional provisions dealing with banking. Many of the convention delegates were small farmers, used to living on the financial edge. They distrusted big, impersonal banks, which might be inclined to foreclose on their property during hard times. Instead, they preferred smaller, locally owned banks whose managers would be more understanding. Consequently, the convention prohibited **branch banking,** a business practice whereby a single, large bank conducts business from several locations. This provision ensured that banks would be locally owned rather than branches of large banks headquartered in Dallas or Houston.

The constitution's deference to local values is also reflected in its provisions dealing with liquor regulation. Although the constitution empowered the legislature to regulate the manufacture, packaging, sale, possession, and transportation of alcoholic beverages, it left the decision to legalize the sale of alcoholic beverages to local voters. **Local-option elections** (also known as wet-dry elections) are held to determine whether an area could legalize the sale of alcoholic beverages. The voters living in a city, a county, or even an area as small as a justice-of-the-peace precinct could vote to keep their area dry, that is, to prohibit the sale of alcoholic beverages. Once an area goes dry, it cannot go wet unless the voters approve. Of the 254 counties in

Branch banking
A business practice whereby a single, large bank conducts business from several locations.

Local-option (wet-dry) elections Elections held to determine whether an area could legalize the sale of alcoholic beverages.

Texas, 51 are totally dry and 39 are entirely wet. The other 164 counties are partially wet, which means that they include some areas where alcohol cannot be sold.[11]

The delegates at the constitutional convention believed in the old adage that a family's home is its castle, and they set about to protect it. They provided that a family **homestead** (that is, legal residence) could not be seized and sold in payment of debt except for delinquent taxes and mortgage payments on a loan taken out to purchase the home itself. The framers added a measure to the constitution requiring that both spouses must give written consent before the homestead could be sold. The constitution also prohibited the garnishment of wages for payment of debt. (A modern constitutional amendment provides an exception—garnishment for the enforcement of court-ordered child support or spousal maintenance.)

In the 1870s, it was not uncommon for states to adopt restrictive constitutions. Although the Texas Constitution written in 1875 reflected the political concerns of rural-oriented Texans, the document was not far out of step with other state constitutions adopted in the late nineteenth century. Many states provided for the

Homestead Legal residence.

Because the Texas Constitution prohibited branch banking, the legislature and the voters had to adopt a constitutional amendment to allow ATM machines.

election of judges and a broad range of executive-branch officials. Short terms of office for governors and judges were common. Furthermore, Texans were not the only Americans who distrusted public officials and worried about the corrupting influences of big banks, corporations, and railroads.[12]

The delegates finished their work in less than three months and, in early 1876, the voters approved the new constitution by a margin of two to one. With amendments, the Constitution of 1876 remains the fundamental law of the state of Texas today.

OVERVIEW OF THE TEXAS CONSTITUTION

To students familiar with the U.S. Constitution, the most striking feature of the Texas Constitution is its length. At 93,000 words, the Texas Constitution is one of the longest state constitutions in the nation. It can be found in most reference libraries, in the *Texas Almanac*, and online.

The Texas Constitution shares a number of features with the U.S. Constitution: a bill of rights, separation of powers with checks and balances, and the creation of a bicameral legislature. A **bill of rights** is a constitutional document guaranteeing individual rights and liberties. As with other provisions of the Texas Constitution, the Texas Bill of Rights is long, considerably longer than its counterpart in the national constitution. The Texas document contains 29 sections and includes most of the guarantees found in the national Bill of Rights, such as the protection of free speech and a free press, the guarantee of the right of trial by jury, and a safeguard against "unreasonable searches and seizures."

Bill of rights
A constitutional document guaranteeing individual rights and liberties.

The Texas Bill of Rights does more than merely restate the guarantees found in the U.S. Constitution. The Texas document phrases the protection of rights positively rather than negatively. Consider the issue of freedom of expression. The First Amendment to the U.S. Constitution prohibits the abridgement of free expression: "Congress shall make no law . . . abridging the freedom of speech, or of the press." In contrast, the Texas Bill of Rights guarantees free expression: "Every person shall be at liberty to speak, write or publish his opinions on any subject . . . and no law shall ever be passed curtailing the liberty of speech or of the press" [Art. 1, Sect. 8]. Professor James C. Harrington believes that the provision in the Texas Constitution is potentially a stronger guarantee of free expression than the First Amendment to the U.S. Constitution. Whereas the U.S. Bill of Rights identifies rights the national government *may not infringe*, the Texas Bill of Rights lists rights state government *must protect*.[13]

The Texas Bill of Rights includes a number of measures not found in the national Bill of Rights. Whereas the U.S. Constitution provides for the right to a jury trial only if defendants face more than six months in jail, the Texas Constitution guarantees the right to trial by jury for persons charged with any offense, even minor traffic violations. The Texas Constitution also contains two guarantees of equal rights more explicit and detailed than any comparable measure included in the U.S. Constitution. Both provisions are found in Article I, Section 3. The first measure is fairly broad: "All free men . . . have equal rights." The second guarantee, which

Texas Equal Rights Amendment (ERA) A provision in the Texas Constitution that states the following: "Equality under the law shall not be denied or abridged because of sex, race, color, creed, or national origin."

Checks and balances The overlapping of the powers of the branches of government so that public officials limit the authority of one another.

was added in 1972, is known as the **Texas Equal Rights Amendment (ERA).** It is a provision in the Texas Constitution that states the following: "Equality under the law shall not be denied or abridged because of sex, race, color, creed, or national origin" [Art. I, Sect. 3a.].

The Texas Constitution establishes a separation-of-powers system with checks and balances. Similar to the national government, Texas state government has three branches: an executive branch headed by the governor; a bicameral legislature, including the Texas House of Representatives and the Texas Senate; and a judicial branch. The term **checks and balances** refers to the overlapping of the powers held by the different branches of government, so that public officials limit the authority of one another. The governor's appointments, for example, must be confirmed by a two-thirds vote of the Texas Senate. Legislation must pass both the House and the Senate before it has passed the Texas legislature. The governor can veto bills passed by the legislature, but the legislature can override the veto by a two-thirds vote of each house.

The Texas Constitution includes features not found in the U.S. Constitution. Some of these provisions involve policy matters of primary concern to state government. One section, for example, deals with voter qualifications and elections. Other sections outline the structures and responsibilities of local governments. Much of the length and detail of the Texas Constitution, though, can be attributed to the inclusion of long sections dealing with substantive policy areas. The framers of the constitution devoted thousands of words to such matters as railroad regulation, education, welfare, and taxation. Subsequent amendments have added thousands of additional words.

CONSTITUTIONAL CHANGE

Constitutions change by means of formal amendment, practical experience, and judicial interpretation. The U.S. Constitution is a relatively brief document of general principles. Although it has been amended 27 times, scholars believe that practical experience and judicial interpretation have been more important means of constitutional change than written amendments. State constitutions are usually longer and more detailed than the national document, providing less opportunity for constitutional growth through practical experience and judicial interpretation. State constitutional change generally occurs through the means of written amendments. This is certainly true for the Texas Constitution.

Change Through Amendment

Constitutional amendment A formal, written change or addition to the state's governing document.

A **constitutional amendment** is a formal, written change or addition to the state's governing document. The detailed style of the Texas Constitution has led to numerous amendments as each successive generation of Texans has attempted to adapt its features to changing times. Some amendments have been trivial, such as an amendment to allow city governments to donate surplus firefighting equipment to rural volunteer fire departments. Other amendments have dealt with weighty policy matters, such as an amendment authorizing the legislature to cap noneconomic damages for pain and suffering awarded in lawsuits. The voters approved both amendments in 2003.

Through the years, amendments have produced several major changes in the Texas Constitution. The legislature and the voters have amended the constitution to strengthen the authority of state officials, especially the governor. Amendments have increased the term of office of the governor, as well as the terms of the state's other elected executive officials, from two years to four years and have empowered the governor to remove his or her own appointees, pending Senate approval. The constitution has also been amended to give the governor limited **budget execution authority,** which is the power to cut agency spending or transfer money between agencies during the period when the legislature is not in session.

The legislature and the voters have amended the Texas Constitution to enable state government to promote economic development. Amendments have eliminated the constitutional prohibition against branch banking, allowed local governments to give tax breaks to businesses relocating to Texas, and provided money for the development and conservation of the state's water resources. Other amendments have provided funds for highway construction, student loans, and college expansion.

The legislature and the voters have periodically approved amendments to enable the state to go into debt by issuing **general obligation bonds,** which are certificates of indebtedness that must be repaid from general revenues. Borrowing enables the state to spread the cost of major projects, such as prison construction and water development, over a period of time. Because the Texas Constitution prohibits the state from incurring debt that must be repaid from general revenues, the legislature has had to propose constitutional amendments to authorize borrowing. In 2010, the bonded indebtedness of the state of Texas was $11.2 billion, with the state paying $342 million a year in principal and interest out of general revenues.[14]

The process of amending the Texas Constitution is fairly straightforward. An amendment must first be proposed by a two-thirds vote of each house of the legislature. Then, it must be ratified by a majority of the voters in an election. Through 2010, the voters had approved 474 amendments to the Texas Constitution out of 656 proposed by the legislature.[15]

However, the amendment process is time-consuming and the electorate apathetic. Even in the most favorable circumstances, the interval between the formulation of a proposed amendment and its ultimate approval or rejection by the voters is measured in years. Furthermore, elections to ratify constitutional amendments generate relatively little voter interest. As Figure 2.1 indicates, the number of Texas voters who decided the fate of the 16 proposed constitutional amendments on the ballot in 2009 was considerably less than the number of Texans who participated in the 2008 presidential election or the 2006 governor's election.

Nearly every state allows its citizens to vote on constitutional amendments, and defenders of the process say that the people should have a voice in the adoption of changes in their state's fundamental law. They frame the issue in terms of democracy. Although the legislature can propose constitutional change, the voters should have the final word on whether changes are adopted.

In contrast, critics argue that most citizens are not well enough informed to make reasonable judgments about the details of state constitutional law. For example, Texas voters have twice rejected efforts to repeal a provision in the Texas Constitution

Budget execution authority The power to cut agency spending or transfer money between agencies during the period when the legislature is not in session.

General obligation bonds Certificates of indebtedness that must be repaid from general revenues.

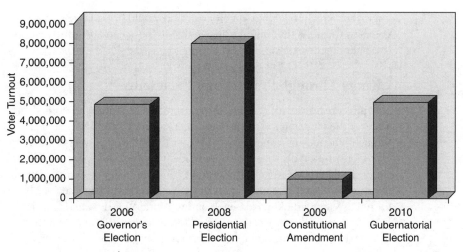

FIGURE 2.1   Voter Turnout, Various Elections.

requiring companies that seek investment from the Texas Growth Fund to disclose whether they do business with the white-minority governments of South Africa and Namibia. With the introduction of democratic, black majority-rule governments in those countries, the original rationale for the requirement no longer applies. Even though there is no organized opposition to repeal the measure, the voters, apparently confused by the issue, have failed twice to ratify amendments repealing the provision.

The Texas legislature sometimes words amendments with an eye toward deceiving the voters. The Texas Constitution requires that the state publish a summary and a brief explanation of proposed constitutional amendments in newspapers at least twice before Election Day. In 1989, the summary for one proposed amendment clearly explained that the amendment would increase the pay for members of the Texas legislature from $7,200 to $23,358 a year. It would raise the salaries of the Speaker of the House and the lieutenant governor even more. On the ballot, however, the description of the measure began as follows: "The constitutional amendment to *limit* the salary. . . ." Poorly informed voters might well have voted to raise legislative salaries while believing they were doing the opposite. In this instance, at least, the legislature's effort at deception failed because the amendment was defeated.

The legislature even manipulates the timing of amendment ratification elections to influence their outcome. In 2003, for example, the legislature passed a constitutional amendment to clarify that the legislature had the constitutional authority to limit the amount of noneconomic damages that a jury could award in a personal injury lawsuit. The legislature adopted the amendment to head off legal challenges against laws restricting the right of individuals to sue over faulty products, personal injuries, or medical malpractice. Instead of scheduling the ratification election for November, when amendment ratification elections are typically held, the legislature set the vote for a Saturday in September. Critics charged that legislative leaders reasoned that the amendment would be more likely to pass if it were held in a low-turnout special election in September than it would in November when a Houston city election would bring large numbers of minority voters to the polls that might vote against it. The plan apparently worked, because the amendment passed.

Change Through Practice and Experience

Not all constitutional changes result from the adoption of formal amendments. Many of the fundamental features of American national government have developed through practice and experience. Consider the military powers of the president. The U.S. Constitution declares that the president is the commander in chief of the armed forces. To determine what this important constitutional power really entails, however, one must look to its practical application by actual presidents, such as Lincoln during the Civil War or Franklin Roosevelt during World War II. When President George W. Bush commanded the American armed forces to attack Iraq to overthrow the regime of Saddam Hussein, for example, no one seriously questioned the president's constitutional authority to order the military into combat, despite the lack of a congressional declaration of war, because previous presidents had taken similar action.

Because of its detail and specificity, the Texas Constitution has not grown as much through practice and experience as the U.S. Constitution, but some informal changes have occurred. For example, the office of lieutenant governor of Texas, as outlined in the state constitution, resembles that of the vice president of the United States, which, historically, has been a relatively weak office. In practice, however, the lieutenant governor has become one of the most important policy leaders in the state, far more important in state government than the vice president has been on the national scene. This is an important development in the fundamental structures of Texas government that resulted not from formal amendment but through the informal processes of practice and experience.

Change Through Judicial Interpretation

Many scholars believe that the most important mechanism through which the U.S. Constitution has changed is judicial interpretation. Federal court rulings have defined constitutional principles in such key policy areas as school integration, voting rights, freedom of expression, freedom of religion, and the rights of persons accused of crimes. Because of the more detailed nature of state constitutions, judicial interpretation has historically been a less significant means for constitutional change at the state level than it has been at the national level. Today, however, this situation may be changing. State courts have begun to play an increasingly important policymaking role through the interpretation of state constitutions, addressing such issues as education funding and gay marriage.

 **WHAT DO YOU THINK?**

Are constitutional amendment ratification elections in Texas so complicated that ordinary citizens cannot make intelligent choices?

Constitutional Revision

Many critics of the Texas Constitution believe that the state should have a new constitution. The League of Women Voters, the Texas Bar Association, some public officials, and many political scientists (including most textbook authors) contend that the document is so long and detailed, and so often amended, that most citizens (and even many public officials) do not understand it. A simpler, more straightforward document, they say, would increase respect for and understanding of state government.

The most telling criticism of the Texas Constitution is that it hinders the formulation, adoption, and implementation of sound public policy. The legislature is periodically forced to deal with serious budget shortfalls, necessitating spending cuts, tax increases, or a combination of the two. The legislature's ability to set spending priorities, however, is limited by constitutionally **dedicated funds,** which are constitutional or statutory provisions that set aside revenue for particular purposes. For example, the **Dedicated Highway Fund** is a constitutionally earmarked account containing money set aside for building, maintaining, and policing state highways. The **Permanent University Fund (PUF)** is money constitutionally set aside as an endowment to finance construction, maintenance, and some other activities at the University of Texas, Texas A&M University, and other institutions in those two university systems. In preparing the budget, legislators did not have the option of cutting highway funds to avoid a tax increase or diverting construction money from the University of Texas and Texas A&M University systems to other colleges and universities because the constitution would not allow it. Similarly, the legislature is limited in its ability to raise revenues by constitutional provisions that prohibit a state property tax, outlaw gambling, and limit the basis for adopting an income tax.

Critics of the Texas Constitution charge that it is loaded with provisions that hinder the operation of efficient government. The governor has insufficient power, they say, to manage the state bureaucracy, the legislature meets too briefly and infrequently to resolve the state's policy problems, and the election of judges makes for a judiciary excessively dependent on interest group campaign contributions. The critics believe that many of the problems facing the state will not be resolved until the Texas Constitution is significantly revised or rewritten entirely.

The most recent efforts at **constitutional revision,** the process of drafting a new constitution, have failed. In 1972, Texas voters approved a constitutional amendment to call a state constitutional convention with members of the legislature serving as convention delegates. The ground rules for the convention required a two-thirds vote of approval for a new constitution, but two-thirds of the legislator-delegates could not agree on a new document. Three years later, the legislature tried to make the best of the situation. After dropping the most controversial items, the legislature divided the rest of the document into a series of amendments to submit to the voters. If the voters approved all of the amendments, the state would effectively have a new constitution.

The campaign for the new constitution was hard fought, with state officials, interest groups, local officeholders, and a host of others getting involved.

Dedicated funds Constitutional or statutory provisions that set aside revenue for particular purposes.

Dedicated Highway Fund A constitutionally earmarked account containing money set aside for building, maintaining, and policing state highways.

Permanent University Fund (PUF) Money constitutionally set aside as an endowment to finance construction, maintenance, and some other activities at the University of Texas, Texas A&M University, and other institutions in those two university systems.

Constitutional revision The process of drafting a new constitution.

The Dedicated Highway Fund is a constitutionally earmarked account containing money set aside for building, maintaining, and policing state highways.

The proponents, including many state officials, newspaper editorial writers, and scholars, argued that the revision would produce a more efficient and effective state government. In response, the opponents, including many local officials and a number of interest groups, warned that the new constitution would increase the power of state government too much and might well lead to the adoption of a state income tax. In the end, the opponents of the new constitution won big as voters rejected all of the amendments by an overwhelming margin.

In the late 1990s, two respected members of the legislature once again raised the issue of constitutional revision. They proposed a new constitution of only 19,000 words that would be a more general statement of fundamental law than the document it would replace. Their proposed constitution would strengthen the powers of the governor, reorganize the executive branch to reduce the number of elected officials, replace the election of judges with a merit selection process, and reorganize the judicial branch of government. The idea never came to a vote in the legislature, however, because most legislators wanted to avoid having to address controversial issues.

Civil union A legal partnership between two men or two women that gives the couple all the benefits, protections, and responsibilities under law as are granted to spouses in a marriage.

INDIVIDUAL RIGHTS AND THE TEXAS CONSTITUTION

Historically, people who believe that their rights have been violated have turned to the federal courts for relief under the U.S. Constitution. During the 1950s and 1960s, in particular, the U.S. Supreme Court acted to protect individuals from racial discrimination, guarantee freedom of expression, and expand the rights of people who

Gay Marriage in Massachusetts

Gay couples have been able to marry legally in Massachusetts since May 2004. Gay marriage is the result of a ruling by the Massachusetts Supreme Judicial Court (SJC) holding that the state cannot discriminate against same-sex couples when it issues marriage licenses. The SJC, which is the state's highest court, acted in response to a lawsuit filed by seven same-sex couples. The court ruled that the state lacked a rational basis for denying the couples a marriage license simply based on their desire to marry a person of the same gender. "The Massachusetts Constitution affirms the dignity and equality of all individuals," declared the court. "It forbids the creation of second class citizens."*

The opponents of the decision immediately began an effort to amend the Massachusetts Constitution to overturn the SJC's ruling. The most commonly used procedure for amending the state constitution begins with the legislature passing an amendment by majority vote in two consecutive legislative sessions. The amendment then goes to the voters for approval. In 2004, the Massachusetts legislature voted 105-92 in favor of a state constitutional amendment that would ban gay marriage and establish civil unions. A **civil union** is a legal partnership between two men or two women giving the couple all the benefits, protections, and responsibilities under law as granted to spouses in a marriage. A year later, however, the legislature rejected the amendment by a lopsided 157-to-39 vote. Over the preceding year, 6,600 same-sex couples had married uneventfully, and the elected officials who supported gay marriage had generally won reelection. In short, the sky had not fallen. A legislator who initially opposed gay marriage but changed his mind to support it explained his decision as follows: "When I look in the eyes of the children living with these couples, I decided that I don't feel at this time that same-sex marriage has hurt the [state] in any way. In fact, I would say that in my view it has had a good effect for the children in these families."[†]

With the failure of the constitutional amendment in the legislature, the opponents of gay marriage turned to the initiative process. An organization called VoteonMarriage.org gathered more than 150,000 signatures to put on the ballot a constitutional amendment to limit future marriages to one man and one woman. (The measure would not annul the same-sex marriages that had already been performed.) The procedure for approving the voter-initiated amendment requires that it receive the votes of at least 50 lawmakers in two consecutive legislative sessions, then voter approval in a referendum. The measure won the votes of 61 legislators in early 2007, but it received only 45 votes in the next session held later in the year. Massachusetts opponents of gay marriage would have to start all over if they hoped to amend the state constitution.[‡]

Gay marriage opponents outside of Massachusetts have proposed an amendment to the U.S. Constitution that would declare that marriage in the United States is limited to the union of a man and a woman. The amendment would overrule any action taken at the state level, including the decision of the SJC. The procedure for amending the U.S. Constitution involves the U.S. House and U.S. Senate voting to propose an amendment by a two-thirds vote. Three-fourths of the states must agree to ratify the amendment. In 2004 and 2006, the marriage amendment fell well short of the two-thirds margin needed in both the House and the Senate. Gay marriage is now well established in Massachusetts and has spread to several other states, either by state court order or through the legislative process.

QUESTIONS

1. The process for amending the Massachusetts Constitution is different from the process for amending the Texas Constitution. Which process do you prefer? Why?
2. Which level of government should decide the issue of gay marriage—the national government or the states? What is the basis of your answer?
3. Do you think gay men and women should be able to marry legally in Texas?

---

*Goodridge et al. v. Department of Public Health, SJC-08860 (2003).

[†]Pam Belluck, "Massachusetts Rejects Bill to Eliminate Gay Marriage," *New York Times*, September 15, 2005, available at www.nytimes.com.

[‡]Pam Belluck, "Massachusetts Gay Marriage to Remain Legal," *New York Times*, June 15, 2007, available at www.nytimes.com.

were accused of crimes. In *Brown v. Board of Education of Topeka* (1954), for example, the U.S. Supreme Court ruled that state laws that required racial segregation in the public schools violated the U.S. Constitution.[16]

Over the last 40 years, state courts have increasingly become a forum for disputes over individual-rights lawsuits filed under the provisions of state constitutions. In America's federal system of government, states must grant their residents all the rights guaranteed by the U.S. Constitution (as interpreted by the Supreme Court). If state governments so choose, however, they may offer their residents *more* rights than those afforded in the U.S. Constitution.[17] Since 1970, state courts around the nation have issued hundreds of rulings providing broader rights than those recognized by the U.S. Supreme Court. The areas in which state courts have been most active are abortion rights, criminal procedure, church/state relations, marriage equality, and gender discrimination.[18]

In Texas, state courts have relied on the Texas Constitution to expand individual rights in several policy areas involving **equal protection of the law,** the legal principle that state laws may not arbitrarily discriminate against persons. The Texas Supreme Court has held that "similarly situated individuals must be treated equally under [state law] . . . unless there is a rational basis for not doing so."[19] In *Edgewood v. Kirby* (1989), for example, the Texas Supreme Court ruled that the state's system of financing public education violated the Texas Constitution because it resulted in unequal treatment for school children residing in different school districts.[20]

The emergence of the Texas Constitution as an instrument for the protection of individual rights is a relatively recent development. Whether it is a lasting development will depend on the state's judges and the voters who elect them. Will the justices serving on the state's two highest courts, the Texas Supreme Court and the Texas Court of Criminal Appeals, dare to make controversial decisions, considering that they must stand periodically for reelection? Election-minded justices may be eager to rule in favor of school children, but will they be just as willing to uphold the rights of gay men and lesbians, atheists, illegal immigrants, persons accused of crimes, or other individuals and groups who may not be popular with the average Texas voter? Because voters are generally uninformed about judges, a single, highly publicized case can have a major import on a judge's electoral fortunes. Research shows that as Election Day approaches judges bring their rulings in line with public opinion.[21]

Equal protection of the law The legal principle that laws may not arbitrarily discriminate against persons.

WHAT WE HAVE LEARNED

1. How do state constitutions compare and contrast with the U.S. Constitution?

State constitutions are similar to the U.S. Constitution in some ways, but they differ in other ways. All state constitutions resemble the U.S. document in that they establish a separation-of-powers system with checks and balances. All but Nebraska are similar to the U.S. Constitution in that they create bicameral legislatures. In contrast to the U.S. Constitution, many state constitutions provide for the election of judges and create a plural executive system. Some state constitutions also include elements of direct democracy. Most state constitutions are younger than the U.S. Constitution. They are more frequently amended and longer than the federal document. State constitutions also generally include numerous miscellaneous provisions that might be called "super legislation."

2. What is the historical background of the Texas Constitution?

Texas has had several constitutions, adopting the first in 1845 and the last, the current document, in 1876. The first Texas Constitution resembled the U.S. Constitution in that it was a general document of basic principles, but other constitutions diverged from the national model. In 1850, Texas amended its constitution to provide for the election of judges, a development that reflected the philosophy of Jacksonian democracy. The Reconstruction era constitution of 1869, the immediate predecessor to the current document, provided for an active government. The Texas Constitution of 1876 was written in reaction to that constitution and E. J. Davis, the governor who served under it.

3. What were the goals of the majority of delegates at the state constitutional convention of 1875, and how did those goals affect the document they drafted?

Most delegates at the constitutional convention of 1875 were white Democrats. Many were former Confederates; many were members of the Grange. The delegates wanted to limit the size and scope of state government and to control the excesses of big business. The constitution they wrote restricted the authority of every branch and unit of government. It limited legislative session length and frequency, diluted the power of the governor with the plural executive, and checked the power of the courts by electing judges and splitting the court system. The constitution restricted the authority of local government as well. The Texas Constitution included a number of provisions limiting the power of big business, such as a prohibition against branch banking. The framers of the constitution also provided that a family's homestead could not be seized and sold in payment of debt except for delinquent taxes and mortgage payments on a loan taken out to purchase the home itself.

4. What are the principal features of the Texas Constitution?

The Texas Constitution, similar to the U.S. Constitution, has a bill of rights, separation of powers with checks and balances, and creates a bicameral legislature. The Texas Constitution is far longer than the U.S. Constitution and includes items not found in the latter document, including details about elections and local government.

5. What are the means through which the Texas Constitution changes?

Constitutions change by means of formal amendment, practical experience, and judicial interpretation. The Texas Constitution has been amended many times more than the U.S. Constitution. Amendments to the Texas Constitution have strengthened the office of governor, enabled the state to promote economic development, and approved the state going into debt. Amendments are proposed by a two-thirds vote of the Texas House and Texas Senate and then ratified by the voters. The means of constitutional change other than amendment have been less important for the Texas Constitution than they are for the U.S. Constitution. Although many critics of the Texas Constitution favor constitutional revision, efforts to write a new constitution for Texas have not been successful.

6. What role do Texas courts and the Texas Constitution play in the protection of individual rights?

Historically, people who believe that their rights have been violated have turned to the federal courts for relief under the U.S. Constitution. Over the last 40 years, state courts have increasingly become a forum for disputes over individual-rights lawsuits filed under the provisions of state constitutions. In Texas, state courts have relied on the Texas Constitution to expand individual rights in several policy areas, including education in the case of *Edgewood v. Kirby*.

KEY TERMS

bicameral legislature

bill of rights

branch banking

budget deficit

budget execution authority

checks and balances

civil union

constitution

constitutional amendment

constitutional law

constitutional revision

dedicated funds

Dedicated Highway Fund

direct democracy

equal protection of the law

general obligation bonds

Grange

homestead

initiative process

Jacksonian democracy

local-option (wet-dry) elections

long ballot

Permanent University Fund (PUF)

plural executive

Radical Republicans

representative democracy *or* republic

separation of powers

statutory law

suffrage

Texas Equal Rights Amendment (ERA)

unicameral legislature

NOTES

1. Enrique Rangel, "Odds Against Passage of Pro-Gambling Bills in Texas," *Lubbock Avalanche-Journal*, April 2, 2011, available at www.lubbockonline.com.

2. Christopher W. Hammons, "Was James Madison Wrong? Rethinking the American Preference for Short, Framework-Oriented Constitutions," *American Political Science Review* 93 (December 1999), p. 837.

3. Lawrence W. Friedman, "An Historical Perspective on State Constitutions," *Intergovernmental Perspective* (Spring 1987): 9–13.

4. Data collected by Janice May, quoted in David C. Saffell and Harry Basehart, *State and Local Government: Politics and Public Policies*, 8th ed. (New York, NY: McGraw-Hill, 2005), pp. 24–26.

5. Alan Greenblatt, "Too Broke to Fix," *Governing*, July 2009, p. 12.

6. Ibid.

7. Friedman, "An Historical Perspective on State Constitutions," pp. 9–13.

8. Hammons, "Was James Madison Wrong?" p. 840.

9. John Walker Mauer, *Southern State Constitutions in the 1870s: A Case Study of Texas*, Ph.D. Thesis, Rice University, Houston, Texas, 1983, p. 152.

10. Ibid.

11. Glenda Taylor, "Going Wet," *Kerrville Daily Times*, February 12, 2005, available at www.dailytimes.com.

12. Friedman, "An Historical Perspective on State Constitutions," pp. 9–13.

13. James C. Harrington, "The Texas Bill of Rights and Civil Liberties," *Texas Tech Law Review* 1487 (1986).

14. Comptroller of Public Accounts, "General Obligation Bonds and Revenue Bonds Payable from General Revenue," available at www.cpa.state.tx.us/treasops/bondapp.html.

15. Legislative Reference Library of Texas, "Constitutional Amendments," available at www.lrl.state.tx.us/legis/constAmends/lrlhome.cfm.

16. *Brown v. Board of Education of Topeka*, 347 U.S. 483 (1954).

17. *Pruneyard Shopping Center v. Robins*, 447 U.S. 74 (1980).

18. Jim Kincaid and Robert F. Williams, "The New Judicial Federalism: The States Lead in Rights Protection," in Thad L. Beyle, ed., *State Government: CQ's Guide to Current Issues and Activities 1993–94* (Chapel Hill: University of North Carolina Press, 1993), p. 183.

19. *Whitworth v. Bynum*, 699 S.W.2d 194 (1985).

20. *Edgewood v. Kirby*, 777 S.W.2d 391 (1989).

21. Gregory A. Huber and Sanford C. Gordon, "Accountability and Coercion: Is Justice Blind When It Runs for Office?" *American Journal of Political Science* 48 (April 2004): 247–263.

Chapter 3

The Federal Context of Texas Policymaking

CHAPTER OUTLINE

WHAT WE WILL LEARN

After studying Chapter 3, you should be able to answer the following questions:

1. What is the role of states in the federal system?

2. How have the U.S. Constitution and the federal courts affected policymaking in Texas, especially concerning the following cases: *Brown v. Board of Education of Topeka*, *Ruiz v. Estelle*, and *Roe v. Wade*?

3. How do federal preemptions and federal mandates affect policymaking in Texas?

4. What are the various kinds of grant programs, and what are the various types of conditions that the federal government places on the receipt of federal funds?

5. How important are federal programs and federal dollars to state and local governments in Texas?

Medicaid A federal program designed to provide health insurance coverage to low-income persons, people with disabilities, and elderly people who are impoverished.

In 2010, Congress passed and President Barack Obama signed the Patient Protection and Affordable Care Act, better known as healthcare reform, with the goals of providing health insurance coverage to millions of uninsured Americans and controlling the spiraling cost of healthcare. The measure is complex and will affect almost every aspect of American healthcare. It is also controversial, with most Democrats in Congress supporting it and every Republican opposing it.

Healthcare reform will have its greatest impact on Texas government through changes in the Medicaid program. **Medicaid** is a federal program designed to provide health insurance coverage to low-income persons, people with disabilities, and elderly people who are impoverished. In 2011, the Texas Medicaid program served 3.5 million people[1] at a cost of more than $25 billion.[2] Even though the federal government covers 60 percent of the cost, Medicaid is the single most expensive program in the Texas state budget, accounting for about a fourth of state spending. Beginning in 2014, the healthcare reform law will extend Medicaid coverage to people with incomes up to 133 percent of the poverty level, significantly higher than the current Medicaid cutoff in Texas, which is 12 percent of the poverty level. The new law will also provide coverage for childless couples and individuals who are currently ineligible for the Texas Medicaid program, regardless of their income.[3]

Healthcare reform is controversial. Reform advocates, including most of the state's Democratic officeholders, welcome the Patient Protection and Affordable Care Act. They note that a million Texans who currently do not have health insurance will be covered by Medicaid. No longer will they be forced to crowd into hospital emergency rooms for medical treatment because they lack insurance coverage. The federal government will pick up the entire cost of the new enrollees for the first three years, injecting $3.7 billion healthcare dollars annually into the Texas economy. Subsequently, the state share will gradually rise until 2020, when Texas will be required to cover 10 percent of the cost, an estimated $370 million, which is less than 1 percent of the state budget. The Congressional Budget Office (CBO) estimates that the total cost of healthcare reform to Texas government between 2010 and 2019 will be $1.4 billion.[4]

Medicare A federal health insurance program for people age 65 and older and for people with permanent disabilities.

Governor Rick Perry and most of the state's other top elected officials, all Republicans, insist that healthcare reform will be a disaster for the state. They believe that the cost of Medicaid expansion will be much greater than the CBO estimates because of increased administrative expenses.[5] They also note that Texas and other states will have to increase Medicaid reimbursement rates to physicians to their level under **Medicare,** which is a federal health insurance program for people age 65 and older. The federal government will pay the difference for the first two years and then leave it to the states to determine whether to continue paying the higher rates. Because it will be politically difficult to cut the higher reimbursement rates after they have been in effect for two years, state government will likely be saddled with an additional expense.

The controversy over healthcare reform and its impact on state government illustrates the importance of the federal system to state government and introduces this chapter on the federal context of policymaking in Texas. The chapter identifies the role of state and local governments in the federal system of American government. It explores the impact of the U.S. Constitution and federal courts on state and local governments by examining three important cases in constitutional law. The chapter studies the influence of federal law on state and local policymaking, considering federal preemption of state authority and federal mandates. The chapter describes federal grant programs and examines their influence on the state and local policymaking process. The chapter concludes with a discussion of the impact of federal programs and federal dollars on Texas.

 WHAT DO YOU THINK?

Will healthcare reform be good or bad for the state of Texas? What is the basis of your opinion?

ROLE OF THE STATES IN THE FEDERAL SYSTEM

Federal system or federation
A political system that divides power between a central government, with authority over the whole nation, and a series of state governments.

Sovereignty The authority of a state to exercise legitimate powers within its boundaries, free from external interference.

National Supremacy Clause
The provision found in Article IV of the Constitution that declares that the U.S. Constitution, the laws made under it, and the treaties of the United States are the supreme law of the land.

Policymaking in Texas takes place within the context of America's federal system of government. A **federal system** or **federation** is a political system that divides power between a central government, with authority over the whole nation, and a series of state governments. In a federal system, both the national government and the states enjoy **sovereignty**, which is the authority of a state to exercise legitimate powers within its boundaries, free from external interference. The national government and the states derive their authority not from one another but from the U.S. Constitution. Both levels of government act directly on the people through their officials and laws, both are supreme within their proper sphere of authority, and both must consent to constitutional change.

The national government is constitutionally the dominant partner in the federal system. Article VI of the U.S. Constitution includes a provision known as the **National Supremacy Clause**, which declares that the U.S. Constitution, the laws made under it, and the treaties of the United States are the supreme law of the land. In short, the National Supremacy Clause states that the legitimate exercise of national power supersedes state action when the two conflict. When state and local government policies conflict with the U.S. Constitution or U.S. law, the latter take precedence.

The powers of state government can be grouped in four broad categories as follows:

1. States exercise **police power,** which is the authority to promote the health, welfare, and safety of the people. States enact criminal laws, establish minimal standards for practicing certain occupations, adopt clean air and water standards, regulate workplace safety, and enforce laws protecting individuals from discrimination. A state's police power includes **eminent domain,** which is the authority to take private property for public use upon just compensation.

2. States provide public services to their residents, including schools, colleges and universities, healthcare, law enforcement, welfare services,

Police power The authority to promote the health, welfare, and safety of the people.

Eminent domain The authority to take private property for public use upon just compensation.

Local governments Subunits of states.

transportation, agricultural support, and conservation. The major budget items for state and local governments in Texas and around the nation are education, healthcare, public safety (police and fire protection), and transportation.

3. States levy taxes and borrow money to finance their operations. The most important tax sources for state and local governments nationwide are sales, property, excise, and income taxes. All of these taxes, except the income tax, are important in Texas. Texas is one of only a handful of states that do not levy a personal income tax.

4. States create and control **local governments,** which are subunits of states. Local governments in Texas include cities, counties, school districts, and special districts.[6]

State governments are sometimes called "laboratories of democracy" because they have the ability to adopt innovative solutions to policy problems. If a creative policy approach adopted by one state is deemed successful, other states and perhaps the national government will likely adopt similar programs. Since 2006, for example, Massachusetts has been experimenting with a state universal healthcare system. The lessons of the Massachusetts approach, both its successes and failures, served as a model for the healthcare reform legislation passed by Congress in 2010.

AROUND THE NATION   Healthcare Reform in Massachusetts

Massachusetts adopted healthcare reform in 2006, several years before Congress enacted the Patient Protection and Affordable Care Act. The Massachusetts plan uses a series of penalties and incentives to close the insurance gap. People who can afford health insurance are required to purchase it much the way drivers in Texas and most other states are required to have automobile liability insurance. Individuals who fail to get health insurance must pay a penalty through the state income tax system. In 2010, the maximum penalty for failing to purchase health insurance was a little more than $1,100.[‡] Businesses with at least 10 employees are required to provide them with health insurance coverage or face

a fine as well. State government subsidizes the cost of health insurance for lower-income people based on a sliding scale. A single person earning $40,000 a year is expected to pay no more than 9 percent of his or her income, about $300 a month, whereas a person making $25,000 a year is expected to pay a smaller percentage, a little more than 3 percent of his or her income, or $70 a month.[§]

The Massachusetts plan has succeeded in expanding healthcare coverage without making much progress on controlling healthcare costs. It has also produced at least a temporary shortage of physicians. The program has reduced the proportion of state residents without insurance to 3 percent of the

[‡]Massachusetts Department of Revenue, "Assessment of Penalties," available at www.mass.gov.

[§]Sharon K. Long and Paul B. Masi, "Access and Affordability: Update on Health Reform in Massachusetts, Fall 2008," available at www.consumerwatchdog.com.

population, the lowest uninsured rate in the nation by far.** As a result, Massachusetts physicians, especially family physicians, have been inundated with new patients. Some patients are waiting as long as 48 days for nonemergency appointments with primary care physicians.†† Furthermore, the Massachusetts plan has failed to control healthcare costs. Although numerous cost-saving initiatives have been adopted, Massachusetts insurance rates are rising more rapidly than national rates.‡‡

QUESTIONS

1. Who should be responsible for providing individual health insurance coverage—the individual, private employers, or the government?
2. Is it right for the government to force healthy young people who do not think they need health insurance to purchase coverage?
3. Would you be willing to wait longer to see your primary care physician in order to provide currently uninsured people with health insurance coverage? Why or why not?

**Charles Wallace, "Is Health Care Reform Working in Massachusetts?" *Daily Finance*, January 25, 2011, available at www.dailyfinance.com.

††Steven Syre, "Doctors in Demand," *Boston Globe*, June 17, 2011, available at www.boston.com.

‡‡Wallace, "Is Health Care Reform Working in Massachusetts?"

STATES, THE COURTS, AND THE CONSTITUTION

The U.S. Constitution is the supreme law of the land. It takes legal precedence over state constitutions, state laws, state administrative procedures, and the actions of local government. State and local officials pledge to uphold the U.S. Constitution, and most of them take that responsibility quite seriously. When the legislature considers changes in the state's capital punishment law, for example, the debate frequently centers on the likelihood that any proposed revision will survive a constitutional challenge. Individuals and groups who believe that the policies of state and local government violate the U.S. Constitution may file suit in federal court, asking the court to intervene. We can illustrate the importance of federal court rulings on policymaking in Texas by examining three historic cases: *Brown v. Board of Education of Topeka*, *Ruiz v. Estelle*, and *Roe v. Wade*.

School Desegregation

Brown v. Board of Education of Topeka (1954) dealt with the constitutionality of state laws requiring racially segregated schools. The Brown family, residents of Topeka, Kansas, wanted their daughter Linda to attend a public school near their home. However, Kansas state law required separate schools for white and African American youngsters. Because the school nearest the Brown home was for whites only, Linda, who was African American, would have to travel across town to another school. With the legal support of the **National Association for the Advancement of Colored People (NAACP),** an interest group organized to represent the interests of African Americans, the Browns filed suit against the state. They charged that the law requiring a racially segregated public school system

National Association for the Advancement of Colored People (NAACP) An interest group organized to represent the interests of African Americans.

Equal Protection Clause The constitutional provision found in the Fourteenth Amendment of the U.S. Constitution that declares "No State shall . . . deny to any person within its jurisdiction the equal protection of the laws."

violated the **Equal Protection Clause,** the constitutional provision found in the Fourteenth Amendment of the U.S. Constitution that declares "No State shall . . . deny to any person within its jurisdiction the equal protection of the laws."

The U.S. Supreme Court ruled that the state law was unconstitutional because it denied equal educational opportunities to African American students. "Segregation of white and colored children in public schools has a detrimental effect upon the colored children," wrote Chief Justice Earl Warren in the Court's opinion. "A sense of inferiority affects the motivation of the child to learn."[7]

Brown v. Board of Education of Topeka ultimately had a profound impact on policymaking in Texas. Even though the case involved a state law in Kansas, the precedent set by the Supreme Court in its ruling applied to all similar statutes throughout the United States. As was true for most southern states, Texas had a **dual school system,** that is, separate sets of schools for white and African American youngsters. Because of the *Brown* case, the state was eventually forced to dismantle its dual school system and adopt policies aimed at achieving racial integration of public schools.

Dual school system Separate sets of schools for white and African American youngsters.

Prison Overcrowding

Ruiz v. Estelle (1972) addressed the issue of living conditions in the Texas Department of Corrections (TDC). In 1972, a group of prison inmates filed suit in federal court, claiming that living and working conditions in Texas prisons constituted "cruel and unusual punishment," forbidden by the Eighth Amendment to the U.S. Constitution. They charged that the state's prison system was severely overcrowded, the prison staff was too small to maintain security, working conditions were unsafe, disciplinary procedures were severe and arbitrary, and medical care was inadequate.

In 1980, U.S. District Judge William Wayne Justice ruled against the state of Texas, ordering sweeping changes in the Texas prison system. Although an appeals court later overturned part of Judge Justice's ruling, it upheld the key points of his decision. Eventually, the state settled the suit by agreeing to limit the inmate population to 95 percent of prison capacity, separate hardcore offenders from inmates convicted of nonviolent crimes, improve the guard-to-inmate ratio, and upgrade inmate medical treatment.[8]

The *Ruiz* case forced Texas to limit its prison population. Initially, the state responded with early release, turning offenders out on **parole,** the conditional release of convicted offenders from prison to serve the remainder of their sentences in the community under supervision. In the long run, the state complied with the court's decision to reduce overcrowding by dramatically increasing the capacity of its prison system.

Parole The conditional release of convicted offenders from prison to serve the remainder of their sentences in the community under supervision.

Abortion

Roe v. Wade (1973) dealt with the issue of abortion. "Jane Roe," an anonymous woman living in Dallas, challenged the constitutionality of a Texas law prohibiting abortion except to save the life of a woman. The U.S. Supreme Court found

Linda Brown and her family were the plaintiffs in the *Brown v. Board of Education of Topeka* case, in which state laws requiring racial segregation in public schools were ruled to be unconstitutional.

the Texas statute unconstitutional, saying that a woman's right to personal privacy under the U.S. Constitution included her decision to terminate a pregnancy within six months of inception.

The Supreme Court explained the ruling by dividing a pregnancy into three trimesters. During the first trimester (a three-month period), state governments could not interfere with a physician's decision, reached in consultation with a pregnant patient, to terminate a pregnancy. In the second trimester, a state could regulate abortion only to protect the health of the woman. In the third trimester, after the fetus has achieved viability (the ability to survive outside the womb), the Court ruled that states could choose to prohibit abortion except when necessary to preserve the life or health of the woman.[9]

In subsequent cases, the Supreme Court modified its ruling in *Roe v. Wade* to allow states greater leeway to limit abortion rights. Although the Court reaffirmed a woman's right to choose to abort a fetus before viability, it ruled that a state could regulate access to abortion as long as the regulations did not place an "undue burden"

GETTING INVOLVED

Contacting Your Representative in Washington, D.C.

In America's federal system of government, individuals are citizens of the United States and citizens of the state in which they live. If you live in the Lone Star State, you are both an American citizen and a citizen of Texas. You receive services, pay taxes, and are subject to the laws and regulations of both the national government and the state of Texas.

American citizens have the constitutional right to participate in the policymaking process of both the national government and their state government. They may vote in both national and state elections and contact their elected representatives at both levels of government to make their policy preferences known.

The names, postal addresses, and e-mail addresses of the people who represent you in Congress are available online. The website for the U.S. Senate is **www.senate.gov.** The website for the U.S. House is **www.house.gov.** Each site has an interactive window that enables you to identify the name of your representatives. You can also find contact information. Write or e-mail your U.S. senators and U.S. representative, expressing your point of view on any federal or national issue about which you have an opinion.

It's your country—get involved!

---

on a woman's right to choose. The Court's majority defined an undue burden as one that presented an "absolute obstacle or severe limitation" on the right to decide to have an abortion. State regulations that simply "inhibited" that right were permissible.[10]

The Texas legislature and the governor have taken advantage of the Supreme Court's flexibility on state abortion regulation by adopting the following measures:

- **Parental consent for minors.** A physician may not perform an abortion on an unmarried girl younger than 18 without the written permission of a parent or guardian. However, the consent requirement can be waived if a judge determines that involving a parent could put the minor at risk of physical or emotional abuse or that the girl seeking an abortion is sufficiently mature to make the decision herself.

- **24-hour waiting period.** Before performing an abortion, a physician must provide a pregnant patient with a state-created packet that includes information on the health risks associated with abortion, alternatives to terminating a pregnancy, and color images of fetal development. The woman must then wait 24 hours before having the abortion.

- **Late-term abortion prohibition.** A physician may not perform an abortion on a woman who has carried a fetus more than 26 weeks unless the woman's life is in jeopardy or the fetus has serious brain damage.

- **Sonogram requirement.** The latest addition to the state's abortion laws is a sonogram requirement. A physician must conduct a sonogram at least 24 hours before an abortion and provide the woman with the opportunity to see the results and hear the fetal heartbeat. The doctor is also required to describe what the sonogram shows, including the existence of legs, arms, and internal organs.

Roe v. Wade and other court cases dealing with abortion rights affected Texas law by restricting the state's ability to adopt policies controlling access to abortion. Before *Roe*, the state was free to adopt any policy ranging from legalization of abortion in most circumstances to the prohibition of abortion in almost all circumstances. Because of *Roe*, abortion is now legal in every state, including Texas, whether legislators and governors like it or not. In 2008, Texas physicians performed 78,330 abortions compared with 405,242 live births.[11]

The data indicate that the Texas parental consent requirement may be reducing the number of abortions performed on minors. After Texas began enforcing the consent requirement, the abortion rate fell by 11 percent for 15-year-olds, by 20 percent among 16-year-olds, and by 16 percent among 17-year-olds. Ironically, the second-trimester abortion rate increased for 18-year-olds who became pregnant within six months of their 18th birthday, suggesting that some 17-year-olds were waiting to seek abortion services until they were no longer covered by the parental consent requirement.[12]

 WHAT DO YOU THINK?

Do you agree with the new Texas law that requires a woman seeking an abortion to undergo a sonogram? Why or why not?

STATES AND FEDERAL LAW

Federal laws apply to state and local governments as long as Congress acts within the scope of its powers under the U.S. Constitution. Article I, Section 8, of the Constitution grants Congress authority to legislate in a range of policy areas, including trade, immigration, patent and copyright law, and national defense. In practice, Congress has made frequent use of the Interstate Commerce Clause as a basis for legislation affecting the states. The **Interstate Commerce Clause** is the constitutional provision giving Congress the authority to "regulate commerce . . . among the several states." Congress has used this constitutional provision as a basis for legislation dealing with such diverse subjects as cable television regulation, agricultural price supports, racial discrimination, and healthcare reform.

The federal laws and regulations that have the greatest impact on state and local policymaking take the form of federal preemption and federal mandates. Federal preemption *prevents* states from adopting their own policies in selected policy areas, whereas federal mandates *require* certain state policy actions.

Federal Preemption

The federal government prevents state and local governments from making policy in some policy areas. An act of Congress adopting regulatory policies that overrule state policies in a particular regulatory area is known as a **federal preemption of state authority.** Through 2008, Congress had passed more than 500 laws preempting state

Interstate Commerce Clause The constitutional provision giving Congress the authority to "regulate commerce . . . among the several states."

Federal preemption of state authority An act of Congress adopting regulatory policies that overrule state policies in a particular regulatory area.

regulation in such policy areas as cellular phone rates, nuclear power safety, pension plans, automobile safety standards, and trucking rates.[13]

Preemption is controversial. The proponents of preemption believe that uniform national regulatory standards are preferable to state-by-state regulation. In contrast, critics of preemption contend that congressional efforts to override state authority violate states' rights principles that hold that state officials know best what policies are most appropriate for their states.

Ironically, business interests, which often oppose regulation in general, frequently support the federal preemption of state regulations. Firms doing business nationwide would rather adapt to a uniform national policy than conform to 50 different state regulations. As one state official put it, "A lot of . . . companies feel it is easier to work with Congress than 50 state legislatures."[14] Business interests would also prefer that Congress adopt a relatively mild nationwide regulatory standard than deal with tough regulations at the state level.

Federal Mandates

Federal mandate
A legal requirement placed on a state or local government by the national government requiring certain policy actions.

A **federal mandate** is a legal requirement placed on a state or local government by the national government requiring certain policy actions. The Americans with Disabilities Act (ADA), Clean Air Act, and No Child Left Behind (NCLB) are examples of federal laws that impose significant mandates on state governments. The **Americans with Disabilities Act (ADA)** is a federal law intended to end discrimination against persons with disabilities and to eliminate barriers preventing their full participation in American society. It mandates that when a new building goes up or an old building undergoes a major renovation, it must be made accessible to people with disabilities, and accommodations must be made for employees with disabilities. Because of the ADA, colleges and universities typically provide special assistance to students with disabilities, such as sign-language interpreters for students who have hearing impairments and additional time to take exams for students with learning disabilities.

Americans with Disabilities Act (ADA) A federal law intended to end discrimination against persons with disabilities and to eliminate barriers preventing their full participation in American society.

Clean Air Act
A federal law that regulates air emissions.

Environmental Protection Agency (EPA)
The federal agency responsible for enforcing the nation's environmental laws.

The **Clean Air Act** is a federal law that regulates air emissions. The **Environmental Protection Agency (EPA),** the federal agency responsible for enforcing the nation's environmental laws, establishes air quality standards to protect the public health. States then develop implementation plans for regulation of emissions from industrial sites, including power plants and oil refineries. The state of Texas and the EPA are at odds over air quality regulation. The Texas Commission on Environmental Quality (TCEQ) has used a flexible permitting process that allows plants to meet clean air requirements based on a ceiling for the entire plant rather than measures for each source within the facility. Although the EPA accepted the approach during the George W. Bush administration, EPA administrators appointed by President Obama have ruled that Texas is violating the Clean Air Act. When the TCEQ refused to change its approach, the EPA took over the permitting process, requiring Texas companies to apply for emissions permits directly from the EPA rather than the TCEQ.[15] The most recent conflict between the EPA and the state of Texas involves federal efforts to regulate greenhouse gas emissions.

The ADA mandates that public buildings be made accessible to persons with disabilities.

Instead of complying with EPA rules to include greenhouse gases in the permitting process, Texas has sued the federal government, arguing that scientific data on global warming are inaccurate.[16]

 WHAT DO YOU THINK?

Do you agree with the decision of Texas officials to sue the federal government over greenhouse gas emissions containment?

No Child Left Behind (NCLB)
A federal law that requires state governments and local school districts to institute basic skills testing in reading and mathematics for students in grades three through eight, and use the results to assess school performance.

No Child Left Behind (NCLB) is a federal law that requires state governments and local school districts to institute basic skills testing in reading and mathematics for students in grades three through eight, and use the results to assess school performance. Schools must assess student progress not just for the entire school but also by subgroups based on race/ethnicity, income level, English proficiency, and special education status. NCLB requires schools to report student progress separately for students in each subgroup, forcing them to be accountable for the progress of all of their students. Even if a school's overall performance is good, it will receive a failing grade under the law if, for example, the performance of Latino or special education students lags.[17] Schools that fail to show adequate yearly progress face an escalating series of sanctions, ultimately including the replacement of faculty and staff, or having the state or a private company take over school management.

State officials complain about the cost of federal mandates. Consider the impact of the Adam Walsh Act, a federal law designed to protect children from sexual predators by creating a national sex offender registry. The law requires states to adopt the federal offender registration system so data can be easily merged into a single national database. States that fail to conform will lose 10 percent of their federal funding under the Bryne Justice Assistance Grants, which provides assistance to crime victims and witnesses. The annual loss to Texas for failing to comply would be $2.2 million. The problem is that the Texas sex offender registry is based on offense and risk level, whereas the federal registration system is based on offenses committed. In order to conform to federal law, Texas would have to change its sex offender registration requirements and reorganize its database at an upfront expense that is estimated at nearly $40 million.[18]

The National Conference of State Legislatures (NCSL) estimates that Congress has shifted $33.7 billion in costs to the states over the last five years.[19] The most expensive programs are the Disabilities Education Act, NCLB, prescription drug costs for people eligible for Medicaid or Medicare, the Help America Vote Act, federal environmental protection requirements, and the cost to states of incarcerating illegal immigrants.[20]

FEDERAL GRANT PROGRAMS

Federal grant program
A program through which the national government gives money to state and local governments to spend in accordance with set standards and conditions.

A **federal grant program** is a program through which the national government gives money to state and local governments to spend in accordance with set standards and conditions. In 2010, the federal government distributed $608 billion in federal grant money to state and local governments, a figure representing 17.6 percent of federal outlays.[21] Most of the funds went directly to state governments rather than localities, although much of that money was passed on by the state to local agencies for health and human services, housing and urban development, transportation, and education.[22]

Program Adoption

Congress and the president adopt federal grant programs through the legislative process. Both houses of Congress must agree to establish a program and the president must either sign the legislation or allow it to become law without signature. If the president vetoes the measure, it can become law only if Congress votes to override the veto by a two-thirds margin in each house.

Authorization process The procedure through which Congress legislatively establishes a program, defines its general purpose, devises procedures for its operation, specifies an agency for implementation, and indicates an approximate level of funding.

Federal programs must be authorized and funds appropriated for their operation. The **authorization process** is the procedure through which Congress legislatively establishes a program, defines its general purpose, devises procedures for its operation, specifies an agency for implementation, and indicates an approximate level of funding. However, the authorization process does not actually allocate money for the program. Congress sometimes specifies that programs be reauthorized periodically. The **appropriation process** is an annual procedure through which Congress legislatively provides money for a particular purpose.

The adoption of the Help America Vote Act of 2002 illustrates the distinction between authorization and appropriation. Congress passed and President

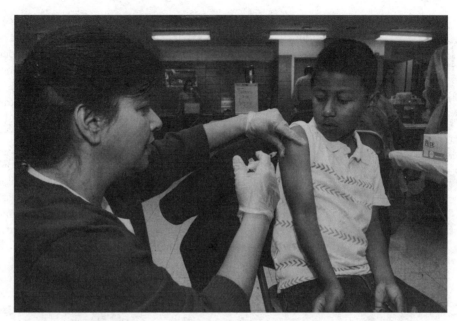

The State Children's Health Insurance Program is a federal program designed to provide health insurance to children from low-income families whose parents are not poor enough to qualify for Medicaid.

Appropriation process An annual procedure through which Congress legislatively provides money for a particular purpose.

Categorical grant program A federal grant-in-aid program that provides funds to state and local governments for a fairly narrow, specific purpose.

Block grant program A federal grant-in-aid program that provides money for a program in a broad, general policy area, such as elementary and secondary education or transportation.

George W. Bush signed the measure to reform state election systems after the debacle of the Florida presidential election controversy in 2000. The law requires states to maintain a database of registered voters, provide voting systems with minimum error rates, set voter identification requirements, provide access for people with disabilities, and adopt procedures for resolving voter complaints.[23] Although the measure authorized $4 billion to cover the cost of new voting machines and other improvements, Congress failed to include the money in the annual appropriation bill, leaving the states to bear the cost of the measure on their own.[24]

Types of Federal Programs

Federal programs come in a variety of forms.

Categorical and Block Grants A **categorical grant program** is a federal grant-in-aid program that provides funds to state and local governments for a fairly narrow, specific purpose, such as removing asbestos from school buildings or acquiring land for outdoor recreation. In this type of program, Congress allows state and local officials little discretion as to how money is spent. Categorical grants comprise more than 90 percent of all federal grants and provide nearly 90 percent of federal grant money to state and local governments.[25] Medicaid is a categorical grant program.

A **block grant program** is a federal grant-in-aid program that provides money for a program in a broad, general policy area, such as elementary and secondary education or transportation. State and local governments have more discretion in spending block grant funds than they have for categorical grant money. For example, **Temporary Assistance for Needy Families (TANF)** is a federal block grant program that provides temporary financial assistance and work opportunities to needy families. The goal of the program is to move welfare families into the workforce. States have considerable leeway in designing their own programs, but if they fall short of federally mandated goals, such as the requirement that half of single parents receiving benefits must participate in a work activity program, they lose some federal funding.

A number of Texas officials, including Governor Perry, would like for Congress to make Medicaid a block grant program. They believe that a block grant would give them the leeway to slow the growth of Medicaid spending by adopting cost savings not allowed under the current categorical grant program framework. In contrast, critics, noting that Texas already has the stingiest Medicaid program in the country, believe that Texas officials want the flexibility to restrict Medicaid benefits even more, making the Texas program even less generous.

Over time Congress tends to attach conditions to the receipt of block grant funds, thus reducing the flexibility of state and local officials. When Congress created the Surface Transportation Program, for example, it gave states a lump sum of money to spend on highways and other transportation projects in accordance with statewide objectives. Subsequently, Congress has added restrictions requiring that 10 percent of the funds be used to improve the safety of state highways and that 10 percent be spent on "transportation enhancement" activities, such as hiking and biking trails.[26]

Policymakers disagree about the relative merits of categorical and block grants. The proponents of categorical grants argue that they enable Congress to identify particular policy problems and ensure that the money that Congress provides targets those problems. Categorical grants, they say, allow Congress to set national goals and apply national standards to achieve those goals. If local officials are given too much discretion, they may use grant money to reward campaign supporters or pay back political debts. In contrast, the proponents of block grants contend that state and local officeholders know better what their residents want and need than do officials in Washington, DC. Block grants enable the officials closest to the people to direct the federal dollars to where they will do the most good.

 WHAT DO YOU THINK?

If you were a member of Congress, would you make Medicaid a block grant or keep it as is?

Entitlement Programs   Some federal programs, such as Medicaid and the School Lunch Program, are **entitlement programs.** These government programs provide benefits to all persons qualified to receive them under law. Congress sets eligibility standards based on such factors as age, income, and disability. Individuals who meet

Temporary Assistance for Needy Families (TANF) A federal block grant program that provides temporary financial assistance and work opportunities to needy families.

Entitlement programs Government programs providing benefits to all persons qualified to receive them under law.

School Lunch Program A federal program that provides free or reduced-cost lunches to children from poor families.

the criteria are entitled to receive the benefits. Medicaid eligibility, for example, is based on income level. The **School Lunch Program** is a federal program that provides free or reduced-cost lunches to children from poor families. Children qualify for free or reduced-cost lunches based on their family income.

Spending for entitlement programs does not go through the appropriation process. The amount of money the federal government spends each year on Medicaid and other entitlement programs depends on the number of eligible recipients who apply for benefits and the cost of providing those benefits. If Congress and the president want to reduce (or increase) spending for an entitlement program, they must pass legislation to change the program.

Entitlement programs are controversial. The proponents of entitlement programs say that they represent a national commitment to address certain important policy issues, including healthcare for the poor and for people with disabilities (Medicaid) and nutritious lunches for low-income school children (the School Lunch Program). Program recipients do not have to depend on Congress and the president to appropriate money each year for their benefits because they are entitled to them by law. In contrast, the critics of entitlement programs charge that they are budget busters. Spending for entitlement programs goes up each year automatically as the number of beneficiaries rises and the cost of providing services increases, regardless of the budgetary situation. For example, state governments are hard pressed to keep up with the rapidly rising costs of the Medicaid program.

Project grant program A grant program that requires state and local governments to compete for available federal money.

Project and Formula Grants Federal grants differ in the criteria by which funding is awarded. A **project grant program** is a grant program that requires state and local governments to compete for available federal money. State and local governments present detailed grant applications, which federal agencies evaluate in order to make funding decisions. The Department of Education, for example, administers project grants dealing with a range of educational initiatives, such as teacher training, math and science education, and the preparation of students for the demands of today's workforce. Public schools, colleges, and universities make application to the agency, which then decides which grant proposals merit funding.

Formula grant program A grant program that awards funding on the basis of a formula established by Congress.

A **formula grant program** is a grant program that awards funding on the basis of a formula established by Congress. In contrast to project grants, formula grants provide money for every state and/or locality that qualifies under the formula. The Clean Fuels Formula Grant Program, administered by the Department of Transportation, allocates money to transit authorities to assist in the purchase and use of low-emissions buses and related equipment. The program awards funds based on a formula that includes area population, the size of the bus fleet, the number of bus passenger miles, and the severity of the area's air pollution problem.[27]

Matching funds requirement A legislative provision that the national government will provide grant money for a particular activity only on the condition that the state or local government involved supply a certain percentage of the total money required for the project or program.

Grant Conditions

Federal grants usually come with conditions. A **matching funds requirement** is a legislative provision that the national government will provide grant money for a particular activity only on the condition that the state or local government

BREAKING NEWS!   States Challenge Constitutionality of Healthcare Reform

Texas and a dozen other states have filed lawsuits against the healthcare reform act, arguing that Congress exceeded its constitutional authority when it enacted the measure. Although the suits raise several issues, their main line of attack is against the individual mandate that requires people who lack health insurance coverage either to purchase a qualifying policy or pay an additional 2.5 percent of their adjusted gross incomes in taxes. The states filing the lawsuit question whether Congress has the power to regulate inactivity by levying a tax on those who do not purchase health insurance. In response, the U.S. Justice Department contends that Congress acted within its constitutional authority and that Congress has taken similar actions before that have been upheld by the courts, such as forcing restaurant and hotel operators to offer services to the public without regard to their race or ethnicity.*

Discussion

Why are states filing suit over the individual mandate? It applies to individuals, not states. This raises an important issue. A basic principle of American law called *standing* holds that a party bringing a lawsuit must show that it has a stake in the outcome of the dispute. The federal government is certain to argue that state governments lack standing to sue because the individual mandate does not affect them. State officials will no doubt respond that healthcare reform taken as a whole has a significant impact on states. They may also assert that they are acting as protectors of state citizens who will be affected by the mandate.

Could a judge throw the case out because states are not directly affected by the individual mandate? That's possible. It is also conceivable that a judge could rule that the case is premature because the individual mandate does not kick in until 2014. If that happens, however, it will likely just delay the controversy because individuals affected by the mandate will be able to file suit once it takes effect.

How does Congress justify healthcare reform and, especially, the individual mandate? Congress based the legislation primarily on the Commerce Clause. The healthcare industry is obviously a huge part of the nation's commerce, and whether people buy or do not buy health insurance significantly affects the industry. People without health insurance who become ill will likely be treated in hospital emergency rooms and the cost of that will be passed on to the taxpayers and consumers through higher hospital fees. Congress also called the fine levied on those who do not purchase health insurance a tax, and the Constitution explicitly gives Congress the authority to tax. Finally, the authors of healthcare reform argued that Congress acted under its general authority to "promote the general Welfare," a phrase found in the preamble to the Constitution.

Why do the state officials who filed the suit think the law is unconstitutional? They believe that healthcare reform is an expansion of federal authority at the expense of the states that goes well beyond anything envisioned by the framers of the Constitution. Furthermore, they regard the individual mandate as an unprecedented intrusion by the federal government into peoples' lives—the equivalent of going beyond regulating automobile safety to requiring people to buy a car.[†]

How have the courts dealt with the issue so far? Several lower federal courts have issued rulings. Because more than one lawsuit was filed, more than one court has been involved. To date, judges appointed by Republican presidents have ruled the law unconstitutional; judges appointed by Democratic presidents have ruled it constitutional. If the U.S. Supreme Court decides to rule on the issue, it will consolidate the various cases into a single suit. For what it's worth, the current court is composed of five justices appointed by Republican presidents and four appointed by Democrats.

*Kevin Sack, "Florida Suit Poses a Challenge to Health Care Law," *New York Times*, May 10, 2010, available at www.nytimes.com.

[†]John Schwartz, "Health Measure's Opponents Plan Legal Challenges," *New York Times*, March 22, 2010, available at www.nytimes.com.

State Children's Health Insurance Program (SCHIP) A federal program designed to provide health insurance to children from low-income families whose parents are not poor enough to qualify for Medicaid.

Supplemental Nutrition Assistance Program (SNAP) Formerly the Food Stamp Program, it is a federal program that provides food vouchers to low-income families and individuals.

involved will supply a certain percentage of the total money required for the project or program. The **State Children's Health Insurance Program (SCHIP),** a federal program designed to provide health insurance to children from low-income families whose parents are not poor enough to qualify for Medicaid, gives money to states based on a 75–25 match. The federal government picks up 75 percent of the cost, leaving only 25 percent to the states.[28] Even federal programs that do not require financial participation by state and local governments often require contributions in-kind. The **Supplemental Nutrition Assistance Program (SNAP),** which was once called the Food Stamp Program, is a federal program that provides food vouchers to low-income families and individuals. The national government covers the entire cost of the program, but state governments must administer its operation.

Congress imposes legislative mandates on the recipients of federal funds. Some mandates apply to grant recipients in general. These include provisions in the area of equal rights, equal access for people with disabilities, environmental protection, historic preservation, and union wage rates for construction workers on federally funded projects. Furthermore, many individual programs have particular strings attached. For example, in order to receive money from the Violent Crime Control and Enforcement Act of 1994 to construct, expand, and operate correctional facilities, states must adopt "truth in sentencing" laws that accurately show the amount of time persons convicted of crimes spend behind bars. States must ensure that violent criminals serve at least 85 percent of their prison sentences. The federal government also requires states to impose stiff penalties for criminal offenders and adopt programs to protect the rights of crime victims.[29]

Congress sometimes uses federal grant money to compel states to adopt policies favored in Washington, although not necessarily in state capitals. In the 1980s, for example, Congress threatened states with the loss of federal highway grant money unless they adopted the 55-miles-per-hour speed limit and raised their minimum legal drinking age to 21. Although Congress dropped the speed limit requirement in 1995, it now requires that states ban open containers in vehicles and revoke the driver's licenses of repeat DUI offenders. If states fail to comply with these requirements, the federal government transfers a portion of their highway construction money into a fund that can be used only for highway safety.[30]

Congress initially took an incentive approach to setting a national standard for blood-alcohol content of 0.08 for determining whether a driver is legally intoxicated. Although some states already followed the 0.08 standard, most states, including Texas, set the drunk-driving level at a blood-alcohol content of 0.10. Instead of penalizing states that failed to adopt the 0.08 standard with the loss of federal money, Congress established a fund to pay a cash bonus to states that voluntarily adopted the tougher blood-alcohol standard. Two years later, however, Congress decided that the incentive plan was not working well enough, so it adopted legislation mandating the loss of highway funds for states that failed to adopt the 0.08 standard. Although most states

The School Lunch Program is a federal program that provides free or inexpensive lunches to children from poor families.

(including Texas) complied with the federal requirement rather than risk the loss of highway funding, state officials complained about Congress forcing its policy preferences on the states. "If states want 0.08, that's fine," said an Iowa legislator, "[but] if Congress says you have to have it, they've [sic] overstepped their bounds."[31]

States that fail to follow federal rules risk the loss of federal funds. The EPA says that the Houston-Galveston, Dallas-Fort Worth, and Beaumont-Port Arthur metropolitan areas fail to meet federal air quality standards for ozone, which is the principal ingredient of smog. Because of new, tougher EPA standards, the Austin, San Antonio, and northeast Texas areas may be out of compliance as well.[32] Regions that fail to meet federal deadlines for ozone standards, which fall between 2013 and 2030, depending on the severity of the problem in an area, can lose funding for transportation projects.[33]

Federal Money and Texas

State and local governments in Texas receive billions of dollars in federal funds annually. In 2011, federal grant money represented one-third of total state revenue, $35 billion out of nearly $103 billion in revenue generated from all sources. Federal dollars helped fund healthcare, highway construction, welfare, and education.[34] Billions of federal dollars flowed to local governments for special education programs, school lunches, urban transit projects, parkland acquisition, neighborhood revitalization, sewerage treatment plants, and other purposes. Figure 3.1 documents the growth in federal aid to state government in Texas between 1990 and 2011. The relative importance of federal funding to state government in Texas grew from 1990 through the early 2000s, increasing from less than 26 percent in 1990 to more than 30 percent in 2002. Since then, the relative importance of federal money has varied between 31 percent and 36 percent of total state revenue. Growth in the Medicaid program accounted for more than 40 percent of the increase in federal grant funds in the 1990s and the first decade of the twenty-first century, but it was not the only federal program to grow. Funding for three-fourths of federal programs has been increasing, including money for programs dealing with natural resources and the environment, transportation, community and regional development, income security, and education and training.[35]

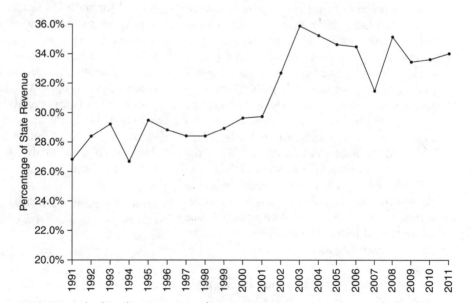

FIGURE 3.1   Federal Funds as Percentage of State Revenue.

WHAT WE HAVE LEARNED

1. **What is the role of states in the federal system?**

   Texas is part of the federal system, which is a political system that divides power between a central government, with authority over the whole nation, and a series of state governments. Although the national government is the dominant partner in the federal system, state and local governments enjoy considerable policymaking authority to provide services, enact regulations, and levy taxes.

2. **How have the U.S. Constitution and the federal courts affected policymaking in Texas, especially concerning the following cases: *Brown v. Board of Education of Topeka, Ruiz v. Estelle,* and *Roe v. Wade*?**

   The U.S. Constitution takes legal precedence over state constitutions, state laws, state administrative procedures, and the actions of local government. Individuals and groups who believe that the policies of state and local government violate the U.S. Constitution may file suit in federal court, asking the court to intervene. *Brown v. Board of Education of Topeka* (1954) dealt with the constitutionality of state laws requiring racially segregated schools. Because of the *Brown* decision, Texas was eventually forced to dismantle its dual school system and racially integrate its public schools. *Ruiz v. Estelle* (1972) addressed the issue of living conditions in the Texas Department of Corrections (TDC). The ruling forced Texas to alleviate overcrowding in the state prison system and make other improvements. *Roe v. Wade* (1973) dealt with the issue of abortion. It restricted Texas's ability to adopt policies controlling access to abortion.

3. **How do federal preemptions and federal mandates affect policymaking in Texas?**

   Federal laws apply to state and local governments as long as Congress acts within the scope of its powers under the U.S. Constitution. Federal preemption *prevents* states from adopting their own policies in selected policy areas, whereas federal mandates *require* certain state policy actions. Congress has passed hundreds of laws preempting state regulation, including preemption of state policies dealing with cellular phone rates, nuclear power safety, pension plans, automobile safety standards, and trucking rates. The ADA, the Clean Air Act, and NCLB are federal programs that contain federal mandates.

4. **What are the various kinds of grant programs, and what are the various types of conditions that the federal government places on the receipt of federal funds?**

   Congress and the president adopt federal grant programs through the legislative process. Programs must be authorized and money appropriated for their operation. Federal programs may come in the form of categorical grants or block grants. Some federal programs, such as Medicaid and the School Lunch Program, are entitlement programs. Programs may be project grant programs or formula grant programs. Federal programs also come with strings attached, including matching funds requirements. States that fail to meet federal standards, such as air quality standards, may lose federal funding.

5. **How important are federal programs and federal dollars to state and local governments in Texas?**

   State and local governments in Texas receive billions of dollars in federal funds annually. About a third of state revenues come from the federal government. Federal dollars help fund healthcare, highway construction, welfare, and education.

KEY TERMS

Americans with Disabilities Act (ADA)

appropriation process

authorization process

block grant program

categorical grant program

Clean Air Act

dual school system

eminent domain

entitlement programs

Environmental Protection Agency (EPA)

Equal Protection Clause

federal grant program

federal mandate

federal preemption of state authority

federal system *or* federation

formula grant program

Interstate Commerce Clause

local governments

matching funds requirement

Medicaid

Medicare

National Association for the Advancement of Colored People (NAACP)

National Supremacy Clause

No Child Left Behind (NCLB)

parole

police power

project grant program

School Lunch Program

sovereignty

State Children's Health Insurance Program (SCHIP)

Supplemental Nutrition Assistance Program (SNAP)

Temporary Assistance for Needy Families (TANF)

NOTES

1. Texas Health and Human Services Commission, "Medicaid Enrollment by Month," October 2010, available at www.hhsc.state.tx.us.
2. Texas Health and Human Services Commission, "Texas Medicaid and CHIP in Perspective," June 2011, available at www.hhsc.state.tx.us.
3. Michael Luo, "Some States Find Burdens in Health Law," *New York Times*, March 26, 2010, available at www.nytimes.com.
4. "Cheap at First, Expensive Later," *Texas Weekly*, March 29, 2010, available at www.texasweekly.com.
5. Emily Ramshaw, "The $27 Billion Question," *Texas Tribune*, April 1, 2010, available at www.texastribune.org.
6. Joseph F. Zimmerman, *Contemporary American Federalism: The Growth of National Power*, 2nd ed. (Albany, NY: SUNY Press, 2008), pp. 34–37.
7. *Brown v. Board of Education of Topeka*, 347 U.S. 483 (1954).
8. *Ruiz v. Estelle*, 503 F. Supp 1265 (S.D. Tex 1980); 679 F 2d 115 (5th Cir. 1982).
9. *Roe v. Wade*, 410 U.S. 113 (1973).
10. *Planned Parenthood of Southeastern Pennsylvania v. Casey*, 505 U.S. 833 (1992).
11. Texas Department of State Health Services, "Vital Statistics," available at www.dshs.state.tx.us.
12. Theodore Joyce, Robert Kaestner, and Silvie Colman, "Changes in Abortions and Births and the Texas Parental Notification Law," *New England Journal of Medicine*, 354 (March 2006): 1031–1038.
13. Zimmerman, *Contemporary American Federalism*, p. 10.
14. Idaho Attorney General Jim Jones, quoted in Martha M. Hamilton, "On Second Thought, We'd Prefer the Feds on Our Backs," *Washington Post National Weekly Edition*, December 14, 1987, p. 32.
15. Dave Montgomery, "EPA Rejects Texas's Flexible Permit System," *Fort Worth Star-Telegram*, June 30, 2010, available at www.star-telegram.com.
16. Matthew Tresaugue, "Greenhouse Gas Curbs Weeks Away for State," *Houston Chronicle*, December 11, 2010, pp. A-1, A-7.
17. Kenneth Wong and Gail Sunderman, "Education Accountability as a Presidential Priority: No Child Left Behind and the Bush Presidency," *Publius: The Journal of Federalism* 37 (Summer 2007): 333–350.
18. Heather Caygle, "New Showdown: Sex Offender List," *Houston Chronicle*, March 7, 2011, pp. A1, A6.
19. National Conference of State Legislatures, "Mandate Monitor," available at www.ncsl.org.
20. Molly Stauffer and Carl Tubbesing, "The Mandate Monster," *State Legislatures*, May 2004, pp. 22–23.
21. Office of Management and Budget, "Summary Comparison of Total Outlays for Grants to State and Local Governments: 1940–2016," *The Budget for Fiscal Year 2012, Historical Tables*, available at www.omb.gov.
22. "Federal Aid to States and Localities," *Governing State and Local Source Book*, 2006, p. 32, available at www.governing.com.

23. Public Law 107-252.

24. Alan Greenblatt, "Squeezing the Federal Turnip," *Governing*, March 2003, p. 29.

25. Larry N. Gerston, *American Federalism: A Concise Introduction* (Armonk, NY: M.E. Sharpe, 2007), p. 69.

26. Transportation Equity Act for the Twenty-first Century, available at www.fhwa.dot.gov.

27. Department of Transportation, "Fact Sheet: Clean Fuels Formula Grant Program," available at www.fhwa.dot.gov/tea21/factsheets/clnfuel.htm.

28. Colleen M. Grogan and Elizabeth Rigby, "Federalism, Partisan Politics, and Shifting Support for State Flexibility: The Case of the U.S. State Children's Health Insurance Program," *Publius: The Journal of Federalism* 39 (Winter 2009): 47–69.

29. Public Law 103-322.

30. Lilliard E. Richardson, Jr. and David J. Houston, "Federalism and Safety on America's Highways," *Publius: The Journalism of Federalism* 39 (Winter 2009): 117–137.

31. Anya Sostek, "Slow to Toe the DUI Line," *Governing*, May 2003, p. 42.

32. Katie Galbraith, "The Pollution Wars," *Texas Tribune*, June 3, 2010, available at www.texastribune.org.

33. Matthew Tresaugue, "EPA's Smog Rules to Get Stiffer," *Houston Chronicle*, March 12, 2008, available at www.chron.com.

34. Texas Comptroller of Public Accounts, "State Revenue by Category, Fiscal Year 2011," available at www.texastransparency.org.

35. Robert J. Dilger, "The Study of American Federalism at the Turn of the Century," *State and Local Government Review* 32 (Spring 2000): 100.

Political Participation

CHAPTER OUTLINE

WHAT WE WILL LEARN

After studying Chapter 4, you should be able to answer the following questions:

1. What is the history of voting rights for women, Latinos, and African Americans in Texas?

2. What are the ways that individuals can participate in the policymaking process?

3. How do voter participation rates in Texas compare with rates in other states, and what is the explanation for the difference?

4. How do political participation rates vary based on income, age, race/ethnicity, and gender?

5. How does the Texas electorate compare with the state's total population in terms of income, education, and age, and how does that affect public policy?

Tea Party movement
A loose network of conservative activists organized to protest high taxes, excessive government spending, and big government in general.

The **Tea Party movement** is a loose network of conservative activists organized to protest high taxes, excessive government spending, and big government in general. The activists take their inspiration from the Boston Tea Party of 1773 when American colonists protested the British tax on tea by dumping three shiploads of tea into Boston Harbor. TEA is also an acronym for "taxed enough already."

The Tea Party movement is an example of a grassroots political organization because it is driven by community activists rather than national organizers. Although Freedom Works, a conservative advocacy group led by former Texas congressman Richard Armey, has provided some organizational support and funding, the Tea Party movement has no professional staff, no official agenda, and no identifiable national leaders. Most of the organization's energy has come from local activists organized into hundreds of local groups who communicate with one another online by e-mail, Twitter, and Facebook.[1]

The Tea Party movement has a strong presence in Texas. Since the Tea Party began in early 2009, more than 200 Tea Party groups have emerged in the Lone Star State.[2] The most important issues for the Texas Tea Party include government spending, tax rates, government regulations, illegal immigration, and governmental responsiveness.

The Tea Party has become an important political force in the state. In the 2010 general election, the energy of the Tea Party movement increased the turnout of conservative voters, helping the Republican Party to dramatically increase its majority in the Texas House and hold on to its majority in the Texas Senate. Republicans gained seats in the U.S. Congress as well. The Tea Party also influenced the work of the Texas legislature in 2011, helping ensure that the legislature balanced the state budget by cutting spending rather than raising revenue or dipping into the state's Rainy Day Fund. State Representative Pete Gallego of Alpine said this about the Tea Party's role in the 2011 session of the legislature: "This session I think the Tea Party was driving the train."[3]

Tea Party activism introduces this chapter on political participation. This chapter examines individual participation, focusing primarily on voting and voting rights. The chapter looks at forms of participation, considers why voter turnout is relatively low in Texas, examines patterns of participation, and evaluates the effect of turnout on the policymaking process.

VOTING RIGHTS AND MINORITY PARTICIPATION

Only white males enjoyed the right to vote when Texas joined the Union in 1845. Much of the subsequent history of the state is the story of the efforts of women and the members of racial and ethnic minority groups to gain the right to vote and participate meaningfully in Texas politics.

Women's Suffrage

In the nineteenth century, politics was a man's world, not just in Texas but in the entire United States. The women's rights movement emerged in the northern states in the 1840s as an offshoot of the abolition movement, a political reform effort in early-nineteenth-century America whose goal was the elimination of slavery. In Texas, the weakness of the abolition movement hindered the cause of women's rights. The drive for women's **suffrage,** the right to vote, did not begin to pick up steam in Texas until 1903 with the founding of the Texas Woman Suffrage Association. In 1915, the state legislature narrowly rejected an amendment to the Texas Constitution calling for women's suffrage. Three years later, the legislature approved a law allowing women to vote in primary elections. Finally, in 1919, the U.S. Congress proposed a constitutional amendment granting women the right to vote nationwide. Texas was the first state in the South to ratify the Nineteenth Amendment, which became law in 1920, giving women in Texas and across America the right to vote.[4]

> **Suffrage** The right to vote.

Minority Voting Rights

Winning the right to vote and having that vote counted was a more elusive goal for Texans of African and Hispanic descent than it was for women.

African American Enfranchisement After the Civil War Before the Civil War, nearly all African Americans who lived in Texas were slaves; none could vote or hold public office. Slavery ended with the Confederate defeat, but the state's white political establishment refused to enfranchise former slaves. (**Franchise** is the right to vote; to **enfranchise** means to grant the right to vote.) The Texas Constitution of 1866, written under President Andrew Johnson's Reconstruction plan, denied African Americans the right to vote and hold public office. The U.S. Congress, however, refused to accept the Johnson plan for Reconstruction. In 1867, Congress passed legislation over Johnson's veto that placed the South under military rule and forced southern states to grant African Americans the right to vote.

> **Franchise** The right to vote.

> **Enfranchise** To grant the right to vote.

African Americans registered to vote for the first time in Texas in 1867. The following year, they cast ballots in an election to select delegates to a state constitutional convention. Of the 90 delegates chosen, 9 were African American men, all of whom were Republicans. In 1869, African American voters helped elect E. J. Davis governor. In the same election, 11 African Americans won seats in the state legislature.

After the early 1870s, Texas politics began to return to the pattern in place before the Civil War. The Democratic Party regained control of the legislature in the 1872 election and recaptured the governor's mansion in the following year. Meanwhile, some white Texans organized chapters of the Ku Klux Klan to threaten and intimidate African American leaders. The Klan sometimes resorted to violence to assert white control.

Nonetheless, African Americans continued to participate in Texas politics. Six African Americans were among the delegates elected to the constitutional convention of 1875. Furthermore, with the exception of the legislature elected in 1887, all legislatures chosen from 1868 through 1894 included African American members. All told, 41 African Americans served in the Texas legislature between 1868 and 1900.[5]

Minority Disfranchisement In the early twentieth century, the white establishment in Texas restricted the voting rights of minorities in order to maintain political power. After Reconstruction, Texas was a one-party state. The Democratic Party, which was controlled by wealthy economic interests, held virtually every elective

Disfranchisement
The denial of voting rights.

office in the state. The political establishment used **disfranchisement,** the denial of voting rights, as a response to the Populist Party's attempt to win power by uniting lower-income voters of all races against the wealthy economic interests that controlled state politics. Conservative political leaders in Texas (and throughout the South) used racial issues to divide the working class along racial lines. They hoped to ensure their long-term control of state government by disfranchising African Americans (as well as many poor whites and Latinos).[6]

Poll tax A tax that prospective voters had to pay in order to register to vote.

The poll tax and the white primary were the main instruments of disfranchisement. The **poll tax,** a tax that prospective voters had to pay in order to register to vote, kept low-income people of all races from voting. In 1902, the Texas legislature proposed and the voters approved a state constitutional amendment requiring a poll tax of $1.50 or $1.75 a year (depending on the county), not an insignificant sum in early-twentieth-century Texas. (In today's value, the poll tax would be $30 to $40.) Before the implementation of the poll tax, more than 60 percent of voting-age Texans typically participated in presidential elections. In contrast, once the poll tax went into effect, election turnout dipped to 30 percent of voting-age adults in 1904.[7]

White primary
An election system that prohibited African Americans from voting in Democratic primary elections.

The **white primary,** an election system that prohibited African Americans from voting in Democratic primary elections, ensured that white voters would control the Democratic Party. In 1903, the state Democratic Party executive committee suggested that all county party committees exclude African Americans from party primary elections. A **primary election** is an intraparty election during which a party's candidates for the general election are chosen. By the 1920s, most counties with significant African American populations were using the white primary, and in 1924 the Texas legislature adopted the procedure statewide. Because the Democratic Party dominated Texas politics in those days, the Democratic primary was the most important election in the state. Whoever won the primary election invariably won the general election. Consequently, the exclusion of African Americans from participation in the Democratic primary barred them not only from influence in Democratic Party politics but also from meaningful participation in Texas politics in general.

Primary election
An intraparty election at which a party's candidates for the general election are chosen.

Boss Control in South Texas Although the white primary did not keep Latinos from the ballot box, political bosses often controlled their votes. In heavily Hispanic South Texas, in particular, ranch owners (some of whom were Latino) controlled both local economies and local politics. The boss would pay the poll tax for his workers (most of whom were Latino) and then instruct them how to vote. With their jobs depending on it, the workers had little choice but to do as they were told.

Many Texans know the story of George Parr, the so-called Duke of Duval County, which is located in South Texas just west of Corpus Christi. For years, Parr ran Duval County as his own political kingdom. The most famous example of Parr's influence occurred in 1948 when a young member of Congress named Lyndon B. Johnson ran for the U.S. Senate against former governor Coke Stevenson. Parr supported Johnson, but the day after the election it appeared that Stevenson had won the statewide vote by a razor-thin margin. One ballot box remained uncounted, however, Box 13 in neighboring Jim Wells County, where Parr's influence extended. Johnson won Box 13 almost unanimously, and "Landslide Lyndon" became an

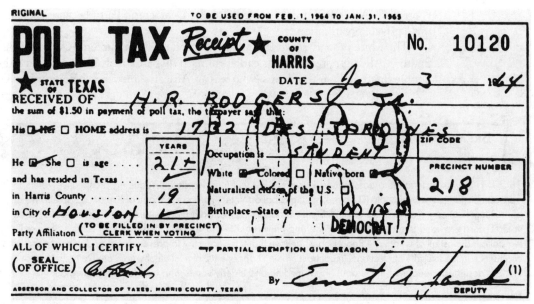

Texans once had to pay a poll tax in order to register to vote.

87-vote winner. Remarkably, 200 voters at Box 13 arrived to cast their ballots in alphabetical order. The affair still inspires deathbed confessions.[8]

The Struggle for Minority Voting Rights African Americans in Texas turned to the federal courts for help in regaining the right to vote. Lawrence A. Nixon, an El Paso physician, challenged the constitutionality of the Texas White Primary Law in federal court. In 1927, the U.S. Supreme Court unanimously struck down the law as a "direct and obvious infringement" of the Equal Protection Clause of the Fourteenth Amendment to the U.S. Constitution.[9]

The Texas legislature responded to the ruling by repealing the White Primary Law and replacing it with a statute allowing the executive committee of each political party to "prescribe the qualifications of its own members." The executive committee of the Texas Democratic Party then declared that only whites could vote in Democratic primary elections. Dr. Nixon again carried the fight to the U.S. Supreme Court and once again the Court invalidated the Texas law. The vote on the Court was close, however, five to four.[10]

Next, the legislature repealed all laws dealing with primary elections, and the Texas Democratic Party declared itself a private organization whose membership was exclusively white. Only party members could vote in Democratic primary elections. African Americans again turned to the federal courts, with Richard R. Grovey, a Houston barbershop owner, filing suit. This time, however, the courts refused to help. In 1935, the U.S. Supreme Court unanimously upheld the white primary on grounds that the state of Texas was not involved. The Court ruled that the

Fourteenth Amendment did not apply to the Democratic Party because the party was a private organization.[11]

The white primary survived until 1944 when the U.S. Supreme Court decided Smith v. Allwright, reversing its earlier ruling. This case involved a suit brought by Lonnie Smith, a Houston dentist who was an African American community leader

Breaking News!

Texas Adopts a Voter ID Law

In 2011, the Texas legislature passed and Governor Perry signed legislation requiring prospective voters to prove their identity with a photo ID before casting a ballot. Voters must present one of five acceptable forms of photo identification—a driver's license, military ID, passport, concealed handgun permit, or a special state-issued voter ID card provided free of charge. College and university IDs are not permitted.* The supporters of voter ID legislation, almost all of whom are Republicans, believe that it is necessary to prevent fraud and enhance public confidence in the integrity of elections. In contrast, voter ID opponents, almost all of whom are Democrats, argue that it is designed to suppress the turnout of low-income and elderly voters who tend to vote Democratic.[†]

Discussion

Why is voter ID such a big deal for Republicans? Many Republican activists and elected officials as well are firmly convinced that voter fraud is a serious problem in Texas, especially in South Texas and minority precincts in the big cities. They believe that Democrats steal elections by bussing unqualified voters to the polls, including, perhaps, illegal aliens. Moreover, they say, showing a photo ID to cast a ballot is not a major inconvenience. After all, people are routinely asked for a photo ID when they pay bills with a check, complete a bank transaction, or board an airplane. Why not require similar identification for something as important as voting?

Why are Democrats so adamantly opposed to voter ID laws? The Democrats believe that the Republicans push voter ID laws in order to suppress Democratic voter turnout. Many low-income people, especially minority citizens who typically vote Democratic, do not have a driver's license or other forms of picture identification and may lack the means to travel to a state office to apply for a state-issued photo ID card. Furthermore, Democrats contend that there is no credible evidence that voter impersonation is a problem in Texas elections.

Are voter ID laws constitutional? In 2008, the U.S. Supreme Court upheld a legal challenge to Indiana's voter ID law. The Court ruled that states have a legitimate interest in ensuring the integrity of the election process and that a voter ID requirement places a minimal burden on the right to vote.[‡] Many of the more recent voter ID laws are more restrictive than the Indiana measure, however, and will likely face legal challenges.

What effect have voter ID laws had in Indiana and other states that have had them for a while? Political scientists have researched the effect of voter ID laws in other states that have adopted legislation similar to that adopted in Texas. Although one study finds that voter ID reduces turnout by 3 to 4 percent, most studies find that the laws have no impact on voter participation. They also indicate that voter ID laws have no effect on reducing fraud or enhancing confidence in election procedures. Ironically, voter ID laws apparently have little impact on the electoral process despite the emotion surrounding their adoption.**

---

* Daniel Setiawan, "After Six-Year Fight, Perry Signs Voter ID into Law," *Texas Observer*, May 27, 2011, available at www.texasobserver.com.

† Tom Curry, "Voter ID Debate Could Change 2012 Landscape," May 25, 2011, available at www.msnbc.com.

‡ *Crawford v. Marion County Election Board*, 553 U.S. 181 (2008).

** Stephen Ansolabehere, "Effects of Identification Requirements on Voting: Evidence from the Experience of Voters on Election Day," *PS: Political Science & Politics* 42 (January 2009): 127–130.

and political activist. The Court ruled eight to one that the Democratic Party acted as an agent of the state when it conducted primary elections. Consequently, the Court declared, the exclusion of African Americans from the Democratic primary was an unconstitutional violation of the Fifteenth Amendment to the U.S. Constitution, which grants African Americans the right to vote.[12]

Although the white primary was history, other forms of voting discrimination remained. In Fort Bend County, for example, white officials arranged a whites-only pre-primary called the Jaybird primary. White voters would cast their ballots for the winner of the Jaybird primary in the regular Democratic primary, thus minimizing the impact of the African American vote. The U.S. Supreme Court overturned this procedure in 1953.[13]

The poll tax was the next barrier to fall. In 1962, the U.S. Congress proposed a constitutional amendment to prohibit poll taxes in elections for the presidency or Congress. When it was ratified as the Twenty-fourth Amendment in 1964, the Texas poll tax could be collected only for state and local elections. Two years later, the U.S. Supreme Court struck that down as well as a violation of the Equal Protection Clause of the Fourteenth Amendment.[14] The poll tax was thus just as dead as the white primary.

The Texas legislature and the governor responded to the loss of the poll tax by establishing the most difficult and restrictive system of voter registration in the nation. Prospective voters had to register between October 1 and January 31 each year. Anyone who lacked the foresight to sign up three months before the spring primaries and nine months before the November general election was out of luck. In practice, this system worked against poor persons of all races. It survived until 1971 when, as with so many other Texas election procedures, it was struck down by the federal courts.[15]

FORMS OF PARTICIPATION

Individual Texans can participate in the policy process in a number of ways: voting, campaigning, joining political groups, contacting public officials, and participating in protest demonstrations and unconventional political acts.

Voting

The federal government and the states jointly establish the ground rules for voting. The U.S. Constitution prohibits voter discrimination based on race or gender and outlaws the poll tax in federal elections. The Constitution also sets 18 as the national minimum voting age. Federal law bans the use of literacy tests as a qualification for voting. The National Voter Registration Act, also known as the Motor Voter Act, requires states to make voter registration available to people who renew their drivers' licenses or apply for social services. The states, meanwhile, establish other voter qualifications, including whether to allow convicted criminals to vote. States also determine most voter registration procedures, choose voting technology, and select the format of the ballot.[16]

To vote in Texas, individuals must be 18 years of age as of the next election, American citizens (native-born or naturalized), and residents of Texas. Newcomers need not wait to establish residency; anyone who has a Texas home address is eligible to vote, including students who may be living in the state temporarily to

Voting is the most common form of political participation.

attend college. Persons who have been declared mentally incapacitated by the final judgment of a court of law are disqualified from voting. Individuals who have been convicted of serious crimes (felonies) lose the right to vote as well, at least temporarily. Convicted criminals in Texas are eligible to vote again after they have fully completed their sentences, including time served on probation or parole. (**Probation** is the suspension of a sentence, permitting the defendant to remain free under court supervision, whereas **parole** is the conditional release of convicted offenders from prison to serve the remainder of their sentences in the community under supervision.)

Individuals must register before they can vote. Registration becomes effective 30 days after an application is received, so prospective voters must apply at least a month before the election in which they want to cast a ballot. Either the county tax assessor-collector's office or, in smaller counties, the county clerk or an election administrator handles voter registration. Voter registration applications are readily available in driver's license offices, libraries, and other government offices and public places. They are printed in both English and Spanish, easy to complete, and require only a person's name, gender, birth date, address, court of naturalization (if applicable), and signature. Voter registration applications are available online as well at the following Internet address: **https://webservices.sos.state.tx.us/vrapp/index.asp**.

Voter registration is permanent as long as citizens keep their addresses current with county election officials. People who change addresses within the same county may return to their old polling place to vote for 90 days after their move. Every two years, however, county election officials mail out new voter registration certificates and purge the voter rolls of the names of people who are no longer at their listed addresses. Consequently, people who move must take the initiative to report changes of address in order to remain registered. Texans who relocate from one county to another must register again in their new county of residence. People who lose their voter certificates can request replacements from county election officials.

Probation The suspension of a sentence, permitting the defendant to remain free under court supervision.

Parole The conditional release of convicted offenders from prison to serve the remainder of their sentences in the community under supervision.

Election precincts
Voting districts.

Voters cast their ballots in **election precincts** (voting districts) near their homes. Rural counties may have only a handful of precincts, but urban counties have hundreds. Harris County, the state's most populous county, has 885 election precincts.[17] Precinct polling places are typically located in public buildings, such as schools or fire stations. Newspapers usually print a list of polling locations a day or so before an election. Prospective voters can also learn the polling place for their election precinct by telephoning the county clerk's office or checking a county website.

Early voting A system that allows citizens to cast ballots before Election Day.

Texas is one of 32 states that permit **early voting,** which is a system that allows citizens to cast ballots before Election Day.[18] State law once limited early voting (formerly called absentee voting) to individuals who planned to be out of town on the day of the election or at least *said* they planned to be out of town—some people voted absentee in order to avoid lines at the polls. In 1987, the legislature revised the election code to allow people to vote early without having to give an explanation, and many Texans now take advantage of no-excuse early voting. The period for early voting begins 17 days before an election and ends 4 days before. Locations for early voting may be limited to the county clerk's office at the courthouse or a handful of branch offices located throughout the county.

It is also possible to vote early by mail. Individuals who expect to be out of the county on the day of the election and during the early voting period may write the county clerk's office and request a mail ballot. People age 65 and older and those who are disabled or ill may vote by mail as well. Students away at school have the option of voting by mail or registering and voting in the county where they attend classes. Two-thirds of Texans who voted in the 2008 presidential election cast their ballots early or in absentee voting, up from 51 percent who voted early in 2004.[19]

Early voting affects both the composition of the electorate and the strategy of election campaigns. Research shows that early voting increases election turnout by less physically active older adults who might have difficulty getting to the polls on Election Day.[20] With so many people casting their ballots early, early voting has turned Election Day into an election period, forcing candidates to advertise earlier and perhaps longer than they did before early voting.[21] Candidates can also take advantage of early voting by organizing early get-out-the-vote (GOTV) drives. Because state law requires election officials to keep a running list of who has voted early and who has not, campaigns can concentrate on getting people to the polls who are most likely to be their supporters. Politically active people are more likely to take advantage of early voting than people who are less involved politically.[22]

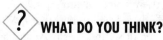 **WHAT DO YOU THINK?**

Can you be a good American and not vote?

Campaigning

People take part in politics by working on election campaigns. Although this is the age of television campaigns and the Internet, volunteers still have a place in election campaigns. In fact, research indicates that the most effective GOTV efforts are best done by volunteers, including door-to-door campaigning and personal telephone calls.[23] Underfinanced campaigns can often compensate for a lack of money with well-organized volunteer efforts. Many local election contests rely almost exclusively on volunteers. Even well-funded campaigns can put volunteers to good use in contacting prospective voters and encouraging them to go to the polls.

Campaigns ask volunteers to do work that demands energy and attention to detail. Volunteers often help with mass mailings. Although campaign professionals believe that direct mail is an effective means for getting a candidate's message across, sending letters and campaign literature to thousands of potential voters is a huge job. Computers can do the work, but that approach is expensive. Consequently, many campaigns use volunteers to fold literature, stuff the literature into envelopes, seal the envelopes, affix address labels, and bundle the envelopes for mailing.

There is almost no end to the work volunteers perform in an election campaign. They assemble yard signs and distribute them to the candidate's supporters. They answer office telephones and deliver soft drinks and snacks to other volunteers. (One of the cardinal rules of a successful campaign is to feed the volunteers.) They build and develop candidate Internet sites and Facebook pages for the candidate. They may even compose Twitter messages on the candidate's behalf. On Election Day, volunteers drive people who lack transportation to the polls and pass out campaign literature outside polling places.

Some Texans participate in political campaigns by giving money to support the political party and the candidates they favor. Money is critical to electoral success. Although the best funded candidates do not always win, poorly funded candidates almost always lose. Candidates can raise the money they need to compete successfully by soliciting small contributions from thousands of individuals or huge sums of money from a few contributors. Wealthy individuals can become major players in Texas politics by giving generously to candidates they favor. In 2010, for example, Houston homebuilder Bob Perry of Perry Homes and his wife Doylene together contributed more than $6 million to various candidates for statewide office and the legislature.[24]

National Rifle Association (NRA) An interest group organized to defend the rights of gun owners and defeat efforts at gun control.

Mothers Against Drunk Driving (MADD) An interest group that supports the reform of laws dealing with drunk driving.

League of United Latin American Citizens (LULAC) A Latino interest group.

Other Forms of Participation

Voting and campaigning are not the only ways individuals take part in politics. People participate by working through a group. One person casting a single ballot or working alone for a candidate is not as effective as a group of people working together. Many Texans make their voices heard by taking part in such political organizations as the National Rifle Association (NRA), Mothers Against Drunk Driving (MADD), and the League of United Latin American Citizens (LULAC). The **National Rifle Association (NRA)** is an interest group organized to defend the rights of gun owners and defeat efforts at gun control. **Mothers Against Drunk Driving (MADD)** is an interest group that supports the reform of laws dealing with drunk driving. The **League of United Latin American Citizens (LULAC)** is a Latino interest group.

People participate in the policy process by contacting government officials. Citizens may send e-mail messages to their state legislators or telephone city council members. Individuals may speak before the board of trustees of the local school district or community college.

Some Americans participate in politics by engaging in protest demonstrations, rallies, and marches. Tea Party activists, for example, have organized demonstrations and rallies in support of lower taxes and less government spending. Americans have a constitutional right to express their political views, and that includes the right to protest publicly. As long as protestors do not break the law (by blocking

AROUND THE NATION

Mail Voting in Oregon

Oregon conducts all of its primary and general elections by mail. Election officials mail ballots to registered voters from 14 to 18 days prior to the election. A voter marks the ballot in blue or black ink and places it in an unmarked envelope; the voter then places the first envelope in a second envelope. The voter signs the outer envelope and either mails it or drops it off at the county election office. Voters have until the day of the election to return their ballots.[*]

Oregon election officials believe that mail balloting has increased voter participation. In 1996, approximately 1.4 million Oregon voters cast ballots for president the old-fashioned way, in person and by traditional absentee ballot. The figure represented 71 percent of the state's registered voters. In contrast, the 2008 presidential election turnout was 1.8 million, 86 percent of registered voters.[†]

Mail balloting is popular with Oregon voters. Nearly three-fourths of the state's voters tell survey researchers that they prefer voting by mail to traditional in-person voting. Younger adults and voters over the age of 50 are the biggest supporters of the new system. They like mail balloting not only because it is convenient, but also because it gives

them time to discuss races with their friends and family before deciding how to vote.[‡] Voting by mail also saves the state from having to hire hundreds of poll workers.[§] Nonetheless, Washington is the only other state to conduct all of its elections entirely by mail.[**]

Research on the impact of mail voting in Oregon finds that it has increased participation by about 10 percent in congressional and presidential elections, without affecting the partisan profile of the electorate. [††] Women, young people, persons with disabilities, and homemakers report that they are more likely to take part in elections with mail voting than they were using traditional voting methods because they find the new system more convenient. The reform has had no apparent effect on the party balance in the electorate or on candidate preferences.[‡‡]

QUESTIONS

1. Do you see any disadvantages to voting by mail?
2. Would you like to vote by mail rather than in person?
3. Why haven't Texas and states other than Washington adopted a mail voting system like the Oregon procedure?

[*]Don Hamilton, "The Oregon Voting Revolution," *The American Prospect*, May 2006, pp. A3–A7.

[†] Oregon Secretary of State, available at www.sos.state.or.us.

[‡] Dave Scott, "Ways to Turn Out Voters," *State Government News*, February 2000, pp. 18–19.

[§]Josh Goodman, "Pushing the Envelope," *Governing*, May 2008, pp. 40–41.

[**]Paul W. Taylor, "Not-So-Priority Mail," *Governing*, March 2011, p. 8.

[††] Sean Richey, "Voting by Mail: Turnout and Institutional Reform in Oregon," *Social Sciences Quarterly* 89 (December 2008): 902–915.

[‡‡] Priscilla L. Southwell, "Five Years Later: A Re-Assessment of Oregon's Vote by Mail Electoral Process," *PS: Political Science & Politics* (January 2004), pp. 89–93.

traffic, for example), they are acting legally within the spirit and the letter of the U.S. Constitution.

Finally, some people go beyond peaceful protest to engage in acts of political violence, including the bombing of abortion clinics and the destruction of property. Although political violence will draw attention to a cause, it is often counterproductive because it provokes a backlash. Most mainstream anti-abortion groups, for example, dissociate themselves from individuals who advocate violence against abortion providers because they believe that violence undermines their cause with mainstream voters. Furthermore, people who commit violent acts or destroy property may face criminal prosecution as ordinary criminals.

Participation Rates in Texas

Voting age population (VAP)
The number of state residents who are 18 years of age or older.

Many adult Texans do not vote, even in high-profile elections. Figure 4.1 summarizes participation in the 2008 presidential election in Texas. The Texas **voting age population (VAP)**, which is the number of state residents who are 18 years of age or older, was 17.7 million people in 2008. The VAP is not the best basis for measuring voter turnout, however, because it includes noncitizens, prison inmates, and others

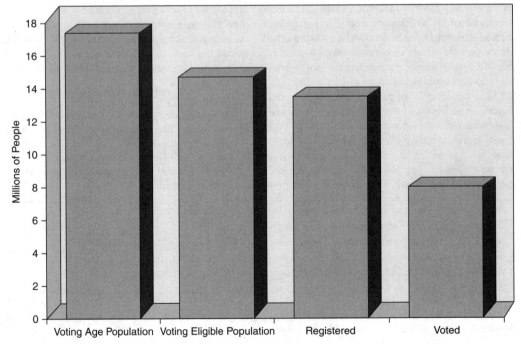

FIGURE 4.1　Participation in 2008 Election in Texas.

who are not eligible to vote. A better measure is the **voting eligible population (VEP)**, which is the number of state residents who are eligible to vote. Professor Michael McDonald estimates that the Texas VEP was 14.8 million people in 2008. Of that number, 13.6 million, 92 percent, were registered to vote. Voter turnout, meanwhile, was 8.1 million, 55 percent of the VEP.

Turnout in lower-profile contests is less than it is in presidential races. Voter participation in the 2009 constitutional amendment election, for example, was less than 7 percent of the VEP. It was only 32 percent in the 2010 statewide election for governor and other offices.[25]

Compared with other states, the level of political participation in Texas is relatively low, at least in terms of voter turnout. Although voting is not the *only* form of participation, it is the most common form and the most easily measured. Figure 4.2 traces voter turnout in Texas and the United States as a percentage of the VEP in the 2000, 2004, and 2008 presidential election years. Voter turnout increased in 2004 and 2008 in Texas and the United States as a whole, but in each year voter turnout in Texas lagged behind the national average by 5 to 7 percentage points. In 2008, Texas had the fifth lowest turnout in the nation.[26]

Political scientists identify several factors that may account for the relatively low rate of political participation in the state. High levels of participation are associated with older, better-educated populations with relatively high incomes. Compared with other states, income levels in Texas are lower, the age distribution is younger, and levels of educational achievement are below average. All of these factors are related to lower levels of political participation.

The weakness of political parties and labor unions in Texas may be associated with relatively low levels of voter turnout. Strong parties and unions are able to

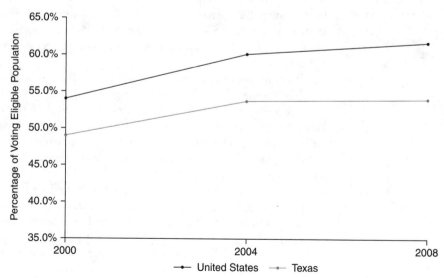

FIGURE 4.2   Voter Turnout, United States and Texas, 2000–2008.

educate citizens about politics and motivate them to participate politically.[27] They recruit voters. Political parties in Texas are generally less well organized than parties in many other states. Furthermore, labor unions in Texas are weaker than unions in the Northeast and Midwest.

The relatively high percentage of recent immigrants to Texas may help account for the state's low participation rates. In general, newcomers to an area need a few years to settle into their new communities before becoming active in state and local political affairs. People vote because they are concerned about their communities, and new residents take time to identify with their new surroundings.[28] Newcomers to an area must also take the time to register to vote. Furthermore, many of the state's immigrants are not yet American citizens and therefore are ineligible to vote.

Finally, in recent presidential elections, Texas has not been a **battleground state,** which is a swing state in which the relative strength of the two major-party presidential candidates is close enough so that either candidate could conceivably carry the state. In 2008, for example, neither the Barack Obama nor the John McCain presidential campaigns devoted resources to turning out the vote in Texas because they both acknowledged that McCain would carry the state, which he did. Many Texans were caught up in the excitement of the campaign because they followed it in the media. However, unlike the residents of battleground states, they were not subjected to aggressive GOTV efforts by the major campaigns.

Battleground state A swing state in which the relative strength of the two major-party presidential candidates is close enough so that either candidate could conceivably carry the state.

PATTERNS OF PARTICIPATION

Exit polls Surveys based on random samples of voters leaving the polling place.

Participation rates vary among individuals based on income, age, and race/ethnicity. Middle- and upper-income groups participate at a higher rate than lower-income groups. According to **exit polls,** which are surveys based on random samples of voters leaving the polling place, 64 percent of Texas voters in 2008 had annual household incomes in excess of $50,000. Nearly half of the Texas electorate earned more than $75,000 a year.[29] In contrast, the median household income in the state is less than $45,000 a year.[30]

Political participation increases with age until advanced age and ill health force the elderly to slow down. National surveys show that voter participation rates among younger adults are 20 or 30 percentage points lower than those for older citizens.[31] Young people have fewer resources and are less interested in the policy process than are older adults. As adults mature, their incomes increase and their skills develop. In addition, older adults establish roots in their communities that increase their interest and awareness of the political process.

The overall participation rates for blacks and whites are similar, whereas the participation rates for Latinos are substantially lower than they are for other racial and ethnic groups. According to the U.S. Census Bureau, the population of Texas is 45 percent white, 38 percent Latino, 12 percent African American, and 4 percent Asian.[32] In contrast, the 2008 electorate in Texas was 63 percent white, 20 percent Latino, and 13 percent African American.[33] Whites are

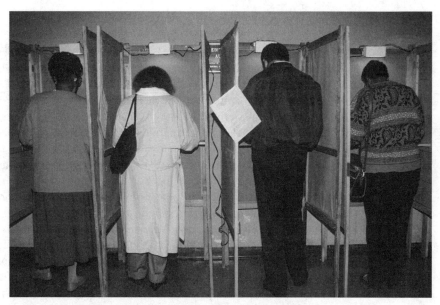

Minority voters made up a third of the Texas electorate in 2008.

significantly overrepresented at the ballot box, whereas Latinos are dramatically underrepresented.

Racial/ethnic patterns of participation reflect the importance of recruitment to political participation. We would expect that participation rates for African American and Latino citizens would be lower than participation rates for whites because of income and age differences. As a group, minority citizens are less affluent and younger than whites. Nonetheless, participation rates for African Americans exceed expectations because of the effectiveness of organizations in the African American community, such as churches and political groups, at stimulating participation. Latino voter turnout, meanwhile, increases when Latino candidates are on the ballot.[34]

Although men and women are equally likely to vote, men are more likely than women to engage in other forms of political participation. Women comprised 53 percent of the Texas electorate in 2008, reflecting the gender distribution of the state's adult population.[35] Women and men are also equally likely to participate in election campaigns. In contrast, women are less likely than men to contribute money to political campaigns, to contact public officials, and to join political organizations.[36]

 ## WHAT DO YOU THINK?

If you were a member of the Texas legislature, would you represent the interests of the people who live in your district or the people who actually vote? What is the basis of your answer?

PARTICIPATION AND REPRESENTATION

The Texas electorate is unrepresentative of the state's population. Table 4.1 compares and contrasts the state's population with the people who turned out to cast ballots in the 2010 statewide election. The population of Texas is young, poorly educated, and, compared with the national population, not especially wealthy. A majority of the state's residents are Latino, African American, or Asian American. In contrast, the Texas electorate is overwhelmingly white, wealthy, well-educated, and older.

The underrepresentation of Texans who are poor and minority is the legacy of the state's long history of public policies designed to limit the right to vote to middle-class and upper-income white people. The white primary, poll tax, and restrictive voter registration requirements all discouraged or prevented poor Texans from registering to vote. Although federal intervention has forced the state to expand its electoral system to broad-based participation, the legacy of exclusion still affects voter turnout today. For example, parents who could not vote were unable to serve as participation role models for their children. Adult Texans who grew up in households with adults who could not vote are less likely to participate politically than are citizens who were raised in families that participated in the political process.

voter mobilization
The process of motivating citizens to vote.

Voter mobilization, the process of motivating citizens to vote, could narrow the participation gap in Texas politics. Although some people are self-starters, the likelihood that individuals will vote increases if those individuals are asked to participate. Political parties, labor unions, interest groups, and other politically oriented organizations can increase turnout by working to mobilize people who might not otherwise turn out to vote. African American turnout in Texas matches the presence of African Americans in the state's population because of the effectiveness of African American churches and political groups at turning out the vote. Outside the African American community, the strongest forces for political mobilization are conservative Christian churches, anti-abortion groups affiliated with the Roman Catholic Church, and the Tea Party. They all make the electorate older, wealthier, and more heavily white than it would be otherwise. In 2010, in particular, Tea Party activism brought to the polls large numbers of older white conservative voters.

TABLE 4.1   The Population of Texas and the 2010 Texas Electorate

Population of Texas	2010 Texas Electorate
• 45 percent white	• 67 percent white
• 10 percent are 65 and over	• 20 percent are 65 and over
• 43 percent are 45 and over	• 77 percent are 45 and over
• 23 percent have college degrees	• 85 percent have college degrees
• Average household income is $50 K	• 73 percent make $100 K or more
	• 66 percent have no children under 18

Data Sources: U.S. Census Bureau, available at www.census.gov; "2010 Exit Polls," available at www.cnn.com.

Tea Party activism helped make the 2010 Texas electorate more unrepresentative of the state's population than was the 2008 electorate.

GETTING INVOLVED

Become a Volunteer Deputy Voter Registrar

You can do more to influence the policymaking process than registering to vote and casting your own ballot. By becoming a volunteer deputy voter registrar, you can register other people to vote—your friends, family, and fellow students; members of your religious group; and even strangers walking through a shopping mall. If you are 18 years old and have never been convicted of failing to deliver a voter application to a voter registrar, you are qualified to become a deputy voter registrar. Visit the voter registrar in your county (whose location can be found online at **www.sos.state.tx.us/elections/voter/votregduties.shtml**) and ask to become a deputy registrar. The clerk will give you voting application materials, swear you in as an official deputy voter registrar, issue you a certificate of appointment, and give you a receipt book. You may then distribute and collect a voter registration application from any resident of the county who is eligible to vote. You may also accept updated registration information from registered voters who have changed addresses. Once you have collected completed voter registration applications, you must deliver them to the voter registrar within five days of receiving them. A conscientious deputy voter registrar can register hundreds of potential voters, more than enough to change the outcome of a close local election.

It's your government—get involved!

The disparity between voters and the electorate impacts public policy. The electorate in Texas is significantly more conservative than the population as a whole. Because elected officials respond to the policy preferences of voters rather than nonvoters, the result is that public policies in Texas are more conservative than they would be if the electorate mirrored the state's population.[37] In 2011, when faced with a $27 billion budget shortfall, the legislature and the governor chose to balance the budget by cutting public education, college financial aid, and healthcare for low-income persons rather than raising taxes. Rather than raise taxes or even dip into the state's multibillion-dollar Rainy Day Fund, the legislature and the governor chose to cut teacher pay and raise class sizes. Higher education suffered budget cuts of 12 to 15 percent.[38] The policy preferences of the legislature and the governor reflected the values of the well-educated, well-to-do, older voters whose children are past school age rather than those of a younger, less well-educated, less well-to-do population with school- and college-age children.

WHAT WE HAVE LEARNED

1. What is the history of voting rights for women, Latinos, and African Americans in Texas?

Texas history records the struggle of women and minorities to gain full participation rates in the state's political process. Women won the right to vote in 1920 with the ratification of the Nineteenth Amendment. Although African American men voted and even won elective office in Texas in the years following the Civil War, they were disenfranchised in the late nineteenth and early twentieth centuries by the poll tax and the white primary. The poll tax affected low-income citizens of all races. Meanwhile, boss control in South Texas limited the effectiveness of Latino participation. The U.S. Supreme Court eventually overturned the white primary. A constitutional amendment coupled with another court ruling eliminated the poll tax as well. Other forms of voting discrimination persisted, but they too were eventually struck down by federal court rulings and, ultimately, the enforcement of the Voting Rights Act.

2. What are the ways that individuals can participate in the policymaking process?

Individual Texans can participate in the policy process in a number of ways: voting, campaigning, joining political groups, contacting public officials, and participating in protest demonstrations and unconventional political acts. To vote in Texas, individuals must be 18 years of age as of the next election, American citizens (either native-born or naturalized), and residents of Texas. People can participate politically by working on election campaigns. Some Texans also participate in political rallies and demonstrations, such as those organized by the Tea Party movement.

3. How do voter participation rates in Texas compare with rates in other states, and what is the explanation for the difference?

In 2008, Texas had the fifth lowest voter turnout in the nation. Compared with other states, income levels in Texas are lower, the age distribution is younger, and levels of educational achievement are below average. All of these factors are related to lower levels of political participation. Political parties and labor unions, which are associated with high levels of voter turnout, are relatively weak in Texas. Texas has a high percentage of recent immigrants, and they are less likely as a group to register and vote than more established residents. Finally, neither political party has campaigned heavily in Texas in recent elections because it has not been a battleground state.

4. **How do political participation rates vary based on income, age, race/ethnicity, and gender?**

Participation rates vary among individuals based on income, age, and race/ethnicity. Middle- and upper-income groups participate at a higher rate than lower-income groups. Political participation increases with age until advanced age and ill health force the elderly to slow down. The overall participation rates for blacks and whites are similar, whereas the participation rates for Latinos are substantially lower than they are for other racial and ethnic groups. Men and women are equally likely to vote, but men are more active than women in other forms of participation.

5. **How does the Texas electorate compare with the state's total population in terms of income, education, and age, and how does that affect public policy?**

The Texas electorate is not representative of the state's population and, because of Tea Party activism, was even less representative than usual in 2010. Voters as a group are wealthier, better educated, older, and less likely to have school-age children than the state's adult population. The state's public policies reflect the values of the electorate, not those of the population as a whole.

KEY TERMS

battleground state

disfranchisement

early voting

election precinct

enfranchise

exit polls

franchise

League of United Latin American Citizens (LULAC)

Mothers Against Drunk Driving (MADD)

National Rifle Association (NRA)

parole

poll tax

primary election

probation

suffrage

Tea Party movement

voter mobilization

voting age population (VAP)

voting eligible population (VEP)

white primary

NOTES

1. Dan Eggen and Philip Rucker, "Loose Network of Activists Drives Reform Opposition," *Washington Post*, August 16, 2009, available at www.washingtonpost.com.
2. "Texas Tea Party Organizations," available at www.teapartypatriots.org.
3. Quoted in Jay Root, "Perry Flexed His Muscles to Influence the Session," *New York Times*, July 2, 2011, available at www.nytimes.com.
4. Elizabeth A. Taylor, "The Woman Suffrage Movement in Texas," *Journal of Southern History* 17 (May 1951): 194–215.
5. Merline Pitre, *Through Many Dangers, Toils and Snares: Black Leadership in Texas, 1868–1900* (Austin, TX: Eakin Press, 1985).
6. V. O. Key, Jr., *Southern Politics in State and Nation* (New York, NY: Alfred A. Knopf, 1949).
7. *Historical Statistics of the United States* (Washington, DC: U.S. Government Printing Office, 1975), pp. 1071–1072.
8. Dudley Lynch, *Duke of Duval* (Waco, TX: Texian Press, 1978).
9. *Nixon v. Herndon*, 273 U.S. 536 (1927).
10. *Nixon v. Condon*, 286 U.S. 73 (1932).
11. *Grovey v. Townsend*, 295 U.S. 45 (1935).
12. *Smith v. Allwright*, 321 U.S. 649 (1944).
13. *Terry v. Adams*, 345 U.S. 461 (1953).
14. *United States v. Texas*, 384 U.S. 155 (1966).
15. *Beare v. Smith*, 321 F. Supp. 1100 (1971).
16. Alec C. Ewald, *The Way We Vote: The Local Dimension of American Suffrage* (Nashville, TN: Vanderbilt University Press, 2009), p. 153.
17. Harris County Tax Office, "Voter Precinct Data," available at www.hctax.net.
18. National Conference of State Legislatures, available at www.ncsl.org.

19. Kelly Shannon, "Texas' Early Vote Increased, Sets Record," *Austin American-Statesman*, November 12, 2008, available at www.statesman.com.

20. William Lyons and John M. Scheb II, "Early Voting and the Timing of the Vote: Unanticipated Consequences of Electoral Reform," *State and Local Government Review* 31 (Spring 1999): 148.

21. Paul Gronke, Eva Galanes-Rosenbaum, and Peter A. Miller, "Early Voting and Voter Turnout," *PS: Political Science & Politics* 40 (October 2007): 639–645.

22. Ibid., pp. 639–645.

23. Donald P. Green and Alan S. Gerber, *Get Out the Vote: How to Increase Voter Turnout*, 2nd ed. (Washington, DC: Brookings Institution Press, 2008), p. 139

24. "Money in State Politics," available at www.followthemoney .org.

25. Texas Secretary of State, "Turnout and Voter Registration Figures (1990–present)," available at www.sos.state.tx.us; Michael P. McDonald, United States Election Project, available at http://elections.gmu.edu.

26. McDonald, United States Election Project.

27. Jan E. Leighley and Jonathan Nagler, "Unions, Voter Turnout, and Class Bias in the U.S. Electorate, 1964–2004," *Journal of Politics* 69 (May 2007): 430–441.

28. André Blais, *To Vote or Not to Vote?* (Pittsburgh, PA: University of Pittsburgh Press, 2000), p. 13.

29. "2008 Exit Polls for Texas," available at www.cnn.com/elections/2008.

30. U.S. Census Bureau, "Household Income—Distribution by Income and State: 2006," *The 2009 Statistical Abstract*, available at www.census.gov.

31. U.S. Census Bureau, "Reported Voting and Registration, by Race, Hispanic Origin, Sex, and Age, for the United States, November 2004," available at www.census.gov.

32. U.S. Census Bureau, "2010 Census Data," available at http://2010census.gov.

33. "2008 Exit Polls for Texas."

34. Matt A. Barreto, "¡Sí Se Puede! Latino Candidates and the Mobilization of Latino Voters," *American Political Science Review* 101 (August 2007): 425–441.

35. "2008 Exit Polls for Texas."

36. Sidney Verba, Kay Lehman Schlozman, and Henry E. Brady, *Voice and Equality: Civic Volunteerism in American Politics* (Cambridge, MA: Harvard University Press, 1995), p. 255.

37. John D. Griffin and Brian Newman, "Are Voters Better Represented?" *Journal of Politics* 67 (November 2005): 1,214.

38. Daniel Seymour, "Spending on Education Is a Business Investment," *Houston Chronicle*, July 1, 2011, p. B9.

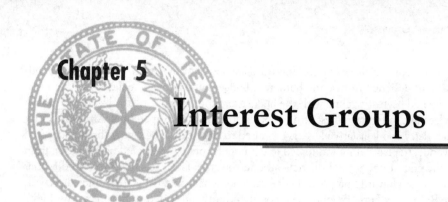

Chapter 5

Interest Groups

CHAPTER OUTLINE

Interest Groups in Texas Politics
    Business Groups and Trade Associations
    Professional Associations
    Organized Labor
    Agricultural Groups
    Racial and Ethnic Minority Groups
    Religious Groups
    Citizen, Advocacy, and Cause Groups

Interest Group Strategies and Tactics
    Electioneering
    Lobbying

Public Relations Campaigns
Litigation
Protest Demonstrations
Political Violence
Alliances

What We Have Learned

WHAT WE WILL LEARN

After studying Chapter 5, you should be able to answer the following questions:

1. What types of interest groups are active in American politics and what are their goals?

2. What strategies and tactics do interest groups use to achieve their goals?

State Representative Donna Howard, a Democrat from Austin, proposed an amendment designed to ease the burden of budget cuts on public education. The legislature had been struggling with the budget for months, working to close a $27 billion budget gap, a figure representing about a fourth of state spending. After Governor Rick Perry and legislative leaders promised to balance the budget without additional revenue, the legislature was forced to cut popular programs, including $4 billion from public education. School districts around the state faced teacher layoffs and higher class sizes. Howard's proposed budget amendment would dedicate surplus money in the Rainy Day Fund beyond the amount currently projected to be sent to the state's school districts to help pay for enrollment growth. The **Rainy Day Fund** is a state savings account funded by a portion of oil and gas production revenues. Some analysts expect the fund to grow faster than the official projection because of rising oil and gas prices. If it does, then Howard's amendment would allocate the additional money, up to $2.2 billion, to public education. Most members of the Texas House liked Howard's proposal, and it passed 101–42, with both Democrats and Republicans voting for it.[1]

Rainy Day Fund
A state savings account funded by a portion of oil and gas production revenues.

The Howard amendment quickly became controversial. Small-government conservative groups such as Texans for Fiscal Responsibility, Empower Texas, Americans for Prosperity, Texas FreedomWorks, and LibertyLinked charged that the Howard amendment was reckless because the money in the Rainy Day Fund might be needed for an emergency or a future shortfall. They also accused the Republican members of the legislature who voted for the amendment of breaking their promise not to use money from the Rainy Day Fund to balance the budget. The groups posted online the names of Republican legislators who voted for the Howard amendment and used social media to alert conservative activists, including many Tea Party supporters, to contact their legislators about the votes. Within days, the tide turned in the legislature against the Howard amendment. The House voted 87–59 against the measure, and it was eventually removed from the final budget.[2] Although numerous liberal groups and pro-education organizations supported the Howard amendment, they were completely outgunned in a legislature dominated by conservative Republicans, many of whom won election with Tea Party support.

Most Texans have probably never heard of Texans for Fiscal Responsibility, Empower Texas, and the other conservative groups. They are not large-membership organizations and are not especially well funded. Nonetheless, the groups had sufficient influence over the legislature in 2011 to convince the House to reverse itself on an important vote. Why were small-government conservative groups able to block the Howard amendment against the opposition of groups supporting public education? This chapter on interest groups in Texas politics examines that question as it explores the role of interest groups in Texas politics. The chapter begins with an overview of the interest groups active in Texas. It then discusses the strategies and tactics they employ to achieve their goals.

Interest group
An organization of people who join together voluntarily on the basis of some interest they share for the purpose of influencing policy.

INTEREST GROUPS IN TEXAS POLITICS

An **interest group** is an organization of people who join together voluntarily on the basis of some interest they share for the purpose of influencing policy. Most Texans have an interest in the policies of state and local government in Texas, but not all Texans have organized to promote and defend their interests. Compare and contrast the position of college students with that of the people who manage large energy companies, such as Reliant Energy and TXU Energy. Both groups have an interest in state and local government. Public policies dealing with college funding, university admissions, course transfer, tuition, and the availability of scholarships and financial aid affect college students. In the meantime, energy company executives have an interest in electricity deregulation, property taxes, alternative energy development, and government regulations dealing with environmental pollution, electric power transmission, and workplace safety. College students and energy company executives are not equally well organized. College students have little, if any, interest group representation. Although student organizations exist at many of the state's colleges and universities, their primary focus is not political. In contrast, energy company executives are organized both by firm and by industry group. They are widely regarded as being among the most influential voices in state and local government.

We begin our study of interest groups by identifying the most important organized interests in Texas politics. Who are the interests, how well are they organized, what do they want from state and local government, and how effective are they at achieving their goals?

Business Groups and Trade Associations

Business groups and trade associations are the most powerful interest groups in Texas politics. Other groups may be influential at particular levels of government, on certain issues, and at certain points in the policy process, but business interests are important everywhere, from the county courthouse to the governor's mansion. Whereas other interests focus on one issue or a narrow range of issues, business voices are heard on virtually every major policy issue, whether education finance, insurance regulation, water development, immigration, or transportation.

Business interests pursue their political goals both as individual firms and through trade associations. Comcast, Reliant Energy, AT&T, State Farm Insurance, and other large business enterprises are major players in state politics. Business groups also work through **trade associations,** which are organizations representing the interests of firms and professionals in the same general field. The **Texas Association of Business (TAB)** is a trade association for business firms ranging from giant corporations to small neighborhood business establishments. The TAB, which includes local chambers of commerce in its organizational structure, is perhaps the single most powerful interest group in the state. Other trade associations include the Texas Association of Builders, a trade association representing the interests of building contractors; the Mid-Continent Oil and Gas Association, a trade association that speaks for the concerns of the major oil producers; and the Insurance Council of Texas, a trade association representing insurance companies.

Business groups and trade associations are effective because they are well organized, well financed, and skilled in advocating their positions. Businesspeople usually know what they want from government and have the financial and

Trade associations
Organizations representing the interests of firms and professionals in the same general field.

Texas Association of Business (TAB)
A trade association for business firms ranging from giant corporations to small neighborhood business establishments.

organizational resources to pursue their goals aggressively. Furthermore, business groups as a whole enjoy a relatively favorable public image. Although the alcohol, gambling, and tobacco industries have public relations problems, most Texans have a favorable image of business in general, especially small business.

Business groups and trade associations generally agree on the need to maintain a **good business climate,** a political environment in which business prospers. In general, a good business environment includes low tax rates on business, laws that restrict union influence, and regulation favorable to business growth. Business interests also support education to train the skilled, well-educated workforce needed for high-technology development.

Texas business interests have largely achieved their goal of promoting the adoption of public policies conducive to business growth. *Chief Executive,* a magazine for corporate executives, conducts an annual survey that asks business executives to evaluate the business climate of each state. For six years in a row, chief executives nationwide have rated Texas as the best state in the nation to do business. The factors most responsible for the state's high ranking are transportation, access to capital, technology, and innovation. Texas also scored highly on tax policy, regulation, and quality of living. The survey ranked North Carolina, Florida, Tennessee, and Georgia just behind Texas for being business friendly. In contrast, California and New York were ranked as the worst and second worst states in which to do business.[3]

Business interests are more influential in Texas politics than they are in national politics because they have fewer competitors in Texas than they do at the national level or in many other states. Organized labor, consumer groups, environmental organizations, and other groups that often oppose business interests on various policy issues are relatively weak in the Lone Star State. California and New York have

Good business climate A political environment in which business prospers.

Texans have a favorable image of business, especially small businesses, such as the Waring General Store pictured here.

extensive environmental and consumer regulations because those states have strong environmental and consumer organizations. In contrast, consumer and environmental organizations in Texas have little influence.

Professional Associations

Texas Medical Association (TMA)
A professional organization of physicians.

Texas Trial Lawyers Association (TTLA)
An organization of attorneys who represent plaintiffs in personal injury lawsuits.

Texas Association of Realtors (TAR)
A professional organization of real estate professionals.

Organizations of doctors, lawyers, realtors, teachers, and other professional are important participants in Texas politics. The **Texas Medical Association (TMA)** is a professional organization of physicians. The **Texas Trial Lawyers Association (TTLA)** is an organization of attorneys who represent plaintiffs in personal injury lawsuits. The **Texas Association of Realtors (TAR)** is an organization of real estate professionals. Professional associations are politically influential because of the relatively high socioeconomic status of their members. Money and political influence are closely tied. Professional associations enjoy an added advantage in that many elected officials come from the ranks of professionals, especially lawyers. Public officials who happen to be lawyers, for example, are more likely to understand and sympathize with the policy perspectives of attorneys than are officials who lack legal training.

Professional associations concern themselves with public policies that affect their members. Doctors and lawyers battle one another over medical damage award caps in malpractice lawsuits. Doctors want the state to limit awards in order to hold down medical malpractice insurance rates. Lawyers oppose caps on damage awards because they assess fees as a percentage of damages awarded. Real estate professionals are primarily concerned with public policies affecting real estate transactions, such as home equity lending and professional licensure. Teacher organizations focus on teacher pay and pensions as well as the whole range of education issues.

Organized Labor

Right-to-work law
A statute prohibiting a union shop.

Union shop A workplace in which every employee must belong to a union.

Organized labor is relatively weak in Texas. State laws make it difficult for unions to organize workers and easy for business to use non-union labor. Texas has a **right-to-work law,** a statute prohibiting a **union shop,** which is a workplace in which every employee must belong to a union. In states without right-to-work laws, the employees in a particular workplace vote whether to create a union shop. If a majority of the workers agrees, everyone employed in the plant must join the union and pay union dues. Union membership becomes mandatory. In a right-to-work state, workers can still join a union and, if a majority of employees in a particular workplace agrees, the union can negotiate with management on their behalf. Workers decide individually, however, whether to join the union and pay union dues. In Texas, unions represent 677,000 workers, negotiating wages and working conditions on their behalf, but only 545,000 of them are union members.[4] Right-to-work laws are controversial. Their defenders argue that no one should be forced to join a union and pay dues. In contrast, the opponents of right-to-work laws contend that it is not fair that non-union workers benefit from union representation when they do not pay union dues.

Nationally, labor unions are strongest in the large, industrialized states of the Northeast and Midwest. In 2010, a fourth of the workforce in New York belonged to unions; the unionization rate in Michigan was 17 percent. In contrast, organized labor is not nearly as well established in the states of the South and Southwest. Only 5.4 percent of Texas workers belonged to unions, less than half the national unionization rate of 11.9 percent. Texas ranked 43rd among the 50 states in the rate of unionization.[5] Labor unions in Texas are too small and too poorly organized to compete effectively against business groups in state politics. In 2010, labor interests contributed $6 million to candidates for various legislative and executive offices, a figure representing just 2 percent of interest group spending.[6]

In Texas, labor unions are strongest in the state's more heavily industrialized areas, such as the Texas Gulf Coast and the Dallas-Fort Worth area. Organized labor has political influence in Houston, Dallas, and Fort Worth, and labor unions may be the single most important political force in the Golden Triangle area of Beaumont, Port Arthur, and Orange. Unions also have influence within the organization of the state Democratic Party.

American Federation of Labor–Congress of Industrial Organizations (AFL–CIO) A national association of labor unions.

Most Texas unions belong to the **American Federation of Labor-Congress of Industrial Organizations (AFL-CIO),** which is a national association of labor unions. The Texas AFL-CIO represents 220,000 workers and includes Texas affiliates of the Communications Workers of America; International Brotherhood of Electrical Workers; Fire Fighters; American Federation of Government Employees; National Association of Letter Carriers; International Association of Machinists; Oil, Chemical, and Atomic Workers Union; American Federation of State, County, and Municipal Employees (AFSCME); and the Texas Federation of Teachers. The fastest growing unions are those representing service-sector workers and government employees.[7] In Houston, for example, the Service Employees International Union (SEIU) and AFSCME have been aggressively organizing janitors, city hall workers, security guards, and medical workers.

Minimum wage The lowest hourly wage that an employer can pay covered workers.

Private-sector unions are concerned with employee compensation, working conditions, job availability, job training, and state laws affecting the ability of unions to organize. The Texas AFL-CIO supports increasing the state minimum wage, which covers farm workers and other employees not covered by the federal minimum wage. The **minimum wage** is the lowest hourly wage that an employer can pay covered workers. Unions also favor public education, job training, and other social programs that benefit working-class families.

Public employee organizations, such as the Fort Worth Firefighters and Houston Police Officers Union, are similar to private-sector unions in that they want higher wages, secure jobs, salaries based on seniority rather than merit, attractive fringe benefits, and good working conditions. Fire and police unions are concerned with state civil service rules for municipal fire and police employees. Public employee organizations also address issues related to the professional concerns of their members. Police organizations take positions on proposals to revise the state's criminal laws. Employees of the Texas Department of Corrections oppose efforts to privatize the state's prison system.

? WHAT DO YOU THINK?

If you were a member of the Texas legislature, would you vote to repeal the state's right-to-work law? Why or why not?

Agricultural Groups

Agricultural interests have long been powerful in Texas politics. In the nineteenth century, the most influential political voices in the state were those of major land-owners, and the rural population was large enough to overwhelm the city vote in statewide elections. Even after Texas became an urban, industrial state, rural inter-ests continued to exercise disproportionate power. Rural areas were overrepresented in the legislature and farm groups were politically skillful.

Texas Farm Bureau An organization that represents the interests of farmers, ranchers, and people living in rural areas.

Urbanization has weakened rural interests in Texas, but farm groups retain influence. The **Texas Farm Bureau** represents the interests of farmers, ranch-ers, and people living in rural areas. Farmers and ranchers are politically astute, organized, and knowledgeable about how to exert influence in state politics. A great deal of agriculture in Texas has become agribusiness, run by corporations that possess all the political skills and advantages of big business in general. Also, many of the policy goals of agricultural interests have long since been achieved and entrenched in law or the state constitution. As a result, agricultural interest groups have the advantage of defending ground already won rather than pushing for new policies.

Agriculture is a tenuous business, and farmers are well aware that government actions can frequently determine whether they make a profit or go broke. Taxes are an area of concern. Farmers on the outskirts of metropolitan areas, for example, can be hurt by rising property taxes. As the big city sprawls in their direction, the value of their land goes up and, consequently, so do their property taxes. Their crops, though, are worth no more. Farm groups have lobbied successfully to have farmland taxed on its value as farmland, not on its value as the site of a future subdivision. Agricultural interests have also won tax breaks on the purchase of farm machinery, seed grain, and fertilizer.

GETTING INVOLVED

Joining a Group

People who want to influence policy in a particu-lar issue area should join a group. This chapter has identified a number of groups active in Texas politics. Many other groups are involved in state and local politics as well, including some student groups. Contact the group whose values and viewpoints most nearly reflect your own and find out how you can join the group and contribute to its work. Add your name to the group's mailing list, give money to the organization, attend meetings, and volunteer.

It's your government—get involved!

League of United Latin American Citizens (LULAC) A Latino interest group.

National Association for the Advancement of Colored People (NAACP) An interest group organized to represent the interests of African Americans.

Hate-crimes legislation Legislative measures that increase penalties for persons convicted of criminal offenses motivated by prejudice based on race, religion, national origin, gender, or sexual orientation.

Racial profiling The practice of a police officer targeting individuals as suspected criminals on the basis of their race or ethnicity.

State Children's Health Insurance Program (SCHIP) A federal program designed to provide health insurance to children from low-income families whose parents are not poor enough to qualify for Medicaid.

Agricultural groups have other interests as well. They are concerned with state laws and regulations affecting agriculture, such as livestock quarantine requirements and restrictions on the use of pesticides. They support generous state funding for agricultural research conducted at Texas A&M University. Water development and conservation are important for agricultural interests needing water for their livestock and irrigation for their crops.

Racial and Ethnic Minority Groups

Racial and ethnic minority groups enjoy some political influence in Texas. The two best-known minority rights organizations in the state are affiliates of prominent national organizations. The Texas **League of United Latin American Citizens (LULAC)** is a Latino interest group, whereas the Texas chapter of the **National Association for the Advancement of Colored People (NAACP)** is an interest group organized to represent the interests of African Americans.

Minority groups are interested in the enforcement of laws protecting the voting rights of minority citizens, the election and appointment of minority Texans to state and local office, college and university admission policies, public services for low-income residents of the state, inner-city development, and, for Latino groups in particular, economic development in South Texas. In recent sessions of the legislature, Latino and African American members have pushed for the passage of legislation concerning hate crimes and racial profiling. **Hate-crimes legislation** refers to legislative measures that increase penalties for persons convicted of criminal offenses motivated by prejudice based on race, religion, national origin, gender, or sexual orientation. **Racial profiling** is the practice of a police officer targeting individuals as suspected criminals on the basis of their race or ethnicity. Most Latino and African American legislators also support funding for public education and healthcare programs targeting low-income residents, such as the **State Children's Health Insurance Program (SCHIP),** which is a federal program designed to provide health insurance to children from low-income families whose parents are not poor enough to qualify for Medicaid.

Racial and ethnic minority groups are considerably more influential in Texas politics today than they were in the early 1960s. More African American and Latino Texans are registered to vote than ever before. In 2008 and 2010, Latino, African American, and Asian Texans constituted more than a third of the statewide vote.[8] No serious candidate for statewide or municipal office in the state's big cities can afford to ignore minority concerns. Latino and African American legislators have also become an important voting bloc in the state legislature.

Nonetheless, racial and ethnic minority groups are not as powerful as the more established interest groups in the state. Racial and ethnic minority groups are sometimes divided among themselves and are almost always short of funds. Many minority residents are not registered to vote; others stay home on Election Day. Furthermore, African American and Hispanic voters do not necessarily follow the political lead of groups such as LULAC and the NAACP.

CALVIN AND HOBBES

Source: Calvin and Hobbes copyright © 1999 Watterson. Distributed by Universal Press Syndicate. Reprinted with permission. All rights reserved.

Religious Groups

Churches and other religious institutions provide the foundation for a number of political organizations. Roman Catholic and Protestant churches in poor and minority areas have helped organize political groups to support healthcare, education, and neighborhood improvement for the state's poor people. These organizations include Communities Organized for Public Service (COPS) in San Antonio, Interfaith Alliance in the Rio Grande Valley, the Metropolitan Organization (TMO) in Houston, and the El Paso Inter-religious Sponsoring Organization (EPISO). They favor expanding SCHIP coverage, increasing funding for public education, and protecting the rights of immigrant workers.

Religious right
Individuals who hold conservative social views because of their religious beliefs.

The most active and probably most influential religiously oriented political groups are associated with the **religious right,** who are individuals who hold conservative social views because of their religious beliefs. Focus on the Family, Eagle Forum, and the American Family Association are national organizations with branches in Texas. Conservative religious organizations oppose abortion, pornography, stem-cell research, gay marriage, and the teaching of evolution in public schools. They favor abstinence-based sex education, prayer in schools, home schooling, and family values in general. Some conservative religious groups also take positions on issues that do not have an obvious family values connection, such as tax rates, immigration, and the United Nations.

Conservative Christian groups are an important part of the base of the Texas Republican Party, and that alliance has enabled them to win some important legislative victories. In recent sessions, the Texas legislature passed a constitutional amendment to outlaw gay marriage, adopted a measure to require couples to attend premarital counseling or pay higher marriage license fees, and defeated efforts to expand legalized gambling in the state. The legislature has also adopted a number of restrictions on access to abortion, including a parental consent requirement for minors and a requirement that women seeking an abortion undergo a sonogram.

BREAKING NEWS!

Legislature Adopts Abortion Sonogram Requirement

In 2011, the Texas legislature passed and Governor Perry signed legislation requiring doctors to administer a sonogram before performing an abortion on a pregnant woman. The physician must make the image of the sonogram available to the woman and allow her to listen to the heartbeat, although she may refuse to look and to listen. The doctor is also required to describe the fetus to the woman, noting the size and condition of the limbs. Women must wait 24 hours after the sonogram before the abortion can be performed unless they live more than 100 miles away, in which case they must wait at least two hours. The law makes exceptions for medical emergencies, fetal abnormalities, and for victims of rape or incest.*

Discussion

What is the purpose of the law? Both pro-life and pro-choice forces agree that the law is intended to reduce the incidence of abortion in the state, but they disagree about the way the law goes about achieving its goal. The proponents of the sonogram law say that it is designed to give women the information they need to make the right decision about whether to have an abortion. State Senator Dan Patrick, a Republican from Houston who authored the measure, says that the law is all about a "woman's right to know."[†] In contrast, the new law's opponents say that the real purpose of the law is to make a woman feel guilty enough about having an abortion that she will change her mind. The law also increases the cost of an abortion by requiring a sonogram. Moreover, the 24-hour waiting period in most cases forces women to take two days off from work for the procedure instead of just one.

The legislature considered the sonogram law in previous sessions, but failed to pass it. Why was it successful in 2011? Governor Perry helped by designating the measure an emergency. Emergency status allowed the legislature to fast-track the bill, reducing the likelihood that opponents would be able to block it in the final days of the session. The most important factor working in the bill's favor was that Republicans held large majorities in both the House and the Senate. Most Republicans are pro-life, and opposition to abortion is a key issue for the Republican Party. In 2011, Republicans had enough votes to push through a sonogram law. Only the details were in doubt and they had to accept some compromises, including the two-hour waiting period for women who live more than 100 miles from the abortion clinic.

Do pro-choice forces have any remaining options to oppose the sonogram law? With abortion, the courthouse is always an option. The Center for Reproductive Rights has filed a lawsuit arguing that (a) the law intrudes on the practice of medicine, (b) forces physicians to deliver government-mandated speeches to patients, and (c) treats women as less-than-competent adults.[‡]

---

* Anna M. Tinsley, "Perry Signs Sonogram Bill That Supporters Say Will Save Lives," *Fort Worth Star-Telegram*, May 25, 2011, available at www.star-telegram.com.

† Dan Patrick, "Abortion Sonogram Bill Will Empower Women," *Houston Chronicle*, February 12, 2011, available at www.chron.com.

‡ Chuck Lindell, "Lawsuit Challenges Texas Sonogram Law," *Austin American-Statesman*, June 13, 2011, available at www.statesman.com.

Citizen, Advocacy, and Cause Groups

Citizen groups
Organizations created to support government policies that they believe will benefit the public at large.

Citizen groups are organizations created to support government policies that they believe will benefit the public at large. For example, Texans for Public Justice (TPJ) and Common Cause are organizations that work for campaign finance reform, ethics regulations for public officials, and other good-government causes. Texas Public Interest Research Group (Tex-PIRG) and Texas Watch are consumer rights organizations.

Advocacy groups are organizations created to seek benefits on behalf of persons who are unable to represent their own interests. The Children's Defense Fund, for

Advocacy groups
Organizations created to seek benefits on behalf of persons who are unable to represent their own interests.

Cause groups
Organizations whose members care intensely about a single issue or a group of related issues.

Texas Right to Life Committee Cause group that opposes abortion.

NARAL Pro-Choice Texas Cause group that favors abortion rights.

Sierra Club Environmental organization.

National Rifle Association (NRA) An interest group organized to defend the rights of gun owners and defeat efforts at gun control.

example, is an organization that attempts to promote the welfare of children. The Texas AIDS Network represents the interests of people with HIV/AIDS.

Cause groups are organizations whose members care intensely about a single issue or a group of related issues. The **Texas Right to Life Committee,** for example, opposes abortion, whereas **NARAL Pro-Choice Texas** favors abortion rights. The **Sierra Club** is an environmental organization. Other cause groups include the **National Rifle Association (NRA), National Organization for Women (NOW),** and **AARP.** The NRA is an interest group organized to defend the rights of gun owners and defeat efforts at gun control. NOW is a group that promotes women's rights. The AARP, which was once the American Association of Retired Persons but now just goes by the acronym, is an interest group representing the concerns of older Americans. Texans for Fiscal Responsibility, Empower Texas, Americans for Prosperity, and the other small-government conservative groups that opposed the Howard amendment are cause groups that advocate lower taxes and less government spending.

Citizen, advocacy, and cause groups vary in political influence, depending on their organizational strength, the power of the opposition, and the popularity of their cause. **Mothers Against Drunk Driving (MADD),** which is an interest group that supports the reform of laws dealing with drunk driving, has been able to overcome the opposition of the liquor industry and driving-while-intoxicated (DWI) defense attorneys because it is well organized and its cause enjoys considerable popular support. In contrast, the Sierra Club and other environmental organizations have been relatively unsuccessful. Even though the environment is a popular cause, environmental organizations in Texas have been no match against the political influence of the oil and gas industry or electric utilities. Small-government conservative groups were a powerful force in the 2011 session of the Texas legislature because of their influence with hardcore conservative voters who dominate Republican primary elections. Save Texas Schools is a cause group created to oppose funding cuts in public education, but its influence was limited because most Republican legislators were more responsive to the small-government conservative groups. Democratic legislators generally supported the goals of Save Texas Schools, but Democrats were almost powerless in the 2011 session of the legislature.

 WHAT DO YOU THINK?

If you were a member of the Texas legislature, would you support the Texas sonogram law? Why or why not?

INTEREST GROUP STRATEGIES AND TACTICS

Interest groups employ a variety of tactics in an effort to achieve their goals.

National Organization for Women (NOW) Women's rights group.

Electioneering

Interest groups attempt to affect public policy by participating in the electoral process. Groups with a large membership and/or influence beyond their ranks try to affect election outcomes by endorsing favored candidates and delivering a

AARP An interest group representing the concerns of older Americans.

Mothers Against Drunk Driving (MADD) An interest group that supports the reform of laws dealing with drunk driving.

Political action committees (PACs) Organizations created to raise and distribute money in political campaigns.

Tort reform The revision of state laws to limit the ability of plaintiffs in personal injury lawsuits to recover damages in court.

Incumbent Current officeholder.

bloc vote on their behalf. Unions, racial and ethnic minority groups, and some citizen groups regularly use this strategy. In 2010, for example, the Texas Right to Life Committee endorsed Republican Governor Perry for reelection, whereas the Texas AFL-CIO threw its support behind Bill White, the Democratic Party nominee for governor.

The most effective tool interest groups have for affecting election outcomes is money. Interest groups contribute to candidates they support through their **political action committees (PACs),** which are organizations created to raise and distribute money in political campaigns. People associated with the interest group, such as union members and business executives, contribute money to the group's PAC, which in turn gives money to candidates for office. Executives with Reliant Energy, for example, contribute to the Reliant Energy PAC. Texas physicians give money to the TMA PAC and trial lawyers contribute to the TTLA PAC.

Texas law does not limit the amount of money individuals, businesses, or PACs can contribute in election campaigns, and some interest groups take advantage of the opportunity to give large amounts of money to the candidates of their choice through their PACs. In 2010, for example, the PAC associated with AT&T, the giant communications company, contributed $1.4 million to various candidates for statewide and legislative office. AFSCME gave more than $900,000 through its PAC.[9]

Interest groups consider several factors in determining which candidates to support. First, groups back candidates who are sympathetic to their policy preferences. For example, trial lawyers typically back Democratic candidates because of their shared opposition to **tort reform,** the revision of state laws to limit the ability of plaintiffs in personal injury lawsuits to recover damages in court. The Mostyn Law Firm of Houston is a personal injury law firm. In 2010, it gave $1.3 million to candidates for office in Texas, with 98 percent of its money going to Democrats. In contrast, Texans for Lawsuit Reform, a business group that favors tort reform, gave 86 percent of its $5.7 million in 2010 donations to Republican candidates.[10]

Second, interest groups consider the likelihood of a candidate's winning the election because groups want to back winners. Interest group leaders would rather give to a strong candidate who is only somewhat supportive of their group than throw their money away on an almost certain loser who is completely behind the group's cause. Consequently, interest groups typically contribute more generously to incumbents than to challengers because they know that an **incumbent,** that is, a current officeholder, is more likely to win than is a challenger. In 2010, for example, the Texas Association of Realtors (TAR) PAC donated $1.6 million to various Texas candidates, with 93 percent going to incumbents.[11]

Finally, interest groups prefer giving to incumbent officeholders who hold important policymaking positions, such as the members of the key policymaking committees in the legislature. Elected officials who hold important posts are in a better position to return favors than are officeholders who have little power. In Texas, the three officials who raised the most money in 2010 were also the three most powerful figures in state politics—Governor Perry ($39 million), Lieutenant Governor David Dewhurst ($9 million), and Speaker of the House Joe Straus ($5 million).[12]

Legal Prostitution in Nevada

Nevada is the only state in the nation with legal prostitution. State law allows every county except Clark County (where Las Vegas is located) to license and regulate brothel prostitution. However, street prostitution is illegal throughout the state. Eight of 16 Nevada counties license brothels to operate in designated areas. As of January 2009, 28 legal brothels employed 300 prostitutes in the state.* Prostitutes must use condoms during sex acts and state law requires weekly checks for certain sexually transmitted diseases and monthly HIV tests.

Prostitutes are independent contractors, living and working for several weeks at a time in a brothel. They seldom leave the premises and cannot have non-paying guests during their contract period. The brothel typically collects half the fee charged by the prostitutes for their room and board. Both the brothel owner and the prostitutes pay taxes to the government.

The Nevada legislature frequently debates whether to outlaw prostitution. Religious groups oppose prostitution on moral grounds, whereas casino operators and business groups favor banning brothel prostitution in order to improve the state's image. U.S. Senator Harry Reid of Nevada recently announced his support for an effort to ban legal prostitution in the state. "Nevada needs to be known as the first place for innovation and investment—not as the last place where prostitution is still legal."† In contrast, the Brothel Owners' Association argues that the issue should be left to local government and that it is safer for prostitution to be legal and regulated

rather than illegal and unregulated. Lawmakers from rural areas typically oppose efforts to outlaw the brothels because they provide jobs in poor counties and local tax revenue. In a good year, legal brothels generate $50 million in total revenue and contribute an estimated $400 million to the state's economy.‡ Some members of the Nevada legislature would like to expand legalized prostitution to Las Vegas and assess a state tax (currently, only counties tax the brothels) in order to generate revenue for the state.§

Public opinion in Nevada is split on the issue. Newcomers to Nevada generally favor outlawing prostitution, whereas long-time residents endorse the status quo. In the meantime, politicians typically play both sides of the issue—they say they are against prostitution but believe that the counties, rather than the state legislature, should decide the issue.

QUESTIONS

1. If you were in the Nevada legislature, would you vote to outlaw the brothels? Why or why not?
2. What does the existence of legalized brothels in Nevada suggest about the nature of interest group influence in the state compared with interest group influence in Texas? In other words, what groups are influential in Nevada but less influential in Texas, and vice versa?
3. If the Texas legislature allowed each county to decide whether to have legal brothels, would you actively support the move in your county, actively oppose it, or stay out of the debate? Why?

---

*"Prostitution in Nevada," available at www.answers.com.

† "Harry Reid's Prostitution Remarks Ignite Debate in Nevada," March 23, 2011, available at www .huffingtonpost.com.

‡ Jessica Ramirez, "Feeling the Pinch: Nevada's Brothels Hit Hard Times," *Newsweek*, June 18, 2008, available at www.newsweek.com.

§ Nick Gillespie, "Paying with Our Sins," *New York Times*, May 16, 2009, available at www.nytimes.com.

Lobbying

Lobbying The communication of information by a representative of an interest group to a government official for the purpose of influencing a policy decision.

Lobbying is the communication of information by a representative of an interest group to a government official for the purpose of influencing a policy decision. More than 1,800 registered lobbyists represented group interests in Texas in 2011.[13] Although some interests hire a single lobbyist to represent them, big companies often employ a small army of high-priced lobbyists. In 2011, AT&T spent as much as $10 million on 113 lobby contracts.[14] (State reporting requirements make it impossible to know the exact amount of lobby expenditures.)

Social lobbying The attempt of lobbyists to influence public policy by cultivating personal, social relationships with policymakers.

The traditional approach of lobbyists in Texas was called **social lobbying,** which is the attempt of lobbyists to influence public policy by cultivating personal, social relationships with policymakers. Cynics referred to the practice as "booze, bribes, and babes." Lobbyists would ply their trade by meeting legislators and executive branch officials at a local barbecue restaurant for an evening of ribs, beer, and storytelling. Even though today's lobbyists are more professional than their predecessors, social lobbying continues to be a big part of the way they do business. In contrast to the national government and 22 other states, Texas places no limit on the amount of money interest groups can spend on meals and entertainment for public officials.

Professional lobbyists are skilled technicians, knowledgeable both in how to approach public officials and in the subject matter vital to their groups. The basic stock in trade of the skilled lobbyist is information. In fact, interest groups are sometimes the main source of information on a piece of legislation. "We have 140 days to deal with thousands of bills," said one state senator. "The lobbyists are providers of information about those issues. I don't know how we could operate without them."[15]

The most effective lobbyists build personal relationships with members of the legislature. Many lobbyists are former members of the legislature or former staff members hired by interest groups to lobby their former colleagues over policy issues that they had worked on together in a previous legislative session. Unlike many states, Texas law allows former members of the legislature and employees of the executive branch to begin work as lobbyists the day after they resign their government positions. For example, State Senator Kipp Averit, a Republican from Waco, resigned from the Texas Senate in 2010 to become a lobbyist. In 2011, he earned as much as $650,000, substantially more money than the $7,200 he earned as a member of the Texas Senate in 2010.[16]

Legislative access An open door through which an interest group hopes to influence the details of policy.

Although legislators all deny that campaign contributions influence their votes, most will admit that groups that give generously to political campaigns enjoy access to lawmakers that other interests do not share. **Legislative access** is an open door through which an interest group hopes to influence the details of policy. Lobbyists for interest groups that contribute heavily to political campaigns usually have the opportunity to make their case to lawmakers. Legislators return their calls, invite them into their offices, and respond to them more quickly than they do for ordinary citizens who are not major campaign contributors.

Interest groups back their legislative lobbyists by mobilizing group members in the home districts of legislators to contact their representatives. The TMA, for example, asks its physician members to personally contact public officials who happen to be their patients. Even though the doctors who make the contacts with policymakers are not professional lobbyists, they are particularly effective because they already have a personal relationship with the public official.

Public Relations Campaigns

Interest groups attempt to influence policy by building public support for their points of view. They recognize that public officials, especially elected officials, are unlikely to jeopardize their political futures by publicly supporting an unpopular cause, regardless of PAC money and lobbying. Interest groups understand that their lobbying efforts will be more effective if policymakers know that the group's goals enjoy public support. Legislators take note when large numbers of their constituents contact them about specific legislative issues. E-mail messages from people who live in a legislator's district written in their own words have a particular impact because legislators believe that people who take the time to write about an issue may also base their voting decision in the next election on how legislators voted on that issue.

Groups attempt to demonstrate popular support for their goals by convincing ordinary citizens to contact members of the legislature about a particular position. For example, the groups supporting tort reform conducted a sophisticated public relations campaign to win support for their point of view. They purchased billboards and ran television and radio advertisements against what they called "lawsuit abuse." They used radio talk shows and other media to publicize examples of what they consider unreasonable jury judgments, such as the story of a woman who sued McDonald's restaurant chain after hot coffee spilled in her lap.

Groups with a large membership base attempt to mobilize their members to take action. Consider the strategy of the Texas Community College Teachers Association (TCCTA) to protect community college funding from major budget cuts during the 2011 legislative session. The TCCTA sent e-mail alerts to its members prior to important votes asking them to contact their state representative and state senator about community college funding. The alerts told members how to look up the names and addresses of their legislators and provided them with talking points that could be included in e-mail messages.

Small-government conservative groups employed a similar strategy to influence legislative decisions on taxes and spending. Texans for Fiscal Responsibility and other groups publish legislative scorecards on their webpages, showing how individual members of the legislature voted on issues important to the group. The groups use e-mail and Twitter to alert their supporters to key votes and urge them to contact legislators. They promote their scorecards at election time, encouraging people to reelect legislators with high scores and defeat those with low scores. In 2011, Republican members of the legislature were especially sensitive to the positions of the small-government conservative groups because they believed the groups carry weight in Republican primary elections.

Groups without substantial membership or financial resources sometimes employ public relations as their primary strategy for influencing public policy. For example, consumer groups, such as Texas Watch, produce research reports on consumer-related issues, such as tort reform and utility rates. They publish the reports on their websites and hold press conferences to call attention to their findings and recommendations.

Litigation

Sometimes interest groups use litigation (i.e., lawsuits) to achieve their goals. In 2009, for example, Shell Oil Company settled a lawsuit filed by Environment Texas and the Sierra Club by agreeing to reduce emissions at its Deer Park refinery.[17] Shell also promised to pay a $5.8 million penalty. The lawsuit was filed under a provision of the federal Clean Air Act that allows private citizens to enforce the act in federal court. The environmental groups filed suit against Shell because they were dissatisfied with what they considered lax enforcement by the Texas Commission on Environmental Quality (TCEQ), which had only issued small fines against Shell and had failed to force the refinery to halt the emissions.[18]

Protest Demonstrations

Some groups attempt to influence public opinion by means of protest demonstrations. Civil rights groups used this technique in the 1960s. Today, it is occasionally employed by a variety of groups pursuing many different goals, ranging from antinuclear groups opposing the construction of a nuclear power plant to Tea Party activists opposing a proposed tax increase. In general, protest demonstrations are a tactic used by groups unable to achieve their goals through other means. Sometimes the protest catches the attention of the general public and pressure is brought to bear on behalf of the protesting group. In most cases, though, protests have only a marginal impact on public policy.

Political demonstrations sometimes backfire. Immigrant rights supporters lost ground when high-school-aged demonstrators waived Mexican flags rather than American flags. In Houston, meanwhile, protestors organized by the SEIU had to pay fines as large as $2,000 and spend several days in jail after illegally blocking intersections in support of a union strike against janitorial companies.[19]

Political Violence

Occasionally, frustrated groups go beyond peaceful protest to violent, illegal activities. During the 1960s, some groups opposed to the war in Vietnam took over college administration buildings or burned Reserve Officer Training Corps (ROTC) offices on campus. The Ku Klux Klan has also been linked to violence. Although political violence usually produces a harsh response from the political establishment, it can occasionally succeed in calling the public's attention to an issue that might otherwise be ignored.

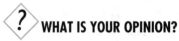 **WHAT IS YOUR OPINION?**

Is violence on behalf of a political cause ever justified?

Immigrant rights supporters demonstrate in support of comprehensive immigration reform.

Alliances

Interest groups find power in alliances with other interest groups and political parties. The Republican Party is currently in firm control of all three branches of Texas government and groups allied with it benefit, including business groups, anti-abortion organizations, small-government groups, and religious conservatives. In contrast, groups allied with the Democratic Party—environmentalists, trial lawyers, minority-rights groups, labor unions, and consumer rights organizations—are on the defensive.

WHAT WE HAVE LEARNED

1. **What types of interest groups are active in American politics and what are their goals?**

Business groups, such as Comcast and Reliant Energy, and trade associations, such as the Texas Association of Business, are the most powerful interest groups in Texas politics because they are well organized, well financed, and skilled in advocating their positions. Business groups and trade associations generally agree on the need to maintain a good business climate. Professional associations, such as the TMA and TTLA, are politically influential because of the relatively high socioeconomic status of their members. They are concerned with public policies that affect their members, such as medical malpractice insurance reform. Organized labor is relatively weak in Texas because of the state's right-to-work law and, in general, its anti-union climate. Unions, such as the Texas AFL-CIO, are concerned with employee compensation, working conditions, job availability, job training, and state laws affecting the ability of unions to organize. Agricultural interests have long been powerful in Texas politics. Farm organizations, such as the Texas Farm Bureau, are concerned with taxes on farm land, state laws and regulations affecting agriculture, water policy, and agricultural research supported by the state. Racial and ethnic minority groups, such as LULAC and the NAACP, enjoy some political influence in Texas. Minority groups are interested in the enforcement of laws protecting the voting rights of minority citizens, the election and appointment of minority Texans to state and local office, college and university admission policies, public services for low-income residents of the state, inner-city development, and, for Latino groups in particular, economic development in South Texas. Churches and other religious institutions provide the foundation for a number of political organizations, including religiously liberal groups such as COPS, Interfaith Alliance, TMO, and EPISO, and religiously conservative organizations such as Focus on the Family, Eagle Forum, and the American Family Association. The religious liberals favor expanding SCHIP coverage, increasing funding for public education, and protecting the rights of immigrant workers; the religiously conservative groups oppose gay marriage and abortion while supporting abstinence-based sex education and prayer in schools. Citizen groups (such as Texans for Public Justice), advocacy groups (such as Children's Defense Fund), and cause groups (such as the Sierra Club and the NRA) focus on a single issue or a group of related issues. Their influence varies, depending on the strength of their organization, the power of the opposition, and the popularity of their cause.

2. **What strategies and tactics do interest groups use to achieve their goals?**

Interest groups attempt to affect public policy by participating in the electoral process. They endorse candidates, encourage their members and supporters to vote for them, and, through their PACs, contribute money to them. Interest groups employ lobbyists to shape the content of legislation and influence the actions of the executive branch of state government. Interest groups attempt to affect policy by building public support for their points of view through public relations campaigns. Some interest groups file lawsuits to achieve their goals. Interest groups attempt to advance their goals through protest demonstrations and even political violence. Groups can also promote their interests by forming alliances with other interest groups and political parties.

KEY TERMS

AARP

advocacy groups

American Federation of Labor-Congress of Industrial Organizations (AFL-CIO)

cause groups

citizen groups

good business climate

hate-crimes legislation

incumbent

interest group

League of United Latin American Citizens (LULAC)

legislative access

lobbying

minimum wage

Mothers Against Drunk Driving (MADD)

NARAL Pro-Choice Texas

National Association for the Advancement of Colored People (NAACP)

National Organization for Women (NOW)

National Rifle Association (NRA)

political action committees (PACs)

racial profiling

Rainy Day Fund

religious right

right-to-work law

Sierra Club

social lobbying

State Children's Health
Insurance Program (SCHIP)

Texas Association of Business
(TAB)

Texas Association of Realtors
(TAR)

Texas Farm Bureau

Texas Medical Association
(TMA)

Texas Right to Life Committee

Texas Trial Lawyers
Association (TTLA)

tort reform

trade associations

union shop *or* closed shop

NOTES

1. Dave Montgomery, "Texas House Backs Allowing Part of Rainy-Day Fund to Go to Education," *Fort Worth Star-Telegram*, June 10, 2011, available at www.star-telegram.com.

2. Morgan Smith, "Measure Providing Extra Money for Schools Dies," *Texas Tribune*, June 24, 2011, available at www.texastribune.org.

3. "Best and Worst States—2011," *Chief Executive*, available at www.chiefexecutive.net.

4. Bureau of Labor Statistics, "Union Affiliation of Employed Wage and Salary Workers by State," available at www.bls.gov.

5. Ibid.

6. National Institute of Money in State Politics, available at www.followthemoney.org.

7. Texas AFL-CIO, available at www.texasaflcio.org.

8. "Exit Polls for Texas," available at www.cnn.com/elections/2010.

9. National Institute of Money in State Politics, available at www.followthemoney.org.

10. Ibid.

11. Ibid.

12. Ibid.

13. Texas Ethics Commission, available at www.ethics.state.tx.us.

14. Texas Ethics Commission, "2011 Lobby List," available at www.ethics.state.tx.us.

15. Quoted in Brent Manley, "Texas Lobbyists' Big Bucks Get Bigger," *Houston Post*, March 18, 1984, pp. 1A, 18A.

16. Texans for Public Justice, "More Lawmakers Hit Lobby; Democrats Work for Food," April 7, 2011, available at www.tpj.org.

17. "Short Arm of the Law," *Houston Chronicle*, May 5, 2009, available at www.chron.com.

18. "Environmental Groups and Shell Oil Company Propose Landmark Settlement of Clean Air Act Lawsuit," available at http://lonestar.sierraclub.org.

19. L. M. Sixel, "Union Protesters Pay Price in City," *Houston Chronicle*, March 25, 2007, pp. D1–D4.

Chapter 6

Political Parties

CHAPTER OUTLINE

WHAT WE WILL LEARN

After studying Chapter 6, you should be able to answer the following questions:

1. What is the party system in the United States?

2. How are the two major parties organized nationally and at the state level in Texas?

3. What is the history of political party competition in Texas?

4. How do the Texas Democratic and Republican Parties compare with one another in terms of voter support and offices held?

5. What groups of voters generally support each of the major political parties based on income, race and ethnicity, age, gender, region, and place of residence?

6. What interest groups are allied with each of the state's major political parties?

7. How do the issue orientations of the state's two major political parties compare and contrast with one another?

8. What factors affect the future of party politics in Texas, and what are the challenges facing both major parties in the state?

The Republican Party dominates all three branches of Texas government. After the 2010 election, every executive branch official elected statewide was a Republican, including the governor, lieutenant governor, attorney general, commissioner of agriculture, comptroller, land commissioner, and all three railroad commissioners. Every member of the state's two highest courts—the Texas Supreme Court and the Texas Court of Criminal Appeals—was a Republican as well. The Republican Party also controlled the Texas legislature. After the 2010 election, Republicans outnumbered Democrats 19–12 in the Texas Senate and 99–51 in the Texas House. When two Democratic members of the House changed parties, the Republican advantage in that chamber ballooned to a 101–49 supermajority. With more than two-thirds of House seats, Republicans could suspend the rules or propose constitutional amendments without Democratic support.

The party balance in Texas introduces this chapter on political parties. The chapter begins by describing the party system in the United States and Texas. It traces the state's party history and examines party organization at the national and state levels. The chapter compares the state's major parties in terms of strength, base of support, interest group alliances, and issue positions. It explores the challenges facing both major parties. The chapter concludes by discussing the role of political parties in the policymaking process.

THE PARTY SYSTEM

Political party An organization that seeks political power.

A **political party** is an organization that seeks political power. Parties are similar to interest groups in that both types of political organizations are interested in election outcomes. The difference is that political parties attempt to win control of the machinery of government by nominating candidates for elected office to run under the party label. If they are successful, they identify with the party while in office. The Republican Party, Democratic Party, Texas Association of Business (TAB), and Texas Trial Lawyers Association (TTLA) all participate in the election process and attempt to influence public policy, but only the Republicans and the Democrats actually put forward candidates for office under their organizational name. They are political parties, whereas the other two organizations are interest groups.

Two-party system The division of voter loyalties between two major political parties, resulting in the near exclusion of minor parties from seriously competing for a share of political power.

Throughout most of its history, the United States has had a **two-party system,** which is the division of voter loyalties between two major political parties, resulting in the near exclusion of minor parties from seriously competing for a share of political power. Since the Civil War era, the Democrats and the Republicans have been the two dominant parties in American national politics. Minor parties, such as the Libertarian, Green, and Reform Parties, have tried to have an impact in Texas politics. However, except for the election of a small number of Libertarian candidates at the local level, minor-party candidates have had little success in the Lone Star State. After the 2010 election, every member of the Texas legislature and every member of the congressional delegation from Texas was either a Republican or Democrat.

Despite a national two-party system, many states have experienced periods of one-party dominance. The most significant example of one-party control took

Party faction An identifiable subgroup within a political party.

place in the South after the end of the Civil War era. The Democratic Party dominated southern politics for nearly a century. Political conflicts still occurred in the South, but they took place within the Democratic Party between factions divided over issues or personalities. A **party faction** is an identifiable subgroup within a political party.

PARTY ORGANIZATION

The Democratic and Republican Parties have both national and state party structures.

National Party Organization

A national committee and a national committee chair head the national party organization. The national committee consists of a committeeman and committeewoman from each state and the District of Columbia, chosen by their state or the district party organization. The national committee elects the national chair. When the party controls the White House, the national chair is usually the choice of the president.

The national political party organizations support party candidates at the state level by spending money on their behalf and providing them with various services. Although federal law limits the amount of money a national party organization can contribute directly to a candidate, the national party organizations can spend unlimited amounts of money on behalf of candidates as long as they do not coordinate directly with a candidate's campaign. In 2010, for example, the Democratic Congressional Committee ($627,000) and the National Republican Congressional Committee ($401,000) invested heavily in the race between Democratic Congressman Chet Edwards and his Republican opponent, Bill Flores, to represent the Seventeenth Congressional District of Texas, which is located in Central Texas. Flores won the race.[1] The national party organizations provide candidates and state parties with polling data and conduct get-out-the-vote efforts. Furthermore, individuals interested in running for state or national office can attend candidate training sessions sponsored by the national party organizations at which they can learn how to build a campaign organization, raise money, deal with the media, identify issues, and present themselves to voters.

Texas Party Organization

Political parties in Texas have both temporary and permanent party organizations. Figure 6.1 depicts the various structures.

Temporary Party Organization The temporary party organization of each party assembles for a few hours or days in general election years (even-numbered years—2010, 2012, etc.) to allow rank-and-file party supporters a chance to participate in the party's decision-making process. On the evening of the March primary after the polls have closed, Texans have the opportunity to attend precinct conventions, usually in the same location as the polling place, with Republicans gathering in one area and

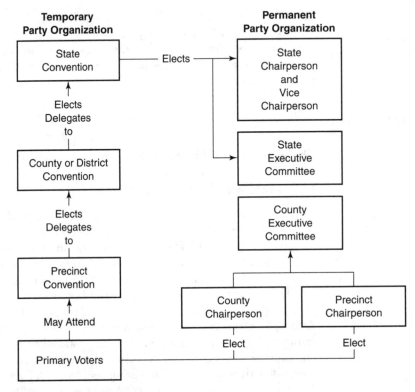

FIGURE 6.1 Texas Party Structures.

Democrats in another. Citizens who voted in a certain party's primary election are eligible to participate in that party's precinct convention. The turnout at precinct conventions is usually light, especially in nonpresidential years. In 2008, however, turnout was especially heavy for the Democratic Party precinct conventions because of the spirited presidential contest between Hillary Clinton and Barack Obama. The main business of precinct conventions is to elect delegates to the county or state senatorial district conventions, which are held on the second Saturday after the primary. In counties with more than one state senatorial district, typically large urban counties, delegates elected at precinct conventions attend state senatorial district conventions. In other counties, they attend a county convention. The number of delegates an election precinct may send to the county or district convention depends on the size of the vote in that precinct for the party's candidate in the last governor's election.

The county and district conventions are larger and more formally organized than precinct conventions, and they generally last longer, sometimes a full day. The convention usually includes speeches by party leaders and officeholders, and the delegates will likely debate and vote on a number of resolutions. Once again, the main business of the meeting is to select delegates to the next highest level—in this case, the state convention. The number of delegates each county or district convention sends to the state convention depends on the size of the vote for the party's candidate in the last governor's election in the county or district.

The Republican and Democratic Parties hold their state conventions in June. This meeting is the largest, most formal, and longest of all, generally lasting most of a weekend. The state convention certifies party nominees for the fall general election, adopts a state **party platform** (a statement of party principles and issue positions), elects the state party chairperson and vice chairperson, chooses members of the state executive committee, and selects individuals to serve on the national party executive committee. The state convention also gives the party the opportunity to showcase itself and its candidates for the upcoming general election.

In presidential election years, the state party convention selects delegates to the national party convention. State law provides that delegates to the national party conventions be pledged to support presidential candidates in rough proportion to the candidates' strength in the spring presidential preference primary. In addition to selecting delegates to the national party convention, each state party convention also names a slate of potential presidential electors to cast the electoral college votes for Texas should the party's presidential candidate carry the state in the November general election. The **Electoral College** is the system established in the U.S. Constitution for the selection of the president and vice president of the United States.

Party platform A statement of party principles and issue positions.

Electoral College The system established in the U.S. Constitution for the selection of the president and vice president of the United States.

Delegates cheer Governor Rick Perry at the Texas Republican State Party convention.

GETTING INVOLVED

Volunteer to Support Your Political Party

Political parties are a means for individuals to influence the policymaking process. The websites of the five most important political parties in Texas politics are as follows:

Democratic Party: **www.txdemocrats.org**

Texas Green Party: **www.txgreens.org/**

Texas Libertarian Party: **www.tx.lp.org/**

Texas Reform Party: **www.texasreformparty.org**

Texas Republican Party: **www.texasgop.org**

Each party website includes information on how Texans can contact the party and participate in its work. Contact the party of your choice and offer to help. Volunteers support their party by registering voters, helping out in the local office, raising money, and researching issues. People who get involved with their party may eventually have the opportunity to attend the county, state, or national convention. Some may even decide to run for office and may be elected. It's your country—get involved!

Permanent Party Organization Each party has a permanent party organization, which operates year-round. Forming the base of the permanent party organization are the precinct chairpersons, elected by party voters in each of the state's precincts, except in those areas where one party is so weak that no one can be found to accept the job. Precinct chairpersons conduct primary elections by staffing the polling place on Election Day. They may also work to organize the precinct for their party.

The county executive committee is the next highest level of permanent party organization. It includes all the precinct chairpersons in the county and the county chairperson, who is elected by party voters countywide. The county executive committee receives filing petitions and fees from primary election candidates for county-wide offices and is responsible for placing candidate names on the ballot. The county executive committee also arranges for county and district conventions.

The state executive committee is the highest level of party organization in the state. It includes the party chair, vice chair, and a committeeman and committee-woman representing each of the 31 state senatorial districts. The State Democratic Executive Committee (SDEC) includes a party treasurer as well. The main duties of the SDEC and the State Republican Executive Committee (SREC) are to certify statewide candidates for the March primary, arrange state party conventions, raise money for party candidates, and, in general, promote the party. In particular, state party chairs serve as media spokespersons for their party.

HISTORY OF THE TEXAS PARTY SYSTEM

Grand Old Party (GOP) A nickname for the Republican Party.

The Civil War and Reconstruction produced the one-party Democratic South. Most native white Southerners hated the Republican Party because of its association with the Union during the Civil War era. In Texas, the **Grand Old Party (GOP),** as the Republican Party was known, could count on the loyalty of African Americans, German Americans living in the Hill Country who had opposed secession before the Civil War, and few others. With the Republican Party in disrepute, the Democrats

Solid South A term referring to the usual Democratic sweep of southern-state electoral votes in presidential election years between the end of the Civil War era and the current party era.

Conservatism The political view that seeks to preserve the political, economic, and social institutions of society against abrupt change. Conservatives generally oppose most government economic regulation and heavy government spending while favoring low taxes and traditional values.

Liberalism The political view that seeks to change the political, economic, or social institutions of society to foster the development of the individual. Liberals believe that the government can (and should) advance social progress by promoting political equality, social justice, and economic prosperity. Liberals usually favor government regulation and high levels of government spending for social programs. Liberals value social and cultural diversity and defend the right of individual adult choice on issues such as access to abortion.

were the dominant party not only in Texas but also throughout the South, so much so, in fact, that political commentators coined the term **Solid South** to refer to the usual Democratic sweep of southern state electoral votes in presidential election years. In Texas, Democrats won nearly every statewide race, most seats in Congress and the state legislature, and the overwhelming majority of local and judicial contests, frequently without Republican opposition.

Large landowners and industrialists controlled the Democratic Party of the late nineteenth and early twentieth centuries. The public policies they favored reflected a political philosophy of **conservatism,** the political view that seeks to preserve the political, economic, and social institutions of society against abrupt change. Conservatives generally oppose most government economic regulation and heavy government spending while favoring low taxes and traditional values.

By the 1930s, an identifiable liberal faction had emerged to challenge conservative dominance of the Democratic Party. **Liberalism** is the political view that seeks to change the political, economic, or social institutions of society to foster the development of the individual. Liberals believe that the government can (and should) advance social progress by promoting political equality, social justice, and economic prosperity. They usually favor government regulation and high levels of government spending for social programs. Liberals value social and cultural diversity and defend the right of individual adult choice on issues such as access to abortion. Liberal Democrats in the Lone Star State supported Democratic President Franklin Roosevelt and his **New Deal,** which was the name of Roosevelt's legislative program for countering the Great Depression. Liberal Democrats called for a more active role for state government in the fields of education, job training, healthcare, and public assistance to the poor. To pay for these programs, liberal Democrats proposed higher taxes on business and industry, as well as on people earning substantial incomes. Liberal Democrats in Texas called for the elimination of the white primary and the poll tax. They also supported an end to discrimination against African Americans and Latinos.

The liberal wing of the Texas Democratic Party achieved some political success during the 1930s as the Great Depression caused many Texans to question the wisdom of the state's conservative public policies. The highpoint for the liberals was the election of James Allred as governor in 1935 and 1937. During the Allred administration, the legislature and the governor enacted several liberal programs designed to combat the Great Depression. Support for the liberal Democrats came primarily from a loose coalition of unemployed persons, working-class whites, labor union members, Jews, university people, some professionals, Latinos, and African Americans. The latter were now beginning a wholesale change of allegiance from the GOP to the party of Franklin Roosevelt.

The conservative Democrats reestablished themselves as the dominant wing of the Democratic Party during the 1940s. With the Great Depression over, the economic issues raised by liberal Democrats were less effective. Conservative Democrats claimed that the return of economic prosperity proved the correctness of their philosophy. Another advantage for conservatives was that they enjoyed easier access to the financial resources needed to wage a modern political campaign in a large and rapidly growing state than did the liberal Democrats. Furthermore, working-class and minority voters who made up the core of support for the liberal Democrats were less likely to vote than the middle- and upper-income white supporters of the conservative Democrats.

New Deal The name of Roosevelt's legislative program for countering the Great Depression.

The period running from the early 1950s through the late 1970s was a time of transition for party politics in the Lone Star State. By the 1950s, the liberal wing of the Texas Democratic Party had become a formidable political force. Although conservative Democrats still held the advantage, liberal challengers had to be taken seriously. Liberal Democrats scored a major breakthrough in 1957 when Ralph Yarborough, a liberal Democrat, won a special election to the U.S. Senate. He held the seat until 1971. Liberal Democrats also captured a few seats in Congress, won a number of positions in the state legislature, and ran credible races for the party's gubernatorial nomination.

BREAKING NEWS!   Democratic Legislators Switch Parties After 2010 Election

Shortly after the 2010 election, two members of the Texas House who had just won reelection as Democrats announced that they were changing parties to become Republicans. Allan Ritter, from Nederland, which is near Beaumont, switched parties after winning reelection running unopposed. He has been a member of the Texas House since 1999. Aaron Peña, from Edinburg in Hidalgo County, changed parties after serving in the House as a Democrat since 2003.*

Discussion

Why do legislators switch political parties? Members of the legislature change party affiliations in hopes of improving their personal political positions. Ritter switched parties because he doubted he could continue to win reelection as a Democrat. Ritter was what is known as a WD 40, a white Democrat over the age of 40. The number of middle-aged and older white Democrats has been dwindling, especially from rural and small-town Texas. Ritter was one of the last ones standing and he figured that he would have been defeated for reelection in 2010 had he faced a Republican opponent.

How about Peña? He obviously wasn't a WD 40. Peña's motivation was less clear. He represented Hidalgo County in the Valley, a heavily Democratic area. His legislative district went 76 percent for Bill White, the 2010 Democratic candidate for governor. Peña probably believed that he would be given better committee assignments in the 2011 session of the legislature as a Republican than a Democrat, considering that the Republicans enjoyed complete control of the House. In fact, Speaker of the House Joe Straus rewarded Peña by appointing him to the redistricting committee.

Does party switching pay off for the legislators who change parties? Sometimes. Although Ritter is more likely to win the next general election in his district as a Republican than a Democrat, he may face an opponent for the Republican nomination who will attack him for being a former Democrat. In the meantime, Peña's decision backfired. Although the legislature created a competitive district for him, a federal court put the legislature's map on hold pending the outcome of a lawsuit based on the Voting Rights Act. A temporary map created by a panel of federal judges for use in the 2012 election put Peña in an overwhelmingly Democratic district and Peña chose not to seek reelection.[†]

---

* Jason Embry, "East Texas Lawmaker Leaving Democrats," *Austin American-Statesman*, December 12, 2010, available at www.statesman.com.

[†] Matt Stiles, "Proposed Peña District Voted 50.1% for Perry in 2010," *Texas Tribune*, April 14, 2010, available at www.texastribune.org.

Liberal Democrats gained strength because the electorate was changing. The legal barriers that had kept many African Americans, Latinos, and poor whites from the polls were coming down, primarily because of the intervention of the federal courts and the U.S. Congress. The liberal wing of the party also benefited from the defection of some conservative voters to the GOP. A poll taken in the mid-1960s found that 37 percent of Texans who said they were once conservative Democrats had left the party to become either Republicans (23 percent) or independents (14 percent).[2] The exodus of conservative voters from the Democratic Party made it easier for liberal candidates to win Democratic primary elections.

In the meantime, the Texas Republican Party was coming to life. The presidential candidacy of General Dwight D. Eisenhower in 1952 brought a flood of new faces into the Republican camp, many of which were former Democrats. Furthermore, many conservative Democrats, including Governor Allan Shivers, deserted their party's presidential nominee, Governor Adlai Stevenson of Illinois, to openly support the Republican presidential candidate. Eisenhower carried the state in both 1952 and 1956.

Texas Republicans built their party throughout the 1960s and 1970s. They elected candidates to the U.S. Congress and the Texas legislature and won a number of local races, particularly in urban areas. Perhaps their most important victory came in 1961, when Republican John Tower, a young college professor at Midwestern State University in Wichita Falls, won a special election to serve the remainder of Lyndon Johnson's U.S. Senate term after Johnson resigned to become vice president. Tower won reelection in 1966, 1972, and 1978.

Surveys of party identification among voters traced the Republican surge. For decades, the most common political animal in the Lone Star State was the Yellow Dog Democrat. This was a Texan, it was said, who would vote for a yellow dog if the dog were the Democratic candidate. In other words, a **Yellow Dog Democrat** was a loyal Democratic Party voter. In 1952, 66 percent of Texans called themselves Democrats, whereas only 6 percent declared allegiance to the Republican Party. Twenty years later, the margin was a bit closer, 57 percent to 14 percent.[3] By 1984, however, Democrats outnumbered Republicans by only 33 percent to 28 percent (with the rest independent).[4]

What accounted for the rise of the GOP as a significant electoral force in Texas? First, the legacy of the Civil War finally began to diminish in importance, especially for younger Texans. Surveys showed that younger voters were more likely to identify with the GOP than were older people.[5] Second, many conservative white Democrats became disenchanted with what they saw as an increasingly liberal national Democratic Party. Whereas some conservative southern Democrats openly defected to GOP ranks, other conservatives remained nominal Democrats but supported Republicans in statewide and national races whenever the Democratic nominee seemed too liberal for their taste. Finally, the Texas Republican Party benefited from the migration of white-collar workers from outside the South. Many of these Republican newcomers identified with the GOP in their old states and simply took their party loyalties with them to their new homes in Texas.

Yellow Dog Democrat A loyal Democratic Party voter.

The 1978 election signaled the emergence of a competitive two-party system in Texas. The spring primary produced the most significant development for the Democrats when Attorney General John Hill, a liberal Democrat, defeated incumbent Governor Dolph Briscoe, a conservative. Hill's victory demonstrated that liberal Democrats could compete with conservative Democrats on an equal footing. The determining political event in 1978 for the GOP came in the fall general election, when Bill Clements defeated Hill to become the first Republican governor in more than a century. The election of Clements demonstrated that well-funded Republican candidates could win statewide elections in Texas, especially against Democrats from the liberal wing of the party.

From 1978 to 1994, Texas party politics was more competitive than ever before. The GOP enjoyed an advantage at the top of the ballot, winning most races for governor and U.S. senator. The Republican presidential nominee also carried the state every time during the period. In contrast, Democrats were considerably more successful in contests below the top of the ballot. Throughout the period, Democrats won most statewide executive offices below the level of governor, enjoyed majorities in the Texas House and Texas Senate, elected most of the state's judges, and held most county offices.

The Republican Party became the clear majority party in the state in 1994 when Republican gubernatorial nominee George W. Bush defeated incumbent Democratic Governor Ann Richards and the GOP won a majority of seats in the Texas Senate. Since that point, no Democrat has won a statewide election for any office. The Democrats lost their last hold on power at the state level in 2002 when the GOP

John McCain won 61 percent of the suburban vote in 2008.

captured a majority of seats in the Texas House. Although Democrats clung to office at the county level in many areas of the state, especially in South Texas, the GOP made significant inroads in the state's urban centers, capturing every local office and judgeship elected countywide in Harris, Dallas, and Tarrant Counties.

THE PARTY BALANCE

Texas Republicans enjoy an edge over Democrats in party identification. A Gallup analysis of survey data collected in 2010 showed that Republicans outnumbered Democrats in the state by 42 percent to 38 percent. Republicans are proportionally more numerous in Texas than they are nationwide, where Democrats held a 44 percent to 40 percent advantage.[6]

Although party identification is an important predictor of an individual's vote, the overall party identification balance does not necessarily forecast election outcomes. People typically vote for the candidates of their preferred political party. In 2008, for example, 89 percent of Texas Democrats backed Obama, whereas 93 percent of Texas Republicans voted for McCain.[7] The party identification balance does not necessarily match the vote because Democrats and Republicans are not equally likely to go to the polls. In Texas (and around the nation), Democratic turnout is typically lower than Republican turnout because Democrats as a group are lower income, and lower-income people are less likely to go to vote than middle- and upper-income individuals. Furthermore, people who call themselves independents may tip the election to one party or the other. In 2008, independents nationwide backed Obama over McCain by a margin of 52 percent to 44 percent. In Texas, however, independents lined up solidly behind McCain, 62 percent to 32 percent for his Democratic opponent.[8] Finally, the Texas Republican Party benefits from the general political climate in the state. Surveys show that self-described conservatives outnumber people who call themselves liberal by a margin of 44 to 17 percent (with the rest moderate or unsure), making Texas the twelfth most conservative state in the nation.[9] Conservatives tend to vote Republican, especially in national elections, giving the Texas GOP a decided advantage over their Democratic opponents.

Table 6.1 compares the electoral strength of the Texas Republican and Democratic Parties. After the 2010 election, the three highest-profile elective office-holders in the state were Republicans: Rick Perry was governor, whereas Kay Bailey Hutchison and John Cornyn represented Texas in the U.S. Senate. The Republican Party held 23 of 32 seats in the U.S. House of Representatives. Every member of the Texas Railroad Commission, Texas Supreme Court, and Texas Court of Criminal Appeals was a Republican. A majority of the members of both houses of the Texas legislature and the State Board of Education (SBOE) was Republican as well.

The 2010 election was a high point for the Texas Republican Party. The Texas GOP not only swept every statewide contest, but Republicans captured more seats in the Texas House than ever before. Republicans also made significant inroads

TABLE 6.1   Party Affiliation of Elected Officials in Texas, 2011

Office	Total Number of Officials	Democrats	Republicans
U.S. Senate	2	0	2
U.S. House	35	9	23
State Executives	6	0	6
Texas Senate	31	12	19
Texas House	150	49	101
Texas Supreme Court	9	0	9
Texas Court of Criminal Appeals	9	0	9
Texas Railroad Commission	3	0	3
Texas State Board of Education	15	4	11

at the county level, especially in East Texas, a region that has historically been a Democratic stronghold. Midterm elections are generally better for Republicans than Democrats because turnout is less than in presidential election years and lower turnout typically advantages Republicans. The 2010 election was particularly good for Texas Republicans because of the unpopularity of Democratic President Obama in the state. Democratic voters were demoralized while Republicans were energized, especially conservatives tied to the Tea Party Movement.

The 2010 election was disappointing for Democrats because it appeared in 2008 that they were closing the gap. After the 2008 election, Democrats were close to a majority in the Texas house, holding 74 of 150 seats in the chamber. Moreover, Democratic candidates for countywide office swept every race in Dallas County. Democrats had hoped to capture a majority of seats in the Texas House in 2010 and that Bill White, the former mayor of Houston, would win the governorship, but their hopes were dashed in the big Republican sweep.

VOTING PATTERNS

Voting patterns in Texas reflect differences in income, race and ethnicity, age, gender, region, and place of residence.

Income

Voting patterns are related to income, with higher-income citizens generally supporting Republican candidates and lower-income voters backing Democrats. Exit polls taken during the 2008 presidential election showed a clear relationship between income and voter choice. The Democratic nominee, Obama, led the Republican nominee, McCain, by a margin of 56 percent to 42 percent among voters with family incomes under $50,000 a year. In contrast, 63 percent of voters with annual family incomes over $50,000 backed McCain compared with 36 percent for Obama.[10]

Race and Ethnicity

Voting patterns vary based on race and ethnicity. Minority voters, especially African Americans, support the Democrats. In 2008, African Americans in Texas supported Obama by an overwhelming margin of 98 percent to just 2 percent for McCain. The Latino vote went for Obama as well, with 63 percent compared with 25 percent for his Republican opponent. In contrast, the white vote in Texas is heavily Republican. In 2008, 73 percent of white voters backed McCain compared with only 26 percent who supported Obama.[11]

Age

Texas Democrats are stronger with younger voters; in contrast, Republicans do better with older voters. In 2008, Obama led McCain among people under the age of 30 by 54 percent to 45 percent. McCain edged Obama among voters in the 30-to-44 age group, 52 percent to 46 percent, and won older voter groups by wider margins, taking two-thirds of the votes of people over the age of 65.[12] The figures provide encouragement to Texas Democrats because the natural turnover of the electorate should produce Democratic gains at the ballot box.

Gender

Gender gap A term that refers to differences in party identification and political attitudes between men and women.

Texas has a **gender gap,** a term that refers to differences in party identification and political attitudes between men and women. Although McCain carried both the women's vote and the men's vote in 2008, his margin was considerably closer with women than with men. McCain outpolled Obama among male voters by 20 percentage points, 59 percent to 39 percent. In contrast, McCain only carried the women's vote by 5 percentage points, 52 percent to 47 percent.[13]

Region

Texas voting patterns have a regional flavor. Republicans are strongest in West Texas and East Texas. In 2008, McCain took 77 percent of the vote in West Texas and 62 percent in East Texas. In the meantime, Democrats are strongest in South Texas. Obama won 60 percent of the South Texas vote in 2008 compared with 38 percent for his Republican opponent. The other three geographic regions of the state—the Dallas-Fort Worth Metroplex, the Houston area, and Central Texas—are closely divided. In 2008, McCain won each of the three regions, but the margins were within 5 percentage points or less.[14]

Place of Residence

Although the Democrats do well in big-city Texas, the Republicans carry the suburbs, small towns, and rural areas of the state. In 2008, Obama outpolled McCain in cities with a population greater than 500,000 by 55 percent to 44 percent, carrying Travis, Dallas, El Paso, Bexar, and Harris Counties. However, McCain won Texas by racking up large margins in the suburbs (61 percent to 37 percent) and the small-town and rural areas of the state (63 percent to 36 percent).[15] McCain's strongest counties in terms of vote margin were Montgomery County, which is just north of Houston, and Collin County, which is just north of Dallas.[16]

INTEREST GROUP–POLITICAL PARTY ALLIANCES

Political parties and interest groups form informal alliances. Interest groups assist political parties by providing campaign funds and organizational support to party candidates. Groups endorse candidates and distribute campaign literature to group members and people who would likely sympathize with the group's goals. Interest groups may also provide lobbying support for policies the party favors. In turn, political parties reward their interest group allies by adopting policies that benefit them.

Table 6.2 lists the interest groups generally associated with the Texas Democratic and Republican Parties. Although the list of groups allied with the Democratic Party is longer than the list associated with the GOP, the groups in the Democratic column are not necessarily more effective politically. With the exception of trial lawyers, who support the Democrats, the groups allied with the Republican Party have more money to devote to political action than do the groups who support the Democratic Party. Many of the groups allied with the Democrats, such as teacher organizations and labor unions, have a large membership base, which can be tapped for volunteer campaign support. Their numbers are somewhat offset, however, by the dedication of anti-abortion activists, conservative religious groups, and small-government conservative organizations, such as the various Tea Party groups, supporting the Republican Party.

Although political parties and interest groups form alliances, groups are not wholly owned subsidiaries of parties. For example, not all African Americans, Latinos, and gay men and lesbians support the Democratic Party; some are Republican. Furthermore, groups and group members may not agree with a political party on every issue or endorse all of its candidates.

TABLE 6.2   Political Party and Interest Group Alliances

Groups Allied with the Democratic Party	Groups Allied with the Republican Party
• Organized labor	• Business groups and trade associations
• Environmental organizations	• Most professional organizations, including doctors and realtors
• Consumer groups	• Farm groups
• African American rights organizations	• Religious conservatives
• Latino rights groups	• National Rifle Association
• Gay and lesbian rights organizations	• Pro-life groups
• Teacher groups	• Tort reform organizations
• Pro-choice groups	• Anti-tax groups
• Trial lawyers	• Small-government conservative organizations
• Women rights groups	

"You can be absolutely certain that every election [to come] in Texas will have a larger percentage of Latino voters." —Sociologist Stephen Klineberg, Rice University

ISSUE ORIENTATION

The two major political parties in Texas agree on the fundamental principles of America's political and economic systems. Neither party wants to rejoin Mexico or establish a monarchy. Both Democrats and Republicans favor good schools, safe streets, healthy families, and a sound economy. However, the two parties disagree on some of the details of policy, particularly on the role of government in society.

Table 6.3 compares the 2010 platforms of the state's two major political parties on selected issues. As the table shows, the two parties agree on some matters. Both the Democrats and the Republicans favor the election of state judges. They both oppose conversion of existing roads to toll roads. Both parties support better border security to stop drug smuggling and stem the flow of illegal immigration.

On other platform issues, the Democrats and Republicans take positions that are clearly different. Whereas the Democrats support a woman's right to choose, the

TABLE 6.3   Texas Democratic and Republican Party Platforms, 2010, Selected Issues

Issue	Democratic Platform Position	Republican Platform Position
State Taxes	Proposes revising the business franchise tax to "provide fairness to all economic sectors." Calls for extending property tax relief to renters. Endorses state constitutional amendment to prohibit a sales tax on food and medicine.	Calls for repealing the business franchise tax and abolishing the property tax. Calls the sales tax the "simplest and most visible, stable, and equitable" tax. Opposes increasing the gasoline tax.
School Finance	Declares that the state should fully fund an exemplary education program in every school district. Favors reducing reliance on the **Robin Hood plan** (a reform of the state's school finance system designed to increase funding for poor school districts by redistributing money from wealthy districts).	Urges state to focus school funding on academics rather than nonacademic activities. Opposes tax increases to fund schools.
School Choice	Opposes private school voucher programs.	Favors giving parents state funding vouchers and then letting them choose among public, private, or parochial schools, contingent on the passage of a state constitutional amendment exempting private and parochial schools from state regulation.
Other Education Issues	Rejects effort to destroy **bilingual education** (teaching of academic subjects in both English and a student's native language, usually Spanish). Endorses a comprehensive sex education program. Calls for increasing teacher and support staff pay to the national average. Supports universal access to pre-kindergarten and kindergarten programs.	Proposes tiered approach to bilingual education that leads to English-only instruction after four years. Favors limiting sex education to abstinence-only before heterosexual marriage. Supports including intelligent design in the science curriculum and allowing teachers to discuss the strengths and weaknesses of all scientific theories.

Robin Hood plan
A reform of the state's school finance system designed to increase funding for poor school districts by redistributing money from wealthy districts.

School choice An educational reform movement that allows parents to choose the elementary or secondary school their children will attend.

Bilingual education Teaching of academic subjects in both English and a student's native language, usually Spanish.

TABLE 6.3   Continued

Issue	Democratic Platform Position	Republican Platform Position
Higher Education	Calls for increased state funding for higher education coupled with a rollback in the increases in college tuition and fees adopted since 2003. Supports giving high school graduates two years of public college or postsecondary technical education tuition free. Calls for fully funded student grant programs. Opposes guns on campus.	Opposes using class rank as the basis for university admissions. Proposes use of the same college textbooks for ten years to reduce costs. Supports charging noncitizens higher tuition and denying noncitizens financial aid. Calls for eliminating faculty tenure at state colleges and universities.
Illegal Immigration	Calls for allocation of sufficient resources to police the border. Supports enforcement of laws against employers who knowingly hire illegal workers at substandard wages. Endorses legislation to create a path to citizenship for undocumented workers living in the United States. Opposes adoption of Arizona-style immigration law.	Declares that all necessary means should be employed to control the border, including building a physical barrier. Opposes any form of amnesty for illegal immigrants and calls for their deportation to their home countries. Opposes allowing the children of illegal immigrants to enroll in public schools.
Healthcare	Supports the implementation of the federal healthcare reform law. Calls for government funding of all types of stem cell research.	Calls for repeal of the federal healthcare reform law. Favors market-based approach to healthcare. Supports government funding for adult stem cell research, but opposes funding research that involves destroying embryos.
Energy	Declares that Texas should reduce global warming pollution by 80 percent by 2050. Supports the development of renewable energy.	Opposes taxes and regulations imposed to counter the "alleged threat of global warming." Favors domestic energy development, including alternative energy sources.
Transportation	Opposes conversion of existing roads to toll roads. Calls for the development of a state rail plan so that Texas will be eligible for federal high-speed rail funding.	Opposes conversion of existing roads to toll roads without voter approval.

continued on next page

TABLE 6.3   Continued

	Issue	Democratic Platform Position	Republican Platform Position
Privatization The process that involves the government contracting with private business to implement government programs.	**Privatization** (the process that involves the government contracting with private business to implement government programs)	Declares that privatization of social services has been a poor use of tax dollars.	Supports the privatization of government services when beneficial to the taxpayer.
Right-to-work law A statute prohibiting a union shop.	**Right-to-Work law** (a law prohibiting a union or closed shop)	Calls for repeal of Texas right-to-work law.	Supports right to work in Texas and calls for a national right-to-work law.
Capital punishment The death penalty.	**Capital Punishment** (the death penalty)	Supports the establishment of a Texas Capital Punishment Commission to study the Texas death penalty system and a moratorium on executions pending action on the commission's findings.	Declares that capital punishment, when "properly applied," is a legitimate form of punishment and a deterrent for serious crime. Says that the death penalty should be a punishment option in rape cases.
	Judicial Selection	Supports the election of state judges while working toward a more diverse judiciary.	Supports the election of state judges.
	Role of Religion	Declares that the separation of church and state allows religion to flourish.	Declares that the separation of church and state is a myth.
Minimum wage The lowest hourly wage that an employer can pay covered workers.	**Minimum Wage** (the lowest hourly wage that an employer can pay covered workers)	Supports increasing the state minimum wage, which applies to farm workers, to keep up with the federal minimum wage.	Calls for the repeal of the minimum wage.
	Abortion	Declares that women should decide when and whether to bear children, "in consultation with their family, their physician, personal conscience, or their God, rather than having these personal decisions made by politicians."	Declares that the unborn child has an individual fundamental right to life that cannot be infringed. Supports a constitutional amendment to ban abortion.
	Divorce	No position.	Calls for repeal of no-fault divorce laws.

TABLE 6.3   Continued

Issue	Democratic Platform Position	Republican Platform Position
Election Reform	Opposes requiring prospective voters to produce a photo ID. Supports same-day voter registration. Endorses public financing of general election campaigns.	Favors requiring the re-registration of voters every four years. Says that prospective voters should produce state or federal photo IDs. Favors full disclosure of campaign contributions.
Gay and Lesbian Rights	Calls for the repeal of all laws that discriminate against members of the gay, lesbian, bisexual, and transgender community. Opposes discrimination in the foster care system.	Calls for the enactment of a constitutional amendment to protect traditional marriage. Opposes laws granting civil rights protection to gay men and lesbians. Declares that homosexuals should not be allowed to adopt, have custody of children, or have visitation with minor children unless ordered by a court. Favors re-institution of laws that criminalize sexual relations between same-sex consenting adults.

GOP platform calls for the adoption of a constitutional amendment to outlaw abortion. Democrats propose increasing the state minimum wage, whereas Republicans want to repeal it altogether. The Democrats favor creating a path to citizenship for undocumented workers, whereas the Republicans demand their deportation. Democrats want to repeal the Texas right-to-work law; Republicans want to keep it.

The party platforms show that the two parties have different perspectives on the role of government. The Democrats believe that government should play a role in addressing social problems. The Democratic platform supports adequate funding for public education, increased state support for higher education, expansion of the **State Children's Health Insurance Program (SCHIP),** the adoption of a universal healthcare program, and a significant reduction in pollution that causes global warming. On social issues, Democrats support abortion rights and oppose laws that discriminate against gay men and lesbians, bisexuals, and people who are transgendered. In contrast, the Republicans believe that government's primary role is to support traditional family values rather than solving social problems. The GOP platform proposes the repeal of the property tax, which is the major source of tax revenue for local governments in Texas, and the business franchise tax. The Republican platform favors private approaches to healthcare and rejects any regulations or taxes adopted to combat global warming, which it calls an "alleged threat."

State Children's Health Insurance Program (SCHIP)
A federal program designed to provide health insurance to children from low-income families whose parents are not poor enough to qualify for Medicaid.

The Republicans believe that government should strengthen traditional marriage by making divorce more difficult, outlawing same-sex marriage, and prohibiting homosexuals from adopting or having the custody of children.

WHAT DO YOU THINK?

Which party's platform more closely matches your political views — the Democratic or the Republican?

THE FUTURE OF PARTY POLITICS IN TEXAS

Despite the 2010 election, Democrats are hopeful that they will soon be able to challenge Republican dominance of state government. Before 2010, they had gained seats in the Texas House of Representatives and done well in county and judicial contests in many urban areas. Dallas County flipped from Republican control to Democratic dominance in 2006 and the trend continued in 2008 and even 2010. Democrats won a majority of races on the ballot in Harris County in 2008 before losing every county race on the ballot in 2010. Democrats already enjoyed the upper hand in county and judicial contests in Travis County, Bexar County, and El Paso County. With the state's minority population growing and white citizens no longer a majority, the future of the Democratic Party seems promising.

When and if Texas becomes a Democratic state again depends on a number of factors:

- **Latino turnout.** In 2008, Latinos accounted for 36 percent of the state's population[17] but only 20 percent of the electorate.[18] As younger Latinos become adults and older noncitizen Latinos gain their citizenship, the potential Latino electorate will grow. Democratic Party gains hinge on the success of its voter registration efforts and get-out-the vote drives.

- **Latino voting patterns.** Latinos supported Obama in 2008 by 63 percent to 25 percent for McCain, a considerably greater margin in favor of the Democratic candidate than in 2004, when political analysts estimated that Republican President George W. Bush ran a close race against John Kerry, perhaps even taking the Latino vote in the Lone Star State.[19] Many political observers believe that the Republican Party has alienated many Latino voters by harsh anti-immigrant rhetoric, especially on talk radio.[20] If Latino voters continue to back the Democrats with 60 percent or more of their votes, Texas will almost certainly become a Democratic state in the next decade.

- **White voters.** Although minority residents represent a majority of the state's population, they do not make up a majority of the electorate. In 2008, the Texas electorate was 63 percent white, 20 percent Latino, 13 percent African American, 2 percent Asian, and 2 percent "other."[21] Obama and other Democratic candidates for statewide office lost because they received only about a fourth of the white vote. McCain trounced Obama among white voters by a margin of 73 percent to 26 percent.[22] Although demographic change may eventually lead the Democrats back into power, their success in the near future depends on doing better with white voters. Democrats can take some comfort from exit polls showing that Obama did better with younger white voters than with older whites, although still trailing badly in each age bracket. Whereas Obama lost the under-30 white vote to McCain by a sizable margin of 30 percent to 69 percent, he lost the over-65 white vote by an even more one-sided margin of 20 percent to 78 percent.[23] As younger white voters mature and older white voters die off, the overall Democratic share of the white vote will likely improve.

Each political party faces challenges. In the long run, the Democratic Party has the advantage because of demographic change. It can begin winning statewide races again sooner rather than later if it can succeed in turning out its base voters, especially Latinos, with aggressive voter registration efforts and get-out-the-vote drives. Democratic success in the near term also depends on increasing the party's share of the white vote.

The challenge for the Texas Republican Party, meanwhile, is to adapt to demographic change. The Republican base is shrinking. Unless GOP candidates can do better with minority voters, especially Latino voters, they will continue to lose elections in urban centers and will sooner or later lose their statewide majority. Republican leaders recognize the need to extend their party's appeal to minority voters. Recent Republican governors, including Bill Clements, George W. Bush, and Rick Perry, have appointed Latinos and African Americans to high-profile positions as secretary of state and to vacancies on the Texas Railroad Commission and the Texas Supreme Court. Bush campaigned hard to win Latino votes, speaking Spanish in campaign appearances and in radio campaign ads. Republicans also hope to attract Latino support by stressing social issues, such as their opposition to abortion and gay marriage.

The dilemma for Republican leaders is that the party's base, especially those voters most likely to participate in Republican primary elections, favors some policy positions that will be a hard sell for minority voters. The 2010 Texas Republican Party platform called for repealing the minimum wage, making American English the state's official language, and deporting undocumented workers. The platform opposed raising any state taxes and fees, even to pay for education, and supported abolishing the property tax, which funds schools and other local governments. It proposed increasing college tuition and denying financial aid for noncitizens, even permanent residents who were in the United States legally. Although those issue positions may appeal to conservative suburban whites, they are unlikely to attract the votes of many African American, Latino, or Asian voters. Republican officeholders who try to broaden the party's appeal by taking moderate positions on immigration or the SCHIP program may be vulnerable to defeat by more conservative challengers in the Republican primary.

Republican efforts to attract Latino voters are also hurt by a primary electorate that appears hostile to Latino candidates. Consider the fate of Railroad Commission

Voters in New York choose from among candidates for the two major parties and several minor parties. State law allows a political party to receive a place on the official ballot if its supporters can collect 20,000 petition signatures. The party holds its ballot slot as long as its candidate for governor receives at least 50,000 votes. In 2010, for example, the New York statewide ballot included not just the Democratic and Republican Parties, but also the Independence, Conservative, Working Families, Green, Rent Is Too Damn High, Libertarian, Taxpayers, Anti-Prohibition, and Freedom Parties.*

Minor parties in New York have been successful at holding their places on the ballot because of the state's cross-endorsement rule. An individual can run for office as the candidate of more than one party. In 2010, for example, Democrat Andrew Cuomo ran for governor of New York as the candidate not just of the Democratic Party, but also the Independence and Working Families Parties. People who want to vote for a minor-party candidate who is cross-endorsed by a major party do not have to worry about throwing their votes away because the candidate receives the sum total of votes cast for that candidate, whether they came from minor-party or major-party voters.

New York's minor parties are more interested in influencing policy than electing candidates. The Conservative Party's primary goal is to make the state's Republican Party more conservative. Most of the Conservative Party's endorsed candidates are

Republicans, but if party leaders believe that the Republican candidate is not sufficiently conservative, the party can run its own candidate or make no endorsement in the race, thereby taking votes away from the Republican nominee.

Some minor parties try to draw attention to their issues by running their own candidates rather than making cross-endorsements. For example, activist Jimmy McMillan was the candidate of the Rent Is Too Damn High Party not only for governor in 2010 but also for mayor of New York City in 2005 and 2009. McMillan and his political party want the government to act to reduce housing costs, end hunger, and eliminate poverty. Kristin Davis, a former madam who ran an escort service, ran for governor as the candidate of the Anti-Prohibition Party. Her issues were legalizing marijuana and prostitution, and taxing them.

QUESTIONS

1. Would you like for Texas to have election laws similar to those in New York that allow minor parties to cross-endorse major-party candidates?
2. If you lived in New York, would you consider minor-party endorsements in deciding which candidate to support?
3. Would you ever vote for a minor-party candidate who was not also endorsed by a major party, knowing that the candidate had no realistic chance of winning? Why or why not?

* New York Board of Elections, available at www.elections.state.ny.us/.

Chairman Victor Carillo in the 2010 Republican primary. Carillo is a petroleum engineer who was appointed to the Railroad Commission in 2003 to fill a vacancy and then elected to the position in 2004. Carillo enjoyed the enthusiastic support of Republican officeholders statewide and spent more than $620,000 on his reelection campaign. Nonetheless, Carillo lost to accountant David Porter who spent little money and barely campaigned. Carillo blamed his loss on his ethnicity. "Given the choice between 'Porter' and 'Carillo,' unfortunately, the Hispanic surname was a serious setback from which I could never recover."[24]

WHAT WE HAVE LEARNED

1. What is the party system in the United States?

A political party is a group of individuals who join together to seek public office in order to influence public policy. Although the United States has had a two-party system for most of its history, many states, including Texas, have experienced long periods of one-party dominance. In those states, political conflicts were fought between party factions.

2. How are the two major parties organized nationally and at the state level in Texas?

A national committee and a national chair head the national party organization. The national political party organizations support party candidates at the state level by spending money on their behalf and providing them with various services. Political parties in Texas have both temporary and permanent party organizations. The temporary party organization allows rank-and-file party supporters a chance to participate in the party's decision-making process in election years by selecting delegates to district, county, and state party conventions. Each party has a permanent organization including a state chairperson and a state executive committee.

3. What is the history of political party competition in Texas?

Texas was a one-party Democratic state from the late nineteenth century through the mid-twentieth century because most native white Southerners were alienated from the Republican Party by its association with the Civil War and Reconstruction. Eventually, identifiable liberal and conservative factions developed within the Democratic Party to contend for political power, with the conservative Democrats usually enjoying the upper hand. Beginning in the 1950s, the Texas Republican Party began to come to life because the legacy of the Civil War began to fade, some conservative Democrats began voting Republican, and the

Texas GOP benefited from the migration of white-collar workers from the north. From 1978 to 1994, party politics was closely competitive in Texas between the two major political parties, and between the liberal and conservative factions within the Democratic Party. Since 1994, the Republican Party has become the dominant party in Texas.

4. How do the Texas Democratic and Republican Parties compare with one another in terms of voter support and offices held?

Surveys indicate that the Republicans outnumber Democrats in party identification. Surveys of party identification do not necessarily predict election outcomes, however, because Republicans are more likely to vote than are Democrats and because independents in Texas lean Republican, especially in national elections. Republicans also benefit from Texas having a relatively conservative electorate. After the 2010 election, the Texas GOP held every statewide elected office and a large majority of state legislative seats and U.S. congressional seats from Texas.

5. What groups of voters generally support each of the major political parties based on income, race and ethnicity, age, gender, region, and place of residence?

The Texas Republican Party typically attracts the support of upper-income voters, whites, older people, men, people living in West Texas and East Texas, suburban residents, and people living in small towns and rural areas. In contrast, the Democrats run more strongly among lower-income voters, minority citizens, younger voters, women, people living in South Texas, and inner-city residents.

6. What interest groups are allied with each of the state's major political parties?

Business and trade groups, most professional organizations, farm groups, religious

conservatives, the NRA, pro-life groups, tort reform organizations, small-government conservative groups, and anti-tax organizations back the
GOP. In contrast, labor groups, environmental
organizations, consumer groups, minority-rights
groups, teacher organizations, pro-choice groups,
trial lawyers, and women's groups are allied with
the Democratic Party.

**7. How do the issue orientations of the state's two
major political parties compare and contrast
with one another?**

The Texas Democratic and Republican Parties
disagree on some of the details of policy,
particularly on the role of government in society.
The Democratic platform is pro-choice, favors
increasing the state minimum wage, and supports
comprehensive immigration reform. The Republican platform is pro-life, advocates the repeal of
the minimum wage, and calls for deporting illegal immigrants. Whereas the Democrats believe
that government should play a role in addressing social problems, the Republicans contend

that government's primary role is to support
traditional family values rather than solve social
problems.

**8. What factors affect the future of party politics
in Texas, and what are the challenges facing
both major parties in the state?**

Despite the 2010 election, Democrats are hopeful that they will soon be able to challenge
Republican dominance of state government
because the Latino population is increasing and
the older white population is decreasing. The
challenge for the Democrats is to increase voter
registration and voter turnout among Latino
citizens and younger people. In the short run,
however, Democrats will make gains only if
they can increase their share of the white vote.
The challenge for Republicans, meanwhile, is
to adapt to demographic change by appealing to
younger voters and minority citizens while sat-
isfying the policy demands of their base, which
is composed primarily of older conservative
suburban whites.

KEY TERMS

bilingual education	minimum wage	Robin Hood plan
capital punishment	New Deal	school choice
conservatism	party faction	Solid South
Electoral College	party platform	State Children's Health
gender gap	political party	Insurance Program (SCHIP)
Grand Old Party (GOP)	privatization	two-party system
liberalism	right-to-work law	Yellow Dog Democrat

NOTES

1. Center for Responsive Politics, available at www.opensecrets
   .org.
2. James A. Dyer, Arnold Vedlitz, and David B. Hill, "New
   Voters, Switchers, and Political Party Realignment in
   Texas," *Western Political Quarterly* 41 (March 1988): 156.
3. Clay Robison, "Texas GOP Beats Dems in Key Areas,"
   Houston Chronicle, November 28, 1989, p. 16A.
4. *Texas Weekly*, July 15, 1991, p. 5.
5. "The Two Souths," *National Journal*, September 20, 1986,
   pp. 2218–2220.
6. "State of the States," February–March, 2011, available at
   www.gallup.com.
7. Ibid.
8. Ibid.

9. Jeffrey M. Jones, "Mississippi Rates as the Most Conservative U.S. State," February 25, 2011, available at www.gallup.com.

10. "Election Results 2008—Texas."

11. Ibid.

12. Ibid.

13. Ibid.

14. Ibid.

15. Ibid.

16. *Texas Weekly*, November 17, 2008, available at www.texasweekly.com.

17. U.S. Census Bureau, "Resident Population by Race, Hispanic or Latino Origin, and State," *The 2011 Statistical Abstract*, available at www.census.gov.

18. "Election Results 2008—Texas."

19. David L. Leal, Matt A. Barreto, Jongho Lee, and Rodolfo O. de la Garza, "The Latino Vote in the 2004 Election," *PS: Political Science and Politics* (January 2005): 46.

20. Wayne Slater, "GOP's Solid Hold in Texas Is Slipping," *Dallas Morning News*, February 20, 2009, available at www.dallasnews.com.

21. "Election Results 2008—Texas."

22. Ibid.

23. Ibid.

24. Brian Thevenot, "The Elefante in the Room," *Texas Tribune*, March 4, 2010, available at www.tribune.org.

Chapter 7

Elections

WHAT WE WILL LEARN

After studying Chapter 7, you should be able to answer the following questions:

1. What are the advantages and disadvantages of the long ballot?

2. What are the various types of elections held in Texas?

3. What factors affect the redistricting process in Texas?

4. What factors affect election campaigns in Texas?

5. How does each of the following factors affect voter choice: incumbency, political party identification, campaigns, retrospective and prospective voting, and national factors?

Texas was the big winner after the 2010 U.S. Census, gaining four seats in the U.S. House to increase its representation from 32 to 36 seats. The U.S. House of Representatives has 435 seats, allocated among the states based on population, with the stipulation that each state, no matter how small, has at least one representative. Every ten years, census data are used to reallocate seats among the states in a process known as **reapportionment.** Rapidly growing states, such as Texas, gain seats; slow-growing states lose seats.

Reapportionment The reallocation of legislative seats.

Members of the U.S. House are elected from districts. Each state is divided into as many districts as it has seats in the House. In Texas, the legislature has the responsibility of drawing U.S. congressional districts. In 2011, the legislature divided the map of Texas into 36 U.S. congressional districts, up from 32 during the previous decade.

Redistricting, the process of redrawing legislative district boundaries to reflect population movement, is highly political. If one political party controls the redistricting process, it can maximize the likelihood of its candidates' success while minimizing the prospects of the other party's candidates. With large majorities in both chambers of the Texas legislature and Republican Rick Perry in the governor's mansion, the Texas Republican Party was able to increase the ratio of Republicans to Democrats in the state's congressional delegation from 23 to 9 in 2011–2013 to a projected ratio of 26 to 10 after the 2012 election. Moreover, only one of the state's 36 congressional districts—congressional district (CD) 23, held by Republican Francisco "Quico" Conseco of San Antonio—was even somewhat competitive between the two political parties. The other 35 districts were either solidly Democratic or solidly Republican.[1]

Redistricting The process of redrawing legislative district boundaries to reflect population movement.

The redistricting process after the 2010 U.S. Census introduces this chapter on Texas elections. The chapter begins by examining the long ballot in Texas, considering which offices are filled by election. It discusses the types of elections conducted in Texas. The chapter then returns to the topic of redistricting, explaining redistricting ground rules and the politics that drive the redistricting process. The chapter looks at election campaigns. It concludes by examining the factors that affect election outcomes.

THE LONG BALLOT

Long ballot An election system that provides for the election of nearly every public official of any significance.

Texas has the **long ballot,** which is an election system that provides for the election of nearly every public official of any significance. A conscientious Texas voter who never misses an election has the opportunity to cast a ballot for each of the following public officials:

- The president and vice president
- Two U.S. senators
- One member of the U.S. House of Representatives
- The governor of Texas and five other state executive officials
- Three railroad commissioners

- One member of the State Board of Education (SBOE)
- One state senator
- One state representative
- Nine members of the Texas Supreme Court
- Nine members of the Texas Court of Criminal Appeals
- At least 2 and perhaps as many as 70 or more state appellate and district court judges, depending on the voter's county of residence
- Numerous local officials, including county executives, county judges, city officials, and members of school district boards of trustees

The ballot is especially long in the state's urban counties, where a large number of state district court judges must stand for election. In 2010, Harris County voters faced a ballot with more than 80 contested races.[2]

The long ballot is not unusual in America, but few states vote on as many officials as Texas. The average state elects six statewide officials. Some states elect only the governor. In contrast, North Carolina chooses 12 statewide officials.[3] Considering the number of candidates and constitutional amendments facing Texas voters, the Lone Star State may well have the longest, most complicated election ballot in the nation.

The long ballot is controversial. Its defenders believe that the electoral process is the best way to ensure that public officials remain accountable to the people. If citizens grow unhappy with some aspect of state government, they can simply vote the responsible officials out of office. In contrast, critics of the long ballot argue that most Texans lack the information necessary to make intelligent voting choices on many down-ballot races. Not knowing the qualifications of the candidates, voters may cast ballots for persons with familiar or catchy names who may be unqualified for the offices they seek.

 WHAT DO YOU THINK?

Is the ballot too long for Texas voters to be able to make informed choices?

TYPES OF ELECTIONS

General election
A statewide election to fill national and state offices held on the Tuesday after the first Monday in November of even-numbered years.

Texans have the opportunity to cast ballots in different types of elections held at various times throughout the year.

General Elections

The **general election** is a statewide election to fill national and state offices held on the Tuesday after the first Monday in November of even-numbered years. In recent years, the Texas statewide general election ballot has included candidates for the Republican Party, Democratic Party, and Libertarian Party. To qualify for the ballot, independents and candidates affiliated with other political parties, such as the Green Party, must gather signatures equivalent to 1 percent of all the votes cast for governor in the last general election. In 2006, Carole Keeton Strayhorn and Kinky Freidman, who each ran for governor as independent candidates, had to collect the signatures of 45,540 registered voters who had not participated in the March primary. Not only that, they had to complete the process within a 60-day period in order to qualify for the general election ballot. Only Texas and North Carolina make it so difficult for independents and third-party candidates to get on the ballot.[4] A party can hold its ballot slot as long as one of its candidates receives at least 5 percent of the statewide vote in at least one race.

Straight-ticket ballot Voters selecting the entire state of candidates of one party only.

Texas is one of 16 states that allow voters to cast a **straight-ticket ballot,** which is the practice of voting for candidates of the same political party for all positions on the ballot. The general election ballot includes a straight-ticket box to enable voters to cast straight-ticket ballots by marking a single box rather than having to vote individually on all of a party's candidates. Straight tickets are more common in urban counties than rural counties because the ballot is longer in urban counties. In 2010, 62 percent of voters in the state's urban counties cast a straight-ticket ballot, with more Republicans voting a straight ticket than Democrats.[5] Citizens who do not cast a straight ticket vote a split ticket. A **split-ticket ballot** occurs when voters cast their ballots for the candidates of two or more political parties during a single election.

Split-ticket ballot Voters cast their ballots for the candidates of two or more political parties during a single election.

The candidate with the most votes wins the general election, regardless of whether that candidate has a majority (more than 50 percent) of the ballots cast. There are no runoffs. The 2006 governor's race featured four major candidates—Republican Rick Perry, Democrat Chris Bell, and independents Strayhorn and Friedman. The outcome of the election was as follows:

Perry	39 percent
Bell	30 percent
Strayhorn	18 percent
Friedman	12 percent

Under the state's election laws, Perry won despite having taken less than a majority of the total votes cast in the election because the candidate with the most votes wins the general election.

Primary election An intraparty election at which a party's candidates for the general election are chosen.

Primary Elections

Although minor parties may select their general election candidates at a state convention, Texas law requires that major parties choose their candidates in a **primary election,** which is an intraparty election at which a party's candidates for the general election are chosen. Democrats compete against other Democrats, and Republicans compete against Republicans. In Texas, primary elections take place on the first Tuesday in March of even-numbered years.

Closed primary An election system that limits primary election participation to registered party members.

The two basic kinds of primary election methods are the closed primary and the open primary. A **closed primary** is an election system that limits primary election participation to registered party members. Many party leaders favor the closed primary because they believe that it prevents the supporters of the opposition party from influencing the selection of candidates for their party. After all, why should Democrats help select Republican nominees and vice versa? In contrast, an **open primary** is an election system that allows voters to pick the party primary of their choice without disclosing their party affiliation. Some party leaders favor the open primary because they believe that it will produce nominees who can appeal to independent voters and supporters of the other party more than the closed primary can. Candidates with broad appeal are more likely to win the general election than are candidates who can attract only the votes of other Democrats or Republicans.

The Texas primary system is a cross between an open primary and a closed primary. In contrast to the practice in many states, Texas does not require that citizens disclose their party affiliation when they register to vote. On primary election day, however, voters must publicly choose the party in whose primary they wish to participate. They cannot vote in both primaries. Once a voter declares a choice, the election judge stamps the voter registration card with the following phrase: "Voted in the Republican (Democratic) primary."

Figure 7.1 compares Democratic and Republican primary election turnout in statewide (nonpresidential) election years from 1978 to 2010. In 1978, Democratic

Open primary An election system that allows voters to pick the party primary of their choice without disclosing their party affiliation.

Texas voters choose among candidates for dozens of offices.

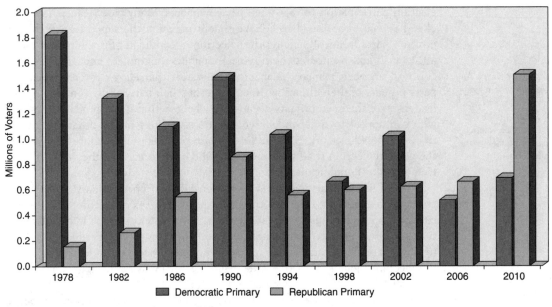

FIGURE 7.1   Primary Turnout in Gubernatorial Election Years.

primary voters outnumbered GOP primary participants by a better than 10-to-1 margin. Subsequently, the Democratic primary electorate shrank while the number of people voting in the Republican primary has increased. In 2010, more than twice as many people voted in the Republican primary than participated in the Democratic primary. Republican primary turnout in 2010 was exceptional because voters were drawn to the polls by a hotly contested race for the Republican gubernatorial nomination between Governor Perry, U.S. Senator Kay Bailey Hutchison, and conservative activist Debra Medina.

Primary turnout in presidential years varies, depending on the level of interest in each party's presidential nomination contest. In 2008, Democratic primary voters outnumbered Republican primary voters 2,874,986 to 1,362,322.[6] The difference in turnout reflected the high level of interest in the Barack Obama–Hillary Clinton race on the Democratic side compared with the level of interest in the Republican contest. By the time of the Texas primary, John McCain had essentially wrapped up the Republican presidential nomination.

To win a primary election, a candidate must receive a majority of the votes cast (50 percent plus one vote). If no one receives a majority in a multicandidate race, the two highest finishers meet in a runoff. For example, suppose that Joe Nava, Elizabeth Jackson, and Lee Chen are running for the Democratic nomination for the office of county sheriff and the vote totals are as follows:

Nava	4,102
Jackson	2,888
Chen	2,009

Nava and Jackson would face one another in the primary runoff because neither received a majority of the votes cast. Chen is eliminated because he finished third.

A **runoff primary election** is an election between the two top finishers in a primary election when no candidate received a majority of the vote in the initial primary. In Texas, the primary runoff takes place in late May, nearly three months after the initial primary. People who voted in the March primary may only vote in the same party's runoff election. They cannot switch parties for the runoff. However, citizens who failed to vote in March can vote in either party's runoff primary. The winner of the runoff is the party's official nominee for the fall general election.

Runoff turnout depends on the level of interest in the contests remaining on the ballot. If the voters have the opportunity to decide a runoff between two high-profile candidates for governor or U.S. senator, turnout will be high, perhaps exceeding turnout in the March primary. In contrast, turnout could be quite low if the only races facing runoffs are low-profile judicial contests or those for county office.

The Presidential Delegate Selection Process

Every four years, Texans have the opportunity to participate in the process through which the Democratic and Republican Parties choose their presidential candidates by selecting delegates to attend the national conventions of the two major parties. The procedure for selecting delegates to the national party conventions varies from state to state. About two-thirds of the states select delegates by means of a **presidential preference primary election,** an election in which party voters cast ballots for the presidential candidate they favor and in so doing help determine the number of convention delegates that candidate will receive. Other states choose national convention delegates by the **caucus method of delegate selection,** a procedure for choosing national party convention delegates that involves party voters participating in a series of precinct and district or county political meetings. The process begins with party members attending precinct conventions, where they elect delegates to district meetings. The district meetings in turn select delegates to the state convention. Finally, the state party convention chooses national convention delegates.

In Texas, the state Republican Party chooses delegates to the national party convention through a presidential preference primary. To receive any delegates, a presidential candidate has to win at least 20 percent of the vote in one or more U.S. congressional districts. Any candidate who gets a majority of the vote in a congressional district claims all of that district's delegates. A candidate who gets more than 20 percent but less than a majority receives a share of the delegates allotted to that district (as long as no other candidate has a majority). In 2008, Senator John McCain won the Republican presidential primary in Texas by taking 51 percent of the total vote compared with 38 percent for former Arkansas Governor Mike Huckabee and 5 percent for Texas Congressman Ron Paul. McCain received 121 delegates; Huckabee was awarded 16.[7]

The Texas Democratic Party selects national convention delegates through a system that combines the primary and the caucus methods—the so-called

Runoff primary election An election between the two top finishers in a primary election when no candidate received a majority of the vote in the initial primary.

Presidential preference primary election An election in which party voters cast ballots for the presidential candidate they favor and in so doing help determine the number of convention delegates that candidate will receive.

Caucus method of delegate selection A procedure for choosing national party convention delegates that involves party voters participating in a series of precinct and district or county political meetings.

Texas Two-Step A system for choosing national convention delegates that combines the primary and the caucus methods.

Texas Two-Step. First, Democrats vote in the primary election, either on primary election day or during the early voting period. Second, they return to their precinct polling place in the early evening of the primary election day to participate in a precinct caucus. Both the primary and the caucus contribute to the delegate selection process in Texas that eventually helps determine who wins the Democratic Party presidential nomination. More than half the state's Democratic delegates are awarded based on the results of the presidential preference primary. Candidates are awarded delegates in rough proportion to the percentage of votes they receive as long as a candidate qualifies by winning at least 15 percent of the statewide vote. Candidates also win delegates based on the results of a caucus process. Finally, the party reserves a number of delegate positions for **super delegates,** Democratic officeholders and party officials who attend the national party convention as delegates who are not officially pledged to support any candidate.

Super delegates Democratic officeholders and party officials who attend the national party convention as delegates who are not officially pledged to support any candidate.

In 2008, Texas was a major battleground in the race for the Democratic presidential nomination between Obama and Clinton. The two contenders traded victories in the early primary and caucus states, almost evenly dividing the delegates between them. Going into the March primary in Texas, Obama had a small delegate lead, but it was by no means large enough to ensure his eventual victory. Consequently, for the first time in modern presidential primary history, Texas was a major focus of campaign activity. Both Clinton and Obama campaigned personally in the Lone Star State and spent heavily on advertising. The excitement of the race produced a record primary turnout, with more than 2.8 million Texans participating in the Democratic primary, the first stage of the Texas Two-Step. Clinton won the primary, earning 51 percent of the votes compared with 48 percent for Obama. Clinton was awarded 65 delegates; Obama received 61 delegates. Meanwhile, Obama won the caucus, the second stage of the Texas Two-Step, with 56 percent of the votes compared with 44 percent for Clinton, giving him 38 delegates compared with 29 for Clinton. Altogether, Obama received 99 Texas delegates, whereas Clinton won 94.[8]

Local Elections

Under state law, local elections for city, school district, and special district officials must be held on either the second Saturday in May or the Tuesday after the first Monday in November. Many local governments conduct their elections in odd-numbered years so they will not coincide with general elections for president, senator, and governor. Most city governments choose officials by majority vote, with a runoff election if no one candidate receives a majority in a multicandidate field. Most school districts choose the members of their boards of trustees by plurality vote—the candidate who receives the most votes wins, regardless of whether it is a majority. The state constitution *requires* majority election for terms of office greater than two years. State law allows cities and school districts to cancel elections if all candidates are running unopposed and no other issues are on the ballot.

Nonpartisan elections Election contests in which the names of the candidates, but not their party affiliations, appear on the ballot.

Most local races in Texas are **nonpartisan elections,** which are election contests in which the names of the candidates, but not their party affiliations, appear on

The Blanket Primary in Louisiana

Louisiana has a unique primary system. Every candidate competes for votes in a blanket primary, regardless of party affiliation. If one candidate wins a majority of the vote, that candidate is elected. Otherwise, the two top finishers face each other in a runoff election, regardless of party affiliation. In theory, the runoff could involve two Democrats, two Republicans, or one candidate from each party. In 2007, for example, 12 candidates competed in the blanket primary for governor, including one Republicans, five Democrats, one Libertarian, and five independents. Bobby Jindahl, the Republican, won without a runoff because he received more than 50 percent of the vote. Louisiana uses the blanket primary, which is also called a jungle primary, in partisan elections for state and local office. The state uses the traditional party primary followed by a general election in races for the U.S. Congress and the U.S. Senate. The proponents of the blanket primary argue that it gives voters more options, whereas opponents of the system contend that it weakens political parties by discouraging party loyalty.

Democratic Governor Edwin Edwards invented the blanket primary in the 1980s and got the state's Democratic-controlled legislature to adopt it as a device to slow the rise of the state's Republican Party. To win office, Democrats had to survive a bruising Democratic primary election and then defeat a Republican opponent in the general election who had usually won the Republican primary without strong opposition. Edwards figured that the blanket primary would erase the Republican advantage by forcing all the candidates into the same set of elections.

Although the open primary has not prevented Republicans from making substantial inroads in Louisiana politics, it probably was responsible for Edwards winning a fourth nonconsecutive term as governor in 1991. The three main contenders, Edwards, Republican state legislator David Duke, and incumbent Republican Governor Buddy Roemer, carried considerable political baggage into the race. Many Louisiana voters thought that Edwards was a crook because he had spent most of his career fighting off corruption charges. (They were apparently right about Edwards because the former governor recently completed a prison sentence for racketeering.) Duke was notorious as a former Nazi sympathizer and leader of the Ku Klux Klan. Finally, Roemer had angered many voters because he broke his promise not to raise taxes. Most experts on Louisiana politics believed that Roemer would have been able to defeat either Edwards or Duke in a runoff, but he finished third. (Raising taxes was apparently a worse political liability than either charges of corruption or ties to the Ku Klux Klan!) Edwards easily defeated Duke in the runoff and became governor of Louisiana once again.

QUESTIONS

1. What are the advantages of a blanket primary system such as the one in Louisiana?
2. What are the disadvantages of a blanket primary?
3. Would you like to see Texas adopt a blanket primary system? Why or why not?

the ballot. The supporters of nonpartisan elections argue that the elimination of political parties from local elections reduces corruption. Furthermore, they say that nonpartisan elections free local politics from state and national political controversies. In contrast, critics of nonpartisan elections believe they work to the advantage of upper-income groups because they reduce the amount of information available to voters about candidates. In partisan elections, the single most important piece of information voters have about candidates is the party label. In nonpartisan elections, voters do not know the party attachments of the candidates. They must study the positions of the candidates if they are going to vote in their own best interest. Upper-income persons are in a better position to determine which candidates best represent their interests because they are better able to learn about candidates than low-income people are.

Scholarly research largely supports the critics of nonpartisan elections. Turnout for nonpartisan elections is generally lower than turnout for partisan elections. Without party labels on the ballot to guide their choice, some potential voters stay home because they are unable to distinguish among the candidates. Furthermore, some people who do cast ballots base their voting decisions on such factors as incumbency, gender, and the perceived ethnicity of the candidates based on their names.[9]

Special Elections

Special election
An election called outside the normal election calendar.

A **special election** is an election called outside the normal election calendar. Special elections may be used to approve local bond issues, which are discussed in the next section, or to fill unexpected vacancies in the legislature or the state's congressional delegation. When a vacancy occurs, the governor calls a special election. Special elections are nonpartisan, although party organizations often get involved. A candidate must receive a majority of the votes cast (50 percent plus one) to win a special election. Otherwise, the two leading candidates meet in a runoff.

Bond A certificate of indebtedness issued to investors who loan money for interest income; in lay terms, a bond is an IOU.

Noncandidate Elections

Texas voters have the opportunity to participate in a number of noncandidate elections, including bond elections, recall elections, and referenda. A **bond** is a certificate of indebtedness issued to investors who loan money for interest income; in lay terms, a bond is an IOU. A **bond election** is an election for the purpose of obtaining voter approval for a local government going into debt. Approval for state government indebtedness is obtained through the adoption of a constitutional amendment.

Bond election
An election for the purpose of obtaining voter approval for a local government going into debt.

Recall election is a procedure allowing voters to remove elected officials from office before the expiration of their terms. If enough signatures can be gathered on petitions, disgruntled citizens can force a recall election to remove the targeted official and let voters decide whether to keep the officeholder or declare the office vacant. The vacancy is then filled in a special election. In 2003, California voters recalled Governor Gray Davis and replaced him with Hollywood actor Arnold Schwarzenegger, but that sort of action could not happen in the Lone Star State because state officials are not subject to recall. In Texas, the power of recall is limited to the citizens of some city governments.

Recall election A procedure allowing voters to remove elected officials from office before the expiration of their terms.

Many cities (but not the state government) provide for the **initiative process,** a procedure whereby citizens can propose legislation by gathering a certain number of signatures on a petition. Election officials then place the measure on the ballot for approval by the voters. Some cities also allow citizens to repeal ordinances passed by the city council through a similar process. In some municipalities, city officials may

Initiative process
A procedure whereby citizens can propose the adoption of a policy measure by gathering a prerequisite number of signatures. Voters must then approve the measure before it can take effect.

place nonbinding referenda on the ballot. Furthermore, the executive committees of the state Republican and Democratic Parties sometimes include nonbinding referendum proposals on their spring primary ballots.

Texans vote on other measures as well. Voters must approve amendments to the state constitution. The legislature typically places amendments on the November ballot, usually in odd-numbered years, so that they will not share the ballot with a general election. Voters must also approve the establishment and dissolution of special districts, such as hospital districts or municipal utility districts. Finally, **local-option (wet-dry) elections** are held to determine whether an area will legalize the sale of alcoholic beverages.

Local-option (wet-dry) elections
Elections held to determine whether an area could legalize the sale of alcoholic beverages.

 WHAT DO YOU THINK?

Does Texas have too many elections?

ELECTION DISTRICTS AND REDISTRICTING

At-large election
A method for choosing public officials in which every citizen of a political subdivision, such as a state or county, votes to select a public official.

Texas voters select public officials in a combination of at-large and district elections. An **at-large election** is a method for choosing public officials in which every citizen of a political subdivision, such as a state or county, votes to select a public official. The president and vice president, two U.S. senators, the governor, the lieutenant governor, the comptroller of public accounts, the land commissioner, the attorney general, the agricultural commissioner, three railroad commissioners, nine justices of the Texas Supreme Court, and nine justices of the Texas Court of Criminal Appeals are all elected in at-large, statewide elections. Furthermore, numerous local officials, including county and district judges, sheriffs, city mayors, some city council members, and some school district trustees, are elected in local at-large elections.

District election
A method for choosing public officials in which a political subdivision, such as a state or county, is divided into districts and each district elects one official.

A **district election** is a method for choosing public officials in which a political subdivision, such as a state or county, is divided into districts and each district elects one official. Members of the Texas legislature, U.S. Congress, and State Board of Education (SBOE) are elected from districts. For example, the 150 members of the Texas House of Representatives are elected one each from 150 state representative districts. The state's 31 state senators are chosen from 31 state senatorial districts. Numerous local officials, including county commissioners, city council members in some cities, and the members of boards of trustees in some school districts, are also elected from single-member districts.

Election districts must be redrawn every ten years to adjust for changes in population. The Texas legislature is responsible for redrawing Texas House districts, Texas Senate districts, U.S. congressional districts, and the districts for the SBOE. Local governing bodies, such as city councils and commissioners courts, redraw the districts of local officials. The national census, which is taken every ten years, provides the population data for redistricting.

Texas Democrats doing the Texas Two-Step, participating in a precinct caucus after first voting in the presidential preference primary.

One Person, One Vote

State legislatures have not always been conscientious about redistricting. During the first half of the twentieth century, the legislatures of a number of states, including Texas, failed to redistrict despite dramatic population movement from rural to urban areas because rural legislators did not want to relinquish control. As a result, the population size of legislative districts sometimes varied dramatically. In 1961, the ratio between the most populous and the least populous U.S. congressional district in Texas was 4.4 to 1. The ratio was eight to one for state senate districts and two to one for state house districts.[10]

The U.S. Supreme Court addressed this issue in a series of cases that established the doctrine of **one person, one vote.** This judicial ruling states that the Equal Protection Clause of the Fourteenth Amendment to the U.S. Constitution requires legislative districts to be apportioned on the basis of population.[11] If one legislative district has substantially more people than another district, then the people living in the less populous district have more political influence than do the residents of the larger district. Suppose an urban district has ten times more people than a rural district. The people in the rural district then have ten times the influence in the election of a legislator or a member of Congress. Compared with the citizens living in the large urban district, the voters in the smaller rural district effectively have ten votes. The Supreme Court ruled that the Constitution requires that citizens have equal political influence regardless of where they live. Consequently, district boundaries have to be drawn to ensure nearly equal population size. Although the Court allows some leeway in state legislative and local district size, it requires that U.S. congressional districts have almost exactly the same number of people. In 2002,

One person, one vote The judicial ruling stating that the Equal Protection Clause of the Fourteenth Amendment to the U.S. Constitution requires legislative districts to be apportioned on the basis of population.

for example, a federal court overturned Pennsylvania's redistricting plan because two U.S. House districts varied in size by 19 people—646,361 compared with 646,380![12]

The Supreme Court's one-person, one-vote doctrine had a significant impact on policymaking in Texas. Because of the Court's ruling, urban areas gained representation, whereas rural interests lost ground. The legislative delegation for Harris County, the state's most populous county, increased from one state senator and 12 members of the Texas House to four senators and 19 House members.[13] African Americans, Latinos, and Republicans, all groups that are numerous in urban areas, increased their representation in legislative bodies. Urban problems such as education, transportation, race relations, crime, and healthcare won a more prominent place on the state's policy agenda.[14]

The Voting Rights Act (VRA)

Voting Rights Act (VRA) A federal law designed to protect the voting rights of racial and ethnic minorities.

The **Voting Rights Act (VRA)** is a federal law designed to protect the voting rights of racial and ethnic minorities. The VRA makes it illegal for state and local governments to enact and enforce election rules and procedures that diminish minority voting power. Furthermore, the pre-clearance provision of the VRA requires that state and local governments in areas with a history of voting discrimination submit redistricting plans either to the U.S. Department of Justice or the U.S. District Court for the District of Columbia for approval *before* they can go into effect. Congress and the president included the pre-clearance requirement in the law in order to stay one step ahead of local officials who would adopt new discriminatory electoral procedures as soon as the federal courts threw out an old procedure. The pre-clearance provision of the VRA applies only to states and parts of states that have substantial racial and language minority populations with relatively low rates of voter participation. Texas is covered, along with all or part of 15 other states: Alabama, Alaska, Arizona, California, Florida, Georgia, Louisiana, Michigan, Mississippi, New Hampshire, New York, North Carolina, South Carolina, South Dakota, and Virginia.

In the late 1980s and early 1990s, the Justice Department in the George H. W. Bush administration interpreted amendments to the VRA adopted in 1982 to require that state legislatures go beyond nondiscrimination to drawing districts designed to maximize minority representation. If a legislature *could* draw a district that would likely elect an African American or Latino candidate, then the legislature *must* draw the district. In other words, state legislatures would have to maximize the number of legislative districts with populations that were more than 50 percent minority.[15]

Why would a Republican administration choose to implement the VRA to increase African American and Latino representation in Congress and state legislatures when most minority lawmakers are Democrats? The reason was simple: The policy also helped the Republican Party gain legislative seats.[16] To construct majority African American and Latino districts, state legislatures redrew district lines to shift minority voters away from adjacent districts into new districts designed to elect minority officeholders. Because most African American and Latino voters are Democrats, the redistricting reduced Democratic voting strength in surrounding districts, threatening the political survival of some white Democratic members of Congress. The Georgia congressional delegation, for example, went from one African

American Democrat, eight white Democrats, and one white Republican before redistricting in 1991 to three African American Democrats and eight white Republicans after the 1994 election. Nationwide, the creation of minority districts after the 1990 census helped white Republicans pick up about ten seats in Congress, defeating white Democrats who were stripped of some of their minority voter support.[17]

In the mid-1990s, the U.S. Supreme Court overruled the Justice Department's interpretation of the VRA. Responding to legal challenges filed against minority districts created in Louisiana, Georgia, and other southern states, the Court declared that state governments cannot use race as the predominant, overriding factor in drawing district lines unless they have a "compelling" reason. The goal of maximizing the number of minority districts was not sufficient to justify race-based redistricting, the Court said, because Congress enacted the VRA to prevent discrimination rather than maximize the number of districts that would elect African American and Latino candidates.[18]

 WHAT DO YOU THINK?

Should state legislatures consider race and ethnicity in drawing legislative districts?

The role of the VRA in the redistricting process has changed considerably since the early 1990s. At the beginning of the decade, the VRA forced legislatures to focus on race and ethnicity during redistricting, and legislatures throughout the South created minority districts whenever possible. By the end of the decade, however, the U.S. Supreme Court made it clear that legislatures could not use race and ethnicity as the primary basis for redistricting unless they had a compelling reason. State legislatures could not regress; that is, they could not adopt redistricting plans that, taken as a whole, would diminish the political influence of minority voters. Legislatures did not, however, have to increase the number of minority districts.

The Supreme Court subsequently held that state legislatures could protect the political interests of minorities not only with districts that have a solid majority of minority voters but also with "influence districts" and "coalitional districts." Although the number of minority voters in an influence district is less than 50 percent, they are numerous enough to have a significant influence on election outcomes. In a coalitional district, one or more minority groups residing in a district can assert their interests by forming coalitions with other groups of minority voters.[19]

The Politics of Redistricting

Redistricting is a highly political process. Legislative districts can be drawn to the advantage of one political party over another or one candidate over another. The drawing of legislative district lines for political advantage is known as **gerrymandering.** In the 1991 redistricting, for example, Democratic State Senator (now U.S. Representative) Eddie Bernice Johnson of Dallas used her position as chair of the Texas Senate redistricting committee to enhance her own chances of winning a seat in Congress. The congressional district she created not only included much of her old state Senate district but also excluded the residences of potential opponents.[20]

Gerrymandering
The drawing of legislative district lines for political advantage.

BREAKING NEWS!

Groups File Suit Against the Texas Redistricting Plan

The Texas congressional redistricting plan is under attack in the courts. Several North Texas voters filed the first redistricting lawsuit even before the legislature had completed its work. Their suit charged that counting undocumented immigrants for redistricting purposes violated the Equal Protection Clause of the Fourteenth Amendment because citizens living in districts that contain large numbers of undocumented residents would have more political influence than citizens in districts with fewer undocumented people.* Subsequently, the National Association for the Advancement of Colored People (NAACP), Mexican American Legal Defense Fund (MALDEF), Texas Democratic Party, and other groups filed suits, arguing that the state's congressional redistricting plan violated the VRA by diminishing minority voting strength.

Discussion

What are the chances of the first lawsuit succeeding? The suit probably won't get very far. The section of the Constitution that discusses the allocation of seats in Congress uses the word *persons*, not *citizens*. The federal courts have always interpreted the passage to apply to everyone who resides in a state, not just its legal residents.

How about the VRA lawsuits? Federal courts regularly force changes in redistricting plans based on the VRA, so it would not be surprising if the courts order at least some modifications in the Texas redistricting plan. The problem for the state is one of perception. Minorities accounted for 89 percent of population growth between 2000 and 2010, yet white voters are expected to control three of the four new seats in Congress.[†]

How will the state of Texas defend its plan? The state will argue that the legislature created a redistricting plan designed to elect Republicans and defeat Democrats, and that's legal. Racial redistricting is illegal; political redistricting is not. The complicating factor is that Latinos and African Americans typically vote for Democrats. How does the state demonstrate that its efforts to hurt Democrats aren't really aimed at hurting Latinos and African Americans? The VRA requires the state to prove that it isn't discriminating.

Is it still necessary for the federal government to police the states to ensure they don't discriminate against their citizens? Governor Perry and Texas Attorney General Greg Abbott argue that the VRA is no longer necessary, certainly not the section that requires Texas and some other states to get prior approval before redistricting plans and other voting changes can take effect. In contrast, civil rights groups believe that the legislature's 2011 redistricting plan is solid evidence that the VRA is still needed.

What happens if the courts find that the state's redistricting plan violates the VRA? The courts could ask the legislature to make certain corrections based on the ruling, or a group of judges could draw their own map.

Was there sufficient time to settle all of these lawsuits before the 2012 election? No. *Even though the Court scheduled a hearing for early January, it seemed likely that the 2012 Texas primary elections for Congress and the Texas legislature would have to be postponed.*[‡]

---

* Ross Ramsey, "Texas Redistricting Lawsuit: Count Citizens Only," *Texas Tribune*, February 11, 2011, available at www.texastribune.org.

[†] *Texas Weekly*, February 21, 2011, available at www.texasweekly.com.

[‡] Ross Ramsey, "Redistricting Orders Throw Texas Politics Into Disarray," *Texas Tribune*, December 12, 2011, available at www.texastribune.org.

Democrats controlled the redistricting process in Texas following the 1990 Census because they held a majority of seats in both chambers of the Texas legislature and Democrat Ann Richards was governor. Republicans accused the Democrats of using their power to create congressional and legislative districts that were unfair to Republican candidates. In 1992, Democratic candidates for the U.S. House won 21 of the state's 30 congressional seats even though they received only 50 percent of the votes cast. Two years later, Republican congressional candidates carried the popular vote 56 percent to 42 percent, but Democrats still won 19 of 30 seats. Similarly, Democrats captured 17 of the 30 seats at stake in 1996 despite once again losing the popular vote, this time by 54 percent to 44 percent.[21]

The political landscape in Texas after the 2000 U.S. Census was considerably different than it was ten years earlier because neither party enjoyed clear control of the redistricting process. Although Democrats still held a majority of seats in the Texas House, Republicans enjoyed a 16–15 advantage in the Texas Senate. In addition, a Republican, Rick Perry, was governor. The result was a legislative stalemate. The 2001 session of the Texas legislature ended without passage of a redistricting plan for either the two houses of the legislature or the Congress.

When the legislature and the governor failed to adopt redistricting plans, the responsibility for drawing new district lines for the Texas legislature fell to the **Legislative Redistricting Board (LRB),** an agency composed of the speaker, lieutenant governor, comptroller, land commissioner, and attorney general that draws the boundaries of Texas House and Texas Senate seats when the legislature is unable to agree on a redistricting plan. In 2001, Republicans held four of the five seats on the LRB and they adopted a plan designed to increase Republican strength in the legislature. As a result, the GOP won a majority of seats in the Texas House for the first time in more than a century and increased its majority in the Texas Senate.

Whereas the Republicans were pleased with the results of legislative redistricting, the Democrats were relieved at the outcome of congressional redistricting. Because the LRB has jurisdiction only over redistricting the legislature, a federal court drew the lines for the state's congressional districts. The court redrew the state's existing 30 congressional districts in such a fashion that incumbent members of Congress from both parties would likely win reelection. It then put one of the state's two new congressional districts in Central Texas and the other in the Dallas suburbs. Although Republicans easily captured the two new congressional districts, the Democrats clung to a 17–15 majority in the state's congressional delegation because Democratic incumbents were able to retain their seats.

The Republican Party attempted to increase its strength in the U.S. House of Representatives by revisiting the issue of redistricting in 2003. Republican Congressman Tom DeLay of Sugar Land, Texas, the House Majority Leader, presented the GOP leadership in the Texas House with a congressional redistricting plan that could produce a congressional delegation from the Lone Star State of 22 Republicans and 10 Democrats. When Tom Craddick, the speaker of the Texas House, pushed for a vote on the plan in the closing days of the legislative session, more than 50 Democratic members of the Texas House of Representatives secretly traveled to Ardmore, Oklahoma, where they would be outside the jurisdiction of Texas law enforcement officials who had been sent to find them and bring them back to

Legislative Redistricting Board (LRB) An agency composed of the speaker, lieutenant governor, comptroller, land commissioner, and attorney general that draws the boundaries of Texas House and Texas Senate seats when the legislature is unable to agree on a redistricting plan.

Austin. The strategy for the Democrats was to prevent the Texas House from having a quorum, the number of members that must be present for the chamber to conduct official business. Because the rules of the Texas House set a quorum at two-thirds of the 150-member body, the absence of more than 50 Democratic legislators blocked the redistricting bill, at least for the time being. Once the deadline for passing legislation expired in the Texas House, the Democrats returned to the state and the legislature resumed its business.

DeLay's redistricting proposal was highly controversial. Republicans said that redrawing the state's congressional district lines to increase the number of Republicans in Congress was fair because Texas is a Republican state. In 2002, Democrats won 17 of the state's 32 U.S. House seats even though 57 percent of Texas voters supported Republicans for Congress. If most Texans vote Republican, DeLay said, most Texas members of Congress should be Republican as well. In contrast, Democrats pointed out that redistricting anytime other than the session after the census is both unusual and unnecessary. They accused DeLay of a power grab aimed at preserving Republican control of the U.S. House of Representatives. Democrats hold a majority of the state's congressional delegation, they said, because Texas voters in a number of districts split their ballots to vote Republican for statewide office while backing Democrats for Congress.

Shortly after the end of the 2003 regular session of the legislature, Governor Perry called a 30-day special session to consider congressional redistricting. The House quickly passed a redistricting plan, but it ran into trouble in the Senate because Senate Democrats held together to block consideration of the plan. The longstanding practice in the Texas Senate is to require a two-thirds vote before a measure can be considered on the floor. With 11 Senate Democrats refusing to agree to debate, the redistricting bill failed. The first special session ended without accomplishing anything.

As the first special session ended, the Republican leadership set a trap for the Democrats. Lieutenant Governor Dewhurst declared that he would not honor the two-thirds rule in a second special session, therefore ensuring that the Republican majority would be able to vote a redistricting plan out of the Senate. While Democrats met in the capital, Governor Perry called a second special session and Dewhurst ordered the doors locked to trap the Democrats inside. Unfortunately for Dewhurst and Perry, the Democrats got word of the scheme just in time and slipped out a side door. They drove to the airport and flew to Albuquerque, New Mexico, out of the reach of Texas authorities. With 11 Democrats in Albuquerque, the Senate lacked the quorum necessary to conduct official business. The second special session accomplished nothing as well.

Before Governor Perry could call a third special session, the Senate Democrats in Albuquerque broke ranks. Senator John Whitmire returned to Texas, declaring that he and his fellow Democrats had made their point and that he would be on the Texas Senate floor when the governor called the next special session, ensuring a quorum. Although the other Democrats were furious with Whitmire, they had no choice but to end their boycott and return to Texas.

Whitmire's return did not mean a quick end to the redistricting battle because the Republicans could not agree on a new map. After several weeks of wrangling,

Congressman DeLay flew to Texas to broker an agreement. The Texas House and Texas Senate passed and Governor Perry signed a redistricting plan that many observers believed would increase the number of Republicans in the U.S. House from 15 to at least 20, and maybe 22.

The predictions proved true. The GOP picked up one seat in the U.S. House even before the next election when Democratic Congressman Ralph Hall of East Texas switched parties. The Republicans added five more seats in the 2004 election, defeating every targeted Democratic incumbent except Congressman Chet Edwards of West Texas, who barely hung on to his seat with 51 percent of the vote. In 2005, the state's congressional delegation included 21 Republicans and 11 Democrats.[22]

As noted in the chapter opener, the Republican Party controlled the redistricting process in 2011. The GOP used its power to claim three of the four new congressional districts and to lock in majorities in the Texas House and Texas Senate for years to come. Barring a major revival of Democratic voting strength, the only threat to Republican dominance of the legislature and the state's congressional delegation would be lawsuits based on the VRA.

More than 50 Democratic legislators spent several days in Ardmore, Oklahoma, in May 2003 in hopes of defeating a congressional redistricting plan that would favor the Republicans.

Reforming the Redistricting Process

Critics believe that the modern redistricting process undermines the quality of democracy in the United States because it reduces electoral competition. State legislators have always tried to create districts that would be safe for their party. Democrats want to draw Democratic districts, whereas Republicans prefer to create Republican districts. Computer technology has enabled legislators to accomplish their goals more efficiently than ever before. As a result, relatively few legislative seats are competitive between the two parties. In the first election after redistricting following the 2000 U.S. Census, the number of elections for seats in the U.S. House nationwide that were decided by less than 10 percentage points fell by 11; the number of seats decided by less than 5 percentage points fell by 15.[23] If elected officials do not have to worry about a serious electoral challenge, critics warn, they have little incentive to represent the interests of their constituents.

The critics of redistricting also believe that it produces legislators who represent the extremes of the political spectrum. Republican primary voters are somewhat more conservative than Republicans in general and much more conservative than the electorate as a whole. Democratic primary voters, meanwhile, are somewhat more liberal than Democrats in general and much more liberal than the electorate as a whole. In competitive districts, candidates recognize the value of appealing to a broad spectrum of voters because they understand that they must win not just the primary election but the general election as well. Primary voters also have an incentive to select more moderate candidates because they have a better chance of winning the general election than do candidates whose views are more extreme. Legislative bodies dominated by members representing the extremes of either party may have difficulty reaching compromise on complex policy issues, instead dissolving into partisan gridlock.

Reformers want to change the redistricting process to make it less political. In Iowa, for example, a bipartisan redistricting commission creates a redistricting plan, which the legislature must accept or reject but not amend. If the legislature rejects the plan, the commission tries a second and even a third time. If the legislature fails to approve any of the commission's plans, a court redistricts for the state. After the 2000 U.S. Census, four of Iowa's five U.S. congressional districts were fairly evenly divided between the two parties. The other district was heavily Republican. A bill designed to change the redistricting process in Texas to resemble the Iowa system was introduced in the last session of the legislature, but it got nowhere.

ELECTION CAMPAIGNS

An **election campaign** is an attempt to get information to voters that will persuade them to elect a candidate or not elect an opponent. Campaigns educate voters about issues and candidates and increase interest in the election campaign. The more familiar citizens are with the candidates, the more likely they are to vote.[24]

Election campaign
An attempt to get information to voters that will persuade them to elect a candidate or not elect an opponent.

The Role of Money

Election campaigns are expensive. The total cost of the campaigns for governor, other statewide executive offices, and the legislature in 2010 was nearly $235 million. Governor Perry spent $39 million winning reelection, more money than any other candidate. Other statewide races were expensive as well. For example, Lieutenant Governor David Dewhurst spent more than $9 million on his reelection campaign. Attorney General Greg Abbott's successful reelection campaign cost nearly $6 million. Legislative races are typically less costly than contests for statewide office because legislators run from districts. On average, candidates for the Texas House spent $236,000 in 2010, whereas the average race for the Texas Senate cost $274,000.[25] Local contests in large metropolitan areas are expensive as well. Candidates for mayor in the state's major cities often spend several million dollars on their campaigns.

Candidates need money to hire a campaign staff, cover overhead expenses, purchase advertising, and pay for travel. They hire consultants to plan strategy, pollsters to assess public reaction to candidates and issues, media consultants to develop an advertising campaign, field organizers to get out the vote, opposition researchers to dig for dirt on opponents, Internet consultants to design websites, and fundraisers to find the cash to pay for it all. Other money goes for campaign literature, office space, postage, telephones, polling, and consulting fees. The largest single item in the big-time campaign budget is media, especially television.[26] A week's worth of television advertising that covers all of the state's major markets costs around $1.5 million.[27]

Advertising costs vary by medium and market size. The average charge for running a 30-second television ad during the late-night news in Dallas is about $5,000. A 60-second radio spot during drive time in a major market is much less expensive, only around $600, but the audience for radio is only a fraction of what television reaches.[28] Candidates for statewide office buy advertising on both radio and television throughout the state if they have the money available. In contrast, candidates for local office or the legislature may focus their efforts on less expensive approaches, such as radio, cable television, billboards, and direct mail.

Candidates who are wealthy can bankroll their own campaigns. In 2002, David Dewhurst invested $24.2 million in his successful campaign for lieutenant governor, counting both contributions and personal loans.[29] Candidates who loan money to their campaigns can often raise money after the election to cover their loans, especially if they won. State law caps the amount of reimbursement for personal loans to $500,000 for candidates for governor and $250,000 for candidates for other statewide offices. Because the law puts no limit on reimbursement for third-party loans personally guaranteed by candidates, none of Dewhurst's loans were subject to the cap.[30]

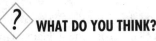 **WHAT DO YOU THINK?**

Should wealthy individuals be allowed to finance their own political campaigns?

Campaign money comes from a relatively small number of contributors. Bob Perry, a Houston homebuilder, and his wife Doylene were the top individual donors, contributing more than $6 million, mostly to Republican candidates and campaign committees. Trial lawyers, real estate interests, various business interests, and labor unions were major contributors as well.[31]

Most states restrict the amount of money individuals and groups can contribute to candidates for office, but not Texas. Two-thirds of the states limit campaign contributions and one-third provides public funding for campaigns in exchange for voluntary spending limits.[32] In contrast, Texas law places no limits on campaign contributions or campaign expenditures for candidates for executive or legislative office. Contribution and expenditure limits on judicial races are voluntary. In short, candidates for executive and legislative office in Texas can raise an unlimited amount of money from individuals or PACs as long as they report the names, occupations, and employers of people who give them $500 or more in campaign contributions. Labor unions and corporations may not contribute directly to candidates for office, although they can fund nonpartisan voter registration drives and get-out-the-vote campaigns.

Money is indispensable to major campaign efforts. In general, candidates who spend the most money get the most votes. Money is especially important for challengers and first-term incumbents who usually are not as well known as long-term officeholders. Once a challenger reaches a certain threshold, the amount of money the incumbent spends is irrelevant.[33] Raising money early in the campaign is particularly important because it gives candidates credibility with potential contributors, making it easier to raise money later in the campaign season. Candidates who amass campaign war chests often scare away potential serious challengers.

 WHAT DO YOU THINK?

Would you support using taxpayer money to finance election campaigns in order to reduce the role of private contributions?

Nonetheless, money does not guarantee victory. In 2010, for example, businessman Farouk Shami spent more than $9 million of his own money trying to win the Democratic nomination for governor.[34] He received less than 13 percent of the vote. Furthermore, a law of diminishing returns may apply to campaign spending. The marginal difference between spending $15 million and spending $13 million is not nearly as great as that between spending $4 million and spending $2 million. After all, if the average Texas voter sees a candidate's commercial 15 times, will it make much difference to see it once or twice more?

The relationship between money and electoral success is complex. Although it is true that well-funded candidates are usually successful, it is perhaps more accurate to say that successful candidates are well funded. Major campaign contributors give money to candidates they believe are likely to win because they hope to gain access to elected officials. Money makes strong candidates stronger; the lack of money makes weak candidates weaker.

Campaign Organization and Strategy

Political campaigns vary in their size and intensity. Many local contests are modest affairs. The candidates, their families, and a few friends shake some hands, knock on a few doors, put up some signs, create a website, and perhaps raise enough money to buy an ad in the local newspaper. The contest may be hard fought, but the stakes are not high enough to support a major-league campaign effort. Not so, however, with statewide races, local elections in big cities, and contests for Congress and the state legislature. These elections feature professional campaign consultants, well-oiled organizations, and big money.

Big-time campaigns are long, drawn-out affairs, beginning years before voters go to the polls. Candidates spend the early months of a race raising money, building an organization, and planning strategy. Candidates who successfully raise money and create a professional organization well before Election Day establish a reputation as serious candidates. In contrast, candidates who fail to raise money and build an organization early in the political season will probably never seriously contend.

An important goal for many campaigns is to improve the candidate's name recognition, especially if a candidate is a challenger who is not already well known.

Julián Castro raised and spent more than a million dollars on his successful 2009 campaign for mayor of San Antonio. Castro was reelected in 2011.

Races for low-profile offices may never move beyond the name-recognition stage. It helps if voters are already familiar with the candidate, or at least the candidate's name. A man named Bruce Wettman once ran for state district judge in Harris County by posting billboards picturing his name written on an umbrella; the strategy must have worked because he won easily.

Sometimes candidates borrow name recognition from better-known namesakes. In 1990, a San Antonio attorney named Gene Kelly won the Democratic nomination for a seat on the Texas Supreme Court despite spending almost no money on the race. Primary voters apparently associated Kelly with the famous entertainer of the same name. "If I had been Fred Astaire, I might have won," joked Kelly's defeated opponent. Kelly's luck ran out in the general election, however, when he lost to Republican nominee John Cornyn, who spent heavily on media advertising that attacked Kelly as unqualified. Ten years later, Kelly repeated his primary success by winning the Democratic nomination for the U.S. Senate to oppose Senator Kay Bailey Hutchison. Once again, Kelly failed to mount a serious general election campaign and Hutchison easily won reelection.

Besides building name recognition, campaigns attempt to create a favorable image for the candidate. In the fall of 1989, advertising firms hired by Clayton Williams ran a series of political commercials that turned Williams from a virtually unknown candidate into the frontrunner for the Republican nomination for governor. Riding on horseback, wearing a white hat, and bathed in golden light, Williams promised to get tough on illegal drugs by teaching teenagers who use drugs "the joys of bustin' rocks."

Campaigns also attempt to create unfavorable impressions of their opponents. In 2010, for example, Governor Perry ran an emotional ad featuring the widow of a Houston police officer who was murdered by a criminal suspect who was in the United States illegally. The grieving widow blamed Bill White, the Democratic candidate for governor, who was mayor of Houston at the time.[35] Research on negative campaigning reveals that challengers are more likely to use it than are incumbents; in addition, Republicans are more inclined to go negative than Democrats. Negative campaigns by challengers are somewhat effective, especially if they are based on policy rather than personality. However, going negative may backfire on incumbents unless they are attacked first. Negative campaigning stimulates election turnout among party loyalists but depresses it among independents.[36]

The last but perhaps most important task for each campaign is to get supporters to the polls. The most popular candidate will not win if his or her supporters stay home on Election Day. Well-organized campaigns identify likely voters and remind them to vote. The campaign distributes early voting materials and telephones likely supporters to urge them to cast their ballots. Getting out the vote is usually more important for Democrats than Republicans. Republicans tend to be better educated and more affluent than Democrats and thus are more likely to participate in elections. Turning out likely Democratic voters, especially African Americans and Latinos, often requires an organized effort.

THE VOTERS DECIDE

Why do voters decide as they do? Political scientists identify a number of factors influencing voter choice.

Incumbency

Incumbent Current
officeholder.

In most election contests, an **incumbent** (current officeholder) enjoys a distinct advantage over a challenger. Nationwide, incumbent members of the U.S. Congress win reelection at a rate that exceeds 90 percent and incumbent state legislators seeking reelection do nearly as well. Furthermore, the advantages of incumbency are apparently growing. Some incumbents win reelection without facing opposition in either the party primary or the general election. Many potential candidates decide not to run against an incumbent because they believe the incumbent will be difficult to beat.[37]

Incumbent success rates are based on several factors. Incumbents have more name recognition than most challengers and they are usually able to raise more money than their opponents can. Incumbent officeholders can often use their positions to generate favorable publicity for themselves through press releases, whereas most challengers, especially in down-ballot races, struggle to generate a meaningful amount of press coverage. Incumbents can make friends by providing services to individual constituents or groups of constituents. Incumbents also benefit from districting schemes that stack most legislative districts for one party or the other.

Political Party Identification

Political party identification is closely related to voter choice.[38] Democrats vote for Democratic candidates; Republicans back Republicans. In 2008, 89 percent of Democratic voters in Texas supported Democrat Barack Obama for president, whereas 93 percent of the Republicans cast their ballots for John McCain.[39]

The relationship between party identification and elections in Texas depends on whether candidates are running from districts or statewide. Most congressional and legislative districts are safe for one political party or the other. Incumbent officeholders running in safe districts may face primary challenges, but will likely escape serious opposition in the general election. If they do face a general election opponent, they can usually win by getting their party supporters to the polls. In contrast, candidates running in competitive districts must work to turn out their fellow party members and to win the support of independents as well.

The challenge for statewide candidates is different for Republicans and Democrats. Because of the GOP edge in party identification, especially among likely voters, Republican candidates start with an advantage. They can win an election based on their party label as long as they avoid embarrassing mistakes that would cost them the votes of people who normally vote Republican. In 2010, for example, Governor Perry played it safe by refusing to debate his Democratic opponent, Bill White, and turning down invitations to interview with the editorial boards of the state's major newspapers. They were not going to endorse him anyway, he said, so why bother to speak with them? Perry's advertising campaign stressed themes that appealed to core Republican voters—opposition to the Obama administration, support for low taxes, and a promise to hold the line on government spending. Democratic candidates running for statewide office have a more difficult challenge. They must turn out the Democratic vote while also winning the support of independents and some Republicans. No Democrat has succeeded in winning statewide office since 1994.

Campaigns

Campaigns educate voters about candidates and issues.[40] Candidates who choose not to conduct a campaign or who lack the necessary funding to get their message across almost never win. Challengers for congressional seats who have less than a quarter million dollars to spend have less than a 1 percent chance of winning.[41]

Research shows that campaign tactics vary in their effectiveness. Campaign advertising affects voters in concert with their party identification, making Democrats more likely to vote Democratic and Republicans more likely to support GOP candidates. The issues that work best for the Democrats are education, childcare, and healthcare. In contrast, Republicans benefit when they can shift the issue focus to taxes, morality, and economic growth.[42]

Retrospective voting The concept that voters choose candidates based on their perception of an incumbent candidate's past performance in office or the performance of the incumbent's party.

Retrospective and Prospective Voting

Citizens make voting decisions based on their evaluations of the past and expectations for the future. **Retrospective voting** is the concept that voters choose candidates

Campaign volunteers staff phone banks to get out the vote for their candidate.

based on their perception of an incumbent candidate's past performance in office or the performance of the incumbent party. If voters perceive that things are going well, incumbent officeholders and their party usually get the credit. In contrast, they get the blame if voters believe that the state or country is on the wrong track. Political science research indicates that the state of the nation's economy is a key element of voter evaluations of incumbent performance. As economic conditions worsen, citizens are more likely to vote against the incumbent party, and vice versa.[43] Similarly, research shows that voters evaluate governors on the state unemployment rate compared with the national average.[44] In 2010, Governor Perry was quick to point out that the Texas unemployment rate was below the national average. Voter evaluations have a prospective as well as a retrospective component. **Prospective voting** is the concept that voters evaluate the incumbent officeholder and the incumbent's party based on their expectations of future developments. One study finds, for example, that voter expectations of economic performance have a strong influence on voter choice.[45]

Prospective voting The concept that voters evaluate the incumbent officeholder and the incumbent's party based on their expectations of future developments.

National Factors

National factors can affect voting decisions in Texas. Presidential popularity and economic conditions can influence the outcome of races in nonpresidential election years. Texas candidates can also be helped by popular national figures. In a presidential election year, for example, a popular presidential candidate can sometimes provide coattails to boost candidates of the same party in other races. The **coattail effect** is a political phenomenon in which a strong candidate for one office gives a boost to fellow party members on the same ballot seeking other offices. In 2008, for example, Texas Democrats may have benefited from an unusually high turnout of core Democratic voters, especially African American voters, because of the Obama candidacy. In contrast, the unpopularity of the Obama administration in Texas helped to doom many Texas Democrats in 2010. Republicans up and down the ballot did their best to link their opponents to President Obama and his policies.

Coattail effect The political phenomenon in which a strong candidate for one office gives a boost to fellow party members on the same ballot seeking other offices.

GETTING INVOLVED

Campaigning

People who volunteer to work in an election campaign can have more of an impact on the outcome than they would by just voting. An individual has only one vote, and it is rare for a single vote to swing the outcome of an election. In contrast, a hardworking campaign volunteer can affect enough votes to make the difference in a close election, especially a low-profile down-ballot race or a local election contest.

Select a candidate to support and contact the candidate's campaign to inquire about volunteering.

All major campaigns and some candidates for local office have websites with contact information for prospective volunteers. Every well-organized campaign will have a telephone number. Contact directory assistance to get the number of the campaign office, call, and volunteer your services. Not only will you have the chance to make a difference in the outcome of the race, but your instructor may also give you extra credit for your volunteer work.

It's your government—get involved!

WHAT WE HAVE LEARNED

1. What are the advantages and disadvantages of the long ballot?

Texas has the long ballot, an election system that provides for the election of nearly every public official of any significance. Defenders of the long ballot believe that the electoral process is the best way to ensure that public officials remain accountable to the people. In contrast, critics of the long ballot argue that most Texans lack the information necessary to make intelligent voting choices on many down-ballot races.

2. What are the various types of elections held in Texas?

Texans have the opportunity to participate in several different types of elections. The general election is a statewide election to fill national and state offices, held in November of even-numbered years. A primary election is an intraparty election at which a party's candidates for the general election are chosen. If no candidate receives a majority in the primary, the two leading contenders meet in a primary runoff. Every four years, Texans have the opportunity to participate in the process through which the Democratic and Republican Parties choose their presidential candidates by selecting delegates to attend the national conventions of the two major parties. Most local elections are nonpartisan. Special elections are held outside the regular election calendar. Texas voters can also participate in a number of noncandidate elections, including constitutional amendment, bond, recall, initiative, and local-option (wet-dry) elections.

3. What factors affect the redistricting process in Texas?

Texas voters select public officials in a combination of at-large and district elections. Election districts must be redrawn every ten years to account for population changes as measured by the U.S. Census. The U.S. Supreme Court held in its one person, one vote rulings that legislative districts must be drawn on the basis of population and be nearly equal in population size. States must also adhere to the Voting Rights Act (VRA), which makes it illegal for state and local governments to enact and enforce election rules and procedures that diminish minority voting power. Even with the limitations of one person, one vote and the VRA, redistricting is highly political. The drawing of legislative district lines for political advantage is known as gerrymandering. If the governor and legislature are unable to agree on redistricting plans, the Legislative Redistricting Board is charged with redistricting state legislative seats. A federal court draws congressional district lines. The Republican Party controlled the redistricting process in 2010 because it had large majorities in both houses of the legislature and Republican Rick Perry was governor. Most observers believe that the legislative and congressional redistricting plans adopted by the legislature will ensure Republican control for years to come, pending a successful lawsuit based on the VRA. Critics believe that the modern redistricting process undermines the quality of democracy in the United States because it reduces electoral competition. State legislatures draw districts that are safe for one party or the other, and these districts tend to produce legislators who represent the extremes of the political spectrum. Reformers want to change the redistricting process to make it less political.

4. What factors affect election campaigns in Texas?

An election campaign is an attempt to get information to voters that will persuade them to elect a certain candidate or not elect that candidate's opponent. Above all else, campaigns are expensive. Candidates need money to hire a campaign staff, cover overhead expenses, and purchase advertising, especially television advertising, which is often the single largest campaign expenditure. Wealthy candidates can fund their own campaigns. Other candidates raise money from PACs and individual contributors. Texas places no restrictions on how much individuals and groups can contribute to candidates for state legislative and executive offices. Money is usually necessary for campaign success, but it does not guarantee victory. Major campaigns are long, drawn-out affairs. An important goal of a campaign is to improve the candidate's name recognition. Campaigns seek to build a favorable image for their candidate while creating an unfavorable image of the opponent. Finally, campaigns work to get supporters to the polls.

5. How does each of the following factors affect voter choice: incumbency, political party identification, campaigns, retrospective and prospective voting, and national factors?

Numerous factors affect voter choice. In most elections, the incumbent enjoys a distinct advantage. Party identification is closely related to voter choice. In Texas, that gives Republican candidates an advantage, at least for statewide office. Campaigns shape the vote by informing voters about candidates and issues. Citizens make voting decisions based on their evaluations of the past (retrospective voting) and expectations for the future (prospective voting). National factors, such as the coattail effect, can influence Texas election results as well.

KEY TERMS

at-large election

bond

bond election

caucus method of delegate selection

closed primary

coattail effect

district election

election campaign

general election

gerrymandering

incumbent

initiative process

Legislative Redistricting Board (LRB)

local-option (wet-dry) elections

long ballot

nonpartisan elections

one person, one vote

open primary

presidential preference primary election

primary election

prospective voting

reapportionment

recall election

redistricting

retrospective voting

runoff primary election

special election

split-ticket ballot

straight-ticket ballot

super delegates

Texas Two-Step

Voting Rights Act (VRA)

NOTES

1. Ross Ramsey, "Maps Ensure Melees in March, Peace in November," *Texas Tribune*, September 16, 2011, available at www.texastribune.org.
2. Chris Moran, "Election 2010: Ballot a Mile Long? No, But It's Lengthy," *Houston Chronicle*, October 12, 2010, available at www.chron.com.
3. Matthew J. Streb, *Rethinking American Democracy* (New York, NY: Routledge, 2008), p. 27.
4. Christy Hoppe, "Independents' 1st Hurdle: Getting on the Ballot," *Dallas Morning News*, February 6, 2005, available at www.dallasnews.com.

5. Aman Batheja, "Straight Ticket Votes Reach 10-Year High in Texas' Largest Counties," *Fort Worth Star-Telegram*, November 8, 2010, available at www.star-telegram.com.
6. Texas Secretary of State, "Turnout and Voter Registration Figures (1970-Present)," available at www.sos.state.tx.us.
7. CNN, "Election Center 2008, Primary Results for Texas," available at www.cnnpolitics.com.
8. Ibid.
9. Marsha Matson and Terri Susan Fine, "Gender, Ethnicity, and Ballot Information: Ballot Cues in Low-Information Elections," *State Politics and Policy Quarterly* 6 (Spring 2006): 49–72.
10. Steve Bickerstaff, "State Legislative and Congressional Reapportionment in Texas: A Historical Perspective," *Public Affairs Comment* 37 (Winter 1991): 2.
11. *Wesberry v. Sanders*, 376 U.S. 1 (1964) and *Reynolds v. Sims*, 377 U.S. 533 (1964).
12. *Vieth v. Commonwealth of Pennsylvania*, 195 F. Supp. 2d 672 (M.D. Pa. 2002).
13. Victor L. Mote, "The Geographical Consequences of Politics in the United States and Texas," in Kent L. Tedin, Donald S. Lutz, and Edward P. Fuchs, eds., *Perspectives on Texas and American Politics*, 4th ed. (Dubuque, IA: Kendall/ Hunt, 1994), p. 10.
14. Mathew D. McCubbins and Thomas Schwartz, "Congress, the Courts, and Public Policy: Consequences of the One Man, One Vote Rule," *American Journal of Political Science* 32 (May 1988): 388–415.
15. Mark Monmonier, *Bushmanders and Bullwinkles: How Politicians Manipulate Electronic Maps and Census Data to Win Elections* (Chicago, IL: University of Chicago Press, 2001), p. 62.
16. David Lublin and D. Stephen Voss, "Racial Redistricting and Realignment in Southern State Legislatures," *American Journal of Political Science* 44 (October 2000): 792–810.
17. David T. Canon, *Race, Redistricting, and Representation: The Unintended Consequences of Black Majority Districts* (Chicago, IL: University of Chicago Press, 1999), p. 257.
18. *Shaw v. Reno*, 509 U.S. 630 (1993) and *Miller v. Johnson*, 515 U.S. 900 (1995).
19. *Georgia v. Ashcroft*, 539 U.S. 461 (2003) and *Bartlett v. Strictland*, 556 U.S. _____ 209 (2009).
20. *Texas Government Newsletter*, July 11, 1994, p. 1.
21. Michael Barone and Grant Ujifusa, *The Almanac of American Politics 1998* (Washington, DC: National Journal, 1997), p. 1339.
22. Seth C. McKee, Jeremy M. Teigen, and Mathieu Turgeon, "The Partisan Impact of Congressional Redistricting: The Case of Texas, 2001–2003," *Social Science Quarterly* 87 (June 2006): 308–317.
23. Michael P. McDonald, "Redistricting and Competitive Districts," in Michael P. McDonald and John Samples,

eds., *The Marketplace of Democracy: Electoral Competition and American Politics* (Washington, DC: Cato Institute, 2006), p. 225.
24. Paul Freedman, Michael Franz, and Kenneth Goldstein, "Campaign Advertising and Democratic Citizenship," *American Journal of Political Science* 48 (October 2004): 723–741.
25. National Institute on Money in State Politics, available at www.followthemoney.org.
26. Paul S. Herrnson, *Congressional Elections: Campaigning at Home and in Washington*, 5th ed. (Washington, DC: CQ Press, 2008), p. 83.
27. *Texas Weekly*, July 19, 2010, available at www.texasweekly.com.
28. *Texas Weekly*, August 15, 2005, available at www.texasweekly.com.
29. R. G. Ratcliffe, "GOP Winners' Coffers Fattened after Election," *Houston Chronicle*, January 16, 2003, available at www.houstonchronicle.com.
30. *Capitol Update*, December 13, 2002, p. 1.
31. National Institute on Money in State Politics, available at www.followthemoney.org.
32. Malcolm E. Jewell and Sarah M. Morehouse, *Political Parties and Elections in American States*, 4th ed. (Washington, DC: CQ Press, 2001), pp. 67–69.
33. Gary C. Jacobson, "Competition in U.S. Congressional Elections," in McDonald and Samples, eds., *The Marketplace of Democracy*, p. 41.
34. National Institute on Money in State Politics, available at www.followthemoney.org.
35. Corrie MacLaggan, "Perry, White Spar over Immigration After Emotional New TV Ad," *Austin American-Statesman*, October 25, 2010, available at www.statesman.com.
36. Richard R. Lau and Gerald M. Pomper, *Negative Campaigning: An Analysis of U.S. Senate Elections* (Lanham, MD: Rowman & Littlefield, 2004), pp. 30–88.
37. Richard G. Niemi, Lynda W. Powell, William D. Berry, Thomas M. Carsey, and James M. Snyder, Jr., "Competition in State Legislative Elections, 1992–2002," in McDonald and Sampels, eds., *The Marketplace of Democracy*, p. 70.
38. Warren E. Miller, "Party Identification, Realignment, and Party Voting: Back to the Basics," *American Political Science Review* 85 (June 1991): 557–568.
39. "Election Results 2008—Texas," *New York Times*, December 9, 2008, available at www.nytimes.com.
40. Thomas M. Holbrook, "Do Campaigns Matter?" in Stephen C. Craig, ed., *The Electoral Challenge: Theory Meets Practice* (Washington, DC: CQ Press, 2006), pp. 12–13.
41. Edward Roeder, "Not Only Does Money Talk, It Often Calls the Winners," *Washington Post National Weekly Edition*, September 26–October 2, 1994, p. 23.

42. Brian F. Schaffner, "Priming Gender: Campaigning on Women's Issues in U.S. Senate Elections," *American Journal of Political Science* 49 (October 2005): 803–817.

43. Alan I. Abramowitz, "Can McCain Overcome the Triple Whammy?" May 29, 2008, Larry J. Sabato's Crystal Ball 2008, available at www.centerforpolitics.org.

44. Jeffrey E. Cohen and James D. King, "Relative Unemployment and Gubernatorial Popularity," *Journal of Politics* 66 (November 2004): 1180–1202.

45. Brad Lockerbie, "Prospective Voting in Presidential Elections, 1956–1988," *American Politics Quarterly* 20 (July 1992): 308–325.

Chapter 8
The Texas Legislature

CHAPTER OUTLINE

WHAT WE WILL LEARN

After studying Chapter 8, you should be able to answer the following questions:

1. What effect do bicameralism, biennial sessions, and limited session length have on legislative policymaking in Texas?

2. What is the job description of a member of the Texas legislature, considering qualifications, background, compensation, turnover, and term limits?

3. How is the Texas legislature organized in terms of leadership, committee organization, and legislative assistance?

4. What are the steps of the legislative process?

5. What affect do the following factors have on the legislative process: legislative leadership, interest groups, constituency, political parties, and political ideology?

Illegal immigration was a hot topic in the 2011 session of the Texas legislature. Although the legislature considered a number of proposals, the one that came closest to passing was a measure designed to outlaw so-called sanctuary cities. The bill would allow police officers to inquire about the immigration status of anyone they arrested or lawfully detained, including people stopped for minor traffic offenses. Any city or other local government with a policy prohibiting officers from asking about immigration status would risk losing state funds.[1]

The sanctuary-cities bill was controversial. Its proponents argued that the measure was necessary to identify criminal aliens engaged in drug trafficking and other offenses for possible deportation by federal officials. In this view, if the federal government is not going to satisfactorily address border security, then the state must take action. In contrast, police chiefs and sheriffs warned that the bill would discourage undocumented residents from reporting crimes to authorities or cooperating in criminal investigations.[2] Furthermore, civil rights advocates worried that all of the state's Latino residents would be forced to prove their immigration status whereas white and African American Texans would be unaffected by the law.

The debate over sanctuary-cities legislation introduces this chapter on the Texas legislature. The chapter traces the progress of sanctuary-cities legislation through the legislative process. It examines the factors that moved the bill toward passage and identifies the reason for the measure's ultimate failure. The chapter begins by outlining the structure of the Texas legislature, including bicameralism, session frequency, and session length. It profiles the membership of the legislature and describes its organization. The chapter traces the legislative process. It concludes by identifying the factors affecting legislative policymaking.

STRUCTURE

The Texas Constitution provides for a bicameral legislature to meet in biennial regular sessions of 140 days in length. The legislative sessions are numbered consecutively, dating from the 1840s, when Texas became a state. The 82nd legislature was elected in 2010 and met in regular session in 2011. The legislature that meets in regular session in 2013 will be the 83rd legislature.

 WHAT DO YOU THINK?

If you were a member of the legislature, would you support the sanctuary cities legislation?

Bicameralism

Bicameral legislature A legislative body with two chambers.

Texas has a **bicameral** (two-chamber) **legislature** consisting of a House of Representatives and a Senate. The Texas House has 150 members elected from various districts to serve two-year terms, whereas the Texas Senate consists of 31 senators elected from districts to serve four-year terms. Senate four-year terms overlap, so half of the senators run for reelection at one time, with the other half running for reelection two years later. The exception to this pattern occurs in the first election after redistricting, when the entire Senate must stand for reelection. In 2012, all 31 Senate seats will be up for election under new district lines drawn after the 2010 U.S. Census. The newly elected senators then draw lots to determine whether they will have to run for election again in 2014 or 2016.

The Texas Constitution assigns each legislative chamber certain powers and responsibilities. The Texas Senate has sole authority to confirm or reject the governor's appointments by a two-thirds vote. Only the Texas House may initiate legislation to raise taxes, even though both chambers must agree before any tax bill can pass. The House alone, by majority vote, has the power of **impeachment,** which is a formal accusation against an executive or judicial officeholder. The Senate tries the impeached official, with a two-thirds vote needed for conviction and removal from office.

Impeachment
The formal process through which the Texas House accuses an executive or judicial branch official of misconduct serious enough to warrant removal from office.

The Texas Constitution requires that the two legislative chambers share certain responsibilities. Both the Texas House and the Texas Senate must concur before any measure can pass the legislature. Both must vote by a two-thirds margin to propose constitutional amendments. Also, two thirds of the members of each chamber must agree to override a governor's veto.

The Texas House and Texas Senate often approach policy issues differently because of structural differences in the two legislative chambers. Compare, for example, Texas House and Senate districts. Each state House member represents approximately 139,000 people, whereas the population of each state Senate district is 673,000. Because state Senate districts are roughly five times larger than House districts, they will probably be more diverse than the smaller House districts. Because they need to please a more diverse constituency, state senators may prove more moderate than state House members, whose districts are more homogeneous. In Texas, the two legislative chambers also differ in the length of their members' terms of office. Texas House members must stand for election every two years, whereas senators serve four-year terms with half the Texas Senate up for election every two years. As a result, Texas senators can evaluate policy issues from a longer-range perspective than state House members, whose next reelection campaign is always just around the corner.

Bicameralism has supporters and critics. Its defenders believe that bicameralism allows one chamber to correct the mistakes of the other. In contrast, the critics of bicameralism believe that a single-chamber legislature is more economical and efficient. Every state has a bicameral legislature except Nebraska, which has a **unicameral** (one-chamber) **legislature.** Nebraska adopted a state constitutional amendment in 1937 to create a unicameral legislature whose members would be chosen in **nonpartisan elections.** These are contests in which the names of the candidates, but not their party affiliations, appear on the ballot. The 49 members of the Nebraska legislature serve four-year overlapping terms.

Unicameral legislature A legislative body with one chamber.

Nonpartisan elections Election contests in which the names of the candidates, but not their party affiliations, appear on the ballot.

The conventional wisdom is that bicameralism has a conservative effect on the policymaking process because two chambers must approve a measure before it can clear the legislature. Nonetheless, Professor James R. Rogers believes that bicameralism is as likely to increase legislative output as to decrease it because both chambers can initiate legislation as well as reject it. Furthermore, he says, the historical evidence from legislative bodies that have switched from unicameral to bicameral or vice versa fails to support the conventional view.[3]

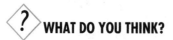

WHAT DO YOU THINK?

Should Texas replace its bicameral legislature with a unicameral legislature?

Session Frequency

The Texas Constitution provides that the legislature meet in regular session every other year, in odd calendar years (2011, 2013, etc.), with sessions beginning on the second Tuesday in January. In the late nineteenth century, when the Texas Constitution was written, biennial legislative sessions were standard practice in most American states. As recently as 1960, 32 states still had biennial sessions. Today, Texas is one of only six states (Arkansas, Montana, Nevada, North Dakota, Oregon, and Texas) whose legislatures do not meet in regular session every year. The Arizona legislature, for example, meets every year for 100 days. The California legislature is in session nearly year-round every year.[4] However, the Texas Constitution empowers the governor to call special sessions of the legislature, which may last a maximum of 30 calendar days. For example, when the legislature failed to adopt a budget in its 2011 regular session, Governor Rick Perry called a special session to begin immediately after the end of the regular session. Although most state legislatures may call themselves into special session, the Texas legislature has no such power.

Annual legislative sessions are near the top of the list of constitutional reforms proposed by those who would like to see a more streamlined state government. Reformers believe that the affairs of state government are too complex to handle in biennial sessions. Budget issues are particularly difficult to address in biennial sessions because the legislature can neither anticipate state spending needs nor estimate tax revenues over so long a period. The most popular proposal for annual sessions would maintain the current 140-day session in odd-numbered years and add a shorter, 60-day session in even years. The 140-day sessions would write a one-year budget and deal with general legislative concerns, whereas the 60-day sessions would be limited to writing a budget, plus any additional matters the governor would want to submit for legislative consideration.

Nonetheless, biennial legislative sessions have their defenders. Give the legislature more time, they say, and Texas will have more laws, more regulations, more spending, and more taxes. Although observers often blame biennial sessions for legislative logjams at the end of a session, legislatures with annual sessions have logjams as well. For example, the New York legislature, which meets annually, has been ridiculed for years because of its inability to pass a budget on time. Furthermore, the citizens of Texas have expressed their support for biennial sessions every time they have had a chance to vote on the issue. In 1930, 1949, 1958, 1969, 1973, and

1975, voters rejected constitutional amendments that would have provided for annual legislative sessions.

Session Length

Constitutional reformers would also like to increase the length of legislative sessions in the Lone Star State. With sessions limited to 140 calendar days, the legislature may not have time to do the state's business. The legislature often falls behind and has to act on a flood of bills in the last few weeks of the session before time runs out. In 2009, for example, the legislature failed to pass measures to continue the operation of the Texas Department of Transportation and the Texas Department of Insurance. Had Governor Perry not called a special session to extend the life of the two agencies, they would have been forced to go out of business in 2010.

Defenders of the 140-day session point out that legislative session limits are common among the states and a useful device for forcing legislators to get down to business. Political scientist Malcolm Jewell believes that session limits force lawmakers to make decisions because they set a deadline for wrapping up business. "When there's no limit," he says, "it drags on. They [legislators] postpone compromise to the last minute; they bargain; they play games."[5]

Research shows that the legislative workload in Texas is not as congested as conventional wisdom suggests. Legislative activity in Texas tends to concentrate at certain times, such as the deadline for submitting bills and the end of the session, but lawmakers work on legislation throughout the session. Although 80 percent of

The membership of the Texas legislature is more diverse today than at any time in its history.

the votes for the final passage of bills comes in the last two weeks of the session, most of the measures passed have been under legislative consideration for months.[6] Furthermore, the Texas House and Texas Senate have adopted rules to prevent a last-minute rush of legislative activity.

WHAT DO YOU THINK?

Should the Texas legislature meet in annual sessions?

MEMBERSHIP

In 2011, the combined membership of the Texas House and Texas Senate included 37 women, 36 Latinos, 16 African Americans, and 2 Asian Americans of 181 members. Although the Texas legislature is a more diverse body than at any time in its history, it does not provide an accurate cross-section of the state's population. The legislature is whiter and more male than the state of Texas as a whole. Most members of the legislature hold college degrees. The most common career fields among House members and senators are business and law. The most common occupations are in business and law.

Compensation

The official salary for members of the legislature, whether they serve in the Texas House or the Texas Senate, is set by the Texas Constitution at $600 a month, or $7,200 a year. Compared with other states, this figure is low. In fact, legislative pay in Texas is lowest among the ten largest states.[7] Several states have full-time, professional legislatures and pay their lawmakers accordingly. Legislators in California, for example, earn $110,880 a year. Even most states whose legislatures meet for limited periods pay their lawmakers more than Texas pays its legislators. For example, members of the Oklahoma legislature receive $38,400 a year. The pay for Louisiana lawmakers is $16,800 a year. Florida legislators earn $29,916 annually.[8]

Should Texas legislators be paid more? The proponents of higher legislative salaries believe that better pay would allow a wide cross-section of Texans to seek office, not just people who are independently wealthy or have careers that permit them time off to attend legislative sessions. Furthermore, higher salaries would help keep legislators independent of interest groups. In contrast, defenders of the current salary structure argue that low salaries ensure the continuation of a citizen-legislature whose members are relatively immune from outside pressures. Because lawmakers are not dependent on legislative salaries, they are more willing to take political chances to do the right thing than they would be if their salaries were higher.

Non-salary compensation for Texas legislators is relatively generous. When the legislature is in session, lawmakers receive a daily expense allowance of $150. The allowance enables legislators to increase their earnings by $21,000 for each regular session and $4,500 for each 30-day special session. Furthermore, legislators have provided themselves with one of the most generous pension plans in the nation. When State Senator Gonzalo Barrientos retired in January 2007 after serving 32 years in the legislature, he immediately began collecting an annual pension of $92,000. Members who serve a minimum of eight years can qualify for a pension of $23,000 a year at age 60. Members serving 12 or more years can begin collecting at 50 years of age. For each year of legislative service, a member receives an annual pension equal to 2.3 percent of the salary of a state district judge, which was $125,000 in 2010. State lawmakers also receive full healthcare benefits, both as active members and in retirement.[9]

Many legislators use excess campaign funds to supplement their incomes and enrich their families. According to a study conducted by the *Dallas Morning News*, more than a third of the campaign spending of North Texas lawmakers goes for non-campaign expenditures, including money for travel, entertainment, living expenses, food, charitable donations, and campaign contributions to other legislators.[10] Critics accuse legislators of using campaign donations as a slush fund. "They're using the lobby's money to enhance their lifestyles, a perk that is technically legal but a clear conflict of interest," says Craig McDonald, the executive director of Texans for Public Justice, a citizen group that focuses on campaign finance reform.[11]

Legislative Turnover

Legislative turnover The replacement of individual members of a legislature from one session to the next.

Legislative turnover refers to the replacement of individual members of a legislature from one session to the next. Over the last decade, the turnover rate in the Texas legislature has ranged from a high of 22 percent to a low of 10 percent. The 82nd session of the legislature, which met in 2011, had the most new members during the period, 40, including 32 new Republican legislators who benefited from the big Republican gains in the 2010 election. In contrast, the 81st session of the legislature, meeting in 2009, had the smallest number of newcomers over the decade, only 19.

Legislative turnover in Texas is more often the result of voluntary retirement than election defeat. Even in 2010, a relatively high turnover election year, 70 incumbent legislators won reelection without a primary election challenge or a major-party opponent in the general election.[12] Some members leave office because they doubt they can win reelection, whereas others quit out of frustration. They complain about low pay, poor staff support, little public appreciation for their efforts, the hectic pace of legislative sessions, and pressure from interest groups and constituents. House members, in particular, often grow cynical about their ability to accomplish their goals. However, not all reasons for leaving are negative. Some legislators attempt to move up the political ladder by running for higher office. Others choose to leave because their law practice has picked up or they receive a business offer they cannot refuse. Some resign to become well-paid lobbyists. Although many states impose a waiting period between the time legislators leave office and the time they can become lobbyists, usually a year, Texas has no such limitation. Members can begin working for interest groups as registered lobbyists the day they leave office, and many do. In fact, 65 former legislators are registered lobbyists in Texas, more

Joe Straus, a Republican from San Antonio, is the speaker of the Texas House.

than in any other state.[13] Moreover, lobbyists earn considerably higher incomes than legislators. The average lobbyist in Texas has contracts worth up to half a million dollars a year.[14]

Term Limits

Term limitation
The movement to restrict the number of terms public officials may serve.

Initiative process
A procedure whereby citizens can propose the adoption of a policy measure by gathering a prerequisite number of signatures. Voters must then approve the measure before it can take effect.

Term limitation is the movement to restrict the number of terms public officials may serve. Fifteen states (but not Texas) limit the terms of state legislators. The limits for members of the House in states that have term limits range from 6 to 12 years. They vary from 8 to 12 years for state senators. The legislature enacted term limits in only one of the states that have legislative term limits.[15] In every other state, the voters adopted term limitation through the **initiative process,** a procedure whereby citizens can propose the adoption of a policy measure by gathering a prerequisite number of signatures. State officials then place the measure on the ballot for approval by the voters. Because Texas does not have an initiative process, most observers think it is unlikely that the state will adopt term limitation. Although polls show that term limits are popular with the voters, many members of the legislature are unwilling to vote themselves out of a job.

The advocates of term limits believe that they improve the capacity of the legislature to do work. They offer the following arguments on behalf of term limitation:

- Members who are not career-oriented can focus on solving the state's problems rather than entrenching themselves in office.

- By forcing veteran lawmakers from office, term limits give new people with fresh ideas an opportunity to have an impact on public policy.
- Term limits reduce the power of interest groups by forcing their favorite lawmakers from office.
- Legislators who know they are term limited are more likely to represent the interests of the voters rather than those of entrenched interest groups.

In contrast, the opponents of term limitation offer the following arguments against term limitation:

- Term limits interfere with the voters' right to elect the individuals they favor.

AROUND THE NATION

Repealing Term Limits in Idaho

In 1994, Idaho voters adopted the most sweeping term-limits law in the country. The measure, which received nearly 60 percent of the vote, restricted the terms of every elected official from the governor down to county commissioners and school board members. It limited most state and local officials to 8 years in office over any 15-year period; county commissioners and school board members could serve no more than 6 years of an 11-year period. Because the term-limit clock did not begin ticking until 1996, term limits would not apply to officials in major offices until 2004; it would not impact local officeholders until 2002.

Opposition to term limits grew as the date for their implementation neared. The Republican Party, the dominant party in Idaho, declared its opposition to term limits because many of its officials, including the legislative leadership, would be forced from office. Party leaders worked behind the scenes to convince Republican legislators to vote to repeal term limits. Local officials and business leaders in rural areas opposed term limits as well because of their potential impact on local government. In sparsely populated rural areas, relatively few people are willing to serve in low-pay or no-pay positions as county officials and school board members. If long-term incumbents were forced from office by term

limits, perhaps no one would be willing to take their places.

In 2002, Idaho became the first state to repeal term limits. (Massachusetts, Oregon, Utah, Washington, and Wyoming have subsequently dropped term limits.)[*] Early in the year, the Idaho legislature voted for repeal, overriding the governor's veto. Term-limit supporters gathered sufficient signatures to put the issue on the ballot to give the voters the chance to "repeal the repeal" in the November 2002 election. By the narrow margin of 1,889 votes of more than 400,000 ballots cast, Idahoans approved the legislature's action and sustained the repeal of term limits, with rural voters providing the margin of victory.[†]

QUESTIONS

1. When the idea of legislative term limits was introduced more than two decades ago, Republicans supported the concept. In Idaho, at least, Republicans switched sides on the issue because of its potential impact on their leadership. Did Republican leaders in Idaho do the right thing or were they being hypocritical?
2. Do you think that Idaho voters would support term limits if local governments were exempted?
3. For which level(s) of government are term limits the most appropriate (if any)?

[*] Russell Nichols, "Termed Out," *Governing*, January 2011, p. 22.

[†] Daniel A. Smith, "Overturning Term limits: The Legislature's Own Private Idaho?" *P.S. Political Science and Politics*, April 2003, pp. 215–220.

- Legislators with valuable experience and expertise will be forced from office.
- Bureaucrats and lobbyists will be more powerful because it will be easier for them to outwit inexperienced lawmakers than it was for the veteran legislators who were forced to retire.
- Legislators will concern themselves only with short-run problems because they serve for limited periods of time.[16]

In practice, term limits have been neither as beneficial as their advocates have hoped nor as harmful as their opponents have warned. On the positive side, state legislators who are term limited place a greater emphasis on the needs of the state as a whole relative to the interests of the districts they represent. In addition, term-limited legislators are less focused on obtaining special benefits for their districts than are other legislators. On the negative side, term limits strengthen the governor and possibly legislative staffers while weakening legislative leaders. Because term-limited legislators are relatively inexperienced, they have not developed the personal relationships that form the basis for legislative compromise and cooperation. Consequently, influence slips away from the legislature toward other political actors, especially executive branch officials and legislative staffers. Furthermore, rather than focusing on legislative business, many term-limited legislators concentrate on lining up their next jobs as elected officials in local government or as lobbyists.[17]

ORGANIZATION

Modern legislatures choose leaders, establish committees, and hire staff assistance in order to facilitate their work.

Leadership

The lieutenant governor and speaker of the House are the presiding officers and foremost political leaders of the Texas legislature. The speaker, who presides in the House, is a state representative who is selected by the members of the House to serve as speaker. The lieutenant governor, who presides in the Senate, is elected state-wide for a four-year term in the same general election year in which the governor is chosen. In contrast to the president and vice president of the United States, the governor and lieutenant governor do not run as a formal ticket. Voters cast ballots for the two offices separately and may choose individuals from different political parties. In 1994, when Republican George W. Bush was initially elected governor, Bob Bullock, a Democrat, was reelected lieutenant governor.

If the office of lieutenant governor becomes vacant, the Senate chooses a successor. For example, when Bush resigned as governor to move to the White House in 2001, Lieutenant Governor Perry moved up to become governor, leaving the office of lieutenant governor vacant. The 31 members of the Texas Senate selected fellow senator Bill Ratliff to replace Perry by majority vote. Ratliff served the remainder of Perry's term as lieutenant governor without resigning his Senate seat. He chose not to stand for election as lieutenant governor in 2002, preferring to run for reelection to the Texas Senate.

The speaker, who presides in the Texas House, is a state representative who is selected by the members of the House to serve as speaker. Because the speaker's powers are extraordinary, the race for the position may be intense. State representatives who hope to become speaker gather signed pledges of support from other House members in hopes of obtaining majority backing well ahead of the actual vote. Usually one candidate wraps up the race early, months or even years ahead of the vote. Because representatives do not want to be on the speaker's bad side, members quickly climb on the bandwagon as soon as it becomes clear that one candidate has the edge. Voting for the speaker is done publicly rather than by secret ballot, so members who vote against the speaker may fear retaliation. Consequently, the actual vote for speaker is usually lopsided.

The 81st session of the legislature began with a speaker fight. Republican Tom Craddick of Midland, the incumbent, had held the position since 2003, the year the Republicans became the majority in the House. Craddick won the position with the support of most Republican members of the House and some Democrats, the so-called Craddick Ds who backed Craddick not because they agreed with him philosophically but because they wanted to be part of his leadership team. Over time, Craddick's support diminished. The opponents of Craddick, including some Republicans and most Democrats, accused the speaker of being dictatorial; they said that he concentrated power in his office rather than sharing it with committee chairs and other legislators. Many members were particularly unhappy with the speaker for forcing votes on controversial issues that could be used against them when they ran for reelection. Moreover, Craddick sometimes supported primary challengers against Republican legislators who dared to vote against the speaker's policy agenda.[18]

Several members of the Texas House declared their intent to seek the office of speaker in 2009. Craddick, who was seeking reelection, had the most signed pledges, but not a majority. In early January, 11 moderate Republicans (the so-called Anybody But Craddick Republicans) met privately to unite behind a speaker candidate. They chose Representative Joe Straus of San Antonio, who was first elected to the House in 2005. Straus promised to run the House in an open, fair manner, dispersing power to the membership, especially committee chairs. Within days, 70 Democrats joined 15 Republicans pledging their votes to Straus, giving him more than enough support to ensure election as speaker.[19]

Two experienced Republican legislators declared their candidacy to challenge Straus for speaker before the 2011 legislative session began. They argued that Straus was insufficiently conservative and too beholden to Democrats for his job. The challengers had the support of Texans for Fiscal Responsibility, Empower Texas, and other conservative grassroots organizations, but business groups backed Straus, and that support proved decisive. Before long, Speaker Straus had more than enough pledges to ensure reelection and his two opponents dropped out. Even though Straus was the only candidate for speaker, a small number of legislators still voted against him. Most of Straus's die-hard opponents were freshman Republicans who had won election with the support of the Tea Party.

The speaker and lieutenant governor are two of the most powerful public officials in the state, exercising extraordinary authority in their respective chambers. The speaker and lieutenant governor control many of the legislative procedures of the Texas House and Texas Senate. They assign bills to committees, and once committees have done their work, the speaker and lieutenant governor have considerable influence over which bills are scheduled for debate. As presiding officers in their respective chambers, the speaker and lieutenant governor recognize members for debate, rule on points of order, and interpret rules.

The speaker and lieutenant governor rarely participate directly in the official deliberations of their respective chambers. As an elected member of the House, the speaker is entitled to participate in debate and vote on every issue before the chamber. In practice, though, the speaker seldom engages in floor discussions and votes only on those matters for which he or she wishes to register strong support. With the exception of Ratliff, who was a state senator, the lieutenant governor is technically not a member of the Senate and may vote only to break a tie.

The speaker and lieutenant governor serve on and make appointments to some of the state's most important policymaking bodies, including the Legislative Budget Board (LBB) and the Legislative Redistricting Board (LRB). The **Legislative Budget Board (LBB)** is an agency created by the legislature to study state revenue and budgetary needs between legislative sessions and prepare budget and appropriations bills to submit to the legislature. The **Legislative Redistricting Board (LRB)**, which is composed of the speaker, lieutenant governor, comptroller, land commissioner, and attorney general, is responsible for redrawing the boundaries of Texas House and Texas Senate seats when the legislature is unable to agree on a redistricting plan. Finally, the speaker and lieutenant governor exercise considerable control over committee membership. They appoint legislative committee chairs, vice chairs, subcommittee chairs, most committee members, and some subcommittee members.

Although the lieutenant governor and the speaker have extraordinary powers, they seldom act in an arbitrary or dictatorial fashion. For the most part, the powers of the speaker and lieutenant governor are not spelled out in the Texas Constitution, and as recently as the 1930s their authority extended little beyond presiding. The powers of the leadership have grown because of changes in House and Senate rules adopted by majority vote in each chamber that could just as easily be withdrawn. The offices of speaker and lieutenant governor have acquired and maintained such broad authority because the people who have held the posts have generally exercised power in a fashion that a majority of legislators approves. Speaker Craddick lost his position because a majority of House members believed that he had abused his power. Speaker Straus held his post in 2011 because most members approved of his leadership.

The speaker and lieutenant governor base their authority on their ability to keep most members of the legislature happy. Both the speaker and the lieutenant governor are in a position to bestow favors on their friends. These favors can be as small as giving a legislator a larger office or as great as appointing a member to chair a prestigious committee. In either case, the lawmaker owes a favor, which the speaker or lieutenant governor can cash when the time is right. If enough members

Legislative Budget Board (LBB) An agency created by the legislature to study state revenue and budgetary needs between legislative sessions and prepare budget and appropriations bills to submit to the legislature.

Legislative Redistricting Board (LRB) An agency composed of the speaker, lieutenant governor, comptroller, land commissioner, and attorney general that draws the boundaries of Texas House and Texas Senate seats when the legislature is unable to agree on a redistricting plan.

are unhappy with the speaker or lieutenant governor, they can face trouble from the membership, as Speaker Craddick discovered. House members have the authority to change leadership. Although senators cannot replace the lieutenant governor, they can strip the lieutenant governor of authority.

The leadership of the speaker and lieutenant governor is collective rather than individual. Each official heads a leadership team made up of supporters in the chamber. This is especially true in the Texas House, where the speaker must first win the backing of a majority of members of the chamber. Both the speaker and the lieutenant governor have a corps of supporters in the chamber that makes up their leadership team. The members of the leadership team advise the speaker or lieutenant governor and work to organize the full chamber to support the leadership's position. The speaker and lieutenant governor appoint the members of their leadership teams to chair the most important committees. In 2009, Speaker Straus rewarded the ten Republicans who were his initial supporters for speaker by appointing each of them to chair a committee, including the most important committees in the House. The speaker and lieutenant governor also punish opponents. In 2011, for example, Speaker Straus named Republican Phil King, one of the leaders of the failed anti-Straus effort, to serve on the Urban Affairs Committee. King is from Weatherford, a town with fewer than 30,000 people.[20]

Committees

Standing committee A permanent committee.

Some of the legislature's most important work takes place in committee. A **standing committee** is a permanent committee. The Texas House had 36 standing committees in 2011, ranging in size from 5 to 27 members. The most common size for House committees was 9 members. The Texas Senate had 19 committees, ranging from 5 to 15 members.

Standing committees are important because they enable members to divide the legislative workload. More than 5,000 bills may be introduced in a regular session, far too many for each member to consider in depth. Committees allow small groups of legislators to examine a bill in detail and then report their evaluation to the full chamber. Committees also permit members to specialize in particular policy areas. Most committees deal with particular substantive policy areas, such as higher education, criminal justice, or agriculture.

Legislators usually have strong preferences regarding committee assignments. In the House, the most coveted committee assignments are the Appropriations, State Affairs, Calendars, and Ways and Means Committees. The committees of choice in the Senate are the Finance, State Affairs, and Jurisprudence Committees. The committees dealing with business interests (Business & Industry in the House, Business & Commerce in the Senate) are popular as well. Legislators may also prefer a particular committee assignment because of personal preference or constituency interest. A state representative from Houston or Dallas, for example, may favor service on the Urban Affairs Committee.

House and Senate rules limit the number of standing committees on which legislators may serve to three. Senators are restricted to membership on no more than two of the three most influential committees: Finance, State Affairs, and Jurisprudence. No House member may serve on more than two of the following three committees: Ways and Means, Appropriations, and State Affairs. No legislator may chair more than one committee.

State senators typically serve on more committees than do state representatives. Because the Senate has only 31 members, individual senators typically serve on three or four committees. In 2011, for example, State Senator Rodney Ellis of Houston chaired the Government Organization Committee and served on the Criminal Justice, State Affairs, and Transportation & Homeland Security Committees. Because the House is larger, with 150 members, individual representatives have more opportunities to specialize on committee assignments. In 2011, most House members served on only one or two committees. Representative Diane Patrick of Arlington, for example, served on the Appropriations Committee and the Higher Education Committee.

The lieutenant governor and speaker make most committee assignments. In the Senate, the lieutenant governor appoints all committee chairs, vice chairs, and committee members at the beginning of each legislative session. The only restriction on the lieutenant governor's assignment power is that three members of each committee with ten or fewer members, and four members of each committee with more than ten members, must be senators who served on the committee during the last regular session.

In the House, the speaker appoints committee chairs, vice chairs, and all of the members of the Appropriations Committee and the Calendars Committee. The speaker also names at least half of the members of each of the other standing committees. House rules allow representatives, in order of seniority, to select one committee assignment, provided that the committee is not already half staffed. **Seniority** refers to the length of continuous service a member has with a legislative body.

An **interim committee** is established to study a particular policy issue between legislative sessions, such as higher education or public school finance. Frequently, an interim committee is also a **select** or **special committee,** which is a committee that is established for a limited period of time to address a specific problem. Interim committees may include private citizens as well as legislators. The speaker, lieutenant governor, and governor may appoint interim committees. Legislative leaders use interim committees as a way to compensate for biennial legislative sessions of limited duration. Because interim committees have more time to study issues and formulate policies than do standing committees, they can lay the groundwork for legislation before the regular session begins.

Legislative Assistance

Staff assistance is important to the Texas legislature because legislators are essentially part-time employees asked to perform a monumental legislative task in a limited period of time. Legislative staff members improve the quantity and quality of information available to legislators, bring insight to issues, and help solve constituent problems. Texas legislators have sufficient funds to employ staff assistance in

Seniority The length of continuous service a member has with a legislative body.

Interim committee A committee established to study a particular policy issue between legislative sessions, such as higher education or public school finance.

Select, or **special committee** A committee that is established for a limited period of time to address a specific problem.

Austin and their home districts. In 2009, the permanent staff of the Texas legislature numbered 2,090, placing the Texas legislature third in the nation in terms of staff resources, after Pennsylvania and New York. Even though the Texas legislature has biennial sessions of limited length, it has staff support equivalent to full-time legislatures in other large states.[21]

The legislature provides members with some institutional assistance as well. Before each session, the Legislative Council conducts a brief orientation for new legislators. During sessions, the staff of the Legislative Council helps members draft bills and assists committees. The Legislative Reference Library fulfills routine requests for research assistance. The House Research Organization (HRO) and Senate Research Center (SRC) research issues, help draft legislation, and prepare technical analyses of bills pending in the legislature. The HRO and SRC also publish daily floor reports explaining and presenting arguments for and against proposed legislation. Standing committees have permanent staffs as well, ranging in size from 2 to 15 staff members in the Texas Senate and from 1 to 6 in the Texas House.[22]

THE LEGISLATIVE PROCESS

The Texas legislative process resembles that of the U.S. Congress but with important differences that affect policy.

Introduction

Bill A proposed law.

During each legislative session, members introduce thousands of bills and hundreds of resolutions. A **bill** is a proposed law, such as a measure to outlaw texting while driving. A **resolution** is a legislative statement of opinion on a certain matter, such as a measure congratulating a Texas sports team for winning a championship. An amendment to the Texas Constitution takes the form of a **joint resolution,** which is a resolution that must be passed by a two-thirds vote of each chamber.

Resolution A legislative statement of opinion on a certain matter.

Introducing bills and resolutions into the legislative process is fairly straightforward. Members of the Texas House or Texas Senate may officially introduce legislation by filing copies in their own chamber with the secretary of the Senate or the chief clerk of the House during a period that begins on the first Monday after the November general election. Legislators introduced 43 bills dealing with immigration for the 2011 session of the legislature to consider, including sanctuary-cities legislation.[23] After the first 60 days of a session, members can introduce only local bills or measures declared an emergency by the governor unless they obtain the approval of four-fifths of the members of their chamber. Once a bill is introduced, the secretary of the Senate or the chief clerk of the House assigns the measure a number, indicating the chamber of origin and order of introduction. HB 45, for example, indicates that the measure is the 45th bill introduced in the Texas House during the session. SR 102 is the 102nd resolution introduced in the Texas Senate. The House version of sanctuary cities was HB 12. The Senate bill was SB 9.

Joint resolution A resolution that must be passed by a two-thirds vote of each chamber.

Committee Action

The lieutenant governor and the speaker, in consultation with the chamber parliamentarian, assign newly introduced measures to committee. With important exceptions, the legislative leadership matches a bill with the committee that specializes in the subject matter it addresses. SB 9, for example, was referred to the Senate Transportation & Homeland Security Committee. The exception to the general practice of matching legislation to the committee that deals with its subject matter involves the House Committee on State Affairs and the Senate Committee on State Affairs, which are general-purpose committees to which the speaker and lieutenant governor regularly assign major pieces of legislation, regardless of their subject matter. For example, HB 12, the House version of sanctuary cities, was referred to the House State Affairs Committee.

Committees do the detailed work of the legislative process. They begin their consideration of proposed legislation by holding public hearings. After the hearings are complete, the committee meets for **mark up,** the process in which legislators go over a piece of legislation line-by-line to revise, amend, or rewrite it. Major legislation is almost always rewritten in committee, with the final product reflecting a compromise among the various groups and interests involved. Eventually, committee members vote whether to recommend the revised measure to the entire House or Senate for passage. If a majority on the committee votes in the affirmative, the measure emerges from committee with a favorable report. The report includes the revised text of the measure, a detailed analysis of the bill, and a **fiscal note,** an analysis indicating a legislative measure's cost to state government, if any. If the majority of the committee votes against the measure, the legislation is probably dead.

Mark up The process in which legislators go over a piece of legislation line-by-line to revise, amend, or rewrite it.

Fiscal note An analysis indicating a legislative measure's cost to state government, if any.

The detailed work of the legislature takes place in committees.

Floor Action

The procedure by which legislation moves from committee to the floor differs in the two chambers of the Texas legislature. In the Texas House, measures recommended favorably by a standing committee go to the Calendars Committee for assignment to a House calendar, which sets the order of priority for considering legislation. In 2011, the House calendars were, in order of priority, the following:

- **Emergency calendar.** This calendar is reserved for legislation declared an emergency by the governor and other measures deemed by the Calendars Committee to merit immediate attention. Tax bills and the **appropriations bill,** a legislative authorization to spend money for particular purposes, are usually assigned to the emergency calendar as well.
- **Major state calendar.** This calendar includes measures of statewide effect that do not merit emergency designation.
- **Constitutional amendment calendar.** This calendar is for proposed amendments to the Texas Constitution or ratification of amendments to the U.S. Constitution.
- **General state calendar.** This calendar is for bills of statewide impact, but secondary significance.
- **Local, consent, and resolution calendar.** This calendar includes bills and resolutions that are not controversial as well as **local bills,** which are proposed laws that affect only a single unit of local government.
- **Resolutions calendar.** This calendar is reserved for resolutions.
- **Congratulatory and memorial resolutions calendar.** This calendar contains resolutions congratulating people, places, and organizations for various accomplishments or honoring individuals who have died.

Although Texas House rules provide for the consideration of measures in order of priority as set by the calendar system, the House may vote by a two-thirds margin to consider a measure outside the sequence established by the calendar system. On Mondays, which are known as Calendar Mondays, members can suspend the rules by a simple majority vote. House members may also decide by a two-thirds vote to suspend the rules on other days to sandwich time for items on the last three calendars between other measures.

The House calendar system becomes more important as a legislative session wears on. During the early months of a session, relatively few bills pass committee for assignment to a calendar and the House typically considers every measure before ending its legislative day. Toward the end of the session, however, the legislative pace quickens and the number of measures on the calendar grows. By the end of the session, measures placed on low-priority calendars risk failure for lack of action.

The Texas Senate does not have a Calendars Committee. Instead, the custom in the Texas Senate is to require a two-thirds vote of the entire membership to consider legislation on the floor, a procedure known as the **two-thirds rule.** Although official Senate rules stipulate that bills emerging from committee must be considered on the

Appropriations bill A legislative authorization to spend money for particular purposes.

Local bills Proposed laws that affect only a single unit of local government.

Two-thirds rule A procedure used in the Texas Senate requiring a two-thirds vote before a measure can be brought to the floor for debate and eventual passage.

floor in the order in which they are received from committee, the official procedure is almost never followed. The first bill reported out of committee at the beginning of a session is invariably a "blocking bill," introduced not to be passed but to rest atop the Senate calendar, preventing consideration of other measures. In recent session, the blocking bill has been a measure proposing the creation of a county park beautification and improvement program. The blocking bill ensures that legislation cannot reach the floor unless the Senate votes by a two-thirds margin to suspend the rules to consider a measure out of order. With the blocking bill firmly in place, the lieutenant governor and other Senate leadership decide which bills to consider on the floor and the order in which to consider them. By prearrangement, the lieutenant governor recognizes a particular senator who then moves that the rules be suspended to allow consideration by the full Senate of a particular bill. The rule suspension requires a two-thirds vote. An important feature of this practice is that 11 senators (one-third plus one) can block Senate action on a bill they oppose. Consequently, measures without the support of at least two-thirds of the members of the Senate do not even come to a vote in the chamber because they are never approved for consideration on the floor.[24]

Lieutenant Governor David Dewhurst and most Republicans in the Senate have made exceptions to the two-thirds procedure for certain highly partisan issues. During a special session in 2003, Dewhurst refused to honor the two-thirds rule to allow congressional redistricting legislation to come to a vote in the Texas Senate. At the beginning of the 2009 legislative session, the Senate membership decided by majority vote to exclude Voter ID legislation from the two-thirds rule. As a result, the measure passed the Senate despite unanimous Democratic opposition. In 2011, the Senate ignored the two-thirds rule for both redistricting and Voter ID measures and dropped the rule altogether for measures in the special session.

Once a bill reaches the floor of either chamber, members debate its merits and perhaps propose amendments. Because Texas House rules limit debate, the measure eventually comes to a vote unless the session ends before action can be taken. In the Senate, members may speak as long as they please, and occasionally senators attempt to defeat a bill through prolonged debate, a practice known as a **filibuster.** However, because debate can be ended by majority vote, the filibuster is not as potent a weapon in the Texas Senate as it is in the U.S. Senate, where 60 of 100 votes are needed to shut off debate. The only time a filibuster can be effective in the Texas Senate is near the end of the session, right before a deadline for passing legislation, when an individual senator can literally run out the clock.

Both the Texas Senate and Texas House set deadlines for the consideration of measures several days in advance of the constitutional end of the session. Senate rules declare that no bill can be considered unless it is reported from committee at least 15 days before final adjournment. In addition, no votes can be taken on the last day of the session except to correct errors. The House has comparable rules.

Ordinary legislation passes the Texas House and Texas Senate by majority vote of those members present and voting. If all 150 House members participate, 76 votes constitute a majority. In the Senate, 16 of 31 senators are a majority if every senator participates. Constitutional amendments require a two-thirds vote of each chamber.

Filibuster An attempt to defeat a bill through prolonged debate.

Members of the House vote electronically and a scoreboard displays each vote. In the smaller Senate, the clerk calls the roll and members shout their preference. The names of members voting for or against a measure are printed in the journal for each chamber. Citizens who are interested in how their representatives voted on a particular measure can find the information online at the website of the Texas legislature (www.legis.state.tx.us/). The website provides a link to the journal page showing the vote breakdown on particular pieces of legislation.

Conference Committee Action

A measure has not cleared the legislature until it has passed both the Texas House and the Texas Senate in identical form during the same legislative session. Sanctuary-cities legislation passed the Texas House in the regular session in 2011. It passed the Texas Senate during a special session called immediately after the 2011 regular session ended. The measure failed because it did not pass both chambers in the same form during the same legislative session. Sometimes legislation passes one chamber and then goes to the other for consideration. At other times, legislators introduce similar or identical measures simultaneously in the Texas House and Texas Senate. Legislation that passes one chamber of the legislature may be rewritten in the other chamber, either during committee mark up or on the floor. By the time a measure that has passed the House has made its way through the Senate (or vice versa), it may differ considerably from the measure originally passed by the other chamber.

What happens when the Texas House and Texas Senate pass similar, but not identical, measures? Frequently, the chamber that initially passed the legislation agrees to the changes adopted by the other chamber. When agreement cannot be reached, and this is often true with major pieces of legislation, the House and Senate form a conference committee to work out the differences. A **conference committee** is a special committee created to negotiate differences on similar pieces of legislation passed by the House and Senate. Separate conference committees are formed to deal with each bill in dispute. In the Texas legislature, conference committees include five members from each chamber, appointed by the presiding officers. A majority of conference members from each house must concur before the conference committee has finished its work.

Conference committee A special committee created to negotiate differences on similar pieces of legislation passed by the House and Senate.

Once conference committee members have reached an agreement, the conference committee returns it to the floors of the Texas House and the Texas Senate for another vote. Each chamber has the option of voting the legislation up or down or returning it to the conference committee for further negotiation. The House and Senate may not amend the measure at this point; rather, legislators must accept or reject the piece of legislation in its entirety.

The legislature passes only a fraction of the measures introduced during a session. In the 2011 regular session, for example, the legislature approved 1,458 bills and resolutions of 10,315 measures that were introduced, for a passage rate of 14 percent.[25] Many of the measures that passed were local bills or other noncontroversial pieces of legislation.

Action by the Governor

Once a bill passes the legislature, it goes to the governor, who has three options. First, the governor may do nothing. If the legislature remains in session, the bill becomes law after 10 days. If the measure reaches the governor's desk within 10 days of adjournment, it becomes law 20 days after the legislative session has ended. Governors generally use this option for bills about which they have mixed feelings. Although they are willing for the measures to become law, they do not want to go on record in favor of them. Second, the governor can sign the bill into law. Governors often sign politically popular bills with great fanfare, staging televised bill-signing ceremonies. Finally, the governor can issue a **veto,** an action in which the chief executive of a state or nation refuses to approve a bill passed by the legislature. In 2011, for example, Governor Perry vetoed 24 bills. Except for appropriations bills, the governor must choose to veto all of a bill or none of it. For appropriations bills, however, the governor has the **line-item veto,** which is the power to veto sections or items of an appropriations bill while signing the remainder of the bill into law. The governor typically vetoes well less than 1 percent of total state spending.

If the legislature is still in session, it can override the governor's veto by a two-thirds vote of each chamber and the bill becomes law despite the governor's opposition. Nonetheless, overrides are rare in Texas. Because most bills that clear the legislature pass in the last two weeks of the session, the governor can wait until the legislature has adjourned before casting a veto, meaning that the veto stands unchallenged.

Laws take effect at different times. The Texas Constitution declares that all laws except the appropriations bill go into effect 90 days after the legislature adjourns unless the legislature by a two-thirds vote designates another date. The appropriations bill takes effect on October 1, the beginning of the state budget year. Sometimes the legislature specifies that a measure take effect immediately upon signature of the governor. At other times the legislature directs that legislation go into effect on September 1.

Veto An action in which the chief executive of a state or nation refuses to approve a bill passed by the legislature.

Line-item veto The power to veto sections or items of an appropriations bill while signing the remainder of the bill into law.

BREAKING NEWS!

Texas Legislature Fails to Pass Guns-on-Campus Legislation

The 2011 session of the Texas legislature failed to pass legislation that would have allowed students, faculty, and staff with concealed handgun licenses to carry their weapons on campus. The measure passed the Senate but failed to come to a vote in the House before time ran out and the session ended. The proponents of guns on campus argued that the measure is designed to give people a chance to defend themselves in case a shooter comes on campus, such as what happened at Virginia Tech in 2007. State Senator Jeff Wentworth, a Republican from San Antonio, said that the students at Virginia Tech were defenseless, enabling the shooter to "pick them off like sitting ducks."* In contrast, the opponents of the legislation argue that more guns on campus would make the environment less safe. Moreover, in case of an incident, the presence of more than one person with a gun could create confusion for law enforcement personnel.[†]

Discussion

Wasn't guns-on-campus legislation expected to pass? Yes. In the 2009 session, a similar measure passed the Texas Senate but failed in the House. With almost every state senator returning in 2011, the likelihood of passage in that chamber was high. Meanwhile, half the members of the 2011 Texas House signed on as coauthors of the guns-on-campus bill. No wonder observers predicted that the measure would pass both chambers and go to the governor, who promised to sign it.

With that level of support, what could go wrong? Keep in mind that the rules of the legislative process make it difficult to pass legislation, even bills with a high level of support. Senator Wentworth, the bill's sponsor in the Senate, was blocked for months by the two-thirds rule. Even though a majority of senators supported guns on campus, Wentworth could not line up the two-thirds support necessary to bring the bill to the floor for debate and eventual vote. Finally, toward the end of the session, Wentworth was able to win approval for the measure by attaching it as an amendment to the appropriations.

What went wrong in the House? The rules of the House limit legislation to a single subject. When the Senate appropriations bill with the guns-on-campus amendment attached came up for debate in the House, opponents made a parliamentary objection and the amendment was removed. That effectively killed the bill for the 2011 session.

So the bill failed without actually losing a vote? Yes, and that's not unusual. Most of the legislation that fails dies without a vote, at least not a floor vote. Because the session is short, the leadership won't generally bring a bill up for a vote on the floor unless its supporters have already lined up majority support. Other legislation fails because time runs out before a vote can be held. Sometimes legislators allow a controversial bill to die without a vote because they don't want to go on record either for or against the measure.

---

* Quoted in Michael Barajas, "State Senator Wentworth Touts His Guns-on-Campus Bill in SA Forum," available at http://blogs@sacurrent.com.

LEGISLATIVE POLICYMAKING

Numerous factors affect the legislative process in Texas.

Legislative Leadership

The speaker of the House and the lieutenant governor are the most powerful figures in the Texas legislature. They appoint members of their leadership team to chair committees and stack key standing committees and conference committees with members who share their political perspectives. They have the power to reward their friends in the legislature and punish their enemies. Their support greatly enhances any measure's chances for passage; their opposition almost certainly dooms a bill to defeat. Although neither Speaker Straus nor Lieutenant Governor Dewhurst openly opposed the sanctuary-cities legislation, the measure nonetheless failed to become law. Some proponents of the measure blame the two leaders for failing to do what was necessary to push it through the legislature in the last days of the special session.[26]

The centralization of legislative power in the hands of the leadership offers both advantages and disadvantages for the policymaking process in the legislature. On the one hand, the centralization of legislative power enables the legislature to act on a fair amount of legislation in a relatively short period of time. Leaders with power are in a position to make things happen. On the other hand, the disadvantage of a centralized power structure is that members who are not part of the leadership team may be left out of the legislative policymaking process. Texas is a diverse state, but that diversity has not always been represented in the outcomes of the legislative process. Historically, the poor, minorities, organized labor, consumers, and other groups not part of the conservative legislative majority have often had little impact on the outcome of policy debates.

Nonetheless, it would be a mistake to regard the speaker and lieutenant governor as legislative dictators. Their considerable powers have been freely given to them by the members of the legislature and could just as easily be withdrawn by majority vote of the membership by simply changing the rules of the House or the rules of the Senate. Historically, the most effective legislative leaders have exercised their authority in a fashion that most members consider fair. The members of the legislature want the opportunity to pass legislation important to their constituents. They also want to avoid, whenever possible, having to cast a vote on a controversial issue that could be used against them in the next election.

Speaker Craddick lost his leadership position in 2009 because most members believed that he neglected their needs in order to advance his policy agenda. They faulted the speaker for failing to share power with the membership, especially the committee chairs, and they resented having to vote on controversial issues that would likely fail in the Senate, anyway. The chamber elected Joe Straus as the new speaker because they believed that he would lead fairly without trying to impose his personal policy agenda on the body.[27]

Interest Groups

Interest groups lay the groundwork for influencing the legislative process by contributing money to candidates. Groups give money to legislative candidates because they want **legislative access,** which is an open door through which an interest group hopes to influence the details of policy. Consequently, interest groups target their contributions to the legislature's most powerful members, including the leadership and members of important committees. The speaker, lieutenant governor, and key committee chairs are able to raise huge amounts of money because they hold positions of influence.

Interest groups attempt to affect the legislative process through **lobbying,** which is the communication of information by a representative of an interest group to a government official for the purpose of influencing a policy decision. Some lobbyists represent a single firm or organization, whereas others contract to lobby on behalf of several clients. In 2011, for example, former state senator David Sibley was a registered lobbyist for 22 interests. Sibley's clients included the City of Harlingen, El Paso Electric Co., State Farm Insurance, Texas Dental Association, and Wholesale Beer Distributors.[28]

Numerous interest groups were concerned with sanctuary-cities legislation. The League of United Latin American Citizens (LULAC) and other Latino rights

Legislative access An open door through which an interest group hopes to influence the details of policy.

Lobbying The communication of information by a representative of an interest group to a government official for the purpose of influencing a policy decision.

Racial profiling
The practice of a police officer targeting individuals as suspected criminals on the basis of their race or ethnicity.

organizations opposed the measure because they worried about the danger of **racial profiling,** the practice of a police officer targeting individuals as suspected criminals on the basis of their race or ethnicity. Business groups, however, were primarily responsible for preventing the passage of sanctuary-cities legislation. The measure passed the Texas Senate in a special session and was moving toward passage in the Texas House when Houston homebuilder Bob Perry (no relation to the governor) and HEB grocery CEO Charles Butt declared their opposition. Immigrant labor helps keep costs down for the construction and agriculture industries. Immigrant families shop at relatively low-cost grocery stores such as HEB. Perry and Butt have considerable influence in the legislature because they are major campaign contributors and have a substantial lobby presence. Over the last decade, Bob Perry has been the single most generous contributor to legislative candidates and Butt is not far behind.[29] Legislative support for the sanctuary-cities bill crumbled and the measure never came to a vote in the House.

Constituency

To what extent do the actions of legislators reflect the wishes of their constituents? The traditional model of representation is that candidates make promises during the election campaign and then keep (or fail to keep) those promises once in office. In this approach to representation, citizens hold legislators accountable for keeping their promises by reelecting or failing to reelect them based on whether lawmakers kept their word. A second model of representation contends that lawmakers do what they think their constituents will approve of at the next election. This approach to representation recognizes that legislators may sometimes address issues that were not discussed during the last election. It also implies that voters worry more about performance than promises. A third model of representation holds that legislators use common sense and good judgment to do what is best for their constituents and the state as a whole. In this approach to representation, voters are less concerned with lawmakers keeping specific promises as they are with elected officials making decisions that improve the quality of life for people in the state as a whole. Finally, another model of representation suggests that lawmakers sometimes represent constituents outside their districts, such as campaign contributors. From this perspective, big money campaign contributors may have as much or more influence over legislative decision making as do the voters. In practice, legislative behavior mixes several forms of representation, depending on the issue. Lawmakers are more likely to vote in accordance with what they perceive as the preferences of their constituents on high-profile issues, but high-profile issues are rare, especially in state government. On most policy matters, legislators have the leeway to make their decisions on other bases.[30]

The debate over sanctuary-cities legislation illustrates both the strengths and weaknesses of constituent pressure compared with the influence of major campaign contributors. Polls showed that a slight majority of all Texans (51 percent) and a large majority (63 percent) of likely voters favored passage of legislation to allow law enforcement personnel to inquire about the immigration status of anyone stopped for an offense.[31] Although members elected from minority districts almost

In 2011, the Texas legislature failed to pass sanctuary-cities legislation that would have empowered police officers to question persons lawfully detained about their immigration status.

universally opposed the measure because their constituents were concerned with racial profiling, legislators representing more conservative districts faced considerable citizen pressure to pass sanctuary-cities legislation. However, business interests succeeded in preventing the legislation from coming to a vote on the floor of the Texas House. Political columnist Lisa Falkenberg summarized the fate of sanctuary-cities legislation as follows: "Popular anti-illegal immigration sentiment may fuel sound bites and symbolic bills, but in the end, big business calls the shots."[32]

Some of the most important constituency-based legislative divisions in the Texas legislature reflect whether a district is predominantly inner city, suburban, or rural. Inner-city residents worry about crime, public school quality, neighborhood restoration, and opportunities for minorities. Suburban voters are concerned about property taxes, crime, annexation, and neighborhood preservation. Rural residents focus on agricultural issues, natural-resource development, and property rights. Consider the controversy over the **Top 10 Percent Rule,** a state law that grants automatic college admission to public high school graduates who finish in the top 10 percent of their class. The legislature passed the measure in hopes of increasing minority enrollment at the state's two flagship universities—the University of Texas at Austin (UT-Austin) and Texas A&M University at College Station. Inner-city

Top 10 Percent Rule A state law that grants automatic college admission to public high school graduates who finish in the top 10 percent of their class.

minority legislators typically defend the rule as a symbol of racial integration, and they are joined by white legislators from small towns and rural areas whose constituents also benefit from the provision.[33] In contrast, suburban lawmakers representing areas with highly competitive high schools have pushed to modify the rule because many of their constituents believe that it limits the opportunity for their youngsters to get into UT-Austin. In 2009, the legislature amended the Top 10 Percent Rule to allow UT-Austin to limit the percentage of top 10 percent students in its freshman class to 75 percent in response to complaints from UT-Austin officials that the rule too severely limited their flexibility in making admissions decisions.

Political Parties

Nonpartisan legislature A legislative body in which political parties play little or no role.

For most of the state's history, Texas had a **nonpartisan legislature,** a legislative body in which political parties play little or no role. Nearly every legislator was a Democrat. As recently as 1970, only two Republicans served in Senate, whereas ten Republicans sat in the House. Neither the Democrats nor the Republicans in the Texas legislature organized formally, nor did they elect party leaders or meet regularly as party groups. Even as the Republican contingent in the legislature grew, partisanship generally remained in the background. The speaker and lieutenant governor included both Republicans and Democrats in their leadership teams and appointed legislators of both parties to chair important committees. In 2001, for example, Republican Lieutenant Governor Bill Ratliff appointed a Democrat, Rodney Ellis of Houston, to chair the important Finance Committee, whereas Democratic House Speaker Pete Laney named a Republican, Delwin Jones of Lubbock, to chair the critical Redistricting Committee.

Partisan legislature A legislative body in which political parties play a defining role.

In contrast, the U.S. Congress is a **partisan legislature,** which is a legislative body in which political parties play a defining role. The members of Congress organize along party lines. The political parties choose committee leaders and floor leaders, with the majority party holding every leadership position both on the floor and in committee. The party leadership acts to advance the party's agenda, and the voting on most pieces of major legislation breaks down along party lines, with a majority of Democrats voting on one side of the issue and a majority of Republicans voting on the other side. Interest group allies and party activists outside of Congress work with the congressional leadership to promote the party's agenda on major issues.

The 78th legislature, which met in 2003, marked the beginning of a turn toward a more partisan legislature, especially in the Texas House. The redistricting plan adopted by the LRB after the 2000 U.S. Census produced legislative districts that were clearly tilted to the advantage of one party or the other. Consequently, most legislators owed their election to primary voters, forcing Democrats to appeal to their liberal base while Republicans targeted their conservative base.[34]

School choice An educational reform movement that allows parents to choose the elementary or secondary school their children will attend.

Craddick, who became speaker in 2003, was the most partisan speaker in the history of the Texas House. He used his power to promote Republican positions on a series of controversial issues, including congressional redistricting, reduced spending for the Children's Health Insurance (CHIP) program, a constitutional amendment to outlaw gay marriage, Voter ID legislation, and **school choice,** which is an educational reform movement that would allow parents to choose the elementary or secondary school their children will attend. Although most Republican members of the House embraced the party's position on these issues, some members resented being pressured by the speaker to support the party position on issues that would be controversial in their districts. Craddick lost his job in 2009 to Joe Straus primarily because Straus promised to be fair and relatively nonpartisan.

Although the Texas legislature is not yet as partisan a body as is the U.S. Congress, it is moving in that direction. On one hand, the legislature retains some elements of a time when decisions were made on bases other than political party affiliation. All of the members of the Texas House select the speaker, not just law-makers who belong to the majority political party, as happens in the U.S. Congress. In 2009, for example, Democrats provided the core of votes needed to ensure Repub-lican Straus the speakership. Furthermore, the speaker and the lieutenant governor name members of both parties to serve as committee chairs, not just those from the majority party, as is the practice in Congress. In 2011, Straus appointed 27 Repub-licans and 11 Democrats to chair committees, a ratio of Republicans to Democrats approximating the two parties' strength in the chamber.

On the other hand, the legislature in some respects is coming to resemble the U.S. Congress. Many of the issues that divide the legislature are fought along party lines, including Voter ID, abortion, immigration, redistricting, school funding for-mulas, and budget priorities. Party members in a legislature frequently vote together because they have similar beliefs and represent similar constituents. Lawmakers from the same political party also have an incentive to work together to promote their party's success because they want their party to have a positive brand identification come election time.[35] In the Texas Senate, partisanship is leading to the erosion of the two-thirds rule, which has historically forced members to work together to seek compromise.

Party politics affected the outcome of the battle over sanctuary-cities legislation. Whereas Democrats opposed the measure, Republicans were split. The Republican base, especially activists associated with the Tea Party, strongly favored the passage of state legislation to crack down on illegal immigration, including sanctuary cities. Moreover, passage of sanctuary cities was a priority for Governor Perry. Had the legislation come to a vote in the House during the special session, it is likely it would have passed because many Republican members of the chamber were concerned that a vote against the bill would be used against them in the next Republican primary election. However, a number of conservative Republican activists opposed the bill because of its potential for long-term damage to the party's image in the Latino com-munity. Some conservative Republican legislators may have secretly preferred that the sanctuary-cities bill die quietly without a vote.

Political Ideology

Political ideology (liberalism/conservatism) influences the legislative process. **Liberalism** is the political view that seeks to change the political, economic, or social institutions of society to foster the development and well-being of the

Liberalism The political view that seeks to change the political, economic, or social institutions of society to foster the development of the individual. Liberals believe that the government can (and should) advance social progress by promoting political equality, social justice, and economic prosperity. Liberals usually favor government regulation and high levels of government spending for social programs. Liberals value social and cultural diversity and defend the right of individual adult choice on issues such as access to abortion.

GETTING INVOLVED

Contacting Your State Legislators

Two people represent you in the Texas legislature—a state senator and a state representative.
You can learn their names and find their e-mail addresses online at the following URL: **www.legis.state
.tx.us/**. Every session, the legislature deals with issues that affect ordinary citizens in general and
college students in particular, including university
tuition, college admission requirements, higher education funding, and guns on campus. Write your
state legislators about these and other issues. Find
out where they stand and let them know how you
feel. They represent you, so they need to hear what
you have to say.

It's your state—get involved!

Conservatism The
political view that
seeks to preserve the
political, economic,
and social institutions
of society against
abrupt change.
Conservatives
generally oppose
most government
economic regulation
and heavy
government spending
while favoring low
taxes and traditional
values.

individual. Liberals believe that government should promote social justice, political
equality, and economic prosperity. Liberals usually favor government regulation and
high levels of spending for social programs. On social issues, such as abortion, liberals tend to support the right of adult free choice against government interference.
In contrast, **conservatism** is the political view that seeks to preserve the political,
economic, and social institutions of society against abrupt change. Conservatives
generally oppose most government economic regulation and heavy government
spending while favoring low taxes and traditional values.

Historically, conservatives have dominated the Texas legislature and legislative
policies have reflected their political values. The legislature has enacted regulatory and tax policies designed to promote business expansion while adopting social
welfare policies that stress personal responsibility. Few states spend less money on
welfare than Texas. The legislature has been tough on crime, building the nation's
largest prison system. The legislature has also created the nation's most prolific capital punishment system, executing more convicted murderers than any other state.
When the legislature faced a $27 billion shortfall in 2011, it chose to balance the
budget without increasing taxes or fees, forcing significant cuts in education and
health services.

WHAT WE HAVE LEARNED

**1. What effect do bicameralism, biennial sessions,
and limited session length have on legislative
policymaking in Texas?**

Texas has a bicameral legislature consisting of
a 150-member House of Representatives and
a 31-member Senate. Members of the Texas
House serve two-year terms; senators serve four-
year terms, with half the Senate membership

standing for election every two years. The Texas
Senate is solely responsible for confirming gubernatorial appointments. The Texas House must
initiate legislation to raise taxes. The House has
the power to impeach; the Senate to remove.
Legislation must be passed in identical form by
both chambers before it can go to the governor. The Texas Constitution provides that the

legislature meet in regular session every other year for no more than 140 calendar days. The governor can call special sessions, which are limited to 30 days. Critics charge that the legislature meets too infrequently and too briefly to do the state's business effectively. In contrast, defenders of the current system say that it forces legislators to get down to business.

2. **What is the job description of a member of the Texas legislature, considering qualifications, background, compensation, turnover, and term limits?**

   Although the membership of the legislature is more diverse today than ever before, white males remain overrepresented while women and minority group members are underrepresented. Legislators earn $7,200 a year, a relatively low salary in comparison with other state lawmakers, but they have given themselves a generous pension plan and other benefits, including the ability to pay some personal expenses from campaign funds. Legislative turnover in Texas is more often the result of voluntary retirement than election defeat. Some states have adopted legislative term limits, usually through the initiative process, but Texas, without an initiative process, has not.

3. **How is the Texas legislature organized in terms of leadership, committee organization, and legislative assistance?**

   Modern legislatures choose leaders, establish committees, and hire staff assistance in order to facilitate their work. The lieutenant governor and speaker of the House are the presiding officers and foremost political leaders of the Texas legislature. The speaker, who presides in the House, is a state representative who is selected by the members of the House to serve as speaker. The lieutenant governor, who presides in the Senate, is elected statewide for a four-year term in the same general election year in which the governor is chosen. The speaker and

lieutenant governor are two of the most powerful public officials in the state, exercising extraordinary authority in their respective chambers. Some of the legislature's most important work takes place in committee. Committee chairs and most committee members are appointed by the speaker in the House; the lieutenant governor makes the appointments in the Senate. Standing committees enable the legislature to divide the legislative workload. Interim committees are established to consider policy issues between legislative sessions. Staff assistance is important to the Texas legislature because state lawmakers are essentially part-time employees asked to perform a monumental legislative task in a limited period of time. Support agencies include the Legislative Council, Legislative Reference Library, House Research Organization (HRO), and Senate Research Center (SRC).

4. **What are the steps of the legislative process?**

   The legislative process begins when a legislator introduces a bill or resolution. The lieutenant governor and the speaker assign newly introduced measures to committee. Committees do the detailed work of the legislative process, conducting hearings and marking up legislative proposals. Bills that pass standing committee in the House go to the Calendars Committee for assignment to a House calendar, which sets the order of priority for considering legislation. In the Senate, the standard procedure for considering bills on the floor that have passed committee is for the chamber to vote by a two-thirds margin to suspend the rules, the two-thirds rule. Ordinary legislation passes the Texas House and Texas Senate by majority vote of those members present and voting. When the House and Senate pass similar but not identical measures, the leadership appoints members to a conference committee to negotiate a compromise measure, which must be voted on again by the two chambers before it has passed the legislature. Once a bill passes the legislature, it goes to the governor. If the governor does nothing, the measure eventually becomes law. The governor can sign the measure into law or veto it. For appropriations measures, the governor has the line-item veto. The legislature can override a veto with a two-thirds vote, but that is rare, primarily because most vetoes are issued after adjournment.

5. **What affect do the following factors have on the legislative process: legislative leadership, interest groups, constituency, political parties, and political ideology?**

Numerous factors affect the legislative process in Texas. The support of the speaker and lieutenant governor greatly enhances any measure's chances for passage; their opposition almost certainly dooms a bill to defeat. Interest groups lay the groundwork for influencing the legislative process by contributing money to candidates. They then attempt to shape the details of legislation through lobbying. Lawmakers are more likely to vote in accordance with what they perceive as the preferences of their constituents on high-profile issues, but high-profile issues are rare, especially in state government. Although the Texas legislature is not as partisan a body as is the U.S. Congress, it is becoming more like Congress. Historically, conservatives have dominated the Texas legislature and legislative policies have reflected their political values.

KEY TERMS

appropriations bill

bicameral legislature

bill

conference committee

conservatism

filibuster

fiscal note

impeachment

initiative process

interim committee

joint resolution

legislative access

Legislative Budget Board (LBB)

Legislative Redistricting Board (LRB)

legislative turnover

liberalism

line-item veto

lobbying

local bills

mark up

nonpartisan election

nonpartisan legislature

partisan legislature

racial profiling

resolution

school choice

select *or* special committee

seniority

standing committee

term limitation

Top 10 Percent Rule

two-thirds rule

unicameral legislature

veto

NOTES

1. Julian Aguilar, "Sanctuary Cities Bill Clears Texas Senate," *Texas Tribune*, June 15, 2011, available at www.texastribune.org.
2. Lisa Falkenberg, "The Bottom Line Prevails," *Houston Chronicle*, June 28, 2011, pp. B1, B3.
3. James R. Rogers, "The Impact of Bicameralism on Legislative Production," *Legislative Studies Quarterly* 28 (November 2003): 509–528.
4. "Texas Legislature Should Meet Every Year," *El Paso Times*, May 22, 2007, available at www.elpasotimes.com.
5. Quoted in Ellen Perlman, "The Gold-Plated Legislature," *Governing*, February 1998, p. 40.
6. Harvey J. Tucker, "Legislative Workload Congestion in Texas," *Journal of Politics* 49 (May 1987): 565–578.

7. W. Gardner Selby, "Another Special Session Gives Rise to Legislative Pay Chatter," *Austin American-Statesman*, April 11, 2006, available at www.statesman.com.

8. Empire Center for New York State Policy, "Legislative Salaries per State," available at www.empirecenter.org.

9. Jay Root, "But the Perks Sure Are Nice," *Fort Worth Star-Telegram*, February 4, 2007, available at www.dfw.com.

10. Emily Ramshaw and Marcus Funk, "For Some Dallas-Area Legislators, Donations Fund the Good Life," *Dallas Morning News*, February 1, 2009, available at www.dallasnews.com.

11. Quoted in Ramshaw and Funk, "For Some Dallas-Area Legislators, Donations Fund the Good Life."

12. "Congratulations," *Texas Tribune*, March 2, 2010, available at www.texastribune.org.

13. "The Ex Files," *Texas Tribune*, June 10, 2011, available at www.texastribune.org.

14. Karen Brooks, "Texas No. 1 in Legislators-Turned-Lobbyists," *Dallas Morning News*, October 13, 2006, available at www.dallasnews.com.

15. U.S. Term Limits, "State Legislative Term Limits," available at www.termlimits.org.

16. Karl T. Kurtz, Bruce Cain, and Richard G. Niemi, *Institutional Change in American Politics: The Case of Term Limits* (Ann Arbor, MI: University of Michigan Press, 2007), pp. 185–192.

17. Russell Nichols, "Termed Out," *Governing*, January 2011, pp. 20–25.

18. Hastings Wyman, "Texas: House Speaker Craddick Gets Runoff Boosts," *Southern Political Report*, April 14, 2008, available at www.southernpoliticalreport.com.

19. Dave Mann, "Fall of the House of Craddick," *Texas Observer*, January 23, 2009, pp. 21–23.

20. *Texas Weekly*, February 4, 2011, available at www.texasweekly.com.

21. National Conference of State Legislatures, "Size of State Legislative Staff: 1979, 1988, 1996, 2003, 2009," available at www.ncsl.org.

22. National Conference of State Legislatures, "Committee Staffing," available at www.ncsl.org.

23. Tim Eaton, "Many Immigration Bills Not Likely to Make It Through Legislature," *Austin American-Statesman*, May 10, 2011, available at www.statesman.com.

24. Bill Hobby, *How Things Really Work: Lessons from a Life in Politics* (Austin, TX: Dolph Briscoe Center for American History, 2010), pp. 133–138.

25. Texas Legislature Online, "Legislative Reports," available at www.legis.state.tx.us/.

26. "Special Session: What Did Not Pass," *Houston Chronicle*, July 3, 2011, p. B7.

27. Jason Embry, "Straus Steered House with a Light Hand," *Austin-American Statesman*, June 7, 2009, available at www.statesman.com.

28. Texas Ethics Commission, "Lobby Lists," available at www.ethics.state.tx.us.

29. Robert T. Garrett, "Top Business Leaders Try to Derail Texas 'Sanctuary Cities' Bill," *Dallas Morning News*, June 23, 2011, available at www.dallasnews.com.

30. Jane Mansbridge, "Rethinking Representation," *American Political Science Review* 97 (November 2003): 515–528.

31. Texas Lyceum Poll, available at www.texaslyceum.org.

32. Lisa Falkenberg, "The Bottom Line Prevails," *Houston Chronicle*, June 28, 2011, p. B1.

33. Polly Ross Hughes and Matthew Tresaugue, "Small-Town GOP Behind Survival of Top 10% Rule," *Houston Chronicle*, May 30, 2007, pp. B1–B2.

34. Bill Bishop, "A Steady Slide Towards a More Partisan Union," *Austin American-Statesman*, May 30, 2004, available at www.statesman.com.

35. Shannon Jenkins, "Party Influence on Roll Call Voting: A View from the U.S. States," *State Politics and Policy Quarterly* 8 (Fall 2008): 239–262.

Chapter 9

Executive Branch

CHAPTER OUTLINE

The Governor
    Qualifications and Background
    Term of Office, Selection, and Removal
    Staff Support
    Powers and Responsibilities
    Measuring Gubernatorial Powers
    The Governor of Texas and the
        Policymaking Process

The Executive Bureaucracy
    Elected Executives
    Appointed Executives

    Elected Boards and Commissions
    Appointed Commissions
    Privatization

Administrative Oversight
    Legislative Oversight
    Gubernatorial Oversight

What We Have Learned

WHAT WE WILL LEARN

After studying Chapter 9, you should be able to answer the following questions:

1. What is the job description for the governor of Texas, including formal qualifications, length of term, impeachment and removal, compensation, staff assistance, powers and responsibilities, strength of office, and role in the policymaking process?

2. How is the executive branch of Texas government structured?

3. How effective are the tools available to the legislature and the governor for overseeing the state's administrative bureaucracy?

The Texas oil and gas industry is booming. Oil companies are drilling thousands of wells in the Eagle Ford shale formation, which runs from South Texas through the center of the state, and in the Barnett shale formation, which is near Fort Worth. Scientists have known for a long time that shale formations contain millions of barrels of oil and huge quantities of natural gas. Until recently, however, shale oil and gas have been considered unrecoverable because they are located in tightly packed rock formations. Oil companies are now able to extract the shale oil and gas because of a drilling technique known as hydraulic fracturing, also known as fracking. Oil companies drill deep underground and then drill horizontally into the shale formation. Fracking penetrates the shale by using a high-pressure mix of water, sand, and chemicals to blast through rocks to release the oil inside. Shale oil and gas production offer great economic promise for the state of Texas and the United States as a whole. The oil industry estimates that shale production will create more than 2 million new jobs, either directly or indirectly, and pump tens of billions of dollars into the economy.[1]

Nonetheless, fracking is controversial. Environmentalists worry about the impact of pumping thousands of gallons of water and chemicals underground. Some of the residents of affected areas have reported the contamination of surface and subsurface water supplies from fracking fluids. Moreover, the volume of water needed for the fracking process, 3 to 8 million gallons per well, places enormous strains on water resources, particularly in drought-parched Texas. Oil industry spokespersons respond that the environmental risks are outweighed by the economic benefits of the new production. Shale oil production in Texas and other states can reduce American dependence on foreign sources of oil. It is also less hazardous than drilling offshore or in the arctic. Furthermore, natural gas produced from shale can fuel power plants, replacing coal, which is much less environmentally friendly than clean-burning natural gas.[2]

Although both the federal government and the states have authority to regulate hydraulic fracking, the responsibility to issue fracking regulations to protect water supplies falls primarily on the states because Congress passed legislation in 2005 to prohibit the federal Environmental Protection Agency (EPA) from regulating fracking under the Safe Drinking Water Act.[3] Some states have been more cautious about fracking than other states. New York, for example, imposed a moratorium on fracking until state environmental officials could conduct a review of the practice. Pennsylvania regulates drilling, casing, cementing, testing, monitoring, and plugging, and has fined companies for water pollution.[4] Texas is in the process of developing a regulatory system for hydraulic fracking. In 2011, the legislature passed and Governor Perry signed legislation that requires oil companies to disclose chemicals used in fracking. The Texas Railroad Commission, the agency charged with regulating oil and gas production in the state, is developing regulations to implement the new law. Meanwhile, the Texas Commission on Environmental Quality (TCEQ) has adopted rules requiring companies to monitor air pollution emissions and follow best practices in controlling harmful emissions.[5]

State regulation of shale oil and gas production introduces this chapter on the executive branch of Texas government. The first part of the chapter examines the office of governor. It considers the qualifications and background of the state's chief executive. The chapter identifies the powers and responsibilities of the governor and assesses the strength of the office in Texas in comparison with governors in other states. The chapter then studies the role of the governor in the policymaking process. The second part of the chapter describes the various agencies and departments that constitute the executive branch of state government. It discusses the elected executive officials other than the governor, appointed executive officials, elected boards and commissions, and appointed boards and commissions. Finally, the chapter discusses the tools available to the governor and legislature for overseeing administrative agencies and assessing their effectiveness.

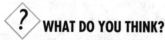 **WHAT DO YOU THINK?**

Do the economic benefits of fracking outweigh the potential impact of the process on the environment?

THE GOVERNOR

The governor is the chief executive officer of the state with important powers to influence the policymaking process.

Qualifications and Background

The Texas Constitution declares that the governor must be an American citizen, a resident of Texas for five years preceding election, and at least 30 years of age. In practice, most of the state's chief executives have come from narrow social circles. Every governor has been a white Anglo-Saxon Protestant. Only two (Miriam Ferguson and Ann Richards) were women. Most governors have been well-to-do, middle-aged lawyers or business executives with prior experience in public affairs. They have also had fairly common, easy-to-pronounce names, such as Perry, Bush, Richards, White, Clements, Briscoe, Smith, and Connally.

Although most recent governors have conformed fairly closely to the traditional image, the election of Ann Richards showed that Texas voters were willing to consider candidates who did not fit the mold in all respects. Not only was Richards a woman, but her political career was based on her own efforts rather than those of her husband. Miriam Ferguson, the first woman governor of Texas, won election as a stand-in for her husband, former Governor Jim Ferguson. Richards, a divorcee, was a schoolteacher before winning election as a county commissioner in Travis County (which includes the city of Austin). In 1982, Richards was elected state treasurer, holding that post until her election as governor in 1990.

Term of Office, Selection, and Removal

The governor's term of office is four years, increased from two years by a constitutional amendment adopted in 1972. Today, only 2 of the 50 states elect their governors for two years instead of four.[6] Elections for governor and other elective state executive officials are held in even-numbered years, timed so that they will not coincide with national presidential elections (e.g., 2010, 2014). The Texas Constitution sets no limit on the number of terms a governor can serve. Rick Perry, who assumed office when George W. Bush resigned in 2001 to become president, holds the record as the state's longest-serving governor.

A governor can be removed from office before a term is ended through the process of impeachment and removal by the legislature. **Impeachment** is the formal process through which the Texas House accuses an executive or judicial official of misconduct serious enough to warrant removal from office. The House votes to impeach the governor by majority vote. The Texas Senate then conducts a trial and may vote to remove the governor by a two-thirds margin. In 1917, for example, the House impeached Governor James Ferguson and the Senate removed him from office over the alleged misuse of public funds. Ferguson is the only Texas governor to date to be impeached. Many of the state's voters apparently did not share the legislature's opinion of Ferguson because they twice elected his wife, Miriam Ferguson, to serve as the state's chief executive after Jim Ferguson was removed from office.

Impeachment
The formal process through which the Texas House accuses an executive or judicial branch official of misconduct serious enough to warrant removal from office.

Staff Support

The governor has a full-time professional staff of 137 people with a two-year office budget of $17 million, including the governor's salary of $150,000. In addition, programs assigned to the governor's office employ 136 full-time staff members with a two-year budget of more than $500 million.[7] The governor appoints staff members without need of Senate confirmation and they serve at the governor's pleasure. The governor has a chief of staff, general counsel, and press secretary. The governor's office also includes administrative units dealing with legislative matters, communications, budgeting and planning, and criminal justice. The size of the governor's staff has increased over the years because state government has grown larger and more complex. The governor today has become a more visible and active participant in

GETTING INVOLVED

Forming a Study Group

A study group is an excellent way for students to learn and retain course material. Studying in a group is more efficient than individual study because the collective knowledge of the group almost always exceeds the knowledge of even the best-prepared student in the class. Consequently, students are less likely to be stumped for an answer to a question and have to waste time looking it up. Study groups are also more fun than studying alone and they motivate students to succeed.

Take the initiative to organize a study group for this course. Identify students who seem serious about their education based on their class attendance and participation and schedule a group study session at a mutually agreed time and place. Coffee shops are a traditional hangout for students preparing for exams. Use the materials in the study guide or the various learning resources in the textbook (review questions, key terms, etc.) to organize your session.

It's your education—get involved!

the state policy process. Furthermore, federal grant programs often require guberna-torial participation in and coordination of program planning and implementation.

Powers and Responsibilities

Although the Texas Constitution grants the governor authority to act in a broad range of policy areas, most of the governor's powers are coupled with limitations.

Legislative Powers The governor's strongest constitutional powers are those used for influencing the legislative process. The Texas Constitution requires that the gover-nor deliver a message to the legislature at the beginning of each legislative session on the condition of the state. The State of the State address, which is comparable to the State of the Union speech the president makes to Congress, enables the gov-ernor to focus attention on issues he or she considers the state's most serious policy needs and offer proposals to meet those needs. The governor can send messages to the legislature at other times as well, both formally and informally. Of course, any legislative measure that the governor proposes must be introduced by a member of the legislature and passed by the Texas House and Texas Senate before it can become a law. The governor can also influence legislative priorities by declaring certain pieces of legislation emergency measures. In 2011, for example, Governor Perry declared sanctuary-cities legislation and an abortion sonogram measure as legisla-tive emergencies. Emergency measures receive priority attention on the floor of the House. Members of the legislature can introduce legislation after the deadline for bill filing if the governor designates the measure as emergency legislation.

Veto An action by the chief executive of a state or nation who refuses to approve a bill passed by the legislature.

The governor has the power to **veto,** an action by the chief executive of a state or nation who refuses to approve a measure passed by the legislature. If the governor objects to a bill passed by the legislature, the governor has ten days to act unless the legislature adjourns during that time. In that case, the governor has 20 days from adjournment in which to decide to issue a veto.

Line-item veto The power to veto sections or items of an appropriations bill while signing the remainder of the bill into law.

The governor also enjoys the power of the **line-item veto,** which is the author-ity to veto sections or items of an appropriations bill while signing the remainder of the bill into law. Keep in mind that the governor's power to issue the line-item veto is limited to the **appropriations bill,** a legislative authorization to spend money for particular purposes. On other pieces of legislation, the governor's options are limited to either accepting or rejecting the measure in its entirety.

Appropriations bill A legislative authorization to spend money for particular purposes.

The Texas legislature can override the governor's veto by a two-thirds vote of each chamber, voting separately. Since Texas became a state, the legislature has successfully overridden only 52 of more than 1,600 gubernatorial vetoes (not count-ing line-item vetoes), for an override rate of 3 percent. Furthermore, since 1941 the legislature has overridden only one veto—a veto cast by Governor Bill Clements in 1979 of a local bill exempting Comal County from the state's game laws.

Why has the legislature so seldom reversed the governor's vetoes? Two-thirds majorities are difficult to attain, of course. More important, most gubernatorial vetoes in Texas come after adjournment, when overriding is impossible. Because much of the legislation introduced during a regular session does not pass until the session's final days, the governor can simply wait until adjournment to issue a veto.

With the legislature gone home, a veto stands unchallenged. Although numerous state constitutions allow the legislature to call itself back into session to consider overriding vetoes, the Texas Constitution does not.

A final legislative power the governor enjoys is the authority to call special sessions. The state constitution empowers the governor to convene the legislature in special sessions that may last no longer than 30 days. In 2011, for example, Governor Perry called a special session immediately after the legislature's regular session ended because the legislature failed to pass the appropriations bill. The Texas Constitution places no limit on the number of special sessions a governor can call. Between May 2003 and January 2007, Governor Perry called seven special sessions to deal with legislative redistricting, school finance, and/or property tax rates. Furthermore, the Texas Constitution declares that in a special session the "legislature may consider only those matters that the governor specifies in the call or subsequently presents to the legislature." The governor can use the power to set the agenda for special sessions as a bargaining tool in negotiations with legislators. In exchange for support on other matters, the governor can offer to expand the call to include issues of particular interest to individual legislators or groups of lawmakers.

Appointive Powers The governor has extensive powers of appointment. The governor is responsible for staffing positions on more than 150 state administrative boards and commissions that set policy for state agencies under their authority. Furthermore, the Texas Constitution empowers the governor to fill vacancies in many

Governor Perry started strong in his race for the White House but quickly faded after a series of embarrassingly poor debate performances highlighted by an "oops" moment when he failed to remember the names of the three federal agencies he wanted to close.

otherwise elective positions, including district and appellate judgeships, should openings occur between elections. A governor makes about 3,000 appointments during a four-year term.[8]

The power of appointment gives the governor an opportunity to influence policy and score political points. As the state's population has grown more diverse, governors of both political parties have sought a diverse set of appointees. Governor Richards named more women and minorities to office than any governor in the history of the state. In fact, 41 percent of her appointees were women, 32 percent Latino, and 12 percent African American. Governor Bush and Governor Perry continued to diversify state government. Among Bush's appointees, 9 percent were African American, 13 percent Latino, and 37 percent women. Governor Perry, meanwhile, has appointed African Americans and Latinos to fill a number of high-profile positions. Perry appointed Wallace Jefferson to be the chief justice of the Texas Supreme Court and named Albert Hawkins the Commissioner of the Texas Health and Human Services Commission. Both Jefferson and Hawkins are African Americans. Perry selected Hope Andrade to be the state's first Latina secretary of state and appointed Eva Guzman to the Texas Supreme Court.

The appointive powers of the governor are limited. Because most administrative board members serve six-year overlapping terms, new governors must work with an administrative structure that was put in place by a predecessor. Although new governors can fill about one-third of administrative positions when they first assume office, they do not have the opportunity to name their own people to a majority of posts for another two years.

The governor has little official removal power. Although the Texas Constitution gives governors the authority to remove their *own* appointees (but not those of a predecessor) with a two-thirds vote of approval by the Texas Senate, this limited procedure has not been used. An incoming governor cannot force the resignation of holdover administrators.

State law allows the governor to appoint a conservator to take over a wayward agency; however, the governor can act only on the recommendation of the Legislative Audit Commission based on a finding that the agency is guilty of gross fiscal mismanagement. In 2007, the procedure was used to take control of the Texas Youth Commission (TYC), the state agency responsible for housing juveniles convicted of criminal offenses. The legislature and the governor acted after the news media reported that TYC officials ignored signs that administrators at a West Texas juvenile prison were sexually abusing inmates.[9]

The governor's appointive powers are often restricted by technical, legal requirements. Consider the make-up of the Texas Racing Commission, which oversees the operation of pari-mutuel wagering on horse and dog racing in the state. The legislature reserved two of the eight positions on the commission for the state comptroller and the chair of the Texas Department of Public Safety (DPS). The governor can appoint the other six members, but only within strict guidelines. Two members of the commission must be experienced in horse racing and two others must be experienced at racing greyhounds. The other two commission members must be veterinarians, one specializing in large animals and the other in small animals.

Furthermore, the legislature specified that all members of the commission must be residents of Texas for at least ten years and file detailed financial statements. Persons with a financial interest in a racetrack or who are closely related to someone with such an interest would be ineligible to serve.

Finally, the governor's appointees must be confirmed by a two-thirds vote of the Texas Senate. In contrast, presidential appointees require only a majority vote of approval in the U.S. Senate. Furthermore, the tradition of senatorial courtesy ensures that the governor's appointees must pass political inspection by their home-area senator or face rejection. **Senatorial courtesy** is a custom of the Texas Senate that allows individual senators a veto over nominees who live in their districts. By tradition, senators will vote against a nominee if the senator from the district in which the nominee lives declares opposition to the nomination.

Gubernatorial appointees who get their positions between legislative sessions serve until the legislature meets again. Then, if the Senate rejects or simply fails to vote on the appointment, the individual loses the position and the governor makes another selection. In 2009, for example, the Texas Senate rejected the nomination of Don McLeroy as chair of the State Board of Education (SBOE) by a vote of 19 in favor to 11 against, just short of the two-thirds vote needed for confirmation. Governor Perry waited until the legislature adjourned and then appointed Cynthia Dunbar to chair the agency. Dunbar would have served until the next regular legislative in session 2011 before facing Senate confirmation, but she chose not to run for reelection in 2010. Perry next appointed Gail Lowe to chair the agency, but she failed to win Senate confirmation in 2011. Once again, Perry waited until the legislature adjourned before making another appointment, Barbara Cargill, who will serve until 2013 when the Texas Senate is back in regular session.

Judicial Powers The Texas Constitution gives the governor some authority in the judicial process. On the recommendation of the Board of Pardons and Paroles, the governor may grant reprieves, commutations, and pardons. A **reprieve** is the postponement of the implementation of punishment for a criminal offense; a **commutation** is the reduction of punishment for a criminal offense. A **pardon** is the exemption from punishment for a criminal offense. In a **capital punishment** (death penalty) case, the governor has authority to grant one 30-day reprieve independently, without recommendation by the Board of Pardons and Paroles, thus postponing a condemned person's execution.

Probably the most effective tool the governor has for influencing judicial policy is the power of appointment. Although judges are elected in Texas, the state constitution empowers the governor to appoint a new judge when appellate and district judges die, retire, or resign during the middle of a term. These appointees serve until the next election, when they must stand for election to hold their jobs. In 2011, 52 percent of the state's appellate judges and 37 percent of district judges had initially taken office through gubernatorial appointment rather than election.[10]

Budgetary Powers The president of the United States and the governors of 47 states enjoy budget-making authority (i.e., preparing a budget to submit to the legislative

Senatorial courtesy The custom of the Texas Senate that allows individual senators a veto over nominees who live in their districts.

Reprieve The postponement of the implementation of punishment for a criminal offense.

Commutation A reduction of punishment for a criminal offense.

Pardon The exemption from punishment for a criminal offense.

Capital punishment The death penalty.

branch).[11] Although the final budget is invariably a negotiated document between the legislative and executive branches of government, the chief executive has the advantage of proposing the initial document. Consequently, the budget debate in the legislature at least begins with the governor's budgetary priorities and policy proposals.

The governor of Texas has no such advantage. Although the Texas Constitution requires the governor to submit budget proposals to the legislature, the Legislative Budget Board (LBB) prepares a budget as well, and its ideas generally carry more weight. The **Legislative Budget Board (LBB)** is an agency created by the legislature to study state revenue and budgetary needs between legislative sessions and prepare budget and appropriation bills to submit to the legislature. As the legislature debates the budget, the point of departure is not the governor's budget but rather the budget proposed by the LBB. In 2011, for example, with the state facing a $27 billion budget shortfall, Governor Perry sent a barebones budget to the legislature that called for major cuts in education and healthcare. For the most part, Perry's budget plan followed the lead of the budget proposal developed by the LBB, with the exception that Perry requested hundreds of millions of dollars in additional spending for projects administered by the governor.[12]

The most important power the Texas governor has for influencing budget priorities is the line-item veto. In contrast to the president, whose only option on an appropriations bill is to accept or reject the measure in its entirety, most state governors can selectively eliminate items while signing the rest into law. This veto and the threat of its use allow a politically skilled governor the opportunity to exercise considerable influence over the final budget document.

Budget execution authority refers to the power to cut agency spending or transfer money between agencies during the period when the legislature is not in session. Much can happen in the two-year interval between legislative sessions. Because of unforeseen events, such as a drought or declining welfare rolls, some budget categories may run short of money, whereas others may have excess cash. Budget execution authority is the power to transfer funds among accounts between legislative sessions. The Texas Constitution allows either the governor or the LBB to propose a reduction in spending or a shift in state funds. Both the governor and the LBB must concur on proposed spending reductions or money transfers before they can take place.

Law Enforcement and Military Powers The governor has some peripheral authority in law enforcement. The governor appoints the three-member board that heads the Department of Public Safety and is empowered to assume command of the Texas Rangers should circumstances warrant, which is rare. The governor is also commander-in-chief of the Texas National Guard, which the governor can call out to assist in situations beyond the control of local law enforcement agencies, such as a natural disaster or civil disorder. In 2005, for example, Governor Perry called several units of the Texas State Guard to active duty to help with people evacuated to Texas from Louisiana after Hurricane Katrina. Guard units subsequently assisted with disaster relief in Texas after Hurricane Rita struck the upper Texas coast. Governor Perry has also ordered several hundred National Guard troops to deploy along the

Legislative Budget Board (LBB) An agency created by the legislature to study state revenue and budgetary needs between legislative sessions and prepare budget and appropriations bills to submit to the legislature.

Budget execution authority The power to cut agency spending or transfer money between agencies during the period when the legislature is not in session.

border to assist local police and federal agents in securing the border against drug smuggling and illegal immigration.

Ceremonial Powers In addition to official powers, the governor is the ceremonial leader of the state. The governor greets foreign leaders, speaks at local chamber of commerce luncheons, issues proclamations on state holidays, and shakes hands with visiting scout troops. Ceremonial activities allow the governor the opportunity to give the appearance of leadership, which can be helpful for a governor attempting to influence the policy process. Leadership depends on the perceptions of the public and other political leaders as much as it depends on official powers.

Governors sometimes use their leadership position to recruit out-of-state companies to relocate to the state. Governor Perry, for example, helped convince Toyota to select San Antonio as the site of a new auto-assembly plant. The legislature did its part by approving the expenditure of state funds to build rail tracks to connect the plant to major rail lines. State and local governments also covered the cost of training 2,000 full-time workers for the plant.[13]

Political Party Leadership The governor is the unofficial leader of his or her political party in the state. The governor sometimes speaks out on partisan controversies and usually campaigns for the party's candidates in state and national elections. Furthermore, as the most visible elected official in a large state, the governor of Texas is often a national political figure. Governor Richards was a prominent figure in Democratic national politics. Her successor, Governor Bush, was elected president of the United States in 2000.

Governor Ann Richards, who died in 2006, was a prominent figure in national Democratic Party politics.

Plural executive
The division of
executive power
among several
elected officials.

Administrative Powers The governor of Texas is probably weakest in the area of administration because of the **plural executive,** which is the division of executive power among several elected officials. Because the land commissioner, attorney general, comptroller, lieutenant governor, and commissioner of agriculture are all elected, they answer not to the governor but to the voters. Elected executive officials do not necessarily share the governor's party affiliation and may be political rivals, even when they belong to the same political party. Comptroller Carole Keeton Strayhorn, for example, challenged Governor Perry for reelection in 2006. Both Strayhorn and Perry were Republicans, although Strayhorn chose to run for governor as an independent.

Nonetheless, a determined governor, especially one who serves more than one term in office, can have an influence over state agencies. By the end of one four-year term, a typical governor has appointed two-thirds of the administrative officials. After six years in office, the governor has had the opportunity to staff the entire executive branch except for those agencies with elected administrators. Many of these officials, especially administrators serving in the most important agencies, are political allies of the governor. As such, they are inclined to listen to the governor's point of view on policy matters and take direction from the governor if the governor wishes to be assertive. Even if the governor cannot force an official out of office, few appointed administrators can withstand the pressure if the governor calls for resignation. For example, every member of the troubled TYC resigned in the face of demands from the governor and legislative leaders to step down.

Governor Perry has attempted to assert influence over the executive branch of state government. He asked the legislature for authority to appoint agency heads, but it turned him down. It also turned down his request to appoint the heads of all the governing boards. Perry then acted on his own to create the Governor's Management Council, which includes the heads of the state's 11 largest agencies as well as representatives of small and medium-size agencies. The purpose of the council, which the governor chairs, is to coordinate the operation of the executive branch.[14]

Executive order
A directive issued
by the governor to
an administrative
agency or executive
department.

Perry has also tried to expand his authority to issue executive orders. (An **executive order** is a directive issued by the governor to an administrative agency or executive department.) Historically, Texas governors have used executive orders to create taskforces or advisory groups or simply to express an opinion on a policy issue. Governors have not used executive orders to make policy.[15] In contrast, Perry has used executive orders as a tool for achieving his policy goals. In 2005, Perry ordered the Texas Education Agency (TEA) to change the state reporting system for school districts to require that districts spend at least 65 percent of their funds on classroom instruction. Education Commissioner Shirley Neely indicated that the agency would implement the governor's order.[16] The governor also directed the TEA to create a limited merit pay program for teachers using $10 million in federal grant money. The program financially rewarded teachers in the 100 campuses that had the most improvement in student performance.[17] In addition to the orders dealing with education, the governor issued an executive order requiring all Texas girls entering the sixth grade to be vaccinated against the human papillomavirus (HPV), the major cause of a sexually transmitted virus that leads to cervical cancer. Furthermore, Governor Perry issued an executive order to the State Office of Administrative Hearings directing it to speed up the permitting process to allow utility companies to build coal-fired power plants in the state.

Governor Perry's efforts to expand the powers of his office through executive orders have met considerable resistance from the legislature, the courts, and other elected officials. The Texas legislature voted overwhelmingly to reverse the governor's effort to mandate HPV vaccinations and a state district judge ruled that Perry exceeded his constitutional authority by ordering faster consideration of power plant permits. Even the Texas Attorney General Greg Abbott weighed in on the matter, at least unofficially. Although the attorney general did not issue a formal opinion, he did

BREAKING NEWS!

Governor Perry Runs for President

In August 2011, Governor Rick Perry announced that he was going to pursue the Republican nomination to oppose Democratic President Barack Obama in the 2012 election. Had Perry succeeded he would have been the fourth Texas politician to live in the White House in the last 50 years. Democrat Lyndon Johnson was president from 1963 to 1969, Republican George H. W. Bush served from 1989 to 1993, and Republican George W. Bush was president from 2001 to 2009.

Discussion

Why is Texas home to so many presidents? Texas has a large population and that provides a good home base for a presidential race. The state is also a good place to raise money, an essential commodity for serious presidential candidates. Because Texas is a big state, Texas politicians typically have a high national profile. The last three Texas governors—Ann Richards, George W. Bush, and Perry—all became national political figures. Moreover, people in other states assume that service as governor of Texas is good preparation for the presidency.

How well prepared is a Texas governor for the presidency? Isn't the office of governor constitutionally weaker than the office of the presidency? Although the governor has a stronger veto power than the president, most of the other official powers of the office of governor are weaker than those of the president. Because of the plural executive, the governor is especially weak in the area of administration. Nonetheless, a governor who has the political skills to achieve his or her policy goal in Texas likely has the ability to navigate Washington politics as well.

Does Texas benefit from having its governor in the presidential election spotlight? Yes and no. Presidential candidates from Texas, especially governors, typically highlight the positive aspects of the state. Governor Perry, for example, noted that Texas created more jobs than any other state during his time as governor. In contrast, Perry's critics were quick to point out that Texas leads the nation in the percentage of residents without health insurance, has a low high-school graduation rate, and a relatively high rate of poverty.

Would Perry have been more successful had he been governor of a state other than Texas? Probably not. Perry's problem wasn't Texas, it was Perry. He started fast, rising to the top of the opinion polls, but then stumbled badly after a series of poor debate performances in which he sometimes appeared uninformed and confused.

indicate to members of the legislature that the governor cannot authorize an agency to do something with an executive order that the agency does not have authority to do and that, in any event, the agency is not obligated to carry out the executive order. In other words, executive orders are advisory opinions without legal weight.[18]

Measuring Gubernatorial Powers

Observers have long held that the constitutional/legal powers of the governor of Texas are among the weakest in the nation. Political scientist Thad Beyle has created an index to measure the official powers of state governors based on the following factors: the number of separately elected officials in the state, the number of years the governor serves and whether the governor can be reelected, the governor's powers of appointment, the governor's power over the state budget, the extent of the governor's veto power, and the governor's authority to reorganize the bureaucracy. Professor Beyle gives the governor of Texas a score of 3.2 on a 5-point scale, placing the powers of the Texas governor in the bottom one-third among the 50 states. The average score is 3.5. The Texas governor scores well on the length of term and opportunity for reelection, the veto, and the governor's power to reorganize the bureaucracy. However, the Texas chief executive scores low on the other measures.

Formal, official powers are an incomplete measure of a governor's authority. Beyle augments his index of official powers with an index measuring each governor's personal power. This index includes the size of the governor's margin of victory in the last election, whether the governor has previously served in lower office and is on an upward career track, whether the governor is early or late in a term, whether the governor can run for reelection, and the governor's standing in public opinion polls. For example, a newly elected governor who won office by a large margin and is perceived as a rising political star is in a better position to be influential than is an unpopular governor nearing the end of a term who is perceived as heading toward retirement. Beyle gives Governor Perry a score of 3.8 of a possible 5. The average score for governors nationwide is 3.9.[19]

Governor Bush's experience in dealing with the legislature illustrates the governor's ability to use unofficial, informal powers to achieve policy influence. In 1995, when Bush first took office, he targeted four policy areas: public education, juvenile justice, welfare, and tort reform. The legislature enacted major reforms in each of these areas. With the exception of welfare policy, the legislature adopted policies that closely reflected the governor's policy preferences.

Governor Bush succeeded because he set limited goals for himself and communicated regularly with legislators. Bush targeted policy areas already high on the official policy agenda because of media attention, the efforts of interest groups, and the recent election campaign. He staked out policy positions on the issues that already enjoyed a good deal of support in the legislature and were popular with the electorate. Bush and his staff communicated directly with individual members of the Texas House and Senate, and the governor spoke regularly with Speaker of the House Pete Laney and Lieutenant Governor Bob Bullock, both of whom were Democrats.

In contrast, Governor Perry is apparently indifferent to his relationship with members of the legislature, even fellow Republicans. In 2011, for example, Perry vetoed SB 1035, a bill that would have allowed counties to require motor vehicle title service companies to operate by permit only. The measure would also have created a state licensing requirement to be administered by the Texas Department of Motor Vehicles (TxDMV). The purpose of the bill was to crack down on title service companies that engage in fraudulent activities and, when caught, set up business in another county and continue their criminal enterprise. Governor Perry vetoed the bill, he said, because the permitting and licensing requirements would be too burdensome for title service companies. The bill's author, State Senator Tommy Williams, a Republican from the Woodlands, responded angrily to the governor's action:

> I am baffled by Governor Perry's unexpected veto of a bill with no opposition. Not a single person testified in opposition or registered concerns during extensive committee hearings. The bill was supported by prosecutors and county tax assessors.[20]

Eminent domain
The authority to take private property for public use upon just compensation.

By and large, Perry has ignored the legislative process until bills have reached his desk. Consequently, the governor had little influence on the details of legislation. Furthermore, Perry's numerous vetoes have angered legislators and other officials who were blindsided by the governor's opposition. In 2007, for example, the legislature passed a politically popular measure dealing with **eminent domain,** which is the authority of the government to take private property for public use. The bill, which passed the House 143-0 and the Senate 29-1, would have limited a city's ability to use eminent domain to take private property for purposes of economic development. Perry surprised almost everyone by vetoing the bill, declaring it would have exposed cities to the possibility of lawsuits. In 2009, legislators bypassed the governor on the eminent domain issue by drafting it in the form of a constitutional amendment, which does not require the governor's approval. They also considered a constitutional amendment that would have empowered the legislature to call itself into special session to consider overriding the governor's vetoes. The proposal easily passed the House and would probably have passed the Senate had it come to a vote in the waning days of the session.[21]

Rainy Day Fund
A state savings account funded by a portion of oil and gas production revenues.

In 2011, however, Governor Perry was able to achieve most of his legislative goals by skillfully using the powers of his office and by making alliances with grassroots conservative Republican groups, including the Tea Party, that pressured legislators to support the governor's policy initiatives. In face of a record setting $27 billion budget deficit, for example, Perry called on the legislature to balance the state budget without raising taxes or spending money from the **Rainy Day Fund,** a state savings account funded by a portion of oil and gas production revenues. Although the governor eventually agreed to use some money from the Rainy Day Fund to cover a shortfall in the current budget, Perry achieved his goal of signing an appropriations bill for 2011-2013 that included no additional tax revenue and did not use funds from the Rainy Day Fund. The issues Perry identified as priorities, by designating them as legislative emergencies, included a crackdown on sanctuary cities, an abortion sonogram requirement, voter ID, and a resolution calling for a balanced budget amendment to the U.S. Constitution. Each of these items was important to one or another important grassroots Republican group—either Tea Party organizations, conservative Christian groups, or small-government conservative organizations. The sanctuary-cities measure was the only one of Perry's legislative priorities that did not pass.

 WHAT DO YOU THINK?

Governor Perry's critics charge that he chose his 2011 legislative priorities with an eye toward advancing his own presidential ambitions rather than in an effort to make Texas a better place to live. Do you agree? Why or why not?

The Governor of Texas and the Policymaking Process

Theodore Roosevelt once said that the presidency was a "bully pulpit." By that phrase, he meant that the office provided its occupants with an excellent platform for making their views widely known. In today's age of modern communications, the phrase "big microphone" might be a more appropriate metaphor. No figure in American politics is better positioned than the president to call public attention to an issue and offer policy proposals to address it.

Similar to the president, the governor is well positioned to influence the official policy agenda. Texas governors are required by the state constitution to make recommendations to the legislature and are empowered to call the legislature into special session for the sole purpose of considering gubernatorial proposals. The governor is the most visible public official in the state, and today's mass media provide the governor with ample opportunity to get messages across to the people.

The governor's powers to affect policy formulation, policy adoption, and policy legitimation are considerable as well. The governor presents a budget to the legislature and may offer policy initiatives on any subject. As the legislature debates policy proposals, the governor can be an effective lobbyist. The governor's veto power, especially the line-item veto for appropriation measures, puts the governor in a powerful position to bargain on behalf of his or her program. At the very least, the veto virtually ensures that the governor can defeat legislation he or she opposes. Governors have the visibility to sell the merits of a policy to the public after it has been adopted.

The governor is weakest in the areas of policy implementation and evaluation. In Texas, public policies are implemented by departments headed by elected executives or appointed boards, all of which are largely independent of direct gubernatorial control. Although the state constitution calls the governor the state's "chief executive," it offers the governor little power to fulfill that role. Furthermore, the governor has no formal mechanism for policy evaluation. Instead, the governor must rely on policy analyses conducted by others, including legislative committees, the LBB, the comptroller, the Sunset Advisory Commission, and the press. Nonetheless, the governor has the visibility effectively to promote policy change.

Although scholars have frequently described the office of governor of Texas as politically weak, the governor has sufficient power to play an important policymaking role. Governors who set realistic policy goals can often achieve them if they are willing to use the resources at their disposal. Governor Bush demonstrated that a politically skillful governor could have influence on at least a range of policy issues. The governor lacks the official powers to coordinate policy implementation effectively, but he or she has ample tools to be a successful leader in agenda setting, policy formulation, policy adoption, and policy legitimation.

THE EXECUTIVE BUREAUCRACY

The executive bureaucracy of Texas government includes more than 150 boards, agencies, offices, departments, committees, councils, and commissions. Some parts of the bureaucracy, such as the Office of the Attorney General and the Railroad Commission, are constitutionally established. The legislature and the governor have created the rest of the state bureaucracy through the legislative process. State government employs 365,700 people.[22]

The executive bureaucracy in Texas is decentralized. In other words, no one official is in charge of the entire structure. Agencies directed by elected executives or elected boards are virtually independent of direction by the governor or other state officials. They respond to the voters, not other officials. Agencies directed by appointed boards operate with a good deal of autonomy as well.

Bureaucratic fragmentation in Texas is a legacy of Jacksonian democracy and the post-Reconstruction distrust of central authority. **Jacksonian democracy** is the view (associated with President Andrew Jackson) that the right to vote should be extended to all adult male citizens and that all government offices of any importance should be filled by election. The influence of Jacksonian democracy in the South led to the creation of the plural executive, in which state executive power was divided among several elected executive branch officials. The framers of the Texas Constitution distrusted central control of government because of their experience with it during Reconstruction. Therefore, they created a decentralized executive branch to guard against the excessive concentration of power in any one person or department.

Jacksonian democracy
The philosophy (associated with President Andrew Jackson) that suggested the right to vote should be extended to all adult male citizens and that all government offices of any importance should be filled by election.

Elected Executives

In addition to the governor, voters elect five state executive officials: the lieutenant governor, attorney general, comptroller of public accounts, commissioner of agriculture, and commissioner of the General Land Office. These officials are elected simultaneously with the governor to serve four-year terms. States differ in how many executive positions they fill by election. Three states (Tennessee, Maine, and New Hampshire) elect only a governor. Most states also elect an attorney general, a lieutenant governor, and a treasurer. Only about one-fourth of the states elect agriculture commissioners or comptrollers, and only one-tenth elect land commissioners.[23] North Dakota, with a total of 11, leads the nation in elected executive officials.[24]

Lieutenant Governor The lieutenant governor is first in the line of succession to the governor's office, should the governor die, resign, or be removed from office. When Governor George W. Bush resigned to become president in 2001, Lieutenant Governor Perry moved up to the office of governor. The lieutenant governor also becomes temporary governor whenever the governor is absent from the state. In practice, the foremost responsibilities of the office lie in the Texas Senate, where the lieutenant governor presides, votes in case of a tie, appoints members of standing and conference committees, helps determine the order of business on the floor, and enforces Senate rules. In addition, the lieutenant governor is a member of several boards and councils, including the LBB and the Legislative Redistricting Board. The **Legislative Redistricting Board (LRB),** an agency composed of the speaker, lieutenant governor, comptroller, land commissioner, and attorney general, is responsible for redrawing the boundaries of Texas House and Texas Senate seats when the legislature is unable to agree on a redistricting plan. These responsibilities make the lieutenant governor one of the most visible and important figures in state government. When the legislature is in town, the lieutenant governor is arguably the most powerful official in the state, more powerful even than the governor.

Legislative Redistricting Board (LRB)
An agency composed of the speaker, lieutenant governor, comptroller, land commissioner, and attorney general that draws the boundaries of Texas House and Senate seats when the legislature is unable to agree on a redistricting plan.

 WHAT DO YOU THINK?

Who is more powerful, the governor or lieutenant governor?

Attorney General Sometimes candidates for attorney general broadcast political advertisements touting their law-and-order credentials and their determination to get tough on crime. Although these kinds of campaign pitches may be politically effective, they are factually misleading. Other than representing Texas in lawsuits challenging the constitutionality of state criminal laws, the attorney general has relatively little to do with fighting crime. That job is primarily the responsibility of city and county law enforcement agencies and county district attorneys.

The attorney general is the state's lawyer, representing state government and its various components in court. In recent years, the attorney general's office has defended the state in federal court against lawsuits over bilingual education, prison overcrowding, the death penalty, and congressional redistricting. The attorney general has broad authority to initiate legal action on behalf of the state. In the late 1990s, for example, Texas Attorney General Dan Morales filed a lawsuit against the tobacco industry to recover the cost of smoking-related illnesses covered by the Medicaid program. Before the case could go to trial, the tobacco industry and the attorney general agreed on a $17.3 billion settlement to be paid out over the next 25 years. The industry also agreed to remove all tobacco billboards in Texas, as well as tobacco advertising on buses, bus stops, taxis, and taxi stands.[25] More recently, Attorney General Greg Abbott has initiated lawsuits on behalf of the state against the federal government over EPA enforcement of the Clean Air Act and federal implementation of healthcare reform. Although suing the federal government gets most of the media attention, the single biggest responsibility of the office of Texas attorney general, at least as measured by staff and budget resources, is collecting child support payments. In 2009, Texas distributed $2.7 billion in child support, more than any other state.[26]

Attorney general's opinion A written interpretation of existing law.

The attorney general gives legal advice to state and local officials and agencies in the form of opinions. An **attorney general's opinion** is a written interpretation of existing law. The attorney general issues opinions in response to a written request from certain state officials who are authorized by law to ask for an opinion. In 2007, for example, Attorney General Greg Abbott responded to a request from State Senator Jane Nelson (R., Lewisville) by issuing an opinion holding that cities can legally pass ordinances prohibiting registered sex offenders from living near schools, parks, or other locations where children typically congregate. State law requires sex offenders to register with authorities but it does not limit where they can live.[27] An attorney general's opinion is not binding on the court system, but in the absence of a court ruling it stands as the highest existing interpretation of law or the Texas Constitution.

Comptroller of Public Accounts The comptroller is the state's chief tax administrator and accountant. The comptroller monitors compliance with state tax laws and collects taxes on behalf of the state. Texans who operate retail businesses work closely with the comptroller's office to collect the state sales tax from their customers and

Attorney General Abbott issued an opinion holding that cities can legally pass ordinances prohibiting registered sex offenders from living near schools, parks, or other locations where children typically congregate.

remit tax receipts to the state. If a retailer fails to pass along sales tax receipts to the state, the comptroller has the power to shut it down and sell off its assets to pay back taxes.

The comptroller is also the state's banker, receiving funds, assuming responsibility for their safekeeping, and paying the state's bills. When tax revenues flow in more rapidly than the state expends funds, the comptroller deposits the money in interest-bearing accounts to generate additional revenue for the state. When the rate of revenue collection lags behind the rate of expenditure, the comptroller borrows money on a short-term basis to ensure that the state will have enough cash on hand to pay its bills.

The comptroller's most publicized task involves the state budget. The Texas Constitution requires the comptroller to estimate state revenues for the next biennium at the beginning of each legislative session. The comptroller may update the revenue estimate during a session to take account of revisions in state tax laws and changing economic conditions. The constitution specifies that no appropriation bill may become law without the comptroller's certification that it falls within the revenue estimate unless the legislature votes by a four-fifths margin to adopt an unbalanced budget.

Commissioner of Agriculture The commissioner of agriculture administers all statutes relating to agriculture and enforces the state's weights and measures law. The agency inspects and regulates a variety of items, including seeds, gasoline pumps, meat market scales, flower and plant nurseries, and the use of pesticides. The commissioner of agriculture promotes the sale of Texas agricultural products. The agency also administers the **School Lunch Program,** a federal program that provides free or reduced-cost lunches to children from poor families.

School Lunch Program A federal program that provides free or reduced-cost lunches to children from poor families.

Commissioner of the General Land Office The treaty of annexation that added Texas to the Union in 1845 allowed the Lone Star State to retain its state lands. Although much of that land was eventually sold, the state still owns at least the mineral rights on more than 20 million acres. The land commissioner is responsible for managing the land, leasing it for mineral exploration and production as well as agricultural purposes. In 2010, state lands generated $760 million, almost 1 percent of total state revenue.[28] That money goes into the **Permanent School Fund (PSF),** a fund established in the Texas Constitution as an endowment to finance public elementary and secondary education. The SBOE invests the money in the PSF to generate investment income known as the Available School Fund (ASF), which is distributed annually to Texas school districts on a per-student basis under laws passed by the legislature. The land commissioner also manages the Veterans' Land Program, which provides low-interest loans to the state's military veterans to purchase land, and the Texas Open Beaches Act, which is designed to ensure public access to the state's beaches.

Permanent School Fund (PSF) A fund established in the Texas Constitution as an endowment to finance public elementary and secondary education.

Appointed Executives

One measure of a governor's power over administration is the number of officials he or she can appoint. In Texas, the most important executive officials are elected, leaving only a handful of executive positions to be filled by the governor, subject to a two-thirds Senate confirmation vote. The most significant of these officials is the Texas secretary of state. As such, he or she is the state's chief election officer, responsible for the uniform application, implementation, and interpretation of election laws. On election night, the office of the secretary of state gathers election returns from around the state, compiles them, and releases running vote totals to the press. Later, the office tabulates and releases final, official returns. In addition to its electoral responsibilities, the secretary of state's office serves as a depository of various agreements, reports, and records of state agencies. The governor appoints a number of other agency heads, including the commissioner of education, who heads the Texas Education Agency (TEA), the adjutant general who heads the Texas National Guard, and the commissioner of insurance.

Elected Boards and Commissions

The Railroad Commission and the State Board of Education (SBOE) are executive agencies headed by elected boards.

The Railroad Commission The Texas Railroad Commission was originally established to enforce state laws concerning railroads. Today, the Railroad Commission regulates the Texas oil and natural gas industry, gas utilities, pipeline transporters, the surface mining of coal and uranium, and the liquefied petroleum (L-P) gas industry. Ironically, the Railroad Commission no longer regulates railroads, which are now under the jurisdiction of the Texas Department of Transportation. The Railroad Commission is composed of three members elected for six-year overlapping terms. In practice, most commission members initially assume office through gubernatorial appointment. When a commission member resigns before the end of a six-year term, the governor names a replacement subject to a two-thirds confirmation vote by the Texas Senate. Although appointed railroad commissioners must face the voters at the next general election, their initial appointment gives them a significant advantage in name recognition and fundraising capability.

The Railroad Commission's regulatory policies fall into three broad categories. First, the commission is a conservation agency. To prevent the waste of natural resources, the commission establishes what is called an *allowable* for each oil and gas well in the state. The **allowable** is the maximum permissible rate of production for oil and gas wells in Texas as set by the Railroad Commission. This rate, which is determined by technical engineering and geological considerations, maximizes current production without jeopardizing long-term output. The Railroad Commission also regulates the drilling, storage, and pipeline transmission of oil and gas to protect the environment. The Railroad Commission's new hydraulic fracking regulations add to the agency's environmental regulation responsibilities.

Second, the commission historically has prorated oil production to conform to market demand. Every month, the commission establishes a percentage of allowable that each well may produce. For example, if a well's allowable is 100 barrels a day and the commission prorates production to 80 percent of allowable, the well can pump only 80 barrels a day for that month. From the 1930s to the 1970s, the

Allowable The maximum permissible rate of production for oil and gas wells in Texas as set by the Railroad Commission.

Railroad Commission used this method to limit the supply of oil to an amount sufficient to fill market demand *at the current price*. If a new oilfield came online, the
commission prevented oversupply by reducing the percentage allowable for wells
across Texas. Because Texas oil was such a big proportion of the national and world
oil supply, the commission effectively controlled oil supplies and, consequently, oil
prices worldwide. Since the early 1970s, the worldwide demand for petroleum has
been so great that the Railroad Commission no longer prorates oil production below
the 100 percent allowable.

Finally, the Railroad Commission protects the rights of producers and royalty
owners, particularly smaller operators. In the early years, the commission established rules on well spacing, transportation, and oil production quotas that generally
benefited small producers at the expense of major oil companies.[29] More recently,
however, hostile court decisions and personnel changes have led the commission to
adopt more evenhanded rules.[30]

State Board of Education (SBOE) The SBOE coordinates education activities and
services below the college level. A 15-member elected board heads the agency. Each
member of the board runs for election from a district to serve a four-year term. The
terms of the board members are staggered, with roughly half the members facing the
voters each general-election year. The SBOE oversees the investment of the money
in the Permanent School Fund to generate income for the Available School Fund.
It sets standards for teacher certification and school accreditation. The SBOE also
approves curricula and selects textbooks for use in the state's public schools.

The SBOE, which is divided between social conservatives and political moder-
ates, has become embroiled in controversy over some of its curriculum decisions.
Even though board members are not required to be professional educators or have
subject-matter expertise, they have the authority to determine the content of the
state's textbooks. Consider the 2009 debate over high school science curriculum
standards, particularly the approach teachers should take toward the theory of evolution. Most scientists and science teachers wanted the curriculum to focus exclusively
on the theory of evolution as the basis of modern biological science. In contrast,
social conservatives favored the inclusion of a requirement that students be taught
the "strengths and weaknesses" of scientific theories. Whereas the social conservatives on the board argued that the approach would promote critical thinking,
scientists and advocates for religious freedom asserted that the real purpose of the
"strengths and weaknesses" provision was "an attempt to bring false weaknesses into
the classroom in an attempt to get students to reject evolution."[31] Ultimately, the
SBOE omitted the "strengths and weaknesses" phrase from the science curriculum
standards, instead including a requirement to have teachers scrutinize "all sides" of
scientific theories. Although the final language was a compromise, social conservatives were happier with the outcome than was the state's scientific community.[32]
Similarly, in 2010, the SBOE drew national attention to itself by rewriting the
social studies curriculum to emphasize the role of Christianity in American history,
deemphasize the negative aspects of American history, and portray conservatives in
a positive light.[33]

The Texas Railroad Commission regulates hydraulic fracking in Texas.

Curriculum and textbook battles in the Lone Star State were once thought to have national implications because publishing companies, eager to sell to the big Texas market, would create textbooks to meet Texas curriculum standards and then market them nationwide. Today's technology, however, enables publishers to create a standard text and then tailor it to particular markets. The publisher can market a conservative text in Texas and a liberal text in California. Furthermore, the Texas approach is out of step with the push toward national curriculum standards, which every state but Texas and Alaska have chosen to join. In the future, publishing companies will likely create textbooks to match national curriculum standards and then modify them for the Texas market.[34]

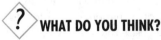 **WHAT DO YOU THINK?**

What approach should high school science classes take to teaching the theory of evolution?

Appointed Commissions

Appointed commissions comprise a substantial part of the executive branch of state government. An unpaid board of 3, 6, 9, or 18 members heads most of the commissions (which may also be called departments, boards, councils, offices, systems, or authorities). The governor appoints board members with two-thirds Senate approval to serve fixed, overlapping terms of six years. Boards meet periodically to set policy. An executive director, who is either appointed by the governor or hired by the board, depending on the agency, manages the professional staff, which does the agency's day-to-day work. The nine-member board of the Texas Department of Parks and Wildlife, for example, hires an executive director who heads a professional staff that carries out the work of the agency.

Agencies perform such a wide variety of functions that they are a challenge to classify. Nonetheless, it is possible to group many of the agencies by form or function.

Administrative Departments The executive branch of Texas government includes a number of administrative departments, which are responsible for implementing policy and carrying out basic state functions. The Texas Department of Criminal Justice runs the state prison system. The Lottery Commission operates the state lottery. The Texas Department of Transportation is responsible for financing, constructing, and maintaining highways, rail stations, airports, and other facilities of public transportation. Other state administrative departments include Parks and Wildlife, State Health Services, and Public Safety.

College and University Boards Appointed boards of regents oversee each of the state's public colleges and university systems. University boards consist of nine members selected by the governor with Senate concurrence to serve overlapping six-year terms. University regents are considered prestige appointments, eagerly sought by well-to-do alumni and often awarded to the governor's major financial backers during the last election campaign. The members of the board of regents of the University of Texas and the Texas A&M University systems in particular read like a "Who's Who" of major political supporters of recent governors. Since taking office, Governor Perry has accepted nearly $5.8 million in campaign contributions from individuals he has named to be regents of college and university boards.[35] For example, Phil Adams, a businessman from Bryan who serves on the Board of Regents of the Texas A&M University System, has given Perry more than $280,000 in political contributions. Steven Hicks, the chair of an investment company in Austin and a member of the Board of Regents of the University of Texas System, has contributed more than $290,000 to Perry. Similarly, Larry Anders and L. Frederick "Rick" Francis, both appointed by Governor Perry to the Texas Tech University Board of Regents, have contributed more than $380,000 and $240,000 respectively to the governor's political campaigns.[36]

Critics suggest that politically connected boards sometimes make decisions that can lead to the politicization of higher education. The Board of Regents of Texas Tech University System, for example, chose Kent Hance as Chancellor of the Texas Tech System. Hance had no background in higher education, but he was a former congressman, former railroad commissioner, and former unsuccessful Republican candidate for governor. In 2009, Chancellor Hance hired former George W. Bush administration Attorney General Alberto Gonzalez for $100,000 a year to teach a class in the political science department and recruit Latino students. Gonzales, an attorney, had no experience in either field. However, he had had trouble finding a full-time legal position because he resigned from the administration under an ethical cloud. Faculty critics at Texas Tech accused Hance of bestowing a political favor rather than acting in the best interests of the university.[37]

Similarly, Mike McKinney and John Sharp, the last two chancellors of the Texas A&M University System, had more political connections than experience in higher education. McKinney, who was chancellor from 2006 to 2011, was Governor Perry's former chief of staff. Texas A&M University faculty members charged McKinney with playing politics in forcing the resignation of Elsa Moreno, the president of Texas A&M University at College Station, at least in part over a dispute concerning control of the research budget.[38] Critics also accused McKinney of steering millions of dollars in contracts to companies owned and operated by big-money contributors to Governor Perry. John Sharp, McKinney's successor as chancellor, was Perry's roommate when the two were students at Texas A&M. After graduation, Sharp and Perry got involved in politics as Democrats. Although Sharp remained a Democrat, Perry switched parties. Sharp was elected comptroller and Perry won election as commissioner of agriculture. In 2000, the two ran against each other for lieutenant governor. Perry won a close race and the two men's relationship was strained for a while. They have subsequently made peace. Journalist Paul Burka warns against politicizing the university system: "The management structure of Texas A&M is of the politicians, by the politicians, for the politicians. The governor's reach into the A&M system is the sort of thing that can make it impossible for A&M to recruit top faculty and administrators."[39]

Licensing Boards Numerous boards and commissions are responsible for licensing and regulating various professions. Some of these include the Department of Licensing and Regulation, Advisory Board of Athletic Trainers, Board of Chiropractic Examiners, Polygraph Examiners Board, and Funeral Service Commission. State law generally requires that licensing boards include members of the professions they are charged with regulating, as well as lay members. The Funeral Service Commission, for example, includes morticians and cemetery owners.

Regulatory Boards Other state agencies regulate various areas of business and industry. The Public Utility Commission (PUC) regulates telephone and electric utilities. The Texas Department of Insurance (TDI) licenses and regulates insurance companies. The Finance Commission regulates banks and savings and loan institutions. The Texas Alcoholic Beverage Commission regulates the manufacture, transportation, and sale of alcoholic beverages in the state. The Texas Racing Commission oversees horse and dog racing.

State regulatory agencies make **rules,** which are legally binding regulations adopted by a regulatory agency. Whenever the PUC sets telephone rates, for example, it does so through **rulemaking,** a regulatory process used by government agencies to

Rules Legally binding regulations adopted by a regulatory agency.

Rulemaking A regulatory process used by government agencies to enact legally binding regulations.

AROUND THE NATION

California Addresses Global Warming

California has taken the lead in the effort to address **global warming,** the gradual warming of the Earth's atmosphere reportedly caused by the burning of fossil fuels and industrial pollutants. In 2006, the California legislature passed and Governor Arnold Schwarzenegger signed legislation to reduce carbon dioxide emissions by 25 percent by 2020. The measure included incentives for alternative energy production and penalties for companies that failed to meet the standard. The legislation calling for a reduction in carbon dioxide emissions was only the most recent attempt by the state to control harmful emissions. California has adopted legislation requiring automobile manufacturers to reduce automobile tailpipe emissions and to mandate that 20 percent of energy sold in the state come from renewable sources, such as wind and geothermal. The state also requires that homebuilders offer buyers the option to have roofs with tiles that convert sunlight into energy.

California political leaders decided to take action to curb greenhouse gas emissions because the federal government had failed to respond to the problem. California is so big that it produces 2.5 percent of the world's total emissions of carbon dioxide. Among the 50 states, only Texas produces more. The California economy is so large that energy companies, automobile manufacturers, appliance manufacturers, and others cannot afford to ignore the California requirements.[*] Furthermore, California officials hoped that other states would follow California's lead, and some have done just that. Numerous states have adopted energy-efficiency requirements for light bulbs and household appliances. Seven states have also agreed on a regional plan to restrict power plant emissions.[†]

Nonetheless, critics warn that the state is taking a huge gamble that it can cut emissions without wrecking the state's economy. Because of the new regulations, California consumers may well have to pay more for energy than consumers in other states and they may face an energy shortage. The new regulations may also place California companies at a competitive disadvantage against firms based in other states without similar environmental regulations.[‡]

QUESTIONS

1. Are you worried about the impact of global warming in your lifetime?
2. Would you be willing to pay more for energy in order to curb emissions that cause global warming?
3. Do you think states should take the lead on issues such as global warming if the federal government fails to act?

[*]Jad Mouadwad and Jeremy W. Peters, "California Plan to Cut Gases Splits Industry," *New York Times,* September 1, 2006, available at www.nytimes.com.

[†]Justin Blum, "Stepping in Where Uncle Sam Refuses to Tread," *Washington Post National Weekly Edition,* January 30–February 5, 2006, p. 18.

[‡]Felicity Barringer, "In Gamble, California Tries to Curb Greenhouse Gases," *New York Times,* September 15, 2006, available at www.nytimes.com.

Global warming
The gradual warming of the Earth's atmosphere reportedly caused by the burning of fossil fuels and industrial pollutants.

enact legally binding regulations. In Texas, the formal rulemaking process has several steps. When a board or commission considers the adoption of a rule, it must first publish the text of that rule in the *Texas Register.* Interested parties may then comment on the rule. State law requires regulatory agencies to hold public hearings if as many as 25 people request one. After a hearing (if one is held), the board votes to adopt or reject the proposed rule. If the rule is adopted, it goes into effect no sooner than 20 days after the agency files two certified copies with the Texas secretary of state.

The rulemaking process in Texas often involves only a minimal amount of public input. Although some regulatory agency actions, such as the adoption of new telephone rates, receive a great deal of media attention, most rulemaking decisions escape notice of all but those parties most directly involved with the particular agency's action. In practice, most proposed rules generate little comment and public hearings are rare.

Agencies have no inherent constitutional power to make rules. Instead, the legislature delegates authority to agencies to make regulations to implement legislative policy. For example, the legislation that required oil companies to disclose the chemicals used in the hydraulic fracking process authorized the Railroad Commission to adopt regulations to implement that disclosure. If the legislature is unhappy with an agency's actions, it can overturn a rule. It can also enact legislation to restrict or even eliminate the agency's rulemaking authority.

Social Service Agencies The legislature has created a number of agencies to facilitate the receipt of federal funds and promote the interests of particular groups in society. The Governor's Committee on People with Disabilities advises state government on disability issues. Other social service agencies include the Texas Department on Aging and Disability Services, Diabetes Council, Council for Developmental Disabilities, and Cancer Prevention and Research Institute. Social service agencies are headed by board members appointed by the governor pending Senate confirmation to serve fixed terms.

Promotional and Preservation Agencies Several state agencies are charged with either promoting economic development or preserving the state's historical heritage. For example, the Texas Film Commission seeks to attract major motion picture and video production to the state. The Texas Historical Commission works to preserve the state's architectural, archeological, and cultural landmarks.

Privatization

Privatization The process that involves the government contracting with private business to implement government programs.

Not all public services are delivered by state agencies. Texas is a national leader in **privatization,** the process that involves the government contracting with private business to implement government programs. For example, thousands of the state's prison inmates are housed in private correction facilities rather than state prisons. Private agencies manage the state's foster care system and private contractors build and repair many state highways.

Privatization is controversial. The advocates of privatization believe that it saves money because private companies operate more efficiently than government bureaucracies. Furthermore, privatization enables the government to gear up or gear down rapidly because private companies do not have to deal with government personnel policies that make it difficult to hire and fire workers. In contrast, the critics of privatization argue that private companies may cut corners at the expense of public service because they are less interested in serving the public than they are in making a profit. The opponents of privatization also worry that elected officials may award contracts to campaign contributors and political cronies rather than to the companies best qualified to deliver government services.

The state's effort to privatize some aspects of the welfare programs administered by the Texas Health and Human Services Commission (HHSC) has stumbled. In 2003, the Texas legislature decided that the state could save hundreds of millions of dollars by outsourcing most of the customer-service functions of the HHSC. Instead of going to a welfare office to meet in person with a case worker, needy Texans would contact a call center to sign up for Medicaid, the Supplemental Nutrition Assistance Program (which was once called the Food Stamp program), the State Children's Health Insurance Program (SCHIP), and other programs. In theory, privatization would save money by allowing the state to close hundreds of government offices, lay off thousands of state workers, and replace them with four call centers staffed by lower-paid privately employed workers hired by the Texas Access Alliance. In practice, the privatization effort was a disaster. Calls were dropped, applications were lost, technology malfunctioned, and thousands of people who qualified for benefits were turned away. The state canceled the contract in 2007 and began hiring state workers to staff the call centers. Instead of saving money, the privatization effort cost the state more than $30 million to pick up the pieces and fix the problems caused by the failed experiment. Despite the setback, the state has not given up on privatization, instead hiring another private company, Maximus, to handle the overall operation of the call centers.[40]

ADMINISTRATIVE OVERSIGHT

State agencies operate with relatively little oversight from the legislature or the governor. Agencies headed by elected executives or commissions are somewhat isolated from legislative or gubernatorial control. Although the legislature determines their budget and can change the laws under which they operate, they are generally free to set policy with no obligation to coordinate their activities with the governor or other agencies. The ballot box provides some accountability. Because the elected officials who head the agencies must periodically face the voters, they have an incentive to ensure that the agencies they head avoid scandal and at least appear to be well run.

The agencies led by appointed boards and commissions are even more independent than agencies headed by elected executives. The multimember boards that typically head these agencies are composed of laypeople selected on the basis of their political ties to the governor rather than their policy expertise. They meet several times a year for a few hours to set basic policy for the agency. In practice, boards typically defer to the leadership of the professional staff.

Legislative Oversight

In theory, the legislature has ultimate authority over most administrative agencies. It can restructure or eliminate a state agency if it chooses or adopt legislation directing an agency to take or refrain from taking particular actions. In practice, however, the legislature sometimes struggles to exert control because of its brief, infrequent sessions. Consequently, the legislature has adopted a number of procedures to provide ongoing oversight and administrative control, including sunset review, committee oversight, and LBB supervision.

Sunset review is the periodic evaluation of state agencies by the legislature to determine whether they should be reauthorized. More than 150 agencies are subject to sunset review. Each agency undergoes sunset review every 12 years, with 20 to 30 agencies facing review each legislative session. The list of state agencies facing sunset review in 2013 included the Texas Education Agency (TEA), Texas Higher Education Coordinating Board (THECB), the Texas Lottery Commission, and the Texas Board of Pardons and Paroles.[41]

Sunset review The periodic evaluation of state agencies by the legislature to determine whether they should be reauthorized.

The sunset review process involves the agency facing review, the Sunset Advisory Commission, the legislature, and, to a lesser degree, the governor. The Sunset Advisory Commission includes five members of the Texas House, five members of the Texas Senate, and two citizens. The speaker of the House appoints the House members and one citizen representative, whereas the lieutenant governor names the state senators and the other citizen representative.

Both the agency under review and the staff of the Sunset Advisory Commission evaluate the agency's operation and performance. The agency conducts a self-study while the Commission staff prepares an independent evaluation. Commission members review the two documents and hold hearings at which agency officials, interest group spokespersons, and interested parties present testimony. After the hearings are complete, the commission recommends whether the agency should be kept as it is, reformed, or abolished. These steps take place before the legislature meets in regular session.

Once the legislative session convenes, lawmakers consider the Sunset Advisory Commission's recommendations and decide the agency's fate. The key feature of the process is that the legislature must reauthorize each agency under review. The reauthorization legislation then goes to the governor for signature or veto. If the legislature fails to act or the governor vetoes the reauthorization measure, the agency dies unless it is a constitutionally created agency, such as the SBOE or the Railroad Commission. Constitutional agencies are subject to review but not abolition. Since the legislature began the sunset process in 1978, it has eliminated 58 agencies and consolidated 12 others. The Sunset Advisory Commission estimates that its recommendations have saved taxpayers nearly $784 million compared with a cost of $29 million to operate the commission and conduct reviews.[42] In practice, the legislature reauthorizes most state agencies while mandating reforms in their procedures. The legislature has added public representation to governing boards, provided for more public input into agency decision making, imposed conflict-of-interest restrictions on board members, and mandated closer legislative review of agency expenditures. In 2009, for example, the legislature used the sunset review process to reform the Department of Public Safety (DPS). It ordered the modernization of the driver's license and vehicle inspection divisions, setting goals for shorter lines at licensing offices and less hold time at call centers. Furthermore, the legislature responded to complaints about the agency's personnel policies by creating an inspector general to investigate complaints.[43]

In addition to the sunset process, the legislature uses the committee system and the Legislative Budget Board (LBB) to oversee the executive bureaucracy. During legislative sessions, standing committees may evaluate agency operations and hold hearings to investigate agency performance. Interim committees may oversee agency operations between sessions. An **interim committee** is established to study a particular policy issue between legislative sessions. The LBB influences agency operations through its role in budget execution. Between legislative sessions, the LBB may propose moving funds from one budget category to another, pending the governor's approval. In practice, budget execution authority gives the LBB power to act as a board of directors for the state bureaucracy. The LBB sets goals for agencies, reviews whether the goals are met, and fine-tunes the budget between legislative sessions to reward (or punish) agencies based on their support of LBB goals.

Interim committee
A committee established to study a particular policy issue between legislative sessions, such as higher education or public school finance.

Gubernatorial Oversight

The Texas governor's legal/constitutional powers for influencing administrative policymaking are relatively weak. Although the line-item veto (and the threat of its use) can be an effective weapon at times, the governor's powers over administration are otherwise limited. The heads of a number of state agencies are independently elected and thus immune from direct gubernatorial control. The governor appoints

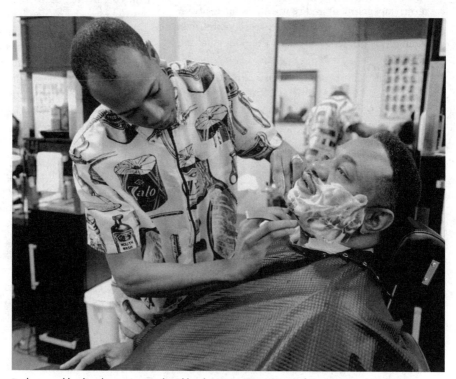

Barbers and barbershops are regulated by the Texas Department of Licensing and Regulation.

the members of most state boards but, because members serve fixed, multiyear terms, a new governor does not usually get to name a majority of the members of any particular agency for several years. Furthermore, board members are not legally obliged to consult with the governor on policy matters or necessarily follow the governor's lead.

Over time, a governor can influence the administrative bureaucracy through the appointment process. A governor can shape an agency's policy perspectives by appointing men and women to agency boards who share a particular point of view. Governor Bush and Governor Perry both tended to name business-oriented conservatives to serve on most boards, especially boards that directly impact business interests. Governor Perry has enjoyed considerable influence over the state bureaucracy because he has been in office long enough to fill every appointed position in the state. His appointees, in turn, have selected agency administrators, sometimes with the direct input of the governor. Consequently, when the legislature proposed major reductions in state programs in 2011 in order to balance the budget, including cuts in education and healthcare, agency administrators offered only muted objections.[44]

WHAT WE HAVE LEARNED

1. What is the job description for the governor of Texas, including formal qualifications, length of term, impeachment and removal, compensation, staff assistance, powers and responsibilities, strength of office, and role in the policymaking process?

The Texas Constitution declares that the governor must be an American citizen, a resident of Texas for five years preceding election, and at least 30 years of age. Every governor has been a white Anglo-Saxon Protestant Christian; and all but two governors have been men. The governor is elected to serve a four-year term without term limits. A governor is subject to impeachment by the Texas House and removal by the Texas Senate. The governor enjoys staff support.

The governor has important powers and responsibilities. The governor can focus legislative attention on policy measures in the State of the State address and by designating certain measures as legislative emergencies. The governor can call special sessions and enjoys the veto power, including the line-item veto for appropriations bills. The governor is responsible for staffing positions on more than 150 state administrative boards and commissions by

appointment subject to a two-thirds confirmation vote by the Texas Senate. The governor has limited removal power. The governor may grant reprieves, commutations, and pardons, but only on recommendation of the Board of Pardons and Paroles. The governor makes appointments to fill judicial vacancies, although appointees must subsequently run for election. The governor can submit a budget to the legislature, but legislators typically ignore it in favor of the budget document prepared by the LBB. The governor's chief budget power is the line-item veto. The governor, along with the speaker and lieutenant governor, plays a role in budget execution. The governor is commander-in-chief of the Texas National Guard and serves as the ceremonial leader of the state. The governor is the unofficial head of his or her political party in the state. Some governors become national political figures. The governor's administrative powers are limited because of the plural executive and because of weak appointive and removal powers. Governor Perry has worked to assert influence over the executive branch of state government through his appointments and executive orders, but his efforts have met considerable resistance from the legislature, the courts, and other executive officials.

Observers have long held that the constitutional/legal powers of the governor of Texas are among the weakest in the nation. Nonetheless, formal, official powers are an incomplete measure of a governor's authority. Governor George W. Bush's experience in dealing with the legislature illustrates the governor's ability to use unofficial, informal powers to achieve policy influence. Bush succeeded in exerting influence because he set limited goals for himself and communicated regularly with legislators. Governor Perry has sometimes stumbled in his dealings with the legislature because he has failed to establish (or perhaps even been indifferent to establishing) positive relationships with members of the legislature. In 2011, however, Perry achieved most of his legislative goals through the skillful use of the powers of his office and his alliances with conservative grassroots Republican groups outside the legislature, including the Tea Party.

The governor is an important participant in the state's policymaking process. Similar to the president, the governor is well positioned to influence the official policy agenda. The governor affects policy formulation by lobbying the legislature. The authority to veto measures, including the line-item veto, enables the governor to affect policy adoption. The governor participates in policy legitimation by using his or her position to explain and defend policies to the public. The governor is weakest in the areas of policy implementation and evaluation. The governor has the visibility to promote policy change.

2. How is the executive branch of Texas government structured?

In addition to the governor, voters elect five state executive officials: the lieutenant governor, attorney general, comptroller of public accounts, commissioner of agriculture, and commissioner of the General Land Office. Although the lieutenant governor becomes governor if that office becomes vacant, his or her most important role is leader of the Texas Senate. The attorney general represents the state in court and issues written interpretations of state law called attorney general's opinions. The comptroller monitors compliance with state tax laws and collects taxes on behalf of the state. The comptroller is also the state's banker, receiving funds, assuming responsibility for their safekeeping, and paying the state's bills. The commissioner of agriculture administers all statutes relating to agriculture and enforces the state's weights and measures law. The land commissioner is responsible for managing the land and enforcing the Open Beaches Act. The governor can appoint a limited number of executive officials, including the Texas secretary of state, who is the state's chief elections official.

The Railroad Commission and the State Board of Education (SBOE) are executive agencies headed by elected boards. The Railroad Commission, which is led by a three-member elected board, regulates the Texas oil and natural gas industry, gas utilities, pipeline transporters, the surface mining of coal and uranium, and the liquefied petroleum (L-P) gas industry. The SBOE, which is a 15-member elected board, oversees the investment of the money in the Permanent School Fund (PSF), sets standards for teacher certification and school accreditation, approves curricula, and selects textbooks for use in the state's public schools.

Appointed commissions comprise a substantial part of the executive branch of state government. An unpaid board of 3, 6, 9, or 18 members appointed by the governor with Senate confirmation heads most of the commissions. Boards meet periodically to set policy, leaving the daily administration of the agency to a professional staff headed by a professional administrator. The appointed commissions include administrative departments such as the Texas Department of Criminal Justice, college and university boards such as the Board of Regents of the University of Texas, licensing boards such as the Board of Chiropractic Examiners, regulatory boards such as the Public Utility Commission (PUC), social service agencies such as the Texas Department on Aging and Disability Services, and promotional and preservation agencies, such as the Texas Film Commission.

Texas is a national leader in privatization, a process that involves the government contracting with private business to implement government programs. The advocates of privatization believe that it saves taxpayers money because private companies operate more efficiently than government bureaucracies. In contrast, the critics of privatization argue that private companies may cut corners at the expense of public service because they are less interested in serving the public than they are in making a profit.

3. How effective are the tools available to the legislature and the governor for overseeing the state's administrative bureaucracy?

State agencies operate with relatively little oversight from the legislature or the governor. Agencies headed by elected officials are accountable to the voters, at least in theory. In practice, most officials below the level of governor are invisible to most voters unless they are involved in some high-profile issue or controversy. Appointed officials are only somewhat accountable to the legislature and governor. The legislature meets too infrequently and too briefly to provide oversight, although it has instituted the sunset review process to assert some control. The governor's legal/constitutional powers for influencing administrative policymaking are relatively weak because of the number of separately elected officials and because the governor has weak removal powers.

KEY TERMS

allowable

appropriations bill

attorney general's opinion

budget execution authority

capital punishment

commutation

eminent domain

executive order

global warming

impeachment

interim committee

Jacksonian democracy

Legislative Budget Board (LBB)

Legislative Redistricting Board (LRB)

line-item veto

pardon

Permanent School Fund (PSF)

plural executive

privatization

Rainy Day Fund

reprieve

rulemaking

rules

School Lunch Program

senatorial courtesy

sunset review

veto

NOTES

1. Clifford Krauss, "Shale Oil Boom in Texas Could Increase U.S. Oil Output," *New York Times*, May 27, 2011, available at www.nytimes.com.
2. Mark Clayton, "Fracking for Natural Gas: EPA Hearings Bring Protests," *Christian Science Monitor*, September 13, 2011, available at www.csmonitor.com.
3. Nicholas Kusnetz, "EPA Proposes New Fracking Emissions Standards," Paltalk News Network, August 23, 2011, available at http://reportergary.com.
4. Steve Kellman and Molly Ramey, "Fracking Regulations Vary Widely from State to State," *Circle of Blue*, August 31, 2010, available at www.circleofblue.org.
5. "TCEQ Goes One Step Forward, Two Steps Back on Air Emissions from Frackin'," Texas Green Report, June 30, 2011, available at http://texasgreenreport.wordpress.com.
6. David M. Hedge, *Governance and the Changing American States* (Boulder, CO: Westview, 1998), p. 93.
7. "The Imperial Governor," *Texas Observer*, April 20, 2007, p. 3.

8. Governor's Appointment Office, available at www .governor.state.tx.us.

9. Clay Robinson, "No Shortage of Blame for TYC's Woes," *Houston Chronicle*, March 5, 2007, available at www.chron .com.

10. "Profile of Appellate and Trial Judges," *Texas Judicial System Annual Report—Fiscal Year 2008*, available at www.courts.state.tx.us.

11. Glen Abney and Thomas P. Lauth, "The Executive Budget in the States: Normative Idea and Empirical Observation," *Policy Studies Journal* 17 (Summer 1989): 829–862.

12. Gary Scharrer, "Perry Wants $500 M for Initiatives in Budget with $15 Billion in Cuts," *Houston Chronicle*, February 8, 2011, available at www.chron.com.

13. "Perry Signs Toyota Rail Legislation," *San Antonio Business Journal*, April 11, 2003, available at www.bizjournals.com/ sanantonio.

14. Mike Ward, "A Quiet Revolution in Governor's Office," *Austin American-Statesman*, January 18, 2005, available at www.statesman.com.

15. Kelly Shannon, "Perry Says He's Not Overstepping His Bounds," *Bryan-College Station Eagle*, February 25, 2007, available at www.theeagle.com.

16. "You're Doing What?" *Fort Worth Star-Telegram*, August 24, 2005, available at www.dfw.com.

17. Janet Elliott, "Gov. Perry Institutes Teacher Merit Pay," *Houston Chronicle*, November 3, 2005, p. A1.

18. *Texas Weekly*, March 19, 2007, available at www .texasweekly.com.

19. Thad Beyle, "Gubernatorial Power: The Institutional Power Ratings of the 50 Governors of the United States, 2007 Updates," available at www.unc.edu~beyle.

20. House Research Organization, Vetoes of Legislation, 82nd Legislature, June 30, 2011, available at www.hro.house .state.tx.us.

21. Christy Hoppe, "Republican Lawmakers Resisting Perry Repeatedly," *Dallas Morning News*, April 8, 2009, available at www.dallasnews.com.

22. *Governing*, "State and Local Sourcebook," available at http://sourcebook.governing.com.

23. Council of State Governments, available at www.csg.org.

24. Alan Ehrenhalt, "A Deep Bench," *Governing*, July 2009, p. 10.

25. *Texas Weekly*, February 2, 1998, p. 6.

26. Theodore Kim, "Texas' Child Support Collection Data Presents Varied Picture," *Dallas Morning News*, August 3, 2010, available at www.dallasnews.com.

27. Opinion #GA-0526, available at www.oag.state.tx.us.

28. Comptroller of Public Accounts, "Texas Net Revenue by Source—Fiscal 2010," available at www.window.state .tx.us.

29. William R. Childs, *The Texas Railroad Commission: Understanding Regulation in America to the Mid-Twentieth Century* (College Station, TX: Texas A&M University Press, 2005).

30. Texas Railroad Commission, available at www.rrc.state .tx.us/.

31. Kevin Fisher, past president of the Science Teachers Association of Texas, quoted in James C. McKinley Jr., "In Texas, a Line in the Curriculum Revives Evolution Debate," *New York Times*, January 22, 2009, available at www.nytimes.com.

32. Laura Heinauer, "State Education Board Approves Science Standards," *Austin American-Statesman*, March 28, 2009, available at www.statesman.com.

33. James C. McKinley Jr., "Texas Conservatives Seek Deeper Stamp on Texts," *New York Times*, March 10, 2010, available at www.nytimes.com.

34. Brian Thevenot, "The Textbook Myth," *Texas Tribune*, March 26, 2010, available at www.texastribune.org.

35. Matt Stiles and Brian Thevenot, "Perry's Appointed Regents Are Big Donors," *Texas Tribune*, August 24, 2010, available at www.texastribune.org.

36. Clay Robison, "Do Political Contributions Equal Choice Appointments?" *San Antonio Express News*, February 15, 2009, available at www.mysanantonio.com.

37. Rick Casey, "Former AG Humiliated Once Again," *Houston Chronicle*, August 2, 2009, pp. B1, B6.

38. Holly K. Hacker, "A&M Power Struggle Raises Questions About Fallout," *Dallas Morning News*, June 22, 2009, available at www.dallasnews.com.

39. Loren Steffy, "Politics Infect A&M Research," *Houston Chronicle*, August 2, 2009, pp. D1, D5.

40. Jonathan Walters, "The Struggle to Streamline," *Governing*, September 2007, pp. 45–48.

41. Sunset Advisory Commission, available at www.sunset .state.tx.us.

42. Sunset Advisory Commission, "Guide to the Sunset Process," December 2009, available at www.sunset.state .tx.us.

43. Victoria Rossi, "Reconstruction," *Texas Observer*, June 26, 2009, p. 16.

44. Jay Root, "Perry Flexed His Muscles to Influence the Session," *New York Times*, July 2, 2011, available at www .nytimes.com.

Chapter 10

Judicial Branch

CHAPTER OUTLINE

WHAT WE WILL LEARN

After studying Chapter 10, students should be able to answer the following questions:

1. What types of legal disputes do Texas courts address?

2. What are the procedures followed by trial and appellate courts in Texas?

3. What are the various courts in Texas, and what types of cases does each court hear?

4. What are the terms of office, method of selection, and qualifications for judges in Texas?

5. How are judges chosen in Texas, and why is judicial selection in the state controversial?

The most important underground natural resource in drought-parched Texas may not be oil or gas but water, and the Texas Supreme Court is poised to decide who controls it. The case before the Court, *Edwards Aquifer Authority v. Day*, pits two landowners, Burrell Day and Joel McDaniel, against a regional groundwater conservation district. Day and McDaniel own a 350-acre ranch in Van Ormy, a small town just south of San Antonio. They want to pump an unlimited amount of groundwater from the Edwards Aquifer to grow crops on their property, but the conservation district granted them a permit for only 14 acre-feet of water.

Day and McDaniel frame their case in terms of private property rights. Since 1904, Texas has allocated groundwater based on the **rule of capture,** the legal principle that each landowner has the right to withdraw an unlimited amount of groundwater from his or her own land by tapping into an underlying aquifer.[1] Day and McDaniel argue that the conservation district, a unit of local government, is depriving them of their property by strictly limiting the amount of water they can pump from the aquifer. It is no different, they say, than the government taking part of their farmland for a public road or a school campus. Day and McDaniel want the court to order the conservation district to compensate them for their lost revenue from not having free access to the water under their land.[2]

Spokespersons for the conservation district argue their position in terms of resource conservation designed to benefit an entire region. If landowners can pump an unlimited amount of underground water from their property, they could deplete the resource, leaving their neighbors' wells dry. The rule of capture would become the "law of the biggest straw." Moreover, the outcome of the Edwards Aquifer case has implications well beyond the San Antonio region. Wealthy oilman Clayton Williams owns land in West Texas where the Ogallala Aquifer is the main source of water. If the Texas Supreme Court rules in favor of the rule of capture, Williams hopes to pump billions of gallons of water from the aquifer and sell it to Midland and other thirsty communities. Critics say that the plan has the potential to make Williams wealthier and West Texas drier.[3]

The controversy over water rights introduces this chapter on the judicial branch of Texas government. The chapter identifies the types of disputes heard in Texas courts, discusses court procedures, and describes the Texas court system. The chapter profiles the state's judges and discusses judicial selection.

Rule of capture
The legal principle that each landowner has the right to withdraw an unlimited amount of groundwater from his or her own land by tapping into an underlying aquifer.

 WHAT DO YOU THINK?

Should landowners have the right to pump as much water as they like from water wells located on their property? Why or why not?

TYPES OF LEGAL DISPUTES

The courts administer justice by settling criminal and civil disputes.

Criminal Cases

A **criminal case** is a legal dispute dealing with an alleged violation of a penal law. A **criminal defendant** is the party charged with a criminal offense, whereas the

Criminal case
A legal dispute dealing with an alleged violation of a penal law.

Criminal defendant The party charged with a criminal offense.

Prosecutor The attorney who tries a criminal case on behalf of the government.

Burden of proof The legal obligation of one party in a lawsuit to prove its position to a court.

Misdemeanor A relatively minor criminal offense, such as a traffic violation.

Felony A serious criminal offense, such as murder, sexual assault, or burglary.

Capital punishment The death penalty.

prosecutor is the attorney who tries a criminal case on behalf of the government. The role of the court in a criminal case is to guide and referee the dispute. Ultimately, a judge or jury rules on the defendant's guilt or innocence and, if the verdict is guilty, assesses punishment.

The **burden of proof** is the legal obligation of one party in a lawsuit to prove its position to a court. The prosecutor has the burden of proof in a criminal case. In other words, the prosecutor must show that the defendant is guilty; the defendant need not demonstrate innocence. Texas law requires that the government prove the defendant's guilt "beyond a reasonable doubt." Unless the evidence clearly points to the defendant's guilt, the law requires that the defendant be found not guilty.

The penal code classifies criminal cases according to their severity. A **misdemeanor** is a relatively minor criminal offense, such as a traffic violation. Texas law classifies misdemeanor offenses as Class A, B, or C. Class A misdemeanors are the most serious, Class C the least serious. Class A misdemeanors can be punishable by a fine not to exceed $3,000 and/or a jail term of a year or less. In contrast, the maximum punishment for a Class C misdemeanor is a fine of $500.

A **felony** is a serious criminal offense, such as murder, sexual assault, or burglary. Texas law divides felony offenses into five categories—capital, and first-, second-, third-, and fourth-degree (state jail) felonies—with fourth-degree felonies being the least serious category of offenses. Convicted felons may be fined heavily and sentenced to as many as 99 years in prison. In Texas and 33 other states, convicted capital murderers may be sentenced to death. The death penalty is known as **capital punishment.**

A relatively minor criminal offense, such as a traffic violation, is called a misdemeanor.

Civil case A legal dispute concerning a private conflict between two or more parties—individuals, corporations, or government agencies.

Plaintiff The party initiating a civil suit.

Civil defendant The responding party to a civil suit.

Property case A civil suit over the ownership of real estate or personal possessions, such as land, jewelry, or an automobile.

Probate case A civil suit dealing with the disposition of the property of a deceased individual.

Domestic-relations case A civil suit based on the law involving the relationship between husband and wife, as well as between parents and children, such as divorce and child custody cases.

Civil Disputes

Courts also settle civil disputes. A **civil case** is a legal dispute concerning a private conflict between two or more parties—individuals, corporations, or government agencies. In this type of legal dispute, the party initiating the lawsuit is called the **plaintiff;** the **civil defendant** is the responding party. The burden of proof in civil cases is on the plaintiff, but it is not as heavy as it is in criminal disputes. With the exception of lawsuits filed to terminate parental rights, the plaintiff is required to prove the case "by a preponderance of the evidence." For the plaintiff's side to win a lawsuit, it need only demonstrate that the weight of evidence in the case is slightly more in its favor. If a judge or jury believes that the evidence is evenly balanced between the plaintiff and the defendant, the defendant prevails because the plaintiff has the burden of proof. A lawsuit to terminate parental rights is a civil action filed by Child Protective Services to ask a court to end a parent-child relationship. The plaintiff has the burden of proof to show by clear and convincing evidence that an individual's parental rights should be terminated because he or she is not a fit parent.

Civil disputes include property, probate, domestic-relations, contract, and tort cases. A **property case** is a civil suit over the ownership of real estate or personal possessions, such as land, jewelry, or an automobile. A **probate case** is a civil suit dealing with the disposition of the property of a deceased individual. A **domestic-relations case** is a civil suit based on the law involving the relationship between husband and wife, as well as between parents and children, such as divorce and child custody cases. A **contract case** is a civil suit dealing with disputes over written or implied legal agreements, such as a suit over a faulty roof repair job. Finally, a **tort case** is a civil suit involving personal injury or damage to property, such as a lawsuit stemming from an automobile accident.

COURT PROCEDURES

The typical image of a court at work is that of a trial with judge, jury, witnesses, and evidence. The parties in the lawsuit, the **litigants,** are represented by counsel engaging in an **adversary proceeding,** which is a legal procedure in which each side presents evidence and arguments to bolster its position while rebutting evidence that might support the other side. Theoretically, the process helps the judge or jury determine the facts in the case.

In practice, most legal disputes are settled not by trials but through a process of negotiation and compromise between the parties involved. In civil cases, litigants usually decide that it is quicker and less costly to settle out of court than to go through the trial process. They agree on a settlement either before the case goes to trial or during the early stages of the trial. Similarly, most criminal cases are resolved through a **plea bargain,** a procedure in which a defendant agrees to plead guilty in

Contract case A civil suit dealing with disputes over written or implied legal agreements, such as a suit over a faulty roof repair job.

Tort case A civil suit involving personal injury or damage to property, such as a lawsuit stemming from an automobile accident.

Litigants The parties in a lawsuit.

Adversary proceeding A legal procedure in which each side presents evidence and arguments to bolster its position while rebutting evidence that might support the other side.

Plea bargain A procedure in which a defendant agrees to plead guilty in order to receive punishment less than the maximum for an offense.

Trial The formal examination of a civil or criminal action in accordance with law before a single judge who has jurisdiction to hear the dispute.

order to receive punishment less than the maximum for an offense. On occasion, defendants may plead guilty to lesser offenses than the crime with which they were originally charged.

Judicial procedures are divided into trials and appeals. A **trial** is the formal examination of a civil or criminal action in accordance with law before a single judge who has jurisdiction to hear the dispute. Trials involve attorneys, witnesses, testimony, evidence, judges, and occasionally juries. In civil cases, the verdict determines which party in the lawsuit prevails. A criminal verdict decides whether the defendant is guilty or not guilty as charged. In general, the outcome of a trial can be appealed to a higher court for review.

Criminal defendants have a constitutional right to trial by jury. The U.S. Supreme Court has held that the U.S. Constitution obligates state governments to offer jury trials to persons charged with felony offenses.[4] The Texas Constitution goes further, granting accused persons the right to trial by jury in *all* cases, misdemeanor and felony, although defendants may waive the right to a jury trial and be tried by a judge alone. Litigants in civil cases have the option of having their case heard by a judge alone or by a jury.

Prospective trial jurors are selected from county voter registration rolls and lists of persons holding Texas driver's licenses and Department of Public Safety (DPS) identification cards. Jurors must be American citizens. Persons who are convicted felons or are under felony indictment are ineligible to serve on a jury. Some groups of people are exempt from jury service if they wish, including full-time students, individuals over 70 years of age, and persons with custody of small children whose absence would leave the children without proper supervision.

An **appeal** is the taking of a case from a lower court to a higher court by the losing party in a lower-court decision. Civil litigants argue that the trial court failed to follow proper procedures or incorrectly applied the law. They hope that an appellate court will reverse or at least temper the decision of the trial court. Parties who lose tort cases, for example, may ask an appellate court to reduce the amount of damages awarded. Criminal defendants who appeal their convictions contend that the trial court committed a **reversible error,** which is a mistake committed by a trial court that is serious enough to warrant a new trial because the mistake could have affected the outcome of the original trial. In contrast, a **harmless error** is a mistake committed by a trial court that is not serious enough to warrant a new trial because it could not have affected the outcome of the original trial. The right to appeal criminal court verdicts extends only to the defendant; the prosecution does not have the right to appeal an acquittal. The constitutional principle that an individual may not be tried a second time by the same unit of government for a single offense if acquitted in the first trial is known as the prohibition against **double jeopardy.**

The procedures of appeals courts differ notably from those of trial courts. In general, trial courts are concerned with questions of fact and the law as it applies

Appeal The taking of a case from a lower court to a higher court by the losing party in a lower-court decision.

Reversible error A mistake committed by a trial court that is serious enough to warrant a new trial because the mistake could have affected the outcome of the original trial.

Harmless error A mistake committed by a trial court that is not serious enough to warrant a new trial because it could not have affected the outcome of the original trial.

to those facts. In contrast, appeals are based on issues of law and procedure. Appellate courts do not retry cases appealed to them. Instead, appeals court justices (juries do not participate in appellate proceedings) make decisions based on the law, the U.S. and Texas constitutions, the written and oral arguments presented by attorneys for the litigants in the lawsuit, and the written record of the lower-court proceedings. Also, appellate court justices usually make decisions collectively in panels of three or more judges rather than singly, as do trial court judges. Appeals court decisions are themselves subject to appeal. Both the prosecution and the defendant have the right to appeal the decisions of appellate courts in criminal cases. However, the constitutional protection against double jeopardy applies only to trial proceedings.

Appeals courts may uphold, reverse, or modify lower-court decisions. An appeals court may direct a trial court to reconsider a case in light of the appellate court's ruling on certain legal issues. If an appeals court overturns a criminal conviction, however, the defendant does not necessarily go free. The district attorney who initially prosecuted the case has the option either to retry the case or to release the defendant. In practice, many defendants are retried, convicted, and sentenced once again. Ignacio Cuevas, for example, was tried three times for capital murder, convicted three times, and sentenced to death three times. Twice the Texas Court of Criminal Appeals overturned Cuevas's conviction, but not a third time. Cuevas was ultimately executed.

THE TEXAS COURT SYSTEM

Double jeopardy The constitutional principle that an individual may not be tried a second time by the same unit of government for a single offense if acquitted in the first trial.

The Texas court system has three levels:

- **Local courts.** Municipal courts, justice of the peace (JP) courts, and county courts hear relatively minor civil cases and misdemeanor criminal disputes.
- **District courts.** State district courts, the general trial courts of the state, hear major civil disputes and try felony criminal cases.
- **Appellate courts.** The Texas Courts of Appeals, Texas Court of Criminal Appeals, and Texas Supreme Court constitute the state's appellate court system.

Local Courts

Municipal, JP, and county courts are local courts operated by cities and county governments.

Municipal Courts The Texas legislature has created municipal courts in every incorporated city in the state. Municipal courts operate in 920 cities, staffed by 1,531 judges.[5] Smaller cities have one municipal court with a single judge; larger cities operate several courtrooms, each with its own judge.

SHOE

City ordinances
Laws enacted by
a municipality's
governing body.

Most municipal court cases involve relatively minor criminal matters. Municipal courts have exclusive jurisdiction over cases involving violations of **city ordinances,** which are laws enacted by the governing body of a municipality. In general, persons convicted of violating city ordinances may be fined no more than $500, except for violators of ordinances relating to litter, fire safety, zoning, public health, and sanitation, who may be fined as much as $2,000. Municipal courts share jurisdiction with JP courts in misdemeanor cases involving violations of Class C misdemeanors within city limits. The maximum fine for a Class C misdemeanor is $500. Municipal courts also have the power to award limited civil monetary penalties in cases involving dangerous dogs.

Traffic cases account for more than 80 percent of the workload of municipal courts. Most municipal court defendants plead guilty and pay a relatively small fine. Almost all of the defendants requesting a trial either before a judge alone or with a jury are found guilty as well. Under state law, municipal court proceedings in all but a handful of the state's largest cities (including Houston, Dallas, Fort Worth, San Antonio, and Austin) are not recorded. Consequently, municipal court defendants in most cities are entitled to a new trial, called trial *de novo*, usually in county court, if they appeal a conviction. In cities whose municipal courts are courts of record, the appeal is done by the record only and is not a trial *de novo*. Nonetheless, less than 1 percent of municipal court defendants found guilty appeal their conviction.[6] Few defendants appeal because the cost of hiring an attorney to handle the appeal usually exceeds the amount of the fine.

Magistrates
Judicial officers.

Municipal court judges serve as **magistrates** (judicial officers) for the state in a range of proceedings involving both misdemeanor and felony offenses. They may issue search and arrest warrants, set bail for criminal defendants, and hold preliminary hearings. Municipal court judges may also conduct driver's license suspension hearings and emergency mental commitment hearings.

Justice of the Peace (JP) Courts The Texas Constitution requires each county to operate at least one JP court and allows larger counties to have as many as 16. In 2011, 819 JP courts operated in counties statewide.[7] JP courts hear both criminal and civil cases, with criminal disputes comprising nearly 90 percent of their caseloads. Most criminal cases heard in JP court involve Class C misdemeanor traffic offenses, with the rest concerning nontraffic Class C misdemeanors, such as game law violations, public intoxication, disorderly conduct, and some thefts. Justice of the peace courts have a civil jurisdiction. Individuals with civil disputes valued at no more than $10,000 can file suit in JP court and present their case to the justice of the peace without aid of an attorney. JP courts also conduct civil proceedings dealing with mortgage foreclosures, property liens, and forcible entry and detainer suits. A **property lien** is a financial claim against property for payment of debt. A **forcible entry and detainer suit** is an effort by a landlord to evict a tenant (usually for failure to pay rent).

Property lien
A financial claim against property for payment of debt.

Forcible entry and detainer suit
An effort by a landlord to evict a tenant (usually for failure to pay rent).

JP court proceedings, similar to most municipal court proceedings, are not recorded. As a result, a person who files an appeal of a JP court decision is entitled to a new trial, generally in county court. In practice, most cases appealed from JP courts are settled by plea bargains or dismissed by county court judges. Appeals of justice court decisions are rare, involving less than 1 percent of the cases disposed by trial in a JP court.[8]

Similar to municipal court judges, justices of the peace are state magistrates. They may issue search and arrest warrants in both misdemeanor and felony cases, set bail for criminal defendants, and conduct preliminary hearings. They also hold driver's license suspension hearings and conduct emergency mental commitment hearings.

County Courts Each of the state's 254 counties has a constitutional county court, so called because it is required by the Texas Constitution. These courts have both criminal and civil jurisdiction. County courts try criminal cases involving violations of Class A and Class B misdemeanors. In practice, criminal cases constitute 77 percent of the cases heard by county courts, with theft, worthless checks, and driving while intoxicated or under the influence of drugs (DWI/DUID) the most common offenses. County courts also try Class C misdemeanor cases appealed from JP or municipal courts.

The civil jurisdiction of the constitutional county courts extends to disputes in which the amount of money at stake is between $200 and $5,000, although these courts may also hear cases involving lesser amounts that are appealed from JP court. The constitutional county courts share their civil jurisdiction with both JP and district courts. An individual bringing a lawsuit for $1,000, for example, can legally file in JP, district, or county court. Lawsuits over debts and personal injury or damage are the most commonly heard civil cases in constitutional county courts.

In addition to their basic civil and criminal jurisdictions, the constitutional county courts fulfill a number of other functions. They probate uncontested wills, appoint guardians for minors, and conduct mental health competency/commitment hearings. The decisions of county courts on mental competency and probate matters may be appealed to district courts, but all other appeals from county court are taken to the courts of appeals.

The Texas legislature has created 233 additional county courts known as statutory county courts (because they are established by statute) and 18 statutory probate courts to supplement the constitutional county courts.[9] These courts, which are sometimes called county courts at law, operate primarily in urban areas where the caseload of the constitutional county court is overwhelming, and the county judge, who presides in the constitutional county court, is busy with the affairs of county government. Some statutory county courts concentrate on civil matters and some handle only criminal cases. The legislature allows many of the statutory county courts to hear civil cases involving as much as $100,000. Appeals from the statutory county courts proceed in the same manner as appeals from constitutional county courts.[10]

District Courts

Texas has 456 district courts.[11] Each court serves a specific geographic area, which, in rural areas, may encompass several counties. In urban counties, the legislature has created multiple courts, many of which specialize in particular areas of the law. Harris County alone has more than 60 district courts, including civil, criminal, family, and juvenile district courts. The 218th District Court, located in Atascosa County, tried *Edwards Aquifer Authority v. Day.*

District courts are the basic trial courts of the state of Texas. They hear all felony cases and have jurisdiction in civil matters involving $200 or more, while

The plaintiff has the burden of proof in a civil trial.

Legal writs Written orders issued by a court directing the performance of an act or prohibiting some act.

Legal briefs Written legal arguments.

Affirm An appeals court upholds the decision of a lower court.

Remand The decision of an appeals court to return a case to a trial for reconsideration.

Majority or **deciding opinion** The official written statement of a court that explains and justifies its ruling and serves as a guideline for lower courts when similar legal issues arise in the future.

Dissenting opinion A written judicial statement that disagrees with the decision of the court's majority.

Concurring opinion A written judicial statement that agrees with the court's ruling but disagrees with the reasoning of the majority.

sharing jurisdiction on smaller sums with JP and county courts. Civil cases comprise 54 percent of the caseload for district courts. Family law disputes, including divorce and child custody cases, are the civil matters most frequently handled by district courts. Personal injury cases, tax cases, and disputes over debts are important as well. The most frequently heard criminal cases are felony drug offenses, thefts, assaults, and burglary.[12] District courts may also issue a number of **legal writs,** which are written orders issued by a court directing the performance of an act or prohibiting some act. Appeals from district court decisions are taken to the courts of appeals, except capital murder cases in which the death penalty is assessed. These cases are appealed directly and automatically to the Texas Court of Criminal Appeals.

Appellate Courts

The courts of appeals, Texas Court of Criminal Appeals, and Texas Supreme Court constitute the state's appellate court system, which considers appeals filed by litigants who lose in lower courts. With the exception of capital murder cases in which the death penalty has been assessed, appellate courts need not hold hearings in every case. After reading **legal briefs,** which are written legal arguments, and reviewing the trial court record, appeals court justices may simply **affirm** (uphold) the lower-court ruling without holding a hearing to consider formal arguments. In practice, appellate courts reject the overwhelming majority of appeals based solely on the legal briefs filed in the case.

When an appeals court decides to accept a case on appeal, the court generally schedules a hearing at which attorneys for the two sides in the dispute present oral arguments and answer questions posed by the justices. Appeals courts do not retry cases. Instead, they review the trial court record and consider legal arguments raised by the attorneys in the case. After hearing oral arguments and studying legal briefs, appeals court justices discuss the case and eventually vote on a decision, with a majority vote of the justices required to decide a case. The court may affirm the lower-court decision, reverse it, modify it, or affirm part of the lower-court ruling while reversing or modifying the rest. Frequently, an appeals court will **remand** (return) a case to the trial court for reconsideration in light of the appeals court decision.

When the court announces its decision, it may issue a **majority** or **deciding opinion,** which is the official written statement of a court that explains and justifies its ruling and serves as a guideline for lower courts when similar legal issues arise in the future. In addition to the court's majority opinion, members of an appellate court may release dissenting or concurring opinions. A **dissenting opinion** is a written judicial statement that disagrees with the decision of the court's majority. It presents the viewpoint of one or more justices who disagree with the court's decision. A **concurring opinion** is a written judicial statement that agrees with the court ruling but disagrees with the reasoning of the majority. Justices who voted in favor of the court's decision for reasons other than those stated in the majority opinion may file concurring opinions.

Courts of Appeals Texas has 14 courts of appeals, each serving a specific geographic area called a court of appeals district. The Court of Appeals for the Fourth District, which meets in San Antonio, heard *Edwards Aquifer v. Day* before it was appealed to the Texas Supreme Court. The number of justices in each court varies from 3 to 13, depending on the workload. Altogether, 80 justices staff the 14 courts of appeals. The justices on each court hear cases in panels of at least three justices, with decisions made by majority vote.

Each of the courts of appeals has jurisdiction on appeals from trial courts located in its district. The courts of appeals hear both civil and criminal appeals, except death penalty appeals, which are considered by the Texas Court of Criminal Appeals. The courts of appeals dealt with more than 11,000 cases in 2010, with criminal cases outnumbering civil cases by a narrow margin. The courts of appeals reversed the decision of the trial court in whole or in part in 8 percent of the cases it heard.[13] The rulings of the courts of appeals may be appealed either to the Texas Court of Criminal Appeals for criminal matters or to the Texas Supreme Court for civil cases.

Texas Court of Criminal Appeals Texas is one of two states (Oklahoma is the other) with two supreme courts—the Texas Supreme Court for civil disputes and the Texas Court of Criminal Appeals for criminal matters. The Texas Court of Criminal Appeals, which meets in Austin, is the court of last resort for all criminal cases in the state. It has nine judges, one presiding judge, and eight additional judges. They sit *en banc* (as a group), with all nine judges hearing a case. As in other appellate courts, the judges of the Texas Court of Criminal Appeals decide cases by majority vote. Decisions of the Texas Court of Criminal Appeals may be appealed to the U.S. Supreme Court when they involve matters of federal law or the U.S. Constitution. However, the Texas Court of Criminal Appeals is the highest court on issues of state criminal law and the state constitution. The U.S. Supreme Court will not accept appeals on state matters unless they involve federal issues.

The Texas Court of Criminal Appeals considers appeals brought from the courts of appeals and death penalty cases appealed directly from district courts. In 2010, the Texas Court of Criminal Appeals disposed of more than 8,200 cases, including 15 death penalty appeals. Although the court is required to review death penalty cases, other appeals are discretionary—the justices have the option to review the lower-court decision or to allow it to stand without review. In 2010, the Texas Court of Criminal Appeals agreed to consider 5 percent of the cases appealed to it. The court reversed the decision of the lower court in 39 percent of the cases it reviewed.[14]

Writ of *habeas corpus* A court order requiring a government official to explain why a person is being held in custody.

The Texas Court of Criminal Appeals is empowered to issue a number of writs. The most important of these is the **writ of *habeas corpus,*** which is a court order requiring a government official to explain why a person is being held in custody. Persons serving sentences in the state's prisons who believe that their rights have been violated may petition the Texas Court of Criminal Appeals for a writ of *habeas corpus* as a means of reopening their case. If the court grants the petition, the state must respond to the prisoner's charges in court. In 2010, the Texas Court of Criminal Appeals granted 170 writs of *habeas corpus* out of 4,149 petitions filed.[15]

Texas Supreme Court The Texas Supreme Court, which sits in Austin, has nine members—one chief justice and eight associate justices—who decide cases *en banc* by majority vote. The Texas Supreme Court is the civil court of highest authority on matters of state law, although losers in cases decided by the Texas Supreme Court may appeal to the U.S. Supreme Court *if* they can demonstrate that an issue under federal law or the U.S. Constitution is involved. The U.S. Supreme Court will not review state court interpretations of state law or the state constitution.

The Texas Supreme Court hears civil matters only. Most of its cases come from the courts of appeals, although appeals may be taken directly to the Texas Supreme Court whenever any state court rules on the validity of a state law or an administrative action under the Texas Constitution. The court is also empowered to issue writs of *mandamus* to compel public officials to fulfill their duties and/or follow the law. A **writ of** *mandamus* is a court order directing a public official to perform a specific act or duty. In 2008, the court acted on a total of 3,757 matters.[16]

The Texas Supreme Court reviews lower-court decisions on a discretionary basis—the justices choose which cases they will consider. In 2008, the Texas Supreme Court granted review to 12 percent of the cases appealed to it. If the court

Writ of mandamus
A court order directing a public official to perform a specific act or duty.

BREAKING NEWS!   **Texas Voters Approve Water Development Bonds**

In November 2011, in the midst of a devastating drought, Texas voters overwhelmingly approved an amendment to the Texas Constitution to authorize the Texas Water Development Board (TWDB) to issue up to $6 billion in bonds to finance water projects around the state. Texas voters had earlier authorized up to $4 billion in bonds.

Discussion

Just what did the voters do in approving this amendment? The TWDB functions as a bank for Texas local governments. Suppose, for example, that Lubbock needs several hundred million dollars to maintain and increase its water supply by drilling additional wells and laying a pipeline to a region with water for sale. Lubbock could borrow the money from the TWDB and repay it over time from locally raised funds. The constitutional amendment approved in 2011 allows the state to borrow money and then authorizes the TWDB to loan that money to local governments for water development projects. Over time, the local governments pay back the money to the TWDB with interest. The interest money is used to cover the cost of borrowing by the state. Money that is paid back can be loaned again.

Does the amendment solve the state's water problems? No, not even close. Unless Texas acts soon to expand its water supply, most Texans will not have adequate water supplies in times of drought in another 30 years. Texas officials have identified more than $50 billion in water projects needed to address the problem. An additional $2 billion in borrowing authority is only a drop in the bucket.*

Not having enough water would be disastrous for the state. Why doesn't the legislature act more aggressively to address the problem than just authorizing a relatively small loan program? The state doesn't have the money to address the problem unless it finds a revenue source. Although some members of the legislature have proposed a small annual tap fee to be charged to every household in the state or a surcharge on bottled water, opponents have labeled the proposals a "water tax." Governor Perry and most members of the legislature have signed a pledge never to raise taxes for any reason.

* Patricia Kilday Hart and Gary Sharrer, "Water Projects for the Future Have Stalled Since '97," *Houston Chronicle*, August 18, 2011, available at www.chron.com.

refuses to grant review, then the lower-court decision stands. The Texas Supreme Court reversed the decision of the lower court in whole or in part in more than 60 percent of the cases it agreed to hear.[17]

In addition to its judicial functions, the Texas Supreme Court plays an important role in administering the judicial branch of state government. It sets the rules of administration and civil procedure for the state court system (as long as those rules do not conflict with state law). It has authority to approve law schools in the state and appoints the Board of Law Examiners, which administers the bar exam to prospective attorneys. The court also has final authority over the involuntary retirement or removal of all judges in the state.

JUDGES

Partisan election
An election contest in which both the names of the candidates and their party affiliations appear on the ballot.

Table 10.1 summarizes the length of term, method of selection, and qualifications for the more than 3,200 judges who staff Texas courts. As the table shows, the term of office for Texas judges ranges from two to six years. Although municipal court judges in some cities serve two-year terms, most trial court judges are elected for four years. Appellate court judges serve six-year terms.

Except for some municipal court judges who are appointed, Texas judges are chosen by **partisan election,** which is an election contest in which both the names of the candidates and their party affiliations appear on the ballot. Elected municipal court judges run citywide, generally in nonpartisan city elections. Justices of the peace are elected from JP precincts. Counties with a population of 18,000 to 30,000 people have two to five JP precincts; larger counties have between four and eight JP precincts. Each JP precinct elects either one or two justices of the peace, depending on the size of the county. County court judges are elected countywide. District court judges and courts of appeals justices run from districts ranging in size from countywide for district courts in metropolitan areas to geographically large, multi-county districts for courts of appeals and district court judges in rural areas. Judges on the Texas Court of Criminal Appeals and the Texas Supreme Court are elected statewide.

The qualifications of judges in Texas depend on the court. The requirements to serve as a municipal court judge vary from city to city, with many municipalities requiring prospective judges to be experienced attorneys. The qualifications of JPs and constitutional county court judges are set in the state constitution. Justices of the peace and constitutional county court judges must be qualified voters, but they need not be attorneys. In fact, most have not even attended law school. Although the Texas Constitution requires that constitutional county court judges "shall be well-informed in the law of the state," it gives no standard for measuring that requirement. Less than 20 percent of the state's county court judges and JPs are lawyers.[18] State law does require, however, that individuals who are elected as judges but who are not attorneys complete a course in legal training before they can serve. The qualifications of statutory county court judges vary, with many courts requiring two to five years of experience as a practicing attorney.

TABLE 10.1   Texas Judges

Court	Length of Term	Method of Selection	Qualifications
Municipal courts	Two or four years, depending on the city	Election or appointment, depending on the city	Set by city government
Justice of the peace (JP) courts	Four years	Partisan election from precincts	Qualified voter
Constitutional county courts	Four years	Partisan election countywide	"Well-informed in the law of the state."
Statutory county courts	Four years	Partisan election countywide	Licensed to practice law. Other qualifications vary.
District courts	Four years	Partisan election countywide or from multicounty districts, with vacancies filled by gubernatorial appointment	Citizen, resident of district for two years, licensed to practice law in Texas, and a practicing attorney or judge for four years
Courts of appeals	Six-year overlapping terms	Partisan election from a court of appeals district, with vacancies filled by gubernatorial appointment	Citizen, 35 years of age, practicing attorney or judge of a court of record for 10 years
Texas Court of Criminal Appeals	Six-year overlapping terms	Partisan election state-wide, with vacancies filled by gubernatorial appointment	Citizen, 35 years of age, practicing attorney or judge of a court of record for 10 years
Texas Supreme Court	Six-year overlapping terms	Partisan election state-wide, with vacancies filled by gubernatorial appointment	Citizen, 35 years of age, practicing attorney or judge of a court of record for 10 years

The Texas Constitution establishes the requirements for judges serving on district and appellate courts. District court judges must be citizens and residents of the district for two years. In addition, they must be licensed to practice law in Texas and have at least four years of experience as a practicing attorney or a judge in a court of record. Appellate court judges are required to be citizens at least 35 years of age and must be practicing lawyers or judges in a court of record for at least ten years.

JUDICIAL SELECTION

Texas and seven other states elect judges on the partisan ballot.[19] Except for municipal court judges, Texas judges are chosen in a fashion that is formally the same as that for electing officials to the legislative and executive branches of government. People who want to become judges run in either the Democratic or the Republican primary, with the primary election winners representing their party on the general election ballot. The candidate with the most votes in November becomes judge.

Research on judicial elections in Texas shows that the outcome of judicial contests depends on political party strength, money, and whether a candidate is involved in a high-profile scandal. Many voters know nothing about judicial candidates other than their party affiliation, so they often back the candidates of their favored party. The Texas Republican Party has consequently held every seat on the Texas Supreme Court and the Texas Court of Criminal Appeals for years as well as many judgeships at the county level. Democrats have won most judicial contests in Travis County (Austin) and in South Texas, and have begun to win again in Dallas County and Harris County after more than a decade of Republican dominance. Democrats prevailed in every judicial contest in Dallas County since 2006. In 2008, Democrats won a majority of judicial races in Harris County. In 2010, however, Republicans returned the favor by sweeping every judicial race in Harris County. Research indicates that well-funded candidates can sometimes overcome a partisan disadvantage, and a high-profile scandal can often cause a judicial candidate to lose despite a partisan advantage. In contrast, incumbency, gender, and race/ethnicity have little effect on the outcome of judicial elections.[20]

Despite the formality of an election system, substantial numbers of the state's district and appellate judges first reach the bench through appointment. The Texas Constitution empowers the governor (with Senate confirmation) to staff newly created courts at the appellate and district levels and fill judicial vacancies on those courts caused by deaths, retirements, or resignations. In 2011, 52 percent of the state's appellate judges and 37 percent of district judges had initially taken office through gubernatorial appointment rather than election.[21] When a vacancy occurs in a county or JP court, the commissioners court of that county fills the vacancy. Although appointed judges must face the voters at the next election, they enjoy the advantage of incumbency.

Is Justice for Sale in Texas?

Critics of the judicial selection system in Texas believe that money plays too prominent a role in the process. Sitting judges and candidates for judicial office raise and spend money in amounts comparable to candidates for other down-ballot statewide and local offices. Successful candidates for the Texas Supreme Court typically raise at least $800,000. Even candidates for district judgeships may raise and spend sums well in excess of $30,000 on their campaigns, especially candidates running in urban counties.

Although Texas law limits campaign expenditures in judicial elections, the limits are ineffective. Candidates for statewide judicial office may spend no more than $2 million for each election. Candidates seeking seats on the courts of appeals or district court judgeships have lower spending limits. In practice, however, the spending limits are too high to have a meaningful impact on judicial elections. Supreme Court candidates, for example, can raise $2 million for the primary election, $2 million more for the primary runoff (if there is one), and another $2 million for the general election. The limits are voluntary. Furthermore, candidates who pledge to adhere to the spending limits are not bound if an opponent exceeds the limits.[22]

Candidates for judicial office in Texas collect campaign contributions from individuals and groups who have a stake in the outcome of cases. From 2000 through the end of the 2008 election season, the nine incumbent members of the Texas Supreme Court collectively raised $14 million in campaign contributions. Chief Justice Wallace B. Jefferson led the way with $2.8 million in contributions. Most of the money came from lawyers, many of whom practice before the court, and business interests with a stake in the outcomes of cases heard by the court.[23]

Ironically, races for seats on the state's other supreme court, the Texas Court of Criminal Appeals, involve less money than many contests for local judicial office. In 2008, no candidate for a seat on the Texas Court of Criminal Appeals raised more than $50,000. In fact, the three winning candidates raised less than $5,000 apiece.[24] Races for the Texas Court of Criminal Appeals are low-budget affairs because the litigants who appear before the court are not as wealthy as the business interests and lawyers whose cases are heard by the Texas Supreme Court. Most criminal defendants have no money and prosecuting attorneys are not especially well paid. Although some criminal defense attorneys earn a good living, they have little incentive to contribute generously to candidates for the Texas Court of Criminal Appeals because, in contrast to trial lawyers, they get paid regardless of whether their clients win or lose.

In 2009, the U.S. Supreme Court weighed in on the issue of campaign contributions and state judicial decision making in a dispute involving a lawsuit between two coal companies in West Virginia. The smaller company, owned by Hugh Caperton, sued the larger company, A. T. Massey Coal Co., charging that the big company unlawfully drove it out of business. A jury agreed and awarded Caperton $50 million. While Massey Coal prepared an appeal, its CEO spent $3 million to persuade voters to replace one of the members of the West Virginia Supreme Court with someone more to his liking. The newly elected justice, Brent Benjamin, then cast the deciding vote in a 3–2 decision in favor of Massey Coal, overturning the $50 million in damages awarded to Caperton. The U.S. Supreme Court held that Benjamin should not have participated in the case because the extraordinary amount of money spent by a litigant on his behalf created an "unconstitutional potential for bias." The U.S. Supreme Court ordered the West Virginia Supreme Court to rehear the case without Justice Benjamin participating in the decision.[25]

The impact of the Caperton case on judicial elections in Texas remains to be seen. Although some proponents of reform are using the case to bolster their argument in favor of changing the way Texas selects judges, the ruling may be too narrow to have any practical impact in the state. The U.S. Supreme Court decided the dispute by the narrowest of margins, 5–4, and the majority opinion was careful to note that the circumstances of the West Virginia case were extreme. The amount of money contributed by the owner of the large coal company exceeded all other contributions to both candidates in the race combined. Furthermore, the money was also given during the period between the jury verdict in the case and the time when the West Virginia Supreme Court heard the appeal. Texas politics features few if any campaign contribution scenarios that are so extreme.[26]

 WHAT DO YOU THINK?

Should judicial candidates and sitting judges be prevented from accepting campaign contributions from potential litigants?

Do Voters Know the Candidates?

Critics believe that many voters are unable to intelligently evaluate the qualifications of judicial candidates. This problem has worsened, they say, as the number of judgeships has increased. In November 2010, for example, the election ballot in Harris County included more than 60 contested judicial races. Many Harris County voters apparently based their voting decision on the one piece of information they knew about the candidates, their party affiliation, because every Republican judicial candidate defeated every Democratic judicial candidate on the ballot. Partisan sweeps for one party or the other have taken place in judicial races in most of the state's large urban counties over the last 20 years.

The election of Steve Mansfield in 1994 to the Texas Court of Criminal Appeals suggests that voters are often uninformed about judicial candidates even in statewide judicial races. Mansfield admitted to having lied in his campaign literature about his place of birth, legal experience, and political background. Nonetheless,

---

GETTING INVOLVED

Volunteer to Become a Court-Appointed Special Advocate

A court-appointed special advocate is a trained volunteer appointed by a juvenile or family court judge to represent the interests of children who appear before the court. Most cases involving an advocate concern children who are removed from their homes because of abuse or neglect. The advocate meets with the child, the child's parents, prospective foster parents, social service caseworkers, and other people involved in the child's life to determine what course of action is in the best interest of the child. The advocate makes recommendations to the court and assists the child in making a transition to a new living situation.

Although the court-appointed special advocacy program is extremely rewarding, it requires a major time commitment and should not be taken lightly.

Volunteers must be at least 21 years old, mature enough to handle difficult situations, and willing to complete a 30-hour training course. They must have their own transportation and be willing to commit to a year or more of volunteer work to see a case through to its resolution.

You can learn more about the Texas child advocacy program at the following website: **www.texascasa.org/**. The website discusses the program and provides contact information for potential volunteers in most of the state's counties. Contact the local organization in your community and inquire about participating in the program. It is your opportunity to play a positive role in the life of a child who needs help.

It's your community—get involved!

the message apparently did not reach many of the voters because they chose the Republican Mansfield over the incumbent Democratic Judge Chuck Campbell. After the election, the press discovered that Mansfield previously had been charged in Massachusetts with the use of marijuana and, in Florida, with the unauthorized practice of law.[27]

Is the Texas Judiciary Representative of the State's Population?

Critics of Texas's system of judicial selection note that it has produced a judiciary that does not reflect the ethnic and racial diversity of the state's population. As Figure 10.1 shows, whites are overrepresented on the Texas bench, whereas Latinos, African Americans, Asian Americans, Native Americans, and people of other ethnicities are underrepresented. More than two-thirds of Texas judges are men and the average age is mid-50s.[28]

Is Partisan Politics Incompatible with Judicial Impartiality?

Can a Republican defendant receive a fair trial from a Democratic judge (and vice versa)? Before going to trial for violating state campaign finance regulations, Republican Congressman Tom DeLay asked that the Travis County district judge assigned to hear the case be removed because the judge was a Democrat who had contributed money to groups that oppose DeLay. After a court granted DeLay's request to change judges, the district attorney responded by challenging the impartiality of the administrative judge appointed to name a new trial judge because the administrative judge had ties to a fundraising group associated with DeLay. When that judge withdrew from the case, the chief justice of the Texas Supreme Court ended the fight over

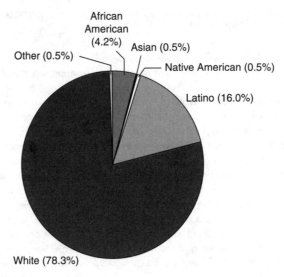

FIGURE 10.1 Profile of Texas Judges.

judges by appointing a Democratic judge from San Antonio to hear the case. The new judge was acceptable to both sides because of his reputation for fairness and his relative dissociation from partisan politics.

Every judge in Texas is either a Republican or a Democrat. If partisan figures, such as Tom DeLay, face trial or if court cases deal with high-profile political issues, such as school finance or abortion, the judges hearing the disputes and deciding the issues will be Democrats or Republicans, elected in the same fashion as executive branch officials or members of the legislature. As long as Texas elects judges on the partisan ballot, at least some people will believe that party politics will determine the outcomes of cases rather than the law and the U.S. and Texas constitutions.

Reforming the Judicial Selection Process

Reformers offer a number of options for changing the state's method for choosing judges. Some reformers propose that the state adopt the so-called merit selection (or Missouri Plan) system of judicial selection, which originated in the state of Missouri in 1941. **Merit selection (or the Missouri Plan)** is a method for selecting judges that combines gubernatorial appointment with voter approval in a retention election. Twenty-five states use merit selection to fill a significant number of judgeships.[29]

Merit selection (or the Missouri Plan) A method for selecting judges that combines gubernatorial appointment with voter approval in a retention election.

 WHAT DO YOU THINK?

How important is it that Texas judges reflect the racial and ethnic diversity of the state?

Former Chief Justice John Hill offered the most detailed proposal for implementing merit selection in Texas. Under Hill's plan, the governor, lieutenant governor, speaker of the House, president of the Texas Bar Association, and chairs of the state Democratic and Republican Parties each choose one or more individuals to serve on a 15-member nominating commission. These 15 individuals include nine lawyers and six nonlawyers who serve six-year staggered terms. When an opening occurs on one of the state's appellate or trial courts, the commission draws up a list of three to five qualified persons from which the governor fills the vacancy, subject to a two-thirds confirmation vote by the state Senate. The newly appointed judge faces the voters in a retention (or confirmation) election in the next general election. The ballot reads as follows: "Should Judge _____ be retained in office?" If a majority of voters approves, the judge continues in office for a full term before facing another retention election. Judges failing to win majority support at a retention election lose their seats. Replacements are selected through the initial procedure of nomination by commission and gubernatorial appointment. Merit selection can be used to choose all or part of a state's judges. Hill proposed separate nominating commissions for appellate and trial courts. He would also permit individual counties to opt out of the plan and continue electing local trial judges if they wished. Other proposals would limit merit selection to appellate justices.

The proponents of merit selection believe that it is an ideal compromise between a system of appointing judges and the election method. Although the governor is able to select the state's judges under merit selection, the bipartisan nominating commission limits the governor's choices to qualified individuals rather than political cronies. Retention (or confirmation) elections allow voters to participate in the process while removing judicial selection from party politics.

Not all Texans favor merit selection, however. Critics dispute the notion that merit selection takes the politics out of judicial selection. Political Scientist David M. O'Brien believes that all methods of choosing judges are political. The difference between election and appointment is that electoral politics are out in the open. In contrast, he says, the selection of appointed judges can be influenced by political considerations and cronyism that are hidden from public view.[30]

The critics of merit selection argue that the system fails to take politics out of the judicial selection process. Interest groups with a stake in judicial decisions jockey to influence the selection of people who serve on the nominating commission. The governor and other officials who make appointments to the nomination commission

In Texas, judges campaign for election just like members of the legislative and executive branches of government.

usually choose their political allies. At least some commission members and the governor may play favorites in the final selection process. Typically, the individuals selected as judges in merit selection states have at least some ties to the governor making the appointment.[31]

Many minority rights advocates prefer the election of district judges from relatively small sub-county districts, perhaps even single-member districts. A **district election** is a method for choosing public officials in which a political subdivision, such as a state or county, is divided into districts, with each district electing one official. The proponents of district elections believe they increase representation for ethnic/racial minorities, make judges more responsive to citizens, and lessen the importance of money in judicial elections. In contrast, opponents of district elections warn that judges chosen from relatively small districts might be partial to litigants from their districts. Furthermore, they point out that many minority judges who now hold office would be defeated under a district system because they live in upper-income neighborhoods that would be unlikely to elect African American or Latino judicial candidates.

District election A method for choosing public officials in which a political subdivision, such as a state or county, is divided into districts and each district elects one official.

WHAT DO YOU THINK?

Should the current system of judicial selection replaced?

Other proposed reforms of the judicial selection process in Texas involve ballot modifications. Some reformers believe that judges should be chosen through **nonpartisan elections,** elections in which candidates run without party labels. Others reformers propose preventing voters from casting a **straight-ticket ballot** for judicial races, which allows voters to select the entire slate of candidates of one party only. The advocates of these ballot reforms argue that they reduce the likelihood of partisan sweeps, such as the Republican sweep in Harris County in 2010. Furthermore, some research indicates that African American and Latino judicial candidates lose not because of their race but because they usually run as Democrats in counties that are leaning Republican.[32] If party labels are removed from the ballot or straight-ticket balloting is made more difficult, minority candidates may have more success. In contrast, other observers point out that these limited reforms do little to lessen the role of money in judicial elections and do nothing to solve the problem of poorly informed voters. In fact, nonpartisan elections reduce the amount of information readily available to voters about the candidates because they remove party labels from the ballot.

Nonpartisan elections Election contests in which the names of the candidates, but not their party affiliations, appear on the ballot.

Straight-ticket ballot Voters selecting the entire slate of candidates of one party only.

Not all Texans oppose the current system of electing judges. Many political leaders, elected officials, both major political parties, and judges (including some of the justices on the state Supreme Court) favor retaining the current system of partisan election of judges. Texans who want to preserve the state's current system of judicial selection argue that election is the democratic way for choosing public officials. Elected judges are more likely to reflect the will of the community than appointed judges. Furthermore, most of the criticisms made against the election of judges could also be made against the election of legislators and executive branch officials. The best way to improve the judicial election process (and the election process in general) is better voter education.

Judicial Retirement and Removal

Judges leave the bench for a variety of reasons. Some die, some are defeated for re-election, and some retire. State law requires district and appellate judges to retire at age 75. However, judges who reach retirement age before the end of a term can finish that term before retiring. In addition, judges can qualify for an increased pension if they retire before reaching age 70.

Judges may be disciplined and removed from office for incompetence or unethical conduct. The Texas Constitution empowers the Commission on Judicial Conduct, a body composed of judges, lawyers, and laypersons, to investigate complaints against judges and recommend discipline. The commission may take any of the following disciplinary actions:

- An admonition is the least serious sanction the commission can impose. It consists of a letter to a judge suggesting that a given action was inappropriate or that another action might have been better. Admonitions may be either private or public.
- A warning is stronger than an admonition. It may be issued privately or publicly.
- A reprimand is more serious than either an admonition or a warning. The Commission on Judicial Conduct issues a reprimand, either publicly or privately, when it believes a judge has committed serious misconduct.
- Recommendation to remove from office is the strongest action the commission may take. When this happens, the chief justice of the Texas Supreme Court selects a seven-judge panel chosen by lot from justices sitting on the various courts of appeals. The panel reviews the report and makes a recommendation to the Supreme Court, which may then remove the offending judge from office.

Address from office A procedure for removing judicial officials that is initiated by the governor and requires a two-thirds vote by the legislature.

In addition to removal by the Supreme Court, Texas judges may be removed through the impeachment process or by a procedure known as address from office. Judges may be impeached by majority vote in the Texas House and removed by a two-thirds vote of the Senate. **Address from office** is a procedure for removing judicial officials that is initiated by the governor and requires a two-thirds vote by the legislature. Neither impeachment nor address from office is used with any frequency. Judges in trouble usually choose to resign rather than undergo the public humiliation of removal.

Problem-solving court A judicial body that attempts to change the future behavior of litigants and promote the welfare of the community.

Visiting Judges

Retirement or election defeat does not necessarily spell the end of a Texas judge's career on the bench. Many judges who have retired or been defeated for reelection continue working as visiting judges, the judicial equivalent of temporary workers.

AROUND THE NATION

Drug Courts in Florida

Over the last decade, states around the nation have been creating a new type of court called a problem-solving court to deal with criminal offenses such as drug use and possession, prostitution, shoplifting, and domestic violence. In contrast to a traditional court, which focuses on facts and legal issues, a **problem-solving court** is a judicial body that attempts to change the future behavior of litigants and promote the welfare of the community. The goal of a problem-solving court is not just to punish offenders but also to prevent future harm.*

The oldest problem-solving court in the nation is the drug court of Dade County (Miami), Florida. The Florida legislature created the drug court in 1989 because of the ineffectiveness of traditional judicial approaches to drug crime. The legislature hoped that the drug court would achieve better results for victims, defendants, and the community than traditional courts had achieved. The drug court sentences addicted defendants to long-term drug treatment instead of prison. The judge monitors the defendant's drug treatment and responds to progress or failure with a system of rewards or punishments, including short-term jail sentences. If a defendant completes treatment successfully, the judge reduces the charges or even dismisses the case altogether.

Research shows that drug court reduce **recidivism,** which is the tendency of offenders released from prison to commit additional crimes and be returned behind bars. Defendants who go through drug court are less likely to be rearrested than are defendants whose cases are heard by a traditional court. Drug court defendants are also more likely to complete treatment than are defendants who enter drug rehabilitation voluntarily.†

Drug courts are now in use in every state.‡ In 2001, the Texas legislature passed and the governor signed a measure requiring counties of more than 550,000 people to set up drug courts and meet minimum enrollment figures in treatment programs. Texas officials hope not only to reduce drug offenses but also to save the state money because it is less expensive to sentence drug defendants to drug rehabilitation than it is to send them to prison.§

QUESTIONS

1. Are drug courts soft on crime?
2. Would you favor the use of a problem-solving court for other sorts of crimes, such as robbery and assault? Why or why not?
3. Are you for or against using drug courts in Texas? Why?

---

*Jeffrey A. Butts, "Introduction: Problem-Solving Courts," *Law & Policy* 23 (April 2001): 121–124.

†Greg Berman and John Feinblatt, "Problem-Solving Courts: A Brief Primer," *Law & Policy* 23 (April 2001): 125–132.

‡Erik Eckholm, "Courts Give Some Addicts Chance to Straighten Out," *New York Times*, October 15, 2008, available at www.nytimes.com.

§Pam Wagner, "Drug Courts on Trial," *Fiscal Notes*, June 2002, pp. 8–9.

Recidivism The tendency of offenders released from prison to commit additional crimes and be returned behind bars.

Visiting judges are especially in demand in the state's rapidly growing urban areas where the number of district courts has not increased fast enough to keep pace with growing caseloads.[33]

The visiting judge system is controversial. The defenders of the practice declare that temporary judges are needed to keep up with crowded court dockets. However, unless the legislature is willing to create dozens of new courts with their own full-time judges, the only alternative to visiting judges is a hopelessly overloaded court system. In contrast, critics charge that visiting judges are unaccountable to the voters, especially visiting judges who were defeated for reelection.

WHAT WE HAVE LEARNED

1. What types of legal disputes do Texas courts address?

Courts administer justice by settling criminal and civil disputes. A criminal case is a legal dispute dealing with an alleged violation of a penal law. Criminal cases are divided into felonies and misdemeanors. In criminal cases in Texas, the prosecutor must prove the defendant's guilt beyond a reasonable doubt. A civil case is a legal dispute concerning a private conflict between two or more parties—individuals, corporations, or government agencies. Civil cases are classified as property, probate, domestic-relations, contract, and tort cases. In civil cases in Texas, the plaintiff must prove his or her case by a preponderance of the evidence.

2. What are the procedures followed by trial and appellate courts in Texas?

The typical image of a court at work is that of a trial with a judge, jury, witnesses, and evidence. In practice, most legal disputes are resolved by plea bargains (for criminal cases) or settled out of court (for civil cases). Judicial procedures include both trials and appeals. A trial is the formal examination of a civil or criminal action in accordance with law before a single judge who has jurisdiction to hear the dispute. An appeal is the taking of a case from a lower court to a higher court by the losing party in a lower-court decision.

3. What are the various courts in Texas, and what types of cases does each court hear?

The Texas court system has three levels: local courts, district courts, and appellate courts. Municipal courts, justice of the peace (JP) courts, and county courts are local courts with limited jurisdiction. Municipal courts hear cases involving violations of city ordinances and Class C misdemeanors. JP courts also hear Class C misdemeanor cases and serve as small claims courts for civil matters involving $10,000 or less. County

courts, which include constitutional county courts and county courts at law, hear Class A and Class B criminal cases, and civil disputes involving larger amounts of money. District courts try all felony criminal cases and hear larger civil cases. The civil jurisdiction of JP, county, and district courts somewhat overlap. With the exception of capital murder cases in which the death penalty is assessed, all trial court appeals go to one of the courts of appeals. Death penalty cases are appealed directly and automatically to the Texas Court of Criminal Appeals, which also hears all criminal appeals brought from the courts of appeals. Civil cases appealed from the courts of appeals are taken to the Texas Supreme Court.

4. What are the terms of office, method of selection, and qualifications for judges in Texas?

Although some municipal court judges serve two-year terms, most trial court judges have four-year terms. Appellate judges serve six-year terms. Except for some municipal court judges who are appointed, Texas judges are chosen by partisan election. Judicial qualifications vary by court, but all must be attorneys except for justices of the peace, county court judges, and some municipal court judges.

5. How are judges chosen in Texas, and why is judicial selection in the state controversial?

Except for municipal court judges, Texas judges are chosen in a fashion that is formally the same as that for electing officials to the legislative and executive branches of government. The outcome of judicial contests depends on political party strength, money, and whether a candidate is involved in a high-profile scandal. Despite the election system, many district and appellate court judges initially reach the bench through appointment. Critics of the judicial selection system in Texas believe that money plays too prominent a role in the process because campaign contributors to judicial candidates are typically individuals and groups who have a stake in the outcomes of court cases. Critics also believe that many voters are unable to evaluate intelligently the qualifications of judicial candidates. Finally, they note that the state's system of judicial selection has produced a judiciary that does not reflect the ethnic and racial diversity of the state's population. Reformers propose a number of alternative systems of judicial selection, including merit selection or the Missouri Plan, nonpartisan judicial elections, or prohibiting the straight ticket in judicial races. Judges leave the bench for a variety of reasons, including death, election defeat, and retirement. Judges may be disciplined and removed from office for incompetence or unethical conduct. Texas judges may also be removed through the impeachment process or by a procedure known as address from office. Many judges who have retired or been defeated for reelection continue working as visiting judges.

KEY TERMS

address from office

adversary proceeding

affirm

appeal

burden of proof

capital punishment

city ordinances

civil case

civil defendant

concurring opinion

contract case

criminal case

criminal defendant

dissenting opinion

district election

domestic-relations case

double jeopardy

felony

forcible entry and detainer suit

harmless error

legal briefs

legal writs

litigants

magistrates

majority *or* deciding opinion

merit selection (*or* the Missouri Plan)

misdemeanor

nonpartisan elections

partisan election

plaintiff

plea bargain

probate case

problem-solving court

property case

property lien

prosecutor

recidivism

remand

reversible error

rule of capture

straight-ticket ballot

tort case

trial

writ of *habeas corpus*

writ of *mandamus*

NOTES

1. Texas Living Waters Project, "Texas Groundwater and the Rule of Capture," available at www.texaswatermatters.org.
2. Morgan Smith, "Lawsuit Could Determine Future of Groundwater," *Texas Tribune*, April 22, 2010, available at www.texastribune.org.
3. Jeannie Kever, "Who Owns Water?" *Houston Chronicle*, November 14, 2011, pp. A1, A6.
4. *Duncan v. Louisiana*, 391 U.S. 145 (1968).
5. Office of Court Administration, "2011 Texas Judicial System Directory," available at www.courts.state.tx.us.
6. "Activity Report for Municipal Courts," *Annual Report of the Texas Judicial System*, Fiscal Year 2010, available at www.courts.state.tx.us.
7. Office of Court Administration, "2011 Texas Judicial System Directory."
8. "Activity Report for Justice Courts," *Annual Report of the Texas Judicial System*, Fiscal Year 2010.
9. Office of Court Administration, "2011 Texas Judicial System Directory."

10. "Court Structure of Texas," *Annual Report of the Texas Judicial System*, Fiscal Year 2010, available at www.courts.state.tx.us.

11. Office of Court Administration, "2011 Texas Judicial System Directory."

12. "District Courts: Summary Activity by Case Type," *Annual Report of the Texas Judicial System*, Fiscal Year 2010.

13. "Activity for the Fiscal Year Ended August 31, 2010," *Annual Report of the Texas Judicial System*, Fiscal Year 2010.

14. "Court of Criminal Appeals Activity: FY 2010," *Annual Report of the Texas Judicial System*, Fiscal Year 2010.

15. Ibid.

16. "Supreme Court Activity: FY 2004-2008," *Annual Report of the Texas Judicial System*, Fiscal Year 2010.

17. Ibid.

18. "Profile of Appellate and Trial Judges," *Annual Report of the Texas Judicial System*, Fiscal Year 2010.

19. American Judicature Society, "Judicial Selection in the States: Appellate and General Jurisdiction Courts," available at www.ajs.org.

20. Kyle Cheek and Anthony Champagne, *Judicial Politics in Texas: Partisanship, Money, and Politics in State Courts* (New York, NY: Peter Lang, 2005), pp. 79–80.

21. "Profile of Appellate and Trial Judges."

22. Sam Kinch, Jr., *Too Much Money Is Not Enough: Big Money and Political Power in Texas* (Austin, TX: Campaign for People, 2000), p. 14.

23. Randy Lee Loftis and Ryan McNeill, "Drive to Choose Texas Judges on Merit Intensifies," *Dallas Morning News*, March 2, 2009, available at www.dallasnews.com.

24. National Institute on Money in State Politics, available at www.followthemoney.com.

25. *Caperton v. A.T. Massey Coal Co.*, No. 08-22 (2009).

26. Tony Mauro and John Council, "Texas's Campaign Finance Laws Could Mute *Caperton's* Impact," *Texas Lawyer*, June 15, 2009, available at www.law.com/jsp/tx.

27. *Texas Weekly*, December 12, 1994, p. 4.

28. "Profile of Appellate and Trial Judges."

29. American Judicature Society, "Judicial Selection in the States: Appellate and General Jurisdiction Courts."

30. Quoted in Adam Liptak, "Rendering Justice, with One Eye on Re-Election," *New York Times*, May 25, 2008, available at www.nytimes.com.

31. David W. Neubauer and Stephen S. Meinhold, *Judicial Process: Law, Courts, and Politics in the United States*, 4th ed. (Boston, MA: Wadsworth, 2007), pp. 188–189.

32. Delbert A. Taebel, "On the Way to Midland: Race or Partisanship? A Research Note on Comparative Voting in Urban Counties in Judicial Elections," *Texas Journal of Political Studies* 12 (Fall/Winter 1989/90): 5–23.

33. Mark Smith, "Business Good for Visiting Judges," *Houston Chronicle*, September 20, 1998, p. 23A.

Chapter 11

City Government

WHAT WE WILL LEARN

After studying Chapter 11, you should be able to answer the following questions:

1. What is the legal status of city governments in Texas?

2. What are the different forms of city government in Texas?

3. What election systems do Texas cities use?

4. What are the most important policies adopted by Texas cities in terms of budgets, annexation, and land use?

5. How has big-city politics in Texas evolved since the 1950s?

Electoral politics in big-city Texas involves coalition building. Houston, Dallas, San Antonio, El Paso, Austin, Fort Worth, and the state's other large cities are multiethnic and multiracial urban centers with numerous interests competing for political influence. Even though most city elections are officially nonpartisan, political parties often operate just behind the scenes. Consequently, candidates for office in big-city Texas have to assemble a diverse coalition of supporters to be successful.

Consider the dynamics of the 2009 mayoralty campaign in Houston, the state's largest city. The race was wide open because Bill White, the incumbent mayor, was term limited. The leading contenders to succeed him were Annise Parker, the city controller, which is the city's financial auditor, and Gene Locke, a former city attorney. Parker was the better known of the two candidates. She had won six consecutive citywide elections, serving on the city council for six years before serving another six years as controller. She was also an experienced community activist, serving two terms as president of the Houston Gay and Lesbian Political Caucus (GLPC), among other activities.[1] Gene Locke, meanwhile, could be described as a former African American student civil rights activist turned corporate lawyer. During the 1970s he was arrested along with another young man for allegedly inciting a riot at Texas Southern University, but a jury failed to convict him and the charges were dismissed. He subsequently earned a law degree, worked as a congressional staffer, and served as city attorney for former mayor Bob Lanier. After leaving city government, Locke took a job as a partner in a prominent Houston law firm, representing Metro (the transit authority) and the Port of Houston Authority.[2]

The challenge for both Parker and Locke was to consolidate their bases of support and reach out to other segments of the community. White liberal Democrats were Parker's primary base, especially inner-city neighborhood activists, members of women's groups, people in the arts community, and the GLPC. Locke hoped to build a base among African American voters to augment his supporters in the business community who knew him from his work as city attorney and as a partner in a major law firm. The winner of the race would be the candidate most successful at gaining the support of voters who were not part of either candidate's base, especially Hispanic voters and white conservatives.

Houston city politics introduces this chapter on the role of cities in the policy-making process. The chapter examines the legal status of Texas cities and describes their political structures and election systems. It discusses three areas of urban policymaking: budgetary policy, annexation and suburban development, and land-use regulation. Finally, the chapter also examines big-city politics in Texas.

LEGAL STATUS OF TEXAS CITIES

City ordinances
Laws enacted by
a municipality's
governing body.

City governments in Texas have broad authority to provide public services, enact regulations, and levy taxes. Texas cities may provide hospitals, libraries, parks, paved streets, police protection, airports, water and sewer service, health clinics, and fire protection for their residents. They may adopt **city ordinances,** laws enacted by a municipality's governing body to regulate such matters as building construction, land-use practices, and driving habits. Cities fund their operations by levying property taxes, sales taxes, and a variety of other taxes, fees, and service charges.

Nonetheless, cities and other units of local government are subordinate units of government, subject to the constitutions and laws of the United States and the state of Texas. Federal laws take precedence over city ordinances and regulations. Cities are dependent on state constitutions and state laws for their creation, organization, and authority. State law controls such matters as city tax rates and exemptions; wages, hours, benefits, and promotion policies for city employees; and annexation procedures.

The Texas legislature and the governor frequently adopt legislation designed to define and limit the policymaking authority of city government. For example, Texas is one of 40 states that prohibit cities from suing the firearms industry.[3] A number of cities in other states have sued gun manufacturers to hold them accountable for manufacturing guns with inadequate safety features that would prevent unauthorized and unintentional shootings, as well as for negligent distribution and marketing practices that contribute to the illegal gun market. The legislature and the governor have also adopted legislation prohibiting city governments from establishing their own **minimum wage,** which is the lowest hourly wage that an employer can pay covered workers.

Interest groups as well as individual citizens who are unhappy with the decisions of a city government can ask the Texas legislature to intervene. Moreover, the legislature and the governor have grown increasingly willing to override the policy decisions of city governments because of a shift in partisanship. Even though most city elections are officially nonpartisan (party labels are not on the ballot), most officials in the state's major cities are Democrats. For example, Parker and Locke, the two major candidates for Houston mayor in 2009, were both Democrats. In contrast, the Republican Party controls both chambers of the Texas legislature and the governorship. On issues that pit city governments against interests usually aligned with the Republican Party, such as suburban residents and developers, the legislature and the governor more often than not intervene against the city.

Incorporation

State law sets the requirements and procedures under which an unincorporated urban area in Texas can become an **incorporated municipality,** a city under the laws of the state. An **unincorporated area,** territory that is not part of a legal city, must have a population of at least 200 people to form a municipality. It must also be outside the legal jurisdiction of other incorporated municipalities unless it receives permission to incorporate from the established city. The proponents of incorporation begin the process by collecting signatures on an incorporation petition. After they have gathered the required number of names, perhaps as many as 10 percent of the registered voters in the prospective municipality, they present their petition to the county judge. The judge then calls an election in which the area's voters may choose either to incorporate or remain unincorporated. The residents of an incorporated city can follow the same procedure if they wish to disincorporate. The voters

Minimum wage The lowest hourly wage that an employer can pay covered workers.

Incorporated municipality A city under the laws of the state.

Unincorporated area Territory not part of a legal city.

City charter
The basic law of a city that defines its powers, responsibilities, and organization.

General-law city A municipality that is limited to those governmental structures and powers specifically granted by state law.

Dillon's rule The legal principle that a city can exercise only those powers expressly allowed by state law.

Home-rule city A municipality that can take any actions not prohibited by state or federal law or the constitutions of the United States or the state of Texas.

Annexation The authority of a city to increase its geographic size by extending its boundaries to take in adjacent unincorporated areas.

Recall election A procedure allowing voters to remove elected officials from office before the expiration of their terms.

of a newly incorporated municipality must also approve a **city charter,** the basic law of a city that defines its powers, responsibilities, and organization. Changes in a city charter must receive voter approval as well.

General-Law and Home-Rule Cities

Texas cities are classified as either general-law or home-rule cities. A **general-law city** is a municipality that is limited to those governmental structures and powers specifically granted by state law. Municipalities with fewer than 5,000 people must be general-law cities.

General-law cities are bound by **Dillon's rule,** the legal principle that states that a city can exercise only those powers expressly allowed by state law. Dillon's rule is named after Judge J. F. Dillon, a member of the Iowa Supreme Court, who wrote an opinion in 1868 concerning the legal status of cities. Dillon concluded that municipalities owe their origins to and derive their power from the state legislature. Therefore, they are totally dependent on and subservient to the legislature. Courts in Texas and in other states have followed Dillon's rule in defining the authority of general-law cities. If a general-law city wants to offer a service or adopt a structure of government not provided for in state law, it must first obtain specific authorization from the legislature.

In 1913, the Texas legislature proposed and the voters approved an amendment to the state constitution to allow a municipality with 5,000 or more people to become a **home-rule city,** a municipality that can take any actions not prohibited by state or federal law or the constitutions of the United States or the state of Texas. In contrast to general-law cities, home-rule cities are not burdened by the limitations of Dillon's rule. A home-rule city can do anything that qualifies as a "public purpose" that does not violate the Texas Constitution or the laws of the state. Compared with general-law cities, home-rule cities enjoy more freedom in the following areas:

- **Organizational structure:** Home-rule cities can adopt any structure of municipal government they choose, whereas general-law cities are limited to a narrow range of options.
- **Annexation:** Home-rule cities can annex without the approval of the people living in the annexed area. General-law cities, in contrast, cannot annex unless the residents of the targeted area vote to accept annexation. (**Annexation** is the authority of a city to increase its geographic size by extending its boundaries to take in adjacent unincorporated areas.)
- **Ordinance-making authority:** Home-rule cities have broader authority to adopt ordinances than do general-law municipalities.
- **Election processes:** Home-rule cities may include both recall and the initiative process in their charters. More than 90 percent of home-rule cities allow citizens the power of **recall,** a procedure for allowing voters to remove elected officials from office before the expiration of their terms. In addition, 85 percent of home rule cities have the **initiative process,** a procedure available in

Initiative process
A procedure whereby citizens can propose the adoption of a policy measure by gathering a prerequisite number of signatures. Voters must then approve the measure before it can take effect.

some states and cities whereby citizens can propose the adoption of a policy measure by gathering a prerequisite number of signatures. Voters must then approve the measure before it can take effect.[4]

More than 340 Texas cities are home rule, including all of the state's big cities. Only 19 cities larger than 5,000 people have chosen to remain general-law cities. Even if a home-rule city falls below the 5,000-population threshold, it maintains its home-rule status.[5]

The legislature has the power to pass laws limiting home-rule authority. For example, the legislature has established uniform election dates, limiting most local elections to either the second Saturday in May or the Tuesday after the first Monday in November. Although the Texas Constitution prevents the legislature from passing local laws regulating the affairs of individual cities, the legislature gets around the restriction by enacting **population bracket laws,** state laws designed to target particular cities based on their population. Houston and Austin are the most frequent targets of population bracket legislation. For example, the legislature could pass a measure that applied to all Texas cities with a population larger than 2 million. It so happens that only one city meets that criterion—Houston. If the legislature wanted to target Austin, it could adopt a bill aimed at cities with populations between 750,000 and 800,000 in 2010. That description applies only to Austin.

Population bracket laws
State laws designed to target particular cities based on their population.

FORMS OF CITY GOVERNMENT

The mayor-council and council-manager forms of city government are the basic structures of municipal government in Texas.

Mayor-Council Form

Mayor–council form of city government A structure of municipal government in which the voters elect a mayor as the chief executive officer of the city and a council that serves as a legislative body.

The **mayor-council form of city government** is a structure of municipal government in which the voters elect a mayor as the chief executive officer of the city and a council that serves as a legislative body. In the mayor-council form of city government, the mayor and council together make policy for the city. They are responsible for raising and spending city revenue, passing local ordinances, and supervising the city's administrative departments.

Being mayor or serving on city council is a full-time job in big cities using the mayor-council form of government, but not in small towns. In Houston, for example, the mayor runs the city government full-time and earns a salary that exceeds $200,000 a year. Although most members of the Houston city council have other jobs, they, too, spend many hours a week on city business, making more than $50,000 a year. In contrast, mayors and council members in small towns using the mayor-council form of city government usually earn only a small salary for a job that normally takes just a few hours a week.

Cities using the mayor-council form of city government differ in the amount of power the mayor enjoys. Figures 11.1 and 11.2 diagram the strong-mayor and

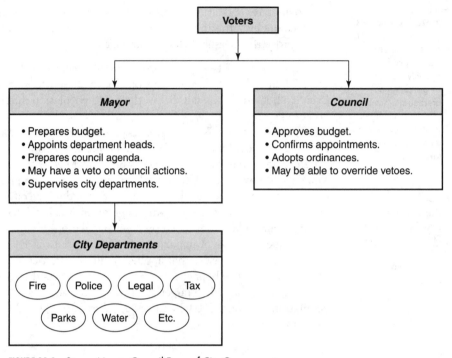

FIGURE 11.1   Strong Mayor–Council Form of City Government.

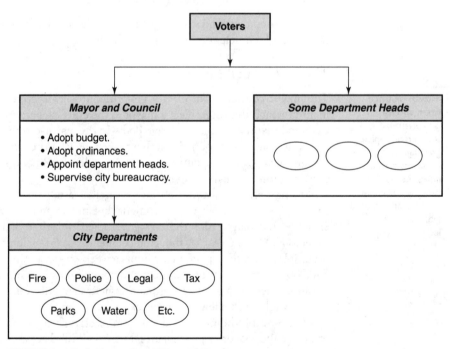

FIGURE 11.2   Weak Mayor–Council Form of City Government.

weak-mayor variations of the mayor-council form of city government. In the strong-mayor variation (Figure 11.1), the mayor is the foremost figure in city government, acting as both a political leader and the city's chief administrative officer. The mayor prepares the budget, enjoys a veto over council actions (with or without possibility of a council override), hires and fires department heads, and essentially runs city government. Although the city council must approve (and thus may reject) many of the mayor's actions, politically skillful mayors can usually win approval of most of their initiatives and appointments. Council members elected from districts will want to stay in the mayor's favor because the mayor oversees the provision of public services to their districts. Furthermore, the mayor and the mayor's financial backers may get involved in council races to elect individuals to council who will be part of the "mayor's team" and to defeat the mayor's opponents on council. Bob Lanier, who was mayor of Houston in the 1990s, lost only three council votes during his six years in office.[6] Former Houston City Council Member Vince Ryan described the strong-mayor system in Houston as "King Kong and the 14 chimps" because of the relative imbalance of power between the mayor and the 14 council members.[7]

The advocates of the strong-mayor variation of the mayor-council form of city government believe that the system provides for efficient city government because it concentrates power and responsibility for policy leadership and policy implementation in the hands of a single elected official, the mayor. The mayor can take the lead in agenda setting, policy formulation, policy adoption, and policy implementation. The voters can then evaluate the mayor on performance. In contrast, the critics of the mayor-council form of city government contend that the strong-mayor variation gives the mayor too much power. They worry that the mayor will build a personal empire and become a political boss. Although the voters elect council members to represent neighborhoods and communities, they have relatively little influence on major policy decisions in the strong-mayor varia-tion. Instead, council members focus on the most mundane details of urban policy implementation, such as abandoned houses, overgrown vacant lots, potholes, and stray dogs.[8]

In contrast to the strong-mayor system, the weak-mayor variation of the mayor-council form of city government (Figure 11.2) fragments political authority by forcing the mayor to share power with the council and other elected officials. These officials may include a tax assessor, treasurer, and even a police chief. The mayor and council together appoint administrative officials, supervise city admin-istration, and adopt the budget. The proponents of the weak-mayor system contend that it prevents the mayor from becoming too powerful by creating a check-and-balance system. Critics of the weak-mayor variation say that it invites corruption and dilutes accountability because it fails to assign policymaking authority to any single official.

The mayor-council system is the traditional form of city government in Amer-ica, and it is still found in most of the nation's larger cities. In Texas, however, Houston is the only large city to use the mayor-council system.[9] The state's other big cities, including Dallas, San Antonio, Fort Worth, Austin, Corpus Christi, and El Paso, have adopted the council-manager form instead.[10]

Council–Manager Form

The **council-manager form of city government** is a structure of municipal government in which the city council/mayor appoints a professional administrator, called a city manager, to act as the municipality's chief executive officer. In this form of city government, the mayor's power is limited to performing ceremonial duties and presiding at council meetings. In fact, in some smaller council-manager cities, voters do not directly choose a mayor at all. Instead, the office may go to the at-large council member receiving the most votes. Alternatively, the council may choose one of its members to serve as mayor. In such cases, the mayor's ability to act as a policy leader depends on personal leadership skills rather than official powers.

The major difference between the mayor-council and council-manager forms of city government concerns the implementation of policy. In both systems, the mayor and council make basic policy decisions. However, in the council-manager form, policy implementation is the responsibility of a professional administrator hired by the city council—a **city manager.** Figure 11.3 diagrams this form of city government.

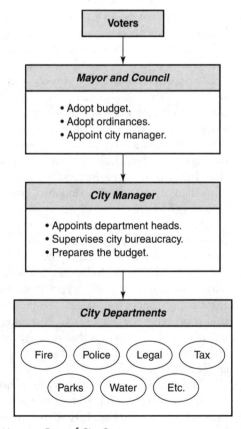

FIGURE 11.3 Council–Manager Form of City Government.

The city manager is the city's chief administrative officer and is generally responsible for hiring and firing department heads, preparing the budget, and overseeing policy implementation. In council-manager cities, the mayor and council members are usually considered part-time officials and are paid accordingly. In Fort Worth, for example, the mayor and council members each receive $75 for every week they attend one or more official meetings. In contrast, the Fort Worth city manager earns $186,513 a year.[11]

The council-manager form of city government has both supporters and detractors. Its advocates believe that it is an efficient system that keeps politics out of administration and administrators out of politics. They argue that a professional city manager can provide more efficient policy administration than a mayor with no administrative experience. Nonetheless, most political scientists believe that city managers inevitably become involved in politics, even in the sense of participating extensively in policy formulation, adoption, and legitimation. Furthermore, policy implementation is inherently political because it determines how the power of government is exercised. City managers act politically when they make recommendations to elected officials and seek to develop support for their positions among public officials and interest groups influential in city politics.

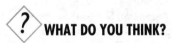 **WHAT DO YOU THINK?**

Would you rather be the mayor of a big city or its city manager? Why?

Critics of the council-manager form of city government argue that it may work fine for mid-size, uncomplicated cities but not for larger cities. They believe that big cities with diverse populations need the policy leadership of a strong mayor. The city manager system is designed to ensure the efficient implementation of policy. What happens, they ask, when city residents and the city council are deeply divided over policy alternatives? Neither the city manager nor the mayor in the council-manager form of government has the political strength to forge a consensus among competing political forces. Critics of city government in Dallas, for example, charge that the city suffers from a council that is divided along ethnic, ideological, and geographic lines and that the mayor has too little power to provide leadership. Nonetheless, Dallas voters turned down a proposal to scrap the council-manager system and replace it with the mayor-council form of city government. The mayor argued that the reform would provide for a more efficient city government, but council members countered that it would give the mayor too much power without checks and balances.

Hybrid Structures

In practice, the structures of city government seldom match the classic mayor-council or council-manager form of municipal government. Many mayor-council cities have added chief administrative officers or deputy mayors who function much

BREAKING NEWS!

Despite the Drought, El Paso Has a Stable Water Supply

While cities around the state are struggling to manage their water supplies in face of a record drought, El Paso, a rapidly growing city in one of the driest parts of the state, has a stable water supply. El Paso gets most of its water from the Hueco Bolson and Mesilla Bolson Aquifers. More than 30 years ago, El Paso city leaders realized that the aquifer would run dry in less than 40 years at the current level of water use. The city removed grass from public spaces, replacing it with gravel, cement, or desert plants. It also paid residents $1 per square foot to replace their grass yards with desert landscapes. This and other conservation measures have been sufficient to stabilize El Paso's water supply, ensuring sufficient supplies for the indefinite future.*

Discussion

Is lawn watering really such a big drag on water supplies? Yes. St. Augustine grass needs a great deal of water to stay green and lush. Other varieties of grass use less water. Even better, desert landscapes need no irrigation.

Was this approach cost effective for the city? It's less expensive to pay people to take out their grass than it is to develop new water supplies for a big city in a desert.

Did everyone replace their grass lawns with cacti and rocks? No, but enough people did to save sufficient water to stabilize the water supply. Keep in mind that homeowners who change their landscapes benefit not just from the cash reward but they also have lower water bills.

Are other Texas cities trying similar approaches? Austin and San Antonio have pilot programs. Houston and Dallas have imposed water restrictions, limiting the days and times when residents can water their yards.

---

* Juan Carlos Llorca, "Texas City Rips up Grass in Effort to Save Water," *Beaumont Enterprise*, August 27, 2011, available at www.beaumontenterprise.com.

---

as city managers do. Furthermore, many council-manager cities have increased the mayor's power to provide greater accountability.[12]

ELECTION SYSTEMS

At-large election system A method for choosing public officials in which every citizen of a political subdivision, such as a state or county, votes to select a public official.

The most popular system for choosing council members in Texas is the **at-large election system,** a method for choosing public officials in which every citizen of a political subdivision, such as a state or county, votes to select a public official. As Table 11.1 indicates, 131 cities use a place system. Candidates must declare for particular seats (or places) on council and voters then select among the candidates for each council seat. Currently, 36 cities elect council members at large without the use of a place system. On Election Day, voters select as many candidates as seats on council. If the city has five council members, for example, a voter chooses five candidates from among the list of people running for council.

In contrast to the at-large election method, a **district election** is a method for choosing public officials in which a political subdivision, such as a state or city, is

TABLE 11.1   Methods of Council Election in Texas Home-Rule Cities

Method of Election	No. of Cities Using System
At-large election by place	131
At-large election	36
District election	74
Combination of district and at-large seats	48
Cumulative voting	1
Total	**290**

Source: Terrell Blodget, "Municipal Home Rule Charters in Texas," Public Affairs Comment 41 (1996): 4.

District election A method for choosing public officials in which a political subdivision, such as a state or county, is divided into districts and each district elects one official.

Cumulative voting system An election system that allows individual voters to cast more than one ballot in the simultaneous election of several officials.

Political machine Entrenched political organization headed by a boss or small group of leaders who hold power through patronage, control over nominations, and bribery.

Political patronage The power of an officeholder to award favors, such as government jobs, to political allies.

divided into districts, with each district electing one official. Seventy-four cities use district election systems. El Paso, for example, elects eight council members from districts.

Not all Texas cities use either at-large or district election systems, however. Forty-eight cities have a combination of at-large and district seats. The Houston city council, for example, has 16 members—11 members chosen from districts and 5 elected at large. Finally, one Texas home-rule city has a **cumulative voting system,** an election system that allows individual voters to cast more than one ballot in the simultaneous election of several officials. The difference between at-large and cumulative voting is that the cumulative system allows voters to cast all of their votes for a single candidate.

Both district and at-large election systems have their proponents. Supporters of district elections believe that they make government more responsive to citizens and increase participation. District elections reduce the role of money in city politics, they say, because candidates need less money to campaign in a district than they would to run a campaign citywide. Furthermore, the advocates of district elections argue that they produce a council that more closely reflects the city's racial and ethnic diversity because they enable geographically concentrated minorities to elect group members to public office.

In contrast, defenders of at-large elections believe that council members chosen at large consider policy issues from a broader perspective than do district council members. Whereas district representatives focus on the particular concerns of their districts, at-large council members must consider what is best for the city as a whole. Furthermore, the supporters of at-large elections believe that citywide campaigns produce better-quality officials than do district elections.

Historically, district (or ward) election systems were associated with big-city **political machines,** which were entrenched political organizations headed by a boss or small group of leaders who held power through patronage, control over nominations, and bribery. **Political patronage** is the power of an officeholder to award favors, such as government jobs, to political allies. In the late nineteenth century, machine politicians in New York City, St. Louis, Cleveland, Chicago, and other big cities won election from districts with the support of geographically concentrated white ethnic minorities, especially Italian, Irish, and Polish Americans.

Well-to-do white Anglo-Saxon business groups who opposed the political machines attacked district elections as corrupt, proposing instead the adoption of nonpartisan at-large council election systems. **Nonpartisan elections** are elections in which candidates run without party labels. Although the business leaders packaged their proposal as a good government reform, it was actually designed to favor the interests of affluent business groups who would have more money to fund candidates for citywide seats than would the working-class ethnic minority groups who supported the political machine.

Nonpartisan elections Election contests in which the names of the candidates, but not their party affiliations, appear on the ballot.

Although most large industrialized cities, including Chicago, St. Louis, and Cleveland, did not adopt nonpartisan at-large election systems, many of the new cities in the South and West did, including most cities in Texas. Dallas, for example, created a nine-member city council with each member elected at large. Houston's eight-member council was chosen at large as well.

The adoption of at-large council elections in Texas cities limited the political influence of ethnic and racial minorities, primarily African Americans and Latinos. Under the at-large council system in Dallas, no African Americans and only one Latino won election to council, and the successful Hispanic candidate was a North Dallas businessman who was endorsed and financed by wealthy white business groups.[13] Similarly, the only minority candidate elected to the Houston city council under that city's at-large election system was an African American real estate investor who had the support of downtown business interests.

Voting Rights Act (VRA) A federal law designed to protect the voting rights of racial and ethnic minorities.

The **Voting Rights Act (VRA)**, a federal law designed to protect the voting rights of racial and ethnic minorities, provides a means that minority rights groups can use to attack election systems they consider discriminatory. The act allows voters to file lawsuits in federal court challenging local election laws and procedures they believe discriminate against minority voters.[14] In 2007, for example, Manuel Benavidez, a longtime resident of Irving, filed suit against the city under the VRA, arguing that Irving's at-large election system prevented Latino residents from winning seats on city council. Even though 40 percent of the population of Irving was Latino, the eight-member city council was all white. Two years later, a federal judge ruled in favor of Benavidez and ordered the city to change its election system. The city responded by creating a mixed election system with six district and two at-large council seats. The majority population of one of the districts was Latino.[15]

In the late 1970s and early 1980s, minority rights groups used the VRA to force Dallas, Houston, San Antonio, El Paso, Fort Worth, and other cities in the state to abandon at-large election systems. Some cities, such as San Antonio, El Paso, and Fort Worth, began electing all council members from districts; other cities adopted mixed systems that combined district seats with at-large positions. Dallas adopted a system with eight district seats and two at-large positions, with the mayor elected at large. In 1991, Dallas settled a VRA lawsuit by changing its city election to provide for a 14-member council with only the mayor elected at large.[16]

The Austin city council meets to consider city business.

The introduction of district election systems led to the selection of city councils in most of the state's big cities that were more ethnically and racially diverse than ever before. In the first election after the implementation of single-member districts, Houston voters chose three African Americans and one Latino to serve on council. In San Antonio, Latinos and African Americans together won a majority on that city's ten-member council. A study of ten Texas cities found that the change from at-large to district election systems led to increases in the number of Latino council candidates, Latinos elected to office, and Latino council members living in predominantly Latino neighborhoods.[17]

 WHAT DO YOU THINK?

What sort of city election system is the best—district, at large, or a mixed system?

PUBLIC POLICIES IN TEXAS CITIES

Political scientist Paul E. Peterson divides urban public policies into three categories: developmental, redistributive, and allocational. **Developmental urban policies** are local programs that enhance a community's economic position in its competition with other communities. They strengthen the local economy, expand the tax base, and generate additional tax revenues for the city. New sports stadiums,

Developmental urban policies
Local programs that enhance the community's economic position in its competition with other communities.

Redistributive urban policies
Local programs that benefit low-income residents of an area.

Allocational urban policies
Local programs that are more or less neutral in their impact on the local economy.

highway expansion, and civic centers are examples of projects that would be part of a developmental urban policy because they could be justified as an investment in a community's economic vitality.

Redistributive urban policies are local programs that benefit the low-income residents of an area. These include such programs as the provision of low-income housing and food assistance to poor families. Although redistributive programs may be desirable from a humanitarian point of view, Peterson says that they retard economic development. Consider the provision of city health clinics for low-income families. City-funded health clinics may discourage businesses and middle-income taxpayers from relocating to the city because they will have to pay more in taxes for this service than they will receive in benefits. Health clinics may encourage the migration of low-income families to the city to take advantage of the service, especially if neighboring ("competing") cities choose not to provide their residents health clinics, instead keeping their tax rates low.

Allocational urban policies are local programs that are more or less neutral in their impact on the local economy. The best examples of allocational policies are urban housekeeping programs such as police and fire protection, garbage pickup, and routine street maintenance. Allocational programs are neither developmental nor redistributive in nature because all members of the community benefit from them without regard for economic status.[18]

Economic factors influence the adoption of urban public policies. Cities concentrate on developmental and allocational programs in order to enhance their tax bases and protect the local economy. Research shows that levels of municipal services and tax rates tend to be lower in cities bordered by other municipalities than they are in cities that are relatively isolated. The study concludes that city officials are forced to keep taxes down and, of course, services low because businesses and middle-income taxpayers have the option of moving to a neighboring municipality with lower tax rates.[19]

City governments frequently adopt developmental policies that entail building entertainment centers, such as sports stadiums and convention centers, designed to attract visitors from out of town and the suburbs. Houston, Dallas, San Antonio, and Arlington have all used tax money to build new sports arenas to keep or attract professional sports teams. Although city officials promise that expensive new sports and entertainment facilities generate tax revenue and increase employment, research indicates that such projects do not pay for themselves. Economists note that most people have fixed entertainment budgets. People who spend money at new sports stadiums would have spent the money on entertainment elsewhere in the city if the stadium had not been built. Furthermore, new stadiums do little to revitalize neighborhoods. Although new stadiums may be symbols of mayoral leadership, they seldom contribute to economic development.[20]

Political factors also play an important role in urban policymaking. Developmental and allocational policies are often characterized by conflict as political forces compete over policy alternatives. In Houston, for example, two sets of business groups opposed one another over the location of a new convention center, whether it would be built east or west of the downtown business district. Similarly, neighborhoods

AROUND THE NATION

Healthcare in San Francisco

The city of San Francisco has a healthcare program designed to provide basic medical services to every city resident without regard for income. The program, which is known as Healthy San Francisco, offers participants comprehensive primary care at any of the city's public and private clinics and hospitals, including lab work, prescription medication, X-rays, hospitalization, and surgeries. The enrollment fee ranges from nothing to $1,800 a year, depending on an individual's income. People earning less than 300 percent of the poverty level have their enrollment subsidized. The cost of the program is covered by savings in city funds that are no longer needed to provide emergency room care for the uninsured, enrollment fees, and mandatory contributions from city businesses. All businesses with 20 or more workers are required to contribute to the program if they do not provide healthcare coverage for their employees.*

Healthy San Francisco has been at least reasonably successful. It has covered 45,000 of the estimated 60,000 uninsured adults living in the city. Furthermore, fears that it would hurt the city's economy have not been fulfilled because employment growth in San Francisco has not lagged behind employment growth in surrounding communities not covered by the program.†

QUESTIONS

1. Is Healthy San Francisco a good idea? Why or why not?
2. Is this an example of a redistributive, developmental, or allocational urban program?
3. Would you expect a city in Texas to adopt something similar anytime soon? Why or why not?

* Laura A. Locke, "San Francisco's Latest Innovation: Universal Healthcare," *Time*, January 23, 2006, available at www.time.com.

† Health Access Blog, August 24, 2009, available at http://blog.health-access.org/.

fought over the timing of the construction of new decentralized police command stations, with each region of town wanting its command station built first.

City officials must balance economic concerns with political demands. Groups representing the interests of disadvantaged constituents in the state's big cities call for the adoption of redistributive programs. They demand home rehabilitation loans, low-interest mortgage loans, small business loans, technical assistance to new businesses, public housing, affirmative action, public transportation in low-income areas, and hiring goals for women and minorities. Research shows that cities become more responsive to the concerns of minority residents as minorities increase their elected representation in city government. One study finds that after city councils experience an increase in minority representation, city governments hire more minorities, award more contracts to minority-owned businesses, and enact programs favored by minority groups.[21]

Budgetary Policy

The state's largest cities are big enterprises with annual budgets greater than a billion dollars. In fiscal (budget) year 2011, for example, the general-fund budget for the City of Houston was $2 billion.[22] The state's largest cities offer their residents

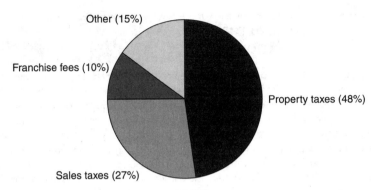

FIGURE 11.4   General Fund Revenues, Houston 2011.

a broad range of services, including police protection, street repair, garbage pickup, libraries, recreational facilities, health clinics, fire protection, emergency medical services (EMS), water and sewer service, airports, sidewalks, and street lighting. In contrast, small towns may provide only a limited number of basic services. Public safety—police, fire, and municipal courts—is typically the largest item in all city budgets because it is labor intensive.

Texas cities generate revenue from property taxes, sales taxes, franchise fees, and other sources. Figure 11.4 shows the relative importance of the various revenue sources for Houston in 2011. As the figure shows, property and sales taxes combined accounted for 75 percent of city revenue. Franchise fees represented 10 percent of revenues, with a variety of other sources supplying the remaining 15 percent.

Property tax (*ad valorem* property tax) A levy assessed on real property, such as houses, land, business inventory, and industrial plants.

The **property tax,** also known as the *ad valorem* **property tax,** is a levy assessed on real property, such as houses, land, business inventory, and industrial plants. State law sets a maximum property tax rate of $1.50 per $100 of valuation for general-law cities and $2.50 per $100 for home-rule cities. In practice, the property tax rates in most cities are well below the maximum. In 2011, the property tax rate for Dallas was $0.797. It was $0.63875 for Houston, $0.56569 for San Antonio, $0.855 for Fort Worth, and $0.4571 for Austin.[23]

City governments may grant property tax breaks, called exemptions, to certain categories of taxpayers, such as homeowners, elderly residents, and veterans with disabilities. Fort Worth, for example, grants exemptions for homeowners, senior citizens, disabled persons, property that is a historic site, and transitional housing for indigent persons. The most common exemption is the **homestead exemption,** which is a property tax reduction granted to homeowners on their principal residence. State law stipulates that property tax exemptions must be at least $5,000 but not more than 20 percent of the property value (unless that figure is less than $5,000).

Homestead exemption A property tax reduction granted to homeowners on their principal residence.

Figuring a property tax bill is relatively easy. Assume, for example, that a home is assessed at $150,000, the city tax rate is $0.60 per $100 valuation, and the city grants a 20 percent homestead exemption. The homeowner's annual property tax bill to the city would be figured as follows:

$150,000	Assessed value
−$30,000	Homestead exemption (20 percent of $150,000)
$120,000	Taxable value
× .60 per $100	Municipal tax rate
$720	Municipal tax due

A property owner's tax bill depends on both the tax rate and the valuation of the property. Property taxes go up (and down) when the local government raises (or lowers) tax rates. Taxes also change when property values change. Texas is *not* one of the 22 states that have **truth-in-taxation laws,** which are laws that block local governments from raising the total amount of property taxes they collect from one year to the next when assessed values go up. When property values increase in these states, local officials have to vote to increase their total tax revenues and advertise their action in the newspaper. Otherwise, the tax rate falls automatically to compensate for rising property values.[24] In contrast, local governments in Texas benefit from rising property values without elected officials having to go on record in favor of raising additional revenue.

The sales tax is the other major tax source for municipal government in Texas. A **sales tax** is a levy on the retail sale of taxable items. State law allows cities to piggyback an extra 1 percent onto the state's general sales tax rate of 6.25 percent. All of the state's larger cities and many smaller towns take advantage of the sales tax option. Cities without transit authorities may seek voter approval to levy a ½ percent additional sales tax to reduce city or county property taxes or help fund law enforcement. Cities of 56,000 or more population that do not want to swap property taxes for sales taxes can ask for voter approval of a ¼ percent sales tax to use for mass transit.

In addition to property and sales taxes, city governments in Texas raise revenue from franchise fees, licenses, permits, fines, and various other sources. Telephone, gas, cable TV, and electric utility companies pay annual franchise fees to city governments for the right to use public rights of way to string wires or lay cable. Cities generate revenue from service charges, such as fees for water and sewer service. Fines for traffic infractions and violations of city ordinances provide cities with revenues as well. Cities raise money from hotel and motel occupancy taxes, rental car taxes, and burglar and fire alarm fees. Federal grant programs offer assistance to municipalities to build sewage treatment plants, acquire parkland, construct airports, treat drug addiction, rehabilitate economically depressed neighborhoods, and provide housing to low-income families.

The recession of 2008–2009 put a serious strain on city budgets. A **recession** is an economic slowdown characterized by declining economic output and rising unemployment. City sales tax revenues fell because consumers made fewer purchases than before the recession. Property taxes declined as well because of falling property values. Most big cities in Texas had less revenue in 2009, 2010, and 2011 than before the recession. Consequently, city leaders were forced to cut spending and/or raise taxes.

Truth-in-taxation laws Laws that block local governments from raising the total amount of property taxes they collect from one year to the next when assessed values go up.

Sales tax A levy on the retail sale of taxable items.

Recession An economic slowdown characterized by declining economic output and rising unemployment.

Bond A certificate of indebtedness issued to investors who loan money for interest income; in lay terms, a bond is an IOU.

Capital expenditure The purchase by government of a permanent, fixed asset, such as a new city hall or highway overpass.

Tax increment financing A program in which a local government promises to earmark increased property tax revenues generated by development in a designated area called a tax increment financing district to fund improvements in the area, such as roads, parks, sidewalks, and street lighting.

Tax abatement A program that exempts property owners from local property taxes on new construction and improvements in a designated tax abatement district for a set period of time.

City governments borrow money by issuing bonds to cover the cost of capital expenditures, such as the construction of buildings, airports, roads, and utility plants. A **bond** is a certificate of indebtedness. A **capital expenditure** is the purchase by government of a permanent, fixed asset, such as a new city hall or highway overpass. City governments levy property taxes to pay back the money they borrow plus interest.

Budgetary policies in urban Texas have historically been allocational and developmental. Police and fire protection, sanitation, and street maintenance—the largest expenditure items for municipal government in the state—are allocational programs. Other allocational expenditures include money for libraries, parkland acquisition, and traffic management. In the meantime, capital expenditures for street construction, sewer trunk line replacement, and new police and fire stations are developmental because they provide infrastructure improvements essential to economic growth.

City governments use tax incentives to promote economic growth, including tax increment financing, tax abatements, and enterprise zones. **Tax increment financing** is a program in which a local government promises to earmark increased property tax revenues generated by development in a designated area called a tax increment reinvestment zone (TIRZ) to fund improvements in the area, such as roads, parks, sidewalks, and street lighting. A city hopes to encourage private investment by promising that any additional tax revenues generated from higher property values resulting from private development in the district will be spent by the city in the area under development. **Tax abatement** is a program that exempts property owners from local property taxes on new construction and improvements in a designated tax abatement district for a set period of time. San Antonio, for example, granted the Sino Swearingen Aircraft Corporation a series of tax abatements to lure the company into agreeing to manufacture a new business jet in San Antonio, a decision that would bring 850 new jobs to the city.[25] **Enterprise zones** are part of a state program that allows local governments to designate certain areas as enterprise zones in which private investors can receive property tax abatements, local sales tax rebates (refunds), and government-backed low-interest loans.

Local officials argue that tax incentives are an important economic development tool. They believe that tax breaks may make the difference between a company deciding to build a plant in Texas or locating it in another state. When businesses establish new facilities in the state, they create jobs that fuel economic growth because their employees purchase goods and services from established businesses. Local governments benefit as well because the increased economic activity generates added tax revenues, which may be sufficient to make up for the revenues lost by the tax incentives.

 WHAT DO YOU THINK?

Should city governments use tax incentives to promote economic development?

Enterprise zones
A state program that allows local governments to designate certain areas called enterprise zones in which private investors can receive property tax abatements, local sales tax rebates (refunds), and government-backed low-interest loans.

The critics of tax incentives charge that they are unnecessary and unfair. Tax breaks are unnecessary, they say, because business managers seldom, if ever, base their relocation decisions on taxes. Businesses decide to expand or relocate based primarily on such factors as transportation and the availability of an educated workforce. Critics charge that tax breaks for new firms are unfair because they shift the cost of government to other taxpayers, including homeowners and established businesses. Businesspeople, in particular, strongly oppose the use of tax incentives to attract potential competitors.

Consider the controversy over Houston's decision to provide millions of dollars in tax breaks to the Embassy Suites hotel chain. The city agreed to rebate up to $1.4 million a year in hotel occupancy taxes for seven years if Embassy Suites built a hotel near the George R. Brown Convention Center and set aside most of the rooms for convention business. The city's goal was to attract more convention business to Houston, but critics questioned the need for the tax rebate. If building another hotel downtown made business sense, they asked, then why did the city have to provide a big tax break that competitor hotels did not receive?[26]

Furthermore, research shows that the developmental policies of city government have little, if any, impact on the location decisions of investors and business managers. One study of the factors influencing the location of manufacturing plants in Texas found that local taxes had little effect on plant location decisions. The research discovered that the availability of skilled labor and the presence of strong colleges and universities were important to **high-technology industries,** those industries based on the latest in modern technology. Some of the other factors important to economic development were the presence of port facilities and the concentration in the area of firms in a similar line of work.[27] Some scholars believe that local officials grant tax incentives because of the political pressure to create jobs. Tax incentive programs give the *appearance* that local officials are doing something to help the economy, even if they have little real impact on economic development. Businesses that accept economic development money typically exaggerate the number of jobs they plan to create and actually expand more slowly than companies that do not accept government subsidies.[28]

High-technology industries Industries that are based on the latest in modern technology, such as telecommunications and robotics.

Annexation and Suburban Development

Traditionally, cities annex to protect their tax bases. Big cities across America have been caught in a financial squeeze as revenues have fallen while demand for services has risen. For decades, the tax bases of the nation's largest cities have declined. Middle-class taxpayers and business establishments have moved to the suburbs in search of safer streets, better schools, and more desirable housing. In contrast, poor people, seriously ill persons who do not have health insurance, and people without places to live have moved to the city to take advantage of health clinics, shelters, and other social services not available in the suburbs. Texas cities have used their power to annex to maintain their tax bases and financial health. The Texas Municipal League, a nonprofit organization that represents Texas cities, calculates that if San Antonio did not have the ability to annex adjacent suburban development, that is, if it still had the same boundaries that it had in 1945, then it would have more poverty and unemployment than Newark, New Jersey, an economically depressed city.[29]

Another reason for annexation is the desire of city officials to prevent encirclement by other incorporated municipalities. Because state law prohibits cities from annexing other cities without their consent, a big city surrounded by smaller incorporated municipalities cannot grow. Many cities located in the Northeast and Midwest find themselves in just such a position. Dallas allowed itself to become ringed by small towns during the early years of its development. In 1976, Dallas broke out of its encirclement by convincing the town of Renner to agree to become part of Dallas. Since the Renner annexation, Dallas has pushed its city limits to the north into Collin and Denton Counties. Other Texas cities have avoided a similar predicament by annexing adjacent unincorporated areas before they could incorporate and by annexing the land around neighboring small towns to prevent their expansion. In Harris County, for example, the municipalities of Bellaire and West University Place are completely surrounded by Houston.

Most city governments provide garbage collection services for their residents.

Finally, cities annex in order to reap the political benefits of a larger population. Federal grant money is often awarded on the basis of formulas that include population. The more people living within a city, the more federal grant money it receives. Because legislative districts are drawn on the basis of population size, increased population also leads to additional representation in Congress and the Texas legislature.

State law permits a city to increase its total land area by as much as 10 percent in any one year. A city that does not annex its full allotment in a year may carry the remaining amount forward to be used in later years, as long as the city does not increase its geographic size by more than 30 percent in any one year. A city of 100 square miles, for example, could add another 10 square miles to its land area this year. Because state law allows municipalities to carry forward unused annexation authority, the city of 100 square miles could wait a few years and then annex up to 30 square miles.

Utility district
A special district that provides utilities, such as water and sewer service, to residents living in unincorporated urban areas.

A city government typically annexes an entire **utility district,** which is a special district that provides utilities, such as water and sewer service, to residents living in unincorporated urban areas. When a city annexes a subdivision, it annexes the utility district that services the subdivision, rather than the development itself. The annexing city takes over the operation of the utility district, similar to a large corporation taking over a small business. The city takes possession of the utility district's physical assets, such as its water and sewer facilities, and assumes its financial assets and liabilities. The city brings police, fire, solid waste, and emergency medical services (EMS) to the area while contracting with a private company to operate the old utility district's water and sewer system.

Historically, Texas cities have annexed aggressively. Between 1950 and 1980, Houston added more than 370 square miles, Dallas more than 230, San Antonio nearly 200, El Paso over 200, Fort Worth nearly 150, Corpus Christi more than 150, and Austin more than 80. During the 1970s alone, Texas cities annexed 1,472 square miles containing 456,000 people. That is an area bigger than Rhode Island and a population almost as large as that of Wyoming.[30]

Since the early 1980s, the pace of annexation by Texas cities has slowed. The annexations of the 1970s produced a political backlash from newly annexed residents who were determined to do their best to vote incumbent mayors and council members out of office. Subsequently, local officeholders grew cautious about adding more angry constituents to their cities. Furthermore, the Texas legislature and the governor have responded to complaints from people living in unincorporated areas near major cities by adopting legislation forcing cities to better accommodate the interests of suburban residents living in unincorporated areas.

In 1999, the legislature passed and the governor signed a measure overhauling annexation policy to require that cities adopt an annexation plan that specifically identifies the areas to be annexed and details how the city will provide those areas with services. The county government may appoint a panel of citizens to negotiate with the city on behalf of area residents. The city cannot complete the actual annexation until the third anniversary of the adoption of the annexation plan, and then it must act within 31 days or lose the opportunity to annex the identified areas for five years. The city must provide police, fire, EMS, solid waste, street repair, water and sewer, and park maintenance services immediately. It has two and a half years to provide full services comparable to those offered to other city residents. If a majority of residents in the newly annexed area believe that the city has failed to provide them with full services, they may petition the city to be disannexed. If the city fails to act, residents may file suit in district court to ask a judge to order disannexation.

WHAT DO YOU THINK?

Do you favor changing state law to require that the people in an area to be annexed must approve before the annexation can take place?

The legislation also gave cities and utility districts the authority to negotiate Strategic Partnership Agreements (SPAs) to provide for limited-purpose annexation. In this case, the utility district gives the city permission to collect sales taxes—but not property taxes—at retail businesses within the district. In exchange, the city provides the district with some city services, such as police and fire service, and a portion of the sales tax revenue collected within its borders. The city also pledges to postpone annexing the district during the period of the partnership.[31] Both units of government benefit from the additional tax revenues, whereas utility district residents avoid annexation, at least in the short run. Houston has moved more aggressively than other cities in the state to negotiate partnership agreements with surrounding utility districts, signing more than 100 agreements. In fact, SAPs have become so popular that some utility districts have approached the city about establishing partnerships in order to share in the sales tax revenue and stave off the possibility of annexation.[32] For example, Houston and The Woodlands signed an agreement in 2007 that enabled the suburban community to eventually incorporate in exchange for a share of local sales tax revenues that would be deposited in a special fund to be used for regional development.[33]

In addition to reforming annexation procedures, the legislature and the governor have revised state laws dealing with **extraterritorial jurisdiction (ETJ),** which is the authority of a city to require conformity with city ordinances and regulations affecting streets, parks, alleys, utility easements, sanitary sewers, and the like in a ring of land extending from one half to five miles beyond the city-limits line. The width of an ETJ depends on the population of the city. Within the extraterritorial area, no new cities may be incorporated without the consent of the existing city. The ETJ is not part of the city; its residents do not pay property or sales taxes to city government and receive no services.

The original purpose of extraterritoriality was to enable a city to control development within the ETJ, thus preparing it for future annexation. When the city eventually annexed subdivisions in the ETJ, they would already conform to city building standards. If the ETJs of two cities overlapped, the cities generally apportioned the area between them.

Extraterritorial jurisdiction (ETJ)
The authority of a city to require conformity with city ordinances and regulations affecting streets, parks, alleys, utility easements, sanitary sewers, and the like in a ring of land extending from one half to five miles beyond the city-limits line.

In 2001, the legislature passed and the governor signed legislation requiring cities and counties to jointly create a single office for dealing with development in the ETJ that would be run by the city, the county, or cooperatively by both units of local government. The legislature's action was a response to complaints from developers that they were sometimes caught between conflicting county and city regulations. In practice, most cities and counties have created a joint office, with a city office the next most popular option.[34]

Land-Use Regulation

Historically, land-use policies in Texas cities have been developmental. Instead of regulating land use, municipalities in the Lone Star State have promoted private development through street construction and the provision of streetlights, drainage, and water and sewer services in undeveloped areas. In the process, city governments left most decisions about land-use policy to private interests—developers, investors, builders, realtors, and architects.

Land-use policy in Texas cities is undergoing a transformation. The introduction of single-member districts has increased the political strength of neighborhood groups concerned about quality-of-life issues, such as traffic congestion, air pollution, and neighborhood revitalization. Neighborhood groups in low-income areas have demanded that city government focus on land-use policies affecting their neighborhoods, such as low-cost housing and urban redevelopment.

Building and Housing Codes Building and housing codes are established by city ordinance to set minimum standards for the construction and maintenance of buildings. **Building codes** are municipal ordinances that set minimum standards for the types of materials used in construction, building design, and construction methods employed in all building projects within the city. Building permits are required for all construction covered by the code. **Housing codes** are local ordinances requiring all dwelling places in a city to meet certain standards of upkeep and structural integrity. City officials enforce the housing codes by making systematic inspections and investigating complaints. Property owners are responsible for structural integrity. Owners and occupants share the responsibility for upkeep. Violators of building codes and housing codes may be fined.

Building and housing codes are designed to promote the health, safety, and welfare of the community, but the results often fall short of the ideal. Critics say that codes are frequently outdated and inconsistent across cities. They believe that enforcement is often lax and too frequently accompanied by graft. The opponents of building codes also charge that they increase building costs, thus encouraging construction outside a city's ETJ, beyond the reach of city authority. Furthermore, the opponents of building and housing codes argue that property owners sometimes fail to repair old, run-down structures because improvements would place them under the building codes, thus forcing owners to undertake more expensive work than they desire and can afford.

Compared with cities in other states, Texas municipalities have been slow to establish code standards. Many Texas cities did not adopt building codes until after

Building codes
Municipal ordinances that set minimum standards for the types of materials used in construction, building design, and construction methods employed in all building within the city.

Housing codes
Local ordinances requiring all dwelling places in a city to meet certain standards of upkeep and structural integrity.

1954 when the federal government made them a condition for obtaining federal funds for public housing, FHA, and urban renewal programs. Houston did not even adopt fire codes until the 1970s.

Zoning and Planning The governmental designation of tracts of land for industrial, commercial, or residential use is known as **zoning.** In 1927, the Texas legislature authorized municipalities to adopt zoning ordinances to restrict the use of privately owned land. Subsequently, many Texas cities adopted local zoning ordinances.

Zoning The governmental designation of tracts of land for industrial, commercial, or residential use.

How does zoning work? Once a city decides it wishes to control land use within its boundaries, it creates a zoning commission. The commission studies land use in the area and makes recommendations concerning appropriate uses of land and the location of commercial and residential districts. After public hearings, the city council considers the proposal and adopts a zoning ordinance based on the commission's recommendation. After the ordinance goes into effect, property owners may not build structures or put property to any use that conflicts with the zoning ordinance applicable to their district.

Proponents of zoning and other types of land-use regulation believe that they help create an orderly city. They say that zoning enables city government to separate districts for residential, commercial, and industrial uses, thus preventing nuisances from developing in residential areas, such as strip shopping centers and trailer parks. Careful planning, they argue, can prevent street congestion, land overcrowding, and the excessive concentration of population by allowing city officials to plan adequately for the provision of transportation, water, sewage, schools, parks, drainage, and other public requirements.

Opponents of zoning and other types of land-use restrictions believe that city planning is inefficient and potentially corrupt because it substitutes the judgment of government bureaucrats for free-enterprise development. Without government controls, they say, cities develop and change in accordance with the dictates of the marketplace. Zoning shifts the basis for deciding how land will be used from economics to politics. As a result, land-use decisions become political, with decisions made on the basis of which developers have made the largest campaign contributions.

Urban land-use policies reflect political conflict between the owners of developed land and the owners of undeveloped property. Homeowners and commercial property owners favor the imposition of strict land-use controls to manage further development in their neighborhoods in order to maintain and enhance their property values. In contrast, persons who own undeveloped tracts of land prefer few land-use restrictions, so that they can develop their property unhindered. Throughout much of the twentieth century, developers held the upper hand in big-city Texas and used their influence to limit land-use controls. Over the last decade or so, however, the political balance has changed in most of the state's large cities. As cities have matured and development has slowed, the owners of developed land have gained political influence. Furthermore, the introduction of single-member districts has enhanced the political influence of neighborhood civic associations concerned about property values.

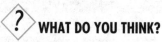 WHAT DO YOU THINK?

Do you favor zoning?

Deed restrictions
Private contractual agreements that limit what residential property owners can do with their houses and land.

Deed Restrictions The opponents of zoning sometimes argue that deed restrictions are preferable to government regulation. **Deed restrictions** are private contractual agreements that limit what residential property owners can do with their houses and land. Almost every modern residential subdivision in the state has deed restrictions. Developers and sometimes the mortgage company draw up deed restrictions to spell out in detail what lot owners may or may not do. Deed restrictions differ from zoning in that they are the result of voluntary contractual agreements between private parties, whereas zoning involves the enactment of city ordinances.

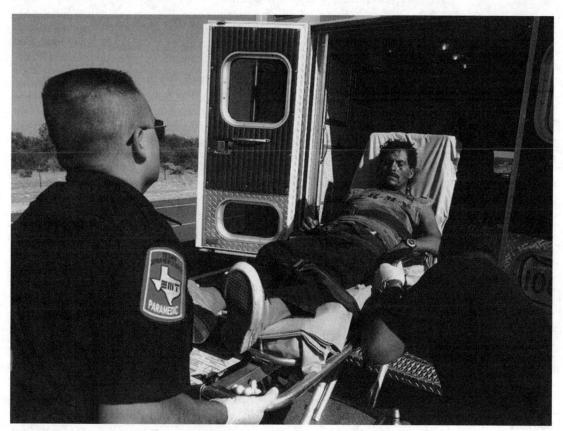

Emergency medical services are also provided by city governments.

GETTING INVOLVED

Contacting City Officials

City governments deal with issues that are close to home—police and fire protection, street repair, garbage pickup, water and sewer service, emergency medical services, parks, libraries, airports, animal control, and local taxes. You can find the name and contact information for the mayor and council members of your city at its homepage, which can be found at the following website: **www.statelocalgov .net/state-tx.cfm**. Contact the people who represent you at city hall and let them know how you feel about city services, taxes, and regulations.

It's your city—get involved!

Deed restrictions typically allow owners to use their property only for specified purposes. They force property owners to observe certain standards and refrain from altering their property without the written approval of the neighborhood civic association's architectural control committee. Deed restrictions cover such issues as where residents can park their vehicles, the color they can paint their homes, and the type of shingles they can put on their roofs. If someone violates the restrictions, the civic association can get a court order directing the offender to stop the violation. Property owners who disobey a court order can be fined or jailed for contempt of court. Deed restrictions that are not enforced may terminate or become unenforceable. This is most likely to occur, of course, in older neighborhoods.

Deed restrictions accomplish some but not all of the goals of zoning. At its best, zoning represents an attempt by government to ensure orderly development. In contrast, deed restrictions provide piecemeal zoning by private developers without resorting to a comprehensive plan. People who live in the suburbs benefit, whereas the residents of older neighborhoods without zoning must live with changes wrought by market forces.

CITY POLITICS IN TEXAS

Elite theory (or elitism) The view that political power is held by a small group of people who dominate politics by controlling economic resources.

Before the mid-1970s, a small group of businesspeople controlled political power in big-city Texas. **Elite theory (or elitism)** is the view that political power is held by a small group of people who dominate politics by controlling economic resources. Growth-oriented business leaders in each of the state's major cities used their economic power to dominate the local policymaking process. In Houston, the elite consisted of a small group of business leaders called the 8-F Crowd because of their practice of meeting informally in Suite 8-F of a downtown hotel. The members of the 8-F Crowd were all wealthy businessmen with interests in real estate, construction, oil and gas, banking, law, and insurance.[35]

Boosters People who promote local economic development.

The overriding goal of the business groups who dominated city politics was economic growth and development. They were **boosters** (people who promote local economic development) who believed that whatever was good for business was also good for their city. The business leaders favored low tax rates, aggressive annexation, and few restrictions on land use. When the occasion arose, they did what was necessary to boost their cities. During the 1930s, for example, Dallas business leaders convinced the legislature to make their city the site for the official celebration of the Texas Centennial, even though Dallas did not exist during the Texas Revolution. In Houston, business leaders promoted the construction of the Ship Channel and the creation of the Johnson Spacecraft Center (JSC).

Business leaders frequently exerted their influence through the vehicle of nonpartisan good government groups, such as the Citizens' Charter Association (CCA) in Dallas, Good Government League (GGL) in San Antonio, Seventh Street in Fort Worth, Citizens for Better Government in Abilene, and Citizens' Committee for Good Government in Wichita Falls. These groups recruited slates of candidates sympathetic with their goals and backed them financially in the at-large nonpartisan elections that were then the norm in most Texas cities. In San Antonio, the GGL won 85 of 97 contested council races between 1955 and 1975. In Dallas, the CCA captured 181 of 211 seats between 1931 and 1975.[36]

Most of the candidates supported by business groups were white businessmen. For example, in Fort Worth, no African Americans were elected to city council before 1967; no Latinos won election before 1977. In fact, most Fort Worth council members lived within blocks of one another on the city's affluent southwest side.[37] In Houston, no women, no Latinos, and only one African American were elected to council before 1981.

Texas cities grew rapidly, but the growth came with social costs. Texas cities developed serious air and water pollution problems. The Environmental Protection Agency (EPA), the federal agency responsible for enforcing the nation's environmental laws, identified four major areas of the state that had failed to meet federal air quality standards for ozone: Dallas-Fort Worth, Houston-Galveston, Beaumont-Port Arthur, and El Paso. In the meantime, air quality in Austin, San Antonio, and Tyler barely met the standard.[38] Texas cities also suffered from traffic congestion, overcrowded schools, and flooding brought on by **subsidence,** the sinking of the surface of the land caused by the too-rapid extraction of subsurface water.

Subsidence
The sinking of the surface of the land caused by the too-rapid extraction of subsurface water.

The costs of rapid development mobilized opposition to the growth-oriented business groups that had long dominated city politics. The business community split between those industries that benefited from development and those that were more concerned with quality-of-life issues. Real estate developers, construction contractors, and other firms that depend on development favored continuing growth-oriented public policies. In contrast, the tourist industry and high-technology firms that employed middle-class professionals were more concerned with the quality of urban life. Neighborhood groups and minority interests demanded that city governments respond to their needs.

By the mid-1970s, the rules of the political game had changed sufficiently to allow the new forces to have an impact on the policy process. The elimination of the poll tax and the liberalization of Texas's once highly restrictive voter registration procedures opened the door to greater political participation by African Americans and Latinos. Furthermore, the extension of the VRA in 1975 to include Texas led

In 2009, Annise Parker was elected mayor of Houston using a deracialization strategy that encompassed not just race and ethnicity but also sexual orientation.

to the introduction of single-member districts in most of the state's largest cities, including Houston, Dallas, San Antonio, El Paso, Lubbock, Corpus Christi, Waco, and, most recently, Irving.

The new voter registration procedures and single-member district elections enabled minority and neighborhood groups to gain a real share of political power in big-city Texas. More African Americans and Latinos won city council seats than ever before, and some Asian Americans won seats on councils as well. The number of women serving on city councils increased. Houston, Dallas, and Fort Worth elected city officials who were openly gay or lesbian. In addition, African Americans, Latinos, and women served as mayor in the state's major cities.[39]

The nature of business groups in big-city Texas also changed. During the 1950s, each city's business establishment was dominated by a fairly small group of strong-willed, fiercely independent, wealthy entrepreneurs, such as Eric Jonsson in Dallas and George Brown in Houston. By the 1980s, the business community in big-city Texas had grown too diverse for any one individual or small group of individuals to speak on its behalf. Furthermore, the days of the individual entrepreneur were past, as management teams now ran the state's major corporations. Before local managers could agree to support a development project, they would have to obtain approval from a corporate board of directors based in New York, San Francisco, or Tokyo.

Pluralist theory (or pluralism) The view that diverse groups of elites with differing interests compete with one another to control policy in various issue areas.

Contemporary urban politics reflects **pluralist theory** (or **pluralism**), which is the view that diverse groups of elites with differing interests compete with one another to control policy in various issue areas. In big-city Texas today, different groups are active on different issues, but no one group is able to dominate policymaking across issue areas. Business groups may control policymaking in one issue area, whereas neighborhood or minority rights groups may have more influence in another issue area.

Deracialization
The attempt of political candidates to deemphasize racially divisive themes in order to garner crossover support from voters of other races/ethnicities while also receiving the overwhelming majority of support from voters of the candidate's own racial/ethnic group.

Political scientists use the term deracialization to describe contemporary urban politics. **Deracialization** is the attempt by political candidates to de-emphasize racially divisive themes in order to garner crossover support from voters of other races/ethnicities while also receiving the overwhelming majority of support from voters of the candidate's own racial/ethnic group.[40] To be successful, candidates running for citywide office in the state's major cities know that they have to attract voters from more than one racial/ethnic group because no one group has an electoral majority. They promote images of themselves that other racial/ethnic groups will perceive as nonthreatening and avoid issues that divide voters along racial/ethnic lines, such as bilingual education, affirmative action, and immigration. In the meantime, they work aggressively to mobilize their own base of support. Political scientist Christian Collet uses the term "toggling" to describe the approach that candidates take to city politics. "Toggling," Collet says, "is a strategy that seeks to build or maintain a victorious electoral coalition in a politically polarized, multicultural environment through the balanced communication of broad- and narrow-cast messages, symbols, issue positions, personal characteristics, and socio-cultural cues to specific racial and ethnic groups."[41] Candidates emphasize broad themes to the general community in order to appeal to as many groups as possible while highlighting points designed to mobilize their own base of support. For example, a candidate can talk about being tough on crime while also promising better representation on the police force for racial and ethnic minority groups.[42]

The 2009 Houston city election illustrates deracialization in Texas urban politics. Annise Parker and Gene Locke, the two leading contenders for mayor, each had strengths and weaknesses. Parker was the better known, having won three consecutive citywide elections for city council and another three elections for controller. Because of her experience, she had a better grasp of the issues than her opponent. She could also count on a small army of campaign volunteers, especially members of the gay and lesbian community. Parker was unable to raise as much money as Locke, however, and some observers questioned whether Houston voters would be willing to elect an openly lesbian mayor.[43] Locke, with strong business backing, was better funded than Parker. Furthermore, as an African American, he could expect majority support from the city's largest voting bloc. The combination of downtown business money and African American voters has historically been a formidable partnership in Houston politics. Locke's weakness was that, having never run for election before, he was an inexperienced candidate who was not well known among Houston voters, not even among African American voters.

The initial challenge for the Parker and Locke campaigns was to do well enough in the November election to make the December runoff. Houston city elections are held in November of odd-numbered years. If no candidate wins a majority of the vote in the first round of voting, the two top finishers meet in a December runoff. With two other serious candidates in the field in addition to Parker and Locke, a runoff was likely. The Parker campaign deployed volunteers to identify supporters and encourage them to vote, using phone banks, direct mail, Facebook, and Twitter. Meanwhile, Locke relied on his financial advantage to build name recognition through radio and television advertising. In particular, Locke wanted to increase his visibility among African American voters.

The November vote set the stage for a December runoff. Parker led with 31 percent followed by Locke with 26 percent, with each campaign doing best with its core supporters. Parker led among liberal white voters while Locke ran best among African Americans. Most of the remainder of the vote was divided between liberal City Councilman Peter Brown and conservative activist Roy Morales. Brown ran second to Parker in liberal white neighborhoods and second to Locke in African American neighborhoods. Most observers expected his vote would split along racial lines in the runoff, with Brown's white voters backing Parker and his African American supporters voting for Locke. The outcome of the runoff election would hinge on the voting decisions of the white conservative voters who supported Morales in the first round. Would they support Parker, the openly gay city controller, or Locke, an African American attorney who was former civil rights activist?

Both runoff candidates worked to turn out their bases of support while appealing to the conservative voters who initially voted for Morales. Parker said that her experience working with city finances better prepared her to guide the city through tough economic times. Locke promised to increase the number of police officers on patrol. Meanwhile, Steven Hotze, an antigay political activist, made sexual orientation an issue by mailing fliers to conservative voters warning about a "gay takeover" of city government and endorsing Locke. Even though Locke was on record as a strong supporter of gay and lesbian rights, he did not reject Hotze's support. In fact, the *Houston Chronicle* newspaper revealed a few days before the runoff election that the two leading members of Locke's finance committee paid for the Hotze mailer.[44]

Houston voters made history in the runoff by electing Parker mayor, 54 percent to 46 percent for Locke. Parker led in every area of the city except for African American neighborhoods, which Locke carried. Her success was built on a deracialization strategy that encompassed not just race and ethnicity but also sexual orientation. Although Parker had always been upfront about her sexual orientation throughout her political career, she focused on issues of concern to Houstonians in general when she ran for mayor. She was a gay candidate but not *the* gay candidate. Whereas many gay and lesbian Houstonians were strongly motivated to contribute money and volunteer their time for her campaign, other Houstonians, including many relatively conservative voters, were not threatened by her. Parker won because most Houston voters consider her the safe choice, safer than Gene Locke.

WHAT WE HAVE LEARNED

1. What is the legal status of city governments in Texas?

Cities are subordinate units of government, subject to the constitutions and laws of the United States and the state of Texas. State law sets the requirements and procedures under which an unincorporated urban area in Texas can become an incorporated municipality. A general-law city is a municipality that is limited to those governmental structures and powers specifically granted by state law. It must follow Dillon's rule. Larger cities may choose home rule, giving them more flexibility than general-law cities in such matters as organizational structure, annexation, ordinance-making authority, and election processes.

2. What are the different forms of city government in Texas?

The mayor-council and council-manager forms of city government are the basic structures of municipal government in Texas. The mayor-council form of city government is a structure of municipal government in which the voters elect a mayor as the chief executive officer of the city and a council that serves as a legislative body. Cities with the mayor-council form of city government vary in the strength of the mayor. Some cities have a strong-mayor variation; others have a weak-mayor variation. Although the mayor-council form of city government is the traditional form for large cities in the United States, Houston is the only big city in Texas that uses it. The state's other large cities have the council-manager form, which is a structure of municipal government in which the city council/mayor appoints a professional administrator, called a city manager, to act as the municipality's chief executive officer. In both systems, the mayor and council make basic policy decisions. In the council-manager form, however, policy implementation is the responsibility of a professional administrator hired by the city council—a city manager.

3. What election systems do Texas cities use?

The at-large election system is the most popular election system used by Texas cities for selecting their city councils. District elections are the next most popular. Historically, district election systems were associated with big-city political machines. For much of the twentieth century, Texas cities elected city councils using nonpartisan at-large election systems, which limited the political influence of ethnic and racial minorities,

primarily African Americans and Latinos. The VRA enabled minority rights groups to attack the at-large election systems in court. As a result, many Texas cities adopted district election systems or systems that combined both district and at-large council seats. The introduction of district election systems led to the selection of city councils in most of the state's big cities that were more ethnically and racially diverse than ever before.

4. What are the most important policies adopted by Texas cities in terms of budgets, annexation, and land use?

Political scientist Paul E. Peterson divides urban public policies into three categories: developmental, redistributive, and allocational. Developmental urban policies are local programs that enhance a community's economic position in its competition with other communities. Redistributive urban policies are local programs that benefit low-income residents of an area. Allocational urban policies are local programs that are more or less neutral in their impact on the local economy.

The state's largest cities are big enterprises with annual budgets well over a billion dollars. Texas cities generate revenue from property taxes, sales taxes, franchise fees, and other sources. City governments borrow money by issuing bonds to cover the cost of capital expenditures. Budgetary policies in urban Texas have historically been allocational and developmental. City governments use tax incentives to promote economic growth, including tax increment financing, tax abatements, and enterprise zones.

Traditionally, cities annex to protect their tax bases. Another reason for annexation is the desire of city officials to prevent encirclement by other incorporated municipalities. Finally, cities annex in order to reap the political benefits of a larger population. Historically, Texas cities have annexed aggressively, but the pace of annexation has recently slowed because of changes in state laws and because of a political backlash from newly annexed residents. Recently passed legislation gives cities and utility districts the authority to negotiate Strategic Partnership Agreements (SPAs) to provide for limited-purpose annexation. State law also gives cities the authority to control development just beyond their city limits, a power known as extraterritoriality.

Historically, land-use policies in Texas cities have been developmental. Building and housing codes are established by city ordinance to set minimum standards for the construction and maintenance of buildings. Many Texas cities (but not Houston) have zoning, the governmental designation of tracts of land for industrial, commercial, or residential use. The opponents of zoning sometimes argue that private deed restrictions are preferable to government regulation.

5. How has big-city politics in Texas evolved since the 1950s?

Before the mid-1970s, big-city politics in Texas was best explained by the elite theory. In one city after another, a small group of wealthy business people dominated politics by controlling economic resources. The overriding goal of the business groups was economic growth and development. Most of the candidates they supported were white businessmen. Economic development and rapid population growth mobilized opposition to the growth-oriented business groups that had long controlled city politics. By the mid-1970s, the rules of the political game had changed sufficiently to allow the new forces to have an impact on the policy process. In particular, the introduction of district elections increased representation for women, minorities, and council members rooted in communities. Contemporary urban politics in Texas reflects pluralist theory or pluralism. Meanwhile, political scientists use the term *deracialization* to describe big-city politics. It is the attempt by political candidates to de-emphasize racially divisive themes in order to garner crossover support from voters of other races/ethnicities while also receiving the overwhelming majority of support from voters of the candidate's own racial/ethnic group. In 2009, Annise Parker was elected mayor of Houston using a deracialization strategy that encompassed not just race and ethnicity but also sexual orientation.

KEY TERMS

allocational urban policies	deed restrictions	housing codes
annexation	deracialization	incorporated municipality
at-large election system	developmental urban policies	initiative process
bond	Dillon's rule	mayor-council form of city government
boosters	district election	
building codes	elite theory (*or* elitism)	minimum wage
capital expenditure	enterprise zones	nonpartisan elections
city charter	extraterritorial jurisdiction (ETJ)	pluralist theory (*or* pluralism)
city manager		political machine
city ordinance	general-law city	political patronage
council-manager form of city government	high-technology industries	population bracket laws
	home-rule city	property tax (*ad valorem* property tax)
cumulative voting system	homestead exemption	

recall election

recession

redistributive urban policies

sales tax

subsidence

tax abatement

tax increment financing

truth-in-taxation laws

unincorporated area

utility district

Voting Rights Act (VRA)

zoning

NOTES

1. Annise Parker for Houston, available at www.anniseparker.com.

2. Gene Locke for Mayor, available at www.genelocke.com.

3. David R. Berman, *Local Government and the States: Autonomy, Politics, and Policy* (Armonk, NY: M.E. Sharpe, 2003), p. 84.

4. Terrell Blodget, "Municipal Home-Rule Charters in Texas," *Public Affairs Comment* 41 (1996): 2.

5. Texas Municipal League, "Local Governments in Texas," available at www.tml.org.

6. Rachel Graves, "In Need of Repairs," *Houston Chronicle*, July 8, 2001, p. 23A.

7. Quoted in T. J. Milling, "'King Kong, 14 Chimps,'" *Houston Chronicle*, October 8, 1995, p. 38A.

8. Rob Gurwitt, "Are City Councils a Relic of the Past?" *Governing*, April 2003, pp. 20–24.

9. Emily Ramshaw, "Strong Mayor Foes Are Diverse," *Dallas Morning News*, January 8, 2005, available at www.dallasnews.com.

10. Texas Municipal League, "Local Governments in Texas."

11. Wayne Lee Gay, "The Salary Survey," *Fort Worth Star-Telegram*, September 12, 2002, available at www.dfw.com.

12. H. George Frederickson, Gary A. Johnson, and Curtis H. Wood, *The Adapted City: Institutional Dynamics and Structural Change* (Armonk, NY: M. E. Sharpe, 2004), pp. 163–167.

13. Steven R. Reed, "Dallas: A City at a Crucial Crossroads," *Houston Chronicle*, December 3, 1990, p. 11A.

14. Joshua G. Behr, *Race, Ethnicity, and the Politics of City Redistricting* (Albany, NY: State University of New York Press, 2000), pp. 97–114.

15. Brandon Formby, "Irving's Single-Member District Plan Unseats Two Officeholders," *Dallas Morning News*, August 21, 2009, available at www.dallasnews.com.

16. Ruth P. Morgan, *Governance by Decree: The Impact of the Voting Rights Act in Dallas* (Lawrence, KS: University of Kansas Press, 2004), pp. 270–273.

17. Jerry L. Polinard, Robert D. Wrinkle, and Tomás Longoria, Jr., "The Impact of District Elections on the Mexican American Community: The Electoral Perspective," *Social Science Quarterly* 72 (September 1991): 608–614.

18. Paul E. Peterson, *City Limits* (Chicago, IL: University of Chicago Press, 1981), Ch. 3.

19. Kenneth K. Wong, "Economic Constraint and Political Choice in Urban Policymaking," *American Journal of Political Science* 32 (February 1988): 1–18.

20. Josh Goodman, "Skybox Skeptics," *Governing*, March 2006, pp. 41–43.

21. *Texas Town and City*, March 1990, pp. 17–35.

22. City of Houston, "Fiscal Year 2011 Budget," available at www.houstontx.gov.

23. Various municipal websites.

24. Alan Greenblatt, "The Loathsome Local Levy," *Governing*, October 2001, p. 36.

25. Sean M. Wood, "Jet Maker to Bring 850 New Jobs to S.A.," *San Antonio Express-News*, June 30, 2006, available at www.mysanantonio.com.

26. Bradley Olson, "Hotel Could Get a Tax Deal," *Houston Chronicle*, April 22, 2009, pp. B1, B3.

27. Helen F. Ladd and John Yinger, *America's Ailing Cities: Fiscal Health and the Design of Urban Policy* (Baltimore, MD: Johns Hopkins University Press, 1989), pp. 287–293.

28. Todd M. Gabe and David S. Kraybill, "The Effect of State Economic Development Incentives on Employment Growth of Establishments," *Journal of Regional Science* 42 (November 2002): 703–730.

29. Texas Municipal League, "Annexation: It Isn't a Four-Letter Word," available at www.tml.org.

30. Arnold P. Fleischmann, "Balancing New Skylines," *Texas Humanist* 6 (January/February 1984): 28–31.

31. Terry Kliewer, "Anxiety over Annexation," *Houston Chronicle*, July 15, 2002, pp. A13–A14.

32. Josh Goodman, "The Tax Grab Game," *Governing*, April 2007, p. 48.

33. Carolyn Feibel and Renee C. Lee, "Council Approves Woodlands Deal," *Houston Chronicle*, October 25, 2007, pp. B1, B4.

34. Jeremy Schwartz, "Cities, Counties Grapple with New Law," *Austin American-Statesman*, April 29, 2002, available at www.statesman.com.

35. Robert D. Thomas and Richard W. Murray, *Pro-Growth Politics: Change and Governance in Houston* (Berkeley, CA: Institute of Government Studies Press, 1991), p. 13.

36. Chandler Davidson and Luis Ricardo Fraga, "Slating Groups as Parties in a 'Nonpartisan' Setting," *Western Political Quarterly* 41 (June 1988): 373–390.

37. Judy Fitzgerald and Melanie Miller, "Fort Worth," in Robert Stewart, ed., *Local Government Election Systems*, Vol. II (Austin, TX: Lyndon B. Johnson School of Public Affairs, 1984), pp. 12–21.

38. Texas Commission on Environmental Quality, "The Quest for Clean Air," available at www.tceq.state.tx.us.

39. Karen M. Kaufmann, *The Urban Voter: Group Conflict and Mayoral Voting Behavior in American Cities* (Ann Arbor, MI: University of Michigan Press, 2004), pp. 197–205.

40. Huey L. Perry, ed., *Race, Politics, and Governance in the United States* (Gainesville, FL: University of Florida Press, 1996), pp. 1–7.

41. Christian Collet, "Minority Candidates, Alternative Media, and Multiethnic America: Deracialization or Toggling?" *Perspectives on Politics* 6 (December 2008): 4.

42. Ibid.

43. Rick Casey, "His Advisers Gave Locke Wrong Key," *Houston Chronicle*, December 13, 2009, pp. A1, A22.

44. Bradley Olson, "Key Locke Backers Gave to Anti-Gay Group," *Houston Chronicle*, December 7, 2009, available at www.chron.com.

Chapter 12

Counties, School Districts, and Special Districts

CHAPTER OUTLINE

County Government
    Legal Status
    Responsibilities
    Organization
    Finances
    Issues in County Government
    County Politics

School Districts
    Administration
    Education Finance

Issues in Educational Policy
Educational Performance

Special Districts
    Reasons for Special Districts
    Creation, Organization, and Operation
    Funding
    Evaluation of Special Districts

What We Have Learned

WHAT WE WILL LEARN

After studying Chapter 12, you should be able to answer the following questions:

1. What is the constitutional/legal status of counties in Texas, how are they structured, how are they funded, what services do they provide, and what issues do they face?

2. How are school districts governed, how are they funded, what issues do they face, and how well do they perform?

3. How are special districts created, organized, operated, and funded, and what are their benefits and liabilities?

The future of Texas looks bleak. Based on current trends, 30 percent of the Texas workforce in 2040 will lack a high school education.[1] The state will not have enough educated workers to move the economy forward. Furthermore, high school dropouts cost the state money because they are more likely than their educated counterparts to collect unemployment, receive welfare benefits, and go to prison. A study conducted by the Bush School of Government and Public Services at Texas A&M University estimates that students in the class of 2012 who drop out of high school will cost the state and its economy $6 billion to $10.7 billion over their lifetimes in lost tax revenues, welfare payments, and prison costs.[2] Texas needs to do a much better job of reducing the high school dropout rate and increasing high school graduation rates, especially for the state's large and growing population of disadvantaged students living in urban areas. Big school districts with large numbers of students from low-income families typically have dropout rates of 50 percent or more.[3]

The controversy over the school dropout rate illustrates the sorts of issues facing local government in Texas. Local government is important, affecting the daily lives of all of the state's residents. The chapter has three sections, one for each major unit of local government except for cities. This chapter begins with county government, then discusses school districts, and concludes with a section on special districts. Each section examines how the particular unit of local government is organized, how it is funded, what services it provides, and the policy challenges it faces.

COUNTY GOVERNMENT

General-law units of local government Units of local government that are limited to those structures and powers specifically granted by state law.

Home rule A unit of local government's authority to take actions not prohibited by the laws or constitutions of the United States or the state.

Texas has 254 counties, ranging in population size from Harris County, with more than four million people, to tiny Loving County, with a population of 65.[4] Some counties are dominated by large cities, such as Harris (Houston), Bexar (San Antonio), Travis (Austin), Tarrant (Fort Worth), El Paso, and Dallas counties. Other counties are predominantly rural, with only a few small towns and no large cities.

Legal Status

Texas counties are **general-law units of local government,** that is, units of local government that are limited to those structures and powers specifically granted by state law. In contrast to Texas cities and the counties in most other states, Texas counties may not adopt home-rule status, which would allow them greater discretion in choosing governmental structures, functions, and tax systems. **Home rule** refers to a unit of local government's authority to take actions not prohibited by the laws or constitutions of the United States or the state. If county officials want to respond to local problems by taking an action not specifically allowed by state law, they must first obtain authorization from the Texas legislature.

Edwards County Courthouse in Rocksprings, Texas.

Responsibilities

County governments in Texas play a dual role of implementing state policies and providing services to residents.

- **Law enforcement** — Counties enforce state laws. The county sheriff's office is the primary law enforcement agency for Texans living in unincorporated areas. Counties also operate county jails, which house people who are awaiting trial and persons convicted of misdemeanor offenses.

- **Courts** — Counties operate justice of the peace, county, and district courts. With the exception of cases tried in municipal court, every state trial that takes place in Texas, both criminal and civil, is held in a court operated by county government.

- **Health** — Counties enforce the state's health laws and provide healthcare services for indigent residents. Under Texas law, counties are required to cover the healthcare costs of residents at or below 21 percent of the federal poverty level ($4,694 a year for a family of four in 2011) if those residents do not qualify for other healthcare programs.[5]

- **Records** — County governments collect and maintain records of births, deaths, marriages, divorces, and deeds.
- **Tax collection** — County governments collect a number of taxes and fees on behalf of the state, including charges for license plates and certificates-of-title for motor vehicles.
- **Elections** — County governments register voters and conduct both primary and general elections for the state.
- **Roads and bridges** — Counties build and maintain roads and bridges.
- **Other services** — State law allows counties to provide a range of additional services. Some counties operate airports or seaports. Counties may also provide their residents with libraries, parks, and recreational facilities. In Houston, for example, Harris County owns and operates Reliant Stadium, the home of the Houston Texans National Football League team.

Organization

Figure 12.1 is the organizational chart of county government in Texas. In many respects, county government is a miniature version of state government in that no single official is in charge. Instead, executive functions are divided among a sizable number of elected and appointed officials.

Commissioners court The board of directors for county government.

Partisan election An election contest in which both the names of the candidates and their party affiliations appear on the ballot.

Commissioners Court The **commissioners court** is the board of directors for county government. It is composed of four county commissioners and the county judge. The members are chosen in partisan elections held concurrently with the biennial statewide general elections. A **partisan election** is an election contest in which both the names and the party affiliation of candidates appear on the ballot. County voters elect the four commissioners, one each from four districts called county commissioner precincts, to serve four-year staggered terms. They elect the county judge countywide to serve a four-year term as well.

Individual commissioners essentially run county government within their precincts. In most counties, the commissioners oversee road repair and construction in their precincts. In fact, roadwork is such an important part of the county commissioners' job in rural counties that residents often refer to them as road commissioners. The commissioners control large road budgets and pick contractors to do county work. Meanwhile, they hire their own crews to do routine maintenance on county roads and in county facilities, such as parks and recreation centers. In Harris County, the state's largest county, the budgets for each of the four commissioners range in size from $40 million to $80 million. They employ full-time staffs of 280 to 380 workers, depending on the geographic size of the precincts.[6] The commissioners also select vendors for the purchase of equipment and supplies.

The responsibilities of the county judge vary, depending on the size of the county. In rural counties, the county judge is the presiding judge in the constitutional county court. In urban counties, the county judge devotes most, if not all, of his or her time to county business and leaves the work of trying cases to the county courts at law. In smaller counties, those with fewer than 225,000 people, the judge is

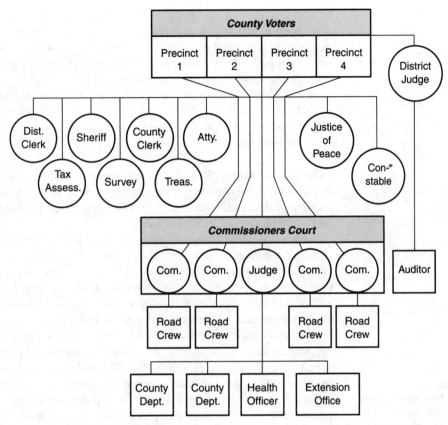

FIGURE 12.1   County Government in Texas.

also the county's chief budget officer. In larger counties, an auditor appointed by the district court judge(s) drafts the budget and oversees county finances.

The powers of the county judge more closely resemble those of a mayor in the council-manager form of city government than a mayor in the mayor-council form of city government with the strong-mayor variation. The county judge presides in the commissioners court but has only one vote and no veto. As the most visible figure in county government, the county judge often serves as the spokesperson for county government. The county judge's ability to provide policy leadership, however, depends more on political skill than official power because the judge lacks the authority to run the commissioners court and has no executive power to manage county government.

The commissioners court has limited authority. It can set the county property tax rate, but it does not have general ordinance-making power. An **ordinance** is a law enacted by the governing body of a unit of local government. Most of the power of the commissioners court comes from its budget-making authority and its power to choose among the optional services county government has available to offer county residents. The commissioners court is empowered to adopt the county budget. This

Ordinance
A law enacted by the governing body of a unit of local government.

authority gives it an important tool to influence policy in county departments not directly under the court's supervision. Also, state law gives the commissioners court authority to determine whether the county will offer residents such local programs/ services as parks, libraries, airports, hospitals, and recreation facilities. In counties that choose to implement these optional programs, the commissioners court appoints administrators to head them. These appointed officials may include a county agricultural agent, home demonstration agent, fire marshal, county health officer, county welfare officer, medical examiner, librarian, county engineer, and, in more populous counties, county purchasing agent.

Other Elected County Officials   The county courthouse houses numerous elected officials in addition to the members of the commissioners court. These officials are chosen in partisan elections to serve staggered four-year terms. All but justices of the peace and constables are elected countywide.

After the county judge, the most visible official is the county sheriff, who is the chief law enforcement officer for the county. The sheriff's department has jurisdiction over the entire county; however, in urban areas, city governments and the county usually agree on a division of responsibilities. City police departments patrol within their cities, whereas the sheriff enforces the law in unincorporated areas. The sheriff also operates the county jail, which holds prisoners awaiting trial for felony offenses and people serving sentences for misdemeanor convictions. In urban counties, in particular, managing the jail consumes a significant proportion of the sheriff department's budget and personnel. Finally, the sheriff assists county courts and state district courts within the county by serving arrest warrants and subpoenas, as well as providing deputies to serve as bailiffs. A **subpoena** is a legal order compelling a person's attendance at an official proceeding, such as a trial.

Subpoena A legal order compelling a person's attendance at an official proceeding, such as a trial.

Larger counties elect both a district attorney and a county attorney. In smaller counties and in Bexar County (San Antonio), the district attorney performs both roles. In counties with both officials, the district attorney's office prosecutes felony criminal cases in state district courts. The county attorney advises the commissioners court and other county officials on legal issues and represents the county in court, mostly in cases of lawsuits to collect delinquent property taxes. The county attorney's office also prosecutes misdemeanor cases in justice of the peace and county courts, except in Harris County, where the district attorney prosecutes both felony and misdemeanor cases.

Two other offices whose titles frequently confuse voters are those of county clerk and district clerk. The county clerk records legal documents, such as deeds, mortgages, and contracts, and keeps vital statistics on births, deaths, marriages, and divorces. The county clerk is also the county election official. He or she conducts early voting, instructs precinct election workers, certifies election returns, and forwards election results to the office of the Texas secretary of state. In a few counties, the county clerk registers voters. The district clerk, meanwhile, maintains legal records for the district courts. In small counties, the county clerk performs the functions of the district clerk.

Justices of the peace (JPs) try Class C misdemeanor cases and hear small claims civil suits. Depending on its population, a county may be divided into as many as eight JP precincts, with each precinct electing one or two JPs. In addition to their judicial duties, JPs in small counties may assume the responsibilities of the county clerk. The JP may also serve as county coroner (although few justices of the peace have medical backgrounds).

Each county elects as many constables as it has justices of the peace. Although constables are certified law enforcement officers, their primary chore in most counties is to assist the JP court(s) by serving legal papers, such as subpoenas and warrants. Constables also handle evictions, execute judgments, and provide bailiffs for the justice courts. In some urban counties, particularly Harris County, constables provide for-hire law enforcement services to subdivisions in unincorporated areas through contract deputy programs.

The tax assessor-collector is the county's chief tax official. The tax assessor collects the county's property taxes, collects fees for automobile license plates, and issues certificates-of-title for motor vehicles. Despite the title of the office, the tax assessor-collector no longer assesses the value of county property for tax purposes. The legislature has assigned that duty to a county tax appraisal district in each county. In small counties, those with fewer than 10,000 people, the sheriff performs the duties of the tax assessor.

Poll tax A tax that prospective voters had to pay in order to register to vote.

In most counties, the tax assessor-collector directs voter registration. This duty is a holdover from the era of the **poll tax,** which was a tax that prospective voters had to pay in order to register to vote. State law allows the commissioners court to transfer voter registration and/or election administration duties to another official, and some urban counties have assigned those responsibilities to the county clerk or to an appointed election administrator.

The county treasurer is responsible for receiving funds and making authorized expenditures. In recent years, the state legislature has proposed and voters have passed constitutional amendments to allow several counties to abolish the office of county treasurer and transfer its duties to the auditor, who is appointed by the district judge(s) in the county.

Two counties, Harris and Dallas, still have county departments of education. These agencies are governed by five-member boards of trustees, with one trustee elected countywide and the other four trustees chosen from the four commissioners court precincts. Historically, county departments of education coordinated relations among the common school districts within the county. Common school districts have now been replaced by independent school districts, and in 1978 the legislature abolished all county education departments except those in Harris and Dallas counties, which successfully argued that they provided important services to county residents. Critics charge that these agencies are expensive bureaucracies whose services can and should be provided by independent school districts.

Finances

Property taxes are the main source of tax revenue for county government. The county tax rate is limited to $0.80 per $100 of valuation, although state law allows county voters to approve as much as $0.15 more for road and bridge operations and

The county jail holds prisoners awaiting trial for felony offenses and people serving sentences for misdemeanor convictions.

TABLE 12.1   Tax Rates in Selected Counties, 2010

County	Tax Rate per $100 Valuation
Bexar (San Antonio)	$0.296187
Dallas	$0.2431
El Paso	$0.361196
Harris (Houston)	$0.388050
Tarrant (Fort Worth)	$0.264
Travis (Austin)	$0.4658

Source: Various county appraisal district websites.

up to $0.30 more to build and maintain farm-to-market (FM) roads. In practice, most county governments set their tax rates well below the allowed maximum. Table 12.1 compares the property tax rates of the largest counties in Texas.

County governments can expand their taxing authority by creating separate but closely allied special districts to provide such costly services as healthcare, flood control, and toll road construction and maintenance. In Harris County, for example, the commissioners court controls three special districts—the Harris County Flood Control District, Hospital District, and Port of Houston Authority. If the property tax rates for these districts were added to the Harris County tax rate, it would jump from $0.38805 to $0.62998. Although that figure would still be well below the state-approved maximum rate for counties, members of the commissioners court find it politically beneficial to spread taxes and occasional tax increases among special districts with their own separate boards of directors, rather than consolidate them under the taxing authority of county government.

Property taxes are not the only revenue source for county governments. Counties that do not have transit authorities or incorporated cities within their boundaries can levy sales taxes. Other revenue sources for county governments include fees for motor vehicle licenses, service charges, and federal aid.

The relative importance of county expenditures varies considerably among counties. Road and bridge construction and maintenance is a major budget item for all counties, but it is particularly prominent in geographically large counties. Rural, sparsely populated counties do little more than maintain the roads, enforce the law, operate a county court, and carry out the basic administrative functions of county government, such as recording deeds and registering voters. In contrast, county governments in metropolitan areas provide a wide range of services, especially if the county has a large population living in unincorporated areas. Although the largest single item in the budget for Harris County is road and bridge construction and maintenance, Harris County government and its related special districts also spend millions of dollars for law enforcement, jail operation, indigent healthcare, the operation of county and district courts, flood control, and parks.

Legislative budget decisions sometimes impact county government. In 2001, the Texas legislature passed and the governor signed legislation requiring counties to establish indigent defense programs to ensure that indigent criminal defendants receive competent legal representation. Although the legislature provided for some funding, county governments were forced to cover more than 90 percent of the program's cost.[7] Similarly, legislative cuts in the State Children's Health Insurance Program increased healthcare costs for counties. The **State Children's Health Insurance Program (SCHIP)** is a federal program designed to provide health insurance to children from low-income families whose parents are not poor enough to qualify for Medicaid. In 2003, legislative cuts in the program left several hundred thousand youngsters from low-income families without health insurance. Without SCHIP coverage, parents often took their ill children to county hospital emergency rooms, forcing county governments to pick up the cost of their healthcare.[8]

State Children's Health Insurance Program (SCHIP)
A federal program designed to provide health insurance to children from low-income families whose parents are not poor enough to qualify for Medicaid.

Issues in County Government

County government has both staunch defenders and harsh critics. The proponents of county government declare that counties are the unit of local government that is closest and most responsive to the people. Counties provide basic government services that citizens want and need. In contrast, critics charge that county government is a relic of the nineteenth century. They believe that county government is inefficient and often corrupt.

To a substantial degree, the validity of the criticism against county government depends on the county's size. For the most part, county government functions effectively in rural and small-town Texas. In rural areas, counties are the primary units of local government. Citizens are aware of county services and know county officials well. In contrast, county governments are almost invisible governments in urban Texas despite employing thousands of persons and spending millions of dollars. Counties operate with little accountability because the media and most citizens are focused primarily on other units and levels of government.

The Long Ballot and Responsibility of the Voters The critics of county government believe that the long ballot makes it difficult for county voters intelligently to choose qualified officeholders, at least in urban areas. The **long ballot** is an election system that provides for the election of nearly every public official of any significance. County elections coincide with state and national primary and general elections held in even-numbered years. Considering all the other races on the ballot in those years, especially in urban counties, many voters may be uninformed about the relative merits of candidates for county clerk, district clerk, or many other county offices. For that matter, most urban voters probably cannot even distinguish between the county clerk and the district clerk.

The theory of democracy is that elections make public officials responsive to the citizens. Public officials do what the voters want because if they do not, they face defeat at the ballot box. However, democracy does not work—or at least does not work well—if the voters are unaware of public officials. Furthermore, elected officials have no incentive to serve the public if the public is unaware of their work. The danger is that public officials who are not likely to be held accountable to the voters will act instead to further their own personal interests and the interests of the individuals and groups that support them politically.

The critics of county government would like to reform the system to make county officials more accountable, at least in urban areas. Reformers would like to reduce the number of elected county officials, either by consolidating positions into a smaller number of offices or providing for the appointment of officials by a single county executive who would be accountable to the voters. Reformers would also like to minimize the role of organized interests in county policymaking.

WHAT DO YOU THINK?

Are too many county officials elected for voters to keep track of the offices and the candidates?

Hiring, Purchasing, Contracting, and Conflict of Interest **Conflict of interest** refers to a situation in which the personal interests of a public official may clash with that official's professional responsibilities. For example, a public official faces a conflict

Long ballot An election system that provides for the election of nearly every public official of any significance.

Conflict of interest A situation in which the personal interests of a public official may clash with that official's professional responsibilities.

of interest in determining whether to award a government contract to a firm owned by family members, as opposed to a company whose management has no personal connection to the official. Public policy analysts generally believe that government works better when public officials avoid decisions in which their personal interests are at stake.

The critics of county government believe that county operations make conflicts of interest inevitable. In general, county commissioners and elected department heads hire and fire employees as they see fit. County governments lack a merit-hiring system and county employees do not enjoy civil service protection. Critics say that county officials often hire and fire employees for political reasons. Furthermore, county employees have an incentive to become campaign workers for their bosses at election time, perhaps even on county time.

Another problem is the absence of centralized purchasing in most counties. Each department contracts for goods and services on its own, often without the benefit of competitive bids. At a minimum, this practice prevents the county from taking advantage of quantity discounts. More seriously, it increases opportunities for corruption by county officials who may be tempted to do business with their friends and political supporters.

The contracting process presents similar problems. County governments contract for services from engineers, accountants, surveyors, architects, and attorneys. Most of these services are provided in connection with road construction projects. Although rural counties are small businesses, urban counties are big businesses. In 2011, general fund expenditures for Harris County totaled $1.4 billion.[9]

Because state law prohibits competitive bidding, individual commissioners decide which firms receive the contracts for work in their precincts, whereas the commissioners court as a whole awards contracts for the entire county. In practice, the firms who win the contracts are also the major election campaign supporters of the county commissioners. Between 2003 and 2007, for example, the five members of the commissioners court in Harris County raised more than $10 million in campaign contributions, with most of the money coming from contractors, engineering firms, law firms, and architectural firms that received millions of dollars in no-bid contracts from the county. The single largest campaign donor, James Dannenbaum of Dannenbaum Engineering, contributed $160,000, while receiving $6.6 million in county contracts.[10]

The contracting process is highly controversial. County commissioners declare that they select the firms best able to provide the services to their constituents. Political contributions have no impact on their decisions, they say, because state law makes it illegal for public officials to accept campaign contributions or anything else of value in return for a contract. In contrast, critics charge that the contracting process is inherently corrupt. Furthermore, they say, the system helps insulate the county commissioners from electoral accountability. County commissioners receive so much campaign money from firms doing business with the county that incumbent commissioners are virtually impossible to defeat for reelection, at least in urban areas. Since 1974, for example, only one incumbent Harris County commissioner has been defeated for reelection.[11]

Some counties use a unit road system, which is a centralized system for maintaining county roads and bridges under the authority of the county engineer. The proponents of the unit road system argue that it allows county government to operate more efficiently and less politically. In contrast, county commissioners, who would suffer a loss of political influence under a unit road system, contend that it would weaken local control of road and bridge maintenance.

Decentralization and Accountability Critics believe that the decentralization of county government makes it difficult for county officials to fulfill the responsibilities of their offices and impossible for voters to accurately evaluate their performance. In many instances, the people who raise revenue and write the budget—the commissioners court—have no direct control over the people who administer county programs—the elected department heads. The sheriff, for example, is the county's chief law enforcement official but does not directly control the budget for law enforcement. If county residents are unhappy with the operation of the county jail, whom do they blame—the commissioners court for not putting enough money in the budget, or the sheriff for being a poor administrator?

 **WHAT DO YOU THINK?**

Is county government too decentralized to operate efficiently?

Structural Inflexibility and the Twenty-first Century Is county government able to respond to contemporary policy problems, especially in urban areas? Anyone driving through an urban county can easily identify where a city's jurisdiction ends and the county jurisdiction begins by the proliferation of roadside vendors, fireworks stands, outsized billboards, portable signs, and automobile junkyards. Cities can pass ordinances to regulate such matters, but counties cannot. Some reformers favor granting county government ordinance-making power, especially county governments in urban areas. If counties could make ordinances, they could better address issues of development in unincorporated areas, such as land use, flood control, environmental protection, and neighborhood integrity. In contrast, the opponents of ordinance-making power for county government are against giving yet another unit of government the power to regulate people's lives.

County Politics

The nature of county politics depends on the county. In rural and small-town Texas, county government is high profile because counties are the primary units of local government. The population is small enough that public officials and county residents often know one another personally. Officials in some counties hold office for decades without facing electoral challenge, sometimes because they are personally popular and sometimes because no one else wants the job. In other counties, political factions form, often on the basis of personalities, and compete for control, usually in the Democratic Party primary. (Despite the growth of the Republican Party in state politics, most rural county courthouses remain Democratic.) The issues of county government in rural Texas are relatively minor; nonetheless, they are important to the people involved. Fixing potholes and paving country roads may not be the most important policy issues facing government in Texas, but they are important issues to the people who live in the region.

In urban areas, county governments are big business but low profile. Most residents of the state's big cities are unaware of county issues and ignorant of county government. The local media typically ignore county issues, preferring instead to cover crime, automobile accidents, and natural disasters. When local media outlets do cover local government, they typically focus on city government and, occasionally, school district politics, but they seldom address county issues.

County government in urban areas is important, especially to selected segments of the population. People without health insurance rely on county health clinics and charity hospitals for healthcare. Residents of unincorporated areas depend on the county sheriff for police protection. Land developers benefit from road construction that provides access to their property. Engineers, contractors, attorneys, surveyors, and other professionals do substantial business with county government.

SCHOOL DISTRICTS

Many Texans consider school districts the most important unit of local government. Public education is the single largest budget expenditure for state and local government in Texas. In fact, many homeowners pay more money in school property taxes than they do in county and city property taxes combined. School districts are major employers, and school activities, especially high school football, are the focus of social life in many communities. Good schools are the foundation for economic growth in a community and the instrument for training young people for success in college and the workforce.

Administration

**Independent
School Districts
(ISDs)** Units of
local government
that provide public
education services to
district residents from
kindergarten through
the 12th grade.

Independent school districts (ISDs) are units of local government that provide public education services to district residents from kindergarten through the 12th grade. The state has more than a thousand school districts, ranging in size from the Houston ISD with just over 200,000 students, to several hundred districts that have fewer than 500 students. In 2011–2012, 4.8 million students attended public schools in Texas.[12]

The governing body for ISDs is the board of trustees, generally composed of seven members (although some of the larger districts have nine members). Trustees may be elected either at-large or from districts to serve terms of two, three, four, or six years. Two-year terms are the most common. School trustee elections, which are nonpartisan, are usually held at times that do not coincide with statewide spring primaries and general elections. **Nonpartisan elections** are elections in which candidates run without party labels. In many urban areas, city elections and school trustee elections take place on the same day, usually the second Saturday in May in odd-numbered years.

**Nonpartisan
elections** Election
contests in which
the names of the
candidates, but not
their party affiliations,
appear on the ballot.

The board of trustees is a body of ordinary citizens that meets periodically to set policy for the district. The members of the board of trustees receive no salary for their services; they are laypeople rather than professional educators. The board approves the budget, sets the property tax rate, and arranges financial audits. It makes personnel decisions, involving such matters as setting the salary schedule and approving personnel contracts. Other board decisions concern the awarding of contracts for the expansion and repair of the district's physical plant.

Perhaps the board's most important decision is the hiring of a superintendent. The superintendent is a professional school administrator who manages the day-to-day operation of the district and ensures that the board's policy decisions are implemented effectively. Board members tend to defer to the superintendent on the basic outline of education policy. Nonetheless, board members, especially in urban districts, frequently make political demands on a superintendent regarding contracts and jobs, especially when it comes to responding to the needs of particular ethnic groups or constituencies. In large urban districts, boards of trustees are sometimes split along racial and ethnic lines, as well as between members representing inner-city areas and members from the suburbs. Consequently, superintendents of urban districts may find themselves caught in the crossfire of a divided board. Nationwide, the average tenure for superintendents in large urban districts is about three years.[13]

Public schools in Texas educate 4.8 million students.

Education Finance

The federal government, state government, and local taxpayers fund public education in Texas. Figure 12.2 shows the relative importance of the three revenue sources for school districts. In 2010, the average ISD received 47 percent of its funds from local tax sources, 43 percent from the state, and 10 percent in federal grant money.[14]

The relative importance of funding sources varies dramatically among school districts. Figure 12.3 compares funding sources for two large, big-city school districts, Houston Independent School District (HISD) and El Paso Independent School District (EPISD). The HISD raises most of its money from local property taxes,

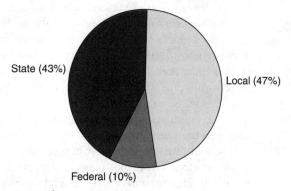

FIGURE 12.2   Education Funding Sources, 2010.
Source: Texas Education Agency.

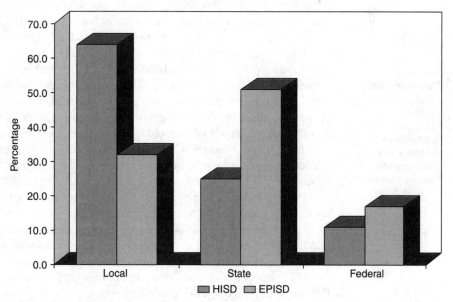

FIGURE 12.3   Funding Comparison, Houston and El Paso.
Source: Texas Education Agency.

Federal grant program A program through which the national government gives money to state and local governments to spend in accordance with set standards and conditions.

School Lunch Program A federal program that provides free or reduced-cost lunches to children from poor families.

Foundation School Program The basic funding program for public education in the state of Texas.

Permanent School Fund (PSF) A fund established in the Texas Constitution as an endowment to finance public elementary and secondary education.

whereas the EPISD gets more of its funding from the state than from any other source. Both districts receive some money from the federal government.

District funding reflects differences in the way the money is raised or awarded. The federal government awards money to school districts through a **federal grant program,** a program through which the national government gives money to state and local governments to spend in accordance with set standards and conditions. Federal grant money targets economically disadvantaged students and students with disabilities. Federal dollars also support the **School Lunch Program,** a federal program that provides free or inexpensive lunches to children from poor families. The amount of federal money a school district receives depends on such factors as the number of district students who are economically disadvantaged or who have limited English-language proficiency. Both the HISD and the EPISD qualify for substantial amounts of federal money under those criteria because a large proportion of their students are poor, have limited English-language proficiency, or need special education. In contrast to the HISD and EPISD, school districts that serve an affluent population, such as the Highland Park ISD in Dallas, receive almost no federal grant money.

The **Foundation School Program** is the basic funding program for public education in the state of Texas. The legislature establishes certain minimum standards that school districts must meet in such areas as teacher compensation and student transportation. The actual amount of money a district receives depends on district wealth, local property tax rates, and a host of other factors. Wealthy districts, such as Highland Park ISD, receive relatively little state money, whereas poor districts, such as the Edgewood ISD in San Antonio, receive most of their money from the state. Because the El Paso ISD is relatively poorer than the Houston ISD, it receives a greater share of its funding from the state than does the HISD.

The state distributes other money to school districts from the Available School Fund. In the 1850s, the legislature set aside a large block of state land to create a trust fund for public education. Income from the sale and lease of that land and from royalties earned from oil and gas production on it goes into the **Permanent School Fund (PSF),** a fund constitutionally established as an endowment to finance public elementary and secondary education. The PSF principal of $24.4 billion cannot be spent.[15] Instead, it must be invested to earn interest and dividends, which go into the Available School Fund (ASF). The ASF is also supported by one-fourth of the taxes collected on motor fuels and natural resources. The state distributes ASF money to school districts based on the number of students in average daily attendance.

Public education in Texas is also funded through local property taxes. School districts use local tax money to participate in the Foundation School Program and for "local enrichment," that is, to pay for services that go beyond the state-mandated minimum standards. Local money pays for building and maintaining school facilities as well and to pay off debt incurred when schools and other district facilities were built.

School tax rates tend to be higher than the property tax rates assessed by counties and cities. A school district's property tax rate includes a maintenance and operations (M&O) rate, as well as an interest and sinking fund (I&S) rate. The M&O rate applies to the district's general operating expenses, whereas the I&S

rate is used to pay off the district's bond debt. Before 2006, the legislature limited the M&O rate to $1.50 per $100 valuation. It capped the I&S rate at $0.50 for debt incurred since 1992 plus whatever rate was needed to pay off debts incurred before 1992.[16] In 2006, the legislature passed and the governor signed a measure that reduced the maximum M&O rate to $1.00 in 2007. The cap for the I&S rate remained unchanged.[17] Local school boards could add another 4 cents to the rate for local enrichment if they wished and, faced with increased enrollment and the rising cost of student transportation, almost every district exercised that option. If local school districts wished to generate more money, they could increase their M&O tax rate as high as $1.17 with voter approval. However, the voter approval requirement has apparently discouraged districts from raising taxes. Between 2006 and 2010, only about a fifth of the state's school districts asked voter authorization to raise taxes, with 70 percent winning approval.[18]

School districts grant property tax breaks to homeowners and people over 65 years of age. The Texas Constitution provides for a $15,000 homestead exemption, reducing the taxable value of a home for school tax purposes. Most school districts grant additional exemptions for persons with disabilities and people over 65 years of age. Furthermore, a homeowner's school property taxes are frozen at age 65. Regardless of increases in tax rates, elderly Texans are assessed the same tax rate they were charged on their current home when they reached their 65th birthday.

The state's system of financing public education has long been controversial because districts with wealthy property tax bases can raise more money than districts that are less affluent, even with lower property tax rates. The Glen Rose ISD in Somervell County benefits from having a nuclear power plant in its taxing district. As a result, the taxable value of property located in the Glen Rose ISD is nearly $2.1 million per student. With a relatively modest tax rate of $0.894, Glen Rose ISD generates $11,118 a year per student locally. In contrast, Crystal City ISD in Zavala County includes no refineries or power plants within its boundaries. The taxable value of property in Crystal City ISD is only $96,677 per student. Even with a relatively hefty property tax rate of $1.510, Crystal City ISD raises just $2,240 per pupil in local revenue. Left to its own financial resources, the Glen Rose ISD would have substantially more money to spend to provide a quality education to its 1,651 students than Crystal City ISD would have to support the education of its 1,924 students.[19]

In 1989, the Texas Supreme Court ruled in the case of *Edgewood ISD v. Kirby* that the state's system of financing public education violated the Texas Constitution. The court ordered the legislature to create a system whereby districts with the same tax rate would have roughly the same amount of money to spend per student.[20] The court focused on equality of tax revenues rather than equality of expenditures. It ordered the state to adopt a system of school funding that ensured that districts would generate similar revenue per student at similar levels of tax effort. If Glen Rose ISD and Crystal City ISD had the same property tax rate, then they would be able to raise the same amount of money per student. The court did not require expenditure equality because it did not force districts to have the same tax rate. The citizens of Crystal City ISD (or Glen Rose ISD) could choose to fund their schools more (or less) generously by adopting a higher (or lower) tax rate than most other districts.

Robin Hood plan
A reform of the state's school finance system designed to increase funding for poor school districts by redistributing money from wealthy districts.

The legislature responded to *Edgewood v. Kirby* by adopting the **Robin Hood Plan,** a reform of the state's school finance system designed to equalize funding among school districts by redistributing money from wealthy districts. Districts that are able to generate more property tax revenue per student than allowed by the state have several choices, but most wealthy districts have complied with the law by either sending money to the state or transferring it to one of the state's poor school districts. In 2011–2012, for example, Glen Rose ISD sent the state more than $14 million out of local property tax revenue of $25 million.[21]

 WHAT DO YOU THINK?

Is the Robin Hood school-finance reform plan fair?

Issues in Educational Policy

Educational issues are an important part of the official Texas policy agenda. We discuss six of the more prominent contemporary educational issues: charter schools, merit pay, school choice, class size, bilingual education, and basic-skills testing.

Charter school A publicly funded but privately managed school that operates under the terms of a formal contract, or charter, with the state.

Charter Schools A **charter school** is a publicly funded but privately managed school that operates under the terms of a formal contract, or charter, with the state. Parents, teachers, private companies, and nonprofit organizations may petition the state for a charter to create a school. The charter spells out the school's educational programs, targets the student population the school intends to serve, defines the school's management style, and identifies its educational goals. Each charter school is independent in that it is not part of an ISD and parents from any district may voluntarily choose to send their children to a particular charter. Charter schools may not discriminate on the basis of race, ethnicity, gender, disability, or educational need, but they may refuse to accept a student who has a history of misbehavior. A charter school may not charge tuition or levy taxes. The state funds charter schools through the Foundation School Program, awarding the same amount of money per student that it gives to traditional public schools. Although the state provides no funding for facilities, it provides loan guarantees to enable financially sound charter schools to qualify for lower interest rates when they borrow money to construct facilities. In 2011, 120,000 students attended one of the state's 390 chapter schools.[22]

Charter schools are exempt from most state education regulations. Although they must conform to health and safety codes and teach the state-mandated curriculum, they do not have to follow state regulations concerning class sizes, teacher qualifications, and the school calendar. Nonetheless, the state evaluates charter schools using the same basis as it judges other schools and on the basis of the goals the schools set for themselves. If a charter school performs poorly and fails to meet its goals, it risks losing its charter and having to close its doors.

BREAKING NEWS!

Another School Funding Lawsuit Filed

Public school districts around the state have filed yet another lawsuit against the state over funding. In *Edgewood v. Kirby* (1973), the Texas Supreme Court ruled that the Texas Constitution requires that school districts with the same tax rate should be able to raise the same amount of money per student. Today, however, the state's poorest school districts have $2,500 less to spend per student than the wealthiest school districts despite levying higher tax rates. School officials believe that this is a clear violation of the funding principle established in the *Edgewood* case. Frustrated with the failure of the Texas legislature to correct the inequity, they are planning to go to court. John Folks, the superintendent of Northside ISD, San Antonio's largest school district, believes that litigation is a certainty. "If the only option that school districts have to force the legislature to do what is right, as far as public education is concerned, is a lawsuit, that's pretty sad."*

Discussion

Why doesn't the legislature fix the problem? The legislature resolved the *Edgewood* case by taking money away from the wealthy districts, the so-called Robin Hood Plan. Robin Hood infuriated voters living in districts that lost funding, but it did not please the people living in poor districts because relatively little new money flowed to the poor districts. Fixing the current funding disparity would require increasing the amount of money that the Robin Hood Plan takes from wealthier districts. Many of the state's voters, especially voters who participate in Republican primary elections, want to repeal Robin Hood, not expand it.

Instead of taking money from wealthy districts, why doesn't the legislature spend more money on education in the poorer districts? What money? In 2011, the legislature faced a $27 billion shortfall and the governor declared his intent to veto any tax increase or any attempt to use the Rainy Day Fund. Instead of adding money to education, the legislature cut $4 billion from what school districts would have gotten under current funding formulas.

So education isn't a priority? In 2011, holding the line on taxes and cutting government spending were the priorities of the legislature and the governor. To be fair, many Republican legislators believe that school districts have enough money to do the job but that they do not use it effectively.

And school districts are likely to file suit because the legislature isn't giving them more money? Yes. School officials are furious with the legislature over budget cuts that have forced them to lay off personnel, including teachers, dip into reserve funds, and increase class sizes. They also know that the only time the legislature has dealt with school funding issues in the past has been when the Texas Supreme Court has given them a deadline to act.

* Gary Scharrer, "Schools Prepare to Sue the State Again," *San Antonio Express News*, July 17, 2011, available at www.mysanantonio.com.

Charter schools are controversial. Their supporters believe that each charter school is an opportunity for educational innovation. Teachers can better do their jobs when freed of red tape, they say. Moreover, the competition from charter schools will force public schools to perform better. In contrast, the critics of charter schools argue that they are a back-door method for funneling taxpayer dollars from public schools to private schools. State funds should be used to improve the existing schools, the critics say, rather than support an unproven educational experiment.

The performance of charter schools has been uneven. Although some charter schools, mostly small, college-preparatory schools, have excelled, other charter schools have failed to make the grade, because of poor test scores, financial mismanagement, or both. A national study of charter school performance conducted by Stanford University found that 17 percent of charters provide outstanding educational opportunities for their students and nearly half of charters achieve results no different from the local public school option. Over a third of charter schools perform worse than their traditional school counterparts. Furthermore, the report singles out Texas for doing a particularly poor job of holding badly run charter schools accountable.[23]

School choice An educational reform movement that allows parents to choose the elementary or secondary school their children will attend.

School Choice The educational reform movement that allows parents to choose the elementary or secondary school their children will attend is known as **school choice.** Under a parental choice program, the state would give parents a voucher that would provide a type of scholarship to be paid to the school that the parents select for their

AROUND THE NATION

Cash for Grades in the District of Columbia

Students in the District of Columbia (DC) can earn money by making good grades. The program, which targets low-income middle school pupils, allows students to collect as much as $100 every two weeks if they behave themselves, wear their school uniforms, go to class, complete their homework, and get good grades. During the fall term of 2008, the average DC student earned $406 of a possible $1,000.*

Cash for grades is controversial. The program's advocates see it as a way to close the performance gap between low-income and middle-class youngsters. Although wealthy families reward their children with trips, parties, and even cash for doing well in school, low-income families do not have the option. In contrast, the opponents of the program contend that students should value learning for learning's sake, not because of a financial reward. Furthermore, the program is expensive to implement.

Research on the effectiveness of cash incentive programs is mixed at best. Studies show that student performance improves during the program, but then falls back after the program ends and the money goes away. Studies find no evidence that cash rewards have a lasting effect on student learning. In fact, cash incentive programs may actually undercut interest in learning.†

QUESTIONS

1. Would you do better in this course if you were promised cash for making a good grade?
2. Are cash-for-grades programs a good use of taxpayer dollars? Why or why not?
3. Do the arguments used in favor of merit pay for teachers also apply to financial incentive programs for students (and vice versa)?

* Theresa Vargas, "Cash Incentives Create Competition," *Washington Post*, March 22, 2009, available at www.washingtonpost.com.

† Zach Patton, "Wage Learners," *Governing*, August 2009, pp. 25–28.

child to attend. Some proponents of parental choice would allow parents to choose not only from among public schools but also from among private schools.

School choice is controversial. The proponents of school choice believe that competition for funding will force schools to improve. If low-quality public schools did not upgrade the quality of their educational programs, they would have to shut down for lack of funding. In contrast, the opponents of school choice question whether lack of competition is the main problem with public schools, believing instead that poverty, lack of parental involvement, and inadequate funding are the primary causes of poor school performance. They fear that vouchers would enable middle-class parents to take their children from public schools, leaving the children of poor families behind in public schools with even less funding. Public schools would get worse, they say, not better.

Texas has a limited school choice program. The parents of students in schools that are judged as low-performing schools for two consecutive years can transfer their children to any other public school in the district that will agree to receive them, including charter schools. The parents of students in low-performing schools are also eligible for free tutoring. In practice, however, few parents and students take advantage of their opportunities.

 WHAT DO YOU THINK?

If you were a parent of a student in a low-performing public school, would you transfer your child to another school?

Merit Pay Texas once had the largest merit pay program for teachers in the nation. In 2009, the Texas legislature appropriated $400 million for merit pay, divided between the 2009–2010 and 2010–2011 school years. The program, called District Awards for Teacher Excellence (DATE), provided money for districts that chose to participate. Although districts established their own reward criteria, the state required that at least 60 percent of the funds be used for bonuses based on student performance. The rest of the money could be used as stipends for teachers working in hard-to-staff schools or in high-demand subjects, such as math and science.[24] In 2011, however, the Texas legislature slashed funding for the merit pay to $40 million, barely enough money to keep the program alive.[25]

Merit pay has both defenders and critics. The advocates of merit pay believe that teachers who work hard and produce positive results should be rewarded financially for their good performance. Merit pay gives all teachers an incentive to do their best and encourages the most effective teachers to remain on the job, rather than leaving the field for higher-paying jobs. The Texas merit pay program also provides districts with money that can be used to reward the best, most experienced teachers for working in schools with large numbers of low-income and minority students.[26] In contrast, teacher unions and other critics of merit pay complain that merit pay is too often based on simplistic measures of performance that fail to grasp the essence of good teaching. Instead of incentive bonuses, the opponents of merit pay favor raising teacher salaries across the board.[27]

Research on the effect of the Texas merit pay program found that it had a small but measurable positive impact on teacher turnover and student test scores. Schools that awarded merit pay bonuses had less teacher turnover than schools that did not participate in the program. The study found that larger bonuses had a greater impact on teacher retention than smaller bonuses. Schools that participated in the merit pay program also recorded greater gains in test scores compared with schools that did not participate. Once again, larger bonuses were associated with greater student achievement gains than were smaller bonuses.[28]

Class Size Does class size matter? Some advocates of education reform believe that the key to improving education is to have smaller classes. The concept is fairly simple: Teachers can do a better job if they have fewer students in a class. In recent years, some state legislatures have mandated smaller class sizes, especially in the early grades. Texas law caps the size of classes in kindergarten through the fourth grade at 22 students, although districts may request a waiver if a school is struggling with rapid growth, lacks facilities, or, beginning in 2011, faces a financial emergency. In fact, most school districts expect larger class sizes in the 2011–2012 and 2012–2013 school years because they will not have sufficient funds to hire additional teachers to keep up with enrollment growth.

Critics argue that the movement to reduce class size may not be a good use of resources. Reducing class size is an expensive reform because it requires school districts to hire additional teachers. Furthermore, research on the effect of smaller class sizes is unclear. Studies show that class sizes must drop to 15–17 students to make much difference, and even then smaller classes seem to make a difference only in student performance in the lowest grades. Critics of the smaller-class movement believe that the money could be better spent on teacher training.

Bilingual education Teaching of academic subjects in both English and a student's native language, usually Spanish.

Bilingual Education **Bilingual education** is the teaching of academic subjects in both English and the student's native language, usually Spanish. About a sixth of the state's public school children have limited proficiency in the English language, including 33 percent in the Dallas ISD, 30 percent in the Houston ISD, and 29 percent in the El Paso ISD.[29] Spanish is by far the most common language spoken by Texas children who have limited English-language ability.

GETTING INVOLVED

Helping a Child Learn

Nothing is more rewarding than helping a child learn. Most school districts have tutoring programs, in which volunteers assist students trying to learn to read or understand mathematics. Call your local school district (the number is in the telephone book) and volunteer to tutor.

It's your community—get involved!

Bilingual education is a controversial educational policy issue. The advocates of bilingual education believe that it enables students whose primary language is not English to learn academic subjects in their own language while they work on their English. Otherwise, they would fall behind, grow frustrated with school, and potentially drop out. Students enrolled in bilingual education programs typically take several years to learn to read, write, and speak English well enough to enter mainstream classes. In contrast, the opponents of bilingual education argue that it retards the English-language development of non-English-speaking students. They believe that students with limited English-language proficiency are better served by a period of intensive English instruction, after which they enter regular academic classes.

Texas schools use a mixture of bilingual education and English-language immersion programs. The legislature has neither mandated bilingual education nor prohibited its use. Instead, each district decides how it can best meet the educational needs of students with limited English-language proficiency.

No Child Left Behind Act (NCLB)
A federal law that requires state governments and local school districts to institute basic skills testing in reading and mathematics for students in grades three through eight, and use the results to assess school performance.

Basic-skills Testing The **No Child Left Behind Act (NCLB)** is a federal law that requires state governments and local school districts to institute basic-skills testing as a condition for receiving federal aid. The results of the tests must be used to assess school performance and track the progress of individual students. Poor-performing schools that fail to improve will eventually lose federal aid money.

Prior to the 2011–2012 school year, Texas used the Texas Assessment of Knowledge and Skills (TAKS) to measure student progress and assess school performance. TAKS testing began in the third grade and continued through high school. Ninth-grade students took TAKS tests in reading and math. Tenth and 11th graders tested in English, math, science, and social sciences. Eleventh graders had to pass all four subjects to earn a diploma, regardless of their course grades. Students who failed in the 11th grade had several more opportunities to pass the test in their senior year and even during the summer after graduation. Students who failed to pass the graduation TAKS could still participate in their high school's graduation ceremony, but they received a certificate of attendance rather than a diploma, unless they eventually passed the test. In 2011, 1 in 12 high school seniors, more than 20,000 students, failed the TAKS and were prevented from graduating.[30] The Texas Education Agency (TEA) used TAKS scores along with four-year high school graduation rates to classify schools and school districts as exemplary, recognized, academically acceptable, or academically unacceptable. In 2010–2011, 5 percent of Texas schools were rated exemplary, 34 percent were recognized, 53 percent were classified as acceptable, and 7 percent were scored unacceptable. (The figures do not add to 100 percent because of rounding.)[31]

In 2011, Texas replaced TAKS with a new basic-skills test called the State of Texas Assessment of Academic Readiness (STAAR). The new test, which is designed to assess college readiness, is tougher than TAKS. High school students will have to average passing scores in end-of-course exams in English, social studies, math, and science in order to graduate. STAAR testing will begin in grades 3–9 in 2011 and then be phased in for high school sophomores, juniors, and seniors over the next several years.

The proponents of basic-skills tests, such as TAKS and STAAR, believe that testing improves public education by holding students, teachers, and school administrators accountable. Students in elementary and middle school must pass the test before they can be promoted to higher grades. High school students must pass in order to graduate. Teachers may face reassignment and school administrators may lose their jobs if their students do poorly on the test. In contrast, the critics of basic-skills testing argue that tests actually undermine educational quality because they force schools to focus on the test rather than student learning. Schools neglect other subjects for weeks before the test is given so they can prepare. Much of their work focuses not on basic skills but on test-taking techniques. Instead of learning to read, write, and do math, students learn how to take multiple-choice exams.

Educational Performance

Independent assessments of the performance of Texas schools indicate that the state's students are less well prepared for college and the workforce than students in many other states. Consider the performance of Texas students on the SAT, which is a standardized exam taken by students planning to apply for admission to a university. In 2010, Texas ranked 45th of 50 states in combined SAT scores.[32] The state ranked 49th in average verbal SAT, 46th in mathematics, and 47th in literacy.[33] Texas does an average job at best in preparing students for college. Half the students entering public colleges and universities in the state are unprepared for college-level work in math, reading, or writing and therefore must take at least one remedial course. Moreover, students who enter college unprepared for college work are much less likely to graduate than are students who have college-level skills.

Educational attainment in Texas lags behind the national average. According to data from the U.S. Census Bureau, 19.3 percent of Texans age 25 and older lacked a high school diploma in 2010 compared with a national figure of 14.4 percent. Meanwhile, the percentage of Texans with a bachelor's degree or higher was 25.9 percent compared with the national figure of 28.1 percent. The relatively low level of educational attainment in Texas helps account for the state's relatively low level of personal income and relatively high poverty rate. Furthermore, Texas businesses are often forced to recruit out of state to find workers with the skills necessary for high-paying jobs. William Flores, the president of the University of Houston-Downtown, notes that many of the highest-paid positions in the Texas Medical Center and NASA are held by people who were educated in other states and countries because Texas residents are not qualified to fill them.[34]

SPECIAL DISTRICTS

A **special district** is a unit of local government created to perform specific functions. Soil and water conservation districts, for example, work to prevent soil erosion and preserve water resources. Levee improvement districts build and maintain levees. Coastal subsidence districts regulate the use of subsurface water resources in order

Special district
A unit of local government created to perform specific functions.

Subsidence
The sinking of the surface of the land caused by the too-rapid extraction of subsurface water.

Utility district A special district that provides utilities, such as water and sewer service, to residents living in unincorporated urban areas.

Hospital district
A special district that provides emergency medical services, indigent healthcare, and community health services.

to minimize **subsidence,** the sinking of the surface of the land caused by the too-rapid extraction of subsurface water. Mosquito control districts spray for mosquitoes to control annoying pests and reduce the danger of encephalitis and other diseases spread by mosquitoes. Groundwater conservation districts work with local landowners to conserve underground water supplies.

Special districts provide important governmental services to millions of Texans. A **utility district** is a special district that provides utilities, such as water and sewer service, to residents living in unincorporated urban areas. Texas has more than 1,100 utility districts, going by such names as Fresh Water Supply Districts (FWSDs), Water Control and Improvement Districts (WCIDs), and Municipal Utility Districts (MUDs), which are the most numerous. In addition to water and sewer services, utility districts may also provide their residents with solid waste collection, fire protection, drainage, parks, and recreation facilities. A **hospital district** is a special district that provides emergency medical services, indigent healthcare, and community health services. The Harris County Hospital District, for example, is the primary medical provider for nearly a million residents in Harris County who do not have health insurance. Its operating budget exceeds $1.3 billion a year.[35] Community/junior college districts enroll more students in higher education than do the state's public universities. Flood control districts are responsible for flood control in many areas of the state.

Reasons for Special Districts

Special districts are created to provide services that other units of local government cannot or will not provide. For example, state law specifies a maximum property tax rate for counties and cities. Local governments can overcome the property tax ceiling by creating special districts with their own taxing authority. Harris County has a flood control district, hospital district, and port authority. Although these districts are separate units of government with their own taxing authority, the Harris County Commissioners Court controls them. Transit authorities and port authorities are other big-budget special districts whose operations could not easily be financed within the budget constraints of existing city and county governments.

Sometimes special districts are an advantageous approach to solving problems that transcend the boundaries of existing units of local government. Flooding, for example, is seldom confined to a single county or city. A countywide or area-wide flood control district offers a regional approach to a regional problem. Similarly, transportation problems may affect several cities and counties. In each of these cases, it is often easier to create a special district that includes the whole area affected by the problem than it is to coordinate the efforts of existing governments.

Other motivations for the establishment of special districts include political expediency and financial gain. At times, existing units of local government refuse to provide certain services because of the opposition of individual officeholders. Special districts can be an effective means of outflanking that opposition. Some problems, such as flood control or mass transit, may become so difficult or controversial that local officials may choose to ignore them. The creation of a special district allows officials to pass the buck while taking credit for having taken the problem "out of politics."

Utility districts enable developers to build subdivisions in rural areas, outside of the coverage of municipal water and sewer services. The utility district borrows money to build water and sewer systems for the development. Homeowners pay off the debt over time through service charges and property taxes. By using a utility district to defer the construction cost of a water and sewer system, developers are able to reduce their upfront construction expenditures, and consumers can buy new homes less expensively than if the utility costs were built into the purchase price. In Denton County, for example, a developer named Realty Capital Belmont Corp. is using two freshwater supply districts to help fund a 4,000-home development project near Argyle and Northlake. In 2006, the developer parked three mobile homes on the property and rented them to employees. The renters filed the necessary paperwork to establish residency and then requested an election to create two freshwater supply districts. In 2007, the seven registered voters living in the three mobile homes cast their ballots to approve the creation of the districts, which would borrow money to pay for roads, water pipes, and a sewage treatment system. The development's future homeowners will pay off the debt with a property tax whose rate could be as high as $1 per $100 of valuation.[36]

Creation, Organization, and Operation

Special districts are created through a variety of procedures. Hospital districts require the adoption of a constitutional amendment. The State Soil and Water Conservation Board creates soil and water conservation districts. The legislature, the Texas Commission on Environmental Quality (TCEQ), or a county commissioners court can establish utility districts. Utility districts that are to be located in a city's extraterritorial jurisdiction must first be approved by that city. The Texas legislature authorizes community/junior college districts, transit authorities, port authorities, and sports authorities.

Most districts require voter approval of area residents before they begin operations. After the legislature authorizes the creation of a utility district, for example, the measure goes on the ballot for approval by voters living within the boundaries of the proposed district. At the same election, voters may also be asked to grant the district authority to sell bonds (that is, to borrow money) and to tax. Utility districts generally issue bonds to finance the construction of sewage treatment plants. Flood control districts use them to pay for drainage improvements. Airport authorities use bond money to build runways and terminals. Sports authorities issue bonds to finance the construction of sports stadiums.

A board of directors, usually consisting of five members, is the governing body for most special districts. The board may be either appointed or elected. District voters elect most water district and community/junior college boards, whereas city mayors appoint housing authority boards. The governor names the directors of river authorities. County commissioners courts select hospital, noxious weed control, and rural fire prevention district boards. In most cases, district board members are unsalaried. They set basic policy but leave the day-to-day operation of the district to a professional staff. Perhaps the most important task for the board of trustees of a community/junior college district, for example, is to hire a chancellor or president to manage the daily affairs of the college.

Funding

Special districts receive funding from a variety of sources. Many districts levy taxes. Utility districts, port authorities, hospital districts, flood control districts, and community/junior college districts all levy property taxes. Suburban utility districts often assess higher property tax rates than do nearby incorporated municipalities. The funding for sports authorities may come from sales taxes, hotel/motel occupancy taxes, property taxes, or taxes on rental cars. Transit authorities levy sales taxes.

Special districts raise revenues from service charges. Utility districts charge residents for water and sewer usage and for garbage pickup. Students in community/junior college districts pay tuition and fees for the classes they take. Transit authorities raise revenues from ticket charges. Toll road authorities collect tolls from drivers. Funding for coastal subsidence districts comes from fees charged for permits to drill water wells. Finally, special districts receive funding from other units of government. Federal mass transit aid supports the state's transit authorities. Community/junior college districts benefit from state funding and federal grant money. Hospital districts receive both federal and state funding to support their programs, including funding from the two huge federal healthcare programs, Medicare and Medicaid.

Evaluation of Special Districts

Special districts have both defenders and critics. Their supporters argue that they provide services that otherwise would not be available. In contrast, critics identify several problem areas. First, special districts often operate in the shadows, with little state supervision and even less public participation. For example, fewer than a dozen voters may participate in utility district authorization elections. Second, special districts generally operate less efficiently than general-purpose units of local government, such as cities and counties.[37] Small districts, particularly utility districts, can be uneconomical. Their operations are often run amateurishly and they are too small to take advantage of economies of scale. Finally, the multiplicity of special districts in Texas complicates the problems of urban government. For example, many observers believe that utility districts are a major cause of land subsidence in the Houston-Galveston area because of their extensive use of subsurface water resources.

WHAT WE HAVE LEARNED

1. What is the constitutional/legal status of counties in Texas, how are they structured, how are they funded, what services do they provide, and what issues do they face?

Texas has 254 counties, ranging in size from the sparsely populated to urban counties with millions of people. As general-law units of local government, counties are limited to the structures of government and powers set by state law. Counties play a dual role in that they provide services to county residents and implement state policies. County governments enforce state laws, operate state and county courts, provide some health services, keep records, collect certain taxes, administer elections, build and maintain roads and bridges, and provide other services.

Counties have numerous elected officials. The commissioners court, with a county judge and four commissioners, is the board of directors for county government. Although the commissioners court sets the property tax rate and adopts a budget, it does not have general ordinance-making power. Other elected county officials, depending somewhat on the size of the county (large counties have more officials than smaller counties), include the sheriff, district attorney, county attorney, district clerk, county clerk, justices of the peace, constables, tax assessor-collector, county treasurer, and, in Harris and Dallas counties, county boards of education.

Property taxes are the main source of tax revenue for county government. County governments can expand their taxing capacity by creating separate but closely allied special districts to provide such costly services as healthcare, flood control, and toll road construction and maintenance. Other revenue sources for county governments include fees for motor vehicle licenses, service charges, and federal aid.

Although road and bridge construction is a major budget item in all counties, it is particularly important in geographically large counties.

County governments in metropolitan areas provide a wide range of services, especially if the county has a large population living in unincorporated areas. These services include law enforcement, jail operation, indigent healthcare, the operation of county and district courts, flood control, and parks.

The issues facing county government depend on the size of the county. In rural areas, county governments are the local government closest to the people. In urban areas, county governments are almost invisible governments despite employing thousands of persons and spending millions of dollars. Issues include the long ballot and accountability to the voters; hiring, purchasing, contracting, and conflicts of interest; decentralization and accountability; and problems created because of structural decentralization.

2. How are school districts governed, how are they funded, what issues do they face, and how well do they perform?

Independent school districts (ISDs) are units of local government that provide public education services to district residents from kindergarten through the 12th grade. Each ISD is governed by an elected board of trustees, a body of ordinary citizens that meets periodically to set policy for the district. The board hires a professional administrator called a superintendent to run the day-to-day affairs of the district.

School districts receive money from the federal government, state government, and from local property taxes. The federal government gives money to school districts through grant programs, such as the School Lunch Program. The Foundation School Program is the basic funding program for K–12 education in Texas. The state's system of financing public education has long been controversial because districts with wealthy property tax bases can raise more money than districts that are less affluent, even if the wealthy districts have lower property tax rates. In *Edgewood v. Kirby* the Texas Supreme Court ordered the legislature to create a system whereby districts with the same tax rate would have roughly the same amount of money to spend per student. The legislature responded by adopting the Robin Hood Plan, a reform of the state's school finance system designed to equalize funding among school districts by redistributing money from wealthy districts. Because of budget cuts adopted in the 2011 session of the legislature, school districts around the state have had to increase class sizes and lay off personnel, including some teachers.

Texas school districts face a number of important issues, involving charter schools, merit pay, school choice, class size, bilingual education, and basic-skills testing. A charter school is a publicly funded but privately managed school that operates under the terms of a formal contract, or charter, with the state. Whereas supporters believe that charter schools are an opportunity for innovation, critics charge that they are a back-door method for funneling taxpayer money to private schools. School choice is the educational reform movement that allows parents to choose the elementary or secondary school their children will attend. The proponents of school choice believe that competition for funding will force schools to improve, but critics warn that choice will weaken public schools by taking funding away from them. Education reformers also debate the merits of class size. Bilingual education, the teaching of academic subjects in both English and the student's native language, usually Spanish, is controversial as well. No Child Left Behind (NCLB) is a federal law that requires state governments and local school districts to institute basic skills testing as a condition for receiving federal aid. Texas recently replaced TAKS with a new, more difficult test called STAAR. The proponents of basic skills testing believe that it improves public education

by holding students, teachers, and school administrators accountable. In contrast, the critics argue that tests actually undermine educational quality because they force schools to focus on the test rather than student learning.

Independent assessments of the performance of Texas schools indicate that the state's students are less well prepared for college and the workforce than students in many other states. Average SAT scores in Texas are below the national average while the dropout rate exceeds the national average. Texas does only an average job at best in preparing students for college. Educational attainment in Texas lags behind the national average. The relatively low level of educational attainment in Texas helps account for the state's relatively low level of personal income and relatively high poverty rate.

3. **How are special districts created, organized, operated, and funded, and what are their benefits and liabilities?**

A special district is a unit of local government created to perform specific functions. Special districts include transit authorities, mosquito control districts, hospital districts, community college districts, flood control districts, port authorities, utility districts, and many more. Special districts are formed to provide services that other units of government cannot or will not provide. They are created through a variety of procedures, including the adoption of amendments to the Texas Constitution or the actions of the Texas legislature, TCEQ, or county commissioners court. Most districts require voter approval of area residents before they begin operations. Special districts receive funding from a variety of sources, including taxes and service charges. The supporters of special districts argue that they provide services that otherwise would not be available. Critics charge that they often operate inefficiently and uneconomically, and that they complicate the problems of local government.

KEY TERMS

bilingual education

charter school

commissioners court

conflict of interest

federal grant program

Foundation School Program

general-law units of local government

home rule

hospital district

independent school districts (ISDs)

long ballot

No Child Left Behind Act (NCLB)

nonpartisan elections

ordinance

partisan election

Permanent School Fund (PSF)

poll tax

Robin Hood Plan

school choice

School Lunch Program

special district

State Children's Health Insurance Program (SCHIP)

subpoena

subsidence

utility district

NOTES

1. Gary Scharrer, "Poverty, Dropout Rates Bode Grim Future for State," *Houston Chronicle*, June 20, 2010, available at www.chron.com.

2. Kate Alexander, "Study: Dropouts Costing Texas Billions," *Austin American-Statesman*, August 23, 2009, available at www.statesman.com.

3. Scharrer, "Poverty, Dropout Rates Bode Grim Future for State."

4. U.S. Bureau of the Census, available at www.census.gov.

5. Melissa del Bosque, "Sick and Tired: How Texas' Healthcare System Bleeds County Coffers and Sends Some to Early Graves," *Texas Observer*, September 4, 2009, pp. 8–14.

6. Rick Casey, "Why Run for Judge If You're King," *Houston Chronicle*, July 8, 2005, p. B1.

7. Equal Justice Center, "Texas Indigent Defense Spending," available at www.equaljusticecenter.org.

8. Glenn Evans, "Counties Concerned over Too Much Control Coming out of Austin," *Longview News-Journal*, April 4, 2004, available at www.news-journal.com.

9. Harris County, FY 2011–2012 Budget, available at www.co.harris.tx.us.

10. Chase David, "Few Rivals But Plenty of Donors," *Houston Chronicle*, November 24, 2007, pp. A1, A9.

11. Chris Moran, "The Most Secure Job in Politics," *Houston Chronicle*, January 12, 2010, p. A1.

12. Texas Education Agency, available at http://ritter.tea.state.tx.us.

13. Council of Great City Schools, available at www.cgcs.org.

14. Texas Education Agency, "Snapshot 2010 Summary Tables," available at www.tea.

15. Office of the Permanent School Fund, *Texas Permanent School Fund, Annual Report, Fiscal Year Ending August 31, 2010*, available at www.tea.state.tx.us.

16. *Financing Public Education in Texas*, 2nd ed., available at www.lbb.state.tx.us.

17. House Research Organization, Focus Report, "Schools and Taxes: A Summary of Legislation of the 2006 Special Session," available at www.hro.house.state.tx.us.

18. Terrence Stutz, "Few Texas School Districts Have Asked Voters to Raise Tax Rates Since 2006 Law Took Hold," *Dallas Morning News*, September 8, 2010, available at www.dallasnews.com.

19. Texas Education Agency, available at www.tea.state.tx.us.

20. *Edgewood v. Kirby*, 777 S.W.2d 391 (1989).

21. Texas Education Agency, available at www.tea.state.tx.us.

22. Thanh Tan, "Lawmakers Help Texas Charter Schools Build, Expand," August 20, 2011, *Texas Tribune*, available at www.texastribune.org.

23. Sam Dillon, "Education Chief to Warn Advocates That Inferior Charter Schools Harm the Effort," *New York Times*, June 22, 2009, available at www.nytimes.com.

24. Terrence Stutz, "Texas Takes Another Crack at Merit Pay," *Dallas Morning News*, August 24, 2009, available at www.dallasnews.com.

25. Terrence Stutz, "Texas Merit Pay Plan for Teachers Among Programs Slashed by Legislature," *Dallas Morning News*, June 23, 2011, available at www.dallasnews.com.

26. Kate Alexander, "Experienced Teachers Not in Neediest Schools, Report Shows," *Austin American-Statesman*, August 5, 2008, available at www.statesman.com.

27. Alan Greenblatt, "Merit Pay Moves Forward," *Governing*, January 2007, p. 51.

28. Terrence Stutz, "Study Shows Texas Teacher Merit Pay Helps Keep Staff, Slightly Helps Test Scores," *Dallas Morning News*, December 6, 2010, available at www.dallasnews.com.

29. Texas Education Agency, "2006 District AEIS+ Report," available at www.tea.state.tx.us.

30. Terrence Stutz, "1 in 12 High School Seniors Fail TAKS, Won't Get Diplomas," *Dallas Morning News*, May 26, 2011, available at www.dallasnews.com.

31. Morgan Smith, "With Change in Formula, Texas School Ratings Drop," *Texas Tribune*, July 29, 2011, available at www.texastribune.org.

32. Gary Scharrer, "Perry's SAT Scores Not as Good as Advertised," *Houston Chronicle*, July 14, 2010, available at www.chron.com.

33. Paul Baskin, "In Texas, Clues to Gov. Perry's Science Agenda," *Chronicle of Higher Education*, September 28, 2011, available at http://chronicle.com.

34. Jeannie Kever, "Census Finds City Lags in Education," *Houston Chronicle*, September 22, 2011, pp. A1, A7.

35. Harris County Hospital District, "Changing Lives Through Health and Wellness: 2009 Annual Report," available at www.hchdonline.com.

36. Dan X. McGraw, "Special Districts Get Voter Approval," *Denton Record-Chronicle*, November 12, 2007, available at www.dentonrc.com.

37. Kathryn A. Foster, *The Political Economy of Special-Purpose Government* (Washington, DC: Georgetown University Press, 1997), pp. 174–183.

Chapter 13

State Budget Policy

CHAPTER OUTLINE

Revenues
    Taxes
    Non-Tax Sources of Revenue

Issues in State Finance
    State Revenue Adequacy
    Tax Incidence
    Tax Fairness
    Tax Elasticity

Policy Options for Reforming
    the State Revenue System
        Adopting a Personal Income Tax
        Broadening the Sales Tax Base
        Expanding Legalized Gambling
        Selling Assets
        Giving Tax Relief to Low-Income Families

State Expenditures

Budget Priorities
    Healthcare
    Elementary and Secondary Education
    Higher Education
    Welfare
    Transportation

The Budget Process

Making Budgetary Policy
    The Context of Budgetary Policymaking
    Agenda Setting
    Policy Formulation, Adoption, and
        Legitimation
    Policy Implementation, Evaluation,
        and Change

What We Have Learned

WHAT WE WILL LEARN

After studying Chapter 13, you should be able to answer the following questions:

1. What are the most important revenue sources for the state of Texas, including both tax and non-tax sources, and how has the relative importance of those sources changed over the last 20 years?

2. What important revenue issues face state government in Texas?

3. What policy options are offered for reforming the state's revenue structure?

4. How do spending levels in Texas compare and contrast with those of other states?

5. What are the most important budget priorities in Texas, and how are those priorities reflected in budget policy?

6. What are the primary steps in the state budgetary process?

7. How are budget policies made in Texas?

Governor Rick Perry wants to reform higher education in Texas by improving teaching and reducing cost. Perry has embraced a set of policy proposals championed by Jeff Sandefer, a member of the board of directors of the Texas Public Policy Foundation, which is a conservative think tank. Sandefer's reforms include the following proposals:

- Universities should give more weight to teaching in making decisions about their budgets and faculty tenure;
- Universities should require senior faculty to teach more classes, especially classes taken by first-year students and sophomores;
- Universities should give large cash bonuses to faculty members with the best student teaching evaluations; and
- Instead of funding universities directly, the state should give vouchers to students who can use them at the public or private institution of their choice within the state of Texas.[1]

Sandefer believes that most senior universities are inefficient because faculty members are unproductive. Although a few senior faculty members win grants and publish valuable research, most of the faculty produces research that has little value while teaching only a handful of small upper-level classes. If unproductive researchers were assigned to the classroom, universities could cut costs while improving the quality of undergraduate education, especially if faculty evaluations and tenure decisions were at least partially based on teaching evaluations.[2] Moreover, Governor Perry has challenged the state's college and universities to offer students a $10,000 bachelor's degree, including the cost of textbooks.[3]

Many university faculty and administrators as well as their allies in the business community believe that Sandefer's approach to higher education will lead to mediocrity. The University of Texas (UT) at Austin and Texas A&M University at College Station are recognized among the nation's elite research institutions. Shifting faculty and budget resources from research to the classroom will diminish their ability to maintain that status. Meanwhile, changing the focus from research to teaching will make it difficult to recruit and retain top-notch faculty members.[4] Basing faculty evaluations and tenure decisions on teaching evaluations will lead to grade inflation. Giving vouchers to students will divert money from state institutions to private schools, including, presumably, the Acton Institute's MBA program, founded by Jeff Sandefer.

The controversy over higher education reform introduces this chapter on budgetary policymaking. The chapter begins with a section examining state revenues. What are the state's most important revenue sources? The next section of the chapter identifies the most important state revenue issues. The chapter then examines proposals for addressing those issues. The next section of the chapter turns to expenditures, comparing expenditure levels in Texas with those of other states. The chapter continues by discussing the most important budget priorities of the state. The chapter reviews the budgetary process before concluding with an overview of budgetary policymaking.

 WHAT DO YOU THINK?

Should universities focus less on research and more on teaching?

REVENUES

Fiscal year Budget year.

During the 2010 **fiscal year** (i.e., budget year), the state of Texas generated $87.4 billion in revenue from all sources, including both taxes and non-tax sources of revenue. Table 13.1 identifies the various sources of state revenue and indicates

TABLE 13.1   State Revenues by Source, Fiscal Years 1990, 2000, and 2010

Tax Sources as a Percentage of Total State Revenue			
Source	1990	2000	2010
General sales tax	32.1%	28.0%	22.5%
Franchise tax	2.5	4.1	4.4
Motor fuels tax	6.4	5.4	3.5
Motor vehicle sales and rental	4.6	5.6	3.0
Taxes on alcohol and tobacco products	3.2	2.1	2.5
Severance taxes on oil and gas production	4.6	2.2	2.0
Insurance company tax	2.2	1.6	1.5
Utility taxes	0.8	0.5	0.5
Other taxes	1.3	1.2	0.6
Total taxes	**57.7**	**50.7**	**40.5**
Non-Tax Sources as a Percentage of Total State Revenue			
Source	1990	2000	2010
Federal funds	25.1%	29.7%	42.2%
Licenses and fees	6.7	8.5	7.9
Net lottery proceeds	–	2.6	1.9
Interest and investment income	7.1	3.8	1.2
Land income	1.2	0.5	0.9
Other non-tax revenue	2.2	5.7	5.4
Total non-tax sources of revenue	**42.3**	**49.3**	**59.5**
Total net revenue (tax and non-tax sources combined)	**100 %** ($23.6 billion)	**100 %** ($49.8 billion)	**100 %** ($87.4 billion)

Source: Texas Comptroller of Public Accounts, "Revenue by Source," various years, available at www.cpa.state.tx.us.

their relative importance. Because the table includes data for fiscal years 1990, 2000, and 2010, it also shows changes in the relative importance of each revenue source across time.

Taxes

In 2010, the state of Texas raised 40.5 percent of its total revenue from taxes. The general sales tax was by far the most important state tax source, generating substantially more money than any other tax. The other major state taxes included a business franchise tax, a motor fuels tax, a tax on motor vehicle sales and rental, and severance taxes on oil and natural gas production.

The relative importance of taxes to the state's revenue picture has declined over the last 20 years. As Table 13.1 indicates, the proportion of state revenue generated by taxes fell from nearly 57.7 percent in 1990 to 40.5 percent in 2010. Taxes have declined as a source of state revenue relative to total revenues because of the rapid growth of non-tax sources of revenue, especially federal funds. Since 1990, federal funds have increased from 25.1 percent of state revenues to 42.2 percent. Most of the growth in federal funds has been through the **Medicaid** program, a federal program designed to provide health insurance coverage to the poor, people with disabilities, and elderly Americans who are impoverished.

Medicaid A federal program designed to provide health insurance coverage to low-income persons, people with disabilities, and elderly people who are impoverished.

General Sales Tax A **sales tax** is a levy on the retail sale of taxable items. Texas levies a sales tax of 6.25 percent on the retail purchase of taxable items. Only eight states have a higher sales tax rate than the Lone Star State.[5] Cities and other units of local government may add as much as 2 percent more to the state tax rate, bringing the total sales tax in many areas of the state to 8.25 percent.

Not all sales are subject to taxation. Although restaurant meals are taxable, food purchased at a grocery store is tax exempt (except for ready-to-eat items). The sale of most agricultural items is tax exempt, including the sale of agricultural machinery and parts, fertilizer, feed for animals, and seed. Drugs and medicine are exempt as well, whether sold over the counter or by prescription. Only some services are taxable. The list of taxable services includes charges for laundry, dry cleaning, cable television service, credit reporting, data processing, debt collection, landscaping, security, telecommunications, car repair, and janitorial services. The sales tax does not apply, however, to charges and fees for many other services, including legal retainers, accounting services, builder and contractor fees, real estate commissions, brokerage fees, and healthcare charges.

Sales tax A levy on the retail sale of taxable items.

The growth of Internet sales is undermining the state sales tax base. State governments cannot legally compel an Internet or mail-order retailer to collect its sales tax unless the retailer has a physical presence in the state. Sears, for example, charges sales tax on Internet purchases made by Texas consumers because Sears has stores throughout the state, but LL Bean, an Internet and mail-order retailer based in Maine, does not because it has no outlets located in the Lone Star State. The Texas comptroller estimates that the Internet sales tax exemption costs Texas state and local governments $600 million annually, a figure representing 3 percent of total sales tax collections.[6]

Franchise tax A tax on businesses chartered or organized in Texas and doing business in the state.

Franchise Tax A **franchise tax** is a tax on businesses chartered or organized in Texas and doing business in the state. It is the primary tax assessed by state government on business, but it is not the *only* tax businesses pay because local governments also levy property taxes on business property, such as land, warehouses, manufacturing plants, stores, inventory, and office buildings. In 2006, the legislature increased the franchise tax rate and expanded its coverage in order to replace the revenue lost by cutting school property taxes. The new franchise tax generated 4.4 percent of state revenue in 2010 compared with 3.6 percent of state revenue in 2006, the year the new tax was adopted.[7]

Severance tax A tax imposed on the removal of nonrenewable resources, such as crude oil and natural gas.

Severance Taxes on Oil and Natural Gas Production A tax imposed on the removal of nonrenewable resources, such as crude oil and natural gas, is known as a **severance tax**. The most important severance taxes in Texas are levied on the production of oil and natural gas. The state collects a 4.6 percent tax on the value of oil produced and 7.5 percent on natural gas, rates that are comparable to those charged by other energy-producing states. Texas also levies severance taxes on the production of cement and the extraction of sulfur. The role of severance taxes in the state's revenue picture fell for years because oil production had been in long-term decline. In 2007, Texas oil production hit bottom at 336 million barrels compared with the peak of

Texans pay one of the highest sales taxes in the nation.

784 million barrels in 1986. Subsequently, Texas oil production has begun to increase, rising to 362 million barrels in 2010.[8] Severance tax collections also fluctuate with the price of oil and gas. In recent years, severance tax collections have increased as the price of oil has risen. In 2010, severance taxes accounted for 2 percent of state revenues, which, despite the recent uptick in oil production and prices, was considerably lower than in 2000 and 1990.

Excise tax A tax levied on the manufacture, transportation, sale, or consumption of a particular item or set of related items.

Excise Taxes An **excise tax** is a tax levied on the manufacture, transportation, sale, or consumption of a particular item or set of related items. It is a selective sales tax. Texas state government levies excise taxes on motor vehicle sales and rentals, motor fuels, alcohol, and tobacco. In 2010, the state's various excise taxes collectively generated 9 percent of state revenue. Excise taxes on alcohol and tobacco products are called sin taxes.

Sin tax A levy on an activity that some people consider morally objectionable, such as smoking or drinking.

A **sin tax** is a levy on an activity that some people consider morally objectionable, such as smoking or drinking. Sin taxes are designed not just to raise revenue but also to discourage the behavior. In 2006, for example, the legislature increased the state's cigarette tax by $1.00 a pack to $1.41, moving the Texas tax rate to the top third among states nationwide. The goal of the tax increase was both to raise revenue to use to fund school property tax cuts and to discourage smoking. The measure is apparently achieving both goals because tobacco tax revenues are up and smoking is down.[9]

 WHAT DO YOU THINK?

Should the government increase taxes on tobacco products and alcohol to discourage smoking and drinking?

Other Taxes In addition to the general sales tax, franchise tax, severance taxes on oil and gas production, and excise taxes, the state of Texas assesses a number of other levies. These other taxes include an insurance company tax and utility taxes. Not one of these taxes accounts for as much as 2 percent of the state's total revenue, but collectively they are an important part of the state's revenue picture.

Pari-mutuel wagering A system for gambling on horse and dog racing.

The state's revenue sources also include taxes on **pari-mutuel wagering,** a system for gambling on horse and dog racing. In this system, the total amount of money wagered on a horse or dog race is pooled and then divided among those who bet on one of the top three finishers, minus percentages that go to the owners of the winning animals, track management, and the government. In 1987, the legislature authorized pari-mutuel gambling on horse and dog racing pending voter approval in a statewide referendum, which passed by a good margin. The legislature permitted the construction of major horse tracks in the Dallas, Houston, San Antonio, and Fort Worth areas, with smaller tracks allowed in other counties pending local voter approval. The legislature permitted the construction of greyhound racetracks in three counties—Galveston, Nueces (Corpus Christi), and Cameron (Brownsville). Although some observers predicted that taxes on pari-mutuel wagering would eventually produce as much as $100 million a year, the payoff for the state has been insignificant. In 2010, pari-mutuel wagering generated $3 million in state revenue, well less than 0.10 percent of total state revenues.[10]

WHAT DO YOU THINK?

Should the state of Texas allow gambling on dog and horse racing?

Non-Tax Sources of Revenue

Non-tax sources of revenue account for a majority of total state revenues.

Federal Funds The federal government is a major funding source for state government in Texas, accounting for more than 40 percent of state revenues in 2010. Medicaid is the largest single source of federal financial aid to state government. Federal money also supports highway construction, a number of welfare programs, and a broad range of other state activities.

Licenses and Fees Texas state government raises money through the sale of licenses and the collection of fees. Texans who wish to drive a motor vehicle, operate a business, practice a profession, go hunting and fishing, attend a state university, or sell

Taxes on pari-mutuel wagering have so far generated relatively little revenue for the state.

alcoholic beverages must purchase licenses or pay a fee for the privilege. In 2010, licenses and fees accounted for 7.9 percent of state revenue.

Interest and Investment Income The state of Texas holds billions of dollars in cash and securities that generate dividend and interest income from their investment. The largest pool of money is the **Texas Teacher Retirement System (TRS) Trust Fund,** a pension fund for the state's public school teachers. The TRS Trust Fund held $108.2 billion in assets in 2011.[11] Similarly, the **Employees Retirement System (ERS) Trust Fund** is a pension fund for state employees. It was worth $20.7 billion at the end of 2010.[12] The TRS and ERS trust funds provide retirement, disability, and death or survivor benefits to their members. Both funds declined in value in late 2008 and early 2009 when the stock market suffered heavy losses.

Although the TRS and ERS trust funds seem flush with cash, they lack sufficient assets to cover future liabilities. The TRS Trust Fund is more than $25 billion short of having enough money to cover promised retirement benefits for current and future retirees, whereas the ERS Trust Fund is $4.8 billion short.[13] Rather than address the trust fund shortfall, the legislature made the problem worse in 2011 by reducing the state contribution rate from 6.5 percent to 6.0 percent. "We didn't have the money," explained State Senate Finance Committee Chair Steve Ogden, a Republican from Bryan.[14]

The Permanent School Fund (PSF) and the Permanent University Fund (PUF) support education. The **Permanent School Fund (PSF)** is a fund established in the Texas Constitution as an endowment to finance public elementary and secondary education. At the end of 2010, the market value of PSF bonds and securities stood at $24.4 billion.[15] The **Permanent University Fund (PUF)** is a fund established in the Texas Constitution as an endowment to finance construction, maintenance, and some other activities at the University of Texas and Texas A&M University. The value of the PUF in 2010 was $12.8 billion.[16] The state's interest and investment income varies, depending on the investment climate. In 2010, interest and investment income accounted for 1.2 percent of state revenue.

Land Income The state of Texas owns more than 20 million acres of land that produce revenue for the state from leases for agricultural use and for oil and gas production. The PSF and PUF hold the largest blocks of land—13 million acres and 2.1 million acres, respectively. Income from land held by the PSF and PUF is invested in stocks, bonds, and other securities, which, in turn, generate interest and investment income. In 2010, land income accounted for 0.9 percent of state revenue.

Lottery Revenue Since the Texas Lottery began operation in 1992 it has generated more than $18 billion for the state.[17] Although that is a great deal of money, it is a relatively small part of the state's total revenue picture. In fact, lottery revenues accounted for just 1.9 percent of state revenues in 2010. Furthermore, most of the money the lottery generates goes for marketing, vendor commissions, and prizes rather than the state treasury. Figure 13.1 shows the distribution of money spent on the lottery. More than 60 percent of the money that Texans pay for lottery tickets goes for prizes. After subtracting money for administration and for compensation to

Texas Teacher Retirement System (TRS) Trust Fund A pension fund for the state's public school teachers.

Employees Retirement System (ERS) Trust Fund A pension fund for state employees.

Permanent School Fund (PSF) A fund established in the Texas Constitution as an endowment to finance public elementary and secondary education.

Permanent University Fund (PUF) Money constitutionally set aside as an endowment to finance construction, maintenance, and some other activities at the University of Texas, Texas A&M University, and other institutions in those two university systems.

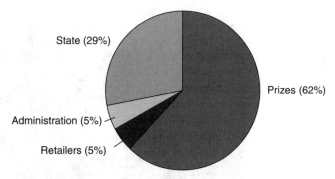

FIGURE 13.1 Distribution of Lottery Proceeds.

retailers for selling lottery tickets, the state realizes 27 percent in revenue of every dollar spent on the lottery.

Most state lottery proceeds go for education, with the rest benefiting the Fund for Veterans Assistance. When the lottery was created, the legislature funneled lottery earnings into the **General Fund,** the state treasury account that supports state programs and services without restriction. In 1997, the legislature amended the law to dedicate lottery proceeds to public education. Because the legislature reduced education spending by a sum equal to the amount of anticipated lottery proceeds, the dedication had no impact on the total amount of money spent for education in Texas. Since 2010, some lottery earnings have gone to benefit veterans.

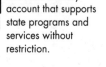

General Fund
The state treasury account that supports state programs and services without restriction.

 **WHAT DO YOU THINK?**

Is it morally wrong for the government to use gambling to raise money?

The history of lotteries nationwide is that they start strong but then decline as the novelty wears off. States attempt to slow or reverse the decline by introducing new or different games and by manipulating how jackpots pile up.[18] Texas is no exception to the pattern. In 1998, Texas Lottery sales dropped after the legislature reduced prizes in order to increase the amount of money going to the state. The Lottery Commission reacted to the situation by making the lottery more difficult to win. Instead of having to pick six numbers correctly from 1 to 50, players had to pick six numbers from 1 to 54. This increased the odds of winning from 15.8 million to 1 to 25.8 million to 1. By making the lottery more difficult to win, the state hoped to increase the size of the jackpots, which would entice more people to spend money on lottery tickets. The strategy worked for a while because lottery sales increased temporarily. When ticket sales slumped again, the state made it even more difficult to win by adding a Bonus Ball, reducing the odds of winning to 47.7 million to 1.[19]

In 2003, the legislature passed, and the governor signed, legislation authorizing the state's participation in a multi-state lottery in hopes of generating additional gambling revenue. The Lottery Commission has decided to participate in both Mega Millions and Powerball, games that are offered in a number of states. Mega Millions

The Texas Lottery generates 1.9 percent of total state revenue.

and Powerball are attractive to bettors because the long odds of winning, more than 100 million to 1, have produced some giant jackpots, including a payout of more than $360 million.[20]

Other Non-Tax Revenue The "other non-tax revenue" category in Table 13.1 groups a number of miscellaneous revenue sources, which in 2010 collectively generated 5.4 percent of total state revenue. For example, the category includes employee benefit contributions, which is money withheld from the paychecks of state workers to cover health insurance for their families and for other benefits. Although the money is technically revenue to the state, the funds are earmarked for employee benefits.

The category also contains revenue from the tobacco lawsuit settlement. In 1996, Texas brought suit against eight large tobacco companies, their public relations companies, and their research firms, accusing them of violating state and federal law by marketing tobacco products to children and adjusting the nicotine levels in tobacco to cause mass addiction. The suit asked for money to cover the state's share of the healthcare costs of Medicaid recipients suffering from smoking-related illnesses. Rather than go to trial, the tobacco industry agreed to a $17.3 billion settlement to be paid out over 25 years.[21]

ISSUES IN STATE FINANCE

Texas policymakers face a number of issues in government finance.

State Revenue Adequacy

The tax burden in Texas is the lowest in the nation. Per capita state taxes are $1,368 compared with a national figure of $2,049.[22] State and local governments in Texas generate less revenue per capita than do their counterparts in other states primarily because Texas is one of only seven states (Alaska, Florida, Nevada, South Dakota, Washington, and Wyoming are the others) without a personal income tax. However, most other state and local taxes in Texas are relatively high.

Recession An economic slowdown characterized by declining economic output and rising unemployment.

Texas government is facing a budget crisis. In the short run, the problem is the lasting effect of the severe recession that began in late 2008 and extended through most of 2009. A **recession** is an economic slowdown characterized by declining economic output and rising unemployment. State revenues fall during a recession because people make fewer purchases that are subject to the state sales tax and the motor vehicle sales and rental tax. Figure 13.2 shows Texas tax receipts each year from 2001 through 2010. As the figure indicates, tax receipts peaked in 2008 before declining substantially in 2009 and 2010, even after the recession officially ended. Meanwhile, state spending increases during a recession because more people can qualify for unemployment benefits and welfare payments.

The Texas legislature was able to balance the budget for 2010–2011 even though it had less state tax money to spend than it had in the previous budget period by using federal stimulus funds and surplus money left over from the previous budget period. In early 2009, Congress passed, and President Barack Obama signed, an $877 billion stimulus package, known as the American Recovery and Reinvestment Act, in order to reduce the impact of the recession.[23] The legislature used part of the money allocated to Texas, $6.4 billion, to help fund state services. The legislature also had available $5.7 billion left over from the previous budget period because strong economic growth generated more tax revenues than anticipated and budgeted.

The budget situation facing the 2011 session of the legislature was much more difficult than that the legislature faced two years prior. Budget analysts estimated the gap between available funds and the amount of money needed to continue state services at their current level at $27 billion, around one-fourth of state spending. The legislature eventually closed the gap with spending cuts and accounting gimmicks.

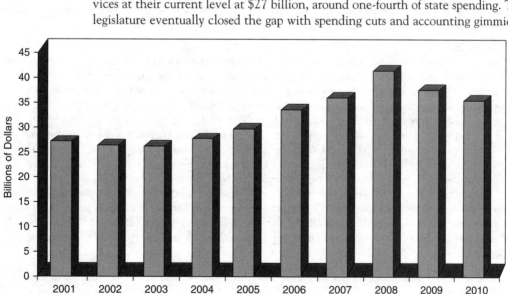

FIGURE 13.2   Texas Tax Receipts, 2001–2010.

Even though the legislature left billions of dollars in the Rainy Day Fund, many budget analysts predicted that the money would be needed to pay for healthcare programs whose cost was deliberately underestimated. The **Rainy Day Fund** is a state savings account funded by a portion of oil and gas production revenues.

Rainy Day Fund
A state savings account funded by a portion of oil and gas production revenues.

Without a robust economic recovery that would generate substantial additional tax revenues, the legislature is likely to face another big budget shortfall in 2013. The cost of state government will continue to increase because more youngsters will enroll in public schools, more students will attend college, a growing population will need more roads and highways, more people may need welfare assistance, and the cost of healthcare and other state services will rise because of inflation. Most of the accounting gimmicks that helped the legislature balance the budget in 2011 will no longer be available because they involved moving up the date revenues are collected and moving back the date bills are paid.[24] Furthermore, the state faces a structural problem caused by its effort to reduce school property taxes. In 2006, the legislature responded to homeowner complaints about rising school property taxes by enacting

BREAKING NEWS!

Legislature Uses Accounting Gimmicks to Help Balance Budget

Although the Texas legislature made big reductions in state programs in 2011, the cuts would have been more than $10 billion larger were it not for various accounting tricks. For example, the legislature saved more than $2 billion, at least on paper, by pushing back a regularly scheduled payment to the state's school districts from the 2012–2013 budget year into the next budget year. Similarly, it increased revenues by moving forward the deadlines for a number of tax payments from the next budget year into 2012–2013. Finally, the legislature "saved" another $4.8 billion in Medicaid spending by intentionally underestimating the number of people who will qualify for services and the cost of those services.*

Discussion

Did the legislature actually save money by moving a payment from one year to the next and then make money by moving the due date for tax payments forward? No. The amounts of the payments and the receipts remain the same. What changes is the time the money is paid out and the time the receipts are taken in. By moving deadlines, the legislature improved the budget picture for 2012–2013 while making the 2014–2015 budget worse. In other words, the legislature borrowed from 2014–2015 to pay bills in 2012–2013.

Is it legitimate to balance the budget with accounting tricks? Keep in mind that the alternative to the accounting gimmicks was to make much larger cuts in education and healthcare spending, because Governor Perry made it clear that he would not sign a tax bill even if one could make it through the legislature. If the economy improves, the legislature will have the money to backfill when it meets in 2013.

How about the decision to underestimate the cost of the Medicaid program? The legislature will have to cover the shortfall when it meets in 2013, probably from the Rainy Day Fund. By underestimating Medicaid costs the legislature was able to pretend that it balanced the budget without raiding the Rainy Day Fund. The truth is that a substantial portion of the Rainy Day Fund will have to be spent in 2013 to fund the Medicaid shortfall.

*Ross Ramsey, "A Businesslike Budget, After a Fashion," *Texas Tribune*, May 27, 2011, available at www .texastribune.org.

a tax shift. The legislature reduced the maximum school property tax rate by nearly one-third. It then revised the state's business tax, which is called the franchise tax, and increased some other taxes to make up the shortfall. Budget analysts estimate the gap between the amount of money raised by the revised franchise tax and the tax cuts adopted in 2006 to be around $10 billion each budget period, leaving the state deep in the whole with an ongoing shortfall.[25]

Tax Incidence

Tax incidence The point at which the actual cost of a tax falls.

The term **tax incidence** refers to the point at which the actual cost of a tax falls. When social scientists and policymakers consider the incidence of a tax, they focus on who actually pays the tax. Sometimes the people who write the check to the government are not the only people who bear the burden of a tax. Consider the franchise tax. Although businesses pay the tax, the actual expense of the tax is borne by people—stockholders who earn smaller dividends, customers who pay higher prices for the company's products, or employees who receive lower wages. Taxes on alcohol and tobacco fall not only on those people who drink and smoke but also on tobacco and liquor companies because higher prices caused by the tax will reduce consumer demand for their products. Tobacco companies oppose efforts to increase cigarette taxes not because they want to shelter their customers from higher prices but because they know that fewer people will smoke if cigarettes cost more.

Progressive tax A levy whose burden weighs more heavily on persons earning higher incomes than it does on individuals making less money.

Proportional tax A levy that weighs equally on all persons, regardless of their income.

Regressive tax A levy whose burden weighs more heavily on low-income groups than wealthy taxpayers.

Social scientists use the terms "progressive," "proportional," and "regressive" to discuss the impact of taxation on different income groups. A **progressive tax** is a levy whose burden weighs more heavily on persons earning higher incomes than it does on individuals making less money. A luxury tax on expensive yachts and jewelry is an example of a progressive tax. If we assume that members of the upper-income groups are the primary people who purchase luxury items, then the tax would obviously represent a greater proportion of the incomes of wealthier individuals than it would the incomes of low-income people. A **proportional tax** is a levy that weighs equally on all persons, regardless of their income. An income tax that charged everyone the same percentage amount without deductions or exemptions would be a proportional tax because each income group would pay the same percentage of its earnings in tax. A **regressive tax** is a levy whose burden weighs more heavily on low-income groups than wealthy taxpayers. Economists generally classify sales and excise taxes as regressive because lower-income persons spend a greater proportion of their earnings on items subject to taxation than do upper-income persons. People in upper-income groups pay more in sales and excise taxes because they purchase more taxable items and the items they purchase tend to be more expensive. However, sales and excise taxes are regressive because lower-income individuals spend a greater proportion of their incomes on taxable items than do members of middle- and upper-income groups.[26]

? WHAT DO YOU THINK?

Do you favor reforming the tax system in Texas to make it more progressive?

The Texas tax structure is regressive because of its heavy reliance on property, sales, and excise taxes. Consider the incidence of the sales tax, the largest source of state revenue. According to a study conducted by the comptroller's office, families earning less than $29,233 annually pay 6 percent of their total household income in sales taxes. As family income rises, the relative burden of the tax declines. Families earning $126,460 or more paid only 1.3 percent of household income in sales taxes. All of the major taxes in Texas are regressive, but some are more regressive than others. The property tax is the least regressive, whereas the gasoline tax is the most regressive.[27] Texas has the fifth most regressive tax system of the 50 states.[28]

Even lottery costs fall more heavily on lower-income groups. Texans earning less than $20,000 a year spend on average nearly twice as much on the lottery as those people who earn $50,000 to $59,000—$76.50 compared with $39.24 a month. Ironically, considering that the lottery helps fund education, high school dropouts spend more than three times as much on the lottery as Texans with college degrees—$173.17 a month compared with $48.61 a month.[29] Furthermore, the state's most expensive lottery tickets, those costing $10, $20, $25, $30, and $50 a game, sell better on a per capita basis in the state's lowest-income areas than they do in the wealthiest neighborhoods.[30]

Tax Fairness

Ability-to-pay theory of taxation
An approach to government finance that holds that taxes should be based on an individual's financial resources.

Although everyone agrees that taxes should be fair, observers define fairness in different ways. Some people favor a tax system based on the **ability-to-pay theory of taxation.** This approach to government finance holds that taxes should be based on an individual's financial resources. They argue that people who earn relatively high incomes should pay more in taxes because well-to-do persons can better afford to pay taxes than can people who make less money. The advocates of the ability-to-pay theory of taxation are critical of the tax system in the state of Texas because it is regressive. They favor the adoption of progressive taxes, such as the personal income tax.

In contrast, some experts on public finance favor a tax system that encourages economic growth. They think that government should keep taxes low, especially taxes on business, in order to encourage investment and business expansion. The advocates of growth-oriented tax systems believe that progressive taxes, such as the personal income tax, are harmful because they reduce the amount of money that middle- and upper-income individuals have to invest in economic development. They also oppose high property taxes because of their impact on business. Instead, they prefer the use of consumer taxes, such as sales and excise taxes. The supporters of growth-oriented tax structures give the Texas tax system mixed reviews. Although they applaud the absence of an individual income tax, they worry that local property taxes are so high that they discourage business expansion. They advocate reducing or evening repealing the property tax in favor of an expanded sales tax.

 WHAT DO YOU THINK?

What sort of tax system is the best? Why?

Tax Elasticity

The term **tax elasticity** refers to the extent to which tax revenues increase as personal income rises. It is a measure of the ability of tax revenues to keep up with economic growth. If tax revenues increase in pace with economic growth, then the government has the funds to address the increased demand for services generated by growth, such as new schools and additional roads. If tax revenues fail to keep up with growth, then state government will lack the resources necessary to meet the demand for services unless the government raises tax rates. The Texas tax system is relatively inelastic.

- The general sales tax is somewhat elastic because retail sales generally increase as personal income rises. Nonetheless, the sales tax is not perfectly elastic because not all goods and services are taxable. As average income rises, people may purchase goods and services that are not taxable, such as stocks, bonds, real estate, accounting services, and legal services. Furthermore, the growth of sales over the Internet is lessening the elasticity of the sales tax.
- Excise taxes on gasoline, alcohol, and tobacco products are inelastic because sales of those products do not necessarily rise as incomes increase. In fact, gasoline tax revenues may fall as income rises because people may trade in their old vehicles for newer-model cars that get better gasoline mileage.
- Severance taxes are inelastic as well. Rising personal income is unrelated to oil and gas production.
- The franchise tax may be elastic if business growth keeps up with the growth in personal income.
- Property taxes are only mildly elastic because property values do not necessarily rise as rapidly as personal income.

Many economists believe that the state's relatively inelastic tax system will be increasingly unable to meet the needs of state government. The healthiest, most rapidly growing sectors of the state's economy are largely exempt from the general sales tax. The sales tax does not cover many service industries, including accounting, legal, medical, and brokerage services. Personal income growth from salaries and investment gains escapes direct taxation as well because Texas does not have a personal income tax.

POLICY OPTIONS FOR REFORMING THE STATE REVENUE SYSTEM

Critics of the Texas tax system offer a number of policy options designed to make the state's tax structure more equitable, efficient, or productive.

Adopting a Personal Income Tax

Most discussions of tax reform in Texas include an examination of the wisdom of a personal income tax. Income tax advocates argue that the state's tax system, which relies heavily on consumer taxes, is incapable of generating sufficient revenue to meet the growing demand for state services. Although some segments of the state's economy are taxed heavily, other sectors of the economy escape taxation almost entirely. As a result, the legislature periodically faces a budget shortfall because the cost of healthcare, public education, criminal justice, higher education, highway construction, and other state services has gone up faster than the revenues have grown to pay for them. Income tax supporters believe that a personal income tax would more accurately mirror growth in the economy, thus producing more revenue for state government.

Tax reformers believe that a personal income tax would be a fairer way to raise revenue than the state's current tax system. The state of Kansas levies a personal income tax with three brackets ranging from 3.5 percent to 6.45 percent of adjusted gross income minus exemptions and deductions. A family of four pays no tax on an income of $24,400. Were Texas to adopt an income tax based on the Kansas model, it would generate $16 billion a year.[31] The adoption of an income tax would also make the state's tax system less regressive.

Income tax opponents question its fairness. Because of loopholes and deductions, they say, wealthy individuals have often avoided paying federal income taxes, leaving the tax burden on the backs of middle- and lower-income people. Who would guarantee that a state income tax would be implemented fairly? Most important, the opponents of a state income tax believe that the real goal of its supporters is to raise revenue to pay for a bigger, more intrusive state government. Instead of replacing or reducing the state sales tax or local property taxes, they predict that a personal income tax would merely supplement other taxes. In the long run, they warn, the adoption of a state income tax would lead to higher taxes for *all* Texans, not just the wealthy.

Conservative economists argue that taxes retard economic growth—the more taxes the government collects, the slower the rate of economic growth. Income taxes are particularly harmful because they discourage people from making the sorts of investments on which business growth depends. High taxes also retard population growth because people generally choose to live and do business in states with lower tax rates.[32]

The Texas Constitution prohibits the legislative adoption of a personal income tax without voter approval. The constitution declares that no personal income tax can take effect unless enacted through the legislative process and then approved by the voters in a referendum election. Furthermore, revenues generated by the tax can be used only for education and for reducing local property taxes for schools.

Broadening the Sales Tax Base

Another proposal for reforming the state tax system is to enlarge the sales tax base to include more services than are currently taxed. Although the legislature broadened the tax base somewhat in the 1980s, many services, including most of the services provided by architects, lawyers, interior designers, advertising agents, insurance companies, investment counselors, accountants, brokers, and physicians, remain untaxed. Eliminating exemptions for all services would have added another

$5.9 billion in sales tax revenue in 2009.[33] The advocates of a widened tax base believe that it would spread the sales tax burden more fairly than it is now. It would also make the tax system more elastic because the service sector is one of the most rapidly growing elements of the state economy. In contrast, critics charge that broadening the sales tax base is just another means of increasing the tax burden on consumers. Regardless of the rhetoric, taxes on services are taxes on people who use the services. Businesses will inevitably pass the tax along to the consumers who purchase their services. Furthermore, extending the sales tax to cover services that are not taxed in other states might make Texas firms less competitive nationwide.

Expanding Legalized Gambling

Some states rely far more heavily on revenues generated by legalized gambling than does Texas. Revenues from taxes on casino gambling, slot machines at racetracks, and lotteries account for more than 10 percent of state revenue in Nevada, South Dakota, Rhode Island, Louisiana, and Oregon. Nevada is by far the state most dependent on gambling revenue, with taxes on games of chance accounting for 27 percent of state revenue.[34] In contrast, gambling proceeds represent less than 2 percent of state revenues in Texas.

Gambling is controversial. The proponents of legalized gambling believe that the legalization of casino gambling or the introduction of slot machines (called video lottery terminals) at racetracks would produce billions in additional state revenue, which could be used to fund education and reduce property tax rates. Gambling is a voluntary tax, they argue; no one pays unless he or she chooses to play. Legalized gambling creates jobs and attracts visitors with money to the state. It also provides a local alternative for Texans who have been traveling to neighboring states to visit casinos. In contrast, the opponents of legalized gambling argue that it creates a morally corrupting climate that is associated with social problems, such as crime, bankruptcy, and gambling addiction. Furthermore, the introduction of casinos and other gambling establishments into an area hurts small businesses because people spend their money gambling rather than purchasing goods and services.

The fate of proposals to expand organized gambling in Texas is uncertain. Although many legislators would prefer an expansion of gambling to a tax increase, opposition to casino gambling and slot machines is substantial. Furthermore, any measure to expand legalized gambling would have to come in the form of a constitutional amendment, requiring a two-thirds vote of the Texas House and Texas Senate, as well as voter approval, a significantly higher hurdle than that required for the passage of ordinary legislation.

Selling Assets

Some state and local governments have sold assets in order to raise money to fund public services. Chicago, for example, sold four downtown parking garages to Morgan Stanley, an investment bank, for more than $500 million. Indiana leased the Indiana Toll Road to private investors for nearly $4 billion. In recent years, pension funds, banks, and other investors have decided that toll roads, lotteries, airports, and other government assets are good long-term investments because they produce steady revenue streams.[35] State and local governments then use the money to finance government operations without having to raise taxes. Governor Perry has proposed selling the Texas Lottery to private investors, but the legislature has not acted on his proposal.[36]

Giving Tax Relief to Low-Income Families

Some states have enacted special tax exemptions and credits for low-income individuals, so that their state tax systems are less regressive. Some states allow property owners a partial rebate on their property taxes if the taxes exceed a certain percentage of income (as certified on Internal Revenue Service tax forms). Iowa, for example, grants property tax relief to those people who are eligible (mostly senior citizens and persons with disabilities) on a sliding scale based on income. New Mexico and Kansas give a sales tax rebate to low-income people.

AROUND THE NATION   Toll Road Privatization in Indiana

In 2006, Indiana leased the 157-mile Indiana Toll Road, which runs east and west between Ohio and Illinois, to a private consortium comprised of Cintra, a Spanish company, and Macquarie, an Australian firm. The consortium gave the state $3.8 billion up front in exchange for the right to collect tolls for the next 75 years. At the end of the lease, the toll road will revert back to the state of Indiana. The state has invested the $3.8 billion and is using the interest to augment its road construction budget. The consortium, meanwhile, has begun increasing tolls to earn a return on its investment.*

The Indiana toll road privatization is controversial. Its supporters, including Indiana Governor Mitch Daniels, argue that the state would never have been able to generate nearly as much cash had its operation remained public because legislators lack the resolve needed to pass regular increases in toll rates. The up-front money from the consortium enables the state to increase its highway budget without increasing taxes. In contrast, opponents criticize the state for turning over control of the toll road to private firms that are accountable to their shareholders rather than the public interest. They argue that the consortium will increase tolls and neglect maintenance in order to maximize its profit.†

QUESTIONS

1. Should state government in Texas consider selling assets, such as toll roads and the lottery, to make money that can be used to finance government services?
2. Would you expect tolls to rise faster if a toll road is controlled by a private firm as opposed to being publicly owned and controlled?
3. Which is preferable—the government selling assets to raise money or increasing taxes?

*Theodore Kim, "After Privatization, Indiana Toll Road's Biggest Difference Is the Price," *Dallas Morning News*, October 19, 2008, available at www.dallasnews.com.

†Tom Coyne, "Indiana Lawmakers at Odds over Toll Road," *Washington Post*, June 27, 2007, available at www.washingtonpost.com.

In Texas, the legislature and the governor have created a sales tax holiday for the third weekend in August. For three days, consumers can purchase clothing, footwear, backpacks, and other back-to-school items costing less than $100 without paying the state sales tax. Most local governments drop their sales tax as well, although they are not required to participate in the tax holiday.

STATE EXPENDITURES

Biennium Two-year budget period.

The state budget for 2012–2013 was $172.3 billion. Because the Texas legislature meets in regular session only once every two years, the legislature and the governor appropriate money for a two-year budget period, which is known as the **biennium.** The 81st legislature, which met in regular session in 2011, approved spending $93.9 billion for 2012 and $78.4 billion for 2013.[37]

Table 13.2 identifies the most important items in the state budget and compares spending priorities in 1990, 2000, and 2010. The largest expenditure categories for state government are health and human services, education, transportation, and public safety and corrections. In 2010, those four categories accounted for more than 87 percent of total state spending. Since 1990, the share of state spending going for health and human services has increased by more than 60 percent. No major expenditure category has grown as rapidly. In contrast, the relative importance of education and transportation to the budget has declined.

Table 13.3 compares and contrasts Texas with other states in terms of state and local government spending. Government expenditures in Texas are well below the national average, $6,707 per capita compared with the national figure of $7,901. Only Arkansas, Arizona, Idaho, Missouri, South Dakota, and Tennessee spend less on a per capita basis than Texas.

Few public services in Texas are well funded, at least in comparison with their funding levels in other states. For example, state and local government expenditures

TABLE 13.2   State Expenditures for Selected Government Functions, 1990, 2000, and 2010

Expenditure	1990	2000	2010
Health and Human Services	24.9%	32.9%	40.1%
Education	44.3	38.4	35.8
Transportation	11.4	9.0	6.6
Public Safety and Corrections	4.6	6.1	5.2
General Government Administration	4.7	3.5	4.0
Natural Resources/ Recreational Services	1.1	2.7	2.0
Other	9.0	7.4	6.3
Total Expenditures	100 % ($22.7 billion)	100 % ($49.7 billion)	100 % ($90.4 billion)

Source: Texas Comptroller of Public Accounts, "Texas Net Expenditures by Function," various years, available at www.cpa.state.tx.us.

TABLE 13.3   State and Local Government Spending, Texas and the United States, FY 2008

Spending Category	Texas	National Average
Total state and local government expenditures per capita	$6,707	$7,901
Elementary and secondary education expenditures per capita	$1,870	$1,858
Higher education expenditures per capita	$772	$734
Welfare expenditures per capita	$934	$1,329
Health and hospital expenditures per capita	$554	$685
Highway expenditures per capita	$589	$504
Police protection expenditures per capita	$231	$295

Source: Tax Policy Center, "State and Local Government Expenditures Per Capita, FY 2008," available at www.taxpolicycenter.org.

per capita for welfare, health and hospitals, and police protection are all below the national average. Although education spending in Texas exceeds the national average, the figures are misleading because they reflect the size of the state's population of school-age children rather than a generous commitment to funding education. During the 2009–2010 school year, Texas spent $9,227 per student, $1,359 below the national average.[38] Education budget reductions adopted by the legislature in 2011 will push Texas further below the national average. However, Texas does exceed the national average in state spending for higher education, both on a per capita and a per student basis.[39]

Texans disagree about the appropriate level of government expenditures. Conservatives favor limited government with low tax rates and low levels of government expenditures. They believe that low tax rates promote economic growth because they leave money in the hands of individual investors and business owners who generate business activity and create jobs. Although government expenditures stimulate economic activity as well, private spending is more economically efficient because of the profit motive. Whereas private employers have an incentive to reduce payrolls and cut costs in order to increase profit margins, government bureaucrats want to enlarge their staffs and increase their budgets. Conservatives favor limiting the growth in state taxes and spending to ensure continued economic prosperity.

In contrast, liberals argue that the state's low-tax, low-spend philosophy fails to address basic social problems. They believe that economic prosperity is built on the presence of an educated workforce whose basic needs are met. According to data from the U.S. Census Bureau, 19.3 percent of Texans age 25 and older lacked a high school diploma in 2010 compared with a national figure of 14.4 percent. Meanwhile, the percentage of Texans with a bachelor's degree or higher was 25.9 percent compared with the national figure of 28.1 percent.[40] In addition, the poverty rate in Texas in 2010 was 18.4 percent compared with a rate of 15.1 percent for the United States as a whole. Texas has the highest percentage of residents without health insurance in the country, and trails the national average in the percentage of children without health insurance coverage as well.[41] Texas liberals advocate tax increases to fund enhanced public services to improve the quality of life for the state's large and diverse population.

BUDGET PRIORITIES

The foremost budget priorities for state government in Texas are healthcare, elementary and secondary education, higher education, welfare, and transportation.

Healthcare

Medicaid and the State Children's Health Insurance Program (SCHIP) are the state's major health programs.

Medicaid The Texas Medicaid program provides medical services to 3.5 million residents of the state who are poor or disabled. It covers such services as inpatient and outpatient hospital care, health screening, dental care, hearing evaluations, physician services, family-planning services, laboratory fees, x-ray work, and

People who do not have health insurance coverage often turn to hospital emergency rooms for healthcare.

prescription drugs. Although two-thirds of the state's Medicaid recipients are children from low-income families, most Medicaid expenditures go to provide services for the blind, persons with disabilities, and impoverished elderly people because their medical needs are greater and therefore more expensive to meet.[42]

Federal grant program A program through which the national government gives money to state and local governments to spend in accordance with set standards and conditions.

Medicaid is a **federal grant program,** a program through which the national government gives money to state and local governments for expenditure in accordance with set standards and conditions. Medicaid is now the nation's largest healthcare program, bigger even than the **Medicare** program, a federally funded healthcare program for the elderly. Medicaid covers the cost of two-thirds of nursing home residents and a majority of all births in the state. The states and the federal government share the cost of Medicaid, with the size of a state's share depending on its level of personal income. The federal government covers 58 percent of the cost of the Texas Medicaid program, with the state paying the other 42 percent.[43]

Medicare A federal health insurance program for people 65 and older.

States enjoy considerable flexibility to design their own Medicaid programs, and Texas has created one of the least generous programs in the nation. Texas is 49th among the states in the percent of poor people covered by Medicaid.[44] Only pregnant women, people with disabilities, and children from low-income families are currently eligible for Medicaid benefits in Texas. The Lone Star State spends $4,555 per year on each Medicaid recipient compared with a national average of $5,163.[45] Furthermore, nursing home reimbursements for Medicaid patients in Texas are the second lowest in the country, $112.79 per patient per day, 30 percent below the national average. Industry experts contend that the low reimbursement rate means that nursing homes in Texas are unable to pay competitive wages. That leads to high staff turnover, which can hurt patient care. About two-thirds of the 90,000 nursing home residents in Texas are on Medicaid.[46]

Medicaid is a large and rapidly growing component of the state budget. Medicaid funding accounted for 25 percent of state spending in 2009, up from 20.5 percent in 1996.[47] Medicaid expenditures have increased because the cost of healthcare services has been going up and the number of recipients has been growing. Prescription drug costs, in particular, have been increasing rapidly, as have long-term care costs for the elderly and people with disabilities.

State governments nationwide are struggling to cover Medicaid costs. Medicaid spending has been increasing by 8 percent a year, much faster than the growth in government revenues.[48] If states cannot control the growth in Medicaid spending, they will have difficulty paying for education, transportation, homeland security, and other budget priorities.

Federal healthcare reform will dramatically change the Texas Medicaid program when it fully takes effect in 2014 (assuming that the U.S. Congress does not repeal or revise the law). The measure, which is officially the federal Patient Protection and Affordable Care Act of 2010, expands Medicaid to cover childless adults earning at least 133 percent of the federal poverty level ($29,726 for a family of four in 2011), adding 10 million to 14 million people to Medicaid rolls nationwide.[49] The Texas Health and Human Services Commission estimates that an additional 1.2 million Texans will become eligible for Medicaid services in 2014 when healthcare reform takes effect. (Another 600,000 Texans are eligible under current guidelines but are

State Children's Health Insurance Program (SCHIP) A federal program designed to provide health insurance to children from low-income families whose parents are not poor enough to qualify for Medicaid.

Matching funds requirement A legislative provision that the national government will provide grant money for a particular activity only on the condition that the state or local government involved supply a certain percentage of the total money required for the project or program.

Foundation School Program The basic funding program for public education in the state of Texas.

Robin Hood plan A reform of the state's school finance system designed to increase funding for poor school districts by redistributing money from wealthy districts.

not enrolled in the program.)[50] The federal government will pick up the entire cost of the new enrollees for the first three years, injecting $3.7 billion healthcare dollars annually into the Texas economy. Subsequently, the state share will gradually rise until 2020, when Texas will be required to cover 10 percent of the cost, an estimated $370 million, which is less than 1 percent of the state budget. The Congressional Budget Office (CBO) estimates that the total cost of healthcare reform to Texas government between 2010 and 2019 will be $1.4 billion.[51]

State Children's Health Insurance Program (SCHIP) The **State Children's Health Insurance Program (SCHIP)** is a federal program designed to provide health insurance to children from low-income families whose parents are not poor enough to qualify for Medicaid. The Texas SCHIP provides health insurance to children and young adults under the age of 19 whose family income does not exceed twice the poverty level, $44,700 for a family of four in 2011.[52] SCHIP is relatively cost-effective for the states because the federal government picks up more than 70 percent of the cost, leaving the rest to the states. Furthermore, SCHIP saves the government money because families with health insurance have fewer visits to hospital emergency rooms. One billion dollars in SCHIP spending over a decade saves $4.4 billion in reduced emergency care, hospital stays, and charity care. SCHIP also reduces school absences.[53]

Texas has consistently failed to take advantage of all the SCHIP money available. Between 1998 and 2003, Texas passed up more than $600 million in federal funds because it failed to meet the federal **matching funds requirement,** a legislative provision in which the national government will provide grant money for a particular activity only on the condition that the state or local government involved supplies a certain percentage of the total money required for the project or program. The state passed up another $550 million in federal funds during the 2004–2005 biennium because the legislature and the governor cut SCHIP funding, so that they could balance the budget without raising taxes. As Figure 13.3 shows, SCHIP enrollment dropped from more than 500,000 in 2003 to less than 350,000 in 2005, 2006, and 2007 before picking up again in 2008 after the legislature relaxed some of the enrollment restrictions added to the program in 2003.

Elementary and Secondary Education

As noted in Chapter 12, state government distributes money to independent school districts through the **Foundation School Program,** the basic funding program for public education in the state of Texas. The amount of money each district receives depends on a complex set of formulas that account for the variable costs of educating different types of students. For example, students with learning disabilities or with limited English proficiency are more expensive to educate than other students. The amount of state funding each district receives also depends on the **Robin Hood plan,** a reform of the state's school finance system designed to increase funding for poor school districts by redistributing money from wealthy districts. The state guarantees that a district will generate a set amount of money per student for each penny of property tax it assesses. The state provides additional aid to districts that

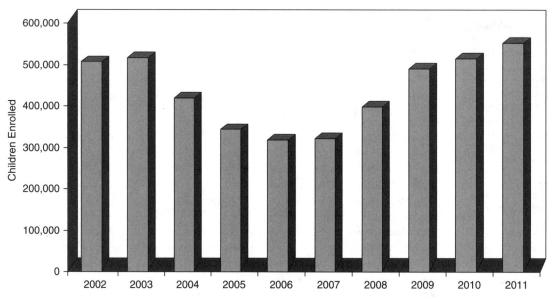

FIGURE 13.3   SCHIP Enrollment in Texas, 2002–2011.

are relatively poor in order to bring them up to the guaranteed yield while forcing wealthy school districts to remit money to the state for redistribution to relatively poor districts.

The importance of education as a budget item has declined. As Table 13.2 shows, education's share of state spending fell from 44.3 percent in 1990 to 35.8 percent in 2010. In part, the change in the relative position of education in the budget reflects the dramatic growth of the Medicaid program. Even though education spending has risen, its relative importance has shrunk because of the explosion in Medicaid expenditures. The decline in the budget share devoted to public education also reflects the failure of state funding to keep pace with the rising cost of public education.

The education finance reforms adopted in 2006 increased the state's share of education spending without significantly increasing total education funding. As discussed in Chapter 12, the legislature cut school property tax rates and increased state funding to make up the difference. To cover the increased state share, the legislature expanded the business franchise tax and increased the cigarette tax. It also changed the method for reporting sales taxes on private used car purchases to increase state revenue.

Nonetheless, many school districts soon faced a financial crisis. The legislature froze spending at 2005–2006 levels, failing to take into account the rising costs of transportation and technology. In fact, the state reimbursement rate to districts for student transportation has not changed in more than 25 years despite a significant increase in fuel costs. Similarly, state technology funding has been $30 per student for more than 20 years, too little to cover the cost of computers and software needed for instruction.[54] In 2009, the legislature provided an additional $1.9 billion in state aid for schools spread over the following two years. With an average funding increase of less than 3 percent per district, the amount barely kept pace with inflation. In 2011, the legislature cut more than $4 billion from public schools, leaving each district not only with less money than before but also without funds to provide services for increased enrollment. School districts responded to the loss of state funds by dismissing teachers and other personnel, increasing class sizes, raising local property taxes, dipping into their reserve funds, and charging fees for extracurricular activities and even bus transportation.[55]

Higher Education

More than 1.3 million students attend one of the state's 38 public universities and upper-division centers, 50 community college districts, nine health-related campuses, and four technical colleges. Only California has more publicly supported colleges and universities than Texas, or more students enrolled in higher education. The University of Texas at Austin (UT-Austin) is the largest center of higher education in the state, registering more than 51,000 students in 2011.[56] Enrollment at Texas A&M University exceeds 50,000 students.[57] Community/junior colleges enroll more than 56 percent of higher education students in the state. In addition, more Latino and African American students attend community colleges than are enrolled in universities.[58]

Higher education governance in Texas is a hodgepodge. Eleven boards of regents appointed by the governor with Texas Senate confirmation oversee management of the state's colleges and universities. The Board of Regents of the University of Texas and the Texas A&M University Board of Regents manage large university systems with campuses located throughout the state. In contrast, Midwestern State University has its own board of regents, even though it has only one campus (in Wichita Falls) and just more than 6,000 students. Each community college district has its own locally elected board of trustees.

Texas has no clear policy on which institutions can offer which degrees. As a result, the education system has a proliferation of doctoral programs. Of the 35 state universities in Texas, 25 offer doctoral degrees, more than any other state. The Texas Higher Education Coordinating Board (THECB) faces considerable pressure from universities to grant requests for doctoral programs because campus administrators, state legislators, and local communities regard them as a sign of prestige. In contrast, higher education specialists generally agree that reserving doctoral education to a relatively small number of campuses ensures depth and quality. Spreading doctoral programs around the state fosters mediocrity because state government lacks adequate financial resources to fund them all sufficiently.[59]

Higher education funding in Texas is near the national average. In 2008, Texas spent $772 per capita on higher education compared with a national average of $734.[60] Colleges and universities in Texas receive funding from a number of sources in addition to the state. Money to support community/junior colleges comes from state funding, student tuition and fees, and local tax support. The state provides

44 percent of the average community college's budget, with local property taxes (30 percent) and student tuition and fees (26 percent) supplying most of the rest. Less than one-half of the funding for state universities in Texas comes from state appropriations, with student tuition and fees, research grants, and private donations making up the rest.[61]

The relative importance of higher education spending in state budgets nationwide has been in decline for years, primarily because the growth of Medicaid has been overwhelming most other budget categories. Between 1990 and 2010, for example, state funding for the University of Texas declined by about 1 percent annually when adjusted for inflation.[62] As the relative importance of state funding for higher education declined, tuition and fees soared and community colleges raised their tax rates. Between fall 2003 and fall 2010, Texas public universities increased their tuition by 72 percent, from an average of $1,934 for 15 semester credit hours in 2003 to $3,328 in fall 2010.[63] Tuition is certain to continue rising because the legislature cut higher education funding by an additional 9 percent in 2011.[64] Furthermore, the legislature slashed funding for the Toward Excellence, Access & Success (TEXAS) grant program, which is available to high school graduates whose families earn less than $40,000 a year.

The University of Texas (UT) at Austin and Texas A&M University at College Station benefit from the Permanent University Fund (PUF). In 1876, the framers of the Texas Constitution set aside a million acres of grassland in West Texas to finance "a university of the first class," including "an agricultural and mechanical branch." A few years later, the legislature added another 1.1 million acres. Income from mineral development on the land and agricultural leasing goes into a Permanent University Fund similar to the Permanent School Fund. The PUF may not be spent but is invested to earn dividends and interest. These earnings constitute the Available University Fund (AUF), two-thirds of which is distributed to the University of Texas, with the other one-third allocated to Texas A&M University. The PUF money is used to guarantee bonds for capital improvements at schools in the UT and A&M University systems. Funds from the AUF cover debt service, including payments on principal and interest. Surplus AUF funds can be used at UT-Austin, Texas A&M in College Station, and Prairie View A&M for "excellence programs," including scholarships, library improvements, and lab equipment.

In 2009, the legislature and the voters approved measures to provide funding aimed at increasing the number of Tier One universities in Texas. A Tier One university is measured by the amount of research it conducts and by membership in the prestigious Association of American Universities. Tier One universities attract the best students and the most research money. In 2006, Texas universities received 5.5 percent of federal funding for research and development in science and engineering compared with 13.6 percent received by schools in California.[65] Whereas California has nine Tier One institutions and New York has seven, Texas has only three—UT-Austin, Texas A&M University at College Station, and Rice University, which is private. The measures set aside more than half a billion dollars in incentive grants that seven state universities can draw upon as they move toward Tier One status. The institutions are the University of Houston, Texas Tech University,

University of Texas at Dallas (UT-Dallas), University of Texas at San Antonio, University of Texas at Arlington, University of Texas El Paso, and the University of North Texas.[66] In 2010, Texas Tech and UT-Dallas qualified for the most funding among the competing schools.[67]

Welfare

The philosophy underlying the nation's welfare system has changed. Before 1996, the unofficial goal of welfare policy was to provide recipients with a minimal standard of living. Low-income families and individuals who met the eligibility requirements could qualify for various federal programs providing healthcare, food vouchers, and cash. In 1996, Congress passed and President Bill Clinton signed sweeping welfare reform legislation that explicitly changed the underlying philosophy of government policy from welfare to work. Instead of attempting to supply low-income individuals and families with cash and in-kind benefits sufficient to meet basic human needs, the new goal of welfare reform was to move recipients from the welfare rolls to the workforce. Able-bodied welfare recipients would have to find work and/or participate in job training programs in order to receive welfare assistance. Furthermore, the government placed lifetime limits on the amount of time welfare recipients could collect benefits before having to leave the welfare rolls forever.

 WHAT DO YOU THINK?

Do you agree with placing lifetime limits on the amount of time over which an individual can collect welfare benefits?

Temporary Assistance for Needy Families (TANF) A federal block grant program that provides temporary financial assistance and work opportunities to needy families.

The welfare reform legislation created **Temporary Assistance for Needy Families (TANF),** a federal program that provides temporary financial assistance and work opportunities to needy families. Low-income families and individuals who meet eligibility requirements receive cash and qualify for other benefits. To maintain eligibility, recipients must comply with a Personal Responsibility Agreement (PRA). The PRA requires recipients to agree to stay free of alcohol or illegal drug use, participate in parenting skills if referred, obtain medical screenings for their children, and ensure that their children are immunized and attending school. They also agree not to quit a job voluntarily. People who fail to comply with their PRA may suffer loss of benefits.

Welfare benefits in Texas are among the least generous in the nation—$934 per capita in 2008 compared with a national average of $1,329.[68] The average TANF recipient in Texas is a 30-year-old African American or Latino woman caring for one or two children under the age of 11. She has neither a high school education nor job training and does not have reliable transportation. Her only income is a TANF grant of $263 a month or less.[69]

Welfare reform has helped reduce the welfare rolls, but it has not eliminated poverty. Although the number of people in Texas receiving a TANF check has declined since 2005, the poverty rate in the state has not fallen. In fact, it has increased. Today, only 2.6 percent of the state's 4.26 million poor children and adults receive TANF checks. The average monthly benefit for the state's 111,040 TANF recipients, 85 percent of whom are children, is only $69 a month.[70] The state has succeeded in moving thousands of single mothers into the workforce, but their average wage is not enough to lift them out of poverty.[71]

Many low-income Texans qualify for the Supplemental Nutrition Assistance Program (SNAP), which is the new name for the Food Stamp Program. In late 2011, 3.5 million Texans received SNAP assistance, with an average monthly benefit of $303 per family paid to recipients through a Lone Star Card, which resembles a debit card. More than one-half of SNAP recipients were children. To qualify for SNAP, families and individuals must be low income and have less than $5,000 in assets, including cash, savings accounts, stocks, bonds, retirement, and even prepaid burial plots. Adults under the age of 50 are limited to three months of benefits unless they have a child living at home.[72]

Texas has one of the worst-administered food assistance programs in the nation. Whereas the federal government covers the cost of the food and half the administrative costs, state governments implement the program and pay the other half of administrative costs. The U.S. Department of Agriculture, the federal agency in charge of the program, estimates that 650,000 Texans qualify for food assistance but are not receiving it, at a cost to Texas grocers of nearly $1 billion a year in food sales. The state routinely fails to process applications within the 30-day federal deadline, leaving many Texas families waiting months for assistance.[73]

Dedicated Highway Fund A constitutionally earmarked account containing money set aside for building, maintaining, and policing state highways.

Transportation

The Texas Good Roads Amendment has been the foundation of Texas transportation funding for more than 60 years. In 1946, the legislature proposed and the voters ratified an amendment to the Texas Constitution creating the **Dedicated Highway Fund,** a constitutionally earmarked account containing money set aside for building, maintaining, and policing state highways. The amendment specified that three-fourths of the motor fuels and lubricants tax be set aside for the construction, policing, and maintenance of state highways.[74] Vehicle license fees support road construction as well. A subsequent amendment to the Texas Constitution allowed the Texas Department of Transportation (TxDOT) to issue bonds secured by future revenue to raise money to support highway construction and expansion. Federal grant money accounts for nearly 40 percent of state transportation funding, with the rest almost evenly divided between the Highway Fund and bond money secured by future revenues.[75]

Texas transportation officials and legislative leaders agree that current funding streams are inadequate to meet the state's transportation needs. Although Texas highway expenditures are above average, $489 per capita compared with a national average of $504, Texas has more highway mileage than any other state and its population is growing rapidly. Gasoline tax revenues have been rising because the number of cars on the road has been increasing steadily, but they have not kept up with the cost of highway construction, especially the cost of building freeways in urban centers. Because automobile engines are more fuel efficient, they consume less gasoline per mile driven than they did in 1991, when the legislature and governor set the current gasoline tax rate of $0.20 a gallon.[76] Furthermore, the state has now borrowed so heavily against future tax revenue (nearly $12 billion as of 2011) that it spends more money to pay off its debt than it spends on new construction.[77] The Texas Transportation Commission, an independent body of Texas business, civic, and academic leaders, has estimated that the state will need to invest $315 billion in highway infrastructure to prevent worsening traffic congestion in urban areas and ensure rural mobility and safety. Current funding streams will cover less than half that amount.[78]

State officials have identified a number of funding options to meet the state's transportation needs:

- **Increase the gasoline tax.** The most straightforward way to generate money to fund the state's transportation needs is to increase the gasoline tax and then index it to the inflation rate so it will go up automatically as costs rise. However, the legislature and the governor have been uninterested in approving any tax increases.

- **Replace the gasoline tax with a vehicle miles traveled (VMT) tax.** Motorists would pay a tax based on the number of miles they drive rather than the amount of gasoline they use. Consequently, the introduction of more fuel-efficient vehicles will not affect tax collections. However, legislators might be reluctant to introduce a new transportation tax system. Furthermore, to address the state's transportation needs, the VMT would have to be designed to raise more revenue than the current gasoline tax, and that would be described by critics as a tax increase.

- **Dedicate all of the gasoline tax to transportation.** The Texas Constitution earmarks only three-fourths of the various fuel taxes to transportation, with the rest allocated to education. Earmarking all of the money for transportation would help considerably, but the change would have to be approved by the voters, who might not support diverting money from education to highways.

- **Build toll roads.** State officials have used toll roads to help address the state's transportation needs. The advantage of toll roads is that they provide funding without raising taxes. Nonetheless, public opposition to toll roads has been building, especially to toll roads built by private companies that may not be accountable to the public interest. Texas residents also complain about proposals to convert formerly free roads into toll roads.

- **Allow local governments to address the problem regionally.** Some legislators from the heavily congested Dallas area have proposed legislation to allow local governments to increase the gasoline tax in their regions with voter approval and then use the additional money for local transportation projects. The advantage of this approach is that it enables lawmakers to take action to address the problem without actually voting on a tax increase. The disadvantage is that it is a piecemeal approach to a statewide problem.

- **Use other state revenue.** The legislature could allocate money from the general fund to support transportation projects, but all of the state's priority programs are underfunded. The move would also be opposed by legislators not wanting to set a precedent of using general fund revenues for highways.

- **Increase vehicle registration fees.** The legislature could raise some money for transportation by increasing registration fees for motor vehicles. Although legislators are reluctant to increase taxes, they have frequently raised fees. However, the amount of money generated by a fee increase would be insufficient to close the funding gap.[79]

 WHAT DO YOU THINK?

Which option or options for meeting the state's transportation needs would you support?

Statewide transportation issues may one day involve railways as well as highways. In 2009, Congress appropriated billions of dollars to assist states in building a network of bullet trains to ease the nation's dependence on automobiles and airplanes to make short trips between major cities. In 2010, the U.S. Department of Transportation awarded Texas a $5.6 million planning grant to study the possibility of a high-speed rail line running from Oklahoma City to the Mexican border.[80]

THE BUDGET PROCESS

The state of Texas uses **performance-based budgeting,** a system of budget preparation and evaluation in which policymakers identify specific policy goals, set performance targets for agencies, and measure results.[81] The governor begins the budget process in the spring of the year before the legislature meets by defining the mission of state government, setting goals, and identifying priorities. Each state agency

Building toll roads is an alternative to increasing the gasoline tax.

Performance-based budgeting
A system of budget preparation and evaluation in which policymakers identify specific policy goals, set performance targets for agencies, and measure results.

Legislative Budget Board (LBB) An agency created by the legislature to study state revenue and budgetary needs between legislative sessions and prepare budget and appropriation bills to submit to the legislature.

develops a strategic plan for accomplishing one or more of the goals. A strategic plan defines the mission of the agency, states its philosophy, and presents a strategy for achieving the goal. The agency also creates a budget to support its strategic plan. In June, July, and August, agencies submit their plans and budgets to the governor and the **Legislative Budget Board (LBB),** an agency created by the legislature to study state revenue and budgetary needs between legislative sessions and prepare budget and appropriation bills to submit to the legislature. Agencies must submit budget requests by the beginning of August.

The philosophy behind performance-based budgeting is that agency budgets are tied to measurable goals. Agencies establish goals, identify quantitative measures to assess progress, and prepare a budget designed to support their efforts. For example, the 2010–2011 performance goals for both state universities and community/junior colleges addressed the issue of student completion, a problem area for higher education in the state. Only 29 percent of students who begin their college careers at a community/junior college earn a bachelor's degree, associate's degree, or certificate in six years. Texas is 42nd in the nation in community college degree and certificate completion.[82] Meanwhile, the six-year graduation rate for university students is 57 percent, again below the national average.[83] The performance goals for state universities included the percentage of beginning students who earn a bachelor's degree within six years and the persistence rate for beginning students after one year.[84] (A student who persists in college is one who does not drop out.) The 2010–2011 performance goals for community colleges included percentage of courses students complete and the number of degrees and certificates awarded.[85] The state rewards managers who achieve their goals by giving them more discretion in the use of funds or allowing them to carry over part of a budget surplus from one budget period to the next.

Professor Thomas Anton identifies three "rules of the budget game" that government agencies follow in making budget requests:

1. Agencies ask for more money than they received the year before and more money than they expect to get, so that they will have room to cut their budget requests later.

2. Agencies insert some items into their budgets that are obvious targets for spending cuts, in hopes that the items they really want included in the budget will survive the cuts.

3. When agencies want large amounts of additional money, they present the requests as extensions of existing programs because it is easier to justify expanding a current program than it is to justify beginning a new initiative.[86]

We could add a fourth rule: When asked to recommend spending reductions, agencies propose cutting programs that are politically popular. Once when the LBB asked the state bureaucracy to prepare budget requests that could be funded without a tax increase, agencies proposed cutting 23,000 poor children from welfare rolls, kicking thousands of elderly Texans out of nursing homes, and leaving newly built prisons to stand unopened.[87] Agency heads wanted to convince state budget makers that it was wiser politically to look elsewhere for budget cuts than to trim their particular piece of the budget pie.

Appropriation bill A legislative authorization to spend money for particular purposes.

After agencies submit their budgets, the LBB and the governor's staff hold hearings, at which agency administrators explain and defend their requests. During the last few months of the year, the LBB drafts an **appropriation bill,** a legislative authorization to spend money for particular purposes. Legislators introduce the LBB draft in the Texas House and Texas Senate as the basis for legislative deliberations on the budget for the upcoming biennium. The governor usually submits budget recommendations as well, but because the legislative leadership—the speaker and lieutenant governor—controls the LBB, its budget serves as the starting point for the legislature, rather than the proposals offered by the governor.

Budget deficit The amount of money by which annual budget expenditures exceed annual budget receipts.

The Texas Constitution, similar to most other state constitutions, prohibits the adoption of a budget that is in deficit. A **budget deficit** is the amount by which budget expenditures exceed budget receipts. The state comptroller estimates state revenues for the upcoming biennium at the beginning of each legislative session. The comptroller may issue periodic updates during the session to reflect changing economic conditions or revisions in tax laws. Any spending bill the legislature approves must fall within the comptroller's revenue projections unless the legislature votes by a four-fifths majority to run a deficit, which, of course, is unlikely.

The Texas Constitution also caps state spending to the rate of economic growth. At the beginning of a legislative session, the comptroller projects the rate of economic growth in the state for the next two-year period. The rate of growth in state spending may be no greater than the projected rate of economic growth unless a majority of legislators will agree that an emergency exists that warrants additional spending. The limit does not affect the expenditure of federal funds or money generated through dedicated funds.

Most spending decisions are predetermined by federal requirements, court orders, or dedicated funds. The U.S. Congress stipulates that most federal dollars fund particular activities, such as highway construction, healthcare for low-income families and children, and vocational education. In order to participate in federal programs, the state must satisfy a matching funds requirement. The national government will provide grant money for a particular activity only on the condition that the state or local government involved supplies a certain percentage of the total money required for the project or program.

The state must also spend money to respond to court orders issued by both federal and state courts. The legislature has appropriated billions of dollars in response to court rulings concerning state hospitals, prisons, public education, and higher education in South Texas, and for people who are mentally ill or mentally retarded. The legislature spent hundreds of millions of dollars to expand educational opportunities in South Texas, for example, because of a lawsuit charging that state higher education funding unconstitutionally discriminated against Latinos living along the border with Mexico. The Texas Supreme Court eventually ruled in favor of the state, at least in part because of the efforts of the legislature to upgrade and expand higher education in South Texas.

Dedicated funds
Constitutional or statutory provisions that set aside revenue for particular purposes.

The legislature's budgetary discretion is also limited by **dedicated funds,** such as the Dedicated Highway Fund and the PUF, which are constitutional or statutory provisions that set aside revenue for particular purposes. The state has more than a hundred dedicated funds setting aside money for highways, parks, university construction, public schools, retirement funds, and other purposes. Constitutional or statutory dedications accounted for 45 percent of general revenue appropriations in the 2010–2011 budget.[88] The advocates of dedicated funds contend that they enable the state to make long-term commitments to goals. Earmarking revenue is also a means of generating public support for a tax increase because it makes budgeting comprehensible to ordinary people and gives the public confidence that tax money will be used as promised. In contrast, critics believe that earmarking contributes to the state budget crises by limiting legislative discretion. Dedicated funds deny legislators the option of cutting certain programs, such as the highway construction budget, in order to avoid a tax increase or to find money for other priorities, such as public education or healthcare. Furthermore, dedicated funds, especially those contained in the state constitution, restrict the legislature's ability to modify budget priorities to reflect the state's changing needs.

The budget must pass the legislature in a fashion similar to that of other bills. In the Texas Senate, the Finance Committee deals with both appropriation and tax

Conference committee A special committee created to negotiate differences on similar pieces of legislation passed by the House and Senate.

Line-item veto The power to veto sections or items of an appropriations bill while signing the remainder of the bill into law.

Incremental model of budgeting A theoretical effort to explain the budget process on the basis of small (incremental) changes in budget categories from one budget period to the next.

Budget execution authority The power to cut agency spending or transfer money between agencies during the period when the legislature is not in session.

bills, making recommendations to the Senate floor. In the Texas House, the Appropriations Committee drafts the budget, whereas the Ways and Means Committee deals with tax measures. In most instances, the final details of the state appropriation bill and most tax packages have to be ironed out by a House-Senate **conference committee,** a special committee created to negotiate differences on similar pieces of legislation passed by the Texas House and Texas Senate. Once legislation receives final legislative approval, it goes to the governor.

On appropriation bills, the governor of Texas (and the governors of most states) has the **line-item veto,** the power to veto sections or items of an appropriations bill while signing the remainder of the bill into law. Although the line-item veto (and the threat of its use) is a potentially potent weapon for influencing the state budget, research shows that it has a relatively small impact on total state spending.[89] In practice, the legislature has limited the governor's ability to knock out objectionable items by lumping millions of dollars of expenditures together in a single line item. In 1941, for example, the appropriation for the University of Texas at Austin included 1,528 line items.[90] Today, the legislature funds each institution of higher education through a single line item or lump-sum appropriation. Governor Perry has criticized this approach to budgeting because it limits his ability to impact the budget process.

Political scientists who study budgeting have developed models to understand the process. The most common approach is the **incremental model of budgeting,** a theoretical effort to explain the budget process on the basis of small (incremental) changes in budget categories from one budget period to the next. Scholars who favor this approach to understanding the budget process believe that agency heads, legislators, and governors all regard an agency's current budget share as its base. Increases or decreases in that base must be justified, whereas maintaining current levels need not be. Consequently, changes in individual budget items tend to be small. Another explanation for incremental budgeting is that an agency's current budget reflects its political strength relative to the strength of other agencies competing for money. Because the relative political influence of various claimants on the state budget is unlikely to change dramatically from one budget period to the next, budget figures are unlikely to change dramatically, either.

Although incremental budgeting may be the norm, not all budget changes are incremental. Between 1990 and 2010, for example, the share of the budget devoted to health and human services grew by more than 60 percent, increasing from 24.9 percent to 40.1 percent of state spending. Spending for health and human services increased because of the growth in Medicaid spending. In contrast, the transportation share of the budget fell by more than 40 percent, from 11.4 percent of spending to 6.6 percent.

The governor and the LBB share **budget execution authority,** the power to cut agency spending or transfer money between agencies during the period when the legislature is not in session. Between legislative sessions, either the LBB or the governor may propose reductions or shifts in state spending. If the LBB proposes a change, the governor must approve the transfer before it can take effect, and vice versa.

MAKING BUDGETARY POLICY

The public policy approach offers a useful mechanism for analyzing budgetary policymaking in Texas.

The Context for Budgetary Policymaking

Environmental and political factors provide the context for budgetary policymaking. Economic development is the single most important factor for explaining state budgetary policies. States with greater levels of personal income have higher tax rates and higher levels of spending for transportation, education, healthcare, criminal justice, and welfare than do states with lower levels of personal income. In short, wealthy states tax their residents more heavily and provide more generous levels of public services than do poor states.[91] Budgetary policies in Texas are consistent with the state's status as a relatively poor state. Compared with other states, tax rates in the Lone Star State are low and spending programs are poorly funded.

States adopt budgetary policies to respond to competition from other states. States offer tax breaks and other subsidies to businesses to encourage them to relocate to the state. In Texas, the legislature has created a multimillion-dollar fund that the governor can use to lure companies to the state, either by providing them with cash subsidies or benefits, such as job training for workers or improved transportation to plant sites. Citgo Petroleum, BP Chemical, Home Depot, Sematech, and Tyson Foods have all benefited from state subsidies.[92] In the meantime, state governments hesitate to increase welfare benefits because they do not want to become welfare magnets, attracting low-income people from other states. Although states attempt to attract companies that create jobs and generate economic activity, they want to repel low-income people who would be a drain on public services.[93]

Short-term economic factors affect budgetary policymaking as well. Economic expansion improves the state's budget picture by fueling the growth of sales tax and excise tax revenues. In the late 1990s, the economy boomed and state officials were able to cut taxes and increase spending at the same time. In contrast, state tax revenues decline during a recession. The recession of 2008–2009 helped produce a budget shortfall that forced the legislature to make some difficult decisions involving spending and state revenues.

 WHAT DO YOU THINK?

Do you favor a small state government that provides relatively modest services but holds down taxes or a larger state government that provides more services but costs more?

Political culture
The widely held, deeply rooted political values of a society.

Texas's budgetary policies of relatively low tax rates coupled with poorly funded public services reflect the state's political culture, interest group environment, and political party balance. **Political culture** is the widely held, deeply rooted political values of a society. Texas's low-tax/low-spend budgetary philosophy is consistent

Individualistic political culture
An approach to government and politics that emphasizes private initiative with a minimum of government interference.

with the state's **individualistic political culture,** an approach to government and politics that emphasizes private initiative with a minimum of government interference. Many Texans believe in small government. When given a choice between higher taxes with more government services and lower taxes with fewer services, they prefer the latter.

The interest group configuration in Texas is consistent with a low-tax/low-spend government. Interest groups that would favor higher taxes to support better-funded public services, such as labor unions, consumer groups, and racial and ethnic minority organizations, are relatively weak in the Lone Star State. In contrast, business organizations, which typically prefer lower tax rates and less generously funded services, are especially strong in Texas. In particular, business interests favor low welfare benefits and strict limits on the amount of time an individual can collect benefits. Low welfare spending not only saves money and helps hold down tax rates, but also helps to hold down wage rates by pushing welfare recipients into the job market and making them more willing to accept low-paying jobs.[94]

The current party balance also supports the state's low-tax/low-spend budgetary policies. The Republican Party, which now controls all three branches of state government, advocates limited government. When faced with a substantial budget shortfall in 2011, Republican leaders in the legislature and the executive branch favored cutting services rather than raising taxes to balance the budget. Republican leaders also chose to save the state's budget surplus in a Rainy Day Fund rather than spend it to support public education. The Democratic Party, which tends to favor a more active government, has limited influence in the state's policymaking process.

Demographic change may eventually affect the environment for budgetary policymaking in Texas. The Latino population is young and growing rapidly, whereas the white population is aging. Population growth will invariably lead to political influence. Because Latinos as a group are more likely to be poor, they are more dependent on public services for healthcare, education, transportation, job training, and welfare than is the white population. As the political influence of Latino voters grows, the state may adopt budgetary policies that shift the tax burden away from consumers and low-income families while increasing spending for government services.

Agenda Setting

Budgetary issues are always near the forefront of the state's official policy agenda because of the biennial budget cycle. Adopting a balanced budget that will meet the needs of the state is typically the overriding issue of each legislative session. Whether legislators will have sufficient funds to enact new initiatives or consider a tax cut or whether they will have to cut programs and raise taxes depends on economic conditions. Boom times produce budget surpluses that can be spent, whereas a recession causes a shortfall that must be addressed.

Public officials and interest groups raise budgetary issues because they hope to see their concerns included in the state's official policy agenda. Public school administrators want the legislature to reform school finance to increase state funding for education. Business interests favor the use of tax breaks and government subsidies to promote business expansion. Medical professionals advocate an increase in the state cigarette tax in hopes of discouraging young people from taking up the smoking habit.

Budgetary issues sometimes arise because of external pressures. Texas absorbed hundreds of thousands of evacuees after Hurricane Katrina. Although the federal government covered some of their food, housing, healthcare, transportation, and other living expenses, state and local governments had to pick up much of the cost. School districts, in particular, faced millions of dollars of unexpected expenses to cover the cost of educating thousands of children from Louisiana. Court decisions can also force budgetary issues on state government. The legislature and governor have had to address school finance in numerous regular and special sessions because of court rulings in *Edgewood v. Kirby* and *Neeley v. West Orange-Cove Consolidated ISD*.

Policy Formulation, Adoption, and Legitimation

A broad range of political actors participates in budgetary policy formulation. State agencies make budget proposals and lobby for their adoption. For example, the THECB lobbies for increased funding for higher education. The agency's strategy is to focus on the gap in educational attainment between whites and the state's two largest minority populations, African Americans and Latinos. THECB officials, joined by allies in higher education and minority rights organizations, argue that closing the educational gap is essential to the state's future. To achieve that goal, they declare, the state must fund higher education more generously.

The members of the legislative leadership are the key players in drafting a budget and formulating tax policy. The speaker and lieutenant governor control the LBB, which prepares the initial budget document. Their closest political allies chair the House and Senate committees that formulate the details of budget policy. The speaker and the lieutenant governor control the conference committee that prepares the final budget document.

The role of the governor in formulating budgetary policy depends on the interest and the skills of the state's chief executive. In 2011, Governor Perry made clear his opposition to raising taxes, calling instead for the legislature to cut spending to eliminate the budget shortfall. The governor also opposed using the Rainy Day Fund, preferring instead that the legislature save it for future budget emergencies. Perry also lobbied legislators to support his spending and funding preferences.

The federal government has a significant impact on policy formulation in Texas because of federal programs. Some of the most important items in the budget rely heavily on federal funds, including welfare, healthcare, transportation, and public education. Federal money, however, comes with strings attached. To ensure the continued flow of federal dollars, state budgetary policies must conform to federal guidelines. They must also appropriate billions of dollars in state money as matching funds.

The legislature and the governor adopt budgetary policies through the legislative process. The appropriation bill and tax bills must be passed by majority vote of both the Texas House and the Texas Senate. The governor must sign them or allow them to become law without signature. If the governor issues a veto, it can be overridden by a two-thirds vote of both chambers of the legislature. In practice, gubernatorial vetoes of tax and spending bills are seldom, if ever, overridden because the legislature invariably gets them to the governor's desk late in the session and the governor allows the legislature to go home before issuing vetoes.

The Texas Constitution establishes special rules for budgetary policymaking that create an atmosphere of budgetary caution. The constitution stipulates that the legislature adopt a balanced budget unless lawmakers agree by a four-fifths majority to run a deficit. The constitution also demands that state spending grow no more rapidly than economic growth unless both chambers vote in favor of greater spending. These two provisions create a bias in favor of spending restraint. The clear message of the Texas Constitution is that public officials should focus on limiting the growth of government rather than providing enough spending to meet the needs of the state and its people.

The governor plays a special role in budgetary policymaking because of the line-item veto. On most legislative measures, including tax bills, the governor faces a take-it-or-leave-it choice. The governor can sign the bill, allow it to become law without signature, or veto it. On appropriation measures, however, the governor can pick out individual provisions to veto while allowing the rest to become law. As a result, the governor can play a more active role in budgetary policymaking than in other sorts of policy issues.

The state officials, interest groups, and political parties that support the adoption of budgetary policies also promote their legitimation. After the 2011 legislative session when lawmakers cut spending rather than increase taxes, Governor Perry and legislative leaders defended the action as evidence of the state's wise budget management. Business groups and Republican officials attribute the state's relatively strong economy to its low-tax/low-spend policies. In contrast, Democrats and their interest group allies warn that the state's economic future is jeopardized by the failure of state government adequately to fund education, healthcare, and transportation.

Policy Implementation, Evaluation, and Change

Private companies, local governments, and state agencies implement budgetary policies. Retail business establishments collect sales taxes and many excise taxes on behalf of the state. State law requires that retailers obtain a sales tax permit from the comptroller, collect taxes on the retail purchase of taxable items, keep records, and remit tax receipts to the state. In return for acting as the state's tax collector, retail establishments can keep a small portion of the money they collect as compensation for their work.

Local governments play a role in administering the state's programs. Most of the state's spending for education goes to independent school districts, which provide educational services for kindergarten through high school. Community/junior colleges implement higher education policies, whereas hospital districts participate in the implementation of the state's healthcare policies. County governments collect a number of taxes and fees on behalf of the state, including charges for license plates and certificates-of-title for motor vehicles.

State agencies implement budgetary policies as well. The comptroller is the state's chief tax collector, sometimes collecting taxes directly and sometimes working through intermediaries, such as retail merchants. The Texas Department of Corrections (TDC) administers the state's correctional programs. The Health and Human Services Commission implements welfare policies. The Texas Department of State Health Services operates mental health facilities. The state's public universities provide higher education services to the state's residents.

Performance-based budgeting ensures that state agencies evaluate at least some aspects of their programs. Agencies set goals, plan strategies, and identify measures to determine whether they are achieving their goals. Each year they produce a report showing their progress at achieving their goals.

The comptroller, LBB, and legislative committees evaluate state programs as well. The websites of the comptroller (**www.cpa.state.tx.us**) and the LBB (**www.lbb .state.tx.us**) include a number of reports evaluating the state tax system and various programs, such as the state's health programs and the Foundation School Program. Legislative committees evaluate state agencies and programs under their jurisdiction. The legislature also evaluates agencies and programs through **sunset review,** the periodic evaluation of state agencies by the legislature to determine whether they should be reauthorized.

Sunset review The periodic evaluation of state agencies by the legislature to determine whether they should be reauthorized.

Budgetary policies change because of changing economic conditions, federal action, and political change. Budgetary policies change as economic conditions change. Whereas a strong economy produces money to fund new programs or expand old ones, a weak economy makes for a tight budget. Some changes in state budget policy occur because of the federal government. Over the next few years, the Texas Medicaid program will expand to cover a million additional Texans because of the federal healthcare reform law adopted in 2010. Finally, policy changes follow political change. The election of a Democratic governor along with Democratic majorities in the legislature would likely lead to an increase in funding for public services along with a reformed tax system that relies less on taxes that affect low- and middle-income residents and more on taxes levied on business and upper-income groups.

WHAT WE HAVE LEARNED

1. **What are the most important revenue sources for the state of Texas, including both tax and non-tax sources, and how has the relative importance of those sources changed over the last 20 years?**

The general sales tax is by far the most important state tax source, generating substantially more money than any other tax. The state sales tax rate is 6.25 percent, and local governments can add 2 percent more. The other major state taxes include a business franchise tax, a motor fuels tax, a tax on motor vehicle sales and rental, and severance taxes on oil and natural gas production. The franchise tax is a tax on businesses chartered or organized in Texas and doing business in the state. Severance taxes are imposed on the removal of nonrenewable resources, such as crude oil and natural gas. Excise taxes are selective sales taxes. The proportion of state revenues generated by tax sources has declined over the last 20 years, whereas non-tax sources, especially federal funds, have grown in importance. Federal money, which represents more than 40 percent of state spending, helps fund healthcare, welfare, highway construction, and a broad range of other state activities. Other non-tax sources of revenue include licenses and fees, interest and investment income, land income, and lottery revenue.

2. What important revenue issues face state government in Texas?

Texas policymakers face a number of issues in government finance. Does the government raise enough money to meet the needs of the state's large and rapidly growing population? Liberals believe that state government generates insufficient funds to address the state's needs, whereas conservatives argue that high taxes limit economic growth. What is the incidence of taxation in Texas? The term *tax incidence* refers to the point at which the actual cost of a tax falls, that is, who actually pays the tax. Tax systems are classified as progressive, regressive, or proportional, depending on the incidence of taxation. The Texas tax structure is regressive because of its heavy reliance on property, sales, and excise taxes. Is the tax system fair? Although everyone agrees that taxes should be fair, observers define fairness in different ways. Some favor income taxes because they reflect the ability-to-pay theory of taxation. In contrast, other experts on public finance believe that government should keep taxes low and focus on consumer taxes, such as the sales tax, in order to encourage economic growth. Finally, to what extent do tax revenues increase as the economy grows (a concept known as tax elasticity)? The Texas tax system is relatively inelastic because of its reliance on excise taxes, severance taxes, and property taxes.

3. What policy options are proposed for reforming the state's revenue structure?

Critics of the Texas tax system offer a number of policy options designed to make the state's tax structure more equitable, efficient, or productive. Most discussions of tax reform in Texas include an examination of the wisdom of a personal income tax. Another proposal for reforming the state tax system is to enlarge the sales tax base to include more services than are currently taxed. Some members of the legislature want to increase revenue by expanding legalized gambling. The state could also raise money by selling assets, such as the lottery, to private investors. Some states have enacted special tax exemptions and credits for low-income individuals, such as the August sales tax holiday.

4. How do spending levels in Texas compare and contrast with those of other states?

The state budget for 2012–2013 was $172.3 billion. The largest expenditure categories for state government were health and human services, education, transportation, and public safety and corrections. State government expenditures in Texas are well below the national average. Few public services in Texas are well funded, at least in comparison with their funding levels in other states.

5. What are the most important budget priorities in Texas, and how are those priorities reflected in budget policy?

The foremost budget priorities for state government in Texas are healthcare, elementary and secondary education, higher education, welfare, and transportation. Medicaid and the State Children's Health Insurance Program (SCHIP) are the state's major health programs. Even though Texas has one of the least generous Medicaid programs in the country, it consumes more than a quarter of total state spending and is growing rapidly. Furthermore, federal healthcare reform legislation adopted in 2010 will expand Medicaid dramatically, eventually increasing the cost to Texas government. SCHIP is a federal program designed to provide health insurance to children from low-income families whose parents are not poor enough to qualify for Medicaid. Texas has consistently failed to take advantage of all the SCHIP money available because it has not met the federal matching funds requirement.

State government distributes money to public schools through the Foundation School Program. The amount of money each district receives depends on a complex set of formulas, including the Robin Hood Plan, which is designed to equalize funding. In 2006, the legislature cut school property tax rates and increased state funding to make up the difference. Nonetheless, many districts soon faced a financial crisis because the legislature froze spending at 2005–2006 levels without taking account of rising costs. The legislature provided additional funding in its 2009 session, but the new money barely kept pace with inflation, leaving many school districts financially strapped. Then, in 2011, the legislature slashed education funding in order to balance the budget without raising taxes or dipping into the Rainy Day Fund.

As the relative importance of state funding for higher education has declined, tuition and fees have soared and community colleges have raised their local property tax rates. The University of Texas (UT) at Austin and Texas A&M University at College Station and some other schools in the UT and A&M systems benefit from the Permanent University Fund (PUF). In 2009, the legislature and the voters approved measures to provide funding aimed at increasing the number of Tier One universities in Texas. Nonetheless, the status of higher education in the state is threatened by continued budget cuts, especially the 2011 cuts.

The philosophy underlying the nation's welfare system has changed from providing recipients with a minimal standard of living to moving recipients to the workforce. Welfare benefits in Texas are among the least generous in the nation. Although welfare reform has reduced the welfare rolls, it has not eliminated poverty. Many low-income Texans qualify for the Supplemental Nutrition Assistance Program (SNAP), which was formerly called the Food Stamp Program.

The Texas Constitution dedicates a majority of the motor fuels tax to construction and maintenance of highways. Nonetheless, Texas transportation officials indicate that current funding is inadequate to meet the state's transportation needs. State officials are considering a number of options for addressing the problem.

6. What are the primary steps in the state budgetary process?

Texas uses performance-based budgeting. The LBB begins the budget process in the year before the legislature meets in regular session by asking agencies to submit their strategic plans and budgets. The LBB drafts an appropriation bill for submission to the legislature by the end of the year. The governor may offer a bill as well, but it is the LBB document that is the starting point for legislative deliberation. The comptroller presents legislators with an estimate of anticipated revenue for the upcoming two-year budget period and the legislature must stay within that estimate unless it votes by a four-fifths margin to run a budget deficit. Most spending decisions are predetermined by federal requirements, court orders, or dedicated funds. The budget must pass the legislature in a fashion similar to that of other bills. The governor has the line-item veto for appropriations measures. Some political scientists explain the budget process using the incremental model of budgeting, but not all budget changes are incremental. The governor and the LBB share budget execution authority.

7. How are budget policies made in Texas?

Environmental and political factors provide the context for budgetary policymaking. Texas's budgetary policies of relatively low tax rates coupled with poorly funded public services reflect the state's political culture, interest group environment, and political party balance. Budgetary issues are always near the forefront of the state's official policy agenda because of the biennial budget cycle. A broad range of political actors participates in budgetary policy formulation, including state agencies, legislative leaders, the governor, and the federal government. The legislature and the governor adopt budgetary policies through the legislative process. The state officials, interest groups, and political parties that supported the adoption of budgetary policies also promote their legitimation. Private companies, local governments, and state agencies implement budgetary policies. Performance-based budgeting ensures that state agencies evaluate at least some aspects of their programs. The comptroller, LBB, and legislative committees evaluate state programs as well. Budgetary policies change because of changing economic conditions, federal action, and political change.

KEY TERMS

ability-to-pay theory of taxation

appropriation bill

biennium

budget deficit

budget execution authority

conference committee

dedicated funds

Dedicated Highway Fund

Employees Retirement System (ERS) Trust Fund

excise tax

federal grant program

fiscal year

Foundation School Program

franchise tax

General Fund

incremental model of budgeting

individualistic political culture

Legislative Budget Board (LBB)

line-item veto

matching funds requirement

Medicaid

Medicare

pari-mutuel wagering

performance-based budgeting

Permanent School Fund (PSF)

Permanent University Fund (PUF)

political culture

progressive tax

proportional tax

Rainy Day Fund

recession

regressive tax

Robin Hood plan

sales tax

severance tax

sin tax

State Children's Health Insurance Program (SCHIP)

sunset review

tax elasticity

tax incidence

Temporary Assistance for Needy Families (TANF)

Texas Teacher Retirement System (TRS) Trust Fund

NOTES

1. "Seven Breakthrough Solutions," available at www.texashighered.com.
2. Jack Stripling, "Conservative Group's Influence on Texas Higher-Education Policy Takes Center Stage Again," Chronicle of Higher Education, May 13, 2011, available at http://chronicle.com.
3. Ross Ramsey, "Perry to Push Texas Colleges to Offer $10,000 Degree," Texas Tribune, February 8, 2011, available at www.texastribune.org.
4. Melissa Ludwig, "New Coalition Pushes Back Against Suggested Reforms," Houston Chronicle, June 17, 2011, p. B3.
5. Sales Tax Institute, "State Sales Tax Rates, State Tax Rates," October 1, 2001, available at www.salestaxinstitute.com.
6. Kevin Sproles, "5 Ways an Internet Sales Tax Will Impact your Business," Entrepreneur Corner, December 22, 2010, available at http://venturebeat.com.
7. Texas Comptroller of Public Accounts, "Revenue by Source," available at www.windows.state.tx.us.

8. Texas Railroad Commission, available at www.rrc.state .tx.us.

9. "Cigarette Tax Increase Pushes Revenue Up, But Sales Are Down," *Dallas Morning News*, March 10, 2007, available at www.dallasnews.com.

10. Texas Racing Commission, *Year 2010 Annual Report*, available at www.txrc.state.tx.us.

11. Teacher Retirement System of Texas, "2010 Actuarial Valuation Report for the Pension Fund," available at http:// trs.state.tx.us.

12. Employee Retirement System of Texas, "FY2010 Annual Report," available at www.ers.state.tx.us.

13. Teacher Retirement System of Texas, "2010 Actuarial Valuation Report for the Pension Fund," and Employee Retirement System of Texas, "FY2010 Annual Report."

14. Patricia Kilday Hart, "Playing with Others' Money," *Houston Chronicle*, October 16, 2011, pp. B1, B3.

15. Texas Education Agency, "Texas Permanent School Fund Annual Report—Fiscal Year Ending August 31, 2010," available at http://ritter.tea.state.tx.us.

16. Texas Permanent University Fund Report, June 30, 2011, available at www.utimco.org.

17. Texas Lottery Commission, available at www.txlottery.org.

18. Ellen Perlman, "Losing Numbers," *Governing*, September 2001, pp. 46–47.

19. "Lotto Texas Jackpot Gets Longer Odds," *Houston Chronicle*, March 27, 2003, available at www.houstonchronicle.com.

20. Mega Millions, available at www.megamillions.com.

21. David W. Winder and James T. LaPlant, "State Lawsuits Against 'Big Tobacco': A Test of Diffusion Theory," *State and Local Government Review* 32 (Spring 2000): 132–141.

22. "Total Tax Burden by State," available at www.statemaster .com.

23. Darren Barbee, "Texas Legislature Used Stimulus Funds to Help Balance Budget," *Fort Worth Star-Telegram*, September 18, 2009, available at www.star-telegram .com.

24. Aman Batheja, "Legislature Still Using Gimmicks to Balance Texas Budget," *Fort Worth Star-Telegram*, October 8, 2011, available at www.star-telegram.com.

25. *Texas Weekly*, February 7, 2001, available at www.texasweekly .com.

26. Texas Comptroller of Public Accounts, "Tax Exemptions and Tax Incidence," February 2011, available at www .window.state.tx.us.

27. Ibid.

28. Dick Lavine, "Who Pays Texas Taxes?" Center for Public Policy Priorities, March 20, 2007, available at www.cppp .org.

29. Ken Rodriguez, "'Pro-Education' Lottery Quietly Fleeces the Poor, Not-So-Educated," *San Antonio Express-News*, September 29, 2006, available at www.mysanantonio .com.

30. Lisa Sandberg and Julie Domel, "So Who's Buying the $50 Scratch-Offs?" *San Antonio Express News*, June 11, 2007, available at www.mysanantonio.com.

31. Dick Lavine, "The Best Choice for a Prosperous Texas," Center for Public Policy Priorities, March 1, 2005, available at www.cppp.org.

32. Richard Vedder, "Taxing Texans," Texas Public Policy Foundation, available at www.texaspolicy.com.

33. Texas Comptroller of Public Accounts, "Tax Exemptions and Tax Incidence."

34. Nevada Department of Administration, "Budget 101: Introduction to State Budgeting," available at http:// nevadabudget.org.

35. Christopher Swope, "Unloading Assets," *Governing*, January 2007, pp. 36–40.

36. John Moritz, "Perry Still Backs Sale of Lottery," *Fort Worth Star-Telegram*, March 27, 2008, available at www .star-telegram.com.

37. "General Appropriation Act for the 2010–2011 Biennium," available at www.lbb.tx.us.

38. Terrence Stutz, "Texas Slips in per Pupil Education Spending Among the States," *Dallas Morning News*, January 28, 2010, available at www.dallasnews.com.

39. College Board, "State Higher Education Finance, FY 2010, available at www.sheeo.org.

40. Jeannie Kever, "Census Finds City Lags in Education," *Houston Chronicle*, September 22, 2011, pp. A1, A7.

41. U.S. Census Bureau, "Income, Poverty and Health Insurance in the United States: 2010," available at www .census.gov.

42. Texas Health and Human Services Commission, "Texas Medicaid Program," available at www.hhsc.state.tx.us.

43. Kaiser Family Health Foundation, "Federal Medical Assistance Percentage (FMAP) for Medicaid and Multi-plier, FY 2007," available at www.statehealthfacts.org.

44. Emily Ramshaw, "Texas Is 'On the Brink,' Legislative Study Group Says," *Texas Tribune*, February 15, 2011, available at www.texastribune,org.

45. Kaiser Family Health Foundation, "Medicaid Payments per Enrollee, FY 2007," available at www.statehealthfacts.org.

46. Bob Moos, "Texas Nursing Homes in a Tight Fix on Medicaid," *Dallas Morning News*, March 4, 2009, available at www.dallasnews.com.

47. "Texas Medicaid in Perspective."

48. John Buntin, "Ending Medicaid as We Know It,"*Governing*, June 2011, p. 46.

49. John Buntin, "Dueling Diagnosis," *Governing*, February 2010, p. 24.

50. "Texas Medicaid in Perspective."

51. "Cheap at First, Expensive Later," *Texas Weekly*, March 29, 2010, available at www.texasweekly.com.

52. U.S. Department of Health and Human Services, "The 2011 HHS Poverty Guidelines," available at www.hhs.gov.

53. Hy Gia Park and Leah Oliver, "Is SCHIP Shipshape?" *State Legislatures*, May 2004, pp. 16–18.

54. John Moritz, "Budget Crunch Coming for Texas School Districts," *Fort Worth Star-Telegram*, July 30, 2008, available at www.star-telegram.com.

55. Morgan Smith, "Fees for Students Redefine 'Free' Public Schools," *Texas Weekly*, July 29, 2011, available at www.texastribune.org.

56. University of Texas News, available at www.utexas.edu.

57. Texas A&M News, available at http://tamunews.tamu.edu.

58. Texas Higher Education Coordinating Board, "Quick Facts 2010," available at www.thecb.state.tx.us.

59. Ralph K. M. Haurwitz, "Spread of Doctoral Programs in Texas Raises Concerns," *Austin American-Statesman*, June 3, 2008, available at www.statesman.com.

60. Tax Policy Center, "State and Local Government Expenditures per Capita, FY 2008," available at www.taxpolicycenter.org.

61. Texas Higher Education Coordinating Board, "Quick Facts 2010."

62. *Capitol Update*, October 2, 2008, available at www.txdirectory.com.

63. Texas Higher Education Coordinating Board, "Overview: Tuition Deregulation," available at www.thecb.state.tx.us.

64. Reeve Hamilton, "Texsplainer: Will Budget Cuts Mean Higher Tuition?" *Texas Tribune*, July 26, 2011, available at www.texastribune.org.

65. Katherine Leal Unmuth, "Texas Colleges' Math-Science Push Falling Short, Board Says," *Dallas Morning News*, August 3, 2009, available at www.dallasnews.com.

66. Holly K. Hacker, "Tier One University Bill Is Signed, Uniting Old Foes," *Dallas Morning News*, June 18, 2009, available at www.dallasnews.com.

67. Reeve Hamilton, "Tier-One Money Up for Grabs in University Competition," *Texas Tribune*, September 6, 2011, available at www.texastribune.org.

68. Tax Policy Center, "State and Local Government Expenditures per Capita, FY 2008," available at www.taxpolicycenter.org.

69. Texas Health and Human Services Commission, "Temporary Assistance for Needy Families," available at www.hhsc.state.tx.us.

70. Texas Health and Human Services Commission, "Texas TANF and SNAP Enrollment Statistics," available at www.hhsc.state.tx.us.

71. Janet Elliott and Terri Langford, "The Cost of Cutting Welfare," *Houston Chronicle*, January 28, 2007, available at www.chron.com.

72. Texas Health and Human Services Commission, available at www.hhsc.state.tx.us.

73. Corrie MacLaggan, "U.S. Food Stamp Official: State Could Be Aiding More Texans," *Austin American Statesman*, January 12, 2010, available at www.statesman.com.

74. Article 8, Section 7a, Texas Constitution.

75. Texas Department of Transportation, at www.dot.state.tx.us.

76. Ryan Holeywell and Russell Nichols, "Street Smarts: Sox Ideas for Untangling the Nation's Infrastructure Problems," *Governing*, June 2011, p. 36.

77. Gary Scharrer, "State Highway Fund Crisis: Are We There Yet?" *Houston Chronicle*, January 30, 2011, pp. B1, B3.

78. Texas Department of Transportation, "Transportation Funding: Understanding State Road and Highway Funding in Texas," January 2011, available at www.dot.state.tx.us.

79. Ibid.

80. Ben Wear, "Texas Awarded High-Speed Rail Grant," *Austin American-Statesman*, October 27, 2010, available at www.statesman.com.

81. Patria da Lancer Julnes, *Performance-Based Management Systems* (Boca Raton, FL: CRC Press, 2009), pp. 3–23.

82. Brian Thevenot, "A Matter of Degrees," *Texas Tribune*, February 2, 2010, available at www.texastribune.org.

83. Texas Higher Education Coordinating Board, "First-Time Degree-Seeking Undergraduates, Fall 2004 Cohort," available at www.thecb.state.tx.us.

84. Legislative Budget Board, "General Academic Institutions Performance Measure Definition: FY 2010 Budget Structure," May 2010, available at www.lbb.state.tx.us.

85. Legislative Budget Board, "Performance Measure Definition for Public Community/Junior Colleges," February 2010, available at www.lbb.state.tx.us.

86. Thomas J. Anton, *The Politics of State Expenditures in Illinois* (Urbana, IL: University of Illinois Press, 1966).

87. Mary Lenz, "$52 Billion State Budget Clears Board," *Houston Post*, December 15, 1990, p. A-1.

88. House Research Organization, "Writing the State Budget, 82nd Legislature," available at www.capitol.state.tx.us/hrofr/.

89. James W. Enderaby and Michael J. Towle, "Effects of Constitutional and Political Controls on State Expenditures," *Publius: The Journal of Federalism* 27 (Winter 1997): 83–98.

90. Pat Thompson and Steven P. Boyd, "Use of the Item Veto in Texas, 1940–1990," *State and Local Government Review* 26 (Winter 1994): 38–45.

91. Thomas R. Dye, *Politics, Economics, and the Public* (Chicago, IL: Rand McNally, 1966).

92. Paul Sweeney, "Texas: The Corporate Welfare State," *Texas Observer*, April 15, 2005, pp. 6–9, 28.

93. Michael A. Bailey and Mark Carl Rom, "A Wider Race? Interstate Competition Across Health and Welfare Programs," *Journal of Politics* 66 (May 2004): 326–347.

94. Carl Klasner, Xiaotong Mao, and Stan Buchanan, "Business Interest Group Power and Temporary Assistance to Needy Families," *Social Science Quarterly* 88 (March 2007): 104–119.

Chapter 14

Criminal Justice

CHAPTER OUTLINE

WHAT WE WILL LEARN

After studying Chapter 14, you should be able to answer the following questions:

1. What methods are used to measure the crime rate, and what do the data indicate about the crime rate in the United States and the state of Texas?

2. What groups of people are most likely to be the victims of crimes, and what groups are most likely to commit crimes?

3. What are the steps of the criminal prosecution process?

4. What is the capital punishment law in Texas, and how is it implemented?

5. How does Texas deal with juvenile offenders?

6. What categories of prisoners are held in county jails, state jails, and state prisons, and how are those facilities managed?

7. How are criminal justice policies made in Texas?

For the first time in the state's history, Texas has closed a prison. In August 2011, the state shut down the Central Unit in Sugar Land, relocating its 900 inmates and 300 employees to other facilities. The land will be sold or leased to developers.[1]

Several factors led to the closure of the Sugar Land prison facility. First, the crime rate has been falling for years, reducing the need for prison beds. Fewer people are committing crimes and fewer people are being sentenced to prison. Second, the local community has been pressing the state to close the facility because it is located in the middle of Sugar Land, an upscale suburb of Houston. No one wants a prison near residential neighborhoods, and the property is more valuable for development than it is as a prison. Finally, the closure allowed the state to save $25 million over two years, enabling the Texas Department of Corrections (TDC) to preserve the treatment/rehabilitation programs for nonviolent offenders that have proved effective at reducing the number of former inmates who commit crimes after their release.[2]

The discussion of the Sugar Land prison closure introduces this chapter on criminal justice in Texas. The chapter begins by reviewing the crime rate in Texas and the United States, examining and assessing recent trends. It then compares and contrasts victims and criminals. The chapter traces the criminal justice process. It reviews the implementation of capital punishment in the state and discusses juvenile justice. The chapter continues by describing the state's system of jails and prisons. Finally, the chapter considers the criminal justice policy process.

CRIME STATISTICS

Crime is a major policy issue in Texas. Many Texans fear becoming victims of crime, local newscasts feature stories of grisly murders, and politicians run for office promising to get tough on crime. How serious is crime in Texas? Is the crime rate going up or down?

 WHAT DO YOU THINK?

How concerned are you about crime?

Measuring Crime

Uniform Crime Report (UCR) A record of offenses known to police compiled by the Federal Bureau of Investigation (FBI) from reports submitted by local law enforcement agencies.

The U.S. Department of Justice uses two complementary measures to assess the incidence of crime in America: the Uniform Crime Reports (UCR) and the National Crime Victim Survey (NCVS). The **Uniform Crime Reports (UCR)** is a record of offenses known to police compiled by the Federal Bureau of Investigation (FBI) from reports submitted by local law enforcement agencies. The UCR includes four violent crimes (murder, forcible rape, robbery, and aggravated assault) and four property crimes (burglary, larceny/theft, motor vehicle theft, and arson). The advantage of the UCR is that it provides crime data for every state and city in the nation, allowing researchers to compare crime rates. The disadvantage of the UCR is that it underestimates the incidence of crime because it only counts offenses known to the police. Some offenses, such as forcible rape, often go unreported because victims may feel ashamed or endangered. Other crimes, such as theft and burglary, may not be reported because victims have little confidence that the police will apprehend the offenders and recover stolen property. In addition, some victims of crime, such as drug dealers or illegal aliens, may not report offenses because they want to avoid contact with the police.

The **National Crime Victim Survey (NCVS)** is a measure of the incidence of crime in the United States based on interviews with people in more than 50,000 households. It estimates the crime rate on the basis of the number of people in the sample who claim to have been victims of crime during the previous year. Although most social scientists regard the NCVS as a better measure of crime than the UCR, it, too, has shortcomings because it relies on individuals' accurately and honestly reporting crimes to an interviewer. Furthermore, the FBI does not break down NCVS data by states and cities because the sample size is too small.

National Crime Victim Survey (NCVS) A measure of the incidence of crime in the United States based on interviews with people in more than 50,000 households.

The Crime Rate

Crime affects many Americans. According to the UCR, the crime rate for the United States in 2010 was 3,346 offenses per 100,000 people, giving the average American 1 chance in 30 of being the victim of a serious crime. Property crimes occur more frequently than violent crimes. In 2010, the violent crime rate was 404 per 100,000 in population compared with a property crime rate of 2,942. Of the eight categories of crime counted by the UCR, larceny/theft was the most frequent. Murder was the least frequent.[3] The incidence of crime in Texas is higher than the national average. The rate of reported crime in Texas in 2010 was 4,236 per 100,000 people, a figure 27 percent higher than the national average.[4] The average Texan had 1 chance in 24 of being a crime victim.

Trends

Figure 14.1 graphs the ups and downs of the crime rate in the United States from 1990 through 2010. As the figure indicates, the crime rate dropped sharply during the 1990s. It rose briefly in 2001 and then began to fall again. The odds of being murdered or robbed are now less than half what they were in the early 1990s when the violent crime rate peaked.

Criminologists have difficulty explaining the continued decline in the crime rate. Many experts expect that the crime rate would fall more slowly or perhaps even increase because of the recession of 2008-2009, but that has not happened. In fact, the crime rate has continued falling despite the recession. Even robberies are down.[5] Criminologists offer several possible explanations for the drop in the crime rate.

- **Prison expansion.** Between 1990 and 2007, the number of people behind bars in the United States nearly tripled, increasing from 773,919 in 1990 to 2,310,980 in 2007. Keeping criminals off the streets holds down the crime rate. In the last couple of years, however, the correctional population has begun to fall without negatively affecting the crime rate.[6]

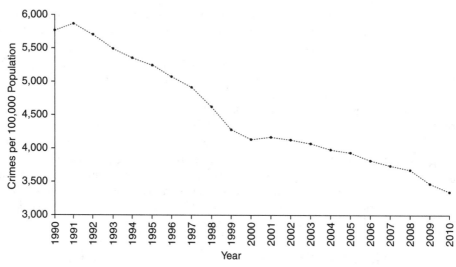

FIGURE 14.1   National Crime Rate, 1990–2010.
Source: FBI, Uniform Crime Reports.

- **Better police work.** Some experts attribute the falling crime rate to better police work, including the introduction of community policing and the implementation of zero-tolerance policies in high-crime areas. **Community policing** is an approach to law enforcement that seeks to reduce crime by increasing the interaction and cooperation between local law enforcement agencies and the people and neighborhoods they serve. The goal of a zero-tolerance policy, meanwhile, is to get lawbreakers off the street by any legitimate means. New York and a number of other cities have aggressively enforced the law in high-crime areas, arresting people not just for serious crimes but also for petty offenses, such as public intoxication, urination in public, traffic-law infractions, and vagrancy.

- **High-tech crime-fighting tools.** Computer technology is giving police the tools to target specific locations and types of crimes minute by minute so they can attack crime before it happens.[7]

Community policing An approach to law enforcement that seeks to reduce crime by increasing the interaction and cooperation between local law enforcement agencies and the people and neighborhoods they serve.

Although crime rates are falling, many Americans do not feel safe. The Gallup Poll regularly asks national samples of Americans the following question: "Is there more crime in your area than there was a year ago or less?" Every year since 1990, more people have said "more" than have said "less," even though the correct answer has almost always been "yes." In 2010, 66 percent of Americans said there was more crime.[8]

Criminologists identify a number of reasons for the disparity between falling crime rates and public apprehension about crime. Police departments continue to warn about the dangers of crime, even when crime rates are falling, because that is their job and their budgets depend on public support for law enforcement. Politicians focus on crime to win votes. Likewise, the media spotlight crime, especially violent crime, to attract viewers and readers. The adage "if it bleeds, it leads" has become the catchphrase for local television news.

VICTIMS AND CRIMINALS

Who are the victims of crime? Although all of us are threatened, some groups of people are more frequent victims of crime. The incidence of crime in urban areas is more than twice as high as in rural areas and is significantly higher than in the suburbs. In addition, low-income persons are more likely to be victims of violent crime than are middle- and upper-income individuals, who, in turn, are more likely to be victims of property crime. Young people are more frequently victimized than are older persons. Except for the crime of forcible rape, men are more likely to be crime victims than are women. Offenses occur more often against racial and ethnic minority groups than against whites. Renters are more likely to become crime victims than are homeowners.[9]

Most criminals are young, poorly educated men. Most people arrested for property crimes and nearly half of individuals arrested for violent crimes are under the age of 25. Three-fourths are male.[10] Criminals and victims often know one another. In fact, a majority of violent crimes occurs between people who know one another. Furthermore, murder typically stays within racial groups. According to official data,

The incidence of crime in Texas is higher than the national average.

most white murder victims nationwide are killed by other whites, whereas most black murder victims are killed by other blacks.[11]

Victims of violent crime in Texas may receive up to $75,000 in financial assistance from the Texas Crime Victims' Compensation fund. This program makes money available to people who are "innocent victims of violent crimes" to cover the loss of earnings, funeral expenses, medical expenses, and the care of minor children. It does not provide compensation for stolen property. The fund is designed to pay expenses not covered by other sources, such as insurance, sick leave, workers' compensation, or Social Security. The fund is financed through fines paid by convicted felons. To receive compensation, a crime victim must report the crime to police within 72 hours, cooperate with law enforcement officials (crime participants are excluded), and file a claim with the Crime Victims' Compensation Division in the attorney general's office within 180 days.[12]

CRIMINAL PROSECUTION PROCESS

The criminal prosecution process begins with an arrest and proceeds through pretrial actions, trial, and sentencing.

Arrest

Probable cause
The reasonable belief that a crime has been committed and that a particular suspect is the likely perpetrator of that crime.

The criminal prosecution process begins with an arrest. Police officers arrest suspects when, in their professional judgment, there is probable cause. **Probable cause** is the reasonable belief that a crime has been committed and that a particular suspect is the likely perpetrator of that crime.

Law enforcement authorities exercise discretion in deciding whether to make an arrest, especially for relatively minor offenses. A police officer may or may not stop a driver traveling at seven miles per hour over the speed limit. A city police officer may warn a pet owner for violating the local leash ordinance, rather than issuing a citation.

Clearance rate The proportion of crimes known to authorities for which an arrest is made.

Law enforcement authorities do not solve every serious crime reported to them. The **clearance rate** is the proportion of crimes known to authorities for which an arrest is made. The clearance rate varies, depending on the offense. It is highest for violent crimes against persons, such as murder, aggravated assault, and robbery. It is lowest for nonviolent crimes against property, such as larceny/theft, motor vehicle theft, and burglary. Victims of violent crimes are often able to identify offenders, whereas property crimes usually occur without witnesses. Furthermore, law enforcement authorities concentrate their resources on violent crime.

Pretrial Actions

Booking An administrative procedure in which law enforcement personnel document a suspect's arrest.

After making an arrest, a police officer takes the suspect to a police station or substation to be booked. **Booking** is an administrative procedure in which law enforcement personnel document a suspect's arrest. While the suspect is fingerprinted

Arraignment A judicial proceeding at which a suspect is formally charged with a crime and asked to enter a plea.

Miranda warning The judicial stipulation that a criminal defendant's confession cannot be admitted into evidence unless police first inform the defendant of the constitutional right to remain silent and to consult an attorney.

Nolo contendere A plea indicating a defendant's decision not to contest a criminal charge.

Bail Money or securities posted by accused persons to guarantee their appearance at later proceedings.

Indictment A formal accusation charging an individual with the commission of a crime.

Grand jury A body of 12 citizens that hears evidence presented by the prosecuting attorney and decides whether to indict an accused person.

and photographed and the paperwork is completed, officials search the records for outstanding arrest warrants against the suspect for other offenses.

An assistant district attorney then determines whether to press charges. Sometimes people arrested for relatively minor offenses such as public intoxication or gambling are not charged. The assistant district attorney may also order a suspect released because of insufficient evidence.

If charges are filed, suspects are brought before a judge for **arraignment,** a judicial proceeding at which a suspect is formally charged with a crime and asked to enter a plea. The judge tells the accused persons of the charges they face and informs them of their constitutional rights. Criminal suspects have the right to remain silent and to know that anything they say may be used against them. They also have the right to discontinue an interview at any time. In addition, they have the right to an attorney and, if they cannot afford to hire one, they have the right to a lawyer appointed by the state. This procedure is known as the **Miranda warning,** which is the judicial stipulation that a criminal defendant's confession cannot be admitted into evidence unless police first inform the defendant of the constitutional right to remain silent and to consult an attorney. Otherwise, any confessions suspects give may not be admitted as evidence at their trials.[13]

At the arraignment, the accused may plead not guilty, guilty, or *nolo contendere,* the Latin phrase for "no contest." **Nolo contendere** is a plea indicating a defendant's decision not to contest a criminal charge. As far as a criminal case is concerned, a plea of *nolo contendere* is the legal equivalent of a guilty plea. At this stage of the criminal prosecution process, most defendants plead not guilty, including many defendants who will eventually plead guilty.

The arraigning judge also sets bail. **Bail** is money or securities posted by accused persons to guarantee their appearance at later proceedings. In general, the amount of bail is based on the seriousness of the criminal offense and the likelihood of the accused returning for trial. If the offense is relatively minor or if the accused has deep roots in the community (a family, job, home, etc.), the judge may release the defendant on personal recognizance (that is, without bail) or at low bail. In contrast, the judge will set a high bond for serious offenses or when there is a strong likelihood that the accused will flee to escape prosecution. In extreme circumstances, the judge may refuse to set bail altogether, requiring the accused to remain in jail until trial. Suspects who make bail are released pending the outcome of their case. In contrast, accused persons without enough money to cover bail must either wait in the county jail or hire a private bail bond company to put up the money for a nonrefundable fee, usually 10 to 15 percent of the bond. If suspects flee, they forfeit their bail and the judge issues a warrant for their arrest. Bail jumping is a crime.

The Texas Constitution requires a grand jury indictment in all felony cases unless the defendant waives that right. An **indictment** is a formal accusation charging an individual with the commission of a crime. A **grand jury** is a body of 12 citizens that hears evidence presented by the prosecuting attorney and decides whether to indict an accused person. Texas has two methods for selecting the members of a grand jury. In the first method, a state district criminal court judge appoints three to five people to serve as jury commissioners. The commissioners, meeting in private, compile a list of 15 to 20 potential grand jurors and present the list to the judge, who selects 12 people to serve as members of a grand jury. In the second method, grand jurors are selected at random from voter registration and driver's license lists, the same pool from which trial jurors are chosen. Grand juries typically meet once or twice a week for a three-month term.

The grand jury works in secret, investigating criminal matters and hearing evidence brought to it by the district attorney. At least 9 of the 12 jurors must agree in order to issue an indictment, also known as a **true bill,** against a defendant. In theory, the grand jury is a screening device that protects innocent persons from unwarranted prosecution by requiring the prosecutor to marshal sufficient evidence to convince a grand jury that there is probable cause of the accused's guilt. Nonetheless, some observers believe that, in contemporary criminal justice systems, grand juries usually act as rubber stamps for the prosecutor. The grand jury hears only the district attorney's view of the case because the defendant does not have the right to present evidence to the grand jury or challenge the information presented by the prosecutor.

However, not all states use the grand-jury system. Many states allow prosecutors to file felony charges directly in the form of an "information." In this method, a judge or a **magistrate** (a judicial official) conducts a hearing to determine if the evidence is sufficient to take the case to trial. Both the prosecutor and the defendant have the opportunity to present evidence to the judge or magistrate, who decides whether the evidence is sufficient to warrant a trial.

The U.S. Supreme Court has ruled that criminal defendants are constitutionally entitled to be represented by an attorney, regardless of their financial status.[14] Texas law empowers district judges to determine whether a defendant is unable to afford an attorney. In practice, judges often assume that a criminal defendant who can afford to make bond has sufficient financial resources to hire an attorney. If the judge determines that a defendant is indigent, the judge assigns the defendant an attorney, who is paid by the county for representing the defendant both at the trial stage and, if necessary, through one round of appeals. Indigent defendants who wish to continue the appeals process beyond this point must obtain private legal assistance or file legal papers themselves. Ten Texas counties, including El Paso and Dallas counties, have public defender offices that employ attorneys full-time to represent indigent defendants. The advocates of the public defender system believe that it provides indigent defendants with better legal representation at less cost to the government.[15] In counties without a public defender office, district judges appoint lawyers in private practice to represent indigent criminal defendants in return for a fee paid by the county government.

Trials

Accused persons have a constitutional right to trial by jury. The U.S. Supreme Court has held that the U.S. Constitution obliges state governments to offer jury trials to persons charged with felony offenses.[16] A **felony** is a serious criminal offense, such as murder, sexual assault, or burglary. The Texas Constitution goes further, granting accused persons the right to trial by jury in *all* cases, misdemeanor and felony.

True bill An indictment issued by a grand jury.

Magistrate Judicial officer.

Felony A serious criminal offense, such as murder, sexual assault, or burglary.

Accused persons without enough money to cover bail must either wait in the county jail or hire a private bond company to put up the money for a nonrefundable fee.

Misdemeanor
A relatively minor criminal offense, such as a traffic violation.

A **misdemeanor** is a less serious offense than a felony. If defendants choose, they may waive the right to a jury trial and be tried by a judge alone.

Prospective trial jurors are selected from county voter registration rolls, lists of persons holding Texas driver's licenses, and Department of Public Safety identification cards. Only American citizens may serve on juries. Persons who are convicted felons or under felony indictment are ineligible to serve on a jury. Some groups of people are exempt from jury service if they wish, including full-time students, individuals over 70 years of age, and persons with custody of small children whose absence would leave the children without proper supervision. A 6-person jury hears misdemeanor cases, whereas a felony-case jury consists of 12 persons.

Adversary proceeding A legal procedure in which each side presents evidence and arguments to bolster its position while rebutting evidence that might support the other side.

A criminal trial is an **adversary proceeding,** that is, a legal procedure in which each side may present evidence and arguments to bolster its position, while rebutting evidence that might support the other side. An assistant district attorney prosecutes the case by presenting evidence and testimony in an effort to prove the defendant's guilt. The defense attorney, meanwhile, cross-examines the prosecution's witnesses to undermine the case against the defendant. After the prosecution has presented its side, the defense has a chance to offer evidence and testimony to show that the defendant is not guilty.

Burden of proof
The legal obligation of one party in a lawsuit to prove its position to a court.

The **burden of proof,** the legal obligation of one party in a lawsuit to prove its position to a court, is on the prosecutor, who must demonstrate the defendant's guilt beyond a reasonable doubt. At least in theory, the defendant need not prove his or her innocence. The judge conducts the trial, ruling on points of law and procedure.

TABLE 14.1   Disposition of Felony Cases in State District Courts, 2008

Disposition	Number of Cases	Percentage
Pled guilty or *nolo contendere*	115,121	71.2%
Tried and convicted	2,590	1.6
Tried and acquitted	961	0.6
Directed acquittal ordered by judge	82	—
Dismissed	42,979	26.6
Total	161,733	100

Source: Office of Court Administration, *Texas Judicial System Annual Report Fiscal Year 2011,* available at www.courts.state.tx.us.

The jury or the judge, if the defendant has waived the right to a jury trial, decides guilt or innocence. The defendant is free to go if acquitted. If the verdict is guilty, punishment must be assessed.

Relatively few individuals indicted for serious crimes ever have a full-blown trial. As Table 14.1 indicates, 71.2 percent of the 161,733 felony cases disposed of by state district courts in 2008 involved the defendant pleading guilty. Most guilty pleas are the result of a **plea bargain,** a procedure in which a defendant agrees to plead guilty in order to receive punishment less than the maximum for an offense. Prosecutors plea bargain because courts are overcrowded—plea bargaining saves money and valuable court time. Also, a plea bargain ensures a conviction. Defendants plea bargain because they fear a harsher punishment or a conviction on a more serious charge.

Plea bargain A procedure in which a defendant agrees to plead guilty in order to receive punishment less than the maximum for an offense.

Most criminal cases that make it to a courtroom conclude with a conviction, through either plea bargaining or a guilty verdict. As Table 14.1 indicates, less than 1 percent of the felony cases heard in Texas in 2008 resulted in the defendant's acquittal. Most defendants pled guilty. Of those who actually went to trial, most were convicted. Furthermore, only about 2 percent of the total number of cases involved jury trials.[17]

 WHAT DO YOU THINK?

Do plea bargains advance the cause of justice?

Sentencing

Except for Class C misdemeanor cases, sentencing is a distinct second phase of the trial proceeding in Texas. Both prosecution and defense may present evidence and arguments in hopes of obtaining a stiffer or lighter sentence for the accused. In jury trials, the defendant may select either the jury or the judge to determine the sentence. In trials without juries, the judge sets the punishment.

Under Texas law, possible sentences vary, depending on the severity of the crime. For misdemeanor offenses, punishment can include a fine and a period of confinement not exceeding a year in jail. For felonies, the fine can be as high as $10,000 and imprisonment, which can range from 180 days to 99 years in prison. Persons convicted of capital murder may be given the death penalty.

With a few exceptions, Texas law permits the judge or jury to grant **probation,** which is the suspension of a sentence, permitting the defendant to remain free under court supervision. The Texas Department of Corrections (TDC) uses the term "community supervision" rather than probation. Instead of going to prison or jail, convicted persons live and work in the community under the supervision of a county probation officer. In granting probation or community supervision, judges may require convicted defendants to hold jobs, support their families, make restitution for their crimes, and stay out of trouble with the law. Should individuals violate the terms of their probation, it may be revoked, and they will be forced to serve time in the county jail or a state prison. Texas has more than twice as many probationers than it has prison inmates, 426,000 offenders in community supervision compared with 155,000 offenders behind bars in 2010.[18]

Persons who plead guilty to relatively minor offenses may be given **deferred adjudication,** a type of probation that can be granted by a judge to a defendant who pleads guilty or *nolo contendere* to certain, relatively less serious offenses. The court defers the judicial proceeding *without* entering the guilty plea in the defendant's record. If the defendant successfully completes the probation, the charges are dismissed and the defendant does not have a conviction on the record, although the defendant will have to file a petition of nondisclosure with a court in order to seal the record of the deferred adjudication from the general public. If the defendant

Probation The suspension of a sentence, permitting the defendant to remain free under court supervision.

Deferred adjudication A type of probation that can be granted by a judge to a defendant who pleads guilty or *nolo contendere* to certain, relatively less serious offenses.

The Texas Constitution guarantees all criminal defendants the right to trial by jury.

violates probation, the case is resumed and the defendant can be convicted and sentenced as if the probation had never taken place. In 2008, state district courts granted deferred adjudication in nearly 50,000 cases, 30 percent of the total number of convictions.[19]

CAPITAL PUNISHMENT

The Texas legislature enacted the state's first capital punishment law in 1923. The first executions took place on February 24, 1924, when five young African American men were electrocuted for murder. Between 1924 and 1964, 503 men and 3 women were sentenced to death in Texas; 361 of the men eventually died in the electric chair. Of those put to death, 229 were African American men, 108 were white men, 23 were Latino men, and one was an American Indian man. None of the three women sentenced to death were executed.[20]

In 1972, the U.S. Supreme Court ruled, in the case of *Furman v. Georgia,* that the death penalty as it was then applied was unconstitutional because it allowed too much discretion to judges and juries, thereby opening the door to discriminatory practices. Getting the death penalty, the Court said, was similar to being struck by lightning.[21] The Court did *not,* however, rule that capital punishment in and of itself was unconstitutional, at least not for the crime of murder.

After the *Furman* decision, many state legislatures adopted new capital punishment laws designed to meet the Supreme Court's objections by reducing discretion in the implementation of the death penalty. The Texas legislature passed a new death penalty statute in 1973, which, with subsequent amendments, defined capital murder to include the following crimes:

- Murdering a peace officer or firefighter, who is acting in the lawful discharge of an official duty and who the person knows is a police officer or firefighter;
- Intentionally committing a murder in the course of committing or attempting to commit kidnapping, burglary, robbery, aggravated sexual assault, or arson;
- Committing a murder for pay or promise to pay or employing another person to commit murder;
- Committing a murder while escaping or attempting to escape from a penal institution;
- Murdering a prison employee while incarcerated;
- Committing a gang-related murder while incarcerated;
- Committing a murder to obstruct justice or in retaliation against a witness in a criminal case;
- Committing serial or mass murder; and
- Murdering a child under the age of six.

The punishment for capital murder is either life imprisonment without possibility of parole or the death penalty. To determine a verdict, the judge or jury must answer three questions:

1. Was the conduct of the defendant that caused the death of the victim committed deliberately and with the reasonable expectation that the victim's death would ensue?
2. Is it probable that the defendant would commit additional criminal acts of violence that would constitute a continuing threat to society?
3. Is there anything in the circumstances of the offense and the defendant's character and background that would warrant a sentence of life imprisonment rather than a death sentence?

Parole The conditional release of convicted offenders from prison to serve the remainder of their sentences in the community under supervision.

The sentence is death if the jury or judge answers *yes, yes,* and *no.* Otherwise, the defendant receives life in prison without **parole,** which is the conditional release of convicted offenders from prison to serve the remainder of their sentences in the community under supervision.

In 1977, the legislature amended the state's capital punishment law to retire "Old Sparky," as the electric chair was nicknamed, and replace it with lethal injection as the means of execution. The law provides that a medically trained individual, whose identity is not revealed, inserts an intravenous catheter into the condemned person's arm. After giving the prisoner the opportunity to make a last statement, the warden orders the introduction of the lethal solution into the catheter. The individual injecting the fatal fluid is visibly separated from the execution chamber by a wall and locked door. A physician makes the final death pronouncement but has no function in the execution. The law allows family members of the convicted murderer and the family of the murder victim to witness the execution.

Because of appeals and other legal delays, no one was executed in Texas from July 1964 until December 1982, when Charlie Brooks, Jr., an African American man convicted of murdering a Fort Worth auto mechanic, died of lethal injection. Between 1982 and mid-2011, Texas carried out 467 executions, substantially more than any other state.[22] In May 2011, death row in Livingston housed 304 men and 10 women.[23]

Capital punishment remains controversial. The opponents of the death penalty charge that the process of trials and appeals is so flawed that innocent people may face execution. A study published by Columbia University law professor James S. Liebman found that two-thirds of the death sentences given by American courts between 1973 and 1995 were overturned on appeal. When death penalty cases were retried, 7 percent of the defendants were found not guilty.[24] Furthermore, the critics of the death penalty argue that it is inefficient because only 5 percent of death sentences are actually carried out and only then after years of appeal.[25] In contrast, the proponents of capital punishment defend the process, saying that it is scrupulously fair. They point out that people given the death penalty are entitled to an appeals process that lasts for years. In Texas, the interval between sentencing and execution for convicted murders is 10.6 years, more than enough time for their cases to be thoroughly examined for error.[26]

Civil Commitment of Sexually Violent Criminals in Kansas

Kansas has adopted a civil commitment procedure to hold sexually violent criminals behind bars after they have completed their prison sentences. In 1994, the Kansas legislature passed and the governor signed the Kansas Sexually Violent Predator Act to provide for the involuntary confinement of sexually violent predators beyond the completion of their prison sentences. Under the law, a sexually violent predator is defined as a person convicted of or charged with a sexually violent offense who suffers from a "mental abnormality" or "personality disorder" that makes the person likely to engage in repeat acts of sexual violence. Once pedophiles and other sexually violent offenders finish their prison sentences, they must be released unless the state can prove to a judge or jury that they meet the criteria to be declared a sexually violent predator. Persons held under the statute are not released until a court certifies that their mental condition has changed and that they no longer qualify as sexually violent predators.

Civil commitment for sexual predators is controversial. The defenders of the procedure argue that it is necessary to protect the community from individuals who are likely to commit horrific crimes. The recidivism rate for sexual offenders is quite high. In contrast, critics contend that the procedure is an unconstitutional mechanism for continuing to punish people who have already served their criminal sentences. They believe the Kansas law violates the Double Jeopardy Clause of the U.S. Constitution, which protects people from being tried twice for the same offense.

The U.S. Supreme Court upheld the constitutionality of the Kansas Sexually Violent Predator Act in *Kansas v. Hendricks.* In a narrow five-to-four decision, the Court compared the civil commitment of sexual predators with the civil commitment of mentally ill persons who are a danger to themselves or others. The Court ruled that the Kansas law does not violate the Double Jeopardy Clause because it is not a criminal penalty. It also ruled that the state is not required to offer treatment for persons held under the statute.*

Nineteen states have adopted civil commitment laws similar to the Kansas statute. In practice, few persons have ever been released because they are no longer considered a threat to offend. Out of 3,000 sexual offenders held in civil commitment facilities nationwide, only 115 have been sent home, most because of technical legal reasons. The program is expensive to operate, especially as the inmates in custody age and require specialized medical care. From 2001 to 2005, the cost of civil commitment in Kansas increased from $1.2 million a year to $6.9 million.†

QUESTIONS TO CONSIDER

1. Should Texas adopt a civil commitment procedure to hold criminally violent sexual offenders in custody after they have completed their prison sentences, similar to the Kansas law?
2. Is it ever safe to release persons convicted of sexually violent crimes from custody?
3. Is civil commitment for violent sexual offenders preferable to longer prison sentences or even the death penalty?

*Kansas v. Hendricks, 521 U.S. 346 (1997).
†Monica Davey and Abby Goodnough, "Doubts Rise as States Hold Sex Offenders After Prison," *New York Times*, March 4, 2007, available at www.nytimes.com.

JUVENILE JUSTICE

The juvenile crime rate has been falling faster than the overall crime rate. In the mid-1990s, juvenile offenders committed about a quarter of all criminal offenses nationwide. By 2010, the percentage of arrestees under the age of 18 had fallen to less than 13 percent.[27] In fact, the recent decline in the crime rate can be attributed entirely to a decrease in juvenile crime. Between 2001 and 2010, the juvenile crime rate fell by 24 percent, whereas the adult crime rate actually increased by 1 percent.[28]

Texas deals with some juvenile offenders as if they were adults. Some juveniles as young as 14 who are charged with serious crimes may be certified to be tried as adults. Judges decide whether to certify a juvenile as an adult depending on the crime's severity and the youngster's maturity. Juveniles below the age of 14 or older juveniles who are not certified as adults are dealt with by the juvenile court system.

Juvenile courts are different from adult courts. Cases tried in juvenile court are heard under the family law code, which is a civil law code rather than criminal law. Juvenile court judges hold hearings to determine if an accused juvenile has engaged in delinquent conduct. The district or county attorney represents the state and must prove the case beyond a reasonable doubt. The juvenile has rights similar to those of adult defendants, including the right to an attorney and the right to cross-examine witnesses. Similar to adult court proceedings, many juvenile court cases are settled through plea bargains. If a juvenile is determined to be delinquent or in need of supervision, the court holds a disposition hearing to determine how the youngster should be handled. The court considers both the safety of the community and the child's best interests.

Juvenile courts enjoy considerable leeway in deciding how to handle youthful defendants. The court can suspend the driver's license of a juvenile offender, order the juvenile to pay restitution to the crime victim, and require the juvenile and the juvenile's parents to perform community service. The court can also order a juvenile to be sent to a community rehabilitation facility or an alternative school. Repeat offenders or juveniles guilty of serious criminal offenses may be held in a state facility operated by the Texas Youth Commission (TYC). Juveniles guilty of certain violent offenses may be transferred to adult prison when they are between ages 16 and 21.

CORRECTIONS

No country locks up as many people and keeps them behind bars as long as does the United States. In the United States, 2.3 million criminals are behind bars.[29] China, with four times the population, imprisons only 1.6 million people. The United States also has the world's highest incarceration rate, with 751 inmates for every 100,000 in population. In contrast, the incarceration rate is 151 per 100,000 in the United Kingdom, 88 in Germany, and 63 in Japan.[30]

The Texas prison system houses 155,000 inmates, making it the largest prison system in the United States.[31] The Texas prison system is more than twice as big as the prison system in New York, even though New York's population is only 12 percent smaller than the Texas population. The incarceration rate in Texas is 683 prison inmates per 100,000 people compared with a national rate of 501 per 100,000. Texas has the second highest incarceration rate in the country, after Louisiana.[32]

County Jails

Except for a few small counties, each of the state's 254 counties has a county jail, built by county tax dollars and staffed by the office of the county sheriff. Jails house people accused of felony and misdemeanor criminal offenses who have not made bail, convicted felons who are awaiting transfer to the Texas Department of Criminal Justice (TDCJ), people charged with federal criminal offenses who are awaiting transfer to a federal facility, and persons convicted of misdemeanor offenses who are serving relatively short sentences. Counties with excess capacity rent space to counties with overcrowded jails. The average daily population of Texas jails in 2010 was 66,064, a figure representing 71 percent of total jail capacity.[33]

State Jails

In 1993, the Texas legislature authorized the creation of a state jail system with an eventual capacity of 22,000 to divert certain nonviolent offenders from the state prison system. State jails house persons convicted of fourth-degree (state jail) felonies. Fourth-degree felonies include forgery, fraud, relatively minor theft, possession or delivery of small amounts of certain illegal drugs, car theft (under $20,000 value), burglary of a building that is not a home, and other nonviolent crimes. Persons convicted of fourth-degree felonies can be given as much as five years' probation or be sentenced to serve as much as two years in a state jail. State jails are designed to keep inexperienced criminals away from hardcore criminals, get them off drugs, and help them finish high school equivalency courses. While in state jails, inmates can receive chemical abuse therapy, job training, and family counseling. State jail inmates serve flat time sentences, with no early release for good behavior. In 2010, 15 state jail facilities housed more than 12,000 offenders.[34]

State Prisons

For years, the Texas prison system was widely regarded as one of the most austere in the nation. More than 90 percent of state prisoners were held in maximum-security prisons, where they were prohibited from having any physical contact with visitors. Inmates were even forbidden from talking with one another in dining areas. Critics called Texas prisons both brutal and brutalizing. However, other observers praised the Texas prison system for its efficiency and effectiveness—the best in the country, they said. Inmates were required to work and attend school. Escapes were rare, the reported rate of inmate violence low, and prison riots unheard of. Furthermore, all of this was achieved at a cost per inmate that was lower than that of any other state in the nation.[35]

In 1972, a group of prisoners filed suit in federal court, claiming that living and working conditions in Texas prisons constituted "cruel and unusual punishment," forbidden by the Eighth Amendment to the U.S. Constitution. The suit, *Ruiz v. Estelle*, charged that the state's prison system was severely overcrowded, the

Texas has the largest prison system in the country.

prison staff was too small to maintain security, working conditions were unsafe, disciplinary procedures were severe and arbitrary, and medical care was inadequate. In particular, the suit attacked the building tender system, in which inmate guards were given authority over their cellblocks to keep them clean and safe. Texas prison officials defended the system for its effectiveness, saying that inmate building tenders were nothing more than glorified janitors. In contrast, critics claimed that inmate guards were dictators who controlled their cellblocks through brute force while guards looked the other way.

In 1980, U.S. District Judge William Wayne Justice ruled against the state of Texas, ordering sweeping changes in the Texas prison system. Although an appeals court later overturned part of Judge Justice's ruling, it agreed with the key points of his decision. Eventually, the state settled the suit by agreeing to limit inmate population to 95 percent of prison capacity, separate hardcore offenders from inmates convicted of nonviolent crimes, improve the guard-to-inmate ratio, upgrade inmate medical treatment, and eliminate the building tender system.[36]

While the state struggled to deal with the impact of *Ruiz v. Estelle*, poor planning by the legislature and the governor made the problem of prison overcrowding considerably worse. During the 1970s and 1980s, the governor and legislature responded to public concerns about crime by getting tough. The legislature passed dozens of anticrime bills, upgrading the seriousness of certain offenses and increasing prison time for offenders. Texas judges and juries began sentencing more people to prison to serve longer terms. The legislature also required that persons convicted of **aggravated offenses** (violent crimes) or crimes using a deadly weapon serve at least a third of a sentence before becoming eligible for parole. As a result, the prison system stacked up with inmates who could not be paroled. In the meantime, the legislature failed to expand prison capacity sufficiently to accommodate the increase in the number of inmates. During the entire decade of the 1970s, the state built only one prison unit with a mere 600 beds. Although the state added 13,000 more beds in the early 1980s, the increase in capacity failed to keep up with the growth of admissions. Prison capacity rose by 50 percent, but admissions increased by 113 percent.[37]

In the late 1980s, the legislature, the governor, and the voters authorized a massive prison construction program to hold the state's rapidly growing prison population. The legislature proposed and the voters approved constitutional amendments to borrow money to build new prison units. Meanwhile, the legislature and the governor appropriated funds to operate the new prison units and begin the long-term process of paying for their construction. The state's prison expansion plans also included the privatization of operations and management at some facilities. **Privatization** is the process that involves the government contracting with private business to implement government programs. In 2008, Texas housed nearly 20,000 inmates at privately managed facilities, 11.5 percent of its inmate population.[38] The proponents of privatization contend that it saves money, and research indicates that the cost of housing prisoners in privately run facilities is about 10 percent less than it is in state-run facilities. In contrast, the critics of prison privatization argue that the savings are illusory because they result from the use of poorly trained, underpaid personnel who pose a security risk.[39]

The Texas prison system is not especially well funded. Despite having the largest prison system in the country, Texas is 21st in per capita spending on corrections. New York, with a prison population less than a third of the size of the Texas inmate population, has a larger corrections budget.[40]

Prison Release

Prisoners leave the prison system through parole or by completing their sentences. In theory, parole is a mechanism for reintegrating offenders into the community because it allows the state to release prisoners to the community conditionally, under supervision. In general, parolees must not associate with known criminals, possess firearms, use illegal drugs, or drink to excess. They are required to report regularly to

Aggravated offenses Violent crimes.

Privatization The process that involves the government contracting with private business to implement government programs.

BREAKING NEWS!   **Texas Prison System Cuts Costs by Dropping Inmate Lunches on Weekends**

The Texas prison system has stopped serving lunch on weekends to save money. Inmates receive three meals a day Monday through Friday, but only breakfast and dinner on weekends. Inmates can buy snacks from the prison commissary, but, critics charge, that puts prisoners from low-income families at a disadvantage. In addition, the prison system is substituting sliced bread for hamburger and hotdog buns and powdered milk for milk cartons. The relatives of prison inmates complain that the measures are unnecessarily harsh.

Discussion

Oh boohoo. Millions of Texas families struggle to put food on the table while prison inmates complain about missing lunch on weekends and having to eat their hamburgers and hotdogs with bread instead of buns. Do you think many Texans care? Prison inmates are not a sympathetic group. Certainly Democratic State Senator John Whitmire from Houston, the chair of the Senate Criminal Justice Committee, isn't sympathetic. "If they don't like the menu," he said, "don't come there in the first place."*

How much money is the state saving with these cutbacks? It can't be much. It isn't. The TDC estimates that skipping lunch on weekends will save $2.8 million in food expenses. Although that sounds like a lot of money, it is a tiny fraction of the state's $27 billion shortfall.

Other than some unhappy inmates, is there a downside to the food cutbacks? There may be. Criminologist Robert Worley of Texas A&M Central Texas calls the food reductions a "very short-sighted idea."[†] Good conditions help keep order. In contrast, angry inmates are less cooperative, more likely to act out, and more dangerous for guards to handle.

Be Served on Weekends," *New York Times*, October 20, 2011, available at **www.nytimes.com.**

---

*Quoted in Manny Fernandez, "In Bid to Cut Costs at Some Texas Prisons, Lunch Will Not Be Served on Weekends," *New York Times*, October 20, 2011, available at www.nytimes.com.
[†]Quoted in Diane Jennings, "Texas Prison System Budget Cuts Stir Up Concerns," *Dallas Morning News*, April 18, 2011, available at www.dallasnews.com.

---

a parole officer and inform that official of a change of residence or a change of jobs. Parole is also cheaper than prison. The cost of parole supervision is $3.74 a day for each offender compared with $47 for each day in prison.[41]

Under state law, most prisoners are eligible for parole after serving one-fourth of their sentence or 15 years, whichever is less. The state determines the amount of time served for inmates convicted of nonviolent offenses by adding together the actual days spent behind bars with good time earned. **Good time** is a prison policy that credits inmates with time off for good behavior. Prisoners can earn a maximum of 75 days of good time for every 30 days actually served if they attend school, work in prison, and generally behave themselves. Violent offenders serve flat time without the opportunity to earn good time. Furthermore, persons found guilty of violent crimes or who used a deadly weapon in the course of committing an offense must serve at least half of their sentence before becoming eligible for parole. In theory, both parole and good time are prison management tools because they give inmates an incentive to cooperate with prison officials. Prisoners who attend classes, develop work skills, and stay out of trouble behind bars earn the opportunity

Good time A prison policy that credits inmates with time off for good behavior.

for parole. If parolees fail to live up to the conditions of their release, they can be returned to prison.

 **WHAT DO YOU THINK?**

Should prison inmates be released early from prison because of good behavior?

Recidivism

Recidivism The tendency of offenders released from prison to commit additional crimes and be returned behind bars.

Many inmates released from prison get in trouble again. **Recidivism** is the tendency of offenders released from prison to commit additional crimes and be returned behind bars. In Texas, 24 percent of inmates released from prison are rearrested for a serious crime within three years of their release.[42] Recidivism is less of a problem in Texas than in many other states. The three-year recidivism rate in California, for example, is 57 percent.[43]

MAKING CRIMINAL JUSTICE POLICY

The most important elements of the policymaking environment for criminal justice policymaking are public opinion, federal court rulings, and the budgetary outlook. The general public has strong views about crime. Elected officials all want to be seen as tough on crime. Whereas public opinion in Texas generally supports a "lock 'em up and throw away the key" philosophy, federal court rulings and the state budget impose constraints on policymakers. Federal court decisions establish the ground rules for the criminal justice process and determine the range of punishments that is constitutionally acceptable. Meanwhile, the state's budget outlook determines the resources policymakers will have available to address criminal justice issues. When the budget is tight, state leaders are more generous with probation and parole than they are in good economic times. In 2007, for example, the legislature passed legislation to expand drug treatment programs and revise parole practices, with the goal of reducing the number of nonviolent offenders behind bars.[44] The approach worked well enough that the state was able to shut down a prison unit in Sugar Land in 2011 during another budget crunch.

Agenda Setting

Numerous political actors set the agenda for criminal justice policymaking. Federal court decisions sometimes force the legislature and the governor to address policy issues. For example, recent decisions of the U.S. Supreme Court on the constitutionality of imposing the death penalty on offenders who were juveniles at the time of their crime[45] or against the mentally retarded[46] have forced the state to revise its capital punishment statute. The legislature and the governor had to address the issue of prison reform because of *Ruiz v. Estelle*, a U.S. district court decision. Media reports of horrific crimes or the possibility that the state has sent an innocent person to prison or even death row set the agenda as well. For example, the legislature and the governor focused on overhauling the operation of the Texas Youth Commission (TYC) after the media revealed allegations of sexual abuse by staff members against juvenile offenders held in TYC custody.

Policy Formulation, Adoption, and Legitimation

The legislature, governor, and some interest groups participate in criminal justice policy formulation. Legislators formulate policy with input from the governor and a number of interest groups that focus on criminal justice issues, such as Mothers Against Drunk Driving (MADD), public employee groups representing police officers and corrections employees, death penalty opponents, and victim rights organizations. For example, MADD lobbies in favor of tougher driving-while-intoxicated (DWI) laws. Unions representing prison employees fought against prison privatization and succeeded in limiting the practice to newly built prisons, rather than privatizing existing units, thus saving the jobs of their members.

The legislature and the governor adopt criminal justice policies through the legislative process. Criminal justice bills must pass the Texas House and Texas Senate and then go to the governor for signature. If the governor vetoes a measure, it dies unless both the Texas House and Texas Senate vote to override the veto by a two-thirds vote.

Interest groups, political parties, and elected officials participate in the policy legitimation process. As the legislature has toughened DWI laws, for example, MADD has supported the action. Many state officials defend the status of Texas as the nation's leading capital punishment state.

Policy Implementation, Evaluation, and Change

State and local law enforcement, district attorneys, the court system, and the TDCJ implement criminal justice policies. Police officers implement criminal justice policies by arresting suspects. District attorneys decide whether to prosecute defendants; courts conduct trials. Ordinary citizens also participate in policy implementation by serving on juries. The TDCJ houses prisoners serving their sentences, whereas the Board of Pardons and Paroles determines whether to grant parole.

Numerous state and federal agencies evaluate criminal justice policies. The Federal Bureau of Investigation (FBI), Federal Bureau of Justice Statistics, Texas Commission on Jail Standards, and the Legislative Budget Board (LBB) all gather criminal justice statistics. The LBB, comptroller, and Texas Sunset Commission prepare analytical reports evaluating the operation of the TDCJ. The legislature and the governor then use these reports as the basis for proposing legislation designed to reform criminal justice policies.

Criminal justice policy change occurs because of the federal government, public opinion, and budget constraints. Many of the state's criminal justice policies have changed because of the actions of the federal government, especially federal court decisions. The decision of lower federal courts in the case of *Ruiz v. Estelle* eventually led to a substantial increase in the state's prison capacity. Public opinion also drives changes in criminal justice policies. During the 1970s, public anger over rising crime rates compelled the legislature to toughen the state's sentencing laws. Finally, budget constraints affect criminal justice policies. Lawmakers in recent sessions of the Texas legislature have reformed sentencing procedures to increase the use of probation and parole in order to save money.

WHAT WE HAVE LEARNED

1. What methods are used to measure the crime rate, and what do the data indicate about the crime rate in the United States and the state of Texas?

The U.S. Department of Justice uses two complementary measures to assess the incidence of crime in America: the Uniform Crime Reports (UCR) and the National Crime Victim Survey (NCVS). According to the UCR, the crime rate for the United States in 2010 was 3,346 offenses per 100,000 people, giving the average American 1 chance in 30 of being the victim of a serious crime. The incidence of crime in Texas is higher than the national average. The rate of reported crime in Texas in 2010 was 4,236 per 100,000 people, 27 percent higher than the national average.[47] The average Texan had 1 chance in 24 of being a crime victim. The crime rate has been falling, both nationally and in Texas, for well over a decade. Criminologists are not certain why the crime rate has been falling, but possible explanations include prison expansion, better police work, and the use of high-tech crime-fighting tools.

2. What groups of people are most likely to be the victims of crimes, and what groups are most likely to commit crimes?

The crime rate is higher in urban areas. Low-income people, young people, racial and ethnic minorities, men, and renters are more likely to be victims of crime than other groups. Most criminals are young, poorly educated men.

3. What are the steps of the criminal prosecution process?

The criminal prosecution process begins with an arrest based on probable cause. Arrests are following by booking and arraignment. Defendants enter a plea, usually innocent at this stage, and may be given the opportunity to make bail. The Texas Constitution requires a grand jury indictment in all felony cases unless the defendant waives that right. Although accused persons have a right to trial by jury, many criminal defendants plea bargain rather than go to trial. Criminal trials are adversary proceedings in which the prosecution has the burden of proof. Except for Class C misdemeanor cases, sentencing is a distinct second phase of the trial proceeding in Texas.

4. What is the capital punishment law in Texas, and how is it implemented?

The Texas death punishment statute defines capital murder to include a distinct set of offenses. The punishment for capital murder is either life imprisonment without possibility of parole or the death penalty. Lethal injection is the method of execution in Texas, which leads the nation in carrying out the death penalty.

5. How does Texas deal with juvenile offenders?

The juvenile crime rate has been falling faster than the overall crime rate. A judge can certify juveniles as young as 14 to be tried as adults. Juvenile courts try younger juveniles and juveniles not certified as adults. Juvenile courts enjoy considerable leeway in deciding how to handle youthful defendants, including referral to the Texas Youth Commission.

6. What categories of prisoners are held in county jails, state jails, and state prisons, and how are those facilities managed?

No country locks up as many people and keeps them behind bars as long as the United States. The Texas prison system houses 155,000 inmates, making it the largest prison system in the United States. County jails house people accused of felony and misdemeanor criminal offenses who have not made bail, convicted felons who are awaiting transfer to the TDCJ, people charged with federal criminal offenses who are awaiting transfer to a federal facility, and persons convicted of misdemeanor offenses who are serving relatively short sentences. State jails hold persons convicted of fourth-degree (state jail) felonies. State prisons house persons convicted of all other felonies. *Ruiz v. Estelle* (1972) forced the state to reduce overcrowding, initially by releasing prisoners and subsequently by building additional prisons. The state has contracted with private firms to operate some of the prisons. Prison officials use good time as a prison-management tool. The tendency of offenders released from prison to commit additional crimes and be returned behind bars is known as recidivism.

7. How are criminal justice policies made in Texas?

The most important elements of the policymaking environment for criminal justice policymaking are public opinion, federal court rulings, and the budgetary outlook. Numerous political actors set the agenda for criminal justice policymaking, including federal judges, legislators, the governor, and the media. The legislature, governor, and some interest groups participate in criminal justice policy formulation. The legislature and the governor adopt criminal justice policies through the legislative process. Interest groups, political parties, and elected officials participate in the policy legitimation process. State and local law enforcement agencies, district attorneys, the court system, and the TDCJ implement criminal justice policies. Numerous state and federal agencies evaluate criminal justice policies. Criminal justice policies change because of the federal government, public opinion, and budget constraints.

KEY TERMS

adversary proceeding	felony	*nolo contendere*
aggravated offenses	good time	parole
arraignment	grand jury	plea bargain
bail	indictment	privatization
booking	magistrate	probable cause
burden of proof	*Miranda* warning	probation
clearance rate	misdemeanor	recidivism
community policing	National Crime Victim Survey (NCVS)	true bill
deferred adjudication		Uniform Crime Reports (UCR)

NOTES

1. Mike Ward, "Texas First: Prison Is Closing," *Austin American-Statesman*, August 3, 2011, available at www.statesman.com.

2. Brandi Grissom, "Budget Writers Agree to First Texas Prison Closure," *Texas Tribune*, May 17, 2011, available at www.texastribune.org.

3. Federal Bureau of Investigation, Uniform Crime Reports, available at www.fbi.gov.

4. Texas Department of Public Safety, "The Texas Crime Report for 2010," available at www.txdps.state.tx.us.

5. Richard A. Oppel Jr., "Steady Decline in Major Crime Baffles Experts," *New York Times*, May 23, 2011, available at www.nytimes.com.

6. Lauren E. Glaze, "Correctional Populations in the United States, 2009," Bureau of Justice Statistics, December 2010, available at www.ojp.usdoj.gov.

7. James Pinkerton and Yang Wang, "Violent Crime in City Takes 12 Percent Dip," *Houston Chronicle*, September 20, 2011, pp. B1, B5.

8. Jeffrey M. Jones, "Americans Still Perceive Crime as on the Rise," November 18, 2010, available at www.gallup.com.

9. "Victimization Rates, by Type of Crime and Characteristics of the Victim: 2009," *2012 Statistical Abstract*, available at www.census.gov.

10. "Arrests by Sex and Age, 2009," *2012 Statistical Abstract*, available at www.census.gov.

11. "Victim-Offender Relationship in Crimes of Violence, by Characteristics of the Criminal Incident," *2012 Statistical Abstract*, available at www.census.gov.

12. Texas Crime Victims' Compensation Fund, available at www.oag.state.tx.us.

13. *Miranda v. Arizona*, 384 U.S. 436 (1966).

14. *Gideon v. Wainwright*, 372 U.S. 335 (1963).

15. Office of Court Administration, "Evidence for the Feasibility of Public Defender Offices in Texas," available at www.courts.state.tx.us.

16. *Duncan v. Louisiana*, 391 U.S. 145 (1968).

17. Office of Court Administration, *Texas Judicial System Annual Report Fiscal Year 2011*, available at www.courts.state.tx.us.

18. Texas Department of Criminal Justice, available at www.tdcj.state.tx.us.

19. Office of Court Administration, *Texas Judicial System Annual Report Fiscal Year 2011*.

20. U.S. Law Enforcement Assistance Administration, *Prisoners in State and Federal Institutions on December 31, 1977*, National Prisoner Statistics Bulletin, SD-NPS-PSF-5 (Washington, DC: U.S. Government Printing Office, 1979); Texas Judicial Council, "Capital Murder Study," in *Forty-Seventh Annual Report 1975* (Austin, TX: Texas Judicial Council, 1976), pp. 89–94; and Rupert C. Koeniger, "Capital Punishment in Texas, 1927–1968," *Crime and Delinquency* 15 (January 1968): 132–141.

21. *Furman v. Georgia*, 408 U.S. 238 (1972).

22. Texas Department of Criminal Justice, "Executions," available at www.tdcj.state.tx.us.

23. Texas Department of Criminal Justice, "Offenders on Death Row," available at www.tdcj.state.tx.us.

24. James S. Leibman, "A Broken System: Error Rates in Capital Cases, 1973–1995," available at www.thejusticeproject.org.

25. Ibid.

26. Texas Department of Criminal Justice, "Execution Statistics," available at www.tdcj.state.tx.us.

27. Federal Bureau of Investigation, "Arrests by Age," *Crime in the United States 2011*, available at www.fbi.gov.

28. Federal Bureau of Investigation, "Ten-Year Arrest Trends 2001-2010," *Crime in the United States 2011*, available at www.fbi.gov.

29. "Adults Under Correctional Supervision," *2012 Statistical Abstract*, available at www.census.gov.

30. Adam Liptak, "Inmate Count in U.S. Dwarfs Other Nations," *New York Times*, April 23, 2008, available at www.nytimes.com.

31. Texas Department of Criminal Justice, "Annual Review 2010," available at www.tdcj.state.tx.us.

32. *Governing*, State and Local Source Book, available at www.governing.com.

33. Texas Commission on Jail Standards, "2010 Annual Report," available at www.tcjs.state.tx.us.

34. Texas Department of Criminal Justice, "Annual Review 2010," available at www.tdcj.state.tx.us.

35. John J. DiIulio, Jr., "Judicial Intervention: Lessons from the Past," in Timothy J. Flanagan, James W. Marquart, and Kenneth G. Adams, eds., *Incarcerating Criminals: Prisons and Jails in Social and Organizational Context* (New York, NY: Oxford University Press, 1998), pp. 81–93.

36. *Ruiz v. Estelle*, 503 F. Supp 1265 (S.D. Tex 1980); 679 F. 2d 115 (5th Cir. 1982).

37. Dianna Hunt, "Justice Delayed: Our State's Criminal Crisis," *Houston Chronicle*, December 2, 1990, p. 24A.

38. Bureau of Justice Statistics, "Prison and Jail Inmates at Midyear 2008," available at www.ojp.usdoj.gov.

39. Douglas McDonald and Carl Patten, Jr., "Governments' Management of Private Prisons," National Institute of Justice, available at www.ncjrs.gov.

40. *Governing*, State and Local Source Book, available at www.governing.com.

41. Legislative Budget Board, "Criminal Justice Uniform Cost Report Tables," available at www.lbb.state.tx.us.

42. Legislative Budget Board, "Statewide Criminal Justice Recidivism and Revocation Rates," January 2011, available at www.lbb.state.tx.us.

43. Office of Adult Research, California Department of Corrections and Rehabilitation, April 2008, available at www.cdcr.ca.gov.

44. *Capitol Update*, March 6, 2008, available at www.txdirectory.com.

45. *Roper v. Simmons*, 543 U.S. 551 (2005).

46. *Atkins v. Virginia*, 536 U.S. 304 (2002).

47. Texas Department of Public Safety, "The Texas Crime Report for 2010," available at www.txdps.state.tx.us.

Glossary

AARP: An interest group representing the concerns of older Americans. (Ch. 5)

Ability-to-pay theory of taxation: An approach to government finance that holds that taxes should be based on an individual's financial resources. (Ch. 13)

Address from office: A procedure for removing judicial officials that is initiated by the governor and requires a two-thirds vote by the legislature. (Ch. 10)

Adversary proceeding: A legal procedure in which each side presents evidence and arguments to bolster its position while rebutting evidence that might support the other side. (Ch. 10, Ch. 14)

Advocacy groups: Organizations created to seek benefits on behalf of persons who are unable to represent their own interests. (Ch. 5)

Affirm: An appeals court upholds the decision of a lower court. (Ch. 10)

Agenda setting: The process through which issues become matters of public concern and government action. (Intro)

Aggravated offenses: Violent crimes. (Ch. 14)

Allocational urban policies: Local programs that are more or less neutral in their impact on the local economy. (Ch. 11)

Allowable: The maximum permissible rate of production for oil and gas wells in Texas as set by the Railroad Commission. (Ch. 9)

American Federation of Labor-Congress of Industrial Organizations (AFL-CIO): A national association of labor unions. (Ch. 5)

Americans with Disabilities Act (ADA): A federal law intended to end discrimination against persons with disabilities and to eliminate barriers preventing their full participation in American society. (Ch. 3)

Annexation: The authority of a city to increase its geographic size by extending its boundaries to take in adjacent unincorporated areas. (Ch. 11)

Appeal: The taking of a case from a lower court to a higher court by the losing party in a lower-court decision. (Ch. 10)

Appropriation bill: A legislative authorization to spend money for particular purposes. (Ch. 8, Ch. 9, Ch. 13)

Appropriation process: An annual procedure through which Congress legislatively provides money for a particular purpose. (Ch. 3)

Arraignment: A judicial proceeding at which a suspect is formally charged with a crime and asked to enter a plea. (Ch. 14)

At-large election: A method for choosing public officials in which every citizen of a political subdivision, such as a state or county, votes to select a public official. (Ch. 7, Ch. 11)

Attorney general's opinion: A written interpretation of existing law. (Ch. 9)

Authorization process: The procedure through which Congress legislatively establishes a program, defines its general purpose, devises procedures for its operation, specifies an agency for implementation, and indicates an approximate level of funding. (Ch. 3)

Bail: Money or securities posted by accused persons to guarantee their appearance at later proceedings. (Ch. 14)

Battleground state: A swing state in which the relative strength of the two major-party presidential candidates is close enough so that either candidate could conceivably carry the state. (Ch. 4)

Bicameral legislature: A legislative body with two chambers. (Ch. 2, Ch. 8)

Biennium: Two-year budget period. (Ch. 13)

Bilingual education: Teaching of academic subjects in both English and a student's native language, usually Spanish. (Ch. 6, Ch. 12)

Bill: A proposed law. (Ch. 8)

Bill of rights: A constitutional document guaranteeing individual rights and liberties. (Ch. 2)

Block grant program: A federal grant-in-aid program that provides money for a program in a broad, general policy area, such as elementary and secondary education or transportation. (Ch. 3)

Bond: A certificate of indebtedness issued to investors who loan money for interest income; in lay terms, a bond is an IOU. (Ch. 7, Ch. 11)

Bond election: An election for the purpose of obtaining voter approval for a local government going into debt. (Ch. 7)

Booking: An administrative procedure in which law enforcement personnel document a suspect's arrest. (Ch. 14)

Boosters: People who promote local economic development. (Ch. 11)

Branch banking: A business practice whereby a single, large bank conducts business from several locations. (Ch. 2)

Budget deficit: The amount of money by which annual budget expenditures exceed annual budget receipts. (Ch. 2, Ch. 13)

Budget execution authority: The power to cut agency spending or transfer money between agencies during the period when the legislature is not in session. (Ch. 2, Ch. 9, Ch. 13)

Building codes: Municipal ordinances that set minimum standards for the types of materials used in construction, building design, and construction methods employed in all building within the city. (Ch. 11)

Burden of proof: The legal obligation of one party in a lawsuit to prove its position to a court. (Ch. 10, Ch. 14)

Capital expenditure: The purchase by government of a permanent, fixed asset, such as a new city hall or highway overpass. (Ch. 11)

Capital punishment: The death penalty. (Intro, Ch. 6, Ch. 9, Ch. 10)

Categorical grant program: A federal grant-in-aid program that provides funds to state and local governments for a fairly narrow, specific purpose. (Ch. 3)

Caucus method of delegate selection: A procedure for choosing national party convention delegates that involves party voters participating in a series of precinct and district or county political meetings. (Ch. 7)

Cause groups: Organizations whose members care intensely about a single issue or a group of related issues. (Ch. 5)

Charter school: A publicly funded but privately managed school that operates under the terms of a formal contract, or charter, with the state. (Ch. 12)

Checks and balances: The overlapping of the powers held by the different branches of government, so that public officials limit the authority of one another. (Ch. 2)

Citizen groups: Organizations created to support government policies that they believe will benefit the public at large. (Ch. 5)

City charter: The basic law of a city that defines its powers, responsibilities, and organization. (Ch. 11)

City manager: A professional administrator hired by the city council. (Ch. 11)

City ordinances: Laws enacted by a municipality's governing body. (Ch. 10, Ch. 11)

Civic culture: A political culture that is conducive to the development of an efficient, effective government that meets the needs of its citizens in a timely and professional manner. (Ch. 1)

Civil case: A legal dispute concerning a private conflict between two or more parties—individuals, corporations, or government agencies. (Ch. 10)

Civil defendant: The responding party to a civil suit. (Ch. 10)

Civil union: A legal partnership between two men or two women giving the couple all the benefits, protections, and responsibilities under law as granted to spouses in a marriage. (Ch. 2)

Clean Air Act: A federal law that regulates air emissions. (Ch. 3)

Clearance rate: The proportion of crimes known to authorities for which an arrest is made. (Ch. 14)

Closed primary: An election system that limits primary election participation to registered party members. (Ch. 7)

Coattail effect: The political phenomenon in which a strong candidate for one office gives a boost to fellow party members on the same ballot seeking other offices. (Ch. 7)

Commissioners court: The board of directors for county government. (Ch. 12)

Community policing: The approach to law enforcement that seeks to reduce crime by increasing the interaction and cooperation between local law enforcement agencies and the people and neighborhoods they serve. (Ch. 14)

Commutation: The reduction of punishment for a criminal offense. (Ch. 9)

Concurring opinion: A written judicial statement that agrees with the court ruling but disagrees with the reasoning of the majority. (Ch. 10)

Conference committee: A special committee created to negotiate differences on similar pieces of legislation passed by the House and Senate. (Ch. 8, Ch. 13)

Conflict of interest: A situation in which the personal interests of a public official may clash with that official's professional responsibilities. (Ch. 12)

Conservatism: The political view that seeks to preserve the political, economic, and social institutions of society against abrupt change. Conservatives generally oppose most government economic regulation and heavy government spending while favoring low taxes and traditional values. (Ch. 6, Ch. 8)

Constitution: The fundamental law by which a state or nation is organized and governed. (Ch. 2)

Constitutional amendment: A formal, written change or addition to the state's governing document. (Ch. 2)

Constitutional law: Law that involves the interpretation and application of the constitution. (Ch. 2)

Constitutional revision: The process of drafting a new constitution. (Ch. 2)

Contract case: A civil suit dealing with disputes over written or implied legal agreements, such as a suit over a faulty roof repair job. (Ch. 10)

Council-manager form of city government: A structure of municipal government in which the city council/mayor appoints a professional administrator, called a city manager, to act as the municipality's chief executive officer. (Ch. 11)

Criminal case: A legal dispute dealing with an alleged violation of a penal law. (Ch. 10)

Criminal defendant: The party charged with a criminal offense. (Ch. 10)

Cumulative voting system: An election system that allows individual voters to cast more than one ballot in the simultaneous election of several officials. (Ch. 11)

Dedicated funds: Constitutional or statutory provisions that set aside revenue for particular purposes. (Ch. 2, Ch. 13)

Dedicated Highway Fund: A constitutionally earmarked account containing money set aside for building, maintaining, and policing state highways. (Ch. 2, Ch. 13)

Deed restrictions: Private contractual agreements that limit what residential property owners can do with their houses and land. (Ch. 11)

Deferred adjudication: A type of probation that can be granted by a judge to a defendant who pleads guilty or *nolo contendere* to certain, relatively less serious offenses. (Ch. 14)

Deracialization: The attempt by political candidates to de-emphasize racially divisive themes in order to garner crossover support from voters of other races/ethnicities while also receiving the overwhelming majority of support from voters of the candidate's own racial/ethnic group. (Ch. 11)

Developmental urban policies: Local programs that enhance the community's economic position in its competition with other communities. (Ch. 11)

Dillon's rule: The legal principle that states that a city can exercise only those powers expressly allowed by state law. (Ch. 11)

Direct democracy: A political system in which the citizens vote directly on matters of public concern. (Ch. 2)

Disfranchisement: The denial of voting rights. (Ch. 4)

Dissenting opinion: A written judicial statement that disagrees with the decision of the court's majority. (Ch. 10)

District election: A method for choosing public officials in which a political subdivision, such as a state or county, is divided into districts and each district elects one official. (Ch. 7, Ch. 10, Ch. 11)

Domestic-relations case: A civil suit based on the law involving the relationship between husband and wife, as well as between parents and children, such as divorce and child custody cases. (Ch. 10)

Double jeopardy: The constitutional principle that an individual may not be tried a second time by the same unit of government for a single offense if acquitted in the first trial. (Ch. 10)

Dual school system: Separate sets of schools for white and African American youngsters. (Ch. 3)

Early voting: A system that allows citizens to cast ballots before Election Day. (Ch. 4)

Election campaign: An attempt to get information to voters that will persuade them to elect a candidate or not elect an opponent. (Ch. 7)

Election precincts: Voting districts. (Ch. 4)

Electoral College: The system established in the U.S. Constitution for the selection of the president and vice president of the United States. (Ch. 6)

Elite theory (*or* elitism): The view that political power is held by a small group of people who dominate politics by controlling economic resources. (Ch. 11)

Eminent domain: The authority to take private property for public use upon just compensation. (Ch. 3, Ch. 9)

Empirical analysis: A method of study that relies on experience and scientific observation. (Intro)

Employees Retirement System (ERS) Trust Fund: A pension fund for state employees. (Ch. 13)

Enfranchise: To grant the right to vote. (Ch. 4)

Enterprise zones: A state program that allows local governments to designate certain areas called enterprise zones in which private investors can receive property tax abatements, local sales tax rebates (refunds), and government-backed low-interest loans. (Ch. 11)

Entitlement programs: Government programs providing benefits to all persons qualified to receive them under law. (Ch. 3)

Environmental Protection Agency (EPA): The federal agency responsible for enforcing the nation's environmental laws. (Ch. 3)

Equal Protection Clause: The constitutional provision found in the Fourteenth Amendment of the U.S. Constitution that declares "No State shall . . . deny to any person within its jurisdiction the equal protection of the laws." (Ch. 3)

Equal protection of the law: The legal principle that laws may not arbitrarily discriminate against persons. (Ch. 2)

Excise tax: A tax levied on the manufacture, transportation, sale, or consumption of a particular item or set of related items. (Ch. 13)

Executive order: A directive issued by the governor to an administrative agency or executive department. (Ch. 9)

Exit polls: Surveys based on random samples of voters leaving the polling place. (Ch. 4)

Extraterritorial jurisdiction (ETJ): The authority of a city to require conformity with city ordinances and regulations affecting streets, parks, alleys, utility easements, sanitary sewers, and the like in a ring of land extending from one-half mile to five miles beyond the city-limits line. (Ch. 11)

Federal grant program: A program through which the national government gives money to state and local governments to spend in accordance with set standards and conditions. (Ch. 3, Ch. 12, Ch. 13)

Federal mandate: A legal requirement placed on a state or local government by the national government requiring certain policy actions. (Ch. 3)

Federal preemption of state authority: An act of Congress adopting regulatory policies that overrule state policies in a particular regulatory area. (Ch. 3)

Federal system or federation: A political system that divides power between a central government, with authority over the whole nation, and a series of state governments. (Ch. 3)

Felony: A serious criminal offense, such as murder, sexual assault, or burglary. (Ch. 10, Ch. 14)

Filibuster: An attempt to defeat a bill through prolonged debate. (Ch. 8)

Fiscal note: An analysis indicating a legislative measure's cost to state government, if any. (Ch. 8)

Fiscal year: Budget year. (Ch. 13)

Forcible entry and detainer suit: An effort by a landlord to evict a tenant (usually for failure to pay rent). (Ch. 10)

Formula grant program: A grant program that awards funding on the basis of a formula established by Congress. (Ch. 3)

Foundation School Program: The basic funding program for public education in the state of Texas. (Ch. 12, Ch. 13)

Franchise: The right to vote. (Ch. 4)

Franchise tax: A tax on businesses chartered or organized in Texas and doing business in the state. (Ch. 13)

Gender gap: A term that refers to differences in party identification and political attitudes between men and women. (Ch. 6)

General election: A statewide election to fill national and state offices held on the Tuesday after the first Monday in November of even-numbered years. (Ch. 7)

General Fund: The state treasury account that supports state programs and services without restriction. (Ch. 13)

General-law city: A municipality that is limited to those governmental structures and powers specifically granted by state law. (Ch. 11)

General-law units of local government: Units of local government that are limited to those structures and powers specifically granted by state law. (Ch. 12)

General obligation bonds: Certificates of indebtedness that must be repaid from general revenues. (Ch. 2)

Gerrymandering: The drawing of legislative district lines for political advantage. (Ch. 7)

Global warming: The gradual warming of the Earth's atmosphere reportedly caused by the burning of fossil fuels and industrial pollutants. (Ch. 9)

Good business climate: A political environment in which business prospers. (Ch. 5)

Good time: A prison policy that credits inmates with time off for good behavior. (Ch. 14)

Grand jury: A body of 12 citizens that hears evidence presented by the prosecuting attorney and decides whether to indict an accused person. (Ch. 14)

Grand Old Party (GOP): A nickname for the Republican Party. (Ch. 6)

Grange: An organization of farmers. (Ch. 2)

Gross state product: The total value of goods and services produced in a state in a year. (Ch. 1)

***Habeus corpus*, writ of:** A court order requiring a government official to explain why a person is being held in custody. (Ch. 10)

Harmless error: A mistake committed by a trial court that is not serious enough to warrant a new trial because it could not have affected the outcome of the original trial. (Ch. 10)

Hate-crimes legislation: Legislative measures that increase penalties for persons convicted of criminal offenses motivated by prejudice based on race, religion, national origin, gender, or sexual orientation. (Ch. 5)

High-technology industries: Industries based on the latest in modern technology, such as telecommunications and robotics. (Ch. 1, Ch. 11)

Home rule: A unit of local government's authority to take actions not prohibited by the laws or constitutions of the United States or the state. (Ch. 12)

Home-rule city: A municipality that can take any actions not prohibited by state or federal law or the constitutions of the United States or the state of Texas. (Ch. 11)

Homestead: Legal residence. (Ch. 2)

Homestead exemption: A property tax reduction granted to homeowners on their principal residence. (Ch. 11)

Hospital district: A special district that provides emergency medical services, indigent healthcare, and community health services. (Ch. 12)

Housing codes: Local ordinances requiring all dwelling places in a city to meet certain standards of upkeep and structural integrity. (Ch. 11)

Impeachment: The formal process through which the Texas House accuses an executive or judicial branch official of misconduct serious enough to warrant removal from office. (Ch. 8, Ch. 9)

Incorporated municipality: A city under the laws of the state. (Ch. 11)

Incremental model of budgeting: A theoretical effort to explain the budget process on the basis of small (incremental) changes in budget categories from one budget period to the next. (Ch. 13)

Incumbent: Current officeholder. (Ch. 5, Ch. 7)

Independent school districts (ISDs): Units of local government that provide public education services to district residents from kindergarten through the 12th grade. (Ch. 12)

Indictment: A formal accusation charging an individual with the commission of a crime. (Ch. 14)

Individualistic political culture: An approach to government and politics that emphasizes private initiative with a minimum of government interference. (Ch. 1, Ch. 13)

Initiative process: A procedure whereby citizens can propose the adoption of a policy measure by gathering a prerequisite number of signatures. Voters must then approve the measure before it can take effect. (Ch. 2, Ch. 7, Ch. 8, Ch. 11)

Interest group: An organization of people who join together voluntarily on the basis of some interest they share for the purpose of influencing policy. (Ch. 5)

Interim committee: A committee established to study a particular policy issue between legislative sessions, such as higher education or public school finance. (Ch. 8, Ch. 9)

Interstate Commerce Clause: The constitutional provision giving Congress the authority to "regulate commerce . . . among the several states." (Ch. 3)

Issue network: A group of political actors that is concerned with some aspect of public policy. (Intro)

Jacksonian democracy: The philosophy (associated with President Andrew Jackson) that suggested the right to vote should be extended to all adult male citizens and that all government offices of any importance should be filled by election. (Ch. 2, Ch. 9)

Joint resolution: A resolution that must be passed by a two-thirds vote of each chamber. (Ch. 8)

League of United Latin American Citizens (LULAC): A Latino interest group. (Ch. 4, Ch. 5)

Legal briefs: Written legal arguments. (Ch. 10)

Legal writs: Written orders issued by a court directing the performance of an act or prohibiting some act. (Ch. 10)

Legislative access: An open door through which an interest group hopes to influence the details of policy. (Ch. 5, Ch. 8)

Legislative Budget Board (LBB): An an agency created by the legislature to study state revenue and budgetary needs between legislative sessions and prepare budget and appropriation bills to submit to the legislature. (Ch. 8, Ch. 9, Ch. 13)

Legislative Redistricting Board (LBB): An agency composed of the speaker, lieutenant governor, comptroller, land commissioner, and attorney general that draws the boundaries of Texas House and Texas Senate seats when the legislature is unable to agree on a redistricting plan. (Ch. 7, Ch. 8, Ch. 9)

Legislative turnover: The replacement of individual members of a legislature from one session to the next. (Ch. 8)

Liberalism: The political view that seeks to change the political, economic, or social institutions of society to foster the development of the individual. Liberals believe that the government can (and should) advance social progress by promoting political equality, social justice, and economic prosperity. Liberals usually favor government regulation and high levels of government spending for social programs. Liberals value social and cultural diversity and defend the right of individual adult choice on issues such as access to abortion. (Ch. 6, Ch. 8)

Line-item veto: The power to veto sections or items of an appropriations bill while signing the remainder of the bill into law. (Ch. 8, Ch. 9, Ch. 13)

Litigants: The parties in a lawsuit. (Ch. 10)

Lobbying: The communication of information by a representative of an interest group to a government official for the purpose of influencing a policy decision. (Ch. 5, Ch. 8)

Local bills: Proposed laws that affect only a single unit of local government. (Ch. 8)

Local governments: Subunits of states. (Ch. 3)

Local-option (wet-dry) elections: Elections held to determine whether an area could legalize the sale of alcoholic beverages. (Ch. 2, Ch. 7)

Lone Star State: A nickname for Texas. (Ch. 1)

Long ballot: An election system that provides for the election of nearly every public official of any significance. (Ch. 2, Ch. 7, Ch. 12)

Magistrates: Judicial officers. (Ch. 10, Ch. 14)

Majority or deciding opinion: The official written statement of a court that explains and justifies its ruling and serves as a guideline for lower courts when similar legal issues arise in the future. (Ch. 10)

***Mandamus,* writ of:** A court order directing a public official to perform a specific act or duty. (Ch. 10)

Mark up: The process in which legislators go over a piece of legislation line by line to revise, amend, or rewrite it. (Ch. 8)

Matching funds requirement: A legislative provision that the national government will provide grant money for a particular activity only on the condition that the state or local government involved supply a certain percentage of the total money required for the project or program. (Ch. 3, Ch. 13)

Mayor-council form of city government: A structure of municipal government in which the voters elect a mayor as the chief executive officer of the city and a council that serves as a legislative body. (Ch. 11)

Medicaid: A federal program designed to provide health insurance coverage to low-income persons, people with disabilities, and elderly people who are impoverished. (Ch. 3, Ch. 13)

Medicare: A federal health insurance program for people 65 and older and people with permanent disabilities. (Ch. 3, Ch. 13)

Merit selection (or the Missouri Plan): A method for selecting judges that combines gubernatorial appointment with voter approval in a retention election. (Ch. 10)

Minimum wage: The lowest hourly wage that an employer can pay covered workers. (Ch. 1, Ch. 5, Ch. 6, Ch. 11)

***Miranda* warning:** The judicial stipulation that a criminal defendant's confession cannot be admitted into evidence unless police first inform the defendant of the constitutional right to remain silent and to consult an attorney. (Ch. 14)

Misdemeanor: A relatively minor criminal offense, such as a traffic violation. (Ch. 10, Ch. 14)

Moralistic political culture: An approach to government and politics in which people expect government to intervene in the social and economic affairs of the state, promoting the public welfare and advancing the public good. (Ch. 1)

Mothers Against Drunk Driving (MADD): An interest group that supports the reform of laws dealing with drunk driving. (Ch. 4, Ch. 5)

NARAL Pro-Choice Texas: Cause group that favors abortion rights. (Ch. 5)

National Association for the Advancement of Colored People (NAACP): An interest group organized to represent the interests of African Americans. (Ch. 3, Ch. 5)

National Crime Victim Survey (NCVS): A measure of the incidence of crime in the United States based on interviews with people in more than 50,000 households. (Ch. 14)

National Organization for Women (NOW): Women's rights group. (Ch. 5)

National Rifle Association (NRA): An interest group organized to defend the rights of gun owners and defeat efforts at gun control. (Ch. 4, Ch. 5)

National Supremacy Clause: The provision found in Article IV of the Constitution that declares that the U.S. Constitution, the laws made under it, and the treaties of the United States are the supreme law of the land. (Ch. 3)

Natural population increase: The extent to which live births exceed deaths. (Ch. 1)

New Deal: The name of Roosevelt's legislative program for countering the Great Depression. (Ch. 6)

No Child Left Behind (NCLB) Act: A federal law that requires state governments and local school districts to institute basic skills testing in reading and mathematics for students in grades three through eight, and use the results to assess school performance. (Ch. 3, Ch. 12)

Nolo contendere: A plea indicating a defendant's decision not to contest a criminal charge. (Ch. 14)

Nonpartisan elections: Election contests in which the names of the candidates, but not their party affiliations, appear on the ballot. (Ch. 7, Ch. 8, Ch. 10, Ch. 11, Ch. 12)

Nonpartisan legislature: A legislative body in which political parties play little or no role. (Ch. 8, Ch. 10)

Normative analysis: A method of study that is based on certain values. (Intro)

Official policy agenda: Those problems that government officials actively consider how to resolve. (Intro)

One person, one vote: The judicial ruling stating that the Equal Protection Clause of the Fourteenth Amendment to the U.S. Constitution requires legislative districts to be apportioned on the basis of population. (Ch. 7)

Open primary: An election system that allows voters to pick the party primary of their choice without disclosing their party affiliation. (Ch. 7)

Ordinance: A law enacted by the governing body of a unit of local government. (Ch. 12)

Pardon: The exemption from punishment for a criminal offense. (Ch. 9)

Pari-mutuel wagering: A system for gambling on horse and dog racing. (Ch. 13)

Parole: The conditional release of convicted offenders from prison to serve the remainder of their sentences in the community under supervision. (Ch. 3, Ch. 4, Ch. 14)

Partisan election: An election contest in which both the names of the candidates and their party affiliations appear on the ballot. (Ch. 10, Ch. 12)

Partisan legislature: A legislative body in which political parties play a defining role. (Ch. 8)

Party faction: An identifiable subgroup within a political party. (Ch. 6)

Party platform: A statement of party principles and issue positions. (Ch. 6)

Performance-based budgeting: A system of budget preparation and evaluation in which policymakers identify specific policy goals, set performance targets for agencies, and measure results. (Ch. 13)

Permanent School Fund (PSF): A fund established in the Texas Constitution as an endowment to finance public elementary and secondary education. (Ch. 9, Ch. 12, Ch. 13)

Permanent University Fund (PUF): Money constitutionally set aside as an endowment to finance construction, maintenance, and some other activities at the University of Texas,

Texas A&M University, and other institutions in those two university systems. (Ch. 2, Ch. 13)

Plaintiff: The party initiating a civil lawsuit. (Ch. 10)

Plea bargain: A procedure in which a defendant agrees to plead guilty in order to receive punishment less than the maximum for an offense. (Ch. 10, Ch. 14)

Plural executive: The division of executive power among several elected officials. (Ch. 2, Ch. 9)

Pluralist theory (*or* pluralism): The view that diverse groups of elites with differing interests compete with one another to control policy in various issue areas. (Ch. 11)

Police power: The authority to promote the health, welfare, and safety of the people. (Ch. 3)

Policy adoption: The official decision of a government body to accept a particular policy and put it into effect. (Intro)

Policy change: The modification of policy goals and means in light of new information or shifting political environments. (Intro)

Policy cycle: The passage of an issue through the policy process from agenda setting through policy change. (Intro)

Policy evaluation: The assessment of policy. (Intro)

Policy formulation: The development of strategies for dealing with the problems on the official policy agenda. (Intro)

Policy implementation: The stage of the policy process in which policies are carried out. (Intro)

Policy legitimation: The actions taken by government officials and others to ensure that most citizens regard a policy as a legal and appropriate government response to a problem. (Intro)

Policy outcomes: The situations that arise as a result of the impact of policy in operation. (Intro)

Policy outputs: Actual government policies. (Intro)

Policymaking process: A logical sequence of activities affecting the development of public policies. (Intro)

Political action committees (PACs): Organizations created to raise and distribute money in political campaigns. (Ch. 5)

Political culture: The widely held, deeply rooted political values of a society. (Ch. 1, Ch. 13)

Political machine: An entrenched political organization headed by a boss or small group of leaders who hold power through patronage, control over nominations, and bribery. (Ch. 11)

Political party: An organization that seeks political power. (Ch. 6)

Political patronage: The power of an officeholder to award favors, such as government jobs, to political allies. (Ch. 11)

Politics: The process that determines who will occupy the roles of leadership in government and how the power of government will be exercised. (Intro)

Poll tax: A tax that prospective voters had to pay in order to register to vote. (Ch. 4, Ch. 12)

Population bracket laws: State laws designed to target particular cities based on their population. (Ch. 11)

Poverty line: The amount of money an individual or a family needs to purchase basic necessities, such as food, clothing, healthcare, shelter, and transportation. (Ch. 1)

Presidential preference primary election: An election in which party voters cast ballots for the presidential candidate they favor and in so doing help determine the number of convention delegates that candidate will receive. (Ch. 7)

Primary election: An intraparty election at which a party's candidates for the general election are chosen. (Ch. 4, Ch. 7)

Privatization: The process that involves the government contracting with private business to implement government programs. (Ch. 6, Ch. 9, Ch. 14)

Probable cause: The reasonable belief that a crime has been committed and that a particular suspect is the likely perpetrator of that crime. (Ch. 14)

Probate case: A civil suit dealing with the disposition of the property of a deceased individual. (Ch. 10)

Probation: The suspension of a sentence, permitting the defendant to remain free under court supervision. (Ch. 4, Ch. 14)

Problem-solving court: A judicial body that attempts to change the future behavior of litigants and promote the welfare of the community. (Ch. 10)

Progressive tax: A levy whose burden weighs more heavily on persons earning higher incomes than it does on individuals making less money. (Ch. 13)

Project grant program: A grant program that requires state and local governments to compete for available federal money. (Ch. 3)

Property case: A civil suit over the ownership of real estate or personal possessions, such as land, jewelry, or an automobile. (Ch. 10)

Property lien: A financial claim against property for payment of debt. (Ch. 10)

Property tax (*ad valorem* property tax): A levy assessed on real property, such as houses, land, business inventory, and industrial plants. (Ch. 11)

Proportional tax: A levy that weighs equally on all persons, regardless of their income. (Ch. 13)

Prosecutor: The attorney who tries a criminal case on behalf of the government. (Ch. 10)

Prospective voting: The concept that voters evaluate the incumbent officeholder and the incumbent's party based on their expectations of future developments. (Ch. 7)

Public policy: What government officials choose to do or not to do about public problems. (Intro)

Racial profiling: The practice of a police officer targeting individuals as suspected criminals on the basis of their race or ethnicity. (Ch. 1, Ch. 5, Ch. 8)

Radical Republicans: Members of the Republican Party that wanted sweeping social change to take place in the South after the Civil War. (Ch. 2)

Rainy Day Fund: A state savings account funded by a portion of oil and gas production revenues. (Ch. 5, Ch. 9, Ch. 13)

Reapportionment: The reallocation of legislative seats. (Ch. 7)

Recall election: A procedure allowing voters to remove elected officials from office before the expiration of their terms. (Ch. 7, Ch. 11)

Recession: An economic slowdown characterized by declining economic output and rising unemployment. (Ch. 1, Ch. 11, Ch. 13)

Recidivism: The tendency of offenders released from prison to commit additional crimes and be returned behind bars. (Ch. 10, Ch. 14)

Redistributive urban policies: Local programs that benefit low-income residents of an area. (Ch. 11)

Redistricting: The process of redrawing legislative district boundaries to reflect population movement. (Ch. 7)

Regressive tax: A levy whose burden weighs more heavily on low-income groups than wealthy taxpayers. (Ch. 13)

Religious right: Individuals who hold conservative social views because of their religious beliefs. (Ch. 5)

Remand: The decision of an appeals court to return a case to a trial court for reconsideration. (Ch. 10)

Representative democracy or republic: A political system in which citizens elect representatives to make policy decisions on their behalf. (Ch. 2)

Reprieve: The postponement of the implementation of punishment for a criminal offense. (Ch. 9)

Resolution: A legislative statement of opinion on a certain matter. (Ch. 8)

Retrospective voting: The concept that voters choose candidates based on their perception of an incumbent candidate's past performance in office or the performance of the incumbent's party. (Ch. 7)

Reversible error: A mistake committed by a trial court that is serious enough to warrant a new trial because the mistake could have affected the outcome of the original trial. (Ch. 10)

Right-to-work law: A statute prohibiting a union shop. (Ch. 5, Ch. 6)

Robin Hood plan: A reform of the state's school finance system designed to increase funding for poor school districts by redistributing money from wealthy districts. (Ch. 6, Ch. 12, Ch. 13)

Rule of capture: The legal principle that each landowner has the right to withdraw an unlimited amount of groundwater from his or her own land by tapping into an underlying aquifer. (Ch. 10)

Rulemaking: A regulatory process used by government agencies to enact legally binding regulations. (Ch. 9)

Rules: Legally binding regulations adopted by a regulatory agency. (Ch. 9)

Runoff primary election: An election between the two top finishers in a primary election when no candidate received a majority of the vote in the initial primary. (Ch. 7)

Sales tax: A levy on the retail sale of taxable items. (Ch. 11, Ch. 13)

School choice: An educational reform movement that allows parents to choose the elementary or secondary school their children will attend. (Ch. 6, Ch. 8, Ch. 12)

School Lunch Program: A federal program that provides free or reduced-cost lunches to children from poor families. (Ch. 3, Ch. 9, Ch. 12)

Select or special committee: A committee that is established for a limited period of time to address a specific problem. (Ch. 8)

Senatorial courtesy: The custom of the Texas Senate that allows individual senators a veto over nominees who live in their districts. (Ch. 9)

Seniority: The length of continuous service a member has with a legislative body. (Ch. 8)

Separation of powers: The division of political authority among the legislative, executive, and judicial branches of government. (Ch. 2)

Severance tax: A tax imposed on the removal of nonrenewable resources, such as crude oil and natural gas. (Ch. 13)

Sierra Club: Environmental organization. (Ch. 5)

Sin tax: A levy on an activity that some people consider morally objectionable, such as smoking or drinking. (Ch. 13)

Social lobbying: The attempt of lobbyists to influence public policy by cultivating personal, social relationships with policymakers. (Ch. 5)

Solid South: A term referring to the usual Democratic sweep of southern-state electoral votes in presidential election years between the end of the Civil War era and the current party era. (Ch. 6)

Sovereignty: The authority of a state to exercise legitimate powers within its boundaries, free from external interference. (Ch. 3)

Special district: A unit of local government created to perform specific functions. (Ch. 12)

Special election: An election called outside the normal election calendar. (Ch. 7)

Split-ticket ballot: Voters cast their ballots for the candidates of two or more political parties during a single election. (Ch. 7)

Standing committee: A permanent committee. (Ch. 8)

State Children's Health Insurance Program (SCHIP): A federal program designed to provide health insurance to children from low-income families whose parents are not poor enough to qualify for Medicaid. (Ch. 3, Ch. 5, Ch. 6, Ch. 12, Ch. 13)

Statutory law: Law made by a legislature. (Ch. 2)

Straight-ticket ballot: Voters selecting the entire slate of candidates of one party only. (Ch. 7, Ch. 10)

Subpoena: A legal order compelling a person's attendance at an official proceeding, such as a trial. (Ch. 12)

Subsidence: The sinking of the surface of the land caused by the too-rapid extraction of subsurface water. (Ch. 11, Ch. 12)

Suffrage: The right to vote. (Ch. 2, Ch. 4)

Sunset review: The periodic evaluation of state agencies by the legislature to determine whether they should be reauthorized. (Ch. 9, Ch. 13)

Super delegates: Democratic officeholders and party officials who attend the national party convention as delegates who are not officially pledged to support any candidate. (Ch. 7)

Supplemental Nutrition Assistance Program (SNAP): Formerly the Food Stamp Program, it is a federal program that provides food vouchers to low-income families and individuals. (Ch. 3)

Tax abatement: A program that exempts property owners from local property taxes on new construction and improvements in a designated tax abatement district for a set period of time. (Ch. 11)

Tax elasticity: The extent to which tax revenues increase as personal income rises. (Ch. 13)

Tax incidence: The point at which the actual cost of a tax falls. (Ch. 13)

Tax increment financing: A program in which a local government promises to earmark increased property tax revenues generated by development in a designated area called a tax increment reinvestment zone (TIRZ) to fund improvements in the area, such as roads, parks, sidewalks, and street lighting. (Ch. 11)

Tea Party movement: A loose network of conservative activists organized to protest high taxes, excessive government spending, and big government in general. (Ch. 4)

Temporary Assistance for Needy Families (TANF): A federal block grant program that provides temporary financial assistance and work opportunities to needy families. (Ch. 3, Ch. 13)

Term limitation: The movement to restrict the number of terms public officials may serve. (Ch. 8)

Texas Association of Business (TAB): A trade association for business firms ranging from giant corporations to small neighborhood business establishments. (Ch. 5)

Texas Association of Realtors (TAR): A professional organization of real estate professionals. (Ch. 5)

Texas Equal Rights Amendment (ERA): A provision in the Texas Constitution that states the following: "Equality under the law shall not be denied or abridged because of sex, race, color, creed, or national origin." (Ch. 2)

Texas Farm Bureau: An organization that represents the interests of farmers, ranchers, and people living in rural areas. (Ch. 5)

Texas Medical Association (TMA): A professional organization of physicians. (Ch. 5)

Texas Right to Life Committee: Cause group that opposes abortion. (Ch. 5)

Texas Teacher Retirement System (TRS) Trust Fund: A pension fund for the state's public school teachers. (Ch. 13)

Texas Trial Lawyers Association (TTLA): An organization of attorneys who represent plaintiffs in personal injury lawsuits. (Ch. 5)

Texas Two-Step: A system for choosing national convention delegates that combines the primary and the caucus methods. (Ch. 7)

Top 10 Percent Rule: A state law that grants automatic college admission to public high school graduates who finish in the top 10 percent of their class. (Ch. 8)

Tort case: A civil suit involving personal injury or damage to property, such as a lawsuit stemming from an automobile accident. (Ch. 10)

Tort reform: The revision of state laws to limit the ability of plaintiffs in personal injury lawsuits to recover damages in court. (Ch. 5)

Trade associations: Organizations representing the interests of firms and professionals in the same general field. (Ch. 5)

Traditionalistic political culture: An approach to government and politics that sees the role of government as the preservation of tradition and the existing social order. (Ch. 1)

Trial: The formal examination of a civil or criminal action in accordance with law before a single judge who has jurisdiction to hear the dispute. (Ch. 10)

True bill: An indictment issued by a grand jury. (Ch. 14)

Truth-in-taxation laws: Laws that block local governments from raising the total amount of property taxes they collect from one year to the next when assessed values go up. (Ch. 11)

Two-party system: The division of voter loyalties between two major political parties, resulting in the near exclusion of minor parties from seriously competing for a share of political power. (Ch. 6)

Two-thirds rule: A procedure used in the Texas Senate requiring a two-thirds vote before a measure can be brought to the floor for debate and eventual passage. (Ch. 8)

Unicameral legislature: A legislative body with one chamber. (Ch. 2, Ch. 8)

Uniform Crime Report (UCR): A record of offenses known to police compiled by the Federal Bureau of Investigation (FBI) from reports submitted by local law enforcement agencies. (Ch. 14)

Unincorporated area: Territory that is not part of a legal city. (Ch. 11)

Union shop: A workplace in which every employee must belong to a union. (Ch. 5)

Utility district: A special district that provides utilities, such as water and sewer service, to residents living in unincorporated urban areas. (Ch. 11, Ch. 12)

Veto: An action in which the chief executive of a state or nation refuses to approve a bill passed by the legislature. (Ch. 8, Ch. 9)

Voter mobilization: The process of motivating citizens to vote. (Ch. 4)

Voting age population (VAP): The number of state residents who are 18 years of age or older. (Ch. 4)

Voting eligible population (VEP): The number of state residents who are eligible to vote. (Ch. 4)

Voting Rights Act (VRA): A federal law designed to protect the voting rights of racial and ethnic minorities. (Ch. 7, Ch. 11)

White primary: An election system that prohibited African Americans from voting in Democratic primary elections. (Ch. 4)

Yellow Dog Democrat: A loyal Democratic Party voter. (Ch. 6)

Zoning: The governmental designation of tracts of land for industrial, commercial, or residential use. (Ch. 11)

Photo Credits

Index

PRACTICE TESTS

NOTE: The first number in parentheses after each question stem indicates the "What We Will Learn" question associated with the particular multiple-choice question. The second is the page number(s) in the text addressed in the question. For example, multiple-choice question one deals with material covered in the first "What We Will Learn" questions. The e information is found on p. 2 of the text.

Introduction: The Policymaking Process

Circle the correct answer.

1. What government officials choose to do or not to do about public problems is a definition of which of the following terms? **(1)** (p. 2)

   (A) Agenda setting
   (B) Public policy
   (C) Policy formulation
   (D) Policy adoption

2. Because of a serious drought, many areas of the state are short of water and some cities must impose water rationing. Agricultural groups initiate a public relations campaign about the need for a state water policy and the news media cover the issue extensively. As a result, the legislature decides to address the issue in its next session. This set of events illustrates which of the following stages of the policymaking process? **(1)** (p. 3)

   (A) Agenda setting
   (B) Policy formulation
   (C) Policy legitimation
   (D) Policy adoption

3. The process through which issues become matters of public concern and government action is a definition for which of the following stages of the policymaking process? **(1)** (p. 3)

   (A) Agenda setting
   (B) Policy formulation
   (C) Policy adoption
   (D) Policy implementation

4. Which of the following issues has recently been part of the state's official policy agenda? **(1)** (pp. 3–4)

   (A) Funding public education
   (B) Electricity deregulation
   (C) Property tax reform
   (D) All of the above

5. A major goal of state legislators is to increase college and university graduation rates. The governor and legislative leaders create a task force of educators, key members of the legislature, business groups, and other interested parties to develop a strategy to achieve the goal. This set of events describes which of the following stages of the policymaking process? **(1)** (pp. 4–5)

   (A) Agenda setting
   (B) Policy evaluation
   (C) Policy formulation
   (D) Policy adoption

6. The development of strategies for dealing with the problems on the official policy agenda is a definition of which of the following stages of the policymaking process? **(1)** (p. 4)

   (A) Agenda setting
   (B) Policy formulation
   (C) Policy adoption
   (D) Policy implementation

7. The Texas House passes a bill to outlaw texting while driving. The Texas Senate passes the bill as well and the governor signs it into law. This set of events describes which of the following stages of the policymaking process? **(1)** (p. 5)

   (A) Policy formulation
   (B) Policy adoption
   (C) Policy implementation
   (D) Policy legitimation

8. The official decision of a government body to accept a particular policy and put it into effect is the definition of which of the following stages of the policymaking process? **(1)** (p. 5)

   (A) Policy change
   (B) Policy formulation
   (C) Policy adoption
   (D) Policy implementation

9. After the state adopted legislation to deregulate electric rates, the governor and legislative leaders held a press conference to praise the action. Meanwhile, utility companies began an advertising campaign promising lower electric rates and better service because of deregulation. This set of events describes which of the following stages of the policymaking process? **(1)** (pp. 5–6)

   (A) Policy implementation
   (B) Policy evaluation
   (C) Policy change
   (D) Policy legitimation

10. The actions taken by government officials and others to ensure that most citizens regard a policy as a legal and appropriate government response to a problem is a definition of which of the following stages of the policymaking process? **(1)** (p. 5)

    (A) Policy legitimation
    (B) Policy adoption
    (C) Policy change
    (D) Policy evaluation

11. The stage of the policy process in which policies are carried out is known as which of the following? **(1)** (p. 6)

   (A) Policy evaluation
   (B) Policy implementation
   (C) Policy change
   (D) Policy formulation

12. After the city passed an ordinance prohibiting the possession of fireworks within the city, the fire marshal stationed patrol cars just inside the city limits on streets where fireworks stands were located to stop and confiscate illegal fireworks from people trying to bring them into the city. This set of events describes which of the following stages of the policymaking process? **(1)** (p. 6)

   (A) Policy adoption
   (B) Policy formulation
   (C) Policy implementation
   (D) Policy evaluation

13. Which of the following statements is true about the death penalty in Texas? **(1)** (pp. 6–8)

   (A) Texas has carried out more executions than any other state.
   (B) People convicted of capital murder can be sentenced either to death or life in prison without possibility of parole.
   (C) The number of death sentences assessed by Texas juries has decreased over the last decade.
   (D) All of the above

14. The assessment of policy is a definition of which of the following? **(1)** (p. 8)

   (A) Agenda setting
   (B) Policy evaluation
   (C) Policy implementation
   (D) Policy change

15. Researchers at Sam Houston State University conduct a study aimed at assessing the effect of the death penalty on the murder rate. Their study illustrates which of the following stages of the policymaking process? **(1)** (p. 8)

   (A) Agenda setting
   (B) Policy formulation
   (C) Policy implementation
   (D) Policy evaluation

16. Which of the following is an example of an empirical analysis of abortion in Texas? **(1)** (p. 8)

   (A) Data from the Department of State Health Services show that about 16 percent of all pregnancies in Texas end in an abortion.
   (B) The Catholic Bishop of Texas has issued a statement condemning abortion and calling for its prohibition because, he says, abortion is taking innocent life.
   (C) A member of the Texas legislature speaks against proposed legislation to require women to view a sonogram before having an abortion. "The government should not intrude into the private decisions of women," she says.
   (D) All of the above

17. The modification of policy goals and means in light of new information or shifting political environments is a definition of which of the following? **(1)** (p. 9)

   (A) Policy implementation
   (B) Policy legitimation
   (C) Policy change
   (D) Policy evaluation

18. The passage of an issue through the policy process from agenda setting through policy change is a definition of which of the following? **(2)** (p. 9)

   (A) Policy change
   (B) Political cycle
   (C) Policymaking process
   (D) Politics

19. Which of the following could be part of an issue network? **(2)** (p. 10)

   (A) Members of the legislature
   (B) Journalists
   (C) Interest groups
   (D) All of the above

20. Which of the following is a reason for studying Texas government and politics? **(3)** (p. 11)

   (A) Everyone living in the state pays taxes to state and local governments.
   (B) State law requires that the core curriculum for public colleges and universities must include the study of the Texas Constitution.
   (C) State and local governments provide a wide range of services.
   (D) All of the above

Circle the correct answer.

1. How does Texas compare with other states in terms of population size? **(1)** (p. 16)

   (A) Texas has the largest population in the country.
   (B) Texas has the second largest population, after New York.
   (C) Texas has the third largest population, after California and New York.
   (D) Texas has the second largest population, after California.

2. How does the rate of population growth in Texas compare with population growth for the nation as a whole? **(1)** (pp. 16–17)

   (A) The population of Texas has consistently increased at a faster pace than national population growth.
   (B) The population of Texas has consistently increased at a slower pace than national population growth.
   (C) The population of Texas has consistently increased at about the same rate as national population growth.
   (D) The population of Texas once grew more slowly than the nation as a whole but in the last two decades Texas has grown more rapidly.

3. Which of the following factors contributed the most to population growth in Texas between 2000 and 2010? **(1)** (p. 17)

   (A) Immigration from abroad
   (B) Natural population increase
   (C) Immigration from other states
   (D) All of the above contributed equally to population growth.

4. Which of the following Texas racial/ethnic groups is the most numerous? **(1)** (p. 19)

   (A) Latinos
   (B) African Americans
   (C) Whites (not Hispanic)
   (D) Asians

5. Which of the following Texas racial/ethnic groups grew the LEAST rapidly between 2000 and 2010? **(1)** (p. 19)

   (A) African Americans
   (B) Asians
   (C) Latinos
   (D) Whites (not Hispanic)

6. In which of the following regions of the state is the population relatively old compared with the state as a whole? **(1)** (p. 21)

   (A) Panhandle
   (B) Rio Grande Valley
   (C) Houston
   (D) The age distribution of the state does not vary from region to region.

7. Which region of the state grew the most slowly between 2000 and 2010? **(1)** (p. 21)

   (A) East Texas
   (B) Gulf Coast
   (C) West Texas
   (D) Rio Grande Valley

8. Which of the following Texas cities is NOT among the ten largest cities in the United States? **(1)** (p. 21)

   (A) Houston
   (B) Fort Worth
   (C) San Antonio
   (D) Dallas

9. Which of the following areas grew the most rapidly between 2000 and 2010? **(1)** (p. 22)

   (A) Suburban counties near major cities, such as Collin County near Dallas
   (B) Counties where major cities are located, such as Harris County
   (C) Rural counties, such as Loving County in West Texas
   (D) All areas of the state grew at a similar rate.

10. Which of the following commodities were most important to the Texas economy in the nineteenth century? **(2)** (p. 23)

    (A) Wheat and corn
    (B) Beans and rice
    (C) Sheep and goats
    (D) Cotton and cattle

11. Spindletop is associated with which of the following? **(2)** (p. 23)

    (A) Cotton
    (B) Cattle
    (C) Oil
    (D) Gold

12. How do wage rates in Texas compare with wage rates in other states? **(2)** (p. 25)

    (A) Wages in Texas are higher than the national average.
    (B) Wages in Texas are lower than the national average.
    (C) Wages in Texas are at the national average.
    (D) Wages in Texas were once below the national average but have recently increased to a level above the national average.

13. Which state has the largest economy? **(2)** (p. 26)

    (A) California; Texas is second.
    (B) Texas; California is second.
    (C) California; New York is second.
    (D) New York; California is second.

14. How does the economic growth rate in Texas compare with the growth rate of the national economy? **(2)** (p. 26)

   (A) The Texas economy grows at roughly the same rate as the national economy.
   (B) The Texas economy grows at a much slower rate than the national economy.
   (C) The Texas economy grows somewhat more slowly than the national economy.
   (D) The Texas economy grows somewhat more rapidly than the national economy.

15. Which of the following statements about wealth, income, and poverty is NOT true? **(2)** (pp. 26–28)

   (A) The average income in Texas is above the national average.
   (B) The poverty rate in Texas is above the national average.
   (C) The growth rate of the Texas economy is above the national average.
   (D) The gap between the top and bottom of the income ladder is greater in Texas than in the nation as a whole.

16. How does Texas compare with other states in terms of the percentage of its residents without health insurance? **(2)** (p. 28)

   (A) Texas has a relatively high level of health insurance coverage.
   (B) Texas leads the nation in the percentage of state residents without health insurance coverage.
   (C) Texas leads the nation in the percentage of state residents with health insurance coverage.
   (D) Texas has a relatively low level of health insurance coverage.

17. Which of the following terms is defined as the widely held, deeply rooted political values of a society? **(3)** (p. 29)

   (A) Civic culture
   (B) Political culture
   (C) Poverty line
   (D) Recession

18. According to Elazar, the Texas political culture is a combination of which of the following political cultures? **(3)** (p. 30)

   (A) Moralistic and individualistic
   (B) Moralistic and traditionalistic
   (C) Traditionalist and individualistic
   (D) Moralistic, traditionalistic, and individualistic

19. A political culture that is conducive to the development of an efficient, effective government that meets the needs of its citizens in a timely and professional manner is known as which of the following? **(3)** (p. 30)

   (A) Moralistic political culture
   (B) Traditionalistic political culture
   (C) Individualistic political culture
   (D) Civic culture

20. A state with a strong civic culture would likely be characterized by which of the following? **(3)** (p. 30)

   (A) High voter turnout
   (B) Tolerance of people with different religions, lifestyles, and points of view
   (C) The presence of large numbers of civic organizations
   (D) All of the above

Circle the correct answer.

1. The Texas legislature has two chambers—the Texas House and the Texas Senate. Which term best describes this arrangement? **(1)** (p. 37)

   (A) Separation of powers
   (B) Checks and balances
   (C) Plural executive
   (D) Bicameral legislature

2. Which of the following features of the Texas Constitution was added specifically to weaken the authority of the governor? **(1)** (p. 37)

   (A) Plural executive
   (B) Bicameral legislature
   (C) Bill of rights
   (D) Separation of powers

3. Which of the following is an expression of direct democracy rather than representative democracy? **(1)** (p. 38)

   (A) The plural executive
   (B) The election of a bicameral legislature
   (C) The initiative process
   (D) The election of judges

4. The voters in a number of states have passed ballot initiatives limiting the terms of office of members of state legislatures. These elections are an example of which of the following? **(1)** (p. 38)

   (A) Checks and balances
   (B) Direct democracy
   (C) Representative democracy
   (D) Jacksonian democracy

5. The long ballot in Texas is a reflection of which of the following constitutional principles? **(2)** (p. 39)

   (A) Jacksonian democracy
   (B) Separation of powers with checks and balances
   (C) Direct democracy
   (D) Bicameral legislature

6. For which of the following reasons was the Texas Constitution of 1869 unpopular with white ex-Confederate Texans? **(2)** (pp. 40–41)

   (A) E. J. Davis, a Republican, was governor when it was in effect.
   (B) It provided for an active state government.
   (C) The governor enjoyed considerable power under the document.
   (D) All of the above

7. Which of the following was a goal of the Grangers at the Texas constitutional convention of 1875? **(3)** (p. 41)

   (A) Ensure racial equality among whites and blacks
   (B) Restrict the size and scope of state government
   (C) Promote the development of the state's cities
   (D) All of the above

8. The framers of the Texas Constitution of 1875 wanted to increase the power of which of the following branches or units of government? **(3)** (pp. 41–42)

   (A) Governor
   (B) Legislature
   (C) Court system
   (D) None of the above

9. What is the purpose of a local-option election? **(3)** (p. 42)

   (A) To determine whether a local government can go into debt
   (B) To set tax rates for local school districts
   (C) To determine whether an area could legalize the sale of alcoholic beverages
   (D) To determine whether the residents of an area want to incorporate and become a municipal government

10. How does the Texas Constitution compare with the U.S. Constitution? **(4)** (pp. 44–45)

    (A) It is shorter.
    (B) It has fewer amendments.
    (C) It is more detailed.
    (D) None of the above

11. Which of the following is an example of a constitutional check and balance? **(4)** (p. 45)

    (A) The Texas Senate must confirm the governor's appointees.
    (B) The governor can veto bills passed by the legislature.
    (C) The legislature can override a governor's veto.
    (D) All of the above

12. A formal, written change or addition to the state's governing document is known as which of the following? **(5)** (p. 45)

    (A) Constitutional amendment
    (B) Constitutional revision
    (C) Checks and balances
    (D) Direct democracy

13. In which of the following ways has the Texas Constitution been amended to increase the authority of the governor? **(5)** (p. 46)

    (A) The governor has been given authority to appoint the lieutenant governor and the speaker of the House.
    (B) The governor's term of office has been increased from two to four years.
    (C) The governor may serve no more than two terms in office.
    (D) All of the above

14. When the state issues general obligation bonds, what is it doing? **(5)** (p. 46)

   (A) Borrowing money
   (B) Giving prison inmates early release
   (C) Giving landowners authority to divert water resources to their own use
   (D) Allowing colleges and universities to set their tuition rates

15. Voter turnout is typically the lowest in which of the following elections? **(5)** (p. 46)

   (A) Presidential
   (B) Gubernatorial
   (C) Constitutional amendment election
   (D) Turnout would not vary substantially among the above elections.

16. Which of the following is NOT a step in the process for amending the Texas Constitution? **(5)** (p. 46)

   (A) The Texas House votes to propose an amendment by a two-thirds vote.
   (B) The Texas Senate votes to propose an amendment by a two-thirds vote.
   (C) The state publishes a summary and brief explanation of proposed amendments in newspapers prior to Election Day.
   (D) Voters approve proposed amendments by a two-thirds margin.

17. Which of the following is a criticism raised against the Texas Constitution by those who favor constitutional revision? **(5)** (pp. 46–47)

   (A) The Texas Constitution gives too much power to the governor.
   (B) The Texas Constitution is too complex and detailed to be easily understood either by citizens or state officials.
   (C) The Texas Constitution does not have a bill of rights.
   (D) The Texas Constitution is too short.

18. The PUF is an example of which of the following? **(5)** (p. 49)

   (A) Dedicated fund
   (B) Checks and balances
   (C) Direct democracy
   (D) General obligation bond

19. Can the Texas Constitution grant Texans more rights than are granted to them by the U.S. Constitution? **(6)** (p. 52)

   (A) No. The U.S. Constitution takes precedence over the Texas Constitution.
   (B) No. The Texas Bill of Rights is the same as the U.S. Bill of Rights, word for word.
   (C) Yes. States can grant their residents more rights than are granted to them by the U.S. Constitution.
   (D) No. The Texas Constitution does not deal with individual rights.

20. *Edgewood v. Kirby* (1989) dealt with which of the following issues? **(6)** (p. 52)

   (A) Abortion
   (B) Illegal immigration
   (C) Gambling
   (D) School finance

Circle the correct answer.

1. Which of the following political arrangements can be described as a federal system? **(1)** (p. 57)

    (A) The Indian legislature has two chambers.
    (B) The members of the British parliament are elected from districts.
    (C) The government of Canada is divided between a national government over the entire nation and a series of provincial governments with authority over particular geographical areas.
    (D) The president of Mexico serves a six-year term.

2. Does the U.S. Congress have the authority to adopt legislation overruling state policies in an area in which the federal government has the power to act, such as interstate commerce? **(1)** (p. 57)

    (A) Yes. The National Supremacy Clause declares that the U.S. Constitution and laws made under it are the supreme law of the land.
    (B) No. States are sovereign governments and the federal government cannot overrule their actions.
    (C) No. State police power supersedes federal authority.
    (D) Yes. The Equal Protection Clause holds that state laws are equal to federal laws. In this case, the state law takes precedence because it was in place first.

3. Which of the following is an example of a state exercising the power of eminent domain? **(1)** (p. 57)

    (A) The state forces a farmer to sell part of his land to the Texas Department of Transportation so a new highway can be built.
    (B) A court rules that landowners have the rights to water under their property.
    (C) A New York judge orders the return to Texas of a fugitive charged with a crime in the Lone Star State.
    (D) The state carries out the execution of a convicted murderer.

4. Which of the following cases eventually led to Texas having to dismantle its dual school system? **(2)** (p. 59)

    (A) *Roe v. Wade*
    (B) *Brown v. Board of Education*
    (C) *Ruiz v. Estelle*
    (D) None of the above

5. The U.S. Supreme Court's decision in *Brown v. Board of Education* was based on which of the following constitutional provisions? **(2)** (pp. 59–60)

    (A) National Supremacy Clause
    (B) Commerce Clause
    (C) Cruel and Unusual Punishment Clause of the Eighth Amendment
    (D) Equal Protection Clause

6. *Ruiz v. Estelle* was based on which of the following constitutional provisions? **(2)** (p. 60)

    (A) National Supremacy Clause
    (B) Commerce Clause
    (C) Cruel and Unusual Punishment Clause of the Eighth Amendment
    (D) Equal Protection Clause

7. *Roe v. Wade* dealt with which of the following issues? **(2)** (pp. 60–61)

    (A) The right of African American youngsters to attend racially integrated schools
    (B) The right of people with disabilities to have access to public places
    (C) The right of persons accused of serious crimes to have a fair trial
    (D) The right of a woman to have an abortion

8. According to the most recent standard set by the U.S. Supreme Court, what is the status of abortion regulation in the United States? **(2)** (pp. 61–63)

    (A) A woman has an absolute right to choose an abortion, and that right may not be restricted by state government.
    (B) States can regulate abortion before viability as long as the regulations do not place an "undue burden" on a woman's right to choose an abortion.
    (C) States can prohibit abortion only during the first two trimesters.
    (D) States can prohibit abortion at any time during the pregnancy.

9. Texas has adopted which of the following abortion regulations? **(2)** (pp. 62–63)

    (A) Women seeking an abortion must wait 24 hours before having the procedure.
    (B) A physician must conduct a sonogram at least 24 hours before performing an abortion and describe to the woman what the sonogram shows.
    (C) Late-term abortions are illegal except to save the life of the woman or if the fetus has serious brain damage.
    (D) All of the above

10. The U.S. Congress has adopted legislation prohibiting states from regulating cellular phone rates. This legislation is an example of which of the following? **(3)** (p. 63)

    (A) Federal mandate
    (B) Federal preemption
    (C) Project grant
    (D) Block grant

11. Because of the ADA, new buildings constructed at a college must be accessible for people with disabilities. This requirement is an example of which of the following? **(3)** (p. 64)

    (A) Federal mandate
    (B) Federal preemption
    (C) Project grant
    (D) Block grant

12. Which of the following has had the greatest effect on individuals with disabilities? **(3)** (p. 64)

    (A) *Roe v. Wade*
    (B) Clean Air Act
    (C) NCLB
    (D) ADA

13. Which of the following has the most direct effect on the TCEQ? **(3)** (p. 64)

    (A) *Roe v. Wade*
    (B) Clean Air Act
    (C) NCLB
    (D) ADA

14. Which of the following has the most direct effect on school districts in Texas? **(3)** (p. 65)

    (A) *Roe v. Wade*
    (B) Clean Air Act
    (C) NCLB
    (D) ADA

15. Which of the following is an example of a federal grant program? **(4)** (pp. 66–69)

    (A) Medicaid
    (B) School Lunch Program
    (C) Temporary Assistance for Needy Families
    (D) All of the above

16. The process through which Congress creates a new program is known by which of the following terms? **(4)** (p. 66)

    (A) Authorization process
    (B) Appropriation process
    (C) Federal mandate
    (D) Federal preemption

17. Why do Governor Perry and other state officials want Congress to make Medicaid a block grant rather than categorical grant program? **(4)** (pp. 67–68)

    (A) States would get more money under a block grant than under a categorical grant.
    (B) States would have more flexibility in designing a program under a block grant program than under a categorical grant program.
    (C) Matching fund requirements are greater under block grant programs.
    (D) All of the above

18. A government program that provides benefits to everyone eligible to receive them under the law is known as which of the following? **(4)** (p. 68)

    (A) Block grant program
    (B) Project grant program
    (C) Entitlement program
    (D) Formula grant program

19. About what proportion of total Texas state revenues comes from the federal government? **(5)** (p. 73)

    (A) One-tenth
    (B) One-fourth
    (C) One-third
    (D) One-half

20. Federal money helps fund which of the following activities in Texas? **(5)** (p. 73)

    (A) Transportation
    (B) Education
    (C) Welfare
    (D) All of the above

Circle the correct answer.

1. Which of the following contributed to the disfranchisement of African Americans in Texas during the late nineteenth and early twentieth centuries? **(1)** (p. 80)

   (A) Nineteenth Amendment
   (B) Voter ID
   (C) Poll tax
   (D) All of the above

2. Because of the white primary, African Americans in Texas were excluded from participating in which of the following elections? **(1)** (p. 80)

   (A) Democratic primary
   (B) Republican primary
   (C) General election
   (D) All of the above

3. George Parr, the so-called Duke of Duval County, was an example of which of the following? **(1)** (pp. 80–81)

   (A) Civil rights activist
   (B) Tea Party activist
   (C) Community organizer
   (D) Political boss

4. The case of *Smith v. Allwright* dealt with which of the following issues? **(1)** (p. 82)

   (A) Poll tax
   (B) White primary
   (C) Women's suffrage
   (D) Voter ID

5. Can a student from Louisiana attending college in Texas register to vote in Texas? **(2)** (pp. 83–84)

   (A) No. Only permanent residents of the state can register to vote in Texas, and students are here temporarily.
   (B) Yes, but only after the student has lived in Texas for six months, the state residency requirement.
   (C) Yes, but because of the new voter ID law, the student must have a Texas driver's license.
   (D) Yes. Students can register to vote in Texas even if they are only temporary residents of the state.

6. Which of the following individuals can legally vote early in Texas? **(2)** (p. 85)

   (A) A woman who is scheduled to be in the hospital on Election Day
   (B) A man with a business meeting scheduled out of town on Election Day
   (C) A man who wants to avoid long lines on Election Day
   (D) All of the above

7. Which of the following is a goal of the Tea Party? **(2)** (pp. 87–88)

   (A) Increased government funding for education
   (B) Lower taxes
   (C) Improved response to the threat of global warming
   (D) All of the above

8. Which of the following terms refers to the number of state residents who are eligible to vote? **(3)** (pp. 88–89)

   (A) VEP
   (B) VAP
   (C) VRA
   (D) GOTV

9. In which of the following years did voter turnout in Texas exceed the national average? **(3)** (p. 89)

   (A) 2000
   (B) 2004
   (C) 2008
   (D) None of the above

10. Which of the following factors helps explain voter turnout rates in Texas? **(3)** (pp. 89–90)

    (A) The age distribution is older than the national average.
    (B) Income levels are higher in Texas than in most other states.
    (C) Education levels in Texas lag behind the national average.
    (D) All of the above

11. Which of the following factors would likely lead to an increase in voter participation rates in Texas? **(3)** (pp. 89–90)

    (A) Increased immigration
    (B) Stronger labor unions
    (C) Closer competition between candidates and parties
    (D) Weaker political parties

12. If median family incomes in Texas were to rise faster than they are rising nationally, how would that affect voter turnout in the Lone Star State? **(4)** (p. 90)

    (A) It would decrease turnout because participation is inversely related to household income.
    (B) It would have no affect because there is no relationship between participation and household income.
    (C) It would increase turnout because participation is related to household income.
    (D) It would decrease turnout except among the wealthier segment of society.

13. Which of the following racial/ethnic groups in Texas has the lowest voter participation rate? **(5)** (p. 90)

    (A) Latinos
    (B) African Americans
    (C) Whites
    (D) Voter participation rates are the same for all three racial/ethnic groups.

14. Which of the following factors helps account for voter participation rates for Latinos in Texas? **(5)** (p. 91)

    (A) Latinos in Texas are better educated as a group than are members of other racial/ethnic groups.
    (B) Latinos in Texas are wealthier as a group than are members of other racial/ethnic groups.
    (C) Latinos in Texas are less likely to be citizens than are members of other racial/ethnic groups.
    (D) All of the above

15. Compared to the state's population, the Texas electorate is which of the following? **(5)** (p. 91)

    (A) Younger
    (B) Less well off financially
    (C) More likely to be minority
    (D) None of the above

16. In which of the following ways is the Texas electorate similar to the state's population as a whole? **(6)** (p. 92)

    (A) The electorate resembles the state's population in terms of education.
    (B) The electorate resembles the state's population in terms of race/ethnicity.
    (C) The electorate resembles the state's population in terms of income.
    (D) None of the above

17. Which of the following groups is overrepresented in the Texas electorate? **(6)** (p. 92)

    (A) Young people
    (B) College graduates
    (C) Latinos
    (D) All of the above

18. Voter mobilization is most closely associated with which of the following terms? **(6)** (p. 92)

    (A) GOTV
    (B) White primary
    (C) Poll tax
    (D) Voter ID

19. In 2010, Tea Party activism helped increase the voter turnout of which of the following groups? **(6)** (p. 92)

    (A) College students
    (B) African Americans and Latinos
    (C) Older whites
    (D) All of the above

20. Even though Texas has the lowest percentage of adults with a college education in the nation, the 2010 legislature chose to cut spending on higher education and college financial aid. Which of the following is the best explanation for the legislature's action? **(6)** (p. 92)

    (A) Texas leads the nation in minimum-wage jobs, and those jobs do not require a college education.
    (B) The Texas electorate is more interested in holding the line on taxes than in funding education.
    (C) Poorly educated people are opposed to the government spending money on higher education.
    (D) Texas already spends more money proportionally for higher education than any state in the nation.

Circle the correct answer.

1. The Texas Association of Business, Texas Association of Builders, and the Mid-Continent Oil and Gas Association are examples of which of the following? **(1)** (p. 99)

   (A) Labor unions
   (B) Trade associations
   (C) Advocacy groups
   (D) Cause groups

2. Which of the following states is/are rated near the top of the list of states with public policies conducive to strong economic growth? **(1)** (p. 100)

   (A) California
   (B) New York
   (C) Texas
   (D) All of the above

3. Which of the following interest groups would be most likely to oppose legislation capping the amount of damages plaintiffs could recover in medical malpractice lawsuits? **(1)** (p. 101)

   (A) TTLA
   (B) TMA
   (C) AFL-CIO
   (D) TAR

4. Which of the following groups would be most likely to support the repeal of the Texas right-to-work law? **(1)** (p. 101)

   (A) TTLA
   (B) TMA
   (C) NAACP
   (D) AFL-CIO

5. Water development is an important issue for which of the following organizations? **(1)** (p. 103)

   (A) LULAC
   (B) Texas Farm Bureau
   (C) NARAL Pro-Choice Texas
   (D) NRA

6. Which of the following groups would be most likely to support the enactment of legislation to prohibit racial profiling? **(1)** (p. 104)

   (A) MADD
   (B) Common Cause
   (C) Texas Farm Bureau
   (D) LULAC

7. Which of the following organizations can most accurately be labeled part of the religious right? **(1)** (p. 105)

   (A) Focus on the Family
   (B) NAACP
   (C) NRA
   (D) NOW

8. Which of the following organization is *least* likely to take a position on the issue of abortion? **(1)** (pp. 106–107)

   (A) Texas Right to Life Committee
   (B) NARAL Pro-Choice Texas
   (C) MADD
   (D) NOW

9. Which of the following organizations would be most interested in local property tax breaks for homeowners age 65 and older? **(1)** (p. 107)

   (A) Sierra Club
   (B) NRA
   (C) NARAL Pro-Choice Texas
   (D) AARP

10. Which of the following organizations would be most interested in state enforcement of clean air laws? **(1)** (p. 107)

    (A) Sierra Club
    (B) MADD
    (C) NOW
    (D) Texas Farm Bureau

11. Which of the following pairs of groups are more often friends than enemies on questions of public policy? **(1)** (pp. 99–107)

    (A) AFL-CIO and TAB
    (B) LULAC and NAACP
    (C) NARAL Pro-Choice Texas and Texas Right to Life Committee
    (D) TTLA and TMA

12. Which of the following organizations is created to raise and distribute money in political campaigns? **(2)** (p. 108)

    (A) Interest group
    (B) Political party
    (C) Political action committee (PAC)
    (D) Trade association

13. What is the maximum amount of money a PAC associated with AFSCME can give to a candidate for the Texas legislature? **(2)** (p. 108)

    (A) $5,000
    (B) $10,000
    (C) $25,000
    (D) There is no limit.

14. Which of the following is an example of social lobbying? **(2)** (p. 110)

    (A) A lobbyist takes a member of the legislature to dinner at one of Austin's nicest restaurants.
    (B) A lobbyist provides a legislator with a detailed report on the possible impact of proposed legislation.
    (C) A PAC contributes $5,000 to a member of the legislature running for reelection.
    (D) A lobbyist provides friendly legislators with arguments in favor of a legislative provision that both the group and the legislator support.

15. Which of the following is an example of legislative access? **(2)** (p. 110)

    (A) State Senator X resigns from the legislature and immediately takes a job as a lobbyist.
    (B) A member of the Texas House agrees to meet with a lobbyist for an interest group that has generously contributed to the legislator's political campaigns.
    (C) A PAC gives most of its contributions to incumbents because most incumbents win reelection.
    (D) State law places no limit on the amount of money an interest group can contribute to legislative candidates.

16. Groups running political ads opposing lawsuit abuse are in favor of which of the following? **(2)** (p. 111)

    (A) Racial profiling
    (B) Hate-crimes legislation
    (C) Tort reform
    (D) Campaign finance reform

17. Which of the following is an example of a group using litigation to achieve its policy goals? **(2)** (p. 112)

    (A) Save Our Schools asks parents to contact their legislators about school finance.
    (B) A Tea Party group holds a rally to call for lower taxes and less government spending.
    (C) NARAL Pro-Choice Texas endorses Bill White for governor.
    (D) The Sierra Club sues the Texas Commission on Environmental Quality over enforcement of the Clean Air Act.

18. Which of the following organizations has sometimes been linked to violence? **(2)** (p. 112)

    (A) Ku Klux Klan
    (B) NAACP
    (C) LULAC
    (D) MADD

19. Which of the following groups is *not* allied with the Republican Party? **(2)** (p. 113)

    (A) Small-government conservatives
    (B) Environmentalists
    (C) Christian conservatives
    (D) Anti-abortion organizations

20. Which of the following groups is allied with the Democratic Party? **(2)** (p. 113)

    (A) Trial lawyers
    (B) Minority-rights groups
    (C) Consumer groups
    (D) All of the above

Circle the correct answer.

1. Which of the following is NOT a political party? **(1)** (p. 118)

   (A) Texas Association of Business
   (B) Texas Democratic Party
   (C) Texas Republican Party
   (D) Texas Libertarian Party

2. Which of the following statements best describes party politics in the South in the decades after the Civil War era? **(1)** (p. 119)

   (A) The Republican Party dominated.
   (B) The Democratic Party dominated.
   (C) The Democratic and Republican Parties competed on nearly equal terms.
   (D) The Populist Party was the strongest party, although both the Democratic and Republican Parties had influence.

3. Which of the following individuals is eligible to participate in a 2012 Republican precinct convention? **(2)** (p. 120)

   (A) Any registered voter
   (B) Anyone who voted in that year's primary election
   (C) Anyone who voted in that year's Republican primary election
   (D) Any resident of Texas

4. How is a county chairperson for the Democratic or Republican Party selected? **(2)** (p. 122)

   (A) Appointed by the county precinct chairpersons
   (B) Appointed by the state party chair
   (C) Appointed by the governor
   (D) Elected by party voters in the county

5. Which of the following statements best explains the nature of party politics in Texas in the decades after the end of the Civil War era? **(3)** (pp. 122–123)

   (A) The Democratic Party dominated because most Texans were poor and the Democrats did well with low-income voters.
   (B) The Republican Party dominated because it benefited from the votes of large numbers of African Americans, who won the right to vote after the Civil War.
   (C) The Republican Party dominated because the Democratic party was associated with a severe economic downturn in the years immediately following the Civil War.
   (D) The Democratic Party dominated because most native white Texans associated the Republican Party with Union victory in the Civil War.

6. Which of the following presidents was an inspiration to liberal Democrats in Texas? **(3)** (p. 123)

   (A) Ronald Reagan
   (B) Abraham Lincoln
   (C) Franklin Roosevelt
   (D) George W. Bush

7. Who was the first Texas Republican to win a state-wide race for a major office (governor or senator) in twentieth-century Texas? **(3)** (p. 125)

   (A) Ralph Yarborough
   (B) John Tower
   (C) Lyndon Johnson
   (D) Ann Richards

8. What is a Yellow Dog Democrat? **(3)** (p. 125)

   (A) A loyal Democratic voter
   (B) A Democrat who changes parties
   (C) A Democrat who votes for Republicans at the top of the ballot and Democrats for local offices
   (D) A Democrat who seldom shows up to vote

9. Which of the following statements best describes the party balance in Texas? **(4)** (p. 127)

   (A) The Democratic Party dominates Texas state politics.
   (B) The Republican Party dominates Texas state politics.
   (C) The two parties are evenly matched.
   (D) The Democratic Party enjoys a majority in the Texas legislature, but the governor is a Republican.

10. Which of the following factors contributes to Republican success in Texas elections? **(4)** (pp. 127–128)

    (A) More people in Texas identify with the GOP than identify with the Democratic Party.
    (B) Independents in Texas are more likely to lean Republican than Democratic.
    (C) Texas is a relatively conservative state.
    (D) All of the above

11. After the 2010 election, Republicans held which of the following offices? **(4)** (p. 128)

    (A) Governor
    (B) Both U.S. senators from Texas
    (C) Every member of the Texas Supreme Court
    (D) All of the above

12. Democratic candidates are typically most successful in winning the support of which of the following groups of voters? **(5)** (p. 129)

    (A) Latinos
    (B) Whites
    (C) African Americans
    (D) Democrats do equally well with voters, regardless of their race/ethnicity.

13. In which of the following regions would you expect a Democratic candidate for statewide office to do best? **(5)** (p. 129)

    (A) South Texas
    (B) Central Texas
    (C) East Texas
    (D) West Texas

14. In which of the following areas do Democratic candidates have their greatest success? **(5)** (pp. 129–130)

    (A) Big cities
    (B) Suburbs
    (C) Rural areas
    (D) Small towns

15. Which of the following groups is allied with the Texas Republican Party? **(6)** (p. 130)

    (A) Trial lawyers
    (B) Anti-abortion advocates
    (C) Civil rights groups
    (D) Labor unions

16. Which of the following policy positions is included in the Texas Democratic Party platform but not the Republican Party platform? **(7)** (pp. 131–136)

    (A) Support for the Texas right-to-work law
    (B) Call for repeal of the state property tax
    (C) Support for repealing laws that discriminate against gay men and lesbians
    (D) None of the above

17. Which of the following policy positions is part of the Texas Republican Party platform? **(7)** (pp. 131–136)

    (A) Opposition to converting existing roads to toll roads
    (B) Support for the election of judges
    (C) Call for repealing the minimum wage
    (D) All of the above

18. Which of the following developments would eventually enable the Texas Democratic Party to again become competitive in statewide elections? **(8)** (p. 136)

    (A) An increase in white voter turnout
    (B) An increase in Latino voter turnout
    (C) Growth of the Tea Party movement
    (D) All of the above

19. About what percentage of the white vote did Obama receive in 2008? **(8)** (p. 137)

    (A) A fourth
    (B) A third
    (C) Half
    (D) Two-thirds

20. Which of the following is a challenge affecting the future success of the Texas Republican Party? **(0)** (p. 000)

    (A) Lack of support among white voters
    (B) Strength among suburban voters
    (C) Increased turnout of Latino voters
    (D) All of the above

Circle the correct answer.

1. In 2010, voters in Harris County had the opportunity to vote on candidates in more than 80 contested races. This situation illustrates which of the following concepts? **(1)** (pp. 144–145)

   (A) Redistricting
   (B) Prospective voting
   (C) Long ballot
   (D) Gerrymandering

2. Which of the following is an argument AGAINST the long ballot? **(1)** (p. 145)

   (A) Citizens lack sufficient information about candidates to make intelligent choices in many races.
   (B) Elections are a means for voters to hold public officials accountable.
   (C) Citizens can vote out elected officials who perform poorly.
   (D) All of the above

3. "It was a long ballot, but I finished voting in just a few seconds. I clicked one button and then I was done. Also, I voted in every race." What did the voter do? **(2)** (p. 146)

   (A) The voter cast a split-ticket ballot.
   (B) The vote cast a straight-ticket ballot.
   (C) The voter cast a retrospective ballot.
   (D) The voter cast a prospective ballot.

4. Which of the following elections is always held in March of even-numbered years? **(2)** (p. 146)

   (A) Local election
   (B) General election
   (C) Special election
   (D) Primary election

5. Which of the following elections is won by the candidate with the most votes, regardless of whether the candidate has a majority of votes cast? **(2)** (p. 146)

   (A) Democratic primary election
   (B) Republican primary election
   (C) General election
   (D) None of the above

6. The Texas Two-Step is most closely associated with which of the following? **(2)** (pp. 149–150)

   (A) The system the Texas Democratic Party uses to participate in the presidential candidate nomination process
   (B) Redistricting in Texas after the census data are made available
   (C) The implementation of the Voting Rights Act in Texas
   (D) The coattail effect on down-ballot candidates in Texas

7. What is the purpose of a bond election? **(2)** (p. 152)

   (A) To fill an unexpected vacancy caused by the death or resignation of a member of Congress or the legislature
   (B) To obtain voter approval for a local government going into debt
   (C) To approve a change in the Texas Constitution
   (D) To remove an official from office before the end of his or her term.

8. A process whereby citizens can propose legislation by gathering signatures is known as which of the following? **(2)** (pp. 152–153)

   (A) Special election
   (B) One person, one vote
   (C) Recall
   (D) Initiative

9. What is the purpose of a local-option election? **(2)** (p. 153)

   (A) To remove an elected official from office
   (B) To allow local voters to legalize casino gambling
   (C) To legalize the sale of alcoholic beverages
   (D) To obtain voter approval for a local government going into debt

10. Which of the following officials running for office in Texas is elected in an at-large election? **(3)** (p. 153)

    (A) Justice of the Texas Supreme Court
    (B) U.S. senator
    (C) Lieutenant governor
    (D) All of the above

11. Which of the following officials running for office in Texas is elected in a district election? **(3)** (p. 153)

    (A) Texas attorney general
    (B) Justice of the Texas Court of Criminal Appeals
    (C) Member of the Texas Senate
    (D) All of the above

12. Which of the following is responsible for drawing the boundaries of U.S. congressional districts in Texas? **(3)** (p. 153)

    (A) Texas legislature
    (B) Texas governor
    (C) Texas Supreme Court
    (D) Legislative Redistricting Board (LRB)

13. Suppose that newly drawn congressional districts from Texas range in population size from 600,000 to 800,000. Would it be legal to have a population variance that great? **(3)** (p. 154)

   (A) No. It would violate the one person, one vote doctrine.
   (B) No. It would violate the Voting Rights Act (VRA).
   (C) No. It would be illegal gerrymandering.
   (D) Yes. A certain amount of population variance is allowed in drawing district lines.

14. What is the purpose of the Voting Rights Act (VRA)? **(3)** (p. 155)

   (A) To prevent gerrymandering
   (B) To protect the voting rights of racial and ethnic minorities
   (C) To ensure that districts have equal population size
   (D) To protect against voter fraud

15. A state legislature draws an oddly shaped congressional district carefully designed to give an advantage to the candidates of the political party that controls the legislature. This action is an example of which of the following? **(3)** (p. 156)

   (A) A coalitional district
   (B) Prospective voting
   (C) Coattail effect
   (D) Gerrymandering

16. Which political party controlled redistricting in Texas after the 2010 U.S. Census? **(3)** (p. 160)

   (A) The Democratic Party had control, because President Obama is a Democrat.
   (B) The Republican Party had control, because it had majorities in both houses of the legislature and the governor was a Republican.
   (C) The two parties shared control because each party had a majority in one house of the legislature.
   (D) Neither political party had control because a nonpartisan commission is responsible for redistricting in Texas.

17. An attempt to get information to voters that will persuade them to elect a candidate or not elect an opponent is the definition of which of the following concepts? **(4)** (p. 161)

   (A) Retrospective voting
   (B) Election campaign
   (C) Reapportionment
   (D) Gerrymandering

18. Why are incumbent officeholders usually able to win reelection? **(5)** (p. 166)

   (A) They are usually better known than their opponents.
   (B) They can usually raise more money than their opponents.
   (C) They often have the advantage of running for re-election from districts that favor members of their political party.
   (D) All of the above

19. "I voted against Governor Perry in the last election because I blame him for my college tuition going up." This statement illustrates which of the following concepts? **(5)** (pp. 167–168)

   (A) Retrospective voting
   (B) Gerrymandering
   (C) Coattail effect
   (D) Straight-ticket ballot

20. Texas Republicans hoped that Governor Perry would win the 2012 Republican presidential nomination because they thought his presence on the ballot would provide a boost to Republicans up and down the ticket. Which of the following terms best describes the phenomenon they were describing? **(5)** (p. 168)

   (A) Retrospective voting
   (B) Prospective voting
   (C) Coattail effect
   (D) Texas Two Step

Circle the correct answer.

1. How frequently and for how long does the Texas legislature meet in regular session? **(1)** (p. 174)

   (A) Every year for 140 days
   (B) Every other year for 140 days
   (C) Every year, for 140 days in odd-numbered years and 60 days in even-numbered years
   (D) Every year with no limit on session length

2. A legislature with two chambers is known by which of the following terms? **(1)** (p. 174)

   (A) Unicameral
   (B) Partisan
   (C) Nonpartisan
   (D) Bicameral

3. Suppose that the regular session of the Texas legislature ends and the legislature has failed to adopt legislation addressing an important matter. What, if anything, can be done to address the situation now? **(1)** (p. 176)

   (A) The governor can call a special session.
   (B) The legislature can call itself back into session.
   (C) The lieutenant governor and the speaker can create an interim committee.
   (D) The legislature will have no option but to wait two years until its next session.

4. What is the salary of a member of the Texas legislature? **(2)** (p. 178)

   (A) $72,000 a year
   (B) $60,000 a year
   (C) $7,200 a year
   (D) Texas legislators are not paid.

5. Do term limits apply to the Texas legislature? **(2)** (p. 180)

   (A) Yes. House members are limited to four terms; senators can serve no more than two terms.
   (B) Yes. No member of the legislature can serve more than eight years.
   (C) Yes. All members are limited to 12 years in office.
   (D) No. Term limits do not apply.

6. How is the lieutenant governor normally chosen? **(3)** (p. 182)

   (A) The lieutenant governor is a state senator selected by the majority party in the Texas Senate.
   (B) The lieutenant governor is elected statewide.
   (C) The lieutenant governor is a state senator selected by majority vote of the Texas Senate.
   (D) The governor appoints the lieutenant governor.

7. Which of the following steps would a member of the Texas House take if that member wanted to become speaker in the next session of the legislature? **(3)** (p. 183)

   (A) He or she would begin gathering signed pledge cards from other members of the House.
   (B) He or she would begin raising money and building an organization to run a statewide election campaign.
   (C) He or she would begin lobbying the governor for the appointment.
   (D) He or she would begin lobbying the lieutenant governor for the appointment.

8. Who presides in the Texas Senate? **(3)** (p. 184)

   (A) Vice president
   (B) Speaker
   (C) Lieutenant governor
   (D) Governor

9. How are committee chairs in the Texas Senate selected? **(3)** (p. 186)

   (A) They are elected by the full Senate.
   (B) They are appointed by the governor.
   (C) They are appointed by the lieutenant governor.
   (D) They are appointed by the speaker.

10. Which of the following committees holds meetings only between legislative sessions? **(3)** (p. 186)

   (A) Standing committees
   (B) Interim committees
   (C) Conference committees
   (D) All of the above

11. Which of the following organizations would be most likely to help a member of the Texas House draft a bill in proper legislative language? **(3)** (p. 187)

   (A) Legislative Budget Board (LBB)
   (B) Legislative Council
   (C) Legislative Redistricting Board (LRB)
   (D) House Research Organization (HRO)

12. In the Texas legislature, a joint resolution would be used for which of the following purposes? **(4)** (p. 187)

   (A) Propose a state constitutional amendment
   (B) Propose a law
   (C) State the opinion of the legislature on a certain manner
   (D) Confirm an appointment

13. What is HB 11? **(4)** (p. 187)

    (A) The 11th bill passed by the Texas legislature.
    (B) The 11th bill introduced in the Texas House.
    (C) The 11th bill signed into law by the governor.
    (D) The 11th bill debated on the floor of the Texas House.

14. At which of the following stages of the legislative process would a bill most likely receive a hearing? **(4)** (p. 188)

    (A) Conference committee
    (B) Calendars committee
    (C) On the floor
    (D) Standing committee

15. Which of the following bodies or procedures determines the order of priority for the consideration of legislation on the floor of the Texas House? **(4)** (p. 189)

    (A) Two-thirds rule
    (B) Conference committee
    (C) Calendars committee
    (D) Legislative Council

16. What is the purpose of the two-thirds rule in the Texas Senate? **(4)** (pp. 189–190)

    (A) To propose constitutional amendments
    (B) To allow for consideration of a bill on the Senate floor
    (C) To approve the governor's appointments
    (D) To override the governor's veto

17. How many votes are needed to pass ordinary legislation in the Texas House? **(4)** (p. 190)

    (A) 76 of 150
    (B) 100 of 150
    (C) 21 of 31
    (D) 16 of 31

18. Is power in the Texas legislature centralized or decentralized? **(5)** (pp. 193–194)

    (A) It is widely decentralized among all the members of the legislature.
    (B) It is somewhat decentralized among the leaders and committee chairs.
    (C) It is centralized in the hands of the speaker and lieutenant governor.
    (D) It is centralized in the hands of the governor and the most senior members of the Texas House and Senate.

19. Which of the following interest groups was most responsible for the defeat of sanctuary-cities legislation in the 2011 session of the Texas legislature? **(5)** (p. 195)

    (A) Latino rights organizations, such as LULAC
    (B) Groups allied with the Tea Party movement
    (C) Labor unions
    (D) Business groups

20. Which of the following political groupings has the most influence in the Texas legislature? **(5)** (p. 197–199)

    (A) Conservative Democrats
    (B) Conservative Republicans
    (C) Liberal Democrats
    (D) Liberal Republicans

Chapter 9: Executive Branch

Circle the correct answer.

1. Which of the following officials is the chief executive of the state of Texas? **(1)** (p. 205)

   (A) Lieutenant governor
   (B) Speaker of the House
   (C) Chief justice of the Texas Supreme Court
   (D) Governor

2. Which of the following governors of Texas LEAST closely conforms to the traditional image of the office's occupant? **(1)** (p. 205)

   (A) Ann Richards
   (B) George W. Bush
   (C) Rick Perry
   (D) Bill Clements

3. Governor Rick Perry was reelected in 2010. When will Texas hold its next governor's election? **(1)** (p. 205)

   (A) 2012
   (B) 2014
   (C) 2016
   (D) If Perry is elected president, the state will hold a special election in 2013. Otherwise, the next governor's election is in 2014.

4. Which of the following is the best explanation of why the Texas legislature has failed to override a governor's veto in more than 30 years? **(1)** (pp. 207–208)

   (A) Governors almost never veto legislation, so there are very few opportunities for overrides.
   (B) The Texas Constitution requires a three-fourths vote of both the Texas House and Texas Senate to override, and the legislature is seldom so united.
   (C) Most vetoes take place after the legislature has adjourned, making an override impossible.
   (D) All of the above

5. Which of the following items can the legislature consider in a special session? **(1)** (p. 208)

   (A) Any measure it wishes to consider
   (B) Only measures considered in the most recent regular session
   (C) Only measures designated by the governor
   (D) Only measures identified by the lieutenant governor and the speaker as priority items

6. The next governor will inherit a state bureaucracy fully staffed with Rick Perry appointees. What can the new governor do to put his or her stamp on the bureaucracy, other than waiting for terms to expire? **(1)** (pp. 208–210)

   (A) The governor can replace all of the holdover officials with his or her own appointees.
   (B) The governor can replace holdover officials with the approval of the Texas Senate by majority vote.
   (C) The governor can replace holdover officials with the approval of the Texas Senate by a two-thirds vote.
   (D) The governor has no power to remove holdover officials appointed by the previous governor.

7. A convicted murderer is facing execution. Which of the following actions can the governor take without the recommendation of the Board of Pardons and Paroles? **(1)** (p. 210)

   (A) The governor can grant a 30-day reprieve.
   (B) The governor can commute the sentence to life in prison without possibility of parole.
   (C) The governor can grant the inmate a pardon.
   (D) All of the above

8. Does the lieutenant governor necessarily work closely with the governor on policy issues? **(1)** (pp. 213–215)

   (A) Yes. The two run for election together as a team and historically have always worked closely together.
   (B) Yes. The governor appoints the lieutenant governor and can remove him or her from office for failure to cooperate.
   (C) No. The lieutenant governor is elected independently from the governor and may be the governor's political adversary.
   (D) No. The Texas Constitution requires that the offices be filled by individuals from different political parties.

9. Which of the following Texas executive branch officials is elected? **(2)** (p. 218)

   (A) Attorney general
   (B) Commissioner of agriculture
   (C) Land commissioner
   (D) All of the above

10. Which of the following officials heads an agency that collects child support payments? **(2)** (p. 219)

    (A) Comptroller
    (B) Attorney general
    (C) Lieutenant governor
    (D) Governor

11. Which of the following officials acts as the state's banker? **(2)** (pp. 220–221)

    (A) Comptroller
    (B) Attorney general
    (C) Land commissioner
    (D) Secretary of state

Copyright © 2013 by Pearson Education, Inc.

PRACTICE TESTS PT-19

12. Which of the following Texas officials heads an agency that administers the school lunch program? **(2)** (p. 221)

(A) Land commissioner
(B) Commissioner of agriculture
(C) Comptroller
(D) Secretary of state

13. Which of the following Texas officials heads an agency that generates revenue for the Permanent School Fund (PSF)? **(2)** (p. 221)

(A) Land commissioner
(B) Commissioner of agriculture
(C) Comptroller
(D) Secretary of state

14. Which of the following agencies regulates the Texas oil and gas industry? **(2)** (p. 222)

(A) Public Utility Commission (PUC)
(B) General Land Office
(C) Railroad Commission
(D) Texas Department of Transportation (TxDOT)

15. Which of the following agencies is headed by a 15-member elected board? **(2)** (p. 223)

(A) General Land Office
(B) Railroad Commission
(C) Public Utility Commission
(D) State Board of Education

16. Which of the following agencies regulates telephone and electric utilities? **(2)** (p. 226)

(A) Railroad Commission
(B) Public Utility Commission
(C) General Land Office
(D) Texas Commission on Environmental Quality

17. What is the purpose of sunset review? **(3)** (p. 230)

(A) To formulate legislative proposals for addressing policy problems between legislative sessions
(B) To review the decision of a lower court to decide whether it should be upheld or reversed
(C) To evaluate state agencies to determine whether they should be restructured or even eliminated
(D) To select a political party's candidates for state office

18. Sunset review is a tool used by which of the following units of government? **(3)** (p. 230)

(A) The Texas legislature
(B) The governor
(C) The Texas Supreme Court
(D) The federal government

19. What happens if the legislature fails to reauthorize an agency that is up for sunset review? **(3)** (p. 230)

(A) It must face sunset review again in the next regular session.
(B) It continues without changes in its operation.
(C) It can continue to operate if the governor, lieutenant governor, and speaker agree.
(D) It must shut down its operation and go out of business.

20. What power does the governor of Texas have over the activities of the General Land Office? **(3)** (pp. 231–232)

(A) The governor has considerable power because he or she appoints the land commissioner and can remove him or her.
(B) The governor has some power because he or she appoints the land commissioner, but the governor has no removal authority.
(C) The governor has some power because he or she controls the agency's budget.
(D) None of the above

Circle the correct answer.

1. Which of the following litigants is a participant in a criminal case but not in a civil case? **(1)** (pp. 238–239)

 (A) Plaintiff
 (B) Prosecutor
 (C) Civil defendant
 (D) All of the above

2. Who has the burden of proof in a criminal case and what is the standard of proof? **(1)** (p. 239)

 (A) The prosecutor must prove the defendant's guilt beyond a reasonable doubt.
 (B) The plaintiff must prove the defendant's guilt by a preponderance of the evidence.
 (C) The defendant must prove his or her innocence by a preponderance of the evidence.
 (D) The prosecutor must prove the defendant's guilt beyond a shadow of a doubt.

3. A legal dispute concerning a private conflict between two or more parties—individuals, corporations, or government agencies—is known as which of the following? **(1)** (p. 240)

 (A) Felony
 (B) Misdemeanor
 (C) Plea bargain
 (D) Civil case

4. A man files a lawsuit to recover damages and pay medical bills after an automobile accident. The case is an example of which of the following? **(1)** (p. 240)

 (A) Misdemeanor
 (B) Contract case
 (C) Tort case
 (D) Contract case

5. A criminal defendant agrees to plead guilty in exchange for a reduced sentence on the charge. This agreement is an example of which of the following? **(2)** (pp. 240–241)

 (A) Settling out of court
 (B) Plea bargain
 (C) Missouri Plan
 (D) Adversary proceeding

6. Which of the following would *not* be part of a trial proceeding? **(2)** (p. 241)

 (A) A panel of three or more judges hears the case.
 (B) A witness testifies as to the facts of the case.
 (C) A lawyer presents an argument to a jury.
 (D) A jury listens to lawyers and witnesses present evidence.

7. Which of the following is an example of a local court? **(3)** (p. 242)

 (A) Municipal court
 (B) Justice of the peace court
 (C) County court
 (D) All of the above

8. A police officer gives a dog owner a citation for violating the city's leash law. Which of the following courts would most likely hear the case? **(3)** (p. 243)

 (A) County court
 (B) JP court
 (C) Municipal court
 (D) District court

9. A motorist driving in West Texas is stopped by a sheriff's deputy and given a ticket for speeding. Which of the following courts would most likely hear the case? **(3)** (p. 244)

 (A) County court
 (B) JP court
 (C) Municipal court
 (D) District court

10. A landlord decides to go to court to evict a tenant who is behind on his rent. Which of the following courts would handle the matter? **(3)** (p. 244)

 (A) JP court
 (B) County court
 (C) District court
 (D) Municipal court

11. Which of the following courts would probate a will when no parties object to its authenticity? **(3)** (p. 244)

 (A) District court
 (B) JP court
 (C) County court
 (D) Texas Supreme Court

12. Which of the following courts would try a case involving an alleged kidnapping and aggravated assault? **(3)** (pp. 245–246)

 (A) County court
 (B) JP court
 (C) Court of Criminal Appeals
 (D) District court

13. Which of the following cases would be heard on appeal from district court by the courts of appeals? **(3)** (p. 246)

 (A) A damage award in a personal injury case
 (B) A decision of a district court concerning the authenticity of a will
 (C) A sentence of life in prison without the possibility of parole in a capital murder case
 (D) All of the above

14. Which of the following cases could be heard on appeal by the Texas Supreme Court? **(3)** (pp. 247–248)

 (A) A damage award in a personal injury case
 (B) A kidnapping conviction and sentence of 50 years in prison
 (C) A death sentence assessed in a capital murder case
 (D) All of the above

15. How are most trial and all appellate judges chosen in Texas? **(4)** (p. 249)

    (A) They are appointed by the governor.
    (B) They are chosen in partisan election.
    (C) They are chosen in nonpartisan election.
    (D) They are chosen through merit selection.

16. Are all Texas judges experienced attorneys? **(4)** (p. 249)

    (A) Yes
    (B) No. The Texas Constitution does not require that any of the state's judges have legal training and experience.
    (C) No. Appellate court judges are required to be experienced attorneys, but trial court judges are not.
    (D) No. Municipal, JP, and county court at law judges are not required to be attorneys, and most are not.

17. Many Texas judges initially reach their positions through appointment. How is that possible? **(5)** (p. 251)

    (A) All Texas judges are selected through appointment pending confirmation by the Texas Senate.
    (B) In Texas, appellate judges are appointed, whereas trial judges are elected.
    (C) The governor fills vacancies in appellate and district judgeships. The newly appointed judges must face the voters at the next election.
    (D) Under merit selection, the governor appoints judges from a list prepared by a nominating commission. The judges then face a retention election.

18. Which of the following statements best describes the campaign finance system for Texas judicial elections? **(5)** (p. 251–252)

    (A) State law limits the amount of money judicial candidates can raise and spend, so fundraising is minimal.
    (B) Candidates for judicial office typically raise campaign money from lawyers and interest groups who have a stake in the outcomes of court cases.
    (C) The state of Texas funds judicial races and candidates for judge are prohibited from raising money on their own.
    (D) Judicial candidates are usually unable to raise more than a minimal amount of money because no one has an interest in judicial election outcomes.

19. Does Texas use merit selection (or the Missouri Plan) to select judges? **(5)** (p. 255)

    (A) No
    (B) Yes, for all judges except local judges
    (C) Yes, but only for appellate judges
    (D) Yes, but only for justices on the Texas Court of Criminal Appeals and the Texas Supreme Court

20. Which of the following is a procedure for removing a Texas judge from office? **(5)** (p. 258)

    (A) Missouri Plan
    (B) Adversary proceeding
    (C) Plea bargain
    (D) Address from office

Circle the correct answer.

1. What is a city ordinance? **(1)** (pp. 264–264)

   (A) The basic law of a municipality that defines its powers, responsibilities, and organization
   (B) A law adopted by a municipality
   (C) A professional administrator hired to run a city government
   (D) A contractual agreement among urban homeowners to manage their subdivision

2. Which of the following statements about general-law cities is/are true? **(1)** (pp. 266–267)

   (A) General-law cities must have city charters.
   (B) General-law cities are bound by Dillon's rule.
   (C) Municipalities with fewer than 5,000 people must be general-law cities.
   (D) All of the above

3. Why does the Texas legislature sometimes enact population bracket laws? **(1)** (p. 267)

   (A) To target individual cities, such as Austin or Houston
   (B) To allow larger municipalities to become home-rule cities
   (C) To prevent any city in the state from adopting its own minimum-wage law
   (D) To increase representation in the legislature for large urban areas

4. Which of the following is/are responsible for setting the tax rate and adopting a budget for a city government in Texas? **(2)** (p. 267)

   (A) The Texas legislature
   (B) The governor
   (C) The mayor and city council
   (D) The city manager

5. Which of the following Texas cities use(s) the mayor-council form of city government? **(2)** (p. 269)

   (A) Houston
   (B) Dallas
   (C) San Antonio
   (D) All of the above

6. In City ABC, voters throughout the city cast ballots for candidates running for all of the city's council seats. What sort of election system does City ABC have? **(3)** (p. 272)

   (A) District election system
   (B) Nonpartisan election system
   (C) At-large election system
   (D) Cumulative election system

7. A minority rights group wants to increase minority representation on the city council of one of the state's major cities. Which of the following electoral reforms would it be most likely to support? **(3)** (p. 274)

   (A) Nonpartisan elections
   (B) District elections
   (C) At-large elections
   (D) All of the above

8. A local program that enhances a community's economic position in its competition with other communities is the definition of which of the following terms? **(4)** (p. 275)

   (A) Allocational urban policy
   (B) Developmental urban policy
   (C) Redistributive urban policy
   (D) Pluralist urban policy

9. City ABC is building a new football stadium in order to keep its NFL team from moving to another city. Building the football stadium is an example of which of the following types of policies? **(4)** (pp. 275–276)

   (A) Elitist urban policy
   (B) Redistributive urban policy
   (C) Pluralist urban policy
   (D) Developmental urban policy

10. Programs that benefit low-income residents of an area are known as which of the following? **(4)** (p. 276)

    (A) Redistributive
    (B) Allocational
    (C) Pluralist
    (D) Developmental

11. Which of the following is NOT a major source of revenue for Texas cities? **(4)** (pp. 277–278)

    (A) Property tax
    (B) Sales tax
    (C) Franchise fees
    (D) Income tax

12. What effect does a homestead exemption have on a homeowner's property tax bill? **(4)** (p. 278)

    (A) It reduces the taxable value of the home by the amount of the exemption.
    (B) It reduces the property tax rate by the amount of the exemption.
    (C) It increases the total tax paid by the amount of the exemption.
    (D) It has no impact on property tax bills.

13. Which of the following is a program in which a local government promises to earmark increased property tax revenues generated by development in a designated area? **(4)** (p. 280)

(A) Zoning
(B) Homestead exemption
(C) Tax increment financing
(D) Pluralism

14. Which of the following actions increases both a city's land area and, possibly, its population as well? **(4)** (pp. 281–282)

(A) Extraterritorial jurisdiction
(B) Zoning
(C) Tax increment financing
(D) Annexation

15. People living in a subdivision just outside the city limits do not pay taxes to the city or vote in city elections, but they must follow city building codes. Why? **(4)** (p. 284)

(A) Because of annexation
(B) Because the subdivision is in the city's ETJ
(C) Because of zoning
(D) Because of deed restrictions

16. A Texas couple hires a contractor to add a room to their house. The contractor applies for and receives a permit from the city. What type of city ordinance forces the contractor to obtain a permit for the work? **(4)** (p. 285)

(A) Building code
(B) Housing code
(C) Zoning
(D) Deed restriction

17. A homeowner discovers that her plan to erect a new chain link fence is unacceptable because her subdivision only allows wooden fences. The fence requirement is most likely the result of which of the following land-use restrictions? **(4)** (p. 287)

(A) Building codes
(B) Housing codes
(C) Zoning
(D) Deed restrictions

18. "A small group of wealthy people dominate politics by controlling economic resources." This statement reflects which of the following concepts? **(5)** (p. 288)

(A) Pluralism
(B) Deracialization
(C) Elitism
(D) Toggling

19. "Diverse groups of elites compete with one another to control policy various issue areas." This statement reflects which of the following concepts? **(5)** (p. 290)

(A) Pluralism
(B) Deracialization
(C) Elitism
(D) Toggling

20. Which of the following statements best describes Annise Parker's strategy for being elected mayor of Houston? **(5)** (pp. 291–292)

(A) She mobilized the gay and lesbian community, who simply outvoted other groups in the city.
(B) She mobilized her base of gay and lesbian voters while simultaneously appealing to other Houstonians, including many relatively conservative voters.
(C) She ran as an outsider promising to shake up the city by putting minorities, including gay men and lesbians, in charge of city departments.
(D) She ran as the candidate of the business community by focusing on economic development.

Circle the correct answer.

1. Which of the following units of local government in Texas has the authority to become a home-rule unit of government? **(1)** (pp. 239–240, 298, 309, 320)

   (A) Cities
   (B) Counties
   (C) School districts
   (D) All of the above

2. County governments in Texas have the authority to provide which of the following services to local residents? **(1)** (p. 299–300)

   (A) Schools
   (B) Roads and bridges
   (C) Community colleges
   (D) All of the above

3. An individual who was born in Texas should contact which of the following units of government in order to obtain a copy of her birth certificate? **(1)** (p. 300)

   (A) City government where she was born
   (B) Office of the Texas Secretary of State
   (C) County government where she was born
   (D) U.S. Social Security Administration

4. Which of the following officials is part of the commissioners court? **(1)** (p. 300)

   (A) County sheriff
   (B) County tax-assessor collector
   (C) County clerk
   (D) None of the above

5. Which of the following county officials oversees road repair and construction? **(1)** (p. 300)

   (A) County judge
   (B) County clerk
   (C) County commissioner
   (D) County sheriff

6. Which of the following county officials prosecutes felony offenses in district court? **(1)** (p. 302)

   (A) County judge
   (B) County attorney
   (C) County sheriff
   (D) District attorney

7. The tax assessor-collector is responsible for which of the following duties in most Texas counties? **(1)** (p. 303)

   (A) Register voters
   (B) Assess property values for tax purposes
   (C) Conduct elections
   (D) All of the above

8. Which of the following is the main source of local tax revenue for county government in Texas? **(1)** (p. 303)

   (A) Sales tax
   (B) Property tax
   (C) Gasoline tax
   (D) Income tax

9. Which of the following officials is responsible for managing the day-to-day affairs of an independent school district? **(2)** (p. 310)

   (A) Mayor
   (B) School board of trustees
   (C) Superintendent
   (D) City manager

10. Which of the following is the most important source of funds for the average Texas ISD? **(2)** (p. 311)

    (A) Local property taxes
    (B) Federal funds
    (C) State funds
    (D) All of the above sources are equally important.

11. The Foundation School Program refers to which of the following? **(2)** (p. 312)

    (A) Basic-skills testing
    (B) A school choice program
    (C) Merit pay
    (D) Basic funding program for public education in Texas

12. What is the most important local funding source for public education in Texas? **(2)** (p. 312)

    (A) Sales tax
    (B) Property tax
    (C) Tuition and fees charged to parents
    (D) Federal aid

13. What was the primary effect of the Robin Hood Plan? **(2)** (p. 314)

    (A) It reduced funding for the state's wealthy school districts.
    (B) It increased funding for the state's poorer school districts to the funding level of the wealthier districts.
    (C) It ended school district reliance on property taxes.
    (D) All of the above

14. The educational reform movement that allows parents to choose the elementary or secondary school their children will attend is known as which of the following? **(2)** (p. 316)

    (A) Charter schools
    (B) Merit pay
    (C) School choice
    (D) Robin Hood Plan

15. STAAR is most closely associated with which of the following concepts? **(2)** (p. 319)

(A) School funding
(B) School choice
(C) Charter schools
(D) Basic-skills testing

16. Which of the following is an example of a special district? **(3)** (pp. 320–322)

(A) Coastal subsidence district
(B) Hospital district
(C) Municipal utility district
(D) All of the above

17. What is the most important local tax source for community/junior college districts? **(3)** (p. 323)

(A) Property taxes
(B) Sales taxes
(C) Hotel/motel occupancy tax
(D) Income tax

18. Which of the following special districts levies a sales tax? **(3)** (p. 323)

(A) Community/junior college district
(B) Transit authority
(C) Hospital district
(D) Port authority

19. Which of the following types of special districts is typically funded by hotel/motel occupancy taxes and taxes on rental cars (among other revenue sources)? **(3)** (p. 323)

(A) Municipal utility districts
(B) Port authorities
(C) Sports authorities
(D) Hospital districts

20. Which of the following types of special districts raises revenue from service charges, including water and sewer usage and garbage pickup fees? **(3)** (p. 323)

(A) Municipal utility districts
(B) Sports authorities
(C) Hospital districts
(D) Port authorities

Circle the correct answer.

1. Which of the following revenue sources for the state of Texas has grown in importance the most over the last 20 years? **(1)** (p. 331)

   (A) General sales tax
   (B) Severance taxes on oil and gas production
   (C) Federal funds
   (D) Land income

2. Which of the following purchases is subject to the Texas sales tax? **(1)** (p. 332)

   (A) Purchase of a bottle of aspirin at the pharmacy
   (B) Purchase of a loaf of bread and a dozen eggs at the grocery store
   (C) Payment to the family doctor for an annual physical exam
   (D) None of the above

3. Which of the following federal programs brings the largest amount of federal money to the state? **(1)** (p. 335)

   (A) Medicaid
   (B) School Lunch Program
   (C) Transportation
   (D) Temporary Assistance to Needy Families (TANF)

4. How does the tax burden in Texas compare with that in other states? **(2)** (p. 339)

   (A) Texas has the highest state taxes in the country.
   (B) Texas has the lowest state taxes in the country.
   (C) Taxes in Texas are just below the national average.
   (D) Taxes in Texas are just above the national average.

5. Economists believe that lower-income families pay a higher portion of their earnings in sales taxes than do middle- and upper-income families because lower-income families spend a greater proportion of their earnings on items subject to taxation. Consequently, the sales tax is an example of which of the following types of taxes? **(2)** (p. 341)

   (A) Regressive tax
   (B) Progressive tax
   (C) Income tax
   (D) Proportional tax

6. The extent to which tax revenues increase as personal income rises is known as which of the following? **(2)** (p. 343)

   (A) Tax incidence
   (B) Tax fairness
   (C) Tax elasticity
   (D) Progressive taxation

7. Which of the following types of taxes does Texas *not* have? **(3)** (p. 343)

   (A) Sales tax
   (B) Cigarette tax
   (C) Severance taxes on oil and gas production
   (D) Personal income tax

8. Which of the following types of legalized gambling does Texas *not* have? **(3)** (p. 345)

   (A) Lottery
   (B) Casino gambling
   (C) Horse racing
   (D) Dog racing

9. Which of the following is *not* a major category of expenditures in the state budget? **(4)** (p. 347)

   (A) Public education
   (B) Transportation
   (C) Healthcare
   (D) Agriculture

10. Which of the following major expenditure categories for Texas state government has grown the most rapidly over the last 20 years? **(4)** (p. 347)

    (A) Health and human services
    (B) Education
    (C) Public safety and corrections
    (D) Transportation

11. Which of the following programs will be most greatly affected by the adoption of federal healthcare reform? **(5)** (pp. 349–350)

    (A) SCHIP
    (B) TANF
    (C) Medicaid
    (D) Food stamps

12. Which of the following is a healthcare program that specifically targets children? **(5)** (p. 351)

    (A) Medicare
    (B) SCHIP
    (C) Medicaid
    (D) School Lunch Program

13. Which of the following institutions benefit(s) from the Permanent University Fund (PUF)? **(5)** (p. 354)

    (A) Community colleges
    (B) University of Houston
    (C) University of Texas at Austin
    (D) All of the above

14. Which of the following programs provides temporary financial assistance and work opportunities to needy families? **(5)** (p. 355)

   (A) SCHIP
   (B) Medicaid
   (C) SNAP (food stamps)
   (D) TANF

15. Revenue raised by which of the following taxes funds highway construction and maintenance in Texas? **(5)** (pp. 356–357)

   (A) Gasoline tax
   (B) Hotel/motel tax
   (C) Insurance tax
   (D) All of the above

16. Which of the following agencies plays the most important role in developing the state budget proposal for consideration by the legislature? **(6)** (p. 359)

   (A) Office of the governor
   (B) LBB
   (C) Comptroller of Public Accounts
   (D) Texas Attorney General

17. What role does the comptroller play in the budget process? **(6)** (p. 360)

   (A) The comptroller prepares the initial budget draft.
   (B) The comptroller, along with the governor, has budget execution authority.
   (C) The comptroller must approve any deficit spending.
   (D) The comptroller projects state revenue for the upcoming budget period.

18. Which of the following is an example of a dedicated fund? **(6)** (p. 361)

   (A) PUF
   (B) TANF
   (C) Medicaid
   (D) SCHIP

19. Which of the following phrases best describes budget policies in Texas? **(7)** (p. 363)

   (A) Low level of taxes, well-funded services
   (B) High level of taxes, poorly funded services
   (C) Low level of taxes, poorly funded services
   (D) High level of taxes, well-funded services

20. Which of the following state officials has/have the greatest influence over the LBB? **(7)** (p. 365)

   (A) Governor
   (B) Speaker and lieutenant governor
   (C) Comptroller
   (D) Attorney general

Circle the correct answer.

1. Which of the following types of crime occurs *least* frequently? **(1)** (p. 375)

    (A) Burglary
    (B) Larceny
    (C) Murder
    (D) Aggravated assault

2. How has the crime rate changed since 1990? **(1)** (pp. 375–376)

    (A) It has been decreasing.
    (B) It has been increasing.
    (C) It increased until 2000 and then began to fall.
    (D) It decreased until 2000 and then began to increase.

3. Which of the following statements about the incidence of crime is/are true? **(2)** (p. 377)

    (A) Renters are more likely to be crime victims than homeowners.
    (B) Men are more likely to be crime victims than women.
    (C) Low-income people are more likely to be crime victims than middle- and upper-income people.
    (D) All of the above

4. Which of the following statements is *not* true of people arrested for crimes? **(2)** (pp. 377–378)

    (A) Most of them are men.
    (B) Most of them are middle aged.
    (C) Most of them are poorly educated.
    (D) At least for violent crimes, most of them know their victims.

5. The clearance rate is lowest for which of the following crimes? **(3)** (p. 378)

    (A) Murder
    (B) Aggravated assault
    (C) Larceny
    (D) Robbery

6. What is the purpose of booking? **(3)** (p. 378)

    (A) To document a person's arrest
    (B) To ensure that an accused person returns for later proceedings
    (C) To monitor a criminal defendant who has been granted probation
    (D) To provide compensation to a crime victim

7. A police officer informs a suspect of his constitutional rights. This action is known as which of the following? **(3)** (p. 379)

    (A) Booking
    (B) Arraignment
    (C) Plea bargain
    (D) *Miranda* warning

8. A grand jury is most closely associated with which of the following actions? **(3)** (pp. 379–380)

    (A) Arraignment
    (B) Indictment
    (C) Bail
    (D) Plea bargain

9. How are most criminal cases resolved in Texas district courts? **(3)** (p. 382)

    (A) The defendant is acquitted after a trial.
    (B) The defendant is convicted after a trial.
    (C) The charges are dismissed.
    (D) The defendant pleads guilty.

10. The case of *Furman v. Georgia* dealt with which of the following issues? **(4)** (p. 384)

    (A) Prison overcrowding
    (B) Confinement of sexual assault offenders after the expiration of their prison terms
    (C) Capital punishment
    (D) Right to legal representation for indigent defendants

11. Under Texas law, which of the following crimes could *not* be charged as capital murder? **(4)** (p. 384)

    (A) A woman is accused of running over and killing her husband after she discovers that he is having an affair.
    (B) A man is accused of killing a store clerk during a botched robbery attempt.
    (C) A man is accused of suffocating his girlfriend's infant child.
    (D) An escaped prison inmate is accused of running over and killing a pedestrian while fleeing from authorities.

12. How does the juvenile crime rate compare with the overall crime rate? **(5)** (pp. 386–387)

    (A) The juvenile crime rate has been increasing much faster than the overall crime rate.
    (B) The juvenile crime rate has been falling much faster than the overall crime rate.
    (C) The juvenile crime rate has been increasing at the same rate as the overall crime rate.
    (D) The juvenile crime rate has been falling at the same rate as the overall crime rate.

13. The TYC deals with which of the following? **(5)** (p. 387)

    (A) Criminal defendants convicted of minor offenses
    (B) Supervising defendants granted probation
    (C) Supervising prisoners released on parole
    (D) Holding juvenile offenders in custody

14. Which of the following countries has the largest prison system? **(6)** (p. 387)

    (A) Germany
    (B) China
    (C) United States
    (D) United Kingdom

15. Which state has the largest prison system? **(6)** (p. 387)

    (A) Texas
    (B) California
    (C) Florida
    (D) New York

16. Which of the following offenders would be the most likely to be held in a county jail? **(6)** (p. 388)

    (A) A death row inmate awaiting execution
    (B) An inmate convicted of a misdemeanor offense serving a three-month sentence
    (C) An inmate convicted of a felony offense serving a 30-year sentence
    (D) None of the above is likely to be held in a county jail.

17. The case of *Ruiz v. Estelle* dealt with which of the following issues? **(6)** (pp. 388–389)

    (A) Capital punishment
    (B) Double jeopardy
    (C) Prison conditions in Texas
    (D) Confinement of convicted sex offenders who have completed their prison sentences

18. The term *recidivism* refers to which of the following? **(6)** (p. 392)

    (A) Exoneration and release of a death row inmate
    (B) A convicted defendant paying back the victim of his or her crime
    (C) The return of a fleeing criminal from one state to another
    (D) The tendency of offenders released from prison to commit additional crimes and be returned behind bars

19. Why does the use of parole and probation go up during times when the state budget is tight? **(7)** (p. 392)

    (A) Parole and probation cost less than prison confinement.
    (B) The unemployment rate is high.
    (C) More people commit crimes during hard budgetary times.
    (D) Public opinion supports getting tough on crime.

20. Which of the following groups would be most interested in DWI laws? **(7)** (p. 393)

    (A) Public employee groups representing correctional employees
    (B) MADD
    (C) Public employee groups representing police officers
    (D) A victim rights organization

ANSWERS TO PRACTICE TEST QUESTIONS

Introduction: The Policymaking Process

1. B	8. C	15. D
2. A	9. D	16. A
3. A	10. A	17. C
4. D	11. B	18. B
5. C	12. D	19. D
6. B	13. D	20. D
7. B	14. B	

Chapter 1: The People, Economy, and Political Culture of Texas

1. D	8. B	15. A
2. A	9. A	16. B
3. B	10. D	17. B
4. C	11. C	18. C
5. D	12. B	19. D
6. A	13. A	20. D
7. C	14. D	

Chapter 2: Texas Constitution

1. D	8. D	15. C
2. A	9. C	16. D
3. C	10. C	17. B
4. B	11. D	18. A
5. A	12. A	19. C
6. D	13. B	20. D
7. B	14. A	

Chapter 3: The Federal Context of Texas Policymaking

1. C	8. B	15. D
2. A	9. C	16. A
3. A	10. B	17. B
4. B	11. A	18. C
5. D	12. D	19. C
6. C	13. B	20. D
7. D	14. C	

Chapter 4: Political Participation

1. C	8. A	15. D
2. A	9. D	16. D
3. D	10. C	17. B
4. B	11. B	18. A
5. D	12. C	19. C
6. D	13. A	20. B
7. B	14. C	

Chapter 5: Interest Groups

1. B	8. C	15. B
2. C	9. D	16. C
3. A	10. A	17. D
4. D	11. B	18. A
5. B	12. C	19. B
6. D	13. D	20. D
7. A	14. A	

Chapter 6: Political Parties

1. A	8. A	15. B
2. B	9. B	16. C
3. C	10. D	17. D
4. D	11. D	18. B
5. D	12. C	19. A
6. C	13. A	20. C
7. B	14. A	

Chapter 7: Elections

1. C	8. D	15. D
2. A	9. C	16. B
3. B	10. D	17. B
4. D	11. C	18. D
5. C	12. A	19. A
6. A	13. A	20. C
7. B	14. B	

Chapter 8: The Texas Legislature

1. B	8. C	15. C
2. D	9. C	16. B
3. A	10. B	17. A
4. C	11. D	18. C
5. D	12. A	19. D
6. B	13. B	20. B
7. A	14. D	

Chapter 9: Executive Branch

1. D	8. C	15. D
2. A	9. D	16. B
3. B	10. B	17. C
4. C	11. A	18. A
5. C	12. B	19. D
6. D	13. A	20. D
7. A	14. C	

Chapter 10: Judicial Branch

1. B	8. C	15. B
2. A	9. B	16. D
3. D	10. A	17. C
4. C	11. C	18. B
5. B	12. D	19. A
6. A	13. D	20. D
7. D	14. A	

Chapter 11: City Government

1. B	8. B	15. B
2. D	9. D	16. A
3. A	10. A	17. D
4. C	11. D	18. C
5. A	12. A	19. A
6. C	13. C	20. B
7. B	14. D	

Chapter 12: Counties, School Districts, and Special Districts

1. A	8. B	15. D
2. B	9. C	16. D
3. C	10. A	17. A
4. D	11. D	18. B
5. C	12. B	19. C
6. D	13. A	20. A
7. A	14. C	

Chapter 13: State Budget Policy

1. C	8. B	15. A
2. D	9. D	16. B
3. A	10. A	17. D
4. B	11. C	18. A
5. A	12. B	19. C
6. C	13. C	20. B
7. D	14. D	

Chapter 14: Criminal Justice

1. C	8. B	15. A
2. A	9. D	16. B
3. D	10. C	17. C
4. B	11. A	18. D
5. C	12. B	19. A
6. A	13. D	20. B
7. D	14. C	